Cisco Certified DevNet Professional
DEVCOR 350-901

Official Cert Guide

JASON DAVIS,
HAZIM DAHIR,
STUART CLARK,
QUINN SNYDER

Cisco Press

Cisco Certified DevNet Professional DEVCOR 350-901 Official Cert Guide

Jason Davis

Hazim Dahir

Stuart Clark

Quinn Snyder

Copyright© 2023 Cisco Systems, Inc.

Published by:
Cisco Press

All rights reserved. No part of this book may be reproduced or transmitted in any form or by any means, electronic or mechanical, including photocopying, recording, or by any information storage and retrieval system, without written permission from the publisher, except for the inclusion of brief quotations in a review.

Library of Congress Control Number: 2022933631

ISBN-13: 978-0-13-737044-3

ISBN-10: 0-13-737044-X

Warning and Disclaimer

This book is designed to provide information about the Cisco DevNet Professional DEVCOR 350-901 exam. Every effort has been made to make this book as complete and as accurate as possible, but no warranty or fitness is implied.

The information is provided on an "as is" basis. The authors, Cisco Press, and Cisco Systems, Inc. shall have neither liability nor responsibility to any person or entity with respect to any loss or damages arising from the information contained in this book or from the use of the discs or programs that may accompany it.

The opinions expressed in this book belong to the author and are not necessarily those of Cisco Systems, Inc.

Trademark Acknowledgments

All terms mentioned in this book that are known to be trademarks or service marks have been appropriately capitalized. Cisco Press or Cisco Systems, Inc., cannot attest to the accuracy of this information. Use of a term in this book should not be regarded as affecting the validity of any trademark or service mark.

Special Sales

For information about buying this title in bulk quantities, or for special sales opportunities (which may include electronic versions; custom cover designs; and content particular to your business, training goals, marketing focus, or branding interests), please contact our corporate sales department at corpsales@pearsoned.com or (800) 382-3419.

For government sales inquiries, please contact governmentsales@pearsoned.com.

For questions about sales outside the U.S., please contact intlcs@pearson.com.

Printed in Great Britain by Bell and Bain Ltd, Glasgow

Feedback Information

At Cisco Press, our goal is to create in-depth technical books of the highest quality and value. Each book is crafted with care and precision, undergoing rigorous development that involves the unique expertise of members from the professional technical community.

Readers' feedback is a natural continuation of this process. If you have any comments regarding how we could improve the quality of this book, or otherwise alter it to better suit your needs, you can contact us through email at feedback@ciscopress.com. Please make sure to include the book title and ISBN in your message.

We greatly appreciate your assistance.

Editor-in-Chief: Mark Taub

Alliances Manager, Cisco Press: Arezou Gol

Director, ITP Product Management: Brett Bartow

Executive Editor: Nancy Davis

Managing Editor: Sandra Schroeder

Development Editor: Ellie Bru

Senior Project Editor: Tonya Simpson

Copy Editor: CAH Editing

Technical Editors: Bryan Byrne, Joe Clark

Editorial Assistant: Cindy Teeters

Cover Designer: Chuti Prasertsith

Composition: Codemantra

Indexer: Cheryl Lenser

Proofreader: Donna E. Mulder

Americas Headquarters
Cisco Systems, Inc.
San Jose, CA

Asia Pacific Headquarters
Cisco Systems (USA) Pte. Ltd.
Singapore

Europe Headquarters
Cisco Systems International BV
Amsterdam, The Netherlands

Cisco has more than 200 offices worldwide. Addresses, phone numbers, and fax numbers are listed on the Cisco Website at **www.cisco.com/go/offices.**

CCDE, CCENT, Cisco Eos, Cisco HealthPresence, the Cisco logo, Cisco Lumin, Cisco Nexus, Cisco StadiumVision, Cisco TelePresence, Cisco WebEx, DCE, and Welcome to the Human Network are trademarks; Changing the Way We Work, Live, Play, and Learn and Cisco Store are service marks; and Access Registrar, Aironet, AsyncOS, Bringing the Meeting To You, Catalyst, CCDA, CCDP, CCIE, CCIP, CCNA, CCNP, CCSP, CCVP, Cisco, the Cisco Certified Internetwork Expert logo, Cisco IOS, Cisco Press, Cisco Systems, Cisco Systems Capital, the Cisco Systems logo, Cisco Unity, Collaboration Without Limitation, EtherFast, EtherSwitch, Event Center, Fast Step, Follow Me Browsing, FormShare, GigaDrive, HomeLink, Internet Quotient, IOS, iPhone, iQuick Study, IronPort, the IronPort logo, LightStream, Linksys, MediaTone, MeetingPlace, MeetingPlace Chime Sound, MGX, Networkers, Networking Academy, Network Registrar, PCNow, PIX, PowerPanels, ProConnect, ScriptShare, SenderBase, SMARTnet, Spectrum Expert, StackWise, The Fastest Way to Increase Your Internet Quotient, TransPath, WebEx, and the WebEx logo are registered trademarks of Cisco Systems, Inc. and/or its affiliates in the United States and certain other countries.

All other trademarks mentioned in this document or website are the property of their respective owners. The use of the word partner does not imply a partnership relationship between Cisco and any other company. (0812R)

Pearson's Commitment to Diversity, Equity, and Inclusion

Pearson is dedicated to creating bias-free content that reflects the diversity of all learners. We embrace the many dimensions of diversity, including but not limited to race, ethnicity, gender, socioeconomic status, ability, age, sexual orientation, and religious or political beliefs.

Education is a powerful force for equity and change in our world. It has the potential to deliver opportunities that improve lives and enable economic mobility. As we work with authors to create content for every product and service, we acknowledge our responsibility to demonstrate inclusivity and incorporate diverse scholarship so that everyone can achieve their potential through learning. As the world's leading learning company, we have a duty to help drive change and live up to our purpose to help more people create a better life for themselves and to create a better world.

Our ambition is to purposefully contribute to a world where

- Everyone has an equitable and lifelong opportunity to succeed through learning
- Our educational products and services are inclusive and represent the rich diversity of learners
- Our educational content accurately reflects the histories and experiences of the learners we serve
- Our educational content prompts deeper discussions with learners and motivates them to expand their own learning (and worldview)

While we work hard to present unbiased content, we want to hear from you about any concerns or needs with this Pearson product so that we can investigate and address them.

Please contact us with concerns about any potential bias at https://www.pearson.com/report-bias.html.

About the Authors

Jason Davis is a distinguished engineer for the DevNet program in the Developer Relations organization at Cisco. His role is technical strategy lead for the DevRel organization as he collaborates with various Cisco business unit leaders, partners, customers, and other industry influencers. Jason is focused on automation, orchestration, cloud-native technologies, and network management/operations technologies. He has a tenured career working with hundreds of customers, worldwide, in some of the largest network automation and management projects and is sought out for consulting and innovative leadership. His former experience as a U.S. Army Signal Corps officer has provided insights to defense, government, and public-sector projects, while his extensive work in professional services at Cisco has spanned commercial, large-enterprise, and service provider segments. Most of his customer engagements have been in automotive, manufacturing, large retail, large event venues, and health care. Jason has achieved Cisco Live Distinguished Speaker Hall of Fame status and is an automation/monitoring lead for the network operations center (NOC) at Cisco Live events in the U.S. and Europe. He resides in Apex, North Carolina, and enjoys IoT projects, home automation, and audio/video technologies in houses of worship. Jason and his wife, Amy, have four children whom they homeschool and cherish daily. Jason is found on social media @SNMPguy.

Hazim Dahir, CCIE No. 5536, is a distinguished engineer at the Cisco office of the CTO. He is working to define and influence next-generation digital transformation architectures across multiple technologies and verticals. Hazim started his Cisco tenure in 1996 as a software engineer and subsequently moved into the services organization focusing on large-scale network designs. He's currently focusing on developing architectures utilizing security, collaboration, Edge computing, and IoT technologies addressing the future of work and hybrid cloud requirements for large enterprises. Through his passion for engineering and sustainability, Hazim is currently working on advanced software solutions for electric and autonomous vehicles with global automotive manufacturers. Hazim is a Distinguished Speaker at Cisco Live and is a frequent presenter at multiple global conferences and standards bodies. He has multiple issued and pending patents and a number of innovation and R&D publications.

Stuart Clark, DevNet Expert #2022005, started his career as a hairdresser in 1990, and in 2008 he changed careers to become a network engineer. After cutting his teeth in network operations, he moved to network projects and programs. Stuart joined Cisco in 2012 as a network engineer, rebuilding one of Cisco's global networks and designing and building Cisco's IXP peering program. After many years as a network engineer, Stuart became obsessed with network automation and joined Cisco DevNet as a developer advocate for network automation. Stuart contributed to the DevNet exams and was part of one of the SME teams that created, designed, and built the Cisco Certified DevNet Expert. Stuart has presented at more than 50 external conferences and is a multitime Cisco Live Distinguished Speaker, covering topics on network automation and methodologies. Stuart lives in Lincoln, England, with his wife, Natalie, and their son, Maddox. He plays guitar and rocks an impressive two-foot beard while drinking coffee. Stuart can be found on social media
@bigevilbeard.

Quinn Snyder is a developer advocate within the Developer Relations organization inside Cisco, focusing on datacenter technologies, both on-premises and cloud-native. In this role, he aligns his passion for education and learning with his enthusiasm for helping the infrastructure automation community grow and harness the powers of APIs, structured data, and programmability tooling. Prior to his work as a DA, Quinn spent 15 years in a variety of design, engineering, and implementation roles across datacenter, utility, and service provider customers for both Cisco and the partner community. Quinn is a proud graduate of Arizona State University (go Sun Devils!) and a Cisco Network Academy alumnus. He is the technical co-chair of the SkillsUSA–Arizona Internetworking contest and is involved with programmability education at the state and regional level for the Cisco Networking Academy. Quinn resides in the suburbs of Phoenix, Arizona, with his wife, Amanda, and his two kids. In his free time, you can find him behind a grill, behind a camera lens, or on the soccer field coaching his daughter's soccer teams. Quinn can be found on social media @qsnyder, usually posting a mixture of technical content and his culinary creations.

About the Technical Reviewers

Bryan Byrne, CCIE No. 25607 (R&S), is a technical solutions architect in Cisco's Global Enterprise segment. With more than 20 years of data networking experience, his current focus is helping his customers transition from traditional LAN/WAN deployments toward Cisco's next-generation software-defined network solutions. Prior to joining Cisco, Bryan spent the first 13 years of his career in an operations role with a global service provider supporting large-scale IP DMVPN and MPLS networks. Bryan is a multitime Cisco Live Distinguished Speaker, covering topics on NETCONF, RESTCONF, and YANG. He is a proud graduate of The Ohio State University and currently lives outside Columbus, Ohio, with his wife, Lindsey, and their two children, Evan and Kaitlin.

Joe Clarke, CCIE No. 5384, is a Cisco Distinguished Customer Experience engineer. Joe has contributed to the development and adoption of many of Cisco's network operations and automation products and technologies. Joe evangelizes these programmability and automation skills in order to build the next generation of network engineers. Joe is a Distinguished Speaker at CiscoLive!, and is certified as a CCIE and a Cisco Certified DevNet Specialist (and a member of the elite DevNet 500). Joe provides network consulting and design support for the CiscoLive! and Internet Engineering Task Force (IETF) conference network infrastructure deployments. He also serves as co-chair of the Ops Area Working Group at the IETF. He is a coauthor of *Network Programmability with YANG: The Structure of Network Automation with YANG, NETCONF, RESTCONF, and gNMI* as well as a chapter coauthor in the Springer publication *Network-Embedded Management and Applications: Understanding Programmable Networking Infrastructure*. He is an alumnus of the University of Miami and holds a bachelor of science degree in computer science. Outside of Cisco, Joe is a commercial pilot, and he and his wife, Julia, enjoy flying around the east coast of the United States.

Dedications

Jason Davis:

When you set off to write a book, how do you quantify the time needed to study, write, and refine? You need time to obtain and configure the lab equipment for examples. There are still family, career, personal health, and welfare activities that demand attention. How can you plan when your job and a global health crisis demand the utmost in flexibility and focus? To all the family and supporters of writers, thank you; there should be a special place in heaven for you. I am indebted to my wife, Amy, and my children, Alyssa, Ryan, Micaela, and Maleah. You provided me with the time and space to do this, especially through the hardships of 2021. Finally, I am thankful that my God has provided opportunities and skills to impact technology in some small part and in a positive way; because He has shown His love for me in innumerable ways, I am motivated to share the same with others.

Hazim Dahir:

To my father, my favorite librarian: I wish this book could have made it to your shelf. I think of you every day. To my mother, with heartfelt gratitude for all your love, prayers, and guidance. I am a better person, husband, father, brother, and engineer because of you two.

To my amazing wife, Angela: no words or pages can grasp how indebted I am to you for your encouragement, patience, and wisdom.

To my children, Hala, Leila, and Zayd. I love watching you grow. Thank you for being such a joy. Never give up on your dreams.

To my sisters, Hana and Dina, and brother Gary. My team.

To Bill, Sylvia, and Karen Moseley. We can do this!

Stuart Clark:

This book is dedicated to my amazing Natalie (Mouse) and our son, Maddox, and our beloved dog, Bailey, who sadly passed while I was authoring this book. Without their love, support, and countless cups of coffee, this book would have never been possible. I would like to thank my father, George, and mother, Wendy Clark, for providing me with the work ethic I have today; and Natalie's father and mother, Frank and Barbara Thomas, for giving me my very first networking book and helping me transition into a new career. A big thank you to my mentors Mandy Whaley, Denise Fishburne, Joe Clarke, and my metaldevops brother Jason Gooley, who have helped and guided me for many years at Cisco.

Quinn Snyder:

Writing a book is an unknown unknown to a first-time author. You have read the products from others, but you don't know what you don't know when you set out to write your own. The only known you have is the support of the people behind you, who make it possible to think, to work, to create, and to inspire you. They are there for your late nights, the constant tapping of the keys, listening to you ramble on about what you've just put to paper. This book would not have been possible without the support of those behind me, propping me up, cheering me along, and believing in me. To my wife, Amanda, you are my rock—my biggest fan and supporter—and the one who has always believed in me, and I wouldn't have been able to do this without you. To my children, Nicolas and Madelyn, you have given me the space to create and do, and have inspired me to show you that anything is possible. To my mother, Cynthia, you have inspired a never-quit work ethic that sticks with me to this day. I thank you all for giving me those gifts, and I dedicate this book to you.

Acknowledgments

Jason Davis:
Most who know me understand that I appreciate telling stories, especially with humor. While that humor may not be recognized, it is mine nonetheless, so thank you to those who have endured it for years. I am thankful for the opportunity to pivot from writing blogs, whitepapers, and presentations to writing this book. It has been an exercise in patience and personal growth. The support team at Cisco Press—Nancy, Ellie, and Tonya—you've been great, valuable partners in this endeavor.

I am thankful to a cadre of supportive managers at Cisco over the years who helped me grow technically and professionally; Mike, Dave, Rich, and Ghaida, you have been awesome! Hazim, Stuart, and Quinn, thank you for joining me on this journey. Besides being wonderful coworkers, our collaboration, though separated by states and countries, has turned into friendship that has made a mark.

Hazim Dahir:
This book would not have been possible without two SUPER teams. The A Team: Jason, Stuart, and Quinn. Thank you for an amazing journey and expert work. "Technically," you complete me! And, the Cisco Press team: Nancy Davis, Ellie Bru, Tonya Simpson, and their teams. Thank you for all your help, guidance, and most importantly, your patience.

Special thanks go to Kaouther Abrougui for her contributions to the Security chapter, Mithun Baphana for his Webex contributions, and to David Wang for his Git contributions. Kaouther, Mithun, and David are experts in their fields, and we're lucky to have them join us.

Many thanks go to Firas Ahmed, for his encouragement, technical reviews, and support.

A great deal of gratitude goes to Hana Dahir, an engineer at heart, who reviewed various content for me.

I am very thankful to the following Cisco colleagues and leaders: Yenu Gobena, Saad Hasan, Carlos Pignataro, Jeff Apcar, Vijay Raghavendran, Ammar Rayes, Nancy Cam-Winget, and many others who supported me throughout my career and encouraged me to break barriers.

Stuart Clark:
Being a first-time author was such a daunting task, but the great people at Cisco Press, Nancy and Ellie; my coauthors, Hazim, Jason, and the BBQ Pit Master Quinn; technical reviewers, Joe Clarke and Bryan Byrne, kept me in check and supporting every chapter. A huge thank you to my leadership at DevNet—Matt Denapoli, Eric Thiel, and Grace Francisco—for always supporting my goals and ambitions. Janel Kratky, Kareem Iskander, and Hank Preston for their vast support and encouragement since joining the DevNet team in 2017. My dearest friends, Patrick Rockholz and Du'An Lightfoot, whose faith in me is always unfaltering.

Quinn Snyder:

I'd like to thank the crew at Cisco Press for wading through my incoherent ramblings and turning them into something worth reading. To Ellie and Nancy, thank you for the patience and dealing with my inane questions. To Joe Clarke, thank you for your technical expertise in the review process.

Thank you to my DevNet leaders—Grace, Eric, Matt, and Jeff—for bringing me into this amazing team and supporting my growth and development to make this work possible.

A special thanks to the guy who taught me "how to DA," John McDonough. You set me on a path for success and showed me the ropes, and for that I am grateful. To Kareem Iskander, thanks for just being there. You always have listened to me, picked me up, and pushed me forward. To my partners in crime (both with and without beards)—Jason, Hazim, and Stuart—you guys believed that I could and gave me a shot. I have appreciated our meetings, our late-night messaging sessions, and the friendship that has developed.

Finally, a special thank you to the man who guided me so many years ago, Barry Williams. Without your Cisco classes, your instruction, your belief, and never accepting "just good enough," I wouldn't have had the foundation that I do today. You helped a kid from rural Arizona see the big world and what was possible if I stuck with it, and because of that, I am where I am today.

Contents at a Glance

Online Elements

Reader Services

Other Features

Register your copy at www.ciscopress.com/title/9780137370443 for convenient access to downloads, updates, and corrections as they become available. To start the registration process, go to www.ciscopress.com/register and log in or create an account.* Enter the product ISBN **9780137370443** and click **Submit**. When the process is complete, you will find any available bonus content under Registered Products.

*Be sure to check the box that you would like to hear from us to receive exclusive discounts on future editions of this product.

Contents

Command Syntax Conventions

The conventions used to present command syntax in this book are the same conventions used in the IOS Command Reference. The Command Reference describes these conventions as follows:

- **Boldface** indicates commands and keywords that are entered literally as shown. In actual configuration examples and output (not general command syntax), boldface indicates commands that are manually input by the user (such as a **show** command).
- *Italic* indicates arguments for which you supply actual values.
- Vertical bars (|) separate alternative, mutually exclusive elements.
- Square brackets ([ ]) indicate an optional element.
- Braces ({ }) indicate a required choice.
- Braces within brackets ([{ }]) indicate a required choice within an optional element.

Introduction

This book was written to help candidates improve their network programmability and automation skills—not only for preparing to take the DevNet Professional DEVCOR 350-901 exam but also for real-world skills in any production environment.

You can expect that the blueprint for the DevNet Professional DEVCOR 350-901 exam tightly aligns with the topics contained in this book. This was by design. You can follow along with the examples in this book by utilizing the tools and resources found on the DevNet website and other free utilities such as Postman and Python.

We are targeting any and all learners who are learning these topics for the first time as well as those who wish to enhance their network programmability and automation skillset.

Be sure to visit www.cisco.com to find the latest information on DevNet Professional DEVCOR 350-901 exam requirements and to keep up to date on any new exams that are announced.

Goals and Methods

The most important and somewhat obvious goal of this book is to help you pass the DevNet Professional DEVCOR 350-901 exam. In fact, if the primary objective of this book were different, then the book's title would be misleading; however, the methods used in this book to help you pass the DevNet Professional exam are designed to also make you much more knowledgeable about how to do your job. Although this book and the companion website together have more than enough questions to help you prepare for the actual exam, the method in which they are used is not to simply make you memorize as many questions and answers as you possibly can.

One key methodology used in this book is to help you discover the exam topics that you need to review in more depth, to help you fully understand and remember those details, and to help you prove to yourself that you have retained your knowledge of those topics. So, this book does not try to help you pass by memorization but helps you truly learn and understand the topics. The DevNet Professional exam is just one of the foundation exams in the DevNet certification suite, and the knowledge contained within is vitally important to consider yourself a truly skilled network developer. This book would do you a disservice if it didn't attempt to help you learn the material. To that end, the book will help you pass the DevNet Professional exam by using the following methods:

- Helping you discover which test topics you have not mastered
- Providing explanations and information to fill in your knowledge gaps
- Supplying exercises and scenarios that enhance your ability to recall and deduce the answers to test questions

Who Should Read This Book?

This book is intended to help candidates prepare for the DevNet Professional DEVCOR 350-901 exam. Not only can this book help you pass the exam, but it can also help you learn the necessary topics to provide value to your organization as a network developer.

Passing the DevNet Professional DEVCOR 350-901 exam is a milestone toward becoming a better network developer, which, in turn, can help with becoming more confident with these technologies.

Strategies for Exam Preparation

The strategy you use for the DevNet Professional exam might be slightly different than strategies used by other readers, mainly based on the skills, knowledge, and experience you already have obtained.

Regardless of the strategy you use or the background you have, the book is designed to help you get to the point where you can pass the exam with the least amount of time required. However, many people like to make sure that they truly know a topic and thus read over material that they already know. Several book features will help you gain the confidence that you need to be convinced that you know some material already and to also help you know what topics you need to study more.

The Companion Website for Online Content Review

All the electronic review elements, as well as other electronic components of the book, exist on this book's companion website.

How to Access the Companion Website

To access the companion website, which gives you access to the electronic content with this book, start by establishing a login at www.ciscopress.com and registering your book. To do so, simply go to www.ciscopress.com/register and enter the ISBN of the print book: **9780137370443**. After you have registered your book, go to your account page and click the **Registered Products** tab. From there, click the **Access Bonus Content** link to get access to the book's companion website.

Note that if you buy the Premium Edition eBook and Practice Test version of this book from Cisco Press, your book will automatically be registered on your account page. Simply go to your account page, click the **Registered Products** tab, and select **Access Bonus Content** to access the book's companion website.

How to Access the Pearson Test Prep (PTP) App

You have two options for installing and using the Pearson Test Prep application: a web app and a desktop app. To use the Pearson Test Prep application, start by finding the registration code that comes with the book. You can find the code in these ways:

- **Print book:** Look in the cardboard sleeve in the back of the book for a piece of paper with your book's unique PTP code.
- **Premium Edition:** If you purchase the Premium Edition eBook and Practice Test directly from the Cisco Press website, the code will be populated on your account page after purchase. Just log in at www.ciscopress.com, click **Account** to see details of your account, and click the **Digital Purchases** tab.
- **Amazon Kindle:** For those who purchase a Kindle edition from Amazon, the access code will be supplied directly from Amazon.
- **Other Bookseller eBooks:** Note that if you purchase an eBook version from any other source, the practice test is not included because other vendors to date have not chosen to vend the required unique access code.

NOTE Do not lose the activation code because it is the only means with which you can access the QA content with the book.

When you have the access code, to find instructions about both the PTP web app and the desktop app, follow these steps:

Step 1. Open this book's companion website, as shown earlier in this Introduction under the heading "How to Access the Companion Website."

Step 2. Click the **Practice Exams** button.

Step 3. Follow the instructions listed there both for installing the desktop app and for using the web app.

Note that if you want to use the web app only at this point, just navigate to www.pearsontestprep.com, establish a free login if you do not already have one, and register this book's practice tests using the registration code you just found. The process should take only a couple of minutes.

NOTE Amazon eBook (Kindle) customers: It is easy to miss Amazon's email that lists your PTP access code. Soon after you purchase the Kindle eBook, Amazon should send an email. However, the email uses very generic text and makes no specific mention of PTP or practice exams. To find your code, read every email from Amazon after you purchase the book. Also do the usual checks for ensuring your email arrives, like checking your spam folder.

NOTE Other eBook customers: As of the time of publication, only the publisher and Amazon supply PTP access codes when you purchase their eBook editions of this book.

How to Use This Book

Although this book could be read cover-to-cover, it is designed to be flexible and allow you to easily move between chapters and sections of chapters to cover just the material that you need more work with. This book was written to include not only reference materials and study guides for the exam but also rich reference material for your day-to-day technical requirements.

The core chapters, Chapters 1 through 17, cover the following topics:

- **Chapter 1, "Software Development Essentials":** This chapter introduces software architecture, architecture requirements, and software development models.
- **Chapter 2, "Software Quality Attributes":** This chapter discusses in detail quality attributes or nonfunctional requirements and discusses in detail modularity, scalability, and high availability in application design.
- **Chapter 3, "Architectural Considerations and Performance Management":** This chapter continues to discuss another set of nonfunctional requirements and how they relate to design trade-offs. It discusses performance, observability, and database selection criteria.
- **Chapter 4, "Version Control and Release Management with Git":** This chapter discusses the basics of version control, Git's way of managing version controls and collaboration, and then covers in detail branching strategies and why they're important for the success of any project.
- **Chapter 5, "Network APIs":** This chapter covers how software developers can use application programming interfaces (APIs) to communicate with and configure networks and how APIs are used to communicate with applications and other software.
- **Chapter 6, "API Development":** This chapter focuses on application programming interface development and covers both API design and API architecture.
- **Chapter 7, "Application Deployment":** This chapter covers the code-to-production process, including organizational structures, responsibilities, and tooling required. Historical as well as current deployment models are discussed, as well as design factors to enable portable applications between hosting locations.
- **Chapter 8, "Security in Application Design":** This chapter discusses security practices for application development. It starts by defining privacy and personally identifiable information and how to protect them. Then it covers the public key infrastructure (PKI), how to secure web applications, and the OAuth Authorization framework.

- **Chapter 9, "Infrastructure":** This chapter covers aspects of network infrastructure management and automation. Some historical context is provided, but exam preparation is focused on newer programmability features that enable automation and orchestration.
- **Chapter 10, "Automation":** This chapter covers topics such as SDN, APIs, and orchestration. Additional helpful context is provided around the impact to IT service management.
- **Chapter 11, "NETCONF and RESTCONF":** This chapter covers the NETCONF, YANG, and RESTCONF technologies with examples that will be helpful in your preparation and professional use.
- **Chapter 12, "Model-Driven Telemetry":** This chapter is focused on model-driven telemetry, its purpose, and how it is implemented. In support of your learning, exam preparation, and professional use, there are also examples for using MDT.
- **Chapter 13, "Open-Source Solutions":** This chapter covers several open-source solutions that are helpful in many environments. Examples for deployment and usage provide insight and help inform your implementation decisions.
- **Chapter 14, "Software Configuration Management":** This chapter discusses software configuration management: what is it, why is it important, and how do you decide which system is best for your project? We also discuss Ansible and Terraform and their strengths and weaknesses.
- **Chapter 15, "Hosting an Application on a Network Device":** This chapter provides insights on how to run containerized workloads on a network device. Some best practices are also shared to encourage your best uses.
- **Chapter 16, "Cisco Platforms":** Finally, this chapter contains a mix of practical API and SDK usage examples across several platforms, such as Webex, Meraki, Intersight, DNA Center, and AppDynamics. If you have some of these solutions, the examples should reveal methods to integrate with them programmatically. If you don't use the platforms, this chapter should reveal the "art of the possible."
- **Chapter 17, "Final Preparation":** This chapter details a set of tools and a study plan to help you complete your preparation for the DEVCOR 350-901 exam.

Certification Exam Topics and This Book

The questions for each certification exam are a closely guarded secret. However, we do know which topics you must know to *successfully* complete this exam. Cisco publishes them as an exam blueprint for the DevNet Professional DEVCOR 350-901 exam. Table I-1 lists each exam topic listed in the blueprint along with a reference to the book chapter that covers the topic. These are the same topics you should be proficient in when working with network programmability and automation in the real world.

Table I-1 DEVCOR 350-901 Exam Topics and Chapter References

DEVCOR 350-901 Exam Topic	Chapter(s) in Which Topic Is Covered
1.0 Software Development and Design	Chapter 1
1.1 Describe distributed applications related to the concepts of front-end, back-end, and load balancing	Chapter 2
1.2 Evaluate an application design considering scalability and modularity	Chapter 2
1.3 Evaluate an application design considering high availability and resiliency (including on-premises, hybrid, and cloud)	Chapter 2
1.4 Evaluate an application design considering latency and rate limiting	Chapter 3
1.5 Evaluate an application design and implementation considering maintainability	Chapter 3
1.6 Evaluate an application design and implementation considering observability	Chapter 3
1.7 Diagnose problems with an application given logs related to an event	Chapter 3
1.8 Evaluate choice of database types with respect to application requirements (such as relational, document, graph, columnar, and time series)	Chapter 3
1.9 Explain architectural patterns (monolithic, services oriented, microservices, and event driven)	Chapter 2
1.10 Utilize advanced version control operations with Git 1.10.a Merge a branch 1.10.b Resolve conflicts 1.10.c git reset 1.10.d git checkout 1.10.e git revert	Chapter 4
1.11 Explain the concepts of release packaging and dependency management	Chapter 4
1.12 Construct a sequence diagram that includes API calls	Chapter 5
2.0 Using APIs	Chapter 5
2.1 Implement robust REST API error handling for timeouts and rate limits	Chapter 6
2.2 Implement control flow of consumer code for unrecoverable REST API errors	Chapter 6
2.3 Identify ways to optimize API usage through HTTP cache controls	Chapter 6
2.4 Construct an application that consumes a REST API that supports pagination	Chapter 6
2.5 Describe the steps in the OAuth2 three-legged authorization code grant flow	Chapter 8

DEVCOR 350-901 Exam Topic	Chapter(s) in Which Topic Is Covered
3.0 Cisco Platforms	Chapter 16
3.1 Construct API requests to implement ChatOps with Webex Teams API	Chapter 16
3.2 Construct API requests to create and delete objects using Firepower device management (FDM)	Chapter 16
3.3 Construct API requests using the Meraki platform to accomplish these tasks 3.3.a Use Meraki Dashboard APIs to enable an SSID 3.3.b Use Meraki location APIs to retrieve location data	Chapter 16
3.4 Construct API calls to retrieve data from Intersight	Chapter 16
3.5 Construct a Python script using the UCS APIs to provision a new UCS server given a template	Chapter 16
3.6 Construct a Python script using the Cisco DNA Center APIs to retrieve and display wireless health information	Chapter 16
3.7 Describe the capabilities of AppDynamics when instrumenting an application	Chapter 16
3.8 Describe steps to build a custom dashboard to present data collected from Cisco APIs	Chapter 16
4.0 Application Deployment and Security	Chapter 8
4.1 Diagnose a CI/CD pipeline failure (such as missing dependency, incompatible versions of components, and failed tests)	Chapter 7
4.2 Integrate an application into a prebuilt CD environment leveraging Docker and Kubernetes	Chapter 7
4.3 Describe the benefits of continuous testing and static code analysis in a CI pipeline	Chapter 7
4.4 Utilize Docker to containerize an application	Chapter 15
4.5 Describe the tenets of the “12-factor app”	Chapter 7
4.6 Describe an effective logging strategy for an application	Chapter 7
4.7 Explain data privacy concerns related to storage and transmission of data	Chapter 8
4.8 Identify the secret storage approach relevant to a given scenario	Chapter 8
4.9 Configure application specific SSL certificates	Chapter 8
4.10 Implement mitigation strategies for OWASP threats (such as XSS, CSRF, and SQL injection)	Chapter 8
4.11 Describe how end-to-end encryption principles apply to APIs	Chapter 8

DEVCOR 350-901 Exam Topic	Chapter(s) in Which Topic Is Covered
5.0 Infrastructure and Automation	Chapters 9 and 10
5.1 Explain considerations of model-driven telemetry (including data consumption and data storage)	Chapter 12
5.2 Utilize RESTCONF to configure a network device including interfaces, static routes, and VLANs (IOS XE only)	Chapter 11
5.3 Construct a workflow to configure network parameters with: 5.3.a Ansible playbook 5.3.b Puppet manifest	Chapter 13
5.4 Identify a configuration management solution to achieve technical and business requirements	Chapter 14
5.5 Describe how to host an application on a network device (including Catalyst 9000 and Cisco IOx-enabled devices)	Chapter 15

Each version of the exam can have topics that emphasize different functions or features, and some topics can be rather broad and generalized. The goal of this book is to provide the most comprehensive coverage to ensure that you are well prepared for the exam. Although some chapters might not address specific exam topics, they provide a foundation that is necessary for a clear understanding of important topics. Your short-term goal might be to pass this exam, but your long-term goal should be to become a qualified network developer.

It is also important to understand that this book is a "static" reference, whereas the exam topics are dynamic. Cisco can and does change the topics covered on certification exams often.

This exam guide should not be your only reference when preparing for the certification exam. You can find a wealth of information available at Cisco.com that covers each topic in great detail. If you think that you need more detailed information on a specific topic, read the Cisco documentation that focuses on that topic.

Note that as automation technologies continue to develop, Cisco reserves the right to change the exam topics without notice. Although you can refer to the list of exam topics in Table I-1, always check Cisco.com to verify the actual list of topics to ensure that you are prepared before taking the exam. You can view the current exam topics on any current Cisco certification exam by visiting the Cisco.com website, choosing Menu, and Training & Events, then selecting from the Certifications list. Note also that, if needed, Cisco Press might post additional preparatory content on the web page associated with this book at http://www.ciscopress.com/title/9780137370443. It's a good idea to check the website a couple of weeks before taking your exam to be sure that you have up-to-date content.

Credits

Figure 4-1 through Figure 4-29, Figure 4-32 through Figure 4-34, Figure 6-8, Figure 6-9, Figure 11-10, Figure 11-11, Figure 12-6, Figure 12-27, Figure 12-28: GitHub, Inc

Figure 5-3 through Figure 5-6, Figure 6-10, Figure 6-11, Figure 6-13: IMDb-API

Figure 5-8, Figure 11-14 through Figure 11-19, Figure 16-16 through Figure 16-19, Figure 16-31, Figure 16-41 through Figure 16-43: Postman, Inc

Figure 6-1 through Figure 6-7: SmartBear Software

Figure 7-3 through Figure 7-5: HootSuite Media Inc

Figure 7-7, Figure 7-8: Weaveworks, Inc

Figure 7-10, Figure 7-11: Jupyter

Figure 7-9, Figure 7-12 through Figure 7-16: Amazon Web Services, Inc

Figure 8-7 through Figure 8-10: DigiCert, Inc

Figure 9-3: Coleman Yuen/Pearson Education Asia Limited

Figure 9-5: vystekimages/Shutterstock

Figure 9-7: faithie/123RF

Figures 9-13 and 9-14, arm icons: De-V/Shutterstock

Figure 10-2: Twitter, Inc

Figure 10-3: Natata/Shutterstock

Figure 10-4: Rawpixel.com/Shutterstock

Figure 10-5: Andrey_Popov/Shutterstock

Figure 10-7 icons: Sergii Korolko/Shutterstock, Vitaly Korovin/Shutterstock, Gazlast/Shutterstock, dodi31/Shutterstock, Stokkete/Shutterstock, Pavel Ignatov/Shutterstock

Figure 10-12: Tribalium/Shutterstock, KJBevan/Shutterstock

Figure 12-21 through Figure 12-25, Figure E-1, Figure E-2: Grafana Labs

Logo in Figure 13-3: Puppet

Figure 13-5: Puppet

Figure 13-6, Figure 14-6 through Figure 14-8: HashiCorp

Figure 16-44, Figure 16-45: AppDynamics

Table 2-2: Permission to reproduce extracts from British Standards is granted by BSI Standards Limited (BSI). No other use of this material is permitted. British Standards can be obtained in PDF or hard copy formats from the BSI online shop: https://shop.bsigroup.com/.

CHAPTER 1

Software Development Essentials

This chapter covers the following topics:

- **A Brief History of the Future:** This section covers network management evolution from basic monitoring to automation and orchestration of complex infrastructures and applications.
- **Software Architecture and Design:** This section covers the basics of software architecture definitions and terminologies.
- **Architecture Requirements:** This section covers functional and nonfunctional requirements and how they affect the overall design.
- **Architectural Patterns:** This section covers common application architectural patterns and their advantages and usage criteria.
- **Software Development Lifecycle (SDLC) Approach:** This section covers SDLC and the basics of the software design, development, testing, and deployment lifecycle.
- **Software Development Models:** This section describes various models like Agile and Waterfall.
- **Architecture and Code Reviews:** This section describes several types of code review, including peer and stakeholder reviews.
- **Software Testing:** This section covers the various types of software testing.

As you start your journey toward DEVCOR certification, it is important to understand that you will be building software for the purpose of automating operational functions that consume several human hours. What you build and automate will be used to reduce human hours and errors while providing a consistent way of conducting various tasks.

In this chapter, we first discuss software development and design in the context of IT operational functions, and then attempt to briefly describe how we got here and why. In addition, we want you to understand the software development concepts from a network domain expertise perspective. We also focus on the architecture design and delivery lifecycle of software products. The keyword here, after design, is *delivery*, which encompasses all aspects of building, testing, and releasing software products. This chapter sets the stage with a brief description of the lifecycle and various processes that most organizations follow to develop, test, and maintain software.

"Do I Know This Already?" Quiz

The "Do I Know This Already?" quiz allows you to assess whether you should read this entire chapter thoroughly or jump to the "Exam Preparation Tasks" section. If you are in doubt about your answers to these questions or your own assessment of your knowledge of the topics, read the entire chapter. Table 1-1 lists the major headings in this chapter and their corresponding "Do I Know This Already?" quiz questions. You can find the answers in Appendix A, "Answers to the 'Do I Know This Already?' Quizzes."

Table 1-1 "Do I Know This Already?" Section-to-Question Mapping

Foundation Topics Section	Questions
A Brief History of the Future	7
Software Architecture and Design	1
Architecture Requirements	3
Architectural Patterns	10
Software Development Lifecycle (SDLC) Approach	2
Software Development Models	4–6
Architecture and Code Reviews	9
Software Testing	8

1. What is software architecture?
   a. A set of structures explaining the software
   b. The components or building blocks and their relations
   c. The single source of truth for all business requirements related to the software being developed
   d. All of these answers are correct.
2. What is SDLC?
   a. Synchronous data link control
   b. Software development lifecycle
   c. Social data language controller
   d. None of these answers are correct.
3. Why do you need functional requirements?
   a. To understand the functionality and business requirements of the application you're building
   b. To specify high availability requirements
   c. To specify development methodology
   d. All of these answers are correct.
4. Which of the following is a type of nonfunctional requirement?
   a. Scalability
   b. Modularity
   c. High availability
   d. All of these answers are correct.
5. How is the Agile software development model different from the waterfall model?
   a. It has individual stages.
   b. It has a higher degree of flexibility and speed.
   c. It has possibly multiple teams working independently with limited collaboration.
   d. All of these answers are correct.

6. Which of the following principles is *not* associated with the Lean software development model?
   a. Fast and frequent value delivery
   b. Continuous learning and innovation
   c. Team empowerment
   d. Holistic, upfront planning
7. Which of the following metrics does DevOps use to assess performance?
   a. Deployment frequency
   b. Lead time
   c. Change volume
   d. All of these answers are correct.
8. Unit testing is considered a type of
   a. Black-box testing conducted with no knowledge of the system
   b. Gray-box testing conducted with some knowledge of the system
   c. White-box testing conducted with full knowledge of the system
   d. None of these answers are correct.
9. An important aspect of software quality assurance is peer code review, which may be looking at
   a. Functionality
   b. Complexity of code
   c. Naming conventions
   d. All of these answers are correct.
10. Why do you need architectural patterns?
   a. Architectural patterns introduce complexity and give the impression of sophisticated programming skills.
   b. Architectural patterns ensure consistency of the code because it is a reusable solution to a commonly occurring problem within a given context.
   c. There so many patterns, and you have to choose one.
   d. All of these answers are correct.

Foundation Topics

A Brief History of the Future

Some of us started programming out of necessity, some out of the desire to simplify routine tasks, some saw an opportunity to improve life around them, and some wanted that job. No matter how you got here, you're now an application developer looking to automate the configuration and orchestration of simple and complex tasks. Over the last few years, a great deal of change has affected the software development world—not necessarily related to software programming as much as it relates to the why, how, and where. The logic, we like to believe, stayed intact. In addition, recent advances in processes in hardware, CPU, and memory and the significant reduction in price point brought an abundance of processing power to a large number of people globally. In return, these changes broke down many barriers and introduced the world to millions of new software developers and a great deal of innovation that accompanied them.

We also like to differentiate between a *software engineer* and a *software developer*. Simply put, we're differentiating between *design* and *execution*, respectively. We think of the software engineer as the person who takes a problem, breaks it down, proposes a solution based on requirements and quality trade-offs, builds an architecture that solves the problem, and then executes a strategy for making that solution happen. The software developer, on the other hand, is a team member of the execution team. Don't get us wrong; there is a lot of creativity in execution, and the differentiation between an engineer and a developer is not meant to show preference or hierarchy.

The Evolution

Many books have been written about the evolution of software development and the many revolutions that have affected various aspects of humanity: engineering, business, health care, and so on. The evolution we want to discuss here is the one that relates to the network and the various tasks for building and managing one. It is also about running a business. How can you bring flexibility to a network, application, and processes to help run your business?

As we discuss the relationship between software development and managing a business, we want to discuss the ever-continuing evolution that has got us here. Without putting timelines and designating specific years as the beginning or end of something, we go through a quick and yet necessary journey of the past to justify (and prepare for) the future.

In the beginning, networks and systems were limited to the four walls of the enterprise. The majority of management tasks were limited to the capabilities provided by the vendor, and some of those were even proprietary. That paradigm was bad for interoperability and simplicity of operations.

Those capabilities mainly were for status and simple configuration and customization functions. Then Simple Network Management Protocol (SNMP) adoption increased, and there was a standard model where an "agent" running on the "managed" system used a standard protocol to communicate with a "manager" or "management server." The adoption of SNMP and network management systems (NMS) provided increased efficiency in network operations and, subsequently, provided some relief for the system administrator who used to configure and maintain various systems individually.

Shortly after, the International Organization for Standardization (ISO) introduced the FCAPS model, which stands for Fault, Configuration, Accounting, Performance, and Security. The FCAPS model provided a standard way for defining and assessing the functions of network management. Security in the form of privilege assignment and information masking was an essential addition as organizations grew in size and grew the adoption of technology, not to forget the staff (internal and external) that manages the growth.

As we discuss the network management evolution that brought software development to the network, we cannot ignore the network's evolution. The network experienced new developments and pressures to expand into remote campuses or branches and to support higher bandwidths reliably for voice and video integration. In addition, as we deployed additional management and visibility systems, we were quick to see clear inefficiencies in the design and utilization of the network.

For example, we saw that 70+ percent of our servers were running at 25 percent utilization of CPU and memory—hence, the birth of "virtualization" and the introduction of another management layer. With virtualization, we were able to improve efficiency at the server level, and we saw that it was good for performance and also for business. Then we moved back to the network and also virtualized it and its main functions, such as routers, switches, firewalls, and load balancers, and we're still doing it.

Having virtualized the majority of the enterprise IT functions, we started observing "ownership" issues: who owns what and who's responsible for where? Why? As the control (or ownership) boundaries were quickly dissolving, it was clear that traditional network management capabilities (and the traditional network manager) were not fully equipped or fast enough to match the speed of business.

The traditional network operations center (NOC) that kept an eye on the network and business applications needed to evolve as well. It needed to utilize software development techniques and technologies to detect network issues better, alert the right people, and possibly take action.

Eventually, we moved up the stack and started looking at business processes and workflows, and through virtualization and APIs, we were able to automate the full enterprise stack and merge (consolidate) the various functions of the enterprise business process management into a single team. The business application developers wanted flexibility deploying their code as frequently as the business desired; the network and systems managers wanted to ensure a higher degree of availability and stability.

Automation, Orchestration, and DevOps

Having the tools to virtualize and multiply resources (e.g., one to many) created the need and the opportunity to empower traditional management tools with new and advanced capabilities. We moved beyond monitoring and alerts into automation of provisioning and eventually into the area of automation of provisioning and orchestration.

Figure 1-1 summarizes the past and gives a simple idea about the evolution of automation and orchestration. This diagram might not fully represent the journey; however, it does describe the various components taking us from monitoring and "reacting" to proactive network improvement, all the way to automation and orchestration. The evolution was simple and fueled by the need for the network operations to be super-efficient and to be able to keep up with the speed of the business. The journey started with simple monitoring of various functions using continuous polling of elements, or "objects," and displaying them in red or green on a management screen. Based on this, we went into the "reactive" mode to investigate the issue and subsequently scheduling a change window to fix the issue. Shortly after that, we attempted to model the network and specific behaviors using the correlation of configuration files from network devices. This type of modeling served its purpose by allowing us to detect gaps in the configuration and architecture before deployment. Understandably, this modeling type also had gaps in modeling interactions beyond the ISO Layer 2 and 3 parameters.

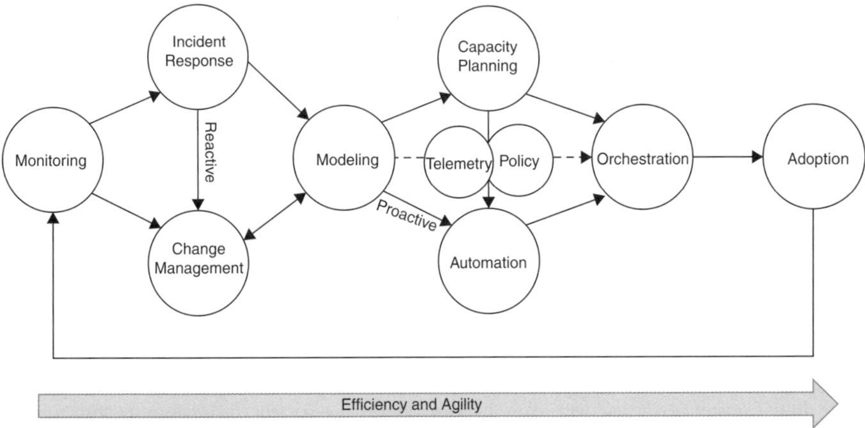

Figure 1-1 *From Monitoring to Automated Orchestration*

With recent advancements in telemetry and programmability, it is much easier to model, predict, and orchestrate the adoption of features and configurations adhering to business functions and operational policies.

The more we represented network functions in software, the easier it became to manage and control them. The better the control, the easier it was to rapidly adapt to situations. The term *situations* here refers to a variety of conditions affecting the proper operation of the network. This could easily mean network outages, security events, hardware/software upgrades, expansions, decommissioning of devices, acquisitions, mergers—anything that affects the business.

It is also worth mentioning that advances in the networking operating systems facilitated a lot of this transition or transformation. Advancements in software-defined networking (SDN) concepts and the separation of the control and data planes allowed us to create and delete networks on the fly, and based on immediate demand, choose optimum paths, create security boundaries, enhance application performance, all with the click of a button.

But wait, aren't we forgetting something? What about the culture?

All enterprises liked the idea of automation for the efficiency and agility it brought to the business, and they wanted that "standardized" approach to managing their IT operations, but what about the cultural paradigm shift and the new processes? This is where the concept of DevOps, which creates and manages the network automation mindset, evolved from.

Without going into too much detail about DevOps and its own evolution, we can safely say that now when the network has become "software functions" or "software-driven," DevOps concepts highlight and manage the relationships among the following functions and personas:

- Application developers
- Network services architects or developers
- Network operations engineers
- Customer or business requirements

The key DevOps practices include the following:

- **Continuous integration/continuous delivery (CI/CD):**
  - Continuous integration and continuous delivery reduce the time required to update or deliver software while improving quality.
  - Continuous integration improves efficiency by allowing team members to work on modules independently before integrating components in a common build area.
  - Continuous delivery (continuous deployment) ensures quality by testing builds in a production environment.
- **Automating processes:**
  - Reduce human error and improve the responsiveness of the development environment.
  - Standardize processes for easy replication.
  - Reduce costs on maintenance, upgrades, or capital expenditures.
  - Shorten lifecycle of software development by reducing implementation time.
  - Improve reliability and reusability of components.
- **Establishing a DevOps culture:**
  - Creates a cultural shift by combining development and IT operations.
  - Facilitates communication among teams.
  - Introduces smaller projects with increased collaboration.
  - Promotes DevOps talent (DevOps engineering team).
  - Utilizes common tools for shared data.
- **Measuring DevOps teams and efforts using the following sample metrics:**
  - Deployment frequency.
  - Change failure rate.
  - Lead time.
  - Change volume.
  - Trouble tickets and service requests.
  - Mean time to recovery (MTTR).

DevOps includes multiple concepts that we cover in the following chapters with clear guidance and examples. The next few sections introduce how to go about building software satisfying your operations.

Software Architecture and Design

Architecture is not unique to software, engineering, or even technology as a whole. It is an essential practice for building anything. It provides the roadmap or blueprint for all elements, and it helps justify various decisions taken through the journey. While building any software or any system, you will find yourself making individual decisions or shortcuts, and you must make sure that those decisions adhere to a set of principles and do not affect the overall goal of the system. In the following few sections, we give you a primer of **software architecture** and all related design pieces that must come together.

Architecture is one of the most critical aspects of building almost anything. Without it, you cannot transform an idea into a product or align a product with a business problem. Architecture, especially a well-documented one, allows you to understand the question, how it relates to the business, and envision a solution that satisfies business requirements.

Of course, various architectures and factors influence and possibly govern software architecture in a business or enterprise environment. For example, the software you're about to design here will be used to perform a task within a system, and that system is built using a collection of software programs that represent a business function within the enterprise. Figure 1-2 is for illustration purposes only, and to make a specific point about software architecture and how it may differ from a system architecture or enterprise architecture.

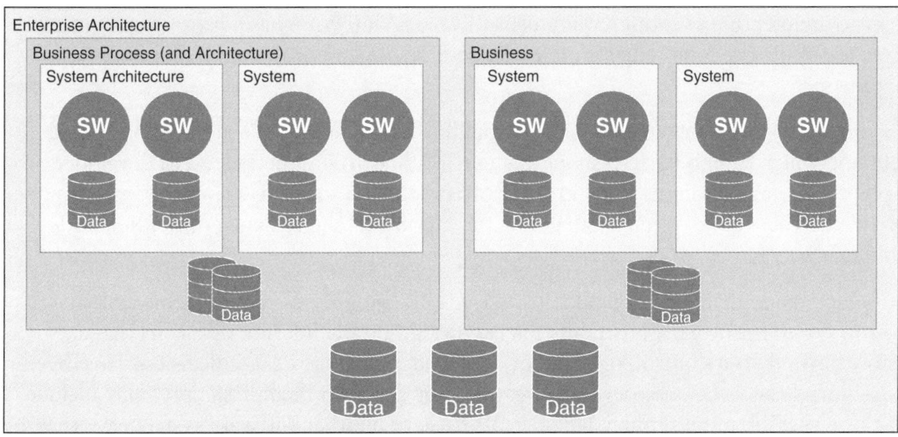

Figure 1-2 *Sample Representation of High-Level Architecture*

I've always liked the simplicity of the software architecture definition given by Carnegie Mellon Software Engineering Institute (SEI) shown in *Software Architecture in Practice*, 4th Edition by Bass et al.:

> The software architecture of a system is the set of structures needed to reason about the system, which comprise software elements, relations among them, and properties of both.

For example, the purpose of Figure 1-2 is to illustrate that the software you're trying to architect has clear relationships (and dependency) on other software as well as on data sources and targets (storage or databases). The relationships can be localized to the system or cross boundaries to other systems or business processes within the enterprise. The relationships among the various components may require different data formats, connectors, and other types of translations that allow heterogeneous systems to communicate or exchange data. You can find more details in Chapter 2, "Software Quality Attributes."

In general, architecture defines the organization of the system, all components, their relationships, interactions, dependencies, and the requirements and principles governing the design. It is also a source of truth when it comes to agreed-upon requirements and design principles, especially as exceptions are made or changes are requested. It also serves as a communication vehicle among stakeholders.

In the next few sections, we look at a few concept frameworks regarding how software is conceptualized, developed, tested, reviewed, and maintained. We follow the general foundational direction by looking at

- Software requirements
- Development lifecycle
- Code review
- Testing
- Version control

The remainder of the book handles these topics with examples and specific use cases.

Architecture Requirements

There is no architecture without requirements. Every architecture has a list of requirements it strives to fulfill. The requirements are discussed, documented, and agreed upon by all stakeholders.

When you're designing software, it is often tough to evaluate how the application should be built and which design pattern should be used. While your experience as a developer and acceptable practices come in handy, it is often better to start objectively by collecting requirements. There are two main categories for capturing requirements: *functional* and *nonfunctional*.

It is not uncommon to see an organization use a third category of requirements called *constraints* or *limitations*. Constraints refer to design or architecture decisions that are somehow beyond your control, or unnegotiable. Some of those design decisions have been previously made and you, as a developer, have to comply with them. Examples may include the use of a specific programming language, the use of another software system (external to your organization), interoperability with a specific system, or possibly, workload movement with a specific cloud provider. We focus on the main two categories.

Functional requirements specify "what" the software in question should do. They describe the functionalities of a system, such as

- Business process
- Data manipulation
- User interaction
- Media processing
- Calculation or computation of data
- Administrative functions

- Audits, reports, and tracking
- Historical data handling, retention, storage, and retrieval
- Compliance or certifications (if any)
- Or any other action that the system can or should perform

Functional requirements can be measured in "yes" or "no" terms and usually include the words *shall* or *can*. For example, some functional requirements for a document editing web application would be

- Users can access documents through a web GUI.
- Users can create, edit, and delete documents.
- Users can save documents to a local drive.
- Users can restore documents to a previous version.
- The administrator can create and delete users.
- Documents can be sent via a GUI to other users.

In addition, there is the concept of nonfunctional requirements. The **nonfunctional requirements** tell you *how* a system should perform those actions or functions. They describe how fast the system should be or how scalable it must be. Nonfunctional requirements are mainly concerned with

- Performance
- Scalability
- High availability
- Modularity
- Interoperability
- Serviceability
- Testability
- Security
- And many more

As you can see from the list, these values are also thought of as the quality attributes of the system. They are often expressed in words like *must* and *should* and are commonly measured over an interval or a range.

NOTE There is always some kind of a trade-off among nonfunctional requirements when considering the final design. Nonfunctional requirements must be considered as a group because they will, most certainly, affect each other. For example, increasing scalability may negatively affect performance.

A few examples of nonfunctional requirements are

- The system should be able to handle 10,000 new sessions concurrently.
- The system should be available at least 99.999 percent of the time.
- The web GUI should take less than two seconds to load.
- Users are required to register before they can use the system.
- Passwords must not show anywhere in the logs or the GUI.
- The GUI system can be translated into all other languages.

When writing the nonfunctional requirements of your system, avoid using nonspecific words. Instead of writing that "the request must be fast," write "the request must be completed in under 300 milliseconds (300 ms)." Instead of "the GUI must be user-friendly," say something like "the GUI must respond in under 500 ms, and the user shall be able to access all main functionalities from the home screen."

Functional and nonfunctional requirements are closely related, and it certainly does not matter where you start the requirement capturing process. In our experience, it is a case-by-case situation. For example, if we were starting a new innovative type of project, we always started at the functional requirement level. However, in other projects where we were reinventing the wheel, and the essence of the project was to build software that superseded or replaced existing software, we tended to start by looking at nonfunctional requirements first. Any way you look at it, at the end of the day, both types of requirements need to be captured in a single document. We just cannot think of any normal situation where a developer is concerned with only one set of requirements. Table 1-2 gives a few examples of differences between the two types.

Table 1-2 Simple Comparison Between Functional and Nonfunctional Requirements

Functional	Nonfunctional
Use case or business process specific	System quality attribute specific
Mandatory	Not mandatory/affected by trade-offs
Functionality specific	Performance or quality specific
User requirements	User experience
Test for functionality	Test for performance, security, etc.
Describe as *can* or *shall*	Describe as *must* or *should*

Another interesting way to look at it is that we would argue that businesses are measured by the revenue they generate, which can be attributed to their success in their business area. In this case, business requirements (that fall under functional requirements) are prioritized.

But what about business requirements that verge on the edge of nonfunctional requirements—for example, scalability and security for a cloud service provider?

As with most things, it is crucial to evaluate requirements to see which ones should be prioritized and which ones impact your application the most. Product owners may focus purely on functional requirements, and it may be up to the development team to take ownership of nonfunctional requirements.

To consider the impact that a requirement has on application quality, assess the requirement by identifying the requirement and creating user stories (for example, users need to have a good experience while browsing), then determining the measurable criteria (for example, round-trip time should be under 500 ms), and finally, identifying the impact (for example, users will not visit your site if it is too slow).

Functional Requirements

Functional requirements are designed to be read by a general, not necessarily technical, audience. Therefore, they are often derived from *user stories*. User stories are short descriptions of functionalities, as seen from the end-user perspective. They focus more on how users interact with the system and what they expect the goal of the interaction to be, rather than what the system does, but because the software is often very domain-specific, they help you to understand the system better as a developer. You will see how significant the user stories are when we discuss the Agile development approach.

Another concept used in the formulation of functional requirements is the *use case*. In contrast to user stories, use cases focus less on a user's interaction and more on the cause and effect of actions. If a user story stated, "A user can save documents by clicking Save," the related use case would state, "When the Save button is clicked, the current document is saved to the server's NoSQL database and to the client's local cache."

Functional requirements should

- Be very concise and to the point. Don't use vague language.
- Be testable.
- Clearly define who is allowed to perform certain actions or access data.
- Fully cover every scenario, including what the system should *not* do.
- Include complete information about data flow in and out of the system.
- Contain only a single functionality per requirement

When you're gathering requirements, consider the business, administrative, user, and system requirements. Business requirements are high-level requirements from a business perspective, such as the users being able to log in with credentials from an existing application. Administrative requirements take care of routine actions, such as logging every change made to a document. User requirements contain the desired outcome of certain actions, like the creation of a new document. System requirements describe software and hardware specifications, like a specific error code being returned when an unauthorized user tries to access a document that is not theirs.

Nonfunctional Requirements

Nonfunctional requirements specify the quality attributes or *technical requirements* of the system. They are more related to the system's architecture than its functionalities and are often constraints on the technical properties of a system. Nonfunctional requirements are often very technical and less thought about than functional requirements. Although functional requirements are commonly defined with the project's stakeholders' help and are more specific, nonfunctional requirements are more implicit and sometimes just assumed. An example of an assumed but not commonly listed nonfunctional requirement is a short loading time for a web page (for example, less than two seconds). Another example of an assumed nonfunctional requirement is a sudden change of underlying technology due to lower licensing costs. If modularity is not included as a nonfunctional requirement from the beginning, this change can cause big delays.

For those reasons, compiling a list of nonfunctional requirements often does not fall on you and your team as software designers or architects. In contrast to functional requirements, which are often isolated features that a single developer can work on, nonfunctional requirements can span the entire application or system and must be considered by all the developers working on the project.

Not all nonfunctional requirements can be implemented and tested at the same time. For example, although a requirement for portability can be considered at the beginning of the implementation, full performance efficiency tests cannot be satisfied until the code is running in an actual production environment. Not all nonfunctional requirements should be taken into consideration when developing because it is easy to go overboard. For example, a web page probably does not need to have 99.999 percent availability and use enterprise-grade security.

Because many different nonfunctional requirements exist, the choice of which nonfunctional requirements to emphasize can have a major impact on further development. Too many nonfunctional requirements can make application development an incredibly long and complicated process, and too few nonfunctional requirements can create an application that does what it is supposed to do but is very slow, insecure, and costly to maintain. In Chapter 2, we cover nonfunctional requirements and quality attributes in greater detail.

Architectural Patterns

Sometimes, the topic of architectural patterns is a philosophical discussion because different patterns have different strengths and usage contexts. Some allow for easier integration; some allow for easier usability. One easy definition we once saw on Wikipedia goes like this:

> An architectural pattern is a general, reusable solution to a commonly occurring problem in software architecture within a given context.

We like this simple definition. The *context*, or the paradigm, is the key word here. It relates to the organization's enterprise architecture and defines the software design schema to be followed. Having a defined pattern allows for collaboration and onboarding of new project participants without jeopardizing efficiency or productivity of the project. In this section we briefly cover a few common patterns in software architecture:

Microservices pattern: It's an architectural approach for breaking an application (a monolithic application) into smaller, independent, and possibly distributed components. Through deterministic interfaces, they interact together to deliver the intended functionality of a monolithic system but with higher flexibility, performance, and scalability. Microservices are discussed in Chapter 2.

Service-oriented architecture (SOA): Distributed applications or components that provide and consume services. The service provider and service consumer don't have to use the same languages or be hosted on the same platforms. They are developed and deployed independently. Every component has interfaces that define the services it provides or the services it requests. In addition to the provider and consumer, there are few important components of this pattern:

- The service registry assists the service provider with offering the services and how they should be offered and with what type of availability, security, or metering (billing), to name a few.

- The service broker provides details about the services to service consumers.

SOA allows for faster deployment, lower cost, and higher scalability. At the same time, because service providers and consumers are built independently and possibly by different organizations, this may introduce limitations in flexibility and scalability when a high level of customization is required.

Event-driven: This model is very common for customer engagement applications where an event (a change in state) is generated, captured, and processed in real time (or near-real time). It is like SOA in the sense that there is an event producer and an event consumer (which listens for the event). When the event is generated, the event producer detects the event and sends it in the form of a message. The producer sends the message not knowing or caring about the consumer and what the consumer may or may not do with it. The event-driven architecture has two different models:

- **Publisher/subscriber (pub/sub) model:** When an event is detected, it is published and sent to subscribers for further analysis (or correlation).
- **Event streaming:** Multiple events or continuous streams of events are detected and logged to a database where consumers or subscribers can read from the database in a customized fashion (e.g., a timestamp or a duration of time).

Event-driven architecture patterns saw a rise with the Internet of Things (IoT) sensors, devices, and applications, especially as streams of data (and events) are analyzed for pattern detection or predictive analysis of events in areas like health care or manufacturing.

Model-view-controller (MVC): This model relies on three components of an application: model, view, and controller:

- **Model:** This component contains core data and all functionality.
- **View:** This component provides a customizable view of the outcome seen by the user. Multiple views can be developed and based on the user interaction (e.g., web page or text message).
- **Controller:** This component receives user input from the view and sends it to the model for processing (or storage).

MVC provides a great deal of simplicity and flexibility because each of the three components can be developed independently by a different group of developers.

Software Development Lifecycle (SDLC) Approach

We've discussed architecture and architecture requirements; now we briefly cover the approach to software development. To keep individual developers and development teams on the same page and to ensure discipline, various lifecycle approaches have been developed and tried. The different approaches we discuss here fit into what is called the **software development lifecycle (SDLC)**.

In general, the SDLC has six distinct phases, as illustrated in Figure 1-3:

- **Planning:** Developing the concept or context; the creation and capture of use cases or user stories.

The narrative: You want to build an application that does this to solve that business problem, and you need to define all stakeholders and define the final product....

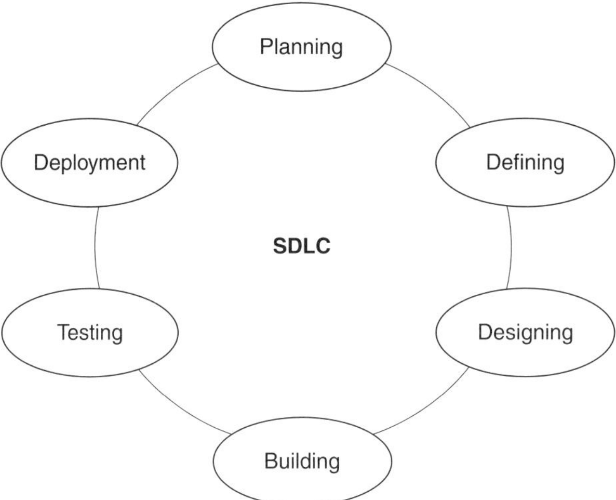

Figure 1-3 *Software Development Lifecycle*

- **Defining:** Defining requirements capture and analysis; building the system specifications.

  The narrative: The app must do ABC using this system or while adhering to this business process enabled by this type of data performing a transaction in no more than 500 ms.

- **Designing:** Converting the high-level conceptual design into technical software specifications.

  The narrative: This step makes sure that all stakeholders are on the same page and are in full agreement on the next steps.

  The outcome of this stage is the "go-to" reference from this moment on.

- **Building/implementing:** Using technical specifications to build the software.

  The narrative: Let's build this thing.

  Often project managers organize milestones and timelines.

NOTE The development models (described in the next section) highlight how this part of SDLC is managed.

- **Testing:** Validating that the software functions as intended. Depending on the organization or the intended use of the system, there may be various phases or certifications of the software. Examples include functional, stress, system, alpha, and beta testing.

  The narrative: The software is almost ready for production deployment, but let's exercise the system and observe how it reacts to certain normal or stressful scenarios.

- **Deployment:** Possibly done in multiple phases or stages—possibly limited rollout or pilot before full-scale production. During the limited deployment phases, you're most likely observing the behavior of the system as well as how it interacts with other software and other business processes.

Some SDLC representations may add a maintenance stage.

Software Development Models

This section could be described in a few paragraphs or in three chapters. Each of the models and methodologies has been previously described in a book on its own, but we give you a summary so that you can understand the topics and be prepared for all related questions on the DEVCOR exam.

The software development process usually is a complex undertaking involving multiple stakeholders, developers, and business owners. Therefore, a model that manages the execution of SDLC is necessary. Over the years, many models have been developed to meet a variety of environmental or process needs; some stood the test of time and evolution, some have become limited in use, others are rarely used. For the DEVCOR exam, it is important to be familiar with the main ones that fulfill the development process of current software environments. The most common models are

- Waterfall
- Iterative
- Agile
- Spiral
- V Model

For the purpose of DEVCOR, two models stand out and are required knowledge: Waterfall and Agile. Agile has several variations that are also understood to stand on their own (Lean, Scrum, Extreme Programming, and so on). For example, the Lean model is considered a variation of Agile, but it is not uncommon to view it as an independent model. In the following sections, we quickly cover a few models and examples.

Waterfall

The waterfall model is considered the simplest and most straightforward model. As the name indicates, this mode is sequential. As shown in Figure 1-4, each stage depends on the one before it. A stage must finish and get the proper signoffs/approvals before the next one can start.

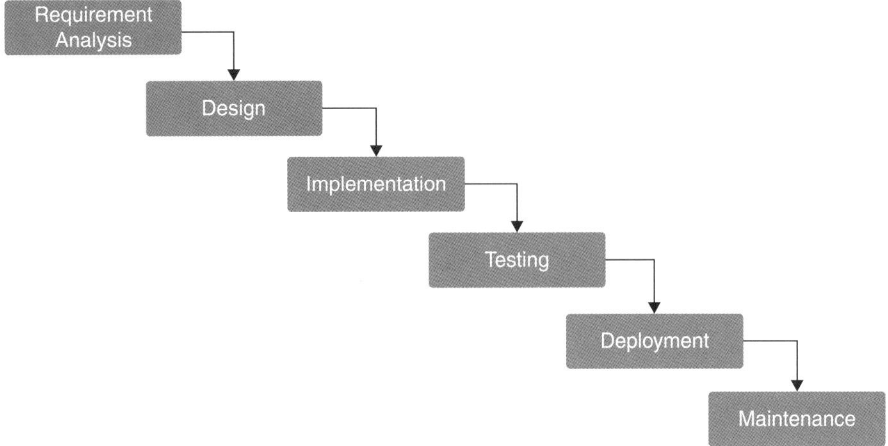

Figure 1-4 *Waterfall Development Model*

In a waterfall model, the flow is sometimes unidirectional (downward or toward the next step). This could be viewed as an advantage because all gates or checks are done at the individual stage before exiting it and starting the next one. It can also be viewed as a disadvantage, or a con, of the system because changes and faults discovered at the following stage are hard to integrate into the system unless the full process is repeated.

Agile Software Development

Agile has been gaining ground as a model, not just for software development only, but also as a project management tool or methodology for a variety of architectures or business problems. It addresses many of the waterfall shortcomings and introduces a high degree of flexibility and speed to the development process. Agile represents a number of methodologies like Scrum, Extreme Programming, or Lean. As seen in Figure 1-5, Agile has the concept of "sprints," which represents short development lifecycles (typically one to four weeks) where small manageable chunks of the software are delivered.

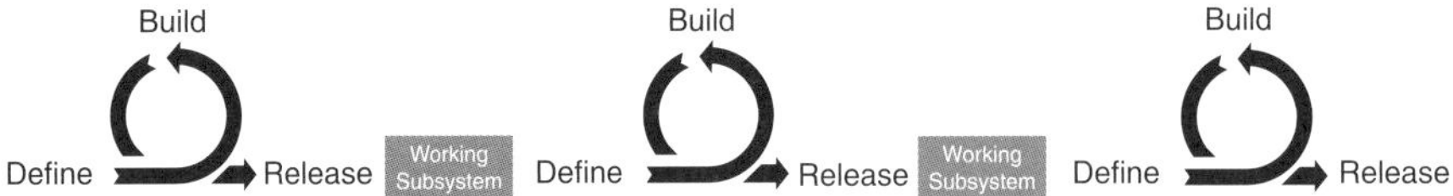

Figure 1-5 *Agile Software Development*

A few years ago, a group of software development experts got together and developed what they called the Agile Manifesto (https://agilemanifesto.org/), which is based on the following principles:

1. Our highest priority is to satisfy the customer through early and continuous delivery of valuable software.
2. Welcome changing requirements, even late in development. Agile processes harness change for the customer's competitive advantage.
3. Deliver working software frequently, from a couple of weeks to a couple of months, with a preference for the shorter timescale.
4. Businesspeople and developers must work together daily throughout the project.

5. Build projects around motivated individuals. Give them the environment and support they need and trust them to get the job done.
6. The most efficient and effective method of conveying information to and within a development team is face-to-face conversation.
7. Working software is the primary measure of progress.
8. Agile processes promote sustainable development. The sponsors, developers, and users should be able to maintain a constant pace indefinitely.
9. Continuous attention to technical excellence and good design enhances agility.
10. Simplicity—the art of maximizing the amount of work not done—is essential.
11. The best architectures, requirements, and designs emerge from self-organizing teams.
12. At regular intervals, the team reflects on how to become more effective, then tunes and adjusts its behavior accordingly.

It's obvious from the list that Agile development emphasizes teamwork, collaboration, and flexibility. As mentioned earlier, Agile represents a variety of methodologies. It is not uncommon to find references or publications internal or external to your organization that deal with the following Agile methodologies as independent models.

Scrum

Scrum uses sprints (short and repeatable development cycles) and multiple teams to achieve success. It is a preferred model where frequent changes or design decisions are made. It requires clear communication of requirements, but teams are empowered to decide on the best ways to fulfill them.

Extreme Programming

Extreme Programming offers high-quality software, frequently and continuously with a typical iteration duration of one to four weeks. It allows for frequent changes, which is considered a plus, but in a poorly managed environment, this could easily degrade the quality of your deliverable.

Kanban

Kanban provides continuous delivery while reducing individual developer burden. In some cases, it focuses on day-long sprints. There is no defined process for introducing changes.

Lean

Lean focuses on "valuable features" and prioritization. Lean is sometimes considered as the origin of Agile or, more like, Agile took the best of Lean and improved upon it. Lean focuses on the following principles:

- Deliver value fast and often.
- Provide continuous learning and innovation.
- Build high-performing and empowered teams.
- Think quality at the design phase.
- Make just-in-time decisions: Always have options but finalize decisions at the right time.
- Eliminate waste and optimize delivery.

In the following section, we provide a brief comparative analysis of the various models. The Agile development model is closely aligned with the DevOps model. DevOps focuses on integration and collaboration among development teams to shorten development and deployment cycles. Agile focuses on frequent and incremental updating and development of systems and subsystems that contribute to the evolution of the final product. We can safely say that both models strive to reduce the time to develop, test, and deploy software.

Which Model?

Agile has been gaining ground as a model, not just for software development only but also as a project management tool for a variety of architectures or business problems. Table 1-3 compares the various development models to help you decide which to use for your project. With the exception of the waterfall model, you will probably observe many similarities among the other models because they're all Agile in nature. The table lists the pros and cons of each. Note that you must make a number of trade-offs between quality, cost, and speed (among other things relevant to your organization).

Table 1-3 Comparative Analysis of the Various Development Models

Model	Pros	Cons
Waterfall	■ Provides simple, easy-to-understand deliverables and stakeholders ■ Rigid ■ Suitable where strict control is needed ■ Good for small or shorter-term projects	■ Possibly higher cost than other models, especially if changes are needed in later stages ■ Not change request friendly ■ Not the best option for large or longer-term projects
Agile	■ Emphasizes frequent and direct communication ■ Friendly to change requests or design improvements ■ Normally yields high-quality iterative development and frequent fixes ■ Good for larger projects where work is distributed over smaller teams	■ Documentation is not emphasized ■ It's easy to lose the big picture if individual teams are controlled with clear milestones or outcomes
Lean	■ Provides for rapid development and eliminates waste ■ Team empowerment ■ Continuous learning ■ Continuous development with functioning systems or subsystems early in the lifecycle	■ Easy to lose focus and the full-system impact ■ Documentation is not emphasized or produced during early development phases

Model	Pros	Cons
Scrum	■ Provides for team empowerment ■ Clear documentation of requirements (especially functional or business ones) is significant ■ Rapid development using a team of experienced developers	■ Easy to lose the big picture ■ Small to medium projects ■ It may be costly (depends on the size and skills of teams)
Extreme Programming (XP)	■ Involves all stakeholders ■ Typically produces high-quality software ■ Dependent on skilled and dedicated developers for high-quality outcomes ■ Short sprints ■ Allows for changes frequently	■ Highly skilled resources add to cost ■ Frequent meetings and checkpoints ■ Visibility into small subsystems and not the big picture or the final outcomes ■ Quality may suffer if the number of changes introduced is high

Architecture and Code Reviews

We won't spend a lot of time on architecture review, although we feel it is very important. Many decisions that the architectures (or architects for that matter) deliver to the developers need to be reviewed or defended. It is also critical that developers understand how coding and implementation errors have performance, security, or quality implications. For all those reasons, code review is an essential step in the development lifecycle.

Three common review types fit in various stages of the lifecycle:

- Peer review
- Customer review (internal stakeholders)
- External or independent review

The unfortunate part is that architecture is hardly ever reviewed or updated after the development lifecycle starts. Code review, on the other hand, cannot be handled that way.

As a software developer, you will typically find yourself very focused on code reviews. Code review, in light of the current requirements and future roadmaps, is extremely essential.

Different organizations have different practices, but reviewers generally look at some common practices. The following is a partial list of examples of what gets checked or verified during a code review:

- Adhering to the architecture
- Following predefined code patterns

- Ensuring nonfunctional requirements are represented:
  - Scalability
  - Efficiency
  - High availability
  - Testability
  - Modifiability/maintainability
  - Security
  - Usability
  - And more
- Using predefined technologies, systems, and subsystems
- Following coding best practices
  - Formatting
  - Naming conventions
  - Documentation

Code review requires collaboration, patience, and documentation of findings. Code review meetings are also a great opportunity for all involved persons or parties to connect and learn from each other.

Software Testing

We could easily dedicate a full chapter to testing, but for the purpose of DEVCOR, we limit the discussion to few paragraphs. Testing can happen at every stage of the development lifecycle, but nothing is more important than the prerelease times. Releases are systemwide releases or subsystem releases as you've seen with the Agile development model.

Your application is as good as your testing process or methodology. You most commonly hear about *alpha* and *beta* type testing, but that type of testing is conducted by customers or other stakeholders outside the development teams. This type of testing is called *acceptance testing*.

The type and frequency of testing is specific to your organization. Figure 1-6 presents a number of testing terminologies; however, the majority of development teams are concerned with four main types of testing:

- **Unit testing:** We like to call this testing at the atomic level (the smallest testable unit), meaning that you conduct this type of testing at the function or class level within a subsystem. Unit testing is conducted mostly by the developers who have full knowledge of the unit under test. It's often advantageous to automate unit testing.
- **Integration testing:** This type tests for integration or interaction among the components of the overall system. Components interact through interfaces, and that's what you're validating here.

- **System testing:** Here, you verify that the full system functionality is as intended or specified in the requirements. It is not uncommon to call this type of testing *functional testing*.
- **Acceptance testing:** Depending on your organization, this category of testing may be customized to whatever functional or nonfunctional requirement you want to test. It is possible to have multiple teams conducting different types of testing under one umbrella testing effort called *acceptance testing*. For example, *performance testing*, *stress testing*, or *usability testing* may be considered types of acceptance testing, or they could stand on their own as individual types of testing.

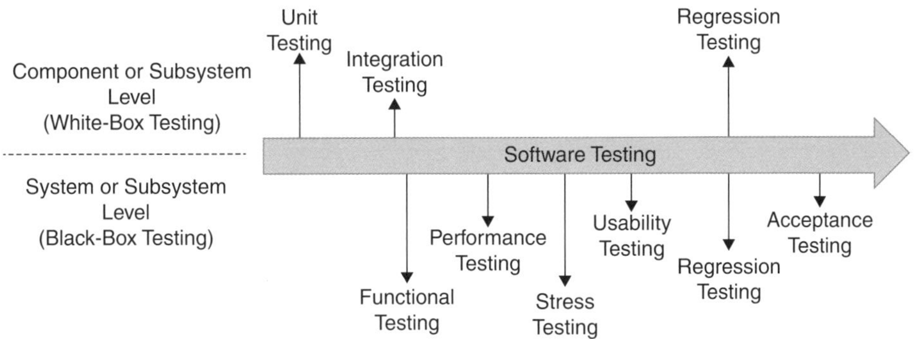

Figure 1-6 *Various Types of Testing Used by Software Developers and Their Customers*

> **NOTE** The terms *white-box testing* and *black-box testing* are mostly seen nowadays in relation to cybersecurity, but they actually originated with software testing. White-box testing indicates that the tester has full knowledge of the subcomponents or inner workings of the system, and it is usually conducted by developers or development test teams. Black-box testing indicates that the testing team has little to no knowledge of the inner workings of the system while testing it. It's worth mentioning that, depending on your organization, the terms *white-box testing* and *black-box testing* might not be widely used in software development.

Testing efforts are normally executed from organized test plans and generate a list of issues to be acted upon in the form of bugs, defects, failures, or errors. The issues are also ranked in severity and priority. It is not unusual to ship the code with bugs or issues included and documented in the "release notes."

Test automation has become a discipline on its own, especially with Agile practices where you're dealing with large systems with small subsystems, continuous updating, and integration.

Exam Preparation Tasks

As mentioned in the section "How to Use This Book" in the Introduction, you have a couple of choices for exam preparation: the exercises here, Chapter 17, "Final Preparation," and the exam simulation questions on the companion website.

Review All Key Topics

Review the most important topics in this chapter, noted with the Key Topic icon in the outer margin of the page. Table 1-4 lists a reference of these key topics and the page numbers on which each is found.

Table 1-4 Key Topics for Chapter 1

Key Topic Element	Description	Page Number
List	The key DevOps practices	8
List	Functional requirements	10
List	Nonfunctional requirements	11
Paragraph	Architectural patterns: MVC and microservices	14
List	SDLC distinct phases	15
Table 1-3	Comparative Analysis of the Various Development Models	20

Complete Tables and Lists from Memory

Print a copy of Appendix C, "Memory Tables" (found on the companion website), or at least the section for this chapter, and complete the tables and lists from memory. Appendix D, "Memory Tables Answer Key," also on the companion website, includes completed tables and lists to check your work.

Define Key Terms

Define the following key terms from this chapter and check your answers in the glossary:

continuous integration/continuous deployment (CI/CD), software development lifecycle (SDLC), functional requirements, nonfunctional requirements, software architecture

References

URL	QR Code
Continuous Architecture in Practice: Software Architecture in the Age of Agility and DevOps https://www.informit.com/store/continuous-architecture-in-practice-software-architecture-9780136523567	
Software Architecture in Practice, 4th Edition https://www.informit.com/store/software-architecture-in-practice-9780136886099	
Manifesto for Agile Software Development https://agilemanifesto.org/	

CHAPTER 2

Software Quality Attributes

This chapter covers the following topics:

- **Quality Attributes and Nonfunctional Requirements:** This section discusses functional and nonfunctional requirements as an essential part of the software development process. Functional requirements describe the business functions and what the software should do, whereas nonfunctional requirements describe how the software should perform these functions.
- **Modularity in Application Design:** This section describes why and how the software should be composed of discrete components such that a change to one component has minimal impact on other components. Cohesive functions with specific functions are the essence of modularity.
- **Scalability in Application Design:** This section covers one of the most important nonfunctional requirements of how to scale your system up and out to meet various growth requirements.
- **High Availability and Resiliency in Application Design:** This section focuses on various strategies for improving the availability and resiliency of the system with various software implementation technologies that affect the availability of the software and hardware alike.

This chapter maps to the first part of the *Developing Applications Using Cisco Core Platforms and APIs v1.0 (350-901)* Exam Blueprint Section 1.0, "Software Development and Design."

In the first chapter, we covered the relationship between functional and nonfunctional requirements. We also determined that writing code that delivers functional or business requirements is the easy part. The part that requires extra attention and careful discussion is the nonfunctional requirements that make your application efficient, scalable, highly available, and modifiable, among other attributes. Our goal is to help you write an application that requires the least amount of work when *changes* are required. It's not efficient if you have to rewrite an application or some of its main components every time you want to enhance a characteristic or feature. Therefore, the quality of the application and its development practices are determined by your ability to enhance it or modify it with the least amount of effort. In this chapter, we focus on the various nonfunctional requirements that describe the quality of the design.

"Do I Know This Already?" Quiz

The "Do I Know This Already?" quiz allows you to assess whether you should read this entire chapter thoroughly or jump to the "Exam Preparation Tasks" section. If you are in doubt about your answers to these questions or your own assessment of your knowledge of the topics, read the entire chapter. Table 2-1 lists the major headings in this chapter and their corresponding "Do I Know This Already?" quiz questions. You can find the answers in Appendix A, "Answers to the 'Do I Know This Already?' Quizzes."

Table 2-1 "Do I Know This Already?" Section-to-Question Mapping

Foundation Topics Section	Questions
Quality Attributes and Nonfunctional Requirements	1–6
Modularity in Application Design	7–9
Scalability in Application Design	10
High Availability and Resiliency in Application Design	11, 12

1. When is a design considered to be of high quality?
   - a. It processes data at high speed.
   - b. It is bug free.
   - c. It is secure.
   - d. Nonfunctional requirements are clearly defined and are measurable.
2. Functional and nonfunctional requirements are
   - a. Independent of each other because they are measured separately.
   - b. Considered in sequence functional then nonfunctional.
   - c. Considered in sequence nonfunctional then functional.
   - d. Considered hand in hand because you cannot measure nonfunctional requirements without understanding the functional or business requirements.
3. The terms *nonfunctional requirements* and *quality attributes* are used interchangeably most of the time.
   - a. True
   - b. False
4. Which of the following is a type of quality attribute?
   - a. Modifiability
   - b. Modularity
   - c. High availability
   - d. All of these answers are correct.
5. Availability can be expressed as
   - a. The number of hours when a system was reachable before it crashed.
   - b. The degree to which a system, product, or component is operational and accessible when required for use.
   - c. When a system was operational but not needed.
   - d. All of these answers are correct.

6. Which of the following attributes are considered part of maintainability according to ISO/IEC 25010?
   a. Modularity
   b. Modifiability
   c. Testability
   d. All of these answers are correct.
7. What do you strive to do with modularity?
   a. Break the architecture into equal-size chunks.
   b. Break the architecture into smaller chunks.
   c. Break the architecture into smaller building blocks with clear functions and interactions.
   d. None of these answers are correct.
8. What is coupling in a modular design?
   a. A degree of independence between modules.
   b. A measure of strength of the relationship among modules.
   c. A degree of independence or dependence among modules.
   d. All of these answers are correct.
9. In modularity, it is considered a best practice when you do which of the following?
   a. Reduce coupling and increase cohesion.
   b. Increase coupling and reduce cohesion.
   c. Reduce coupling and improve comprehension.
   d. None of these answers are correct.
10. What is horizontal scalability?
    a. Scaling out.
    b. Adding additional servers to handle additional load.
    c. Similar to server load balancing.
    d. All of these answers are correct.
11. To improve availability in a design, what type of redundancy should you use?
    a. Hot standby
    b. Warm standby
    c. Cold standby
    d. Any of these answers are correct based on requirements and capabilities.
12. Heartbeats or "hello packets" are usually exchanged between redundant systems
    a. To help detect a failure.
    b. To alert the standby system that the active system is no longer available.
    c. And may require special processing and prioritization.
    d. All of these answers are correct.

Foundation Topics

Quality Attributes and Nonfunctional Requirements

What defines the quality of a design?

Processing of input data is high speed?

It is bug free?

It applies security checks or tasks?

It can scale up to 100,000 concurrent connections when only 10,000 are required?

All these qualities are great, but do they really indicate that the system is of high quality? Maybe. Regardless of what system you're working with, when discussing quality, you must be specific about the quality attribute being investigated or discussed. Quality attributes or nonfunctional requirements must be measurable and testable. The best or easiest example is security. You can never say that a system is "secure," but you can say that the system is secure under a set of conditions, inputs, or stimuli. The same applies to availability. You must specify the failure type before you can judge the system to be available.

The message we want to deliver here is that quality attributes and functional requirements are connected. You cannot consider one without the other. You cannot assess performance or availability if you're not observing them against the system performing a functional or business requirement task. In other words, you cannot measure nonfunctional quality attributes without considering the functions the system is performing.

Another message that shines in the preceding paragraph is *measure*. For the most part, quality attributes should be measurable and testable. As mentioned, you can quickly define quality attributes as measurable indicators of how well a system responds to certain stimuli or how it performs functional requirements. Quality attributes need to be precise and specific. When discussing performance, you have to use specific parameters such as time or CPU cycles or time-out values.

In addition, you have to keep in mind that trade-offs exist among the various attributes. A high-level example would be the inverse relationship between performance and scalability. As scalability or capacity requirements increase, there is a high probability that performance would suffer.

Brief Overview of the Most Common Quality Attributes

If you have not noticed yet, we've been using the terms *nonfunctional requirements* and *quality attributes* interchangeably.

> **NOTE** Remember that, as specified in Chapter 1, "Software Development Essentials," the terms *quality attributes* and *nonfunctional requirements* are used interchangeably.

The following are quality attributes by which you can judge the quality of a given system:

- **Performance:** This attribute is mostly measured by time. Transactions per second is a good indicator of performance. However, the same description can be used to discuss the reliability of the system, such as how much load it can handle per second before the intended performance begins to degrade.
- **Security:** This attribute is possibly the simplest or hardest quality attribute to fulfill. It can be summarized as the capability of the system (and its subcomponents) to protect data from unauthorized access.
- **Availability:** This attribute is the system's capability to recover from subcomponent failure and continue to be operational.
- **Resiliency:** This attribute is often combined or confused with availability. A system is resilient if it continues to provide the same level of operation after a failure event. With high availability, the system recovers from a failure; with resilience, the system recovers fast enough to maintain the services it was offering.
- **Modifiability:** Simply put, this attribute addresses how the system handles change. There are many types of change. Change can come as an enhancement, a fix, or the inclusion of a new technology or business process. Can you integrate the new changes without having to rewrite the system or subsystems?
- **Reliability:** This attribute asks how long a system can perform specific functions under specific load or stress. For example, a system designed to handle 10,000 new connections per second is hit with a failure scenario that causes the 12,000 existing users to connect at once. How does the system handle this unforeseen load and for how long?
- **Usability:** This attribute determines the ease or difficulty with which a system's user can accomplish a task and how much support (help) is available. One organization we worked with called this attribute *serviceability*. Both terms are concerned with the same outcome.
- **Testability:** This attribute determines how a system handles normal or erroneous input at execution time. The system is testable when it can handle various inputs and conditions representing a variety of test cases. For example, the system asks users to input a birthdate in the form *mm/dd/yyyy*. How does that system react when a user enters March 10, 2021? That test case can be tried to test how the system handles abnormal input patterns.
- **Interoperability:** This attribute addresses how the system interacts with other systems. How does a system exchange information and using what interfaces? Interoperability relies on understanding the system interface, sending a request to it, and seeing how the request is handled.
- **Serviceability:** This attribute addresses the ability of users to install, configure, and monitor the software. Serviceability is also referred to as *supportability*, where users (or test teams) can identify and debug exceptions and faults.

NOTE The ISO/IEC 25010 standard publication presents a more generic, or standard, definition of a more comprehensive list of quality attributes. Notice how it creates subcategories of quality attributes. The ISO/IEC 25010 is good to know if you're helping your organization build a standard list of attributes for internal software projects. See System and software engineering—System and software Quality Requirements and Evaluation (SQuaRE)—System and software quality models.

The standard document explains the various quality characteristics.

Table 2-2 shows how ISO/IEC 25010 describes each of the quality characteristics or attributes. The highlighted categories are essential to DEVCOR development and are handled in some detail.

Table 2-2 Quality Attributes Described by ISO/IEC 25010

Quality Attribute	Subcategory	Definition
Functional Suitability	Functional completeness	The degree to which the set of functions covers all the specified tasks and user objectives
	Functional correctness	The degree to which a product or system provides the correct results with the needed degree of precision
	Functional appropriateness	The degree to which the functions facilitate the accomplishment of specified tasks and objectives
Performance Efficiency	Time behavior	The degree to which the response and processing times and throughput rates of a product or system, when performing its functions, meet requirements
	Resource utilization	The degree to which the amounts and types of resources used by a product or system, when performing its functions, meet requirements
	Capacity	The degree to which the maximum limits of a product or system parameter meet requirements
Compatibility	Co-existence	The degree to which a product can perform its required functions efficiently while sharing a common environment and resources with other products, without detrimental impact on any other product
	Interoperability	The degree to which two or more systems, products, or components can exchange information and use the information that has been exchanged

Quality Attribute	Subcategory	Definition
Usability	Appropriateness recognizability	The degree to which users can recognize whether a product or system is appropriate for their needs
	Learnability	The degree to which a product or system can be used by specified users to achieve specified goals of learning to use the product or system with effectiveness, efficiency, freedom from risk, and satisfaction in a specified context of use
	Operability	The degree to which a product or system has attributes that make it easy to operate and control
	User error protection	The degree to which a system protects users against making errors
	User interface aesthetics	The degree to which a user interface enables pleasing and satisfying interaction for the user
	Accessibility	The degree to which a product or system can be used by people with the widest range of characteristics and capabilities to achieve a specified goal in a specified context of use
Reliability	Maturity	The degree to which a system, product, or component meets needs for reliability under normal operation
	Availability	The degree to which a system, product, or component is operational and accessible when required for use
	Fault tolerance	The degree to which a system, product, or component operates as intended despite the presence of hardware or software faults
	Recoverability	The degree to which, in the event of an interruption or a failure, a product or system can recover the data directly affected and re-establish the desired state of the system
Security	Confidentiality	The degree to which a product or system ensures that data are accessible only to those authorized to have access
	Integrity	The degree to which a system, product, or component prevents unauthorized access to, or modification of, computer programs or data
	Nonrepudiation	The degree to which actions or events can be proven to have taken place so that the events or actions cannot be repudiated later
	Accountability	The degree to which the actions of an entity can be traced uniquely to the entity
	Authenticity	The degree to which the identity of a subject or resource can be proved to be the one claimed

Quality Attribute	Subcategory	Definition
Maintainability	Modularity	The degree to which a system or computer program is composed of discrete components such that a change to one component has minimal impact on other components
	Reusability	The degree to which an asset can be used in more than one system, or in building other assets
	Analyzability	The degree of effectiveness and efficiency with which it is possible to assess the impact on a product or system of an intended change to one or more of its parts, or to diagnose a product for deficiencies or causes of failures, or to identify parts to be modified
	Modifiability	The degree to which a product or system can be effectively and efficiently modified without introducing defects or degrading existing product quality
	Testability	The degree of effectiveness and efficiency with which test criteria can be established for a system, product, or component and tests can be performed to determine whether those criteria have been met
Portability	Adaptability	The degree to which a product or system can effectively and efficiently be adapted for different or evolving hardware, software, or other operational or usage environments
	Installability	The degree of effectiveness and efficiency with which a product or system can be successfully installed and/or uninstalled in a specified environment
	Replaceability	The degree to which a product can replace another specified software product for the same purpose in the same environment

NOTE The highlighted quality attributes are necessary for the DEVCOR exam and are given detailed attention. We consider them independently and not necessarily as main or subcategories as shown in the table. For example, *modularity* and *modifiability* are discussed in independent sections and not under the main header "Maintainability." Similarly for *availability* and *reliability*.

It's clear from Table 2-2 how important it is to have a clearly defined list of nonfunctional or quality attributes. For example, as a developer, what more do you need than to have your code highly available, modular, and secure? Therefore, it becomes clear that a focus on these attributes achieves what every developer is looking to deliver on the code they're working on:

- **Quality:** Good and standardized coding practices create easy-to-understand and well-documented code.
- **High performance:** Deploying modularity alongside efficient coding practices allows for high-speed processing of information at various load levels.
- **Security:** Security cannot be an afterthought, and it cannot be assumed. Use defense-in-depth or multilayer security practices and technologies.
- **Low errors:** A clear understanding of both functional nonfunctional requirements such as testability, availability, and usability can reduce the number of bugs and errors in an application.
- **Unplanned outages:** Availability and resiliency at the component level can increase uptime of the overall system even when failure occurs at the component level.
- **Low maintenance:** Modularity and modifiability lower maintenance costs and future-proof your system.
- **Customer satisfaction:** User experience is a make-or-break for anything, let alone software applications. Users often expect usability and responsiveness, and these attributes should be prioritized.

As you build software applications, it is important to have the end goal in mind. There are several important points that, as a developer, you need to consider every time:

- Change is constant. It will always happen.
- Functional or business requirements will always change or grow.
- Software support is expensive.
- Your name is on it. Guard your reputation.
- Document your work. You will save yourself and others valuable time.
- Try to understand the full system architecture, not just your component.
- Collaborate and learn from others.
- Reinvent yourself. Evolve your development practices if you can.
- Learn new tools and technologies.
- Keep it simple.
- Ask questions. If requirements are not clear, don't make assumptions that may affect the whole system or affect those who are on the receiving end from you.

Measuring Quality Attributes

As seen from the definition of quality attributes, to be able to measure them, you almost always have an "event" and a "response." Some software architecture publications go further into qualifying them into multiple stages:

1. **Source** of the event (How is the event generated?)
2. **Stimulus** or condition that affects the system
3. **System**, subsystem, or function affected by the condition
4. **Environment** or condition when the stimulus arrived
5. **Response** or activity invoked or resulted
6. **Measure** of the response (e.g., time)

These six stages are very important, especially when you look at network events. Consider Figure 2-1, which shows availability with a switch-failover scenario. This example demonstrates the concept using a scenario familiar to network engineers. We expand into software high availability functions later in this chapter.

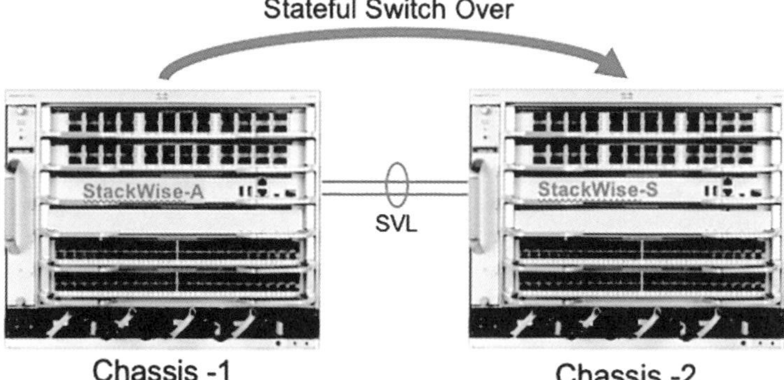

Figure 2-1 *A High Availability Scenario Used to Demonstrate Quality Attributes Stages*

We use the devices in Figure 2-1 to demonstrate the stages described. For these two redundant switches, one is Active (StackWise-A), and the other is Standby (StackWise-S). The StackWise Virtual Link (SVL) is used to synchronize state between the Active and Standby and for transmitting the *heartbeat* informing both switches of the state of each switch. Let's assume that the failure event here is loss of power at Chassis-1 (meaning StackWise-A); then the processor is no longer available and no longer transmitting heartbeats to Chassis-2. Then Chassis-2 becomes the Active switch within 50 ms. Table 2-3 demonstrates each of the stages and the event associated with it.

Table 2-3 Measuring Attributes (and Example for Measuring Availability)

Stage	Value or Description Associated with the Stage
Source	Power connectivity of a Cisco Catalyst Switch is lost.
Stimulus	Keep-alive packets are lost between the Master and Backup StackWise virtual pair.

Stage	Value or Description Associated with the Stage
System	StackWise Virtual subsystem experiences a fail-over event.
Environment	Active switch is affected by loss of power.
Response	The StackWise virtual invokes the stateful switch over (SSO).
Measure	Chassis-2 becomes Active in 50 ms.

More advanced high availability concepts are discussed later in the chapter.

Modularity in Application Design

One of your first tasks as an architect is to break your architecture into smaller building blocks with clear functions and interactions. This way, it is easier to understand, explain, and build. This is what modularity is all about: building small functional modules (subsystems) that can come together to build a full or larger-scale system. Modularity and reusability are also similar in the way that the individual modules are functions that are reusable to improve efficiency and readability of code.

As applications grow in size and functionality, modularity becomes a must-have practice, not just a nice-to-have good-coding practice. The ability to build modular code demonstrates the difference between a software developer and a software engineer. Writing reusable modules with clear and specific interfaces is necessary in large-scale projects and is also an essential object-oriented skill. Figure 2-2 gives a simple example of Module 2 fulfilling a requirement for both System A and System B.

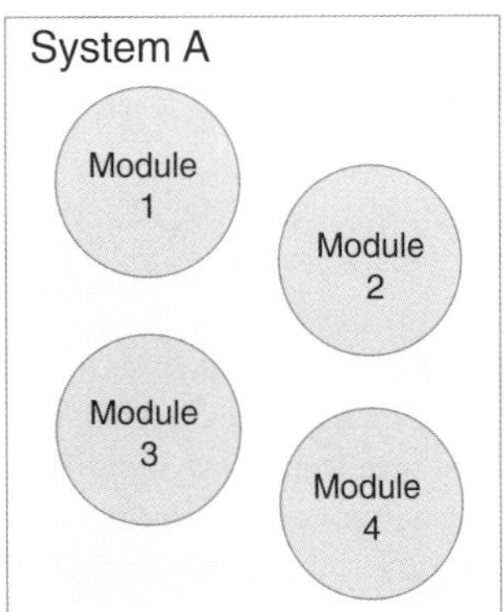

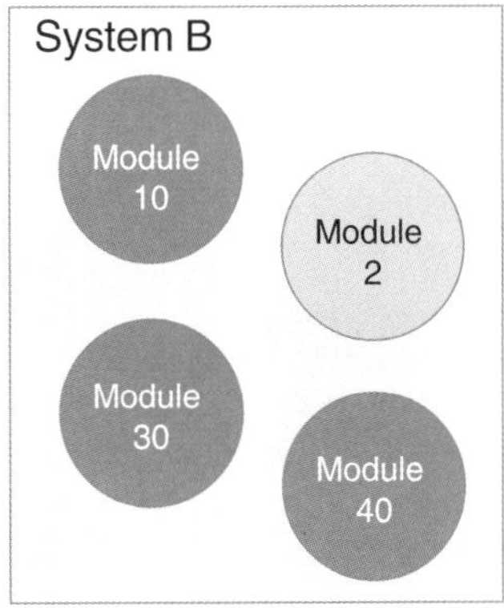

Figure 2-2 *Modularity and Reusability*

Benefits of Modularity

The most important benefits of modularity are as follows:

- Maintaining and modifying the individual modules and the overall system are easier. Updating or enhancing functionality of the system may easily be done through simple modification to one or multiple modules without having to touch the entire code base.

- Reading, understanding, and following the code logic are easier. Modularity also makes code review and debugging easier.
- Team collaboration, especially within an Agile model, is improved. Individual modules can easily be developed by multiple teams.
- Modularity enables scalability. An example would be to deploy or reuse modules for additional processing of additional data concurrently, allowing for scalability of the system.
- Security is improved. It's easier to focus on secure coding practices when you're dealing with smaller chunks.

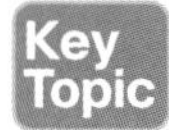

Modularity Coding Best Practices

A good software design uses these leading modularity practices:

- **Reduce coupling and increase cohesion:** Individual independent modules of specific functionality can be easily changed, modified, exploded (separated into two or more modules), or even imploded (combining multiples into one) without affecting the overall structure of the system or code. High **cohesion** means that the elements of a specific module are functionally well related, whereas **coupling** is a measure of the strength of the relationship among modules. Low coupling states that the modules are largely independent from one another (that's a positive thing). Interactions between modules should be kept to a minimum but should be plentiful inside a module, as shown in Figure 2-3.

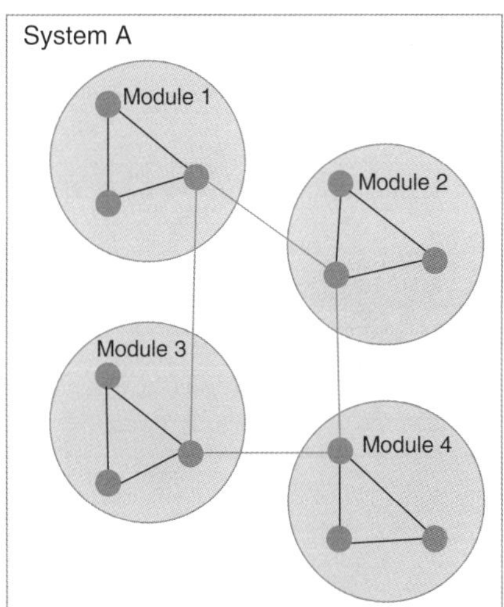

Figure 2-3 *Coupling and Cohesion*

In contrast, modules with low cohesion often make function calls to other modules, while rarely using the module's internal functions and classes, as displayed in Figure 2-4.

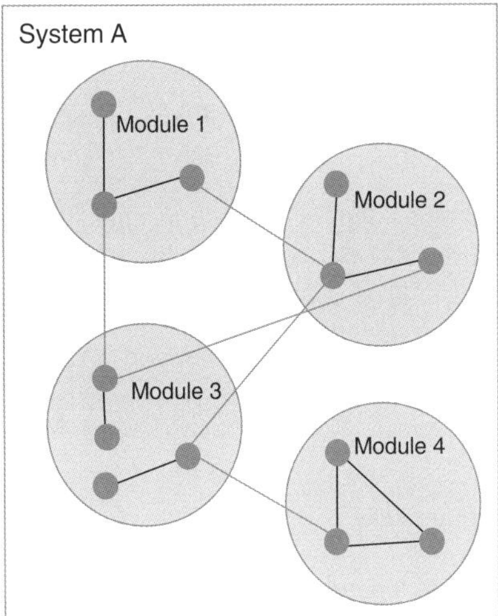

Figure 2-4 *Low Cohesion*

- **Control the scope (dependencies outside the scope of the module):** Almost always, try to keep the scope of control of a module to those modules that are directly related to it and are considered subordinate to it in sequence (you can call this sequential cohesion, if you like). It's not uncommon to see dependencies among modules; however, a module cannot be dependent on data from another module that has no direct interaction or adjacency. To illustrate this point, Figure 2-5 shows that Module 2 cannot generate data that affects Module 10. Module 10 is outside the span of control or effect of Module 2.

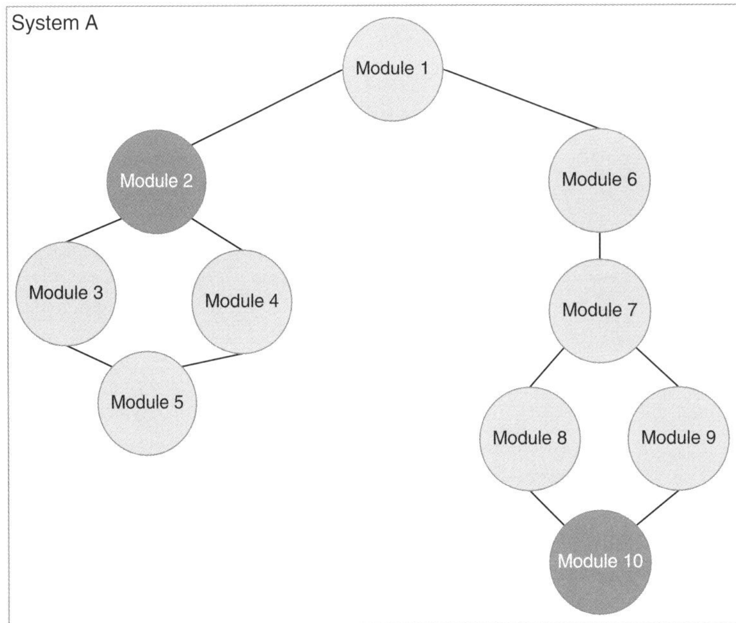

Figure 2-5 *Scope of Effect or Control*

- **Think black-box design:** Modules should have predictable or clear functions with consistent outputs. Modules that maintain local data (through memory) and that do not reset variables will have inconsistent outputs. With black-box design, you expect to have the same output generated for the same input introduced, as shown in Figure 2-6.

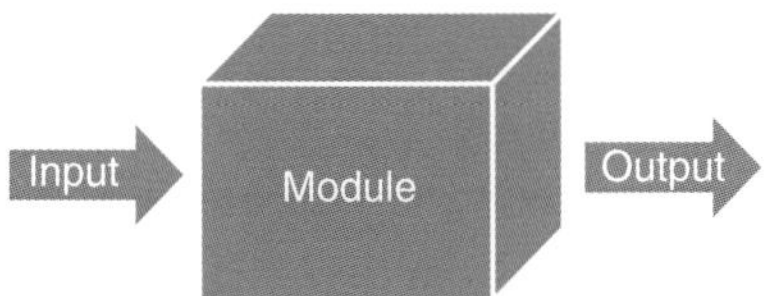

Figure 2-6 *Input and Output Are Consistent in a Module; No Data Executed by a Module Should Impact Subsequent Ones*

NOTE Try to make your application components as stateless as you can, especially for modules of generic functions being used multiple times within your application.

- **Pay attention to interfaces:** Typically, every module has a function and an interface. The function is easy to understand because it is the body or purpose of why the module exists and how it is implemented. The interface, on the other hand, is what data, properties, or executable actions, specific to the module, you're willing to share with anyone or anything that interacts with the module.

  As you look at the leading practices for building efficient modules, you also have to pay close attention to best practices for building and assigning interfaces. Refer to Table 2-4 for a list of best practices and how to use them.

Table 2-4 Modular Design Best Practices

Modular Design Best Practice	Benefits
Reduce coupling and increase cohesion	Maintain clear, functional relationships and the strength of interaction
Monitor scope or span of control	Watch for interdependencies and how data generated by one module affects other modules downstream or upstream from it in sequence
Address consistency	Provide consistency in execution. Don't maintain data or "memory" within a module that is not properly being reset. The same input must always generate the same output.
Interface design is vital	Simple (avoid complexity) Small interfaces (limit information exchange between modules) Avoid redundant interfaces (the smaller, the better) Overall architecture alignment
Align to overall architecture	Avoid "lost-in-translation" scenarios where modules significantly deviate from design principles of the overall system

Complex and redundant interfaces defeat the purpose of modularity or make it altogether confusing. You need to control and restrict interfaces to the surface or edge of the module, as shown in Figure 2-7. Reaching into the middle of the module is not clean and may create issues of coupling. In addition, reducing the number of interfaces is key to consistency and reduction of coupling.

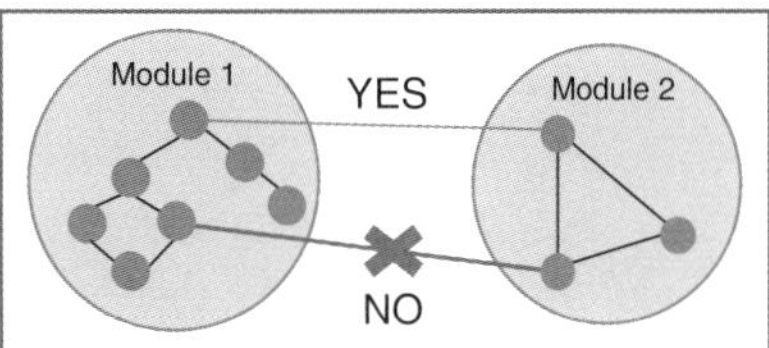

Figure 2-7 *Control the Number of Interfaces and Where They're Provided*

Microservices and Modular Design

A microservice is an architectural approach for breaking an application (a monolithic application) into smaller and independent components. Through deterministic interfaces, they interact together to deliver the intended functionality of a monolithic system but with higher flexibility, performance, and scalability. Modularity is at the code, subsystem, or system level. The way microservices are implemented today exemplifies what modularity at the system level looks like.

A microservice at the end of the day is a service that you tap into for a particular outcome or context. That service can be used to perform the same task for multiple systems and does not necessarily belong solely to that system (we're generalizing here).

To illustrate the point, consider the simple representation of an e-commerce or shopping application in Figure 2-8. This application is composed of a number of microservices, or modules, that are autonomous (loosely coupled), independently developed and maintained, have a specific interface, and have a specific context or outcomes.

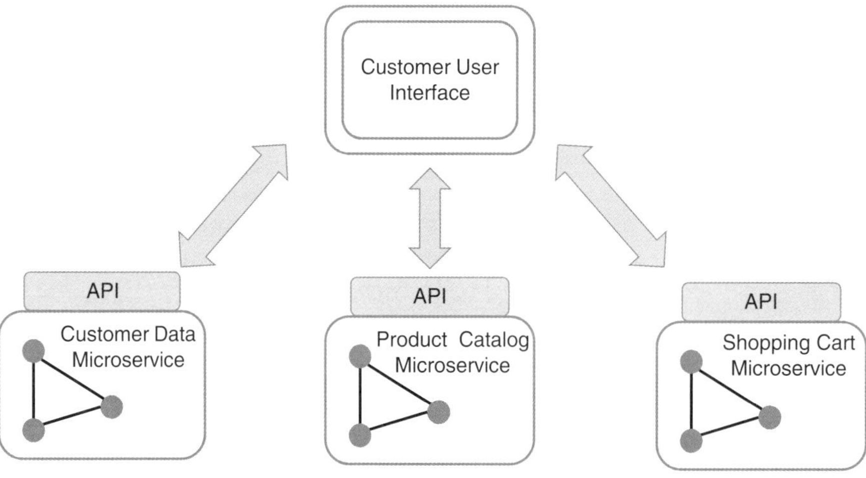

Figure 2-8 *Microservices*

The following points demonstrate how microservices contribute to modularity in application design:

- Microservices are loosely coupled.
- Each microservice has a unique purpose within the context of the overall system.
- Each microservice has a specific interface.
- Microservices are reusable across multiple systems delivering the same outcomes across various systems.
- Microservices can interact through the interfaces to deliver a higher level of meaningful outcome.
- Microservices are mainly agnostic to underlying hardware architecture, making them reusable across a variety of platforms.
- You can easily develop and maintain microservices independently of other microservices. In return, you can support DevOps processes with rapid and frequent deployments.

Scalability in Application Design

A close relative of modularity and one of its biggest beneficiaries is scalability. As you scale a system horizontally or vertically, you discover that modularity (when utilized) plays a great role in allowing you to achieve scalability goals with the least amount of change in the system. Scalability is about utilizing or deploying additional resources to handle additional load. Additional load could be in the form of any sizing up of the application's requirements as described in the following examples:

- **Functionality:** Adapt to newer requirements without disrupting existing services.
- **Geographical reach:** Reach customers or users across wider geographies. Of course, this requirement brings a number of challenges for your application, especially if you have to worry about data sovereignty, caching, and storage across international boundaries.
- **Load:** Increase load on individual components and/or the overall system.
- **Administrative or user capacity:** Support more users or tenants locally or at the cloud level.
- **Future-proofing or multi-generations:** Be able to adapt to future components, features, or releases of dependencies outside of your control (e.g., legacy systems).
- **Multivendor support:** Be able to adapt to different vendors with various requirements. Your application's adaptability to other vendors with different interfacing or interoperability requirements may also influence scalability.

Horizontal Scalability

Horizontal scaling (a.k.a. scaling out) is concerned with adding resources or processing power to an application or logical/virtual system. For example, this might mean adding additional servers to handle additional load to a single system or application. An even simpler definition is that multiple physical servers in a cluster support a single application. Adding additional servers or machines to a single application should also lead to load distribution. For example, if a single machine is running at 80 percent capacity, after scaling out, you should end up with two machines running as close as possible to 40 percent each (ideally but not always the case). The most common tool for distributing the load over multiple servers is called **load balancing** or *server load balancing* or *clustering* (some exceptions may apply).

The left side of Figure 2-9 clearly demonstrates that a single server is handling the entire load and is a single point of failure. With load balancing, the right side of the figure clearly demonstrates that the load balancer creates a virtual server that responds to client requests and passes them to one of the physical servers representing the virtual server.

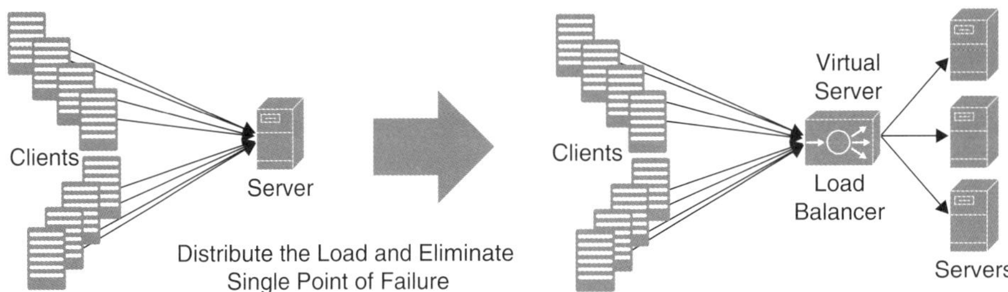

Figure 2-9 *Horizontal Scaling*

Vertical Scalability

In contrast to horizontal scaling, vertical scaling (a.k.a. scaling up) is concerned with adding resources to a single node or physical system. For example, this means adding memory or storage to a single server to allow it to support an application. A single node is upgraded with additional power to do more. One of the most common ways to do this in application development is multithreading. As you scale up the number of available processors (or cores, as commonly used nowadays), the application automatically utilizes the additional processors. It is also not uncommon to see multiple single-threaded modules or instances utilizing the presence of additional number of processors.

In Figure 2-10, the two scalability scenarios of scaling up and scaling out are clearly demonstrated.

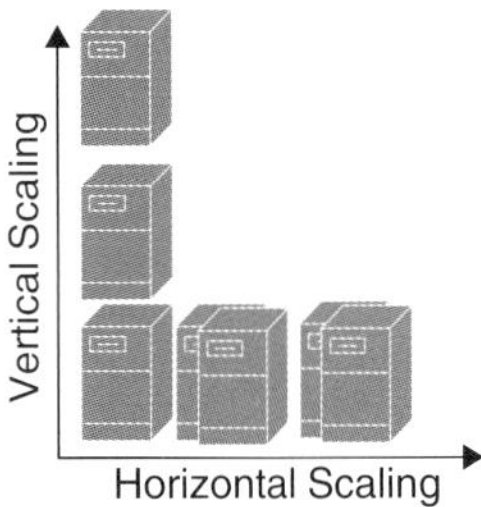

Figure 2-10 *Horizontal vs. Vertical Scalability*

Some publications refer to *hybrid scaling* or *autoscaling*, which means using both approaches to keep the system or application healthy. This means that the system (through automation and prediction) scales up or out depending on the need of the application.

It's worth noting here that the term *elasticity*, which you commonly hear in relation to cloud resource management, is also a type of scaling up/down or in/out based on predetermined policies or based on system demands. For example, you might have seen systems add resources to a web application based on time-of-day policy. More resources can be added during known or predicted high-demand hours, and subsequently, the resources can be released outside the high-demand hours.

NOTE Points to keep in mind:

- For a solution to be considered scalable, it has to allow for scaling (up or out) with little to no changes to the original architecture.
- Scalability is easiest if considered at the time the solution is architected. True, you may not know that you need it, but certain considerations with threading, modularity, and other attribute trade-offs may help you in the long run. Everything is related to everything.
- Horizontal scaling is better suited for environments and applications with varying high-demand or high-peak periods. It is easier to improve capacity of an application using additional hardware or virtual machines.
- Remember, nonfunctional requirements or quality attributes need to be measurable. Scalability can be measured in multiple ways and depending on where or what function you're trying to enhance. They include concurrent sessions, users, throughput, and resource usage like CPU, memory, disk-space, and link/network bandwidth.

Practical Scalability in Application Design

As mentioned earlier, modularity and scalability are closely related. Successful modularity techniques forced loose coupling among application components. Components or modules were designed to be independent with defined input/output and clear interfaces, allowing interaction among the various application components. Subsequently, the industry moved toward distributed execution of application modules. Doing this required that no state is maintained by the various modules and that data shared across the system may be available to the proper module without strict routing and without paying attention to the span of control or scope of the module's data (see the "black-box design" and "span of control" descriptions in the section "Modularity Coding Best Practices").

Why are we saying all this? Simple, because in practice, scaling an application is very much dependent on its capability to be modular, with the modules being as independent or autonomous as possible, as stateless as possible, and with interfaces and APIs for interaction. Only then can you scale the application in, out, up, or down with the fewest changes to the underlying architecture. The following examples are practical ways of improving scalability through modularity:

1. Understand your application's memory and CPU requirements and enable your system to utilize the addition of resources effectively. For example, how many bytes or kilobytes of RAM do you need per 100 concurrent users? How many more users can you handle by increasing memory? It's most probably not a linear relationship. Scalability

is measured by how easy or effective it would be to add resources to improve performance. One issue to also keep in mind here is the cost. CPUs, GPUs, memory space, or virtual machines can be costly. Understanding your overall cost per transaction is essential for working through your design trade-offs.

2. Remember what we said earlier about modularity enabling scalability. The use of microservices, containers, and virtual machines allows for greater flexibility and elasticity of resources for your application.
3. Optimize data access. Building stateless modules does improve scalability and performance but requires data access from centralized databases and memory. Optimize your database choice and how data is accessed. For example, *indexing* or *sharding* helps you scale the data set size and the overall system. Sharding in databases is a type of horizontal partitioning where a dataset is distributed over multiple databases (possibly even over multiple physical machines), allowing you to scale out your system.
4. As your application grows and covers larger geographies, caching data close to your user base becomes a great scalability tool. The use of **content delivery networks (CDNs)** and edge computing can help you achieve this goal.
5. Server or traffic load balancing distributes the load across multiple machines, allowing for great scalability. We discussed server load balancing earlier. Traffic or network load balancing is in the form of path optimization with **software-defined networks (SDN)** or through equal cost multipath (ECMP) routing supported by the major network routing protocols.
6. As a last resort, when all fails, you may find yourself having to redesign your application to allow for greater scalability.

High Availability and Resiliency in Application Design

Countless issues affect the availability of an application or a system. These issues are not always associated with failures, outages, or errors within the application itself. Sometimes they are environment-related, host-system-related, cloud-related—you get the point. There is a lot beyond the control of the developer that can affect the application. However, a few excellent design and development practices can help increase the availability and resiliency of your system or application.

The applications we're talking about in this book are mostly related to programmability and IT DevOps management and probably have high availability goals and are "always on." Therefore, the concept of availability becomes of high importance because it is closely related to dependability, reliability, and security. Various types of security issues affect the availability of an application. For example, a distributed denial-of-service (DDOS) attack can drain the system's resources and cause it to fail, hence, affecting its availability.

Availability is about maximizing uptime or minimizing downtime of a system through fault mitigation, self-healing, or repair.

How does an application react to the loss of connectivity to its subsystems or databases?

What happens when host systems fail?

How does a system handle the hardware failure of one of the nodes in a cluster?

You can measure the availability of a system as the time it is fully operational in a given period. Although the following formula was initially used for hardware systems, it is an excellent example to illustrate this point:

Availability = MTBF / (MTBF + MTTR)

MTBF refers to the **mean time between failures**, and **MTTR** refers to the **mean time to repair** (or resolution, or recovery). As a software developer, when you're thinking about availability, you should think about what will make your system fail, the likelihood of it happening, and how much time will be required to repair it.

Every system has an availability goal that includes all planned and unplanned outages, and we sometimes call this a **service-level agreement (SLA)**. The SLA is a commitment made by the system architect (owner or operator) that the system will be up for a specified period (e.g., a billing cycle or a year). For example, an SLA of 99 percent means that the system will be available 99 percent of the time it is needed. If you use one year as a time of operation, then the SLA specifies that the system will be available 362 days and 8 hours. Also, 99 percent availability means that there is a 1 percent probability that the system will not be available when it is needed, and that translates to 3 days and 16 hours.

You commonly see terms like *three nines* to describe 99.9 percent availability or *five nines* to describe 99.999 percent availability. Table 2-5 lists yearly values of availability.

Table 2-5 Availability Requirements

Availability	Also Known As	Probability of Downtime per Year
99%	Two nines	3 days, 15 hours, 36 minutes
99.9%	Three nines	8 hours, 46 seconds
99.99%	Four nines	52 minutes and 34 seconds
99.999%	Five nines	5 minutes and 15 seconds
99.9999%	Six nines	32 seconds

NOTE The availability rating of a system is constrained by the lowest availability number of any of its components. For example, in an application that uses three interdependent systems where two of them are considered to have 99.999 percent availability and a third has 99.9 percent availability, the system's availability is 99.9 percent.

Recently, the focus has been shifting to high availability of five or six nines or even higher (eight nines), especially as some of the software applications discussed in this book are concerned with running enterprise or service provider networks or business services at a global level. Certain instances of businesses require being as close to "always on" as possible.

There is a great deal that we could discuss about availability, but we limit the discussion to these main points:

- Detection
- Recovery
- Prevention

Failure or Fault Detection

In practice, the terms *failure* and *fault* are used interchangeably. In reality, and especially in software practices, a failure is caused by the presence of a fault in the software or one of the system components that alter the behavior of the system or degrade its performance without actually causing a full-system outage.

NOTE IEEE defines the following terms:

- **Failure:** Observable incorrect behavior
- **Fault:** Incorrect code (sometimes called a *bug*)
- **Error:** The cause of the fault

Regardless of how you want to look at it, the following are common ways of detecting a fault and alerting you to a failure that is about to happen or has already happened:

- **Monitoring:** Monitoring, sometimes known as continuous monitoring, is essential in informing you about the current state or health of the system. Monitoring, whether at the software level or the underlying hardware components, has come a long way. Alongside monitoring up/down scenarios, monitoring also informs you of the current state of resources being used by the system and the possibility of certain thresholds that could lead to system performance degradation or failure. For example, continuous monitoring and reporting (or trending) of memory utilization can inform you about the presence of memory leak scenarios where processes are not releasing memory back after completion.
- **Self-testing or self-monitoring:** Individual systems or subsystems perform tests on themselves or possibly have a testing or monitoring subsystem that tests the overall system for operational accuracy or health checks. This process is different from monitoring in that it is performed internally by the system instead of an external system.
- **Heartbeat or "hello packets":** Cisco loyalists or experts commonly see this process used in the majority of network operating systems. This is probably one of the most important components of achieving high availability. A heartbeat is usually exchanged between two or more redundant system components or between a software/hardware system and a monitoring system. Sending, receiving, and processing heartbeats requires system resources. There are a few things that you can do to prioritize heartbeats between components using special tags or quality of service (QoS) marking on a network link. This way, you can guarantee (to a certain extent) that heartbeat messages are not dropped or discarded during high system utilization periods. Figure 2-11 demonstrates the concept of heartbeats informing the server load balancer of their availability:
- **Simple ping or ICMP echo/echo-reply:** We use the term *simple* in describing this method because it only informs you that the system or subsystem component is up or down and nothing else about the overall behavior. However, you can read something

into the latency numbers generated by the echo/echo-reply. If the latency (or round-trip time) is high, then this could tell you something about the state of the network or the underlying hardware architecture.

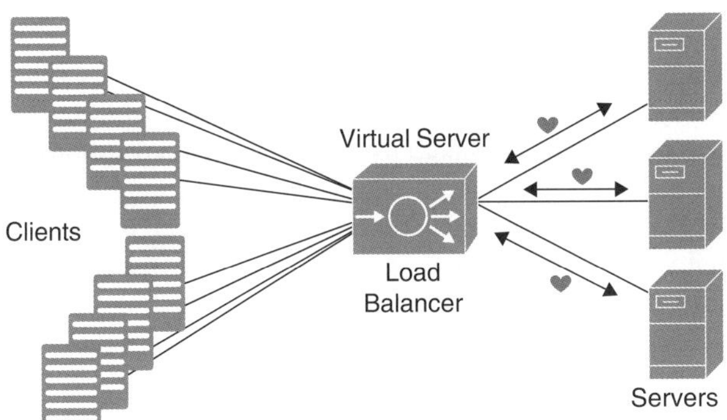

Figure 2-11 *Heartbeats or Hello Packets in a Server Load-Balancing Scenario*

- **Sanity checks:** These processes check the validity of important output values. Understanding certain operations with high dependencies and checking the validity of the operations are very important. For example, if you perform an operation and store the result in a variable that gets used in a subsequent operation, and all you check is that the stored value exists without validating the "operation," then you have a fault that is very hard to find. Sanity checks are simple and should not stress the system resources.

Recovery: High Availability in Practice

Remember the term *mean time to repair (MTTR)*? We address a few important concepts in this section. Dealing with network infrastructure, you're likely used to the term *disaster recovery*, and you use that for various aspects of the network and system failure scenarios. These concepts are also used in software systems and affect software and hardware recovery mechanisms. When failures occur, there are a few things that you can do, and as expected, they're mostly around redundancy and/or self-healing:

- **Redundancy:** Redundancy is the most common way to deal with failure. In essence, redundancy strives to remove single points of failure and ensure fast recovery from faults. Having additional resources capable of performing the task of the failing device is essential. There are various ways to configure redundant resources. The decision of which one to use depends on the availability requirements of the system or business process. Redundancy types include the following examples:
  - **Active (hot standby):** Redundant systems or nodes receive and process input at the same time; however, only one system replies back to the request. The standby system maintains the same state (or data) as the active system and will be available to take over in a very short time. With the recent advancements in processors and software development practices, you can expect to see failover or switchover times in the single or low double-digit milliseconds (e.g., 10–90 ms). Consider,

for example, the high availability feature of the Cisco Catalyst switching platform called StackWise. Without going into too much detail on how it works, Figure 2-12 demonstrates the hot standby concept mentioned here. The Active switch has both the control and data planes active, which means that the Active switch will receive requests (network packets), perform the destination lookup, make a forwarding decision, and update its lookup tables (databases). The Standby switch, on the other hand, being in hot standby mode, synchronizes state and lookup tables with the Active processor but does not perform any lookup or make forwarding decisions because its control plane is in standby. However, it does forward packets on its physical ports using decisions made by the Active processor. At failover and after a number of heartbeats (hello packets) are not received from the Active switch over the StackWise virtual link, the Standby switch declares itself as Active and continues the operation using the lookup tables it has already synchronized with the previously active switch without having to rebuild the lookup tables.

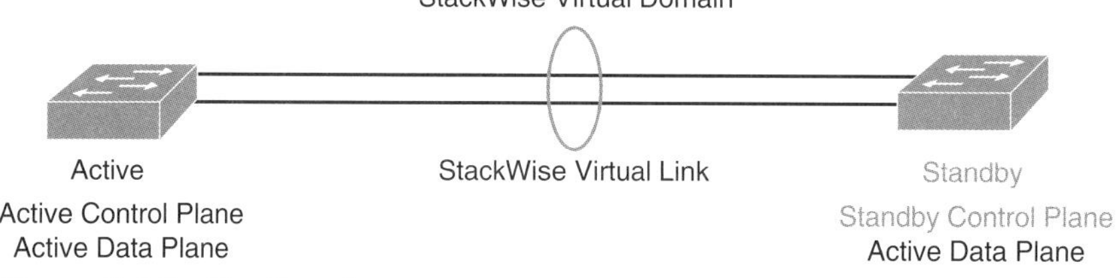

Figure 2-12 *Hot Standby*

- **Passive (warm standby):** In this type of redundancy, there are two or more redundant systems; one of them is fully active (hot) and processing all input, and one or more are in standby mode. The warm standby system is preconfigured and powered up but does not have the necessary data to continue the operation. When a failover event is triggered, the standby system becomes active and starts the learning process to create the proper state. Figure 2-13 provides an example of warm standby and how the Spanning Tree Protocol (STP) provides path redundancy at the Layer 2 level by blocking one path and unblocking it at the time of failure. But after unblocking the path, the device that has just become the owner of the active path must go through a learning period before it can build the tree and provide a forwarding path. The learning period may reach as high as 50 seconds.

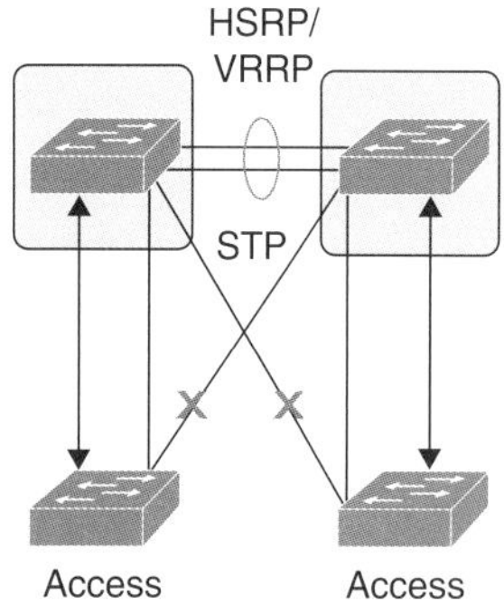

Figure 2-13 *Warm Standby Using Spanning Tree Protocol (STP)*

- **Spare (cold standby):** The spare system may or may not be operational; it possibly is not even powered up and, in some cases, may require a manual process to become effective. In Figure 2-14, the Cisco Catalyst 9600 switch supports the presence of a second supervisor module leading to what's known as the redundant supervisor module (RSM). If you deploy two redundant switches with two redundant processors installed in each of the chassis, then you end up with an active processor in one chassis and a standby in the other chassis. The two remaining ones (one in each chassis) are called in-chassis standby (ICS). The two supervisor modules use route processor redundancy (RPR) technology to establish an RPR cold-standby relationship within each local chassis and stateful switchover (SSO) technology to establish an active/hot-standby redundancy relationship across the chassis. In the unlikely event that the active supervisor should fail within the chassis, the standby cold supervisor will transition to the active role. This transition occurs by fully booting up the ICS supervisor; it remains nonoperational until the SSO redundancy is reestablished with the new StackWise virtual active supervisor across the chassis. In a way, Figure 2-14 illustrates a good example of cold and warm standby configurations. The StackWise Virtual Link (SVL) is used to synchronize state between the active and standby switches and for transmitting the heartbeat informing both switches of the state of each switch, and the Dual-Active Detection (DAD) link ensures that you do not end up with two active switches.

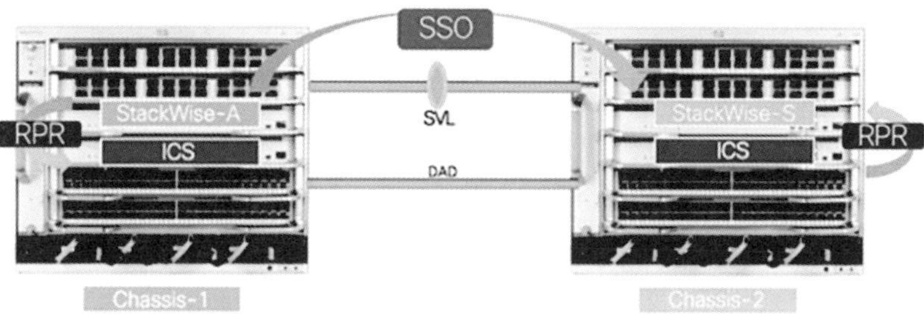

Figure 2-14 *Cold Standby (Catalyst 9600 Quad-Supervisor Support)*

- **Retries:** Retries are another type of redundancy. This type of redundancy is in retrying the operation to confirm that it is an actual failure or just high-demand situation that prevented normal operations at the first try. Like retransmission, retries consume additional resources and should be handled with care and should have longer intervals between retries and should also be bound to a finite set. As you've already seen in the majority of networking protocols, we've limited retries to three before we declare a system failure.

- **Timeouts:** Timeouts are a close relative to heartbeats and retries. Timeout values are given to processes that wait for responses from retries or retransmissions. Every time a retry or a heartbeat is sent, a timer is set and decrements until either a response is received or it times out. When it times out, then a failure is declared.

- **System upgrade:** Using this method, you upgrade the system software during operations and without significantly affecting the performance of the system. Of course, there is a reason for the upgrade, and that is a failure. The failure may have occurred or may have only been known to affect similar systems, so this is why an in-service software upgrade (ISSU) or hit-less upgrade is needed. Cisco routers and switches have been supporting this type of upgrade for quite some time, especially on systems where multiple processors or supervisor cards exist.

- **Rollback:** This method has proven to work well especially after changes in configuration or after upgrades. The system maintains a copy of a previously working state or dataset and reverts back to it in case the new configuration experiences complications or does not pass certain checks.

Prevention

A great deal of time and effort has been dedicated to failure prevention, and that effort seems to be paying off. There is a technology element to prevention, which we discuss here, but there is also an operational process level that should not be ignored. Following a standard procedure of maintenance and upgrades is essential to preventing unplanned outages.

- **Isolation:** At the detection of a fault and to prevent a potential failure, you can remove the system from service to allow for further analysis or mitigation. This type of prevention is also used for periodic maintenance cycles.
- **Predictive analytics:** A great deal of historical data is available for analysis and to train statistical models to identify patterns or trends that led to a failure. Using telemetry, logs, and monitoring, you can understand the system's normal behavior and also how it behaved before, during, or after a failure. By observing or learning these events, you can predict failures before they occur.
- **Automation:** Automation not only improves provisioning and configuration but also improves consistency and eliminates human error.

High Availability Planning and the Responsibilities of the Developer

In high availability design, business continuity planning (BCP) and disaster recovery planning (DRP) are two important concepts. BCP is a type of strategy or document with three main areas of focus, each with an implication on applications as well as the underlying IT infrastructure:

- **High availability planning:** These functions and processes harness the power of redundancy at all levels such as servers, databases, storage, replication, routers, and switches. In a way, this includes everything we've discussed in this chapter alongside the business processes and the physical infrastructure hosting the business applications. An example of something that you need to keep in mind as related to SLAs is the storage and replication requirements.
- **Continuous operations:** These operations are a continuation of HA planning because they focus on maintenance and unplanned outage scheduling and ensuring that the backup plan continues to operate the business application during an outage.
- **Disaster recovery planning:** DRP is concerned with the facilities (i.e., the data center) and ensuring connectivity between redundant sites and ensuring adequate distance between the active and standby data centers (a.k.a. disaster recovery data center).

Several standards bodies and government entities specify what are called *disaster zones* and subsequently designate disaster radiuses. For example, if your active data center is an area prone to earthquakes, then your DR site should be outside that zone or outside the disaster radius.

High Availability Deployment Models

As mentioned before, you need to make a few important decisions before you decide on your high availability deployment, and they depend on the service-level agreement (SLA) or other mechanisms that allow you to measure the importance of an application to the success of your business, customer experience, and the cost of maintaining them. Keeping these items in mind will help you decide on your deployment models and how much time and money you're willing to spend.

As seen from previous discussions, clustering, server load balancing, network load balancing, and general redundancy practices are part of the overall high availability and continuous operations deployment. In addition, the following are extremely important deployment practices:

1. **Data backup and replication:** This is probably the most important high availability deployment concept. No redundancy or high availability design is complete (or even useful) without a proper backup, retrieval, and replication system or process. Data integrity is key.
2. **Clustering:** We briefly touched on clustering and server load balancing earlier. With clustering, multiple servers share or access data through common storage or memory systems. The addition or removal of a server (or virtual server) does not affect the cluster.

   Figure 2-15 illustrates how the applications represented by the cluster will continue to operate normally as long as one server is active. Traditionally, clustering does not necessarily require a load balancer to be involved. The load balancer in Figure 2-15 could easily be substituted by a switch, and clustering would not be affected.

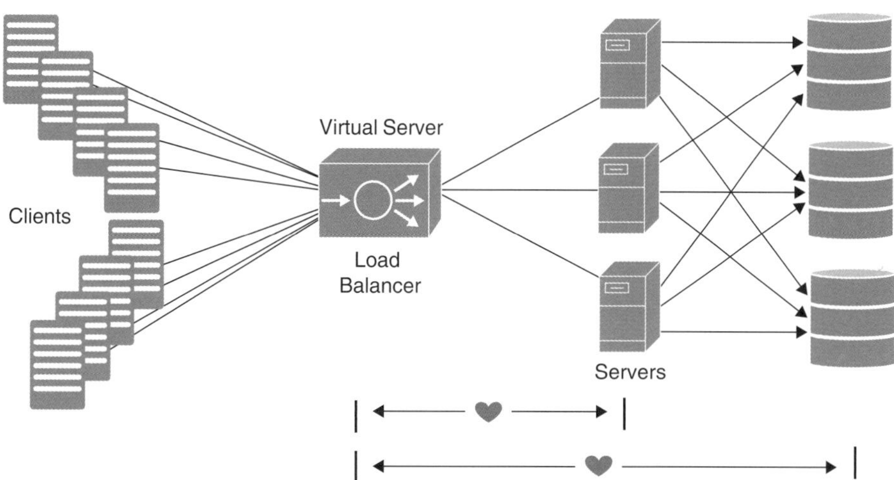

Figure 2-15 *Clustering Is an Essential Deployment Model for High Availability in Application Design*

The storage and servers, as shown in Figure 2-15, exchange heartbeats with the load balancer or cluster manager in-band or out-of-band (on a dedicated network). With the recent advancement in network and cloud technologies, clusters started expanding beyond a single data center into other enterprise data centers or into the cloud.

The Cisco DNA Center, for example, supports a three-node cluster configuration, which provides both software and hardware high availability. A software failure occurs when a service on a node fails. Software high availability involves the ability of the services on the node or nodes to be restarted. For example, if a service fails on one node in a three-node cluster, that service is either restarted on the same node or on one of the other two remaining nodes. A hardware failure occurs when the appliance itself malfunctions or fails. Hardware high availability is enabled by the presence of multiple appliances in a cluster, multiple disk drives within each appliance's redundant disk drive configuration, and multiple power supplies. As a result, a failure by one of these components can be tolerated until the faulty component is restored or replaced.

NOTE As you start designing your HA solution, the decision to keep your application completely on-premises (e.g., served from one or two enterprise data centers), move it to the cloud, or even use a hybrid of both, highly depends on a choice between latency, performance, efficiency, and quality of experience.

Table 2-6 lists a few advantages and disadvantages of the models described previously:

Table 2-6 Availability Deployment Models

Deployment Model	Advantages	Disadvantages
On-premises	Full control of your data Own and control SLA Ability to customize	Relatively costly to acquire, ramp up, and maintain Not easily scalable
Cloud	Elasticity in scale and performance Low maintenance Low cost (few exceptions apply) Ability to place apps and data as close as possible to your users or customers Mobility and easy access regardless of location High availability and disaster recovery built into the infrastructure (Make sure your application is able to utilize the features)	Functionality is limited by cloud provider capabilities Security is still an issue, especially if access is through the Internet Technical support. Of course, it all depends on your application and its functionality, but this is an important aspect to keep in mind.

Deployment Model	Advantages	Disadvantages
Hybrid	Workload mobility between on-premises and cloud based on demand or resource utilization thresholds Flexibility to utilize both models based on demand or customer requirements	Complexity in configuration Difficult to maintain

Exam Preparation Tasks

As mentioned in the section "How to Use This Book" in the Introduction, you have a couple of choices for exam preparation: the exercises here, Chapter 17, "Final Preparation," and the exam simulation questions on the companion website.

Review All Key Topics

Review the most important topics in this chapter, noted with the Key Topic icon in the outer margin of the page. Table 2-7 lists a reference of these key topics and the page numbers on which each is found.

Table 2-7 Key Topics for Chapter 2

Key Topic Element	Description	Page Number
Section	Modularity Coding Best Practices	37
Section	Microservices and Modular Design	40
Section	Horizontal Scalability	41
Section	Vertical Scalability	42
Note	Points to keep in mind	43
Section	High Availability and Resiliency in Application Design	44

Complete Tables and Lists from Memory

Print a copy of Appendix C, "Memory Tables" (found on the companion website), or at least the section for this chapter, and complete the tables and lists from memory. Appendix D, "Memory Tables Answer Key," also on the companion website, includes completed tables and lists to check your work.

Define Key Terms

Define the following key terms from this chapter and check your answers in the glossary:

cohesion, coupling, cold standby, content delivery networks (CDNs), clustering, load balancing, mean time to repair or mean time to recovery (MTTR), mean time between failures (MTBF), software-defined networking (SDN), service-level agreement (SLA)

References

URL	QR Code
https://www.cisco.com/c/en/us/products/collateral/switches/catalyst-9000/nb-06-cat-9k-stack-wp-cte-en.html	
https://www.cisco.com/c/en/us/td/docs/cloud-systems-management/network-automation-and-management/dna-center/2-1-2/ha_guide/b_cisco_dna_center_ha_guide_2_1_2.html	
Continuous Architecture in Practice: Software Architecture in the Age of Agility and DevOps https://www.informit.com/store/continuous-architecture-in-practice-software-architecture-9780136523567	
Software Architecture in Practice, 4th Edition https://www.informit.com/store/software-architecture-in-practice-9780136886099	
ISO/IEC 25010:2011: *Systems and software engineering—Systems and software Quality Requirements and Evaluation (SQuaRE)—System and software quality models*	

CHAPTER 3

Architectural Considerations and Performance Management

This chapter covers the following topics:

- **Maintainable Design and Implementation:** This section describes best practices for building maintainable software using modularity, proper documentation, and object-oriented design.
- **Latency and Rate Limiting in Application Design and Performance:** This section covers various performance enhancements or degradation parameters and best architectural practices.
- **Design and Implementation for Observability:** This section describes best practices for application performance monitoring and user experience management using observability concepts.
- **Database Selection Criteria:** This section describes how application performance and flexibility depend on proper database selection criteria. We also discuss architectural decisions for database selection.

This chapter maps to the *Developing Applications Using Cisco Core Platforms and APIs v1.0 (350-901)* Exam Blueprint Section 1.0, "Application Deployment and Security," specifically subsections 1.4, 1.5, 1.6, and 1.8.

In this chapter, we continue to discuss a few other nonfunctional requirements and how they affect the application's quality and performance. As you learned in Chapter 2, "Software Quality Attributes," quality attributes intersect in many ways, either in a complementary fashion or as trade-offs. You saw how modularity positively contributes to scalability. In this chapter, you get exposed to application performance and what trade-offs that may have to be made to improve it. For example, will increasing system capacity impact the performance of the system?

This chapter also includes topics related to observability and maintainability of applications and what software development principles you need to be aware of to improve your visibility into your overall environments and application-related parameters through full stack observability.

The concepts discussed throughout Chapter 2 enable you to build scalable and highly available software. In this chapter, you learn how to optimize for performance and detectability through visibility.

"Do I Know This Already?" Quiz

The "Do I Know This Already?" quiz allows you to assess whether you should read this entire chapter thoroughly or jump to the "Exam Preparation Tasks" section. If you are in doubt about your answers to these questions or your own assessment of your knowledge of the topics, read the entire chapter. Table 3-1 lists the major headings in this chapter and their corresponding "Do I Know This Already?" quiz questions. You can find the answers in Appendix A, "Answers to the 'Do I Know This Already?' Quizzes."

Table 3-1 "Do I Know This Already?" Section-to-Question Mapping

Foundation Topics Section	Questions
Maintainable Design and Implementation	1, 2
Latency and Rate Limiting in Application Design and Performance	3–8
Design and Implementation for Observability	9, 10
Database Selection Criteria	11

1. What is it essential to have for software maintainability?
   - **a.** A modular design
   - **b.** Proper documentation
   - **c.** Coding standards
   - **d.** All of these answers are correct.
2. Which item is *not* a characteristic of object-oriented programming?
   - **a.** Encapsulation
   - **b.** Inheritance
   - **c.** Polymorphism
   - **d.** Structured programming
3. What is SOLID?
   - **a.** Single Object Language ID
   - **b.** A type of programming language
   - **c.** Software design principles for building maintainable code
   - **d.** None of these answers are correct.
4. "Modules should be open for extension but closed for modification" is a definition of which of the SOLID principles?
   - **a.** Single responsibility principle (SRP)
   - **b.** Open-closed principle (OCP)
   - **c.** Liskov's substitution principle (LSP)
   - **d.** Interface segregation principle (ISP)
   - **e.** Dependency inversion principle (DIP)

5. Which SOLID principle states that higher-level modules should not depend on lower-level modules?
   a. Single responsibility principle (SRP)
   b. Open-closed principle (OCP)
   c. Liskov's substitution principle (LSP)
   d. Interface segregation principle (ISP)
   e. Dependency inversion principle (DIP)
6. Which of the following is used as an indicator of software performance?
   a. Latency
   b. Round-trip time (RTT)
   c. Throughput
   d. All of these answers are correct.
7. Network congestion or packet drops are side effects of what network condition?
   a. Wireless systems
   b. Network overload or oversubscription
   c. Slow software
   d. All of these answers are correct.
8. Which performance enhancements are commonly used in application design? (Choose two.)
   a. Caching
   b. Rate limiting
   c. Echo replies
   d. Open Shortest Path First
9. What is observability, in simple terms?
   a. A way to monitor the performance of a system through its users' experience
   b. A way to detect system issues through the observation of its output
   c. A way to manage and monitor distributed applications
   d. All of these answers are correct
10. Observability is said to have which three pillars?
    a. Logging, balancing, and multiprocessing
    b. Tracing, routing, and switching
    c. Logging, metrics, and tracing
    d. Routing, switching, and multithreading
11. What are the differences between relational and nonrelational databases? (Choose two.)
    a. Relational databases can be key-value stores where each key is associated with one value.
    b. Relational databases store data in rows and columns like a spreadsheet.
    c. Nonrelational databases are also known as NoSQL, where one type can be a document-oriented store.
    d. There are hardly any differences between the two except that relational databases are commercial and nonrelational are mostly open source.

Foundation Topics

Maintainable Design and Implementation

Change is constant. You've surely heard this phrase before, and we're sure that it holds true for all software or code. If you're sure that, indeed, change is constant, then you can prepare for it and design your applications to be modifiable and maintainable. By doing so, you will save yourself and your customers a lot of time. Research has repeatedly shown that a larger part of the cost of an application is incurred after an application is released. That cost is spent on maintenance, new functionality, and bug fixes, among other things. Designing for maintainability is the area where you should put your thought process early in the design or development process. Focus on questions such as "What can possibly change?" "How likely are these changes?" and "What will these changes impact?" Future-proof your design by anticipating change.

As we mentioned in Chapter 2, proper modular design allows you to make changes within a small module or subcomponent without having to redesign or rewrite the entire system. Modularity is one of the many leading practices that allows for easier and more effective maintainability of your application. The following factors contribute to that goal:

- **Modular design:** Modularity allows for updates, modifications, and fixes without having to redesign the application.
- **Proper documentation and proper naming conventions:** Maintaining these factors improves compliance and observability and allows you to integrate additional developers into the project with the least amount of onboarding time.
- **Common toolset:** Closely related to the previous point—and equally as important—is using a common toolset. Which toolset to use is a decision that needs to be made early in the process. Having a common toolset significantly improves migration and integration of various functions among developers.
- **Software configuration management and version control:** Tracking changes and maintaining overall version control are helpful on many fronts, including traceability of changes and individuals contributing to changes. Managing this issue may be your best friend when it comes to maintenance and bug fixes.
- **Coding standards:** The use of coding standards simplifies both initial development and subsequent maintenance. It also keeps the developer's thought processes within a predefined set of rules and limitations.
- **Object-oriented design (OOD):** Object-oriented design is natural and intuitive, and subsequently makes it easy for others to follow the logic of a piece of code. Therefore, OOD leads to shorter cycles of development time and a reduction in resources related to maintaining the code. In Chapter 2, we discussed how independent modules or classes contribute to this end as well.

Software developers change and subsequently introduce additional cost to the lifecycle of a project for various reasons or factors:

- **Bug fixes:** Whether bugs or errors are detected during a test cycle, code review, or the production use of an application, at the end of the day, changes have to be introduced to the code. In some cases, such changes may require a major redesign of modules, objects, or classes. Modular and well-documented code speeds up this cycle.
- **New features and upgrades:** If your code or application is being used and continuously exercised, it is a matter of time before new features and upgrades are needed so that you can stay competitive. New features address customer efficiency or performance requirements that extend the life of your application and subsequently its shelf life. If the guidelines detailed in the previous section are followed, then introducing new features is simple and fast.
- **Code refactoring:** Refactoring is a DevOps feature that strives to improve the structure and quality of code without changing the functionality. It is often performed after the initial deployment, most often to improve efficiency and maintainability.
- **Performance optimization:** There is always room for improvement, and performance usually get the most attention. Performance improvements can be related to the efficiency of the code or the underlying hardware infrastructure (network, compute, or storage).
- **Code adaptation to new environments:** This is closely related to the previous point, and it is mostly related to adapting your code to new computing or hosting environments to improve performance, reduce cost, or gain more market share.
- **Problem prevention or future-proofing:** As you optimize your code for new environments or for performance, you also should lean on lessons learned to future-proof it for anticipated changes to the runtime environment or the release of new hardware capabilities.

Maintaining a SOLID Design

Based on the preceding section, one of the best guidelines for composing code that allows for maintainability is to use the well-known **SOLID** principles for object-oriented design. These five principles together combine to give guidelines for composing and maintaining software code:

- Single responsibility principle (SRP)
- Open-closed principle (OCP)
- Liskov's substitution principle (LSP)
- Interface segregation principle (ISP)
- Dependency inversion principle (DIP)

Single Responsibility Principle (SRP)

A class or a module should have only a single responsibility. The single responsibility principle was originally stated as: "A class should have one, and only one, reason to change." This means that it has one job, and it would be easy to modify and maintain a module with a single job. If a module has multiple jobs or functions, then modifying one function affects other functions and the overall system they compose. Consider Figure 3-1, where a class has multiple responsibilities:

```
class NetworkSwitch:
      def __init__(self, model, port_density):
            self.model = model
            self.port_density = port_density

1     def set_model(self, model):
            self.model = model

      def set_port_density(self, port_density):
            self.port_density = port_density

2     def deploy_switch(self):
            datacenter.deploy(self.model, self.port_density)
```

Figure 3-1 *Not-Easy-to-Maintain Code*

In Figure 3-1, you first set the class (labeled "1") and parameters (**model** and **port_density**) and then deploy the switch (labeled "2") with **deploy_switch**. Any change to the deployment service (**deploy_switch**) affects the **NetworkSwitch** class. This is exactly what SRP is trying to prevent.

A simple fix is to decouple the responsibilities into independent single responsibility classes (as shown in Figure 3-2). This approach produces efficient and easily maintainable code. The **NetworkSwitch** class (labeled "1") sets the data for the service, and the new class **Switch-DeployerService** (labeled "2") deploys the switches (or service for that matter). Changing or evolving the one class does not affect the other.

```
      class NetworkSwitch:
            def __init__(self, model, port_density):
                  self.model = model
                  self.port_density = port_density

1           def set_model(self, model):
                  self.model = model

            def set_port_density(self, port_density):
                  self.port_density = port_density


      class SwitchDeployerService:
2           def deploy_switch(service):
                  datacenter.deploy(service.model, service.port_density)
```

Figure 3-2 *Recommended and Easy-to-Maintain/Modify Code*

Open-Closed Principle (OCP)

Components (classes, modules, or functions) should be open for extension but closed for modification. They should be open for different uses or implementations through interfaces (loose coupling) but also closed for modifications.

Extensibility is an interesting concept in software design in that it allows a system to extend its capabilities or features without major modifications or rewriting. This is what the open-closed principle recommends: open for extending capabilities, closed for rewriting or modifications. Subsequently, OCP says that you should not have to rewrite classes, functions, or interfaces to add new functionality.

To demonstrate the point of OCP, consider the previous **SwitchDeployerService** example with a mission to deploy network switches and types in different network segments. In Example 3-1, the **SwitchDeployerService** supports the MoR (middle of row) data center switches.

Example 3-1 *Deployment Illustrating the Open-Closed Principle*

```
    class NetworkSwitch:
         def __init__(self, type, model, config):
              self.type = type
              self.model = model
              self.config = config
    class SwitchDeployerService:
def deploy_switch(self, service):
    if service.type == 'MoR'  # Middle of Row Switch
              datacenter.deploy(service.config, '192.168.100.0/24')
```

Let's say you want to add support for an out-of-band management network. Is that easily done? Not really! Adding such support requires rewriting or modifying the original code.

However, if you had already written the code using the single responsibility principle, then you would definitely be able to add support for as many network types as needed by adding additional classes and eventually conforming to OPC as well. A possible solution for this would be to build a static or common **NetworkSwitch** and **SwitchDeployerService**. Then build additional classes or features into the classes. In Example 3-2 the **segment** parameter is added and the **if** statement is converted into the extended classes, one for the user and one for management: **NetworkSwitchMoR** and **NetworkSwitchOOB**. No if or but.

Example 3-2 *Example Illustrating the Open-Closed Principle*

```
class NetworkSwitch:
    def __init__(self, type, model, config):
         self.type = type
         self.model = model
         self.config = config
```

```
class NetworkSwitchMoR (NetworkSwitch):
    def __init__(self):
        super().__init__(self)
        self.segment = '192.168.100.0/24'

class NetworkSwitchOOB (NetworkSwitch):
    def __init__(self):
        super().__init__(self)
        self.segment = '192.168.200.0/24'

class SwitchDeployerService:
    def deploy_switch(self, service):
        datacenter.deploy(service.config, service.segment)0
```

If, in the future, another network type requires the deployment of the same services, all you need to do is create and extend the class. For example, if you have a top-of-rack (ToR) data center switch, all you have to do is create the class **NetworkSwitchToR** and specify the segment (in this case, you use the IP subnet for definition).

NOTE The **super()** function is used to invoke the **__int__** function of the **NetworkSwitch**, which can be thought of as the super class. It initializes the inherited instance **self._xxx.**

Liskov's Substitution Principle (LSP)

Liskov's substitution principle requires that objects of subclasses be substitutable for objects of their super classes and the application or super classes should continue to function properly. Substitutability is a fact of life in object-oriented programming, and LSP states that if A is a subclass of B then objects of type B may be replaced by objects of type A without causing errors.

To demonstrate the point, let's continue with the previous example using the super class **NetworkSwitch** (see Example 3-3).

Example 3-3 *LSP Violation and How It Can Be Avoided*

```
class NetworkSwitch:
    def get_model(self):
        return self.model

Then consider the following Subclass NetworkSwitchMoR:

class NetworkSwitchMoR(NetworkSwitch):
    def get_model(self, switch_name):
        model = db.get_switch(switch_name)
        print(model)
        return None
```

In this example, the subclass **NetworkSwitchMoR** changes what's intended by **get_model** from the super class, and that is a violation of LSP.

Interface Segregation Principle (ISP)

The name of the interface segregation principle tells the story. ISP requires interfaces to be independent of (or should not rely on) interfaces they do not use. For example, having a super class with many interfaces reduces its flexibility and maintainability. It is better to have many subclasses than to have one large subclass. In other words, clients should not depend on interfaces they don't use.

Consider Example 3-4, where unnecessary interfaces are implemented and then flagged with an error message (e.g., **NotAvailableError**). Developers call these *fat interfaces*. This practice produces complex, hard-to-read, and hard-to-maintain code. Example 3-4 shows the complex way. Example 3-5 shows the cleanest and ISP-compliant coding practices.

Example 3-4 *Inefficient, Unclean, and Unreadable Code That Violates ISP*

```
class NetworkSwitchMoR(NetworkSwitch):
    def get_MoRmodel(self):
        return db.get_MoRmodel(self)
    def get_ToRmodel(self):
        raise NotAvailableError

class NetworkSwitchToR(NetworkSwitch):
    def get_MoRmodel(self):
        raise NotAvailableError
    def get_ToRModel(self):
        return db.get_ToRmodel(self)
```

Example 3-5 is simpler, easier to read, and easier to maintain and gives the freedom of "on an as-needed basis." There's no need to generate errors without reason; it's simpler to not use an unnecessary interface.

Example 3-5 *Clean and Efficient Code with ISP*

```
class NetworkSwitch:
    def get_model(self):
        return self.get_model()

class NetworkSwitchMoR(NetworkSwitch):
    def get_model(self):
        return db.get_MoRmodel(self)
class NetworkSwitchToR(NetworkSwitch):
    def get_model(self):
        return db.get_ToRmodel(self)
```

NOTE The interface segregation principle and Liskov substitution principle are closely related. You can think of ISP as the client's perspective, where you want the client interaction to be simple and efficient. LSP is the developer's perspective, where unnecessary types generate errors like the one seen previously: **NotAvailableError.**

Dependency Inversion Principle (DIP)

The dependency inversion principle, in a way, is the essence of modularity, and it states that higher-level modules should not depend on lower-level modules. Going back to the "coupling" discussion in the previous chapter, DIP encourages loosely coupling lower-level modules for the purpose of modifying, rewriting, or removing.

In his design paper, "Design Principles and Design Patterns," Robert C. Martin defines DIP as follows:

1. High-level modules should not depend on low-level modules. Both should depend on abstractions.
2. Abstractions should not depend on details. Details should depend on abstractions.

Compliance to DIP produces modular code because it allows for modifying or rewriting lower-level modules without affecting higher-level modules (loosely coupled).

In Figure 3-3, you can easily see the dependency among the various components of the system or service. It is hard to maintain this system because any change to any of the components needs to be considered across the entire system.

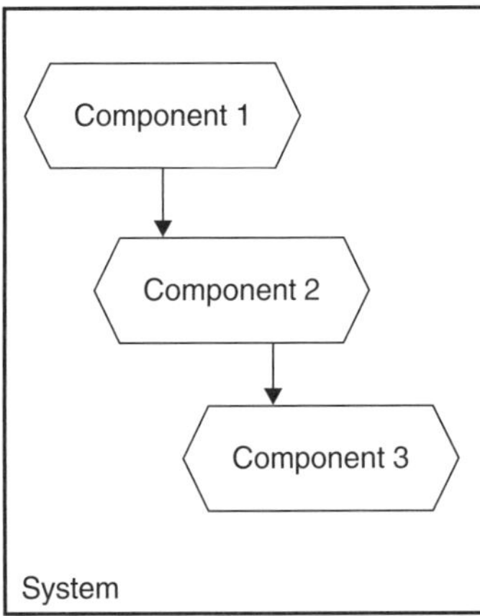

Figure 3-3 *Dependency of Higher-Level Components on Lower-Level Ones*

Programming "direct" interaction between modules or components could prove to be problematic from a maintainability and modifiability perspective. It is highly recommended to program interaction to interfaces and provide flexibility, as shown in Figure 3-4.

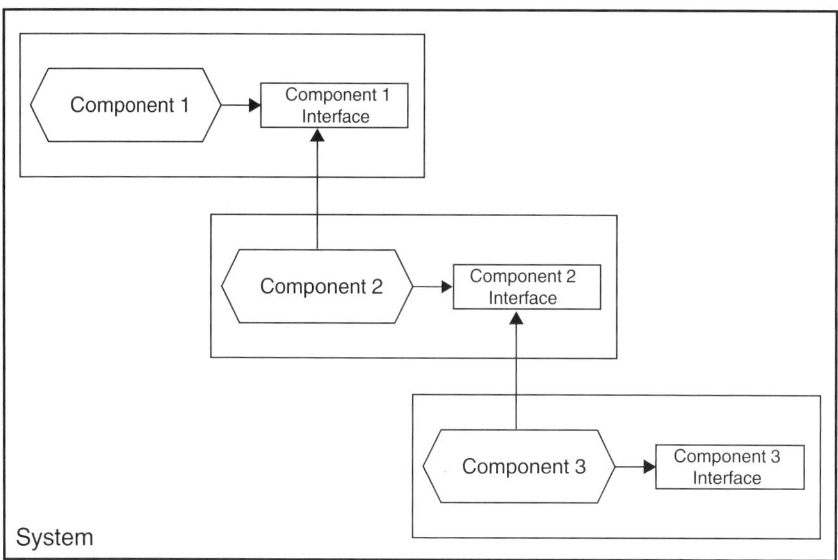

Figure 3-4 *Programming to an Interface, Not to the Implementation of the Component*

As a best practice, allow higher-level classes to use an abstraction of lower-level classes.

High-level classes should manage decisions and orchestrate lower-level classes but not do any system-specific functions. However, lower-level classes should contain little decision-making but implement the actual interaction functions, such as API calls, database writes, view updates, and data manipulations.

NOTE To get more in-depth knowledge of the SOLID principles, we highly recommend that you read Robert Martin's white paper about the subject: "Design Principles and Design Patterns by Robert C. Martin," https://www.academia.edu/40543946/Design_Principles_and_Design_Patterns.

Latency and Rate Limiting in Application Design and Performance

Performance of a system is highly dependent on its ability to manage resources needed to meet requirements. The longer you keep resource utilization within the constraints, the longer the performance is manageable and predictable. Predictable and manageable performance leads to good customer experience.

Latency and **throughput** are the most common ways of measuring performance, but as systems become more distributed, you can start considering additional factors like **round-trip time (RTT)** and bandwidth. It is not uncommon to think of bandwidth as a factor or a contributor to round-trip time. A simple definition of bandwidth (BW) is the capacity of the communication path or the maximum rate at which information can be transferred through that path or medium.

In computer systems and application design, latency may also be referred to as response time (RT), but we stick to the term *latency* to avoid confusing you with the difference between RTT and RT. This book is mainly concerned with building software that automates networks, so it is fitting to understand what parameters affect performance for both the network and the software or computer systems. Table 3-2 provides a simple definition from both points of view.

Table 3-2 Performance Parameters from Networking and Software Perspectives

Performance Indicator	Computer Networking or Communication Design	Software or Application Design
Latency	Length of time taken for a packet to traverse a system. This could be in/out a single system or the total time between a sender and receiver.	Length of time taken for a system to complete a specified task.
Round-trip time	Time taken for a round-trip travel between two network nodes (from, to, and back).	Length of time taken to complete a set of tasks.
Throughput	The rate at which packets (or any unit of information) are being transferred in a time period (e.g., packets per second or bits per second).	The amount of load (utilization) a system is capable of handling during a time period (e.g., transaction per second, or, user requests per second).

Figure 3-5 is a simple attempt to put all of the definitions found in Table 3-2 in one diagram.

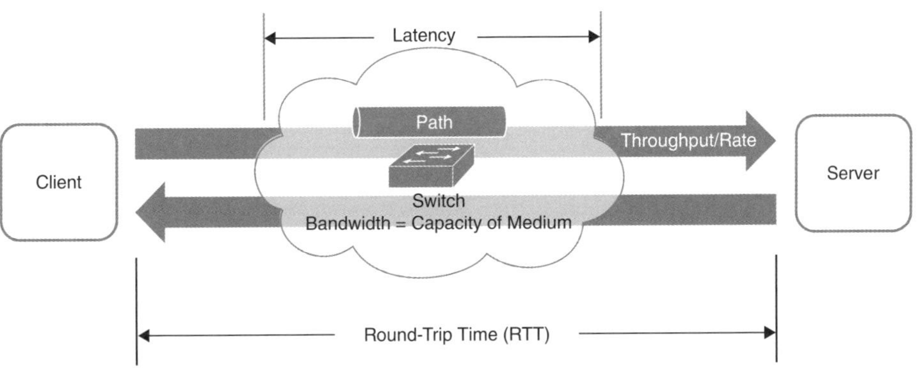

Figure 3-5 *Performance Parameters: Latency, Throughput, and RTT*

In a communication system, multiple factors affect latency of the system. Of course, one of the most important factors is the medium used and its capacity. However, even if you're using a high-capacity or high-bandwidth medium (e.g., Ethernet), latency is negatively impacted by other factors related to the overall system and the type of data being transmitted. For example, overhead plays a factor, especially when it comes to processing, encapsulation, encryption/decryption, and other similar factors.

It's worth mentioning that the overall system never lacks impurities and imperfections, and therefore, other factors play a huge role in performance. For the purpose of this discussion, if you think of the overall system as communication between a client (or an application) and a server over some communication path that most probably has routers, switches, firewalls, and an intrusion prevention system (IPS), then you need to consider a few other factors:

- **Network congestion and packet drops:** This is a side effect of network overload or oversubscription.
- **Hardware resource utilization:** Hardware interfaces, CPUs, and memory utilization are all factors in which resource demand and resource availability need to be balanced.
- **Hardware malfunctions:** Hardware failures are a fact of life, but when they come, they don't always lead to complete failure. Sometimes failure comes intermittently or sporadically. That sometimes puts the system in a fuzzy state.
- **Software issues:** Software issues can negatively affect performance. Here are a few examples:
  - Suboptimal software versions
  - Use of outdated libraries
  - Faults and bugs
- **Network device misconfigurations:** In a practical sense, this factor is probably the biggest culprit of performance degradation. Misconfiguration comes in many shapes and forms:
  - Restricting the use of available resources
  - Suboptimal traffic routing that forces traffic to high latency or congested paths, causing packet drops and frequent retransmissions
  - Operator error where wrong values for resources are manually and erroneously entered
- **Wired versus wireless communication:** Wireless communication has a lot of limitations, including interference, distortion, and laws of physics that contribute to packet loss. Wireless does bring flexibility and agility to today's environments, making packet loss an acceptable design trade-off. High-performance computing environments remain highly dependent on wired communication.
- **Geographically distributed users and data centers:** For many business, mobility, and disaster recovery reasons, applications may be geographically disbursed, eventually creating significant distances between them and their users. Even with the most advanced fiber-optic networks and with a minimum number of hops, the laws of physics contribute enough latency that affects performance.

With the deployment of software-defined networking (SDN) and the use of automation and orchestration, user or operator errors are significantly reduced. Successful SDN deployments highly depend on programmability and automation of various network functions and policies.

Different types of traffic react differently to latency or packet loss. For example, with TCP traffic, where traffic acknowledgment is part of the process, packet loss causes lower performance, but all lost traffic is retransmitted. UDP traffic, used for video streaming and IP telephony, has quality of service or quality of experience consequences. For UDP streams, dropped packets cause low-resolution videos or choppy voice. The following are side effects of high-latency, low-throughput systems:

- Application performance issues; slow response times or slow loading of web pages
- Longer transaction times for applications
- Audio and video quality issues; quality of experience impact
- Frequent retransmission and processing of packets that increase load and resource utilization and possibly starve other processes
- Unsatisfactory user experiences

Designing for Application Low Latency and High Performance

Architecture decisions play a huge role in how resources are distributed and utilized. The key to high performance is the balance maintained between supply and demand of resources.

Architecture Trade-offs

As mentioned in Chapter 2, nonfunctional requirements are closely related, and you almost always have to decide or prioritize one over the other based on the business requirements. This is also true for performance. Consider the following points:

- **Availability and performance:** Improving availability through redundancy of resources may affect latency and negatively impact performance.
- **Scalability and performance:** This point is a clear one. Scaling your system or network up or out affects resource utilization and may impact performance. As you distribute resources among multiple servers or networks, you introduce the need for "communication" among the resources, and that in itself introduces additional latency.
- **Cost:** This one is also obvious. Having to use cost-effective networks and resources may not always provide you with the highest-performance systems.

Improving Performance

As mentioned earlier, low-latency, high-performance systems are highly dependent on configurations that optimize the utilization of resources and create a balance between resource demands and resource supplies. Various technologies and methodologies for improving performance can be built into the software or operating systems for prioritizing requests or increasing available resources. For this discussion, we focus on caching and rate limiting as possibly the most frequently used ways for improving performance and enhancing the user experience.

Caching

Caching enables you to store or position frequently accessed data as close as possible to the user (or server, depending on the performance problem you're trying to solve). In Figure 3-6, **caching** is used to offload the servers by caching responses and replying on behalf of the server.

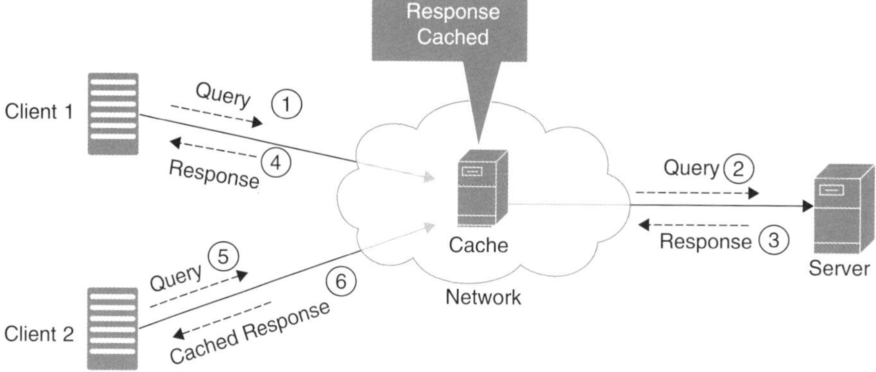

Figure 3-6 *A Cache Device Capturing Responses and Replying on Behalf of the Server to Subsequent Queries*

Immediate benefits of caching are improved response time, user experience, and the potential saving of network bandwidth and processing power. We've commonly used content delivery networks (CDNs) for caching static content like web pages or various media types like videos or training material. Using CDNs is an effective way of caching or storing content close to the user base.

Caching strategies differ depending on the design decision. The following are a few examples:

- **Caching of paginated results (a.k.a. pagination):** This strategy is most commonly used for requests or API calls that have multiple pages or rows in the response; for example, a request from a messaging server to view the last 100 text messages of a conversation of 1000 messages. The response is split into, say, 10 pages of 10 messages each. The user views the first 10, and if they want to see the next 10, then another request is generated to fetch the next 10.
- **Lazy loading:** The name tells the story. The resources or data is cached when necessary or when needed, not at initialization time. This strategy saves on resources and bandwidth and also reduces loading time. Example 3-6 demonstrates the difference between loading data when needed using *lazy loading* and loading the data at initialization time. The latter form is called *eager loading* or *forced loading* of resources.

In Example 3-6, resources are loaded when needed for **GetRecords**, rather than at initialization, as seen in Example 3-7.

Example 3-6 *Lazy Loading Is a Type of Caching That Loads Data Only When Necessary*

```
class LazyLoading() :
     def __init__(self) :
          self.resource = None
     def GetRecords (self, resource)
          self.resource = resource <- Load when needed
          execute (self.resource)
```

Example 3-7 *Eager or Forced Loading Forces the Preloading of Resources at Initialization Time*

```
class EagerLoading ():
     def __init__ (self, resource) :
          self.resource = resource <- Load at Initialization
     def GetRecords (self) :
          execute (self. resource)
```

As with any other design decision, trade-offs exist, and the cost-effectiveness of caching should be analyzed against its benefits, especially if the dynamic retrieval requirements outweigh the placement of static content. For example:

1. What's required for executing the query or operation at the back end? Network utilization limitations? Server resource utilization limitations?
2. What is the cost-effectiveness of the caching system or service?
3. What is the type of data and the effectiveness of caching? What are the hits versus misses? If the cache misses are a higher percentage and requests are having to pass through to the back-end server, maybe the system needs further adjustment or maybe it is not needed altogether.

Rate Limiting

Another frequently used strategy for improving performance by managing the load on the system is called **rate limiting.** Figure 3-7 demonstrates how rate limiting enables you to control the rate at which requests or data is passed to the system (or processor) to avoid overloading it.

Figure 3-7 *Rate Limiting External to the Server That Limits the Number of Requests Reaching the Server and Possibly Overloading*

The purpose of Figure 3-7 is only to demonstrate a point about how rate limiters work. The rate limiters are not always external to the system receiving the requests. The network connecting the client (the source) to the server (destination) could possibly have rate limiters to control the rate at which the server is receiving requests. The server itself may also have rate limiters implemented to control how many of the requests it should process.

Rate limiting can be applied in many places and for various purposes:

- **Number of requests:** This can mean requests for an echo/echo reply as in the ICMP (ping of death) or for requests against an API. API metering or billing systems may provide this type of rate limiting as an external mechanism to the system (cloud level) or locally and internally to the system.
- **User actions:** The purpose is to limit how many actions a user can take per web exchange or experience. A user may be allowed to enter their password three times to avoid overutilizing network or systems resources (but most importantly for security reasons).
- **Server-bound traffic:** This type of rate limiting is similar to the number of requests, but you can also use other parameters to control traffic directed toward a specific server, like the geography from which the request is coming or time of day.
- **Concurrent connections:** In various scenarios, you want to control how many concurrent sessions or connections a system can have. This type of rate limiting is used to prevent overload of the system where user experience or security may be at stake.

Parallel Processing

Serial or sequential processing systems process data in sequence and mostly one task during a time period. With parallel processing, multiple tasks are executed concurrently and in parallel, reducing latency and improving performance. There are two main types of parallel processing:

- **Multithreading:** You can design your software in a way that allows for dividing your tasks or requests into threads that can be processed in parallel. Multithreading is complex and must be decided at development time and most of the time adheres to specific system requirements.
- **Multiprocessing:** You can add additional processors to execute the tasks in parallel. This approach can also be looked at as processing multiple user requests as they arrive concurrently and processing them independently. This means that every session or concurrent user is provided independent memory space and processing timeslot.

Exponential Backoff

Backoff techniques rely on system feedback for rate limiting. When requests arrive and are not processed in a timely manner and retries are executed, they overload the system and may eventually increase the latency. In Internet of Things (IoT) implementations, for example, if you have an application monitoring temperature and you're unable to get readings, instead of continuing to poll the sensors for data and overload them, you can use exponential backoffs to limit the number of requests sent. This way, you allow the sensor various random time periods between requests.

Design and Implementation for Observability

Architecture decisions play a huge role in how resources are distributed and utilized. As we mentioned earlier, the key to high performance is the balance maintained between supply and demand of resources. Software systems have become large, complex, and continuously evolving. This creates the need and the opportunity for continuous monitoring of performance or the inner workings of the system by how it is experienced by its users (determining system issues through the observation of its output).

Applications and networks have profoundly changed. Networks are seeing increased adoption of cloud environments and a rise in distributed applications or cloud-based microservices. This, in turn, presents a few issues for the DevOps and engineering teams around monitoring, troubleshooting, visibility, and development. The traditional logging and monitoring may not deliver the full picture. Traditional monitoring may not be able to report on the application's proper operation. In addition, development teams may not have full visibility into what applications are operating where and for what business function, leading to inefficient environments with duplicating services.

For the reasons provided, an advanced or a comprehensive way for managing distributed applications is needed. You can think of it as **observability** for applications. Observability helps you

- Eliminate application performance blind spots (in distributed environments)
- Address application availability and uptime
- Measure response times
- Identify memory utilization (or leaks)
- Monitor database response times
- Observe the user or client experience
- Watch mobile application performance
- Monitor API usage and responses
- Decrease MTTR by predicting issues before they occur

Observability has three pillars or telemetry types that you, as application developer or designer, need to take into consideration:

- **Logging:** Logging tracks events and their timestamps. Logs and log types are also important.
- **Metrics or time-series metrics:** These metrics can simply be defined as system performance parameters (or application health measures) and are usually measured within a unit in time. As mentioned in "Latency and Rate Limiting in Application Design and Performance," response time, sessions per second, transactions per second—all are examples of metrics.

- **Tracing:** Tracing is the ability to track multiple events or a series of distributed events through a system.

When designing and building an application, you need to keep in mind that failures or faults will happen. The failures may be related to a software bug, a hardware issue, the network, misuse, or many other reasons. Having the right type of telemetry capabilities and the right instrumentation to collect is important and must be considered in the design phase. In addition, planning for telemetry or observability could influence your choice of hardware, operating system, or even your choice of programming language. Always design with the end goal in mind and coordinate your workflows to include the three types of telemetry.

Logging

Logging has been deployed for tens of years and has proven, if used correctly, to be one of the most useful telemetry tools. Logging is easy and straightforward, and it provides a great deal of information about the application's (a process) state or health.

Logging could be as simple as using a **print()** statement in various locations of your code to display some variable's value. However, using **print()** everywhere you want to log an event or a value may complicate your code and render it as inefficient or "unclean." For that reason, you should consider (and understand) logging capabilities of your programming language. Doing that provides a clean standard for logging with consistent logging levels and message formats.

Python, for example, provides a Logging module that is enabled like this:

```
import logging


logging.basicConfig(level=logging.INFO, format='%(asctime)s -
%(levelname)s - %(message)s')

logging.info('Welcome to DEVCOR')
```

When displayed, it looks like this, with day and timestamps:

```
2021-10-29 07:08:27,192 - INFO - Welcome to DEVCOR
```

That is an informational (INFO) example, but Python defines a few other levels like the following ones:

```
logging.critical('your favorite CRITICAL message')

logging.error('your favorite ERROR message')

logging.warning('your favorite WARNING message')

logging.debug('your favorite DEBUG message')
```

Table 3-3 gives a brief explanation of each of the logging levels.

Table 3-3 Python Logging Levels with Explanation of Severity

Level	Used to Indicate	Function
CRITICAL	High severity or fatal errors that may cause the application to crash or stop working	**logging.critical()**
ERROR	Server errors that affect a subset of operations but may not cause a crash	**logging.error()**
WARNING	A warning or a potential issue	**logging.warning()**
INFO	Informational messages indicating normal behavior while displaying status	**logging.info()**
DEBUG	Used to diagnose issues and is the lowest severity function	**logging.debug()**

NOTE Logging is just like any other function or process; it requires careful design and implementation consideration. For example, is it used as a development aid or for exception logging? Will logging of the various levels and message formats tax the CPU? How granular do you want your debugging to be?

Having a logging framework (or standard) is important for consistency, efficiency, and documentation across multiple development teams. On the other hand, if you've been working with Cisco devices and you need to capture system messages, then it is good to familiarize yourself with Cisco's System Message Logging, which uses the IETF RFC 5424 (The Syslog Protocol) definitions shown in Table 3-4.

Table 3-4 Syslog Message Severities as Defined by the IETF RFC 5424

Severity Keyword	Level	Description	Syslog Definition
emergency	0	System unusable	LOG_EMERG
alert	1	Immediate action needed	LOG_ALERT
critical	2	Critical conditions	LOG_CRIT
error	3	Error conditions	LOG_ERR
warning	4	Warning conditions	LOG_WARNING
notification	5	Normal but significant condition	LOG_NOTICE
informational	6	Informational messages only	LOG_INFO
debugging	7	Debugging messages	LOG_DEBUG

As a generic example, the Cisco IOS XR message looks like this:

```
node-id : timestamp : process-name [pid] : % message category
-group -severity -message -code : message-text
```

NOTE Logging is an important part of good programming practices that require efficient, readable, and well-documented code. Be sure to make your messages informative, clear, specific, and timestamped. You also need to think about where to capture and store the logs and how long they should be retained.

Metrics

Metrics are system performance parameters (or application health measures) and are usually measured as a unit in time. Simple and common examples are application response time, requests per second, sessions per second, and transactions per second.

Defining the right metrics to be measured or monitored for your project should be based on the goal, function, or problem you're trying to solve with your application. Whenever you're executing software, you must measure CPU usage, memory usage, swap space, and a few other things related to the environment.

Network and application performance monitoring has seen major improvements and advancements in the last two decades, and it is still improving as computer and network hardware includes advanced diagnostics and telemetry embedded into the system. But there are a few limitations that arise as you start looking at distributed and cloud-based environments where physical and virtual boundaries restrict metric monitoring.

Application-level monitoring has become an extreme necessity, allowing you to monitor all parameters affecting application performance throughout the path from the client to the application, wherever it may be. Another important function of observability should be the ability to correlate events captured across all services, all paths, hardware, and software. Figure 3-8 shows a small subset of services and components affecting application performance and subsequently affecting business performance.

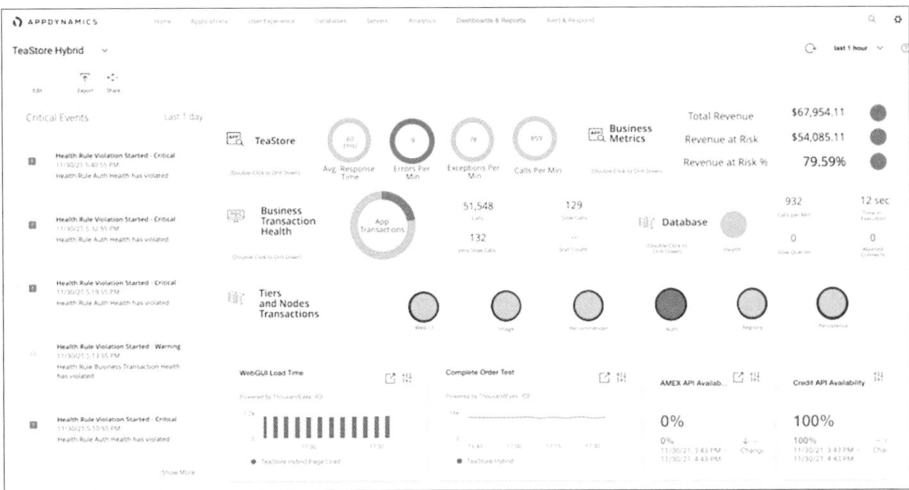

Figure 3-8 *AppDynamics Display of Various Dashboards*

Monitoring various parameters at a granular level has been the focus of a new generation of tools called **application performance monitoring (APM) applications.** AppDynamics is an example of an APM. AppDynamics utilizes agents (plug-ins or extensions) sitting across the entire application ecosystem that monitor the performance of application code, runtime environments, and interactions. The agents send real-time data to the controllers for visualization and further instructions. The data is used for mapping dependencies, business transaction monitoring, anomaly detection, root cause diagnostics, and analytics. Figure 3-8 shows the TeaStore application with AppDynamics monitoring various aspects about the application, including the business context and therefore allowing the business to prioritize what's important.

AppDynamics exposes various APIs for customizing and extending the feature set on the platform side, which are served by the Controller and Events Service, and on the agent side.

3

Tracing

Traces are an important part of observability because they provide information about the structure of a transaction and the path or route taken (requests and responses). In the previous section, we discussed APMs and how they may be able to provide you with application dependency mapping. With tracing, you can understand the various services used for a transaction or a request. In the world of networking, ICMP echo and echo reply as well as Layer 2 traces enable you to discover the path taken for a trace and what network nodes or devices are used to deliver the trace. Application tracing is similar.

With cloud or distributed environments, you see the term *distributed tracing* more often than just *tracing*; however, conceptually they are the same. With tracing, you can determine

- What parts or services of the system are slow
- What calls are redundant
- What call patterns can be optimized
- What routes or paths are affected by failing services (what if type modeling?)
- Trace queries
- And more

Figure 3-9 is a generic example of what devices, networks, servers, or services can possibly be in the path between the users and their applications. Many factors can affect the performance of an application and subsequently the user experience.

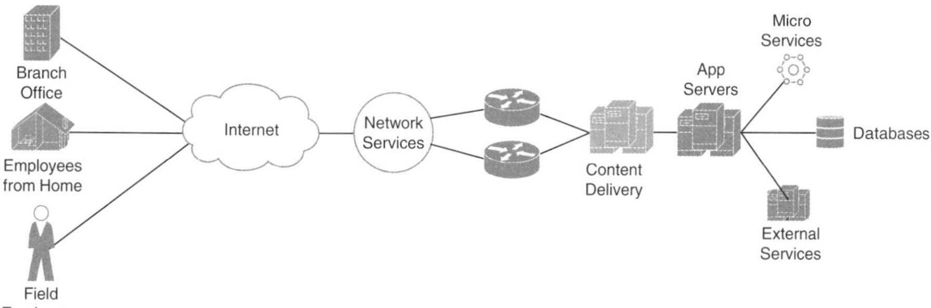

Figure 3-9 *Internet and Network Path That Connects Users and User Services*

You will probably not see deep level tracing being emphasized during your DEVCOR studies, but it is good to practice when developing distributed applications and microservices.

AppDynamics (explained earlier), combined with digital experience monitoring systems like ThousandEyes, can give you the best view of the application and business parameters with the least amount of work. Figure 3-10 shows an application analysis display using the ThousandEyes platform of services.

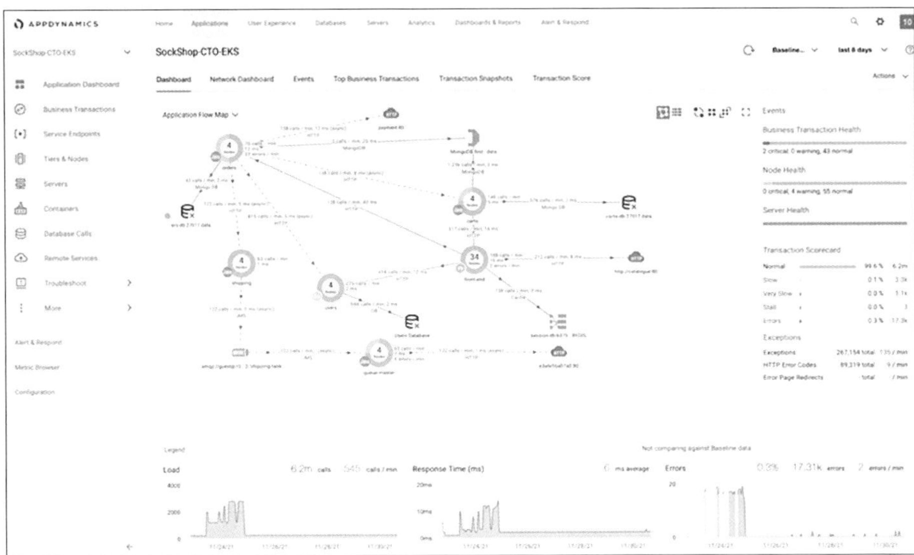

Figure 3-10 *Sock-Shop Application Analysis Using ThousandEyes*

Figure 3-11 shows a small subset of services and components affecting application performance, the digital experience, and subsequently business performance. It is not uncommon to see the combination of AppDynamics and ThousandEyes referred to as full stack observability (FSO).

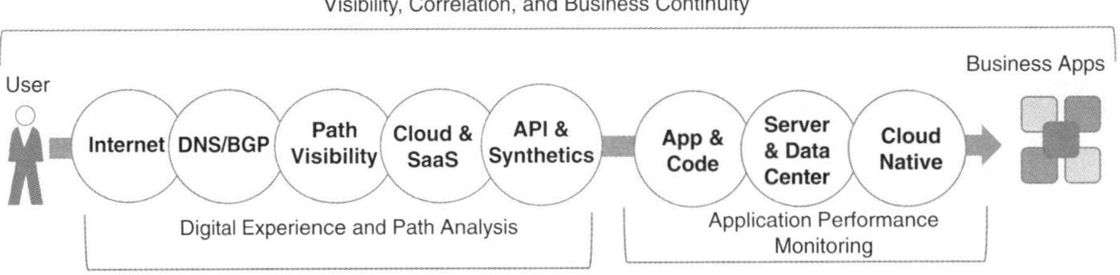

Figure 3-11 *Full Stack Observability as Serviced by the Cisco Platforms*

Good Documentation Practices: An Observability Reminder

We touched on good documentation practices in Chapter 2, and we think it is as relevant to observability as the "three pillars" discussed earlier. In distributed environments or environments where workloads are consistently moving between the cloud and on-premises computing environments, good (or rather, excellent) documentation practices become very essential.

NOTE Because modules are a part of the overall system, all modules should describe how they participate in the overall system and what part or service they provide and how it relates to other parts. Sound familiar? This sounds like a combination of monitoring and tracing but in text format.

As documented in "Software Architecture in Practice," you should emphasize the following practices for every module or function developed within the overall system. The following are quick reminders of what every module or component should have:

- Name
- Responsibility
- Interfaces
- Implementation information
- Mapping to source code units
- Test information
- Management (or monitoring) information
- Implementation constraints
- Revision history

The list, of course, is at the module level, but you cannot forget code comments or low-level documentation.

NOTE Code comments and low-level documentation are as important as all higher-level documentation, if not the most important. They give you a window into the developers' thought processes at the time of writing. They also simplify troubleshooting and speed up modifiability.

Database Selection Criteria

It has been said that the global economy is powered by data more than any other item in the world. Whether it's the storage of archival data to be found at a later date, analysis of data across different sets looking for patterns, or access to lots of data for training of AI/ML models, without the storage and retrieval of information—everything that occurs within the world would be based on the subjective nature of people's memory. Out of these requirements, databases were developed to hold all of the information required for a given use case. Over time, requirements for how and what was stored have evolved, leading to a seemingly confusing number of database types that need to work all the way to web scale and be able to interface with one or more applications depending on the user and use case.

While much emphasis is generally placed on the code being written for an application, the data that the application gathers or generates can be argued to be the reason the application was generated in the first place, and without proper storage of the data, the application has no real purpose. In addition to proper storage, the data needs to be accessed quickly, survive potential failures, and be robust to grow as the data collected becomes larger and larger. Looking through these points of consideration, you can easily see that the selection of a proper database for the application and potential dataset can make or break the success of an application.

Database Requirements Gathering

While databases are generally lumped into a single category, there are many different classifications of databases, depending on the application and data being stored within them. Each different type of database is optimized for a certain structure or set of data, maximum data set size, and response time to queries. For performant applications, a close understanding of all of them is critical (which is why so many database platforms exist). However, for simple applications or systems, simply understanding the type of data being ingested by the database is sufficient (scale problems generally arise at the many hundreds of gigabytes of data, making them less of an issue for hobbyist or small-scale applications).

The first step in gathering database requirements is determining the type of database to use, based on the data being gathered by the application. While not exhaustive, the following list outlines some of the common database types and provides a brief description and some names of databases that fit that type. Also, note that each type of database exists within all the major cloud providers, allowing customers to benefit from the same levels of abstraction in databases that exist within application deployment and management (see Chapter 7, "Application Deployment").

- **Relational:** Relational databases are typically referred to as SQL databases, for their use of Structured Query Language (SQL) to gather information from the store. Relational databases are constructed of one or more tables of information, with each table containing rows of information defined by a key, or unique identifying value. To gather information from the database, you might be required to join multiple tables together, based on relational attributes shared between the tables (such as a database that needs to query the transaction logs for an item [one table] along with the inventory records of that same item [another table] for audit purposes). These types of databases are best used with structured data, due to the way the data must be split to align within a given table.

  Examples: PostgreSQL, MySQL

- **Nonrelational (NoSQL):** Nonrelational databases are a broad category of databases in which the data is not structured or does not easily fit into the format of a traditional relational database (it helps to visualize a relational database as formatted similarly to a standard spreadsheet). Each category of NoSQL database is optimized for the storage of different types of data, such as key-value pairs, documents, or big data warehousing. These databases also provide an easier framework to scale across clusters of machines as well as the flexibility to change the database in real time.

  Examples: MongoDB, CouchDB

- **Time series:** On the surface, time series databases (TSDB) can almost be considered relational databases because they provide unique keys (driven by the timestamps of the data being ingested into the database) and the data being stored is very uniformly structured in nature. However, time series databases are unique in that there is rarely a relational component or specialized linked tables within a TSDB. The uniformity of the data (composed of a timestamp and some payload of data) allows for specialized compression and storage algorithms not possible in other databases. TSDBs also generally hold onto data only for a predetermined time, rather than forever, allowing them to be deployed in smaller footprints than traditional databases.

Examples: InfluxDB, Prometheus

You might be able to place information in a database to which it was not fully intended and have everything function as normal during proof of concept, or even at small scale. Issues may arise only after running the database in production at scale for some time, at which point, cracks may develop and must be patched, moved around, or just accepted. The option of moving to another database type isn't something that can be undertaken lightly, either. Applications needing to push data to or pull data from the database often rely on SDKs to map the data to the database location and schema. For applications with tens or hundreds of different functions or methods that utilize this database, the code migration is no small undertaking. This is added to the fact that the data that resides in one database (say, a relational database) will need to undergo some transformation and mutation to ensure that the fields from each entry are mapped correctly (and align with the new code being developed in parallel to utilize the new fields). Finally, during a migration event, most databases must be locked to prevent new records from being written during the migration, requiring a downtime/outage for the application. It's easy to see how poor planning or a lack of database knowledge can bring on a lot of technical debt to be fixed later.

This is not to say that the decision of which database platform to use should create analysis paralysis and bottleneck an application's design and creation; at some point, decisions must be made based on the best information at hand. However, knowing and understanding different types of databases, at least at a high level, are important to your overall knowledge of software design.

Aside from the characteristics of the different types of databases provided, additional existing considerations can help narrow the choices for which database platform should be used. These are generally referred to as the "three *V*s" of databases: volume, velocity, and variety. Some materials reference these considerations specifically in the context of big data, but big data is a specific set of large data set warehousing, meant to operate at the bounds of scale, speed, and types of data. However, by planning out the rough requirements in each of the three following points, the database selection process can be streamlined.

Data Volume

Data volume is self-explanatory on the surface; it's the amount of data required to be held within a given database. Certain databases can perform up until a given threshold of size, at which point they either become unstable (at best) or unusable (at worst). This is due to the structure in which the data is stored and the ability of the data to be queried after it resides inside the database. If the data cannot be extracted after it has been placed within a database, it's no longer a database, but more like a vault. This can be a factor for the raw amount of data being stored (especially for NoSQL databases, particularly ones focused on documents) or the amount of RAM being dedicated to the store (in the case of Redis, which is an in-memory database). However, regardless of database, queries will eventually become slower (if only marginally so) as the size grows due to the bounds on the speed at which queries can occur.

However, volume isn't just about the raw amount of data being stored in terms of bytes. Databases are composed of records, and as the number of records grows, the system's ability to query and find the information quickly decreases. While optimized search algorithms exist, there is a finite bound for which those algorithms can search through hundreds of millions of records, even if the size of said set of records is only in the tens of gigabytes. Although it is impossible to predict the size of a long-running application's database, this becomes a critical aspect of database selection.

Data Velocity

Much like data volume, data velocity is also self-explanatory, and refers to the speed at which the database must be able to ingest data from the various sources of the application. While this seems like a simple metric (faster is always better, right?), velocity isn't just a product of how fast records can be processed but must also consider the patterns in which the data is sent. In some instances, like those that use TSDBs, data is sent at relatively consistent intervals, and performance is scaled through optimizing the database for the data being ingested and the underlying subsystem supporting the database (CPU, RAM, and disk).

However, if a database is supporting an application with a bursty traffic profile, it may be impossible to find a database that is performant enough, depending on the overall load to the system. In this case, some sort of front-end cache system to the database may be required to ensure that records are not dropped or lost before they are committed to the database. In other cases, the choice of database may allow for distribution/sharding of the overall database to ensure scale, with the idea that the database peers will update themselves or find quorum on the data written at some point in the future (in the case of NoSQL-based databases that support horizontal scale-out). Anticipating the baseline and peak traffic profiles for the database, along with ways to mitigate growth in velocity requirements, will help ensure that a selected database will have the ability to scale with growth.

Data Variety

While the preceding two considerations are applicable to all databases, variety has a limited applicability to most databases, outside of those meant for document archival or big data. Variety refers to how much the incoming data will differ from the previous set. In most instances, the data received from the application is of a normalized set: time-series data from an IoT sensor or a standard entry from a webform entry. Although these sets of data may have varying levels of structure and payload, they are generally considered uniform in the presentation and can be easily handled within a semi-rigid database structure and be indexed and queried properly. Because of the separation possible for different input sources to a database, the normalization must occur only per source—say, adding a new IoT sensor to a TSDB needing a new bucket within InfluxDB, rather than a new database or complete pre-filter of the sensor data to have it align with what exists.

In the case of a document database, the types and structures of the inputs could vary drastically. In the cases of some of the largest databases supporting social media platforms, indexing of images, video, and audio must occur within the same database. With corporate document databases, the file types could be endless, including PDFs, word processor documents, spreadsheets, presentations, and even archived emails of several different formats. Understanding the potential variety of data (if there needs to be any) can serve as a very powerful filter for database selection.

Exam Preparation Tasks

As mentioned in the section "How to Use This Book" in the Introduction, you have a couple of choices for exam preparation: the exercises here, Chapter 17, "Final Preparation," and the exam simulation questions on the companion website.

Review All Key Topics

Review the most important topics in this chapter, noted with the Key Topic icon in the outer margin of the page. Table 3-5 lists a reference of these key topics and the page numbers on which each is found.

Table 3-5 Key Topics for Chapter 3

Key Topic Element	Description	Page Number
Section	Maintaining a SOLID Design	60
Table 3-2	Performance parameters from networking and software perspectives	67
Figure 3-5	Performance Parameters: Latency, Throughput, and RTT	67
Section	Architecture Trade-offs	69
Section	Improving Performance	69
Section	Caching	70
Section	Rate Limiting	71
Table 3-3	Python Logging Levels with Explanation of Severity	75
Table 3-4	Syslog Message Severities as Defined by the IETF RFC 5424	75
Paragraph	Application performance monitoring	77
Section	Good Documentation Practices: An Observability Reminder	78
Section	Database Requirements Gathering	80

Complete Tables and Lists from Memory

Print a copy of Appendix C, "Memory Tables" (found on the companion website), or at least the section for this chapter, and complete the tables and lists from memory. Appendix D, "Memory Tables Answer Key," also on the companion website, includes completed tables and lists to check your work.

Define Key Terms

Define the following key terms from this chapter and check your answers in the glossary:

application performance monitoring (APM), caching, latency, logging, metrics, multi-threading, multiprocessing, observability, rate limiting, round-trip time (RTT), SOLID, throughput, tracing

References

URL	QR Code
"Design Principles and Design Patterns," Robert C. Martin https://www.academia.edu/40543946/Design_Principles_and_Design_Patterns	
IETF RFC 5424 https://datatracker.ietf.org/doc/html/rfc5424	
Continuous Architecture in Practice: Software Architecture in the Age of Agility and DevOps https://www.informit.com/store/continuous-architecture-in-practice-software-architecture-9780136523567	
Software Architecture in Practice, 4th Edition https://www.informit.com/store/software-architecture-in-practice-9780136886099	

CHAPTER 4

Version Control and Release Management with Git

This chapter covers the following topics:

- Version Control and Git: This section briefly discusses version control for managing code or file changes and how Git is a widely used version control system (VCS). It also discusses Git basics and advanced features for managing code changes from multiple concurrent developers.
- Git Workflow: This section discusses Git basic workflow agreement, how to manage access to the code, and who contributes and who is trusted to manage the workflow. Basics of branching and forking are also discussed.
- Git Branching Strategy: This section discusses a strategy for managing the code development and stabilization teams and processes. This is a strategy that all developers must understand and agree upon.

This chapter maps to the first part of the *Developing Applications Using Cisco Core Platforms and APIs v1.0 (350-901)* Exam Blueprint Section 1.0, "Infrastructure and Automation," specifically subsections 1.10 and 1.11.

This chapter describes version control, version control systems (VCSs) in general, and then goes on to describe Git as a version control system. The concept of version control is simple and used in every aspect of our lives: documents, applications, operating systems, webpages, standards, frameworks—you get the idea. The code you build for automating and orchestrating your network is no different. We're confident that you're not building the code by yourself, and we're confident you're not building it in one sitting. You're collaborating with others and most probably in an agile development process where various releases and sprints are in order. This chapter teaches you how to keep track of the development process.

"Do I Know This Already?" Quiz

The "Do I Know This Already?" quiz allows you to assess whether you should read this entire chapter thoroughly or jump to the "Exam Preparation Tasks" section. If you are in doubt about your answers to these questions or your own assessment of your knowledge of the topics, read the entire chapter. Table 4-1 lists the major headings in this chapter and their corresponding "Do I Know This Already?" quiz questions. You can find the answers in Appendix A, "Answers to the 'Do I Know This Already?' Quizzes."

Table 4-1 "Do I Know This Already?" Section-to-Question Mapping

Foundation Topics Section	Questions
Version Control and Git	1
Git Workflow	2, 3
Git Branching Strategy	4, 5

1. What is version control used to track?
   a. Code changes
   b. Configurations
   c. Releases
   d. All of these answers are correct.
2. What is the difference between Git and GitHub?
   a. There is no difference.
   b. GitHub is used for hosting Git projects.
   c. GitHub has a hub, and Git does not.
   d. GitLab, GitHub, and Git are different names for the same thing.
3. The main benefit of a VCS is your ability to do what?
   a. Manage code for multiple development projects.
   b. Streamline the development cycle or process.
   c. Track and save all changes.
   d. All of these answers are correct.
4. Which scenario is more likely to cause a merge conflict?
   a. Two developers open the same file.
   b. A file gets deleted by one developer while it's being modified by another developer.
   c. Two merges are performed back-to-back.
   d. All these scenarios are easily handled by Git.
5. Which statements are correct about branching? (Choose two.)
   a. Branching is important only if you plan to merge changes from two independent projects.
   b. A branching strategy needs to define types of branches and all rules governing usage by the developers.
   c. Every developer must understand the strategy and agree to follow it.
   d. Branching strategies must be agreed upon only by development team leads, not all developers.

Foundation Topics

Version Control and Git

When we discussed maintainability and modifiability in the preceding chapter, we started with a statement that is super fit to use here: "Change is constant." Therefore, a system or methodology for tracking changes to a code, who made them, and for what purpose becomes a very important component of a project. **Version control**, or simply *versioning*, can be at all levels of the development process: a module, function, feature, system, or application.

A number of popular systems are in use today, and most of the time the one you use will be the one that your company supports and that your development team is currently using. Git is such a system; it has gained a lot of popularity recently for its ease of use (at least the latest versions) and simplicity, and because it's open source. In the next few sections, we describe Git and look at some of its basic and advanced features.

Git differentiates itself in being fast and efficient, and also by having the following interesting features:

- A typical VCS stores *deltas*, or file changes, over a period of time (delta-based version control), whereas Git stores *snapshots* of files and the filesystem.
- Almost all operations are local to your system or computer. All related history is stored locally and can be accessed regardless of whether you're online or offline.
- Data in Git is verified for integrity through a checksum algorithm. A checksum is produced before storing a file, and the checksum is used to refer to the file or data.

For more information about Git and how it works, we highly recommend you refer to the free book written by Scott Chacon and Ben Straub and contributed to by the Git developer community: *Pro Git, Version 2.1.240*. It was used as a reference for this book. You can refer to the book and to online documentation for installing and learning Git.

Git Workflow

When multiple people need to collaborate and contribute to the same Git repository for a project, there needs to be a working agreement on how that work will be done. A team must agree on an operating model for coordinating their contributions to a shared, source-of-truth code repository.

The Git Workflow that a team selects depends on the following:

1. Shared repo access policies
   - Will all contributors have read-write access to the shared repository?
   - Or will some contributors have read-only access to the shared repository?
2. Untrusted contributors
   - Are all contributors known up front and trusted with repository read-write access?
   - Or will some contributors be untrusted or from the public?

3. Novice versus intermediate Git users

    - Will users follow a more complex workflow that is used by the vast majority of open-source projects?
    - Or will they follow a simpler workflow that novice users of Git may easily understand?

The following sections detail the two primary workflows that teams use: the Branch and Pull Workflow and the Fork and Pull Workflow.

Branch and Pull Workflow

The Branch and Pull Workflow is the simpler of the two options for Git workflows. It works best with the following properties:

- **Shared repo access policies:** All contributors have read-write access to the shared repository.
- **Trusted contributors:** All contributors are known up front and trusted with repository read-write access.
- **Novice versus intermediate Git users:** The team requires a simpler workflow that novice users of Git may easily understand.

The Branch and Pull Workflow has the following pros and cons.

Pros

- This model requires only simple knowledge of Git, only incrementally different from working solo on a Git repository because only a single Git repo is involved.
- It does not require a contributor to be aware of the concept of *forking*.
- Because there are no forks, the user does not need to understand how to manage working with distributed Git repos (that is, synchronizing the same source code among many repos).

Cons

- This model diverges from the way that the vast majority of open-source software works (most open-source software uses the Fork and Pull Workflow).
- All code contributors *must* have read-write access to the shared, source-of-truth repository.
- This workflow is less safe because all team members have read-write access and are pushing to the same source of truth, allowing the possibility of overwriting each other's branches, especially shared branches such as the main or master.
- This model cannot work for untrusted contributors who do not have write access to the shared repository.

Sample Setup

Next, let's look at a sample setup, followed by the actual Branch and Pull example.

1. Assume that you have configured your github.com user profile with an SSH key.
   - This allows you to execute remote Git operations such as **clone** and **push** using SSH-key authentication.
   - Otherwise, Git defaults to using password authentication, which requires you to frequently type in a username and password.
2. Assume that **bluecodemonks** is your team name.
   - Thus, your team has already created a GitHub organization named **bluecodemonks**.
   - See https://github.com/bluecodemonks.
3. Assume that **go-hello-world** will be a team collaboration project.
   - Thus, your team has already created a shared, source-of-truth repository named **go-hello-world**.
   - See https://github.com/bluecodemonks/go-hello-world.
4. Assume that you have already been added as a read-write contributor to the project. Figure 4-1 shows the go-hello-world project.

Figure 4-1 *Branch and Pull: Origin Repository*

Sample Branch and Pull Workflow

NOTE You cannot follow along with this exercise using this specific repository because you don't have write access to the repo at https://github.com/bluecodemonks/go-hello-world. This illustrates the limitations of the Branch and Pull Workflow. The counter Fork and Pull Workflow does not have this limitation, however, as you will see in a subsequent exercise.

Step 1. Clone the project repository to your local computer:

```
$ mkdir ~/Dev
$ cd ~/Dev
$ git clone git@github.com:bluecodemonks/go-hello-
  world.git
```

```
Cloning into 'go-hello-world'...
[snipped]
```

Step 2. You now have a local copy of the project repository on your filesystem, as seen in Figure 4-2, where the local clone of go-hello-world was created.

Step 3. Look around the newly cloned repository:

```
$ cd ~/Dev/go-hello-world
$ tree
.
├── LICENSE
├── README.md
├── go.mod
└── main.go
0 directories, 4 files
```


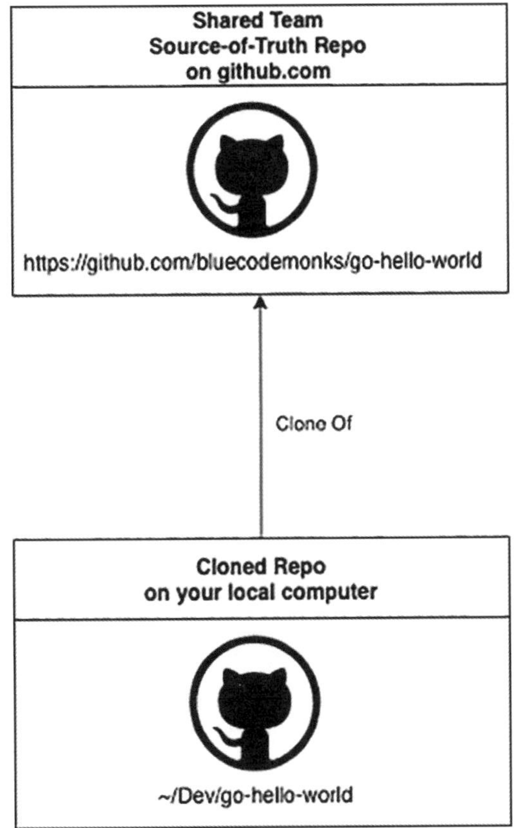

Figure 4-2 *Branch and Pull: Locally Cloned Repo*

Step 4. Notice that a Git remote repository configuration has already been set up because you cloned from a remote repository.

- This repository is named **origin** (by default).
- It refers to the original URI from which this repo was cloned.
- Your team's shared, source-of-truth remote repo is now labeled **origin**:

```
$ git remote -v
origin git@github.com:bluecodemonks/go-hello-world.git
(fetch)
origin git@github.com:bluecodemonks/go-hello-world.git
(push)
```

Step 5. Look at what branch you are currently on and what branches are available.

- You are on the main branch, denoted by the asterisk (*) character.
- Your local main branch is at the same commit as the remote origin/main branch. It is set to track the origin/main remote upstream by default (see Figure 4-3). Thus, if you execute commands such as **git push** without fully qualifying where to push, it assumes the target is the default origin/main remote upstream. To push to a specific git remote and specific branch on that remote, you may fully qualify the target **git push** ***<remote>/<branch>***.

```
$ git branch -avv
* main ad0bbc5 [origin/main] Added install and run
instructions
 remotes/origin/HEAD -> origin/main
 remotes/origin/main ad0bbc5 Added install and run
instructions
```

Step 6. Now it's time to make a contribution. First, create a local branch to store your local changes. Because you are currently on the main branch, your new branch will be created from main. Example 4-1 shows the CLI commands, and Figure 4-4 illustrates the logical results.

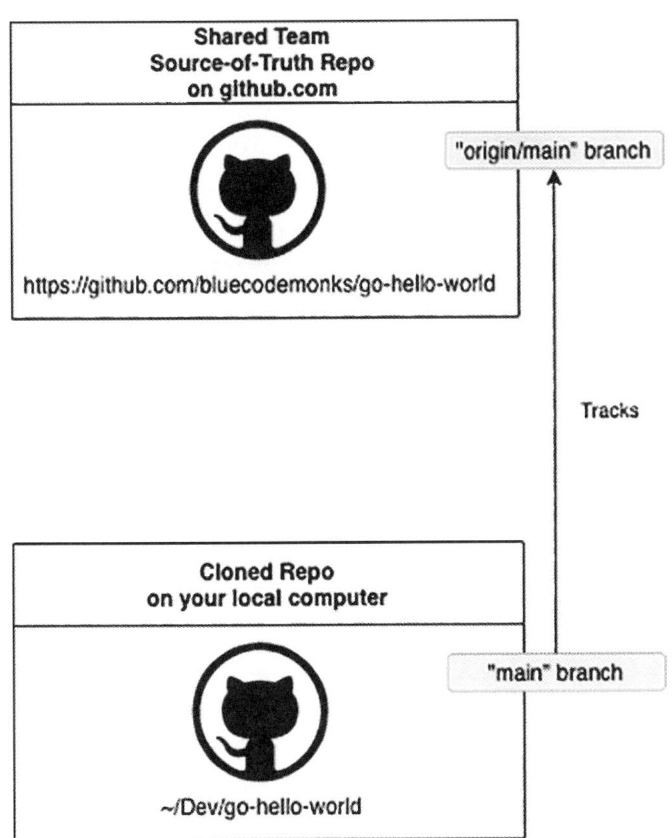

Figure 4-3 *Branch and Pull: Main Branch Tracking*

4

Example 4-1 *Creating a Branch*

```
# Check what branch we are on
$ git branch
* main
# Create a new feature-branch from "main" and switch to it
$ git checkout -b update-readme
Switched to a new branch 'update-readme'
# View your branch status
$ git branch -avv
 main ad0bbc5 [origin/main] Added install and run instructions
* update-readme ad0bbc5 Added install and run instructions
 remotes/origin/HEAD -> origin/main
 remotes/origin/main ad0bbc5 Added install and run instructions
```

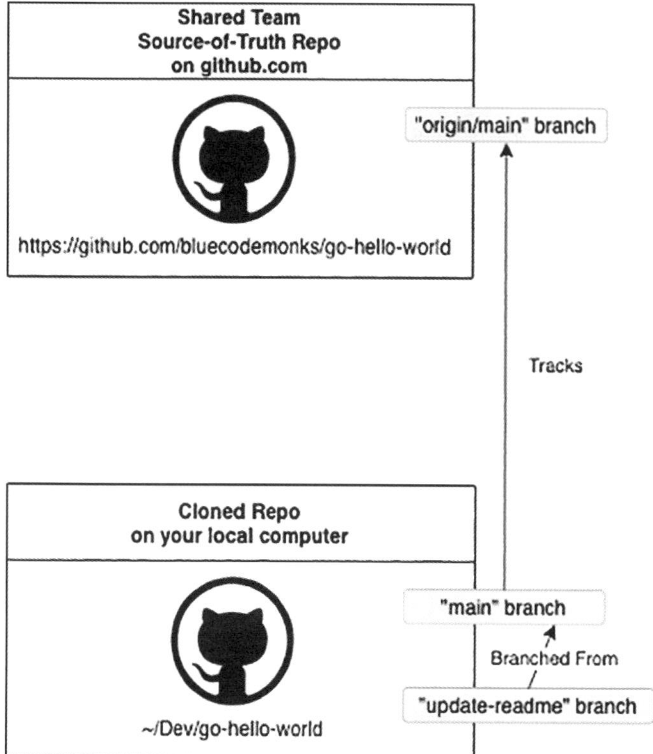

Figure 4-4 *Branch and Pull: Creating a Branch*

Step 7. Now, make some edits to the README.md file. You can enhance the README.md with uninstall instructions:

```
$ vi README.md
Uninstall
```
$ rm $GOPATH/bin/go-hello-world
```
```

Step 8. Assess your changes before you stage them.

This step is not required but is extremely good practice to evaluate your changes before you stage them. The steps are described in Example 4-2.

Example 4-2 *Branch and Pull: Reviewing Current Changes*

```
$ git status
On branch update-readme
Changes not staged for commit:
 (use "git add <file>..." to update what will be committed)
 (use "git restore <file>..." to discard changes in working directory)
 modified: README.md
```

~~~~
no changes added to commit (use "git add" and/or "git commit -a")

$ git diff
diff --git a/README.md b/README.md
index f272b4d..8e86322 100644
--- a/README.md
+++ b/README.md
@@ -11,4 +11,10 @@ Run
 ```
 $ go-hello-world
 Hello World
-```
\ No newline at end of file
+```
+
+Uninstall
+
+```
+$ rm $GOPATH/bin/go-hello-world
+```
~~~~


Step 9. Stage your changes:

~~~~
$ git add README.md
~~~~

Step 10. Assess your staged changes to double-check your edits.

This step is not required but is extremely good practice to evaluate your changes before you commit them. The steps to review changes before committing are described in Example 4-3.

Example 4-3 *Branch and Pull: Reviewing Staged Changes*

~~~~
$ git diff --cached
diff --git a/README.md b/README.md
index f272b4d..8e86322 100644
--- a/README.md
+++ b/README.md
@@ -11,4 +11,10 @@ Run
 ```
 $ go-hello-world
 Hello World
-```
\ No newline at end of file
+```
~~~~

```
+
+Uninstall
+
+```
+$ rm $GOPATH/bin/go-hello-world
+```
```

Step 11. Commit the changes to the local branch:

```
$ git commit -m "Update README.md with uninstall
instructions"
[update-readme bb63877] Update README.md with uninstall
instructions
 1 file changed, 7 insertions(+), 1 deletion(-)
```

Step 12. Push a copy of your local branch update-readme to the shared source-of-truth repo. The **git push** command is illustrated in Example 4-4 and logically represented in Figure 4-5.

- The source-of-truth repo is named origin in your git remotes:

```
$ git remote -v
origin git@github.com:bluecodemonks/go-hello-world.git
(fetch)
origin git@github.com:bluecodemonks/go-hello-world.git
(push)
```

- Notice that you are currently on the update-readme local branch and that the origin git remote has no such branch:

```
$ git branch -avv
 main ad0bbc5 [origin/main] Added install and run
instructions
* update-readme 8144024 Update README.md with uninstall
instructions
 remotes/origin/HEAD -> origin/main
 remotes/origin/main ad0bbc5 Added install and run
 instructions
```

- Thus, you must push the current branch to the origin remote, specifying a fully qualified branch name in the format *<remote> <branch>*.

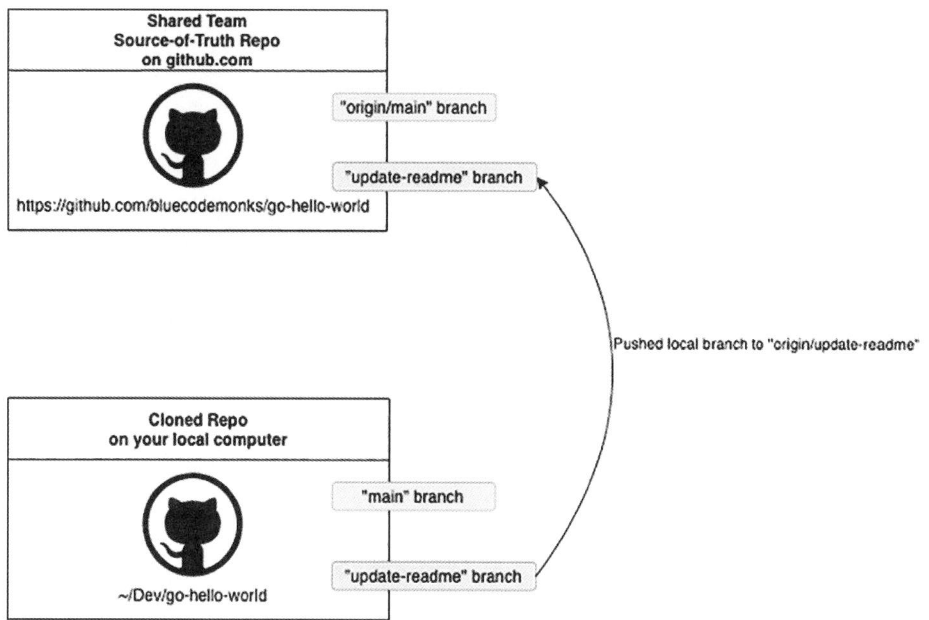

Figure 4-5 *Branch and Pull: Listing All Branches*

Example 4-4 *Branch and Pull: Pushing a Branch to the Origin Repo*

```
$ git push origin update-readme
Enumerating objects: 5, done.
Counting objects: 100% (5/5), done.
Delta compression using up to 12 threads
Compressing objects: 100% (1/1), done.
Writing objects: 100% (3/3), 367 bytes | 367.00 KiB/s, done.
Total 3 (delta 2), reused 2 (delta 2), pack-reused 0
remote: Resolving deltas: 100% (2/2), completed with 2 local objects.
Remote:
remote: Create a pull request for 'update-readme' on GitHub by visiting:
remote: https://github.com/bluecodemonks/go-hello-world/pull/new/update-readme
remote:
To github.com:bluecodemonks/go-hello-world.git
 * [new branch] update-readme -> update-readme
```

- Now, verify that the remote origin has a new branch named **updated-readme**:

```
$ git branch -avv
 main ad0bbc5 [origin/main] Added install and run
instructions
* update-readme bb63877 Update README.md with uninstall
instructions
 remotes/origin/HEAD -> origin/main
 remotes/origin/main ad0bbc5 Added install and run
instructions
 remotes/origin/update-readme bb63877 Update README.md
with uninstall instructions
```

Step 13. Initiate a pull request (PR) through the repo on the GitHub UI by clicking the **Compare & Pull Request** button shown in Figure 4-6.

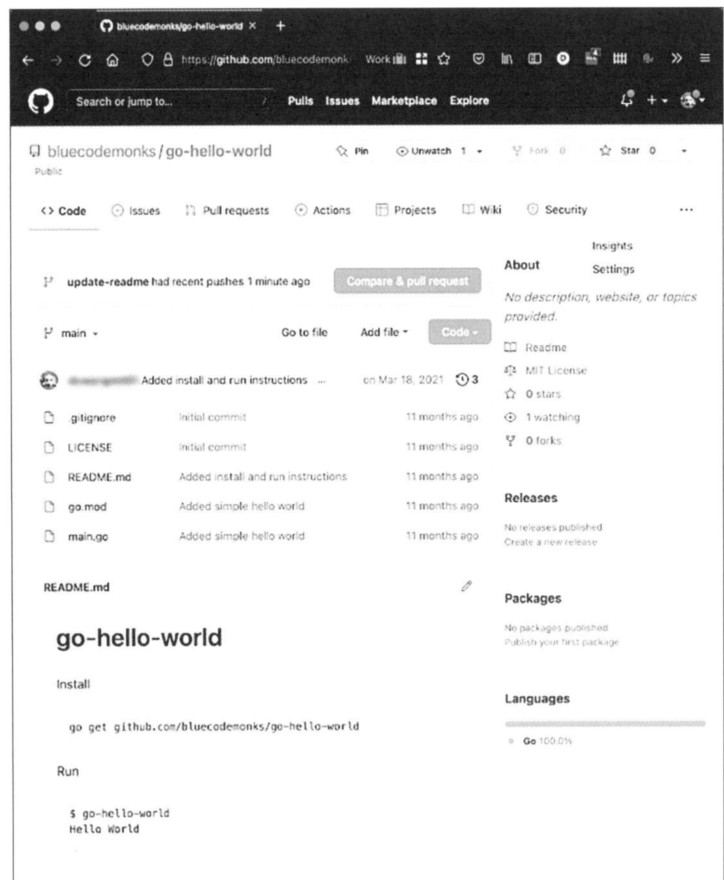

Figure 4-6 *Branch and Pull: GitHub Origin Repo Page*

You are taken to the Open a Pull Request page (as shown in Figure 4-7).

- Notice that you are asking to merge the update-readme branch into the main branch.
- This is your opportunity to provide a name for the pull request, as well as add additional comments if necessary.

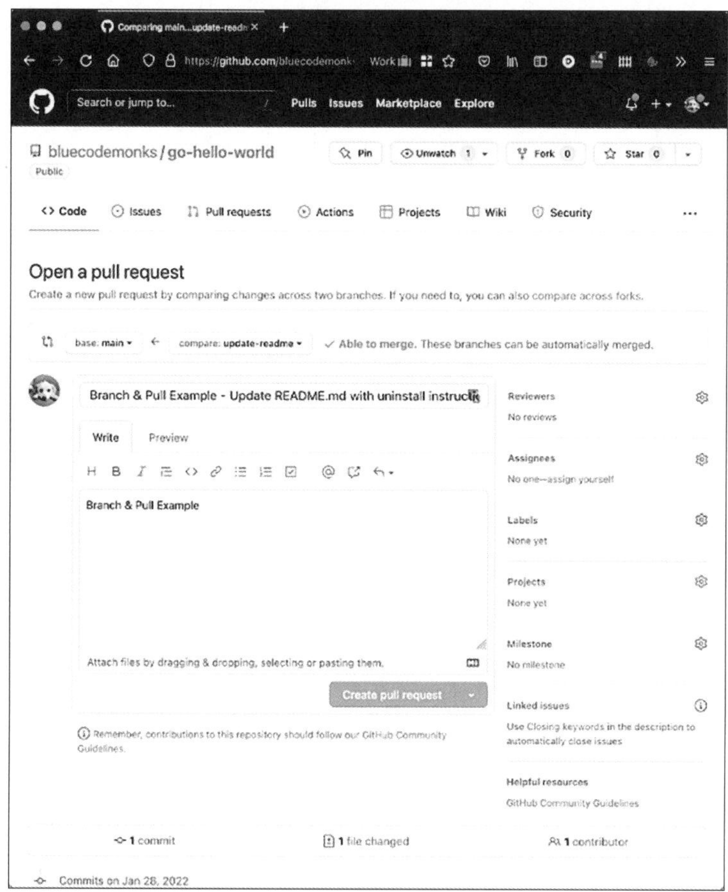

Figure 4-7 *Branch and Pull: Opening a Pull Request*

Step 14. Scroll down and inspect the proposed code changes. In Figure 4-8, notice the changes in the lower window, shown as "showing 1 changed file with 7 additions and 1 deletion."

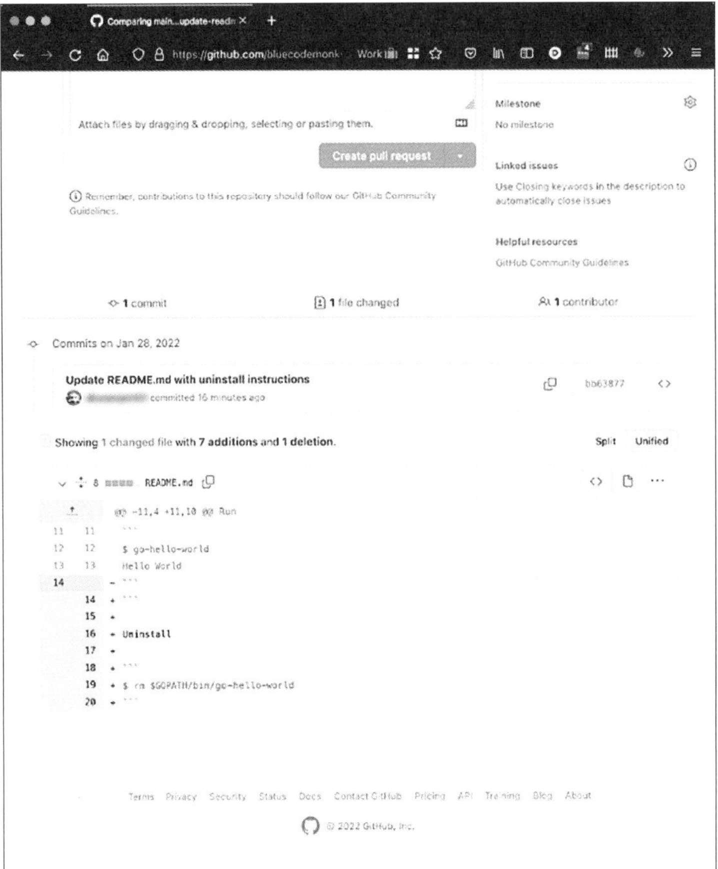

Figure 4-8 *Branch and Pull: Reviewing Pull Request Changes Before Submitting*

- If the code changes are not what you expected, you may make additional commits in your local update-readme branch and then push the additional commits to the origin/update-readme branch, which will then automatically update the pull request.

Step 15. Click the **Create Pull Request** button. Figure 4-9 clearly illustrates the pull request, and Figure 4-10 shows that the pull request is complete and ready for review.

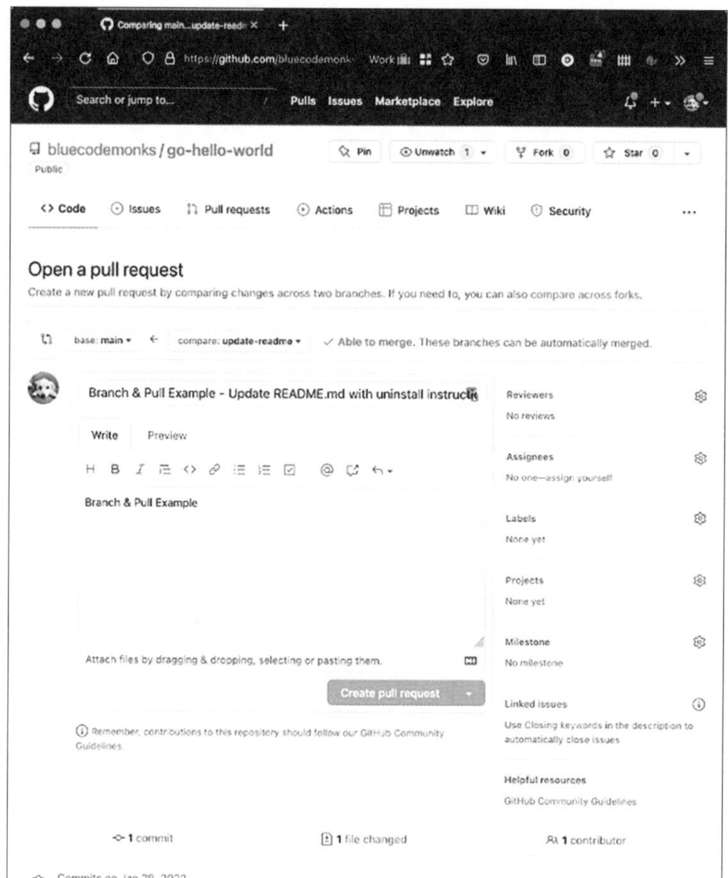

Figure 4-9 *Branch and Pull: Submitting Pull Request*

Step 16. Get your PR code reviewed by a friend or colleague:

- The code reviewer should signal that the pull request is in an acceptable/mergeable state by providing an approval signal or comment (shown as thumbs up in Figure 4-11).
- If the code reviewer requests changes, the reviewer can comment on the code, and you may fix the identified issues by making additional commits in your local update-readme branch and then pushing the additional commits to the origin/update-readme branch, which then automatically updates the PR.

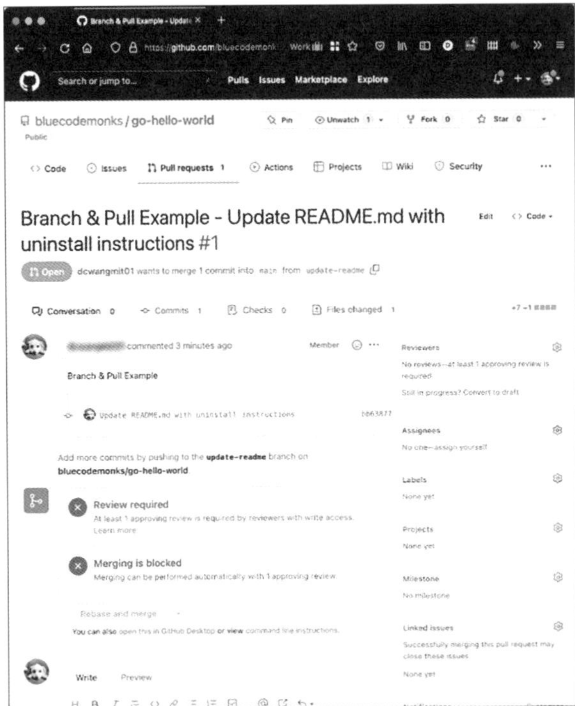

Figure 4-10 *Branch and Pull: Submit Pull Request Complete*

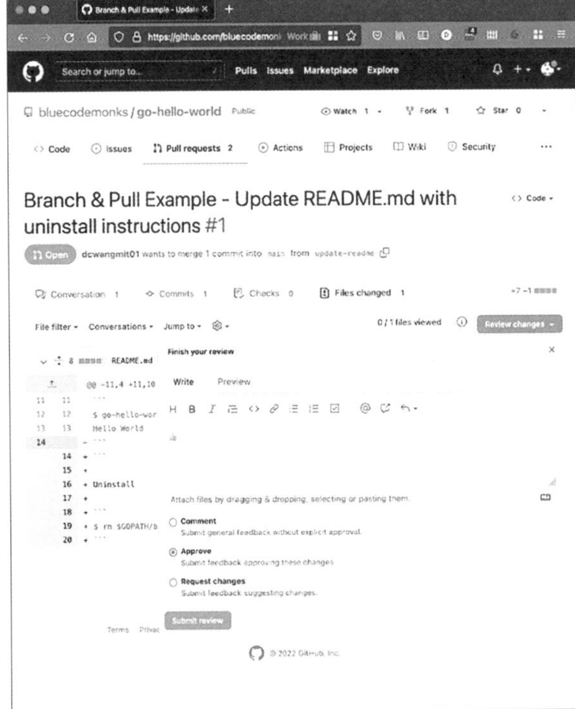

Figure 4-11 *Branch and Pull: Code Review Approval*

Step 17. Now that your pull request has been code reviewed and approved, you may merge your PR by clicking the **Merge Pull Request** button. Figure 4-12 shows the approval.

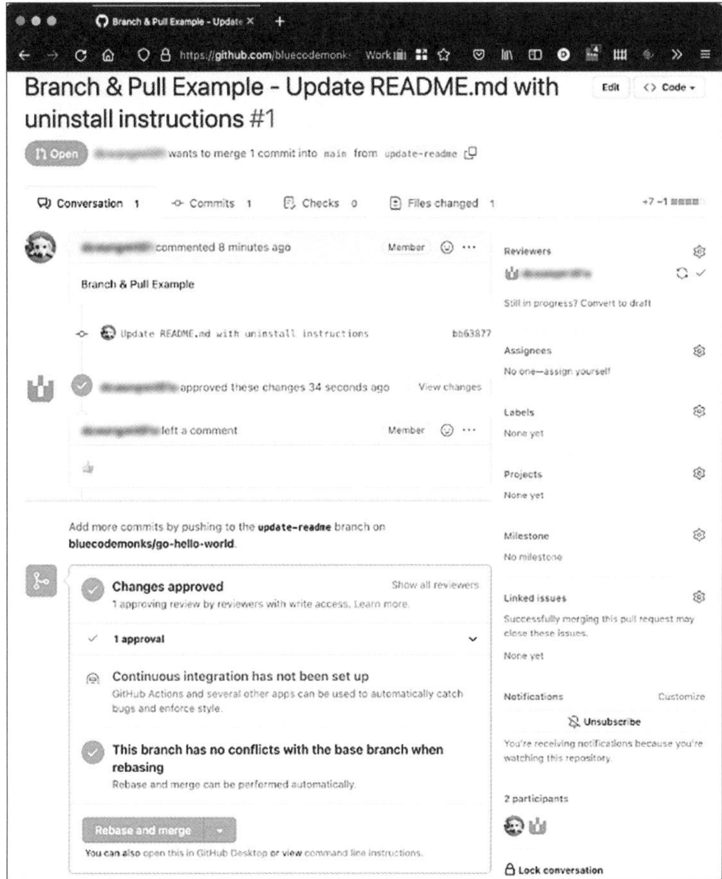

Figure 4-12 *Branch and Pull: Approved for Merge*

- Subsequently, confirm the merge, as shown in Figure 4-13.

Step 18. The PR will be fully merged after the Confirm button is clicked. For the purposes of maintaining this sample repository, do not merge this PR; instead, leave it in the open state for people to inspect.

Step 19. Because you pushed your branch update-readme to a shared repository, common courtesy is to delete your branch from the shared repository.

- Note that this step is unnecessary in the Fork and Pull Workflow.

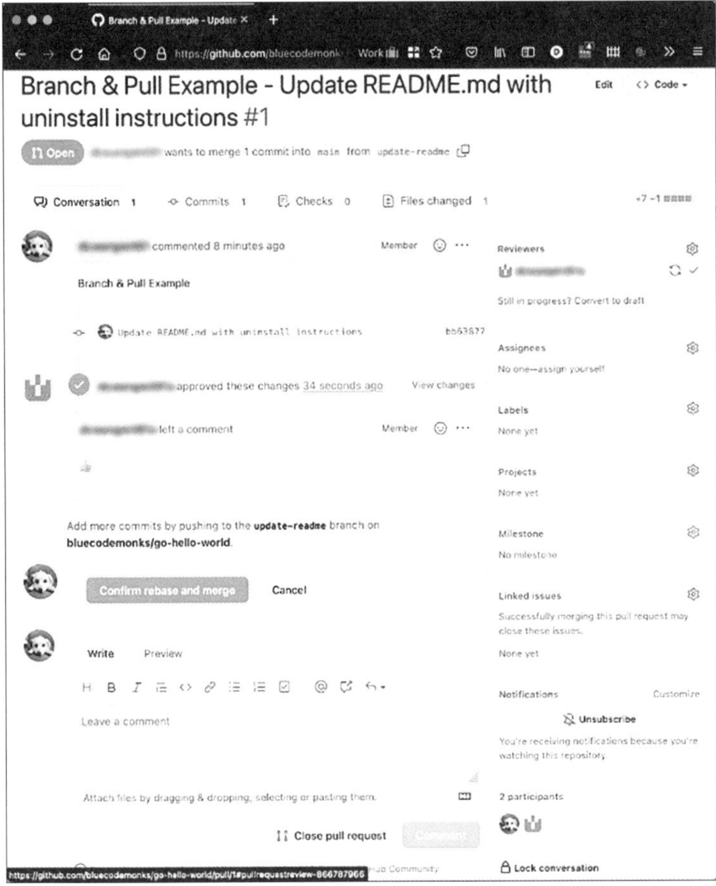

Figure 4-13 *Branch and Pull: Confirm Merge*

Fork and Pull Workflow

The Fork and Pull Workflow is the more complex of the two options for Git workflows, but it works in all use cases. In addition, it is the most popular Git workflow in the open-source and commercial worlds because it enables contributions from untrusted contributors without read-write access to the shared, source-of-truth repo.

It works when

- **Shared repo access policies:** Contributors have a minimal read-only access to the shared repository.
- **Untrusted contributors:** Unknown, untrusted, or public contributors.
- **Novice versus intermediate Git users:** The team is capable of following a more complex workflow, especially if they are already familiar with the open-source model.

This Fork and Pull Workflow has the following pros and cons.

Pros

- This model matches the workflow of the vast majority of open-source software.
- All code contributors follow the same workflow:
  - Whether a contributor is a complete stranger
  - Whether a contributor has read-only or read-write access to the shared, source-of-truth repository
- This workflow is safer because team members with write access by default push changes to their own forks before PR (instead of to a shared repository).
- This model can work for untrusted contributors who do not have write access to the shared repository.

Cons

- This model requires a higher competence of Git, beyond working in a solo repository.
- It requires a contributor to be aware of the concept of forking.

Sample Setup

Let's look at a sample setup, followed immediately by the actual Fork and Pull Workflow.

Step 1. Assume that you have configured your github.com user profile with an SSH key.

- This allows you to execute remote Git operations such as **clone** and **push** using SSH-key authentication.
- Otherwise, Git defaults to using password authentication, which requires you to frequently type in a username and password.

Step 2. Assume that **bluecodemonks** is a GitHub organization that has a code repository that you would like to contribute to.

- Assume also that the organization already exists, regardless of whether or not you are a member.
- See https://github.com/bluecodemonks.

Step 3. Assume that you would like to contribute to the **go-hello-world** repository.

- The community has agreed to use this repository as the shared, source of truth for the go-hello-world project.
- See https://github.com/bluecodemonks/go-hello-world.

Step 4. Assume that you have read-only access to this project, which has been enabled publicly readable by the project maintainers so that anyone on the Internet may view the source code. Figure 4-14 shows the bluecodemonks organization's project called go-hello-world.

- This organization might not know you, but you are still able to contribute!

Figure 4-14 *Fork and Pull: Origin Repo*

Sample Fork and Pull Workflow

Step 1. From the shared, source-of-truth repo, fork the project repository to your personal GitHub organization (shown in Figure 4-15).

- The shared repository is located at https://github.com/bluecodemonks/go-hello-world.
- After clicking the **Fork** button, you might be prompted to specify the target location for the fork. If this is the case, choose your personal GitHub organization: https://github.com/<*your-gitub-id*>.
- This places the fork at https://github.com/<*your-github-id*>/go-hello-world.

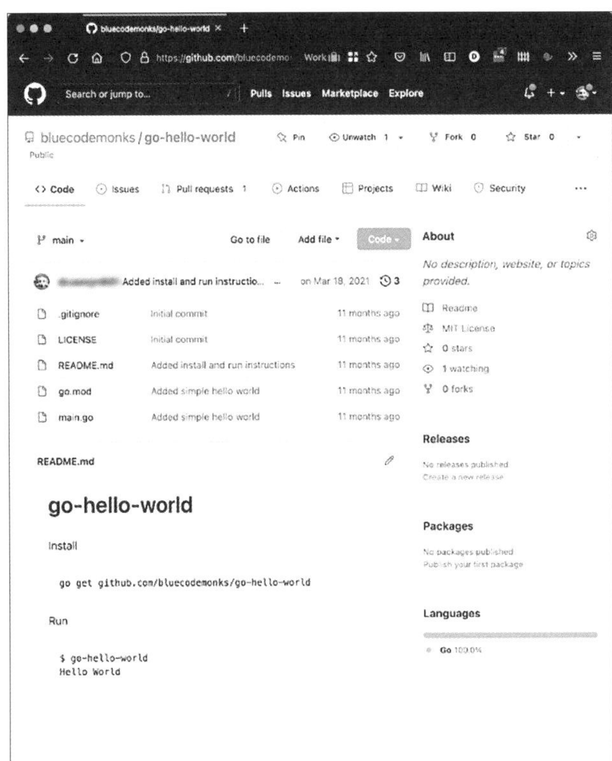

Figure 4-15 *Fork and Pull: GitHub Origin Repository*

Step 2. Go to your forked repository in your personal GitHub organization:

- It should be found at https://github.com/<*your-github-id*>/go-hello-world.
- For the purposes of illustrating the rest of this example, as shown in Figure 4-16, the repo has been forked to https://github.com/dcwangmit01/go-hello-world.

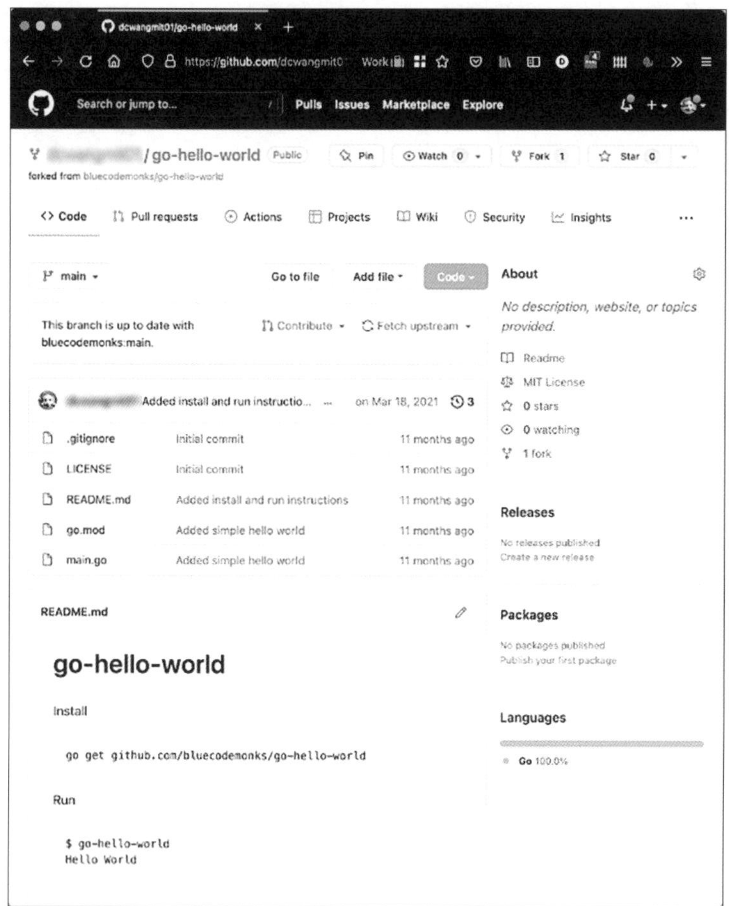

Figure 4-16 *Fork and Pull: GitHub Forked Personal Repo*

Step 3. Your fork is now tracking the shared, source-of-truth team repo.

- A *fork* is essentially a clone of the original GitHub repo but is stored in a different GitHub organization than the original rather than your local disk. GitHub tracks the parent of the fork, to set defaults such as default targets for pull request initiation. Notice the difference between the original and the clone (fork) in the logical representation shown in Figure 4-17.

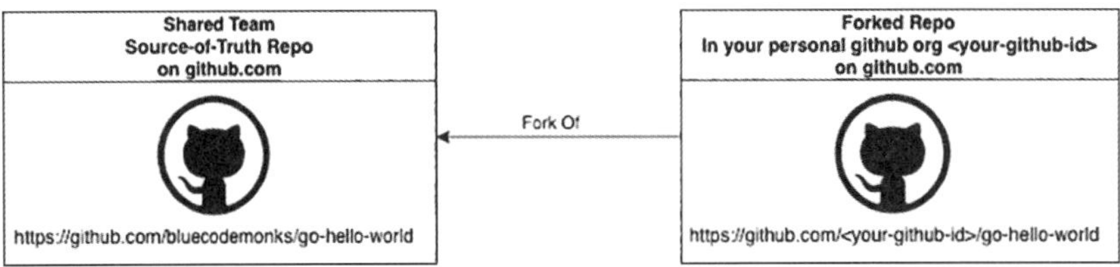

Figure 4-17 *Fork and Pull: Forked Personal Repo*

Step 4. Clone the project repository to your local computer:

```
$ mkdir ~/Dev
$ cd ~/Dev
$ git clone git@github.com:dcwangmit01/go-hello-world.git
Cloning into 'go-hello-world'...
[snipped]
```

Step 5. You now have a local copy of the project repository on your filesystem. The local copy is shown in Figure 4-18.

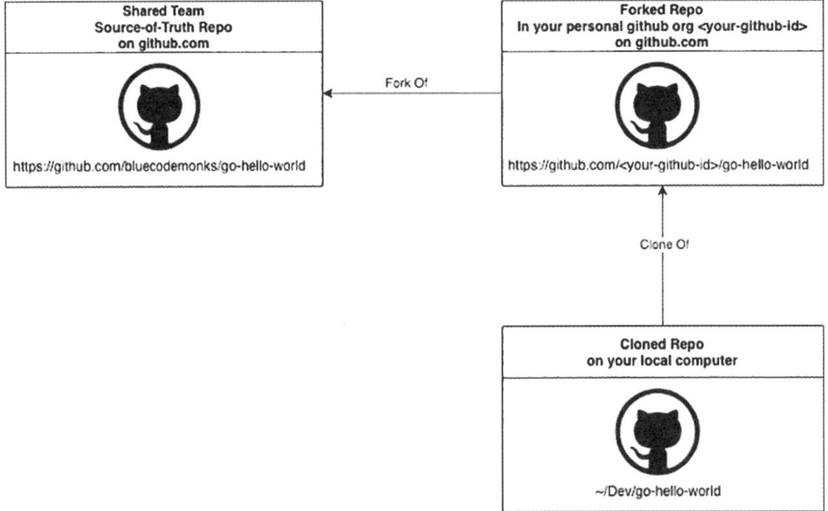

Figure 4-18 *Fork and Pull: Locally Cloned from Fork of Origin Repo*

Step 6. Look around the newly cloned repository:

```
$ cd ~/Dev/go-hello-world
$ tree
.
├── LICENSE
├── README.md
├── go.mod
└── main.go
0 directories, 4 files
```

Step 7. Notice that a Git remote repository configuration has already been set up because you cloned from a remote repository.

- This repository is named **origin** (by default).
- It refers to the original URI from which this repo was cloned, which is the personal repository fork, instead of the shared, source-of-truth bluecodemonks.

```
$ git remote -v
origin git@github.com:dcwangmit01/go-hello-world.git
(fetch)
origin git@github.com:dcwangmit01/go-hello-world.git
(push)
```

Step 8. Add an additional Git remote repository configuration for the original shared, source-of-truth repository.

- Explicitly name the remote repository **upstream**, as in the original repo that has been forked.

```
$ git remote add upstream git@github.com:bluecodemonks/
go-hello-world.git
$ git remote -v
origin git@github.com:dcwangmit01/go-hello-world.git
(fetch)
origin git@github.com:dcwangmit01/go-hello-world.git
(push)
upstream git@github.com:bluecodemonks/go-hello-world.git
(fetch)
upstream git@github.com:bluecodemonks/go-hello-world.git
(push)
```

- Note that you may name these Git remotes however you choose. An alternate configuration may be to name the original shared, source-of-truth forked repository **origin** and then name any other remote to be the name of the GitHub organization. This helps if you need to access the personal forks of people you are collaborating with. Your configuration might look like this:

```
$ git remote -v
origin git@github.com:bluecodemonks/go-hello-world.git
(fetch)
origin git@github.com:bluecodemonks/go-hello-world.git
(push)
jack git@github.com:jack/go-hello-world.git (fetch)
jack git@github.com:jack/go-hello-world.git (push)
jill git@github.com:jill/go-hello-world.git (fetch)
```

```
jill git@github.com:jill/go-hello-world.git (push)
you git@github.com:you/go-hello-world.git (fetch)
you git@github.com:you/go-hello-world.git (push)
```

- The rest of this example assumes the more common naming convention that the original, shared source-of-truth repository is named **upstream**.

Step 9. Look at what branch you are currently on and what branches are available.

- You are on the main branch, denoted by the asterisk (*) character.
- Your local main branch is at the same commit as the remote origin/main branch. It is set to track the origin/main remote upstream by default. Thus, if you execute commands such as **git push** without fully qualifying where to push, it assumes the target is the default origin/main remote upstream. To push to a specific Git remote and specific branch on that remote, you may fully qualify the target **git push** *<remote>/<branch>*. Note the logical representation in Figure 4-19.

```
$ git branch -avv
* main ad0bbc5 [origin/main] Added install and run
instructions
 remotes/origin/HEAD -> origin/main
 remotes/origin/main ad0bbc5 Added install and run
instructions
 remotes/origin/update-readme bb63877 Update README.md
with uninstall instructions
```

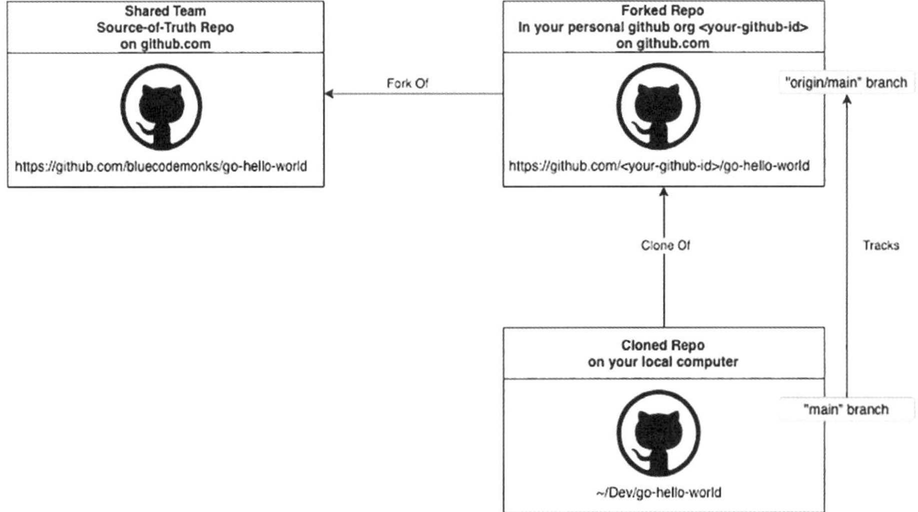

Figure 4-19 *Fork and Pull: Main Branch Tracking*

Step 10. Now it's time to make a contribution. First, create a local branch to store your local changes. Because you are currently on the main branch, the new branch is created from main. The steps are illustrated in Example 4-5 and logically represented in Figure 4-20.

Example 4-5 *Fork and Pull: Creating a Branch*

```
# Check what branch we are on
$ git branch
* main

# Create a new feature-branch from "main" and switch to it
$ git checkout -b update-readme-2
Switched to a new branch 'update-readme-2'

# View your branch status
$ git branch -avv
 main ad0bbc5 [origin/main] Added install and run instructions
* update-readme-2 ad0bbc5 Added install and run instructions
 remotes/origin/HEAD -> origin/main
 remotes/origin/main ad0bbc5 Added install and run instructions
 remotes/origin/update-readme bb63877 Update README.md with uninstall instructions
```

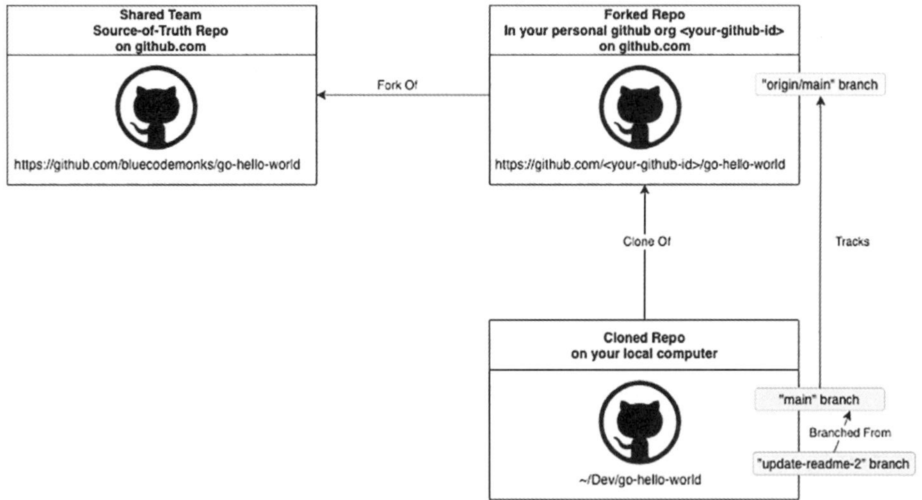

Figure 4-20 *Fork and Pull: Creating a Branch*

Step 11. Now make some edits to the README.md file. You're going to enhance the README.md with details:

```
$ vi README.md
This is an example repo.
```

Step 12. Assess your changes before you stage them.

The step represented in Example 4-6 is not required but is extremely good practice to evaluate your changes before you stage them.

Example 4-6 *Fork and Pull: Reviewing Current Changes*

```
$ git status
On branch update-readme-2
Changes not staged for commit:
 (use "git add <file>..." to update what will be committed)
 (use "git restore <file>..." to discard changes in working directory)
 modified: README.md

no changes added to commit (use "git add" and/or "git commit -a")

$ git diff
diff --git a/README.md b/README.md
index f272b4d..567f23b 100644
--- a/README.md
+++ b/README.md
@@ -1,5 +1,7 @@
 # go-hello-world

+This is an example repo.
+
 Install

 ```
```

Step 13. Stage your changes:

```
$ git add README.md
```

Step 14. Assess your staged changes to double-check your edits.

This step, illustrated in Example 4-7, is not required but is extremely good practice to evaluate your changes before you commit them.

```
$ git diff --cached
```

Example 4-7 *Fork and Pull: Reviewing Staged Changes*

```
diff --git a/README.md b/README.md
index f272b4d..567f23b 100644
--- a/README.md
+++ b/README.md
@@ -1,5 +1,7 @@
```
```

~~~
 # go-hello-world

+This is an example repo.
+
 Install

 ```
~~~

Step 15. Commit the changes to the local branch:

```
$ git commit -m "Update README.md with details"
[update-readme-2 de7b443] Update README.md with details
 1 file changed, 2 insertions(+)
```


Step 16. Push a copy of your local branch update-readme-2 to your personal fork repo (instead of the shared source-of-truth repo).

- The personal fork repo is named **origin** in your Git remotes:

```
$ git remote -v
origin git@github.com:dcwangmit01/go-hello-world.git (fetch)
origin git@github.com:dcwangmit01/go-hello-world.git (push)
upstream git@github.com:bluecodemonks/go-hello-world.git (fetch)
upstream git@github.com:bluecodemonks/go-hello-world.git (push)
```

- Notice that you are currently on the update-readme-2 local branch and that the origin Git remote has no such branch:

```
$ git branch -avv
 main ad0bbc5 [origin/main] Added install and run instructions
* update-readme-2 de7b443 Update README.md with details
 remotes/origin/HEAD -> origin/main
 remotes/origin/main ad0bbc5 Added install and run instructions
 remotes/origin/update-readme bb63877 Update README.md with uninstall instructions
```

- Thus, you must push the current branch to the origin remote, specifying a fully qualified branch name in the format *<remote> <branch>*.
- The configuration steps are shown in Example 4-8 and illustrated in Figure 4-21.

Example 4-8 *Fork and Pull: Pushing a Branch to Forked Repo*

```
$ git push origin update-readme-2
Enumerating objects: 5, done.
Counting objects: 100% (5/5), done.
Delta compression using up to 12 threads
Compressing objects: 100% (3/3), done.
Writing objects: 100% (3/3), 380 bytes | 380.00 KiB/s, done.
Total 3 (delta 1), reused 0 (delta 0), pack-reused 0
remote: Resolving deltas: 100% (1/1), completed with 1 local object.
Remote:
remote: Create a pull request for 'update-readme-2' on GitHub by visiting:
remote: https://github.com/dcwangmit01/go-hello-world/pull/new/update-readme-2
remote:
To github.com:dcwangmit01/go-hello-world.git
 * [new branch] update-readme-2 -> update-readme-2
```

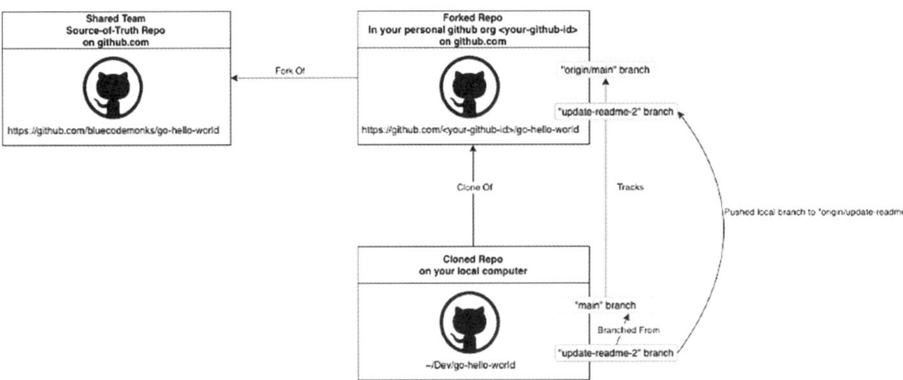

Figure 4-21 *Fork and Pull: Listing All Branches*

- Now verify that the remote origin has a new branch named **updated-readme:**

```
$ git branch -avv
 main ad0bbc5 [origin/main] Added install and run
instructions
* update-readme-2 de7b443 Update README.md with details
 remotes/origin/HEAD -> origin/main
 remotes/origin/main ad0bbc5 Added install and run
instructions
 remotes/origin/update-readme bb63877 Update README.md
with uninstall instructions
 remotes/origin/update-readme-2 de7b443 Update README.md
with details
```

Step 17. Now initiate a pull request from your personal fork to the shared, source-of-truth repo on the GitHub UI by clicking the **Compare & Pull Request** button. You may initiate this pull request from either your personal fork or the shared, source-of-truth repo. In the example, shown here in Figure 4-22, the latter is chosen.

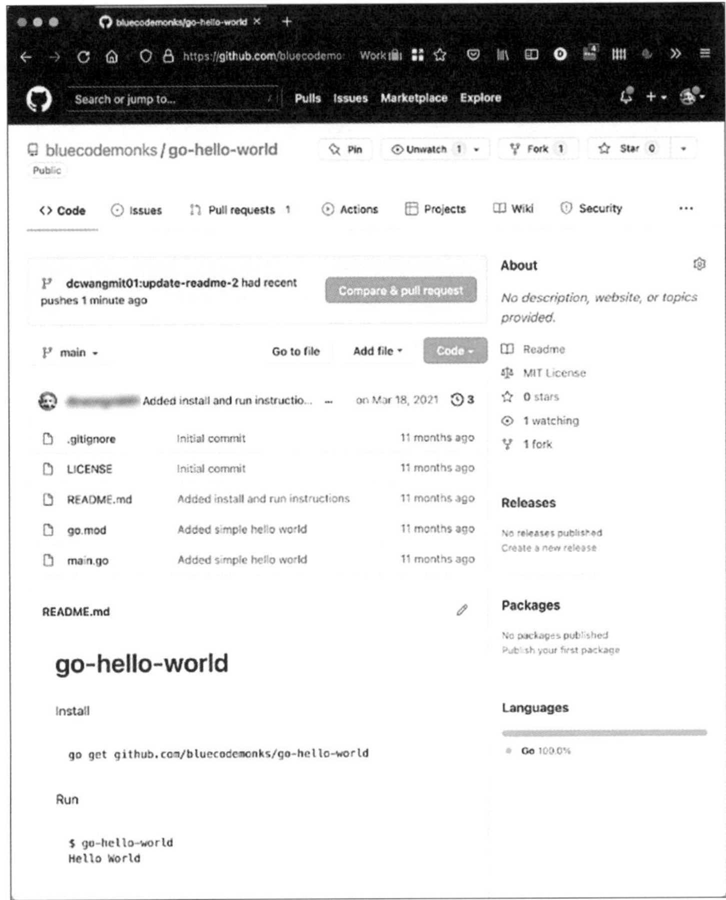

Figure 4-22 *Fork and Pull: GitHub Origin Repo Page*

Step 18. You are taken to the Open a Pull Request page.

- Notice that you are asking to merge the update-readme-2 branch into the main branch.
- This is your opportunity to provide a name for the pull request, as well as add additional comments if necessary.
- Figure 4-23 shows the Open a Pull Request page and the text box for adding your comments.

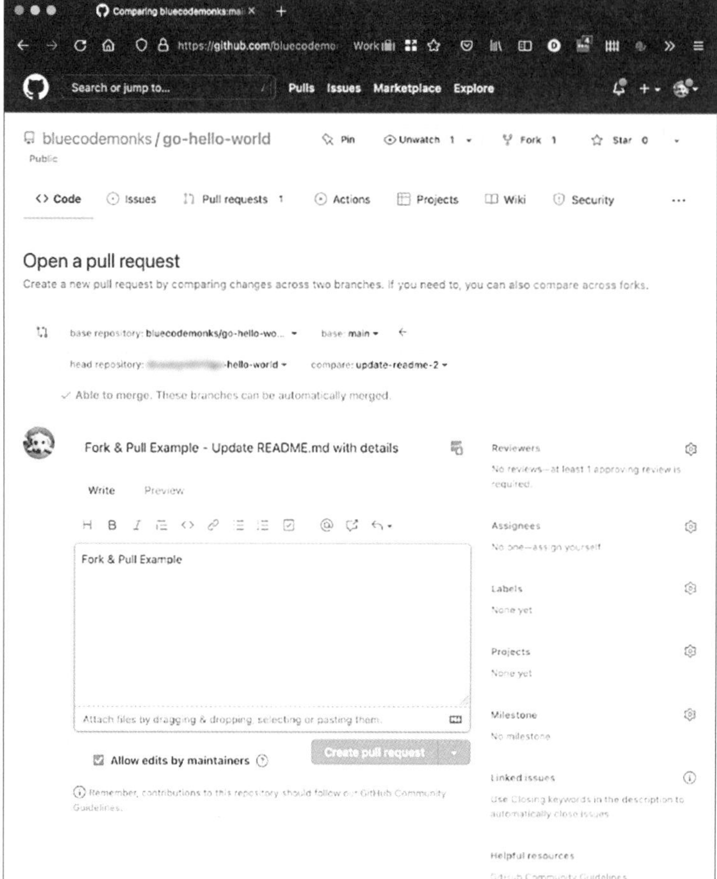

Figure 4-23 *Fork and Pull: Opening a Pull Request*

Step 19. Scroll down and inspect the proposed code changes. Figure 4-24, which is a continuation of Figure 4-23, shows the proposed code changes for review before submitting.

- If the code changes are not what you expected, you may make additional commits in your local update-readme branch and then push the additional commits to the origin/update-readme branch, which then automatically updates the PR.

Step 20. Click the **Create Pull Request** button. Figure 4-25 shows the Create pull request step, and it is immediately followed by Figure 4-26 showing the pull request complete.

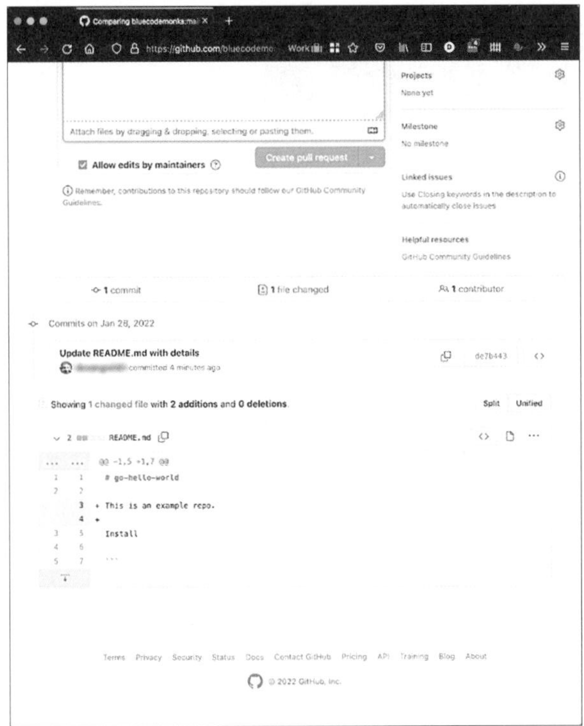

Figure 4-24 *Fork and Pull: Reviewing Pull Request Changes Before Submitting*

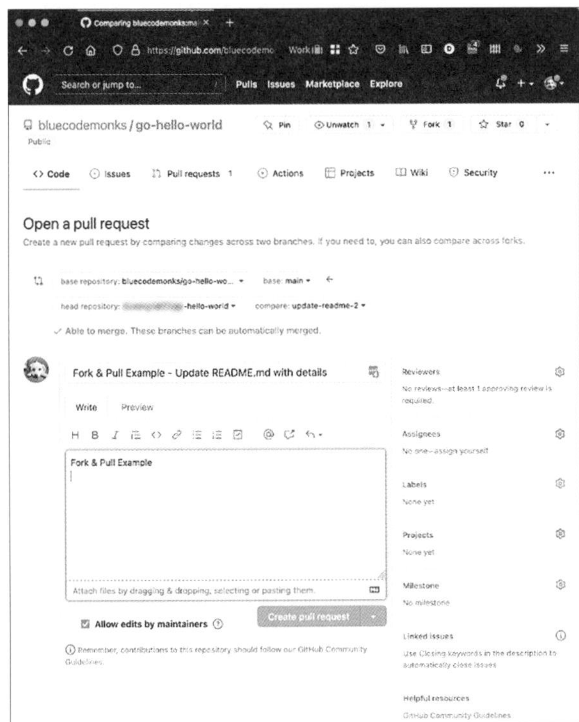

Figure 4-25 *Fork and Pull: Submitting Pull Request*

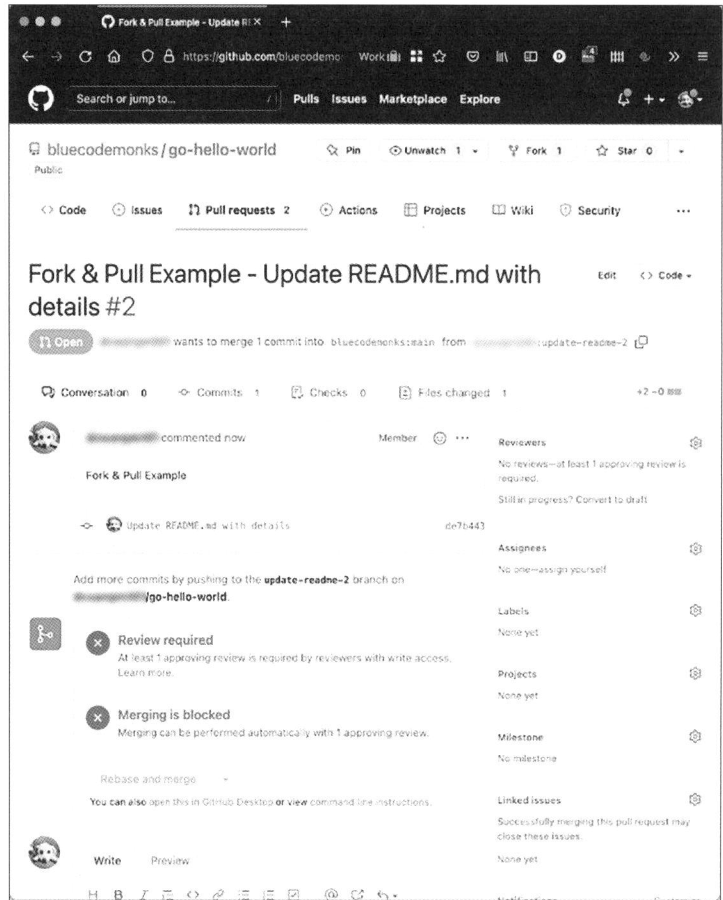

Figure 4-26 *Fork and Pull: Submit Pull Request Complete*

Step 21. Get your PR code reviewed by a friend or colleague.

- The code reviewer should signal that the pull request is in an acceptable/mergeable state by providing an approval signal or comment. See Figure 4-27 for more details.

- If the code reviewer requests changes, the reviewer can comment on the code, and you may fix the identified issues by making additional commits in your local update-readme branch and then pushing the additional commits to the origin/update-readme branch, which then automatically updates the PR.

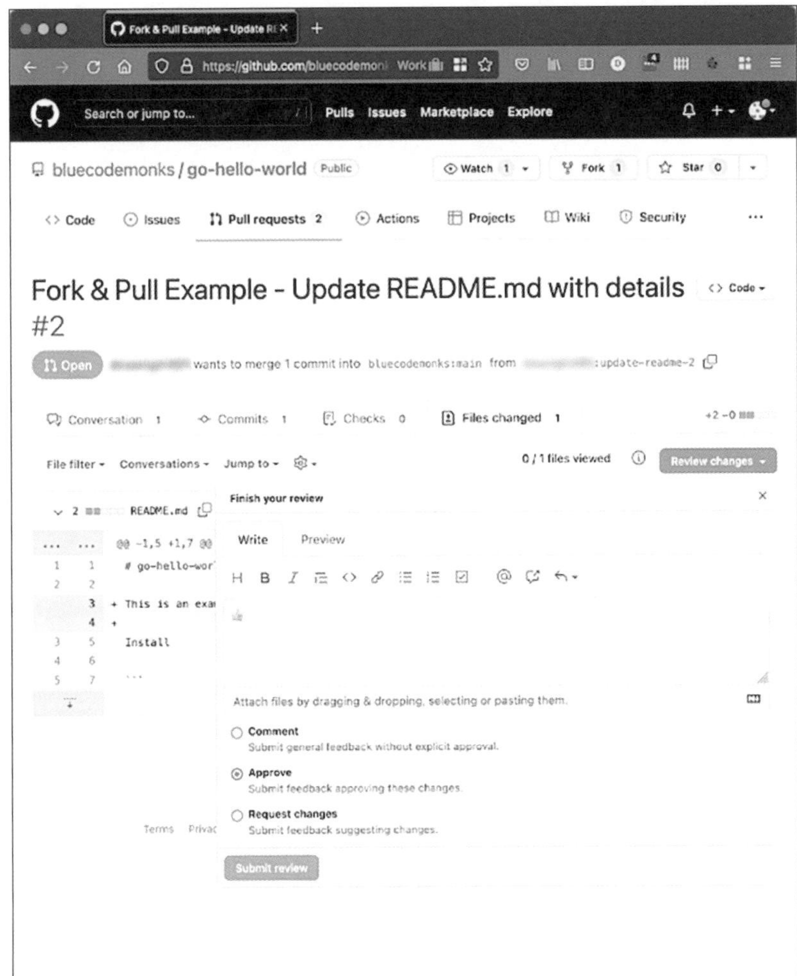

Figure 4-27 *Fork and Pull: Code Review Approval*

Step 22. Now that your pull request has been code reviewed and approved, you may merge your PR by clicking the **Merge Pull Request** button. Figure 4-28 shows that the approval has been obtained (for example, 1 approval), and now it is ready for Merge.

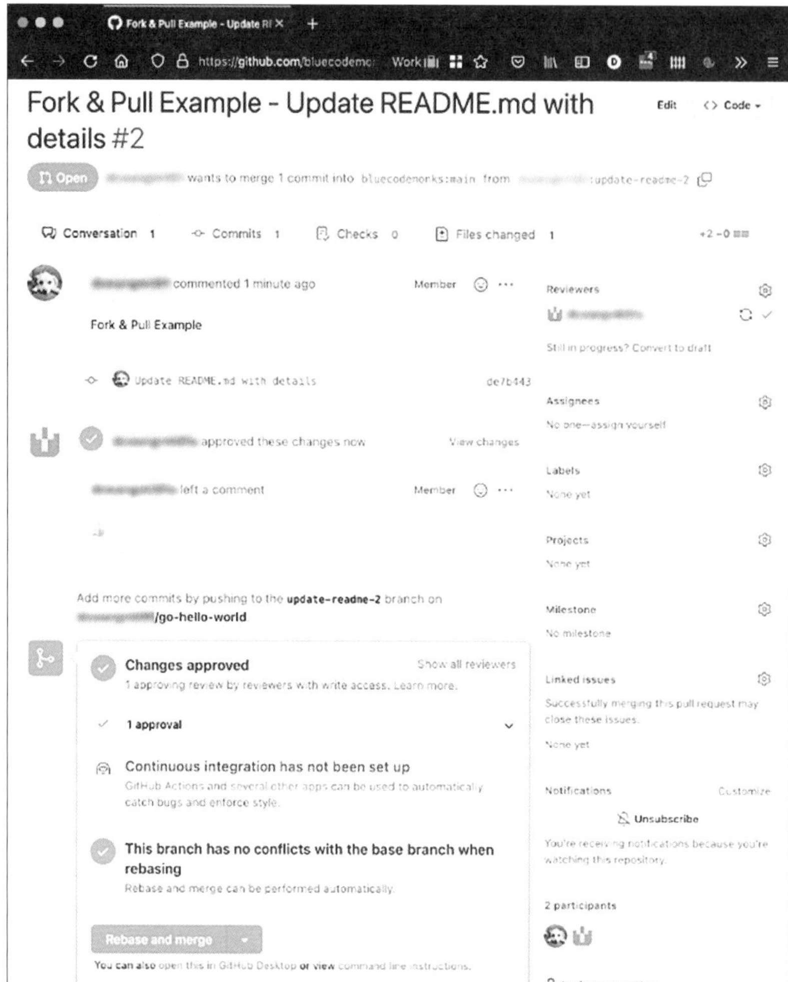

Figure 4-28 *Fork and Pull: Approved for Merge*

- Subsequently, confirm the merge, as shown in Figure 4-29.

Step 23. Now the pull request will be fully merged after the **Confirm** button is clicked. For the purposes of maintaining this sample repository, do not merge this PR; instead, leave it in the open state for people to inspect.

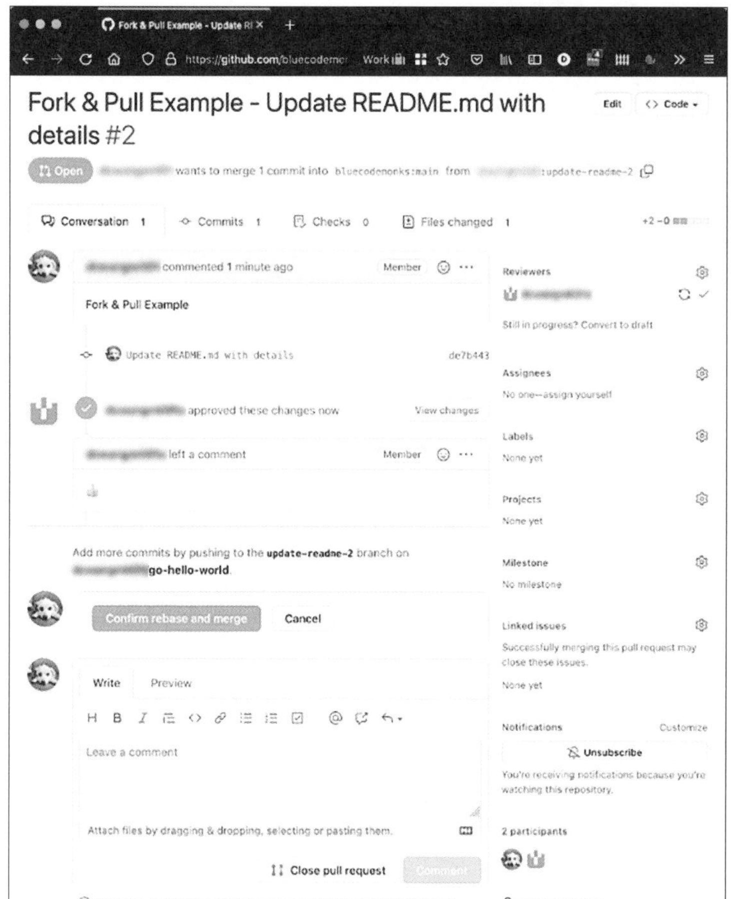

Figure 4-29 *Fork and Pull: Confirm Merge*

Git Branching Strategy

Branching is easy to understand and is a powerful tool when dealing with larger projects involving multiple developers. However, all powerful tools can be useless if the team does not agree on a common workflow and a branching strategy. The following sections discuss the most common branching strategies and how to use them.

What Is a Branching Strategy?

A branching strategy is a team working agreement that enables the management of

- **Developing code:** Destabilizes code because development introduces code changes
- **Stabilizing code:** Stabilizes code through reducing the rate of code changes

The need for code development for new features versus stabilizing code for release is a constant push and pull. Thus, a team needs a working agreement on managing this process.

The Most Important Factor When Selecting a Git Branching Strategy

When you're deciding on a branching strategy, the most important question that influences the outcome is, Do you trust your automated tests?

If your automated tests are comprehensive enough where a pass result on its own is trusted evidence that the code is deployable to production, your team is a shining example of modern software development.

Popular Git Branching Strategies

If you do a web search on Git branching strategies, you'll find a large collection of documented strategies. The most popular ones are as follows:

- **GitHub Flow:** https://guides.github.com/introduction/flow/
- **Git Flow:** https://nvie.com/posts/a-successful-git-branching-model/
- **GitLab Flow:** https://docs.gitlab.com/ee/topics/gitlab_flow.html

When to Use GitHub Flow

GitHub Flow is the recommended branch strategy for all software projects that are disciplined and adhere to comprehensive automated test coverage. New software projects should always start with this modern-day approach.

If you answered "yes" to the question "Do you trust your automated tests?" it enables a lot of good things:

1. You are able to keep a stable main branch because tests can block the PR merge.
2. You are able to release to production several times a day.
3. You can tag versions of your release directly from the main branch.
4. You have no need for release branches to stabilize your product.
5. You have no need for code freezes to stabilize your product.
6. You have no dependencies on manual quality assurance (QA) to stabilize your product.

Here's a visualization of the GitHub Flow model. Notice that a single, linear main branch exists with only feature branches and without the existence of release branches. This example (shown in Figure 4-30) is the simplest of the Git branching strategies; it keeps a single main branch stable.

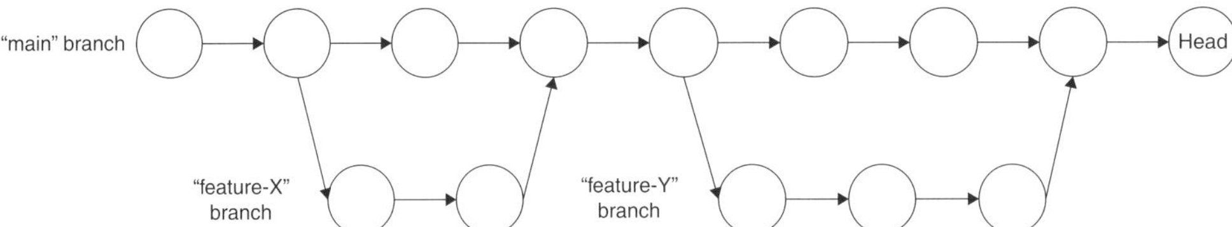

Figure 4-30 *GitHub Flow Branch Visualization*

If you're not able to trust your automated tests because they are not comprehensive, then GitHub Flow does not work. Instead, use a different model called Git Flow.

Most of the open-source world uses GitHub Flow.

When to Use Git Flow

Git Flow is the recommended branch strategy for software projects that are not disciplined with comprehensive automated test coverage. Typically, legacy software development projects that rely on days, weeks, or months of manual QA testing should follow the Git Flow branch strategy. Git Flow uses release branches to allow development and quality assurance teams to stabilize code for a release, while allowing code development to proceed on the main branch.

Git Flow is not recommended as a first choice for branch strategy, unless your project falls into this legacy category. In fact, the original author of Git Flow now recommends GitHub Flow. You can read the original article at https://nvie.com/posts/a-successful-git-branching-model/.

If you answered "no" to the question "Do you trust your automated tests?" your project may have a lot of legacy qualities:

1. You are unable to keep a stable main branch because your automated tests are not comprehensive enough to block PR merges based on test results.
2. You are unable to release to production several times a day.
3. You cannot tag versions of your release directly from the main branch because main is not kept stable.
4. You must use release branches to stabilize your product, and you tag your releases off the release branches.
5. You need code freezes to stabilize your product.
6. You have dependencies on manual QA to stabilize your product.

Figure 4-31 shows a visualization of the Git Flow model.

The Git Flow branching strategy allows teams to stabilize code in release branches that are code-frozen for bug fixes only. In addition, development may continue to move forward and allow destabilized code to continue to be merged into the develop branch. The main branch would only receive merges from stabilized release branches.

When to Use GitLab Flow

GitLab Flow is a Git branching strategy that is centered around a main branch as the base branch and requires maintaining a separate branch per environment (development, staging, production). As changes occur in the environment branches, they must be cherry-picked back into the main branch.

This branching strategy is complicated. We cannot recommend this Git branching strategy, but it may be good for your use cases. Read more at https://docs.gitlab.com/ee/topics/gitlab_flow.html.

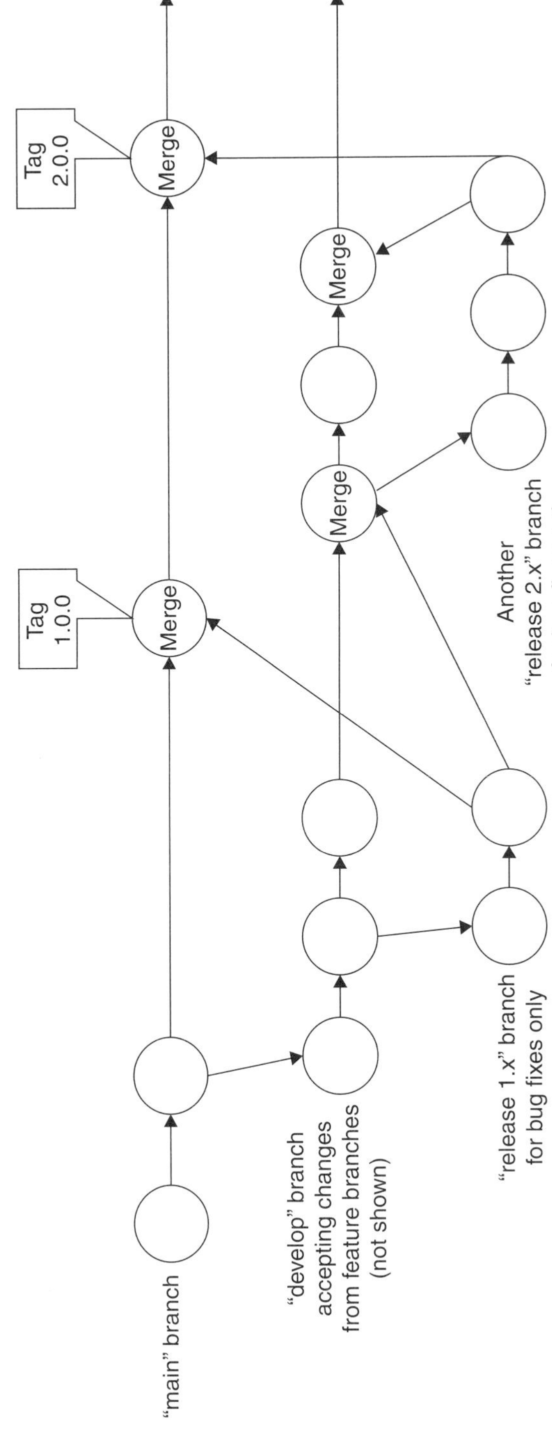

Figure 4-31 *Git Flow Branch Visualization*

Recommended GitHub Settings

Shared, source-of-truth GitHub repositories should be configured for team access and code reviews. These settings are available via the repo settings page. In this example, the settings page, which is found at https://github.com/bluecodemonks/go-hello-world/settings, is accessible only by repository owners.

Configuring the PR Merge Button

Merge button settings are found under **Options > Merge Button.** To keep a clean Git commit history, we recommend that you rebase merging and thus disable the other options (see Figure 4-32).

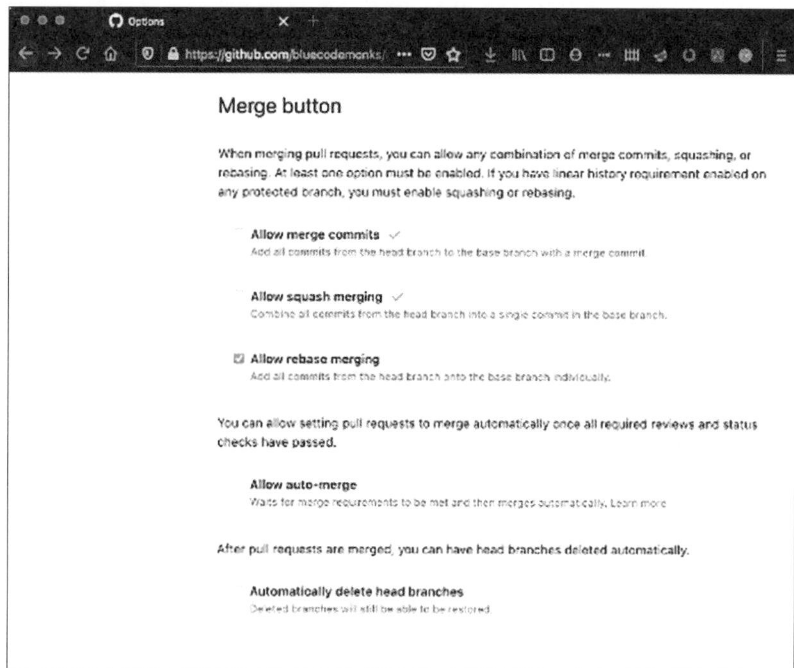

Figure 4-32 *GitHub Repo Merge Button Settings*

Rebase merging enables a team to keep a clean, linear Git history.

Configuring a Branch Protection Rule to Require Code Reviews

In GitHub, a branch protection rule may be used to disallow contributors to push directly to a shared branch without certain prerequisites, such as code reviews. Configuration is done at the page shown in Figure 4-33.

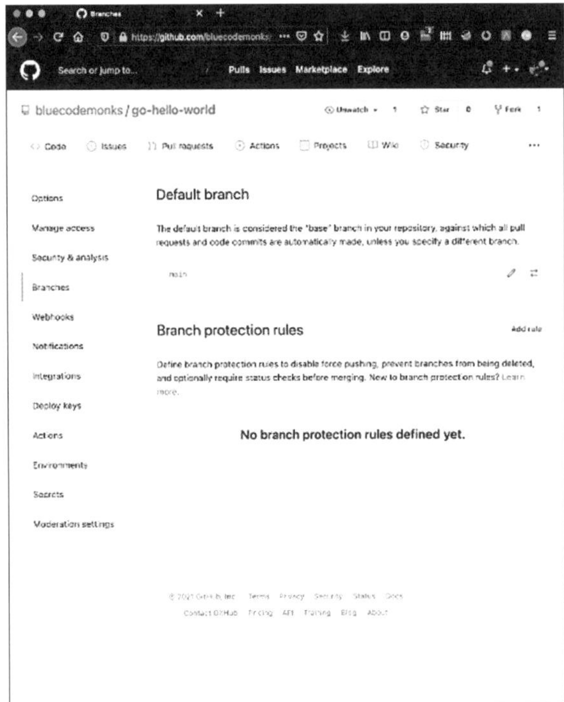

Figure 4-33 *GitHub Repo Branch Protection Rules*

From the main page shown in the figure, an administrator may add a branch protection rule. A common practice is to add a branch protection rule for the main branch.

The main shared branch is often a branch that needs protection, affecting important practices such as

- Disabling the ability to directly push to a branch without a code review
- Requiring one or more code review approvals before enabling PR merges
- Enforcing a linear commit history

The settings are shown in Figure 4-34.

In this chapter we provided you with frequently used commands, techniques, and workflows for version control. As your projects grow in size and the number of developers and testers, your **version control system** also grows in complexity. Depending on your organization, we highly recommend you take a deeper look at Git through practice and use the *Pro Git* book mentioned at the beginning of this chapter.

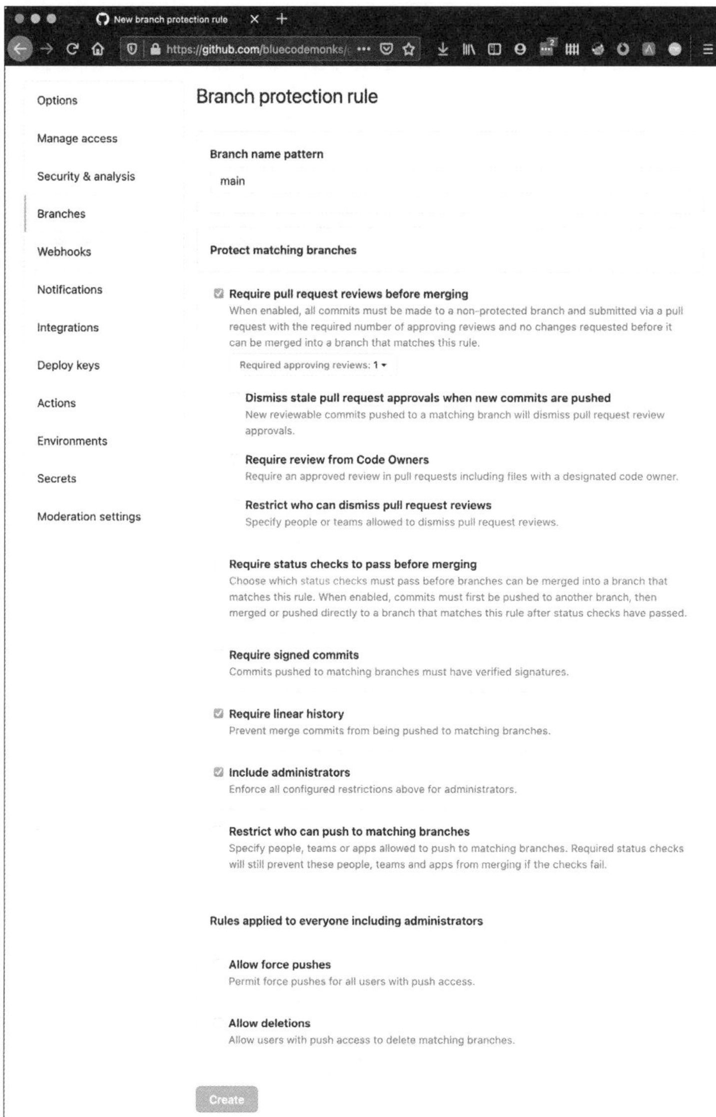

Figure 4-34 *GitHub Repo Branch Protection Rule*

Exam Preparation Tasks

As mentioned in the section "How to Use This Book" in the Introduction, you have a couple of choices for exam preparation: the exercises here, Chapter 17, "Final Preparation," and the exam simulation questions on the companion website.

Review All Key Topics

Review the most important topics in this chapter, noted with the Key Topic icon in the outer margin of the page. Table 4-2 lists a reference of these key topics and the page numbers on which each is found.

Table 4-2 Key Topics for Chapter 4

Key Topic Element	Description	Page Number
Step list	Sample branch and pull workflow	90
Section	Fork and Pull Workflow	104
List	Popular Git branching strategies	122
Section	When to Use Git Flow	123
Section	Recommended GitHub Settings	125

Complete Tables and Lists from Memory

There are no memory tables or lists in this chapter.

Define Key Terms

Define the following key terms from this chapter and check your answers in the glossary:

version control, version control system

References

URL	QR Code
ProGit: Everything You Need to Know About Git https://github.com/progit/progit2	
github.com	

CHAPTER 5

Network APIs

This chapter covers the following topics:

- **What Are APIs?:** This section describes what application programming interfaces (APIs) are and what they are used for.
- **Calling an API:** This section covers how to call an API using Cisco platforms or others by using its Uniform Resource Identifier (URI).
- **Selecting an API Style:** This section discusses using either Open API (Swagger) or JSON (JavaScript Object Notation) when making design decisions and doing so in a machine-parsable format.
- **Network API Styles:** This section covers both REST and YANG styles, addressing web APIs and network device APIs and the differences in the main abstractions they build on.

This chapter maps to the *Developing Applications Using Cisco Core Platforms and APIs v1.0* (350-901) Exam Blueprint Section 3.0, "Cisco Platforms."

Software developers use application programming interfaces (APIs) to communicate with and configure networks. APIs are used to communicate with applications and other software. They are also used to communicate with various components of a network through software. This chapter focuses on what APIs are used for, how to use them, and the different API styles including data types and REST/RPCs. You learn how to keep the consumer in mind when you're designing an API so that developers who are not familiar with your product can easily understand your API. In addition, you see the importance of consuming and visualizing RESTful web services.

"Do I Know This Already?" Quiz

The "Do I Know This Already?" quiz allows you to assess whether you should read this entire chapter thoroughly or jump to the "Exam Preparation Tasks" section. If you are in doubt about your answers to these questions or your own assessment of your knowledge of the topics, read the entire chapter. Table 5-1 lists the major headings in this chapter and their corresponding "Do I Know This Already?" quiz questions. You can find the answers in Appendix A, "Answers to the 'Do I Know This Already?' Quizzes."

Table 5-1 "Do I Know This Already?" Section-to-Question Mapping

Foundation Topics Section	Questions
What Are APIs?	1, 2
Calling an API	3, 4
Network API Styles	5–7
Selecting an API Style	8–10

1. When you issue an API call using the PATCH method, what does the request method supported by Hypertext Transfer Protocol (HTTP) do to the current resource?
   a. PATCH modifies the current resource.
   b. PATCH retrieves the resource details.
   c. PATCH cancels the current resource.
   d. PATCH removes all the resources.
2. Which of the following statements is correct regarding the HTTP PUT method?
   a. The HTTP PUT method is safe and does not impact resources.
   b. The HTTP PUT method is idempotent; it is not safe and it impacts resources.
   c. The HTTP PUT method is nonidempotent and it impacts resources per changes.
   d. PUT removes all the resources and does not replace the data.
3. The Content-Type header attribute specifies the format of data in the request body so that the receiver can parse it into the appropriate format. When you're specifying the content types of the request body and output, what does using the Content-Type application/x-www-form-urlencoded do?
   a. It indicates that the request body is encoded in key-value tuples.
   b. It indicates that the request body format is multipart/form-data.
   c. It sets the output type to XML.
   d. It indicates that the request body format is XML.
4. What is the Swagger UI?
   a. The Swagger UI can be used to generate API documentation that can be used only via Python or Ansible.
   b. The Swagger UI can be used to generate isolated API documentation that lets your users try out the API calls directly in the browser.
   c. The Swagger UI can be used to generate interactive API documentation that lets your users try out the API calls directly in the browser.
   d. The Swagger UI can be used to generate API code that lets your users try out the API calls directly in Postman.
5. What are REST and RESTful? (Choose two.)
   a. REST represents Representational State Transfer.
   b. REST is an HTTP-based protocol that provides a programmatic interface for accessing data defined in YANG.
   c. RESTful refers to web services written by applying REST architectural concepts; they are called RESTful services.
   d. RESTful refers to web services that perform an RPC by sending an HTTP request to a server that implements XML-RPC and receives the HTTP response.
6. What are the ACID properties?
   a. Atomicity, consistency, isolation, and durability
   b. Atomicity, consistency, isometric, and duration
   c. Atomicity, consistency, isolation, and duration
   d. Atomicity, composite, isolation, and durability

7. Which statement is most accurate when describing SOAP web services?
   a. SOAP is defined as a JSON- and XML-based protocol.
   b. SOAP is defined as an XML-based protocol.
   c. SOAP has no error handling method.
   d. SOAP is defined as an XML-based protocol and is stateless only.
8. Which statement describes NETCONF/YANG?
   a. NETCONF/YANG provides a standardized way to programmatically update and modify the configuration of a network device.
   b. NETCONF/YANG provides a nonstandardized way to programmatically update and modify the configuration of a network device.
   c. NETCONF/YANG provides a standardized way to programmatically update and modify only the startup configuration of a network device.
   d. NETCONF/YANG provides an irreplaceable way to programmatically update and modify the configuration of a network device.
9. What are some architectural styles for creating a Web API? (Choose all that apply.)
   a. HTTP for client/server communication
   b. XML/JSON as a formatting language
   c. Simple URI as the address for the services
   d. Stateless communication
10. Which statement describes the advantages of gRPC? (Choose all that apply.)
   a. It provides low-latency, highly scalable, distributed systems.
   b. gRPC is a framework for implementing RPC APIs via HTTP/2.
   c. A newly designed protocol needs to be accurate, efficient, and language independent.
   d. Layered design enables extension; for example, authentication, load balancing, logging, and monitoring.

Foundation Topics

What Are APIs?

Most of today's automation workflows and integration use application programming interfaces for deployments, validation, and pipelines. All applications expose some sort of API that governs how an application can be accessed by other applications. An API provides a set of routines, protocols, tools, and documentation that can be leveraged for programmatic interaction. The API represents a way in which elements or applications can be programmatically controlled and described. It can also allow external applications to gain access to capabilities and functions within another application.

APIs have the following primary components:

- Methods
- Objects
- Formats

Methods

The major or most commonly used Hypertext Transfer Protocol verbs (or **methods**, as they are correctly termed) are HTTP methods that indicate the intent of the API call, although they also can be nouns. A RESTful architecture API can describe the operations available, such as GET, POST, PUT, PATCH, and DELETE. These operations are described in more detail here:

- The GET request enables you to retrieve information only. The GET request does not modify or update any information. Because the GET request does not update or change the state of the devices, it is often referred to as a safe method. GET APIs typically are idempotent. An idempotent operation is one in which a request can be retransmitted or retried with no additional side effects; this means that making multiple identical requests must produce the same result every time until another API (POST or PUT) has changed the state of the device on the server. For example, you need an application to retrieve all the users who are listed as Admin on a device or devices. The GET request would return the same data repeatedly until only a new user or users remain.

- A POST request enables you or your application to create some added information or update current information. This would not be on your devices or in your application or if you are wishing to update this information with newer or correct information. A POST request is neither safe nor idempotent. This means that if you create a new user called Bob on your application and send this as a POST request, the new user Bob would be created. If you run the same code several times after this, you would have five users all called Bob. Always using POST to create operations is considered best practice.

- The PUT request enables you to update a piece of information that is already present on your device or application. The PUT method is idempotent. If you retry a request several times, that should be comparable to sending a single request modification. After you create Bob as a new user, for example, you want to update his address. Sending a PUT with these details would add his address to his information. If you send this request again, the PUT replaces Bob's address in its entirety and overwrites the current resource.

- The PATCH request can be used when you require partial resources or need to modify an existing resource. The PATCH request is neither safe nor idempotent. The main difference between the PUT and PATCH requests is in the way the server processes the enclosed entity that will modify the resource, identified by the Request-URI. For example, Bob bought a new phone, and you need to update just his phone number records with his new number. In this case, you would use PATCH to request updates on part of the resource.

- A DELETE request, to no one's surprise, is not a safe request, but it is idempotent. Of all the HTTP requests, the DELETE method is the most self-explanatory. After you issue a DELETE request, the resource you wish to delete is removed. Further DELETE requests to the same resources would not yield any different results because the resource is no longer present. However, it is worth noting that trying to delete a resource that is not present would yield a Not Found message because there is nothing to delete. Sadly, you learn that Bob has decided to leave the company and you are asked to remove all of Bob's information and details, so you complete the task and go to lunch. Another member of the team picks up the request while you are at lunch and runs an API call to delete Bob's details. That team member is then met with a 404 Not Found error message.

Table 5-2 summarizes the API methods and whether they are idempotent and considered safe or not safe.

Table 5-2 A Summary of API Methods, Idempotency, and Safety

HTTP	Idempotent	Safe
GET	Yes	Yes
POST	No	No
PUT	Yes	No
PATCH	No	No
DELETE	Yes	No

Objects

An **object** is a resource that a user is trying to access. In the RESTful architecture, this object is often referred to as a noun, and it is typically a Uniform Resource Identifier (URI).

A URI can be described in the same way that an IP address is described. It is unique—just like your home address or your office address, with a number or name; street; city; and depending on the country, a state, county, or province. The URI is a digital version of your address or location. Details can be sent to this address, and the sender knows this is a valid address. Using the URI is like going to a coffee shop and requesting a coffee, but in the URI's case, this is a resource you are asking for and not a steaming hot beverage—that would be a GET request.

Formats

A **format** is how data is represented, such as JavaScript Object Notation (JSON) or Extensible Markup Language (XML).

Whether you are sending or receiving data, APIs use machine-readable formats such as JSON or XML. These formats allow APIs to be represented as semistructured data. The main reason for their use is that semistructured data is significantly easier to analyze than unstructured data. This is the reason that both are known as "self-describing" data structures also. Unlike JSON, which does not have a data binding contract, XML uses data binding and data serialization. This distinction can be key because most APIs use structured data, not structured documents. The biggest majority of APIs today use JSON, but some do use XML.

Figure 5-1 shows the workflow for an API request to a server and the API response.

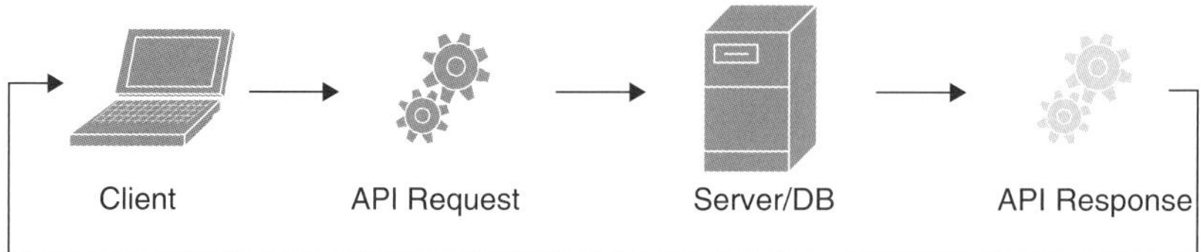

Figure 5-1 *Workflow for an API*

APIs are also used to communicate with various components of a network through software. In software-defined networking (SDN), northbound and southbound APIs are used to describe how interfaces operate between the different planes—the data plane, control plane, and application plane.

The northbound interface can provide such information as network topology and configuration retrieval and provisioning services, and it facilitates the integration with the operations support system (OSS) for fault management and flow-through provisioning. The southbound interface defines the way the SDN controller should interact with the data plane (aka forwarding plane) to modify the network so that it can better adapt to changing requirements. For example, here are some examples of how the Meraki API can be leveraged to use both northbound and southbound APIs:

- Adding new organizations, admins, networks, devices, VLANs, and SSIDs
- Provisioning new sites with an automation script
- Automatically onboarding and offboarding new employees' teleworker devices
- Building a dashboard for a store manager, field techs, or unique use cases

APIs vs. No API

All the Cisco controller-based platforms, such as Cisco SD-WAN vManage (software-defined wide-area network), Cisco DNA Center, and Cisco Application Centric Infrastructure (ACI), have a robust collection of APIs. This allows developer and engineering teams to build code and integrate Cisco APIs into the workflow, CI/CD pipeline testing, and monitoring.

However, APIs are not just limited to Cisco controllers and devices. Cisco has APIs for gathering data, such as the CCW Catalog API and Cisco PSIRT openVuln API. You can access them at https://apiconsole.cisco.com/. They allow Cisco partners, customers, and internal developers who need to access APIs to get Cisco data and services.

APIs can certainly be helpful for developers when they are maintained and supported, but not every website or service has the ability to do so. Some websites and services do not provide an API, or some have had an API and have chosen to take down their API services from their websites. Providers such as Twitter, Facebook, and Google are known to have powerfully built and well-documented APIs as they see the value for developers, and this way, they can provide an interface and keep their services secure at the same time. Whereas some providers get this right, numerous service providers have exposed an API to their services, and this has led to a data breach and their company details being leaked, along with their customers' information too (not good!). But even the big players of the tech world get this wrong too sometimes; some of the bigger companies have either significantly scaled down their APIs' functionality or changed their API terms of service. Some companies have even shut down their APIs altogether when there is serious risk of attack or data leaks, or they are not making enough profit. But what if the service you want to consume does not provide an API?

Web Scraping

One of the most common gripes about APIs is that they are subject to change (as mentioned previously for company policy, security, or an update). Such changes can leave developers frustrated and with nonworking code or integrations. Another case is that there is no API, the company has no desire to build one, or it just does not have the resources to do so.

When no API is present or you wish to grab data in a reliable way, **web scraping** provides a reliable alternative to assembling data. Here are some of the pros of web scraping:

- **Rate limiting:** A well-designed API has rate limiting; web scraping, in contrast, does not. You can access the data swiftly, and as long as you are not generating vast amounts of traffic to the website, setting off alarm bells to the provider's DDOS service, you will be fine.
- **Updates and changes:** APIs are subject to changes over time. As much as a provider does not wish to remove an API resource, it does happen. This is one reason that using an undocumented API resource is not recommended because this capability can be taken away at any time and without any notice! Web scraping can be done at any given point and on any website or URL.
- **Data format and reliability:** A well-designed and well-built API provides customers access to the services they need and in a structured data format. However, some APIs lack investment and might not provide the best format, so you might find yourself spending more time cleaning up the data than you wished or receiving old data back because the API has not been updated. In both cases, web scraping can be custom driven, giving you good data back.

Figure 5-2 shows web scraping, web harvesting, or web data extraction, which is data scraping used for extracting data from websites.

Figure 5-2 *Web Scraping Extraction Is Data Scraping Used for Extracting Data from Websites*

Web scraping does require some knowledge of automation and coding. Most web scraping is done via software tools, but when you have the data, you need to know what do with it. Web scraping is typically "low code." A good example might be Selenium IDE, which is popular because testing can be written in Python, Java, Ruby, and other programming languages. The alternative to this is "no code." This method can be highly effective in creating APIs for any website that might not have one; in most cases, it is as simple as clicking the data you want to extract. The general flow of web scraping is shown in Figure 5-2. The web scraping is provided with a URL. The scraper loads the complete HTML code from the web page, and the scraper extracts all or some of the data (typically defined by the user). The data can be output in a format to a file such as an Excel or CSV file.

Jeff Bezos's API Mandate: How the AWS API-Driven Cloud Was Born

Cloud computing and Amazon Web Services (AWS) changed the way that a lot of companies built their infrastructure. The huge surge in moving to the cloud prompted a change in businesses and the way they updated their delivery model and their engineering team's structure, and with this, the way they deployed, engineered, and designed their solutions.

In a cloud-first world, APIs were one of the key attributes at the forefront. In the early 2000s, Jeff Bezos's API mandate was born. In his API mandate, he outlined the principles and foundation as to how AWS could be more agile. He did not say what technologies his team must use but defined only the outcomes of the systems. Here is the mandate he wrote in the early 2000s.

All teams will henceforth expose their data and functionality through service interfaces.

By providing an external API so that customers can have access to data and connect their systems, less guiding is needed for the customer and less handholding. This is one of the foundations for the huge success of Amazon and AWS; it helped build greater collaboration and was a big money maker for the company.

Teams must communicate with each other through these interfaces.

There will be no other form of inter-process communication allowed: no direct linking, no direct reads of another team's data store, no shared-memory model, no backdoors whatsoever. The only communication allowed is via service interface calls over the network.

Imagine that the support and operations team would like customer data from the network or the infrastructure because a customer has reported slow data loading and service page timeouts. The customer wants to know the state of the load balancer—for example, how many devices are in the VIP pool and which servers and VMs are taking the loads. For a lot of companies, these teams do not have access to such devices (not even read-only access!), which means they must find the owners or team for the devices and create a support request ticket for this information. Creating a self-serve format can resolve many of these challenges.

Providing an API is only part of the puzzle; ensuring a standard and keeping to it can be even harder. The expression "throwing it over the fence" is commonly heard when building infrastructure; this means that after the team has built it, their work is done. Often, in this method, getting support or help becomes almost impossible, so you or your customer is left to figure out the details on your own. When you're designing APIs, the format and the schema become your own company's mandate. Without this, how would you know whether what you are designing and building works and delivers the correct level of details or when an error is raised? If your company doesn't form a standard methodology, the process can get very complex and fast. When all teams adhere to the same process and take ownership of documenting, this produces value for all the company.

It doesn't matter what technology you use.

Technology moves fast. The way the engineering team did things 10 years go might not be compatible with today's technology. APIs should change, grow, and be adaptable, just as your business does. As much as you can learn from other teams within an organization and as much as you often try to use the same tools to get great consistency, this is often not possible for several reasons, such as team skill, different platform requirements, and even budgets.

All service interfaces, without exception, must be designed from the ground up to be externalize-able. That is to say, the team must plan and design to be able to expose the interface to developers in the outside world. No exceptions.

By reading this far, you likely have gathered that Bezos's mandate is that of an "API First World" or that APIs are "first-class citizens." In an API First World, this assumes the design and development of an API come before the implementation itself, not as an afterthought. This method is built with developers in mind because the thinking is "How will developers use this API?" Later, as feedback is provided from the consumers of the API, the functionality of the API can be expanded and grown.

The mandate ended with this message:

"Anyone who doesn't do this will be fired. Thank you; have a nice day!"

The lessons learned from the mandate are that changes do not always come from the top, but when they do, they send a very powerful message to an organization that this is the direction to take. Such lessons greatly help clarify situations and provide clear guardrails for engineering teams and developers alike. Jeff Bezos was clearly passionate about APIs and saw their value for Amazon. Building an API-first culture allowed a singular stance and position in which his API mandate could serve to structure Amazon's API organizations effectively.

Calling an API

Now that we have established the principles behind APIs and where they are used in today's systems and organizations, we can investigate how to call an API and the steps required. In this example, you can assume that the API call is being made by a user to an external API.

- **User:** The person who makes a request. The user makes a call to the API via its URI.
- **Client:** The computer that sends the request to the server, giving a request verb, headers, and optionally, a request body in a Python script.
- **Server:** The computer that replies to the request. The API gives the data to the initial requesting program.

To construct an API request, you need to know the following information for the API you are calling. Good API documentation provides all these steps and details to successfully use and consume the API resources. One of the key elements of API documentation is the methods and which methods can be used with the API's resources.

The URL is the endpoint you are intending to call; the endpoint is the API point of entry in this most pivotal piece of an API.

This example uses a GET request to send an API call to the Cisco DNA Center. The client's health is part of the client's API. It returns the information by client type: wired and wireless. The API call being made is **'/dna/intent/api/v1/network-health'**. Response details are parsed to provide the information.

```
NETWORK_HEALTH = '/dna/intent/api/v1/network-health'

response = requests.get(BASE_URL + NETWORK_HEALTH,

                        headers=headers, verify=False)

network_health = response.json()['response']

print('Good: {0}, Bad: {1}, Health score: {2}'.format(

            network_health[0]['goodCount'],
```

```
              network_health[0]['badCount'], network_health[0]
['healthScore']
))
```

If authentication is used when you're making the request, you need to know the type to use; basic and OAuth are two common types of authentications. This example uses basic authentication. The format of the credentials could be **'USERNAME:PASSWORD'**, and it needs to be Base64-encoded.

If the API requires any HTTP headers to be sent, the headers represent the metadata associated with the API request and response. As an example, here are some of the most common API headers:

- **ACCEPT:** Application/XML or Application/JSON indicates to the server what media type(s) this client is willing to accept.
- **Authorization:** "Basic", plus username and password (per RFC 2617), identifies the authorized user making this request.
- **Content-Type:** Application/XML or Application/JSON describes the representation and syntax of the request message body.

5

In this example, basic authentication is used along with a request to retrieve a token from the API **'/dna/system/api/v1/auth/token'**. The device URL, API call, username, and password are passed in through a YAML file (not shown). The Content-Type, **application/json**, indicates that the request body format is JSON:

```
BASE_NoteURL = 'https://<IP Address>'

AUTH_URL = '/dna/system/api/v1/auth/token'

USERNAME = '<USERNAME>'

PASSWORD = '<PASSWORD>'

response = requests.post(BASE_URL + AUTH_URL,
auth=HTTPBasicAuth(USERNAME, PASSWORD), verify=False) token =
response.json()['Token']

headers = {'X-Auth-Token': token, 'Content-Type': 'application/
json'}
```

When you use the POST, PUT, or PATCH method, you might be required to send request body parameters, which describe the action that will take place. This data might be in the format of JSON or XML and contain data that is needed to complete the request being sent.

The following example shows a JSON-formatted "object" that is an unordered set of name/value pairs. When you're sending JSON data, it is important to ensure the format is correct. Often a plug-in or software tool can be used to serialize a resource into JSON API-compliant format.

```
{
  "templateId": "3f7c91b6-4a17-4544-af59-390e51f1de45",
  "targetInfo": [
```

```
        {
          "id": "10.10.21.80",
          "type": "MANAGED_DEVICE_IP",
          "params": {"description": "Updated today DNAC -mooncat",
"interface":"TenGigabitEthernet1/0/25"}
        }
    ]
}
```

Several public APIs (public APIs are also known as open APIs) are available. The HTTP/JSON API is an application programming interface made publicly available to developers. These APIs are published on the Internet and often shared for free or with a limited free tier use. Lists and GitHub repositories provide many links to public APIs; for example, see https://github.com/public-apis/public-apis. Here, developers can browse and build recommendation systems, classifiers, and many other machine-learning algorithms and tools on top of these APIs.

The IMDb API has a free tier service that enables developers to query the database of movies and TV shows. The free tier allows 100 API calls per day (24 hours). Once you reach the limit, you cannot make further calls unless you upgrade or wait until the next day. The IMDb API provides access to more than three million data items, including cast and crew information, plot summaries, release dates, and ratings. The IMDb provides all IMDb API documentation and online testing; API documentation is also presented in Swagger documentation.

NOTE To use the IMDb API documentation, you need an API key for testing APIs.

Figure 5-3 shows the online documentation and online testing for the IMDb API.

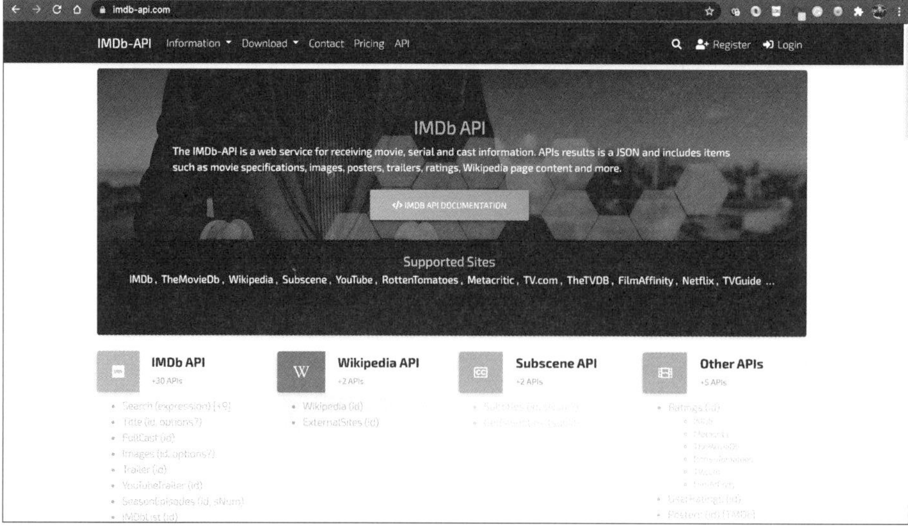

Figure 5-3 *IMDb Online Documentation Page for API Testing and Reference*

IMDb also provides Swagger-based testing and documentation of its APIs, as shown in Figure 5-4.

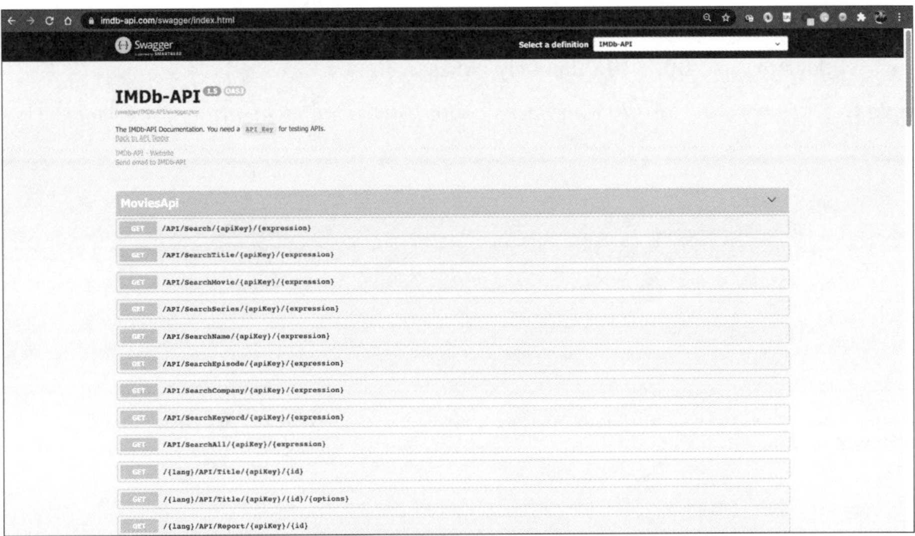

Figure 5-4 *IMDb's Swagger-Based Testing and API Documentation*

To start using the API, you must register and create an account to get an API key; go to https://imdb-api.com/Identity/Account/Register (see Figure 5-5). The API key is attached to each request sent as a string and is stored with the user profile.

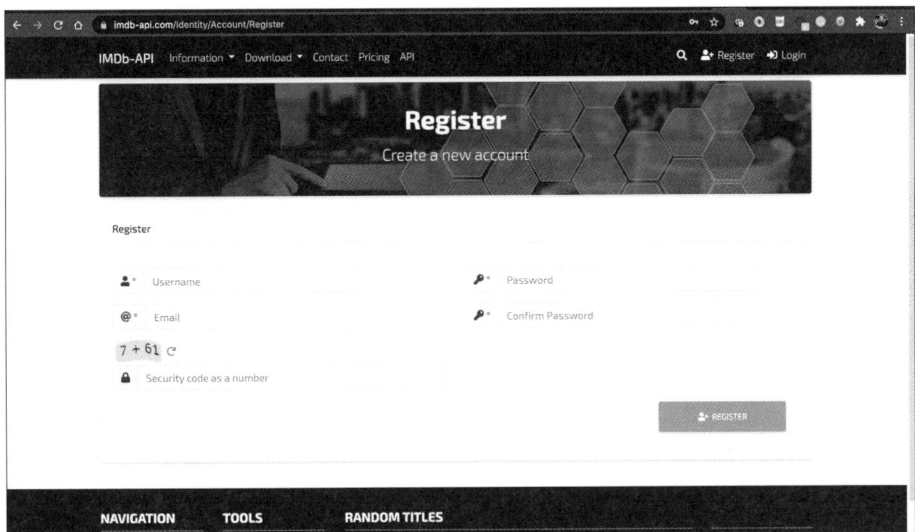

Figure 5-5 *IMDb's API Registration Page*

After the user account is created, you can send API calls through the documentation pages or code formats such as cURL (client URL), Python, or Postman. The IMDb API uses unique identifiers for each of the entities referenced in IMDb data. For example, "Name IDs" identifies name entities (people), and "Title IDs" identifies title entities (movies, series, episodes, and video games). IMDb's identifiers always take the form of two letters, which signify the type of entity being identified, followed by a sequence of at least seven numbers that uniquely identify a specific entity of that type.

In Example 5-1, "**tt0075148**" is the unique identifier for the movie *Rocky*, where **tt** signifies that it's a title entity and **0075148** uniquely indicates *Rocky*.

Example 5-1 *Performing an API Call Based on an IMDb Unique Identifier for a Movie Title*

```
{
  "searchType": "Title",
  "expression": "tt0075148",
  "results": [
    {
      "id": "tt0075148",
      "resultType": "Title",
      "image": "https://imdb-
      api.com/images/original/MV5BMTY5MDMzODUyOF5BMl5BanBnXkFtZTcwMTQ3NTMyNA@@._V1_
Ratio0.6762_AL_.jpg",
      "title": "Rocky",
      "description": "1976"
    }
  ],
  "errorMessage": ""
}
```

Example 5-2 shows an API call based on an actor's name.

Example 5-2 *Performing an API Call Based on an IMDb Unique Identifier for an Actor*

```
actorList: [
{
        id: "nm0000230",
        image: "https://imdb-
      api.com/images/original/MV5BMTQwMTk3NDU2OV5BMl5BanBnXkFtZTcwNTA3MTI0Mw@@._V1_
Ratio0.7273_AL_.jpg",
      name: "Sylvester Stallone",
       asCharacter: "Rocky"
},
```

Using Python and the IMDb API, you can access resources with the Python Requests library. To gather all details on the Top 250 movies of all time, use the URL https://imdb-api.com/en/API/Top250Movies/{API_KEY}, as shown in Example 5-3. IMDb's APIs data set is provided in JSON Lines file format. The files are UTF-8 encoded text files, where each line in the file is a valid JSON string. Each JSON document, one per line, relates to a single entity, uniquely identified by an IMDb ID (see Example 5-4).

Example 5-3 *Python Code Using the IMDb API Resource to Get the Top 250 Movies*

```
import requests
import json
API_KEY = '[add_user_key]'
URL = "imdb-api.com"
url = f"https://{URL}/en/API/Top250Movies/{API_KEY}"
response = requests.request("GET", url)
pretty json = json.loads(response.text)
print (json.dumps(pretty_json, indent=2))
```

Example 5-4 *Python Output in JSON Format Showing APIs for the Top 250 Movies*


```
{
  "items": [
    {
      "id": "tt0111161",
      "rank": "1",
      "title": "The Shawshank Redemption",
      "fullTitle": "The Shawshank Redemption (1994)",
      "year": "1994",
      "image": "https://m.media-amazon.com/images/M/MV5BMDFkYTc0MGEtZmNhMC00ZDIzLW-
FmNTEtODM1ZmRlYWMwMWFmXkEyXkFqcGdeQXVyMTMxODk2OTU@._V1_UX128_CR0,3,128,176_AL_.jpg",
      "crew": "Frank Darabont (dir.), Tim Robbins, Morgan Freeman",
      "imDbRating": "9.2",
      "imDbRatingCount": "2435338"
    },
    {
      "id": "tt0068646",
      "rank": "2",
      "title": "The Godfather",
      "fullTitle": "The Godfather (1972)",
      "year": "1972",
      "image": "https://m.media-amazon.com/images/M/MV5BM2MyNjYxNmUtYTAwNi00MTYx-
LWJmNWYtYzZlODY3ZTk3OTFlXkEyXkFqcGdeQXVyNzkwMjQ5NzM@._V1_UX128_CR0,1,128,176_AL_.
jpg",
      "crew": "Francis Ford Coppola (dir.), Marlon Brando, Al Pacino",
      "imDbRating": "9.1",
      "imDbRatingCount": "1685910"
    },
[output shortened for brevity]
```


Because this code is not very easy to read, you can use a Python library called Tabulate to put the information into a grid format (see Example 5-5 and Figure 5-6). Tabulate can be installed with PIP.

Example 5-5 *Python Code Using the IMDb API Resource to Get the Top 250 Movies Formatting Output in Table Format*

```
import requests
import json
from tabulate import tabulate
API_KEY = '[add user key]'
URL = "imdb-api.com"
url = f"https://{URL}/en/API/Top250Movies/{API_KEY}"
response = requests.request("GET", url)
response = response.json()
headers = ["ID", "Rank", "Full Title", "Year", "Crew", "IMDb Rating", "Certificate"]
table = list()
for item in response['items']:
    info = [item['id'], item['rank'], item['fullTitle'],
    item['year'], item['crew'], item['imDbRating']]
    table.append(info)
print(tabulate(table, headers, tablefmt="fancy_grid"))
```

```
> python imdb_tabulate.py
```

ID	Rank	Full Title	Year	Crew	IMDb Rating
tt0111161	1	The Shawshank Redemption (1994)	1994	Frank Darabont (dir.), Tim Robbins, Morgan Freeman	9.2
tt0068646	2	The Godfather (1972)	1972	Francis Ford Coppola (dir.), Marlon Brando, Al Pacino	9.1
tt0071562	3	The Godfather: Part II (1974)	1974	Francis Ford Coppola (dir.), Al Pacino, Robert De Niro	9
tt0468569	4	The Dark Knight (2008)	2008	Christopher Nolan (dir.), Christian Bale, Heath Ledger	9
tt0050083	5	12 Angry Men (1957)	1957	Sidney Lumet (dir.), Henry Fonda, Lee J. Cobb	8.9
tt0108052	6	Schindler's List (1993)	1993	Steven Spielberg (dir.), Liam Neeson, Ralph Fiennes	8.9
tt0167260	7	The Lord of the Rings: The Return of the King (2003)	2003	Peter Jackson (dir.), Elijah Wood, Viggo Mortensen	8.9
tt0110912	8	Pulp Fiction (1994)	1994	Quentin Tarantino (dir.), John Travolta, Uma Thurman	8.8
tt0060196	9	The Good, the Bad and the Ugly (1966)	1966	Sergio Leone (dir.), Clint Eastwood, Eli Wallach	8.8
tt0120737	10	The Lord of the Rings: The Fellowship of the Ring (2001)	2001	Peter Jackson (dir.), Elijah Wood, Ian McKellen	8.8

Figure 5-6 *The Top 250 Movies Formatting Output in Table Format*

What Is API Development?

More and more engineering teams are creating and making both external and internal APIs available for their services. By doing so, their company, its customers, and other developers can consume resources, update current services, and create net-new resources. All of these capabilities help support the growth and success of the company. As per Jeff Bezos's mandate "It doesn't matter what technology you use," not all teams will design and build their APIs the same way. Numerous technologies can be used for developing APIs, such as HTTP, REST, SOAP, OpenAPI, gRPC, GraphQL, and Kafka. Each has its own merits. Which one your team decides on will depend on what style of API you want to develop and your overall business goals and constraints.

- **Internal APIs:** Internal APIs are closed from external access and not accessible by anyone outside the organization. These APIs often contain information that the company would wish to keep secure, such as employee details and internal services. An example of an internal API might be to provide new services on the company infrastructure to book meeting rooms or access employee directory information. Internal APIs can be event-driven APIs (or streaming APIs); they are also referred to as asynchronous

APIs or reactive APIs. These APIs do not wait for interaction; instead, they use a "push architecture." Like the push model in model-driven telemetry, event-driven API clients subscribe and receive event notifications when an event happens or something changes.

- **External APIs:** External APIs are created for external consumption outside the organization and use by third-party companies, software teams, and developers. An example is the Spotify API, which is based on the REST architecture. In it, the API endpoints can return JSON metadata about music artists, albums, and tracks directly from the Spotify Data Catalogue. Like Internal APIs, external APIs can be asynchronous APIs or reactive APIs. One example where you might see event-driven APIs is a stock tracker displaying price changes in stock chat applications. A lot of social media sites use event-driven APIs to push out the latest content from companies or people you follow via their platforms.

- **Partner APIs:** Partner APIs are a hybrid of internal and external APIs and are designed for an organization's partners. This means that the consumer must have some form of relationship to the organization. Special permissions and security procedures, such as onboarding registration, are often required to access partner API resources. Cisco's API Console is an easy-to-use resource for Cisco partners, customers, and internal developers (see https://apiconsole.cisco.com/). External and internal users who are not signed in can only access publicly available documentation, and partners and registered users can access Cisco data and services.

- The Cisco API Console, shown in Figure 5-7, allows Cisco partners and customers to access and consume Cisco data in the cloud.

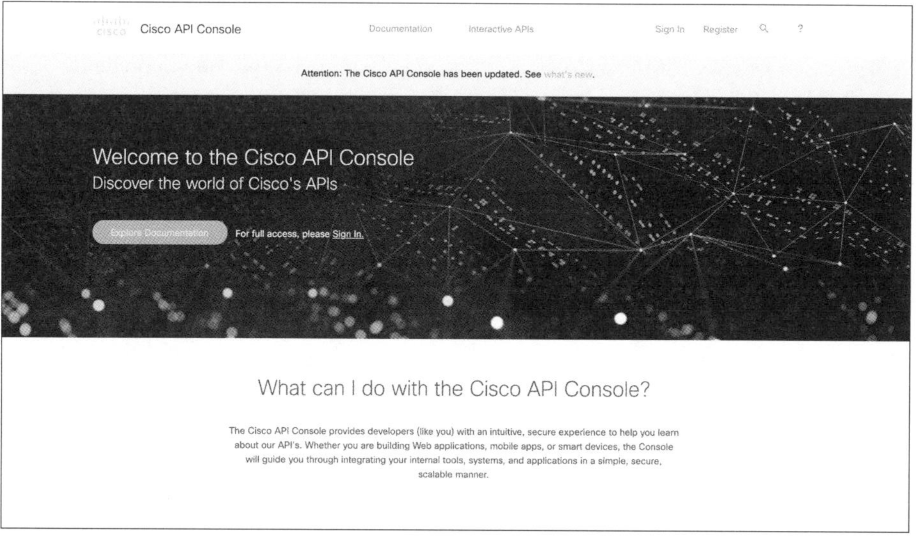

Figure 5-7 *Cisco API Console, Where Cisco Partners and Customers Can Access and Consume Cisco Data in the Cloud*

API Architectural Styles

When you're developing an API, various API styles are considered common designs, and there are different formats for each style, depending on the use case and purpose of the API architecture, the developer consumption, and the systems or services that will be connecting to the API. As covered in the previous sections, the reasons for developing and building an API should be kept at the forefront when designing an API. The main four are

- **Performance:** Providing a library of resources and reusable APIs helps speed up development and ongoing production of services.
- **Security:** Providing a secure connection and content sharing both inside and outside a company enables the API to securely expose systems.
- **Engagement:** Publishing APIs can lead to software companies and other teams writing software and services to interact and consume API resources.
- **Monetization:** If the company's API is external facing, the API's design can be to make money, either directly or indirectly via subscription or pay-per-service.

Some command tools for building and developing an API include the following:

- **Postman:** Postman is a collaboration platform for API development. Postman enables API-first development, automated testing, and developer onboarding. It enables you to write, edit, or import schema formats including RAML, WADL, OpenAPI, and GraphQL. Then you can generate collections directly from the schema. A feature of Postman is mock servers, which allow you to generate mock APIs from collection servers to simulate your API endpoints. Postman can also help create documentation for individual requests and collections. Cisco DevNet provides a number of Postman collections, which you can access through the Postman workspace (see https://www.postman.com/ciscodevnet).

  The Cisco DevNet Postman Collection, shown in Figure 5-8, provides a prebuilt collection of Cisco APIs.

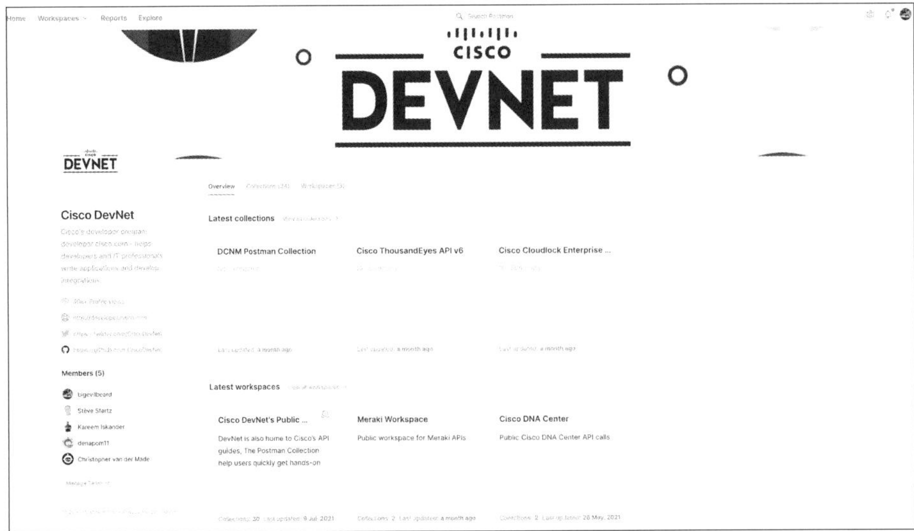

Figure 5-8 *Cisco DevNet Postman Collection's Prebuilt Collection of Cisco APIs*

- **Apigee:** Apigee, from Google Cloud, is a cross-cloud API testing tool that enables you to measure and test API performance and supports, and to build APIs using other editors like Swagger. Apigee has several features that enable you to design APIs to create API proxies and visually configure or code API policies as steps in the API flow. Security APIs can administer security best practices and governance policies. Other features, such as Publish APIs, Monitor APIs, and Monetize APIs, are also available.
- **Swagger:** Swagger is a set of open-source tools for writing REST-based APIs. It enables you to describe the structure of your APIs so that machines can read them. In Swagger, you can build and design your APIs according to specification-based standards. You also can build stable, reusable code for your APIs in almost any language and help improve the developer experience with interactive API documentation. Swagger can also perform simple functional tests on your APIs without overhead and provide governance settings and enforce API style guidelines across your API architecture.
- **Fiddler:** The Fiddler Everywhere client can intercept both insecure traffic over HTTP and secure traffic over HTTPS (administrative privileges are required to capture secure traffic). The client acts as a man-in-the-middle to capture traffic and can ensure the correct cookies, headers, and cache directives are conveyed between the client and the server. The Fiddler's Composer allows you to compose requests to APIs. You can organize, group, and test your APIs, which is very helpful when creating and testing API requests.

Selecting an API Style

Choosing the API style when preparing to design, deploy, and manage an API is critical. Here are the most common API styles:

- *Representational state transfer (REST)* is an architectural style that specifies constraints, such as the uniform interface, from the API provider by using commands that are built into the underlying networking protocol. HTML is the most recognizable style of REST; other formats include JSON for Linked Documents (JSON-LD) and Hypertext Application Language (HAL). REST was defined in 2000 by Roy Fielding in his dissertation, "Architectural Styles and the Design of Network-Based Software Architectures," at https://www.ics.uci.edu/~fielding/pubs/dissertation/top.htm.
- *Remote-procedure call (RPC)* blocks of code are executed on another server. XML-RPC uses Extensible Markup Language (XML) to encode commands. In XML-RPC, a client performs an RPC by sending an HTTP request to a server that implements XML-RPC and receives the HTTP response. JSON- RPC uses the JSON format to transfer data. RPCs can be seen in standard API technologies such as SOAP, GraphQL, and gRPC.
- *GraphQL* is a query language. To make it easy to recall, remember that this is what the *QL* in the name means. GraphQL prioritizes client details to provide the exact data it needs. This helps to simplify data aggregation, which can be retrieved from multiple sources, allowing the developer to use one API call to limit the number of requests. This capability is very useful in mobile applications because it can help save battery life and CPU cycles being consumed by applications. GraphQL uses a *type system* to describe data. The type system defines various data types that can be used in a GraphQL application.

NOTE GraphQL was originally created by Facebook in 2012 for internal use and was made external in 2015. Now GraphQL is an open-source tool with more than 13,000 GitHub stars and 1,000 GitHub forks. More than 14,500 companies are said to use GraphQL in their tech stacks to power their mobile apps, websites, and APIs; they include Twitter, Shopify, Medium, and the *New York Times*.

- The *Simple Object Access Protocol (SOAP)* is a lightweight standards-based web services access protocol. It is XML-based and uses HTTP/HTTPS for accessing web services. (SMTP can also be used as a transport.) Although SOAP provides basic structural elements of the message, you can tailor what you put into the headers and body as needed. SOAP has three conceptual components: protocol concepts, encapsulation concepts, and network concepts. SOAP has built-in security and reliability functions because it supports SSL and supports Web Services Security (WS Security). SOAP is mostly used when exchanging sensitive information within enterprises such as financial institutions when security is more critical than performance of the application.

A SOAP interface supports the atomicity, consistency, isolation, and durability (ACID) properties:

- **Atomicity:** A transaction must be completed in its entirety or not at all. If a transaction aborts in the middle, all operations up to that point must be completely invalidated. This is called the "all-or-none" approach.
- **Consistency:** A transaction must transform a database from one consistent state to another consistent state. In other words, if something fails, the system is rolled back to the beginning state.
- **Isolation:** Transactions must occur independently of each other.
- **Durability:** If there is a system failure, the completed transaction will remain, and committed transactions must be fully recoverable in all but the most extreme circumstances.

Table 5-3 provides a summary of API specifications/protocols.

Table 5-3 A Summary of API Specifications/Protocols

	REST	gRPC	GraphQL	SOAP
Style	Architectural Style	RPC	Query Language	Protocol
Protocol	HTTP/1	HTTP/2	HTTP/1	HTTP/1
Format	XML, JSON, HTML, Plaintext	JSON, XML, Protobuf	JSON	XML
Security	TLS/ SSL / HTTPS	TLS / SSL	TLS / SSL	WS security / SSL
State	Stateless	Stateless	Stateless	Stateful/Stateless
ACID Compliant	No	No	No	Yes

HTTP/JSON

Where would we be today without the Internet? A high-performing Internet connection is at the top of the priority list when someone is looking to purchase a new home or to relocate. This is with the huge adoption of remote working, hybrid working, social media, online gaming, and media data streaming, typically all running at the same time in the home. A lot of this information is driven using HTTP. When you're making HTTP requests, this format is used to structure requests and responses for effective communication between a client to a named host, which is located on a server. The goal is for the client request to access resources that are located on the server. When requests are sent, clients can use various methods for this process. The request process is documented in RFC 2616 as part of Hypertext Transfer Protocol, or HTTP/1.1.

Figure 5-9 shows an example of an HTTP GET request and the response.

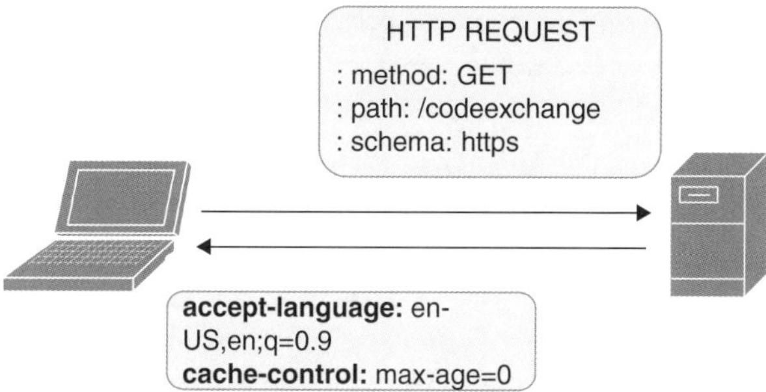

Figure 5-9 *An HTTP GET Request and Response*

A request line starts with a method; the method is a one-word command that instructs the server what it should do with the resource. This could be GET, POST, PUT, PATCH, or DELETE. The path identifies the resources on the server and then the protocol, scheme, and version (for example, the HTTP version number).

When you open a web browser to https://developer.cisco.com/codeexchange, Example 5-6 shows that the method is a GET request, the path is /codeexchange, and the schema is HTTPs.

Example 5-6 *Using https://developer.cisco.com/codeexchange*

```
: method: GET
: path: /codeexchange
: schema: https
```

The HTTP headers allow the client and the server to communicate and in which way they do so. The headers are *not* case sensitive, header fields are separated by a colon, and key-value pairs are in clear-text string format. The HTTP protocol specifications outline the standard set of HTTP headers and describe how to use them correctly.

The following headers show the accepted language and the amount of time a resource is considered fresh:

`accept-language:` `en-US,en;q=0.9`

`cache-control:` `max-age=0`

The Accept-Language request HTTP header advertises which languages the client can understand. If none is found, a 406 error could be sent back. The **max-age** defines, in seconds, the length of time it takes for a cached copy of this resource to expire. After the copy expires, the browser must refresh its version of the resource by sending another request.

The message body is also known as the request body. The message body data is transmitted in an HTTP transaction message immediately following the headers. The body can be made of JSON or XML formats containing data; it can be sent on the body of the request if it is needed to complete the request. The message body is optional; depending on the method being used, they may be appropriate for some request methods and unsuitable for others.

NOTE The acronyms *URL*, for Uniform Resource Locator, and *URI*, for Uniform Resource Identifier, are often interchangeable. However, they do have different meanings:

- A URL is a type of identifier that informs you how you can access a resource—for example, https, http, or ftp.
- A URI is an identifier of a special resource.
- Simply stated: All URLs can be URIs, but not all URIs can be URLs. You often hear or read the two terms; in the same way, some people might say *jacuzzi* when they mean *hot tub*.

REST/JSON

REST on its own is not a standard; however, RESTful implementations do make use of standards. They include HTTP, URI, JSON, and XML. Generally, with REST APIs, JSON is the most popular programming language used when sending data for request payloads and sending responses. JSON is a data representation format just like XML or YAML, which, as you may recall, means YAML Ain't Markup Language. JSON is small and lightweight; it can also be incorporated into JavaScript because JSON is a superset of JavaScript, and anything written in JSON is acceptable JavaScript. JSON also is language agnostic; it is easily readable by humans and machines. A big bonus with JSON is that it's easy to parse. Every programming language has a library that can parse JSON objects or strings in data or classes.

JSON can represent the following types: strings, numbers, Booleans, null (or nothing), arrays, and objects. When you're creating APIs, JSON objects are the most-used formats because an object in JSON uses *key-value* pairs. The key-value pairs can be any of the other types too, such as strings and/or numbers. Example 5-7 provides an example of a JSON object.

Example 5-7 *JSON Object*

```
{
  "id": "L_62911817269526195",
  "organizationId": "62911817269526195",
  "name": "Site Number 1",
  "productTypes": [
    "appliance",
    "switch",
    "wireless"
```

```
  ],
  "timeZone": "America/Los_Angeles",
  "tags": [
    "tag1",
    "tag2"
  ],
  "enrollmentString": null,
  "url": "https://n22.meraki.com/Site-Number-1-ap/n/_VGdgdw/manage/usage/list",
  "notes": null
}
```

JSON opens with a curly brace and closes with a curly brace. Within the curly braces are the key-value pairs that make up the object. For this to be a valid JSON format, the key must be enclosed by double quotation marks and a colon, followed by the value for that key. In Example 5-7, there are multiple key-value pairs; they need to be separated by a comma. In this example, **"id"** is the key, and **"L_575334852396597311"** is the value. Because there is another key-value pair after this, the line ends with a comma. Here, this value is a number. The **"name"** key has a string as its value, and **"productTypes"** has an array as its value. Finally, you can see this example ends with a key of **"notes"** and the value is set to **null**. It's the same way with empty objects using opening and closing braces ({}).

5

Cache-Control

RESTful APIs are very efficient and can perform very quickly because caching was built into the REST architectural style. As you saw previously, caching is added to the Cache-Control header in the HTTP response. As such, the data is returned from the local memory cache instead of having to query the database to get the data every time. Caching helps with REST performance by reducing the number of calls made to an API endpoint and lowering the latency of requests.

The drawback to this is that the data retrieved could be stale, and debugging stale data often leads to many problems. Cache constrictions do require that a data response to a request should be identified as cacheable or noncacheable. Other rules state that lowercase formatting is preferred over uppercase or mixed case, and when there is more than one directive, they should be separated by a comma.

RFC 7234 defines the syntax and semantics of the cache-control standard. However, this RFC does not cover the extended cache-control attributes.

The following snippet shows some of the standard cache-control directives that are used by a client in an HTTP request:

```
Cache-Control: no-cache

Cache-Control: no-store

Cache-Control: no-transform

Cache-Control: max-age=<seconds>

Cache-Control: max-stale[=<seconds>]

Cache-Control: min-fresh=<seconds>

Cache-Control: only-if-cached
```

Cache-response directives, which are used by the server during an HTTP response, include the following:

```
Cache-Control: max-age=<seconds>

Cache-Control: s-maxage=<seconds>

Cache-Control: must-revalidate

Cache-Control: no-cache

Cache-Control: no-store

Cache-Control: no-transform

Cache-Control: public

Cache-Control: private

Cache-Control: proxy-revalidate
```

REST vs. RPC

If you have worked in software or programming for any length of time, you will be accustomed to choosing the right execution. This effort does require weighing the pros and cons and what the result will look like. REST and RPC designs have their own values and use cases. It's critical to choose a design that works best for your given situation. In this section, we compare HTTP and RPC and the different methodologies you can use for web APIs with both architectures.

As you learned previously, REST APIs are resource-oriented, whereas RPC APIs are action-oriented. In REST, the GET, POST, PUT, and DELETE methods are performed via so-called CRUD (Create, Read, Update, and Delete) operations, whereas RPC uses GET for fetching information and POST for the rest. For example, in REST you would issue **"DELETE /devcore/2"**. However, in RPC, you might use **"/deleteDevCore"**, with a body of **{"id": 2}**. This approach can make the RPC API much easier to read because the action is part of the URL itself, making it self-explanatory. Notice that the **"id"** is wrapped in curly braces in this example. If you're thinking that the body is JSON, you would be correct here because RPC supports JSON-RPC. The example with the **"id"** has a special meaning depending on the version of JSON-RPC. At the time of writing, there are two versions: 1.0 and 2.0. When you use version 2.0, this must be specified in the payload.

NOTE **JSON-RPC 1.0 id** is the request ID. It can be of any type. It is used to match the response with the request that it is replying to.

JSON-RPC 2.0 id is an identifier established by the client that *must* contain a string, number, or null value if included. If it is not included, it is assumed to be a notification. The value *should* normally not be null, and numbers *should not* contain fractional parts.

The following example uses a Cisco Nexus 9000 Series device. (The NX-API CLI supports **show** commands, configurations, and Linux Bash. It also supports JSON-RPC.)

The following code snippet shows the payload in JSON format:

```
cat show_version.json
```

```
[{ "jsonrpc": "2.0", "method": "cli", "params": { "cmd": "show
version", "version": 1 }, "id": 1 }]
```

The following code snippet shows Cisco Nexus command output in JSON format:

```
curl -k -v -u admin:Admin_1234! -H "Content-Type: application/
json-rpc" -H "Cache-Control: no-cache" -d @show_version.json POST
https://sandbox-nxos-1.cisco.com/ins
```

In this example, the payload uses JSON-RPC version 2.0. The method is listed as **cli** (the command-line interface) for **show** or **configuration** commands. The **params** specify the **cmd** **'show version'** (**show** commands can also be chained together on NX-OS if they are separated with a colon). In this example, the ID is set to 1. In the reply shown in Example 5-8, the version has been matched and the output formatted in JSON; the last line again shows the ID of 1. Notice that although you are simply gathering data, in RPC this is a POST request.

Example 5-8 *Expected Output When Performing a cURL Request for JSON-RPC*

```
{
  "jsonrpc": "2.0",
  "result": {
    "body": {
      "header_str": "Cisco Nexus Operating System (NX-OS) Software\nTAC support:
http://www.cisco.com/tac\nDocuments: http://www.cisco.com/en/US/products/ps9372/
tsd_products_support_series_home.html\nCopyright (c) 2002-2019, Cisco Systems, Inc.
All rights reserved.\nThe copyrights to certain works contained herein are owned by\
nother third parties and are used and distributed under license.\nSome parts of this
software are covered under the GNU Public\nLicense. A copy of the license is avail-
able at\nhttp://www.gnu.org/licenses/gpl.html.\n\nNexus 9000v is a demo version of
the Nexus Operating System\n",
      "bios_ver_str": "",
      "kickstart_ver_str": "9.3(3)",
      "nxos_ver_str": "9.3(3)",
      "bios_cmpl_time": "",
      "kick_file_name": "bootflash:///nxos.9.3.3.bin",
      "nxos_file_name": "bootflash:///nxos.9.3.3.bin",
      "kick_cmpl_time": "12/22/2019 2:00:00",
      "nxos_cmpl_time": "12/22/2019 2:00:00",
      "kick_tmstmp": "12/22/2019 14:00:37",
      "nxos_tmstmp": "12/22/2019 14:00:37",
      "chassis_id": "Nexus9000 C9300v Chassis",
      "cpu_name": "Intel(R) Xeon(R) CPU E5-4669 v4 @ 2.20GHz",
      "memory": "16409064",
     "mem_type": "kB",
      "proc_board_id": "9N3KD63KWT0",
      "host_name": "N9K_1",
      "bootflash_size": "4287040",
      "kern_uptm_days": "8",
      "kern_uptm_hrs": "2",
```

```
        "kern_uptm_mins": "3",
        "kern_uptm_secs": "30",
        "rr_reason": "Unknown",
        "rr_sys_ver": "",
        "rr_service": "",
        "plugins": "Core Plugin, Ethernet Plugin",
        "manufacturer": "Cisco Systems, Inc.",
        "TABLE_package_list": {
          "ROW_package_list": {
            "package_id": "mtx-openconfig-all-1.0.0.0-9.3.3.lib32_n9000"
          }
        }
      }
    },
    "id": 1
}
```


Like REST, RPC also supports additional formats: they are XML-RPC and Protocol Buffers (Protobuf). Protobuf is similar to the data serializing protocols JSON and XML. Whereas JSON and XML are quite friendly to human eyes, Protobufs are not because they are compiled in bytes.

gRPC

You are likely familiar with the acronym *gRPC* if you have used or investigated model-driven telemetry. Originally designed by Google, today Google Remote Procedure Call is a free open-source project with an open spec and roadmap. Many Cisco platforms, such as Cisco Nexus switches, introduced telemetry over gRPC using a Cisco proprietary gRPC agent from NX-OS Release 7.x.

gRPC can be used as a framework for working with remote-procedure calls. This allows you to write code as if it was designed to run on your computer, even though what you may have written will be executed elsewhere.

gRPC is built on HTTP/2 as a transport. The main goals for using HTTP/2 are to improve performance, enable full request and response, initiate multiple requests in parallel over a single TCP connection, multiplex, minimize protocol overhead via efficient compression of HTTP header fields, and add support for request prioritization and server push.

By default, gRPC uses the Protocol Buffer (Protobuf) Interface Definition Language (IDL) for describing both the service interface and the structure of the payload messages. Protobuf is an open-source mechanism used to serialize structured data for efficient binary encoding (or machine readability), which can be used to exchange messages between services and not over a web browser, unlike REST. By using binary encoding rather than text, the payload is kept compact and very efficient.

The latest version of Protocol Buffer is proto3, and the advantage of the Protobuf IDL is that it enables gRPC to be completely language and platform agnostic, supporting code generation in Java, C++, Python, Java Lite, Ruby, JavaScript, Objective-C, and C#. Example 5-9 provides an example.

Example 5-9 *Using Protobuf*

```
syntax = "proto3";
message House {
        int32 id = 1;
          string name = 2;
          float cost = 3;
}
message Houses {
         repeated House houses = 1;
}
```

To start a .proto file, you need to specify which version you are running. In Example 5-9, version three is defined. The house message definition specifies three fields (name/value pairs)—one for each piece of data that you want to include in this type of message. Each field has a name and a type. This example creates a single detail about one house. You can use this code again if you add an array. If you use the **repeated** field, this field can be repeated any number of times (including zero) in a well-formed message.

OpenAPI/Swagger

The OpenAPI Specification (OAS) was originally known as the Swagger Specification. OpenAPI documents are both machine- and human-readable, which enables you to easily determine how to consume and visualize RESTful web services. There is, however, a difference between OpenAPI and Swagger.

The OAS is an API specification defined and maintained by the OpenAPI initiative. The OAS was donated by Swagger to the Linux Foundation under the OpenAPI Initiative in 2015. OAS sets a standard, programming-language-agnostic interface description for HTTP APIs. This allows for both machines and humans to discover and comprehend the capabilities of an API service without the need to access the source code, any additional documentation, or an inspection of network traffic (tools such as Fiddler and Developer Tools in Chrome are often used to do this). One benefit of using OpenAPI is that it helps when you're designing an API.

OAS can use either JSON or YAML file formats for an API to provide these functions:

- Defining the API's endpoints and available operations (GET, POST, PUT, PATCH, DELETE).
- Outlining the parameters required for the input and output of each operation. OpenAPI 3.0 distinguishes between parameter types—path, query, header, and cookie.
- Describing APIs protected using security schemes such as Basic and Bearer.

Because OpenAPI is language agnostic, you can define an API in generic terms so that feedback can be given before anything can be implemented and added to the design. OpenAPI provides service-side stubs to build the API; this also allows client SDKs to be generated by client or third-party systems. Several companies use OpenAPI, including Atlassian, MuleSoft, Netflix, and PayPal.

Swagger is built by SmartBear Software, the leader in quality software tools for teams. Here's a great way to think about Swagger: say you have built an API, but without documentation and accessibility your API might not be consumable. One reoccurring piece of feedback from developers is that API documentation isn't very good, and this is where Swagger enters the picture. It helps you build, document, test, and consume RESTful web services. It can do this from the source code by requesting the API to return a documentation file from its annotations. In short, Swagger can take the code written for an API and generate the documentation for you.

Swagger has several services and tools:

- **Swagger Editor:** With the Swagger Editor, you can design, describe, and document new and existing APIs in JSON or YAML formats within a browser and preview your documentation in real time. The Swagger Editor is open source, and you can contribute to the project via GitHub.
- **Swagger UI:** The user interface can use an existing JSON or YAML document and make it fully interactive. The tool can arrange the RESTful methods (such as GET, PUT, POST, and DELETE) categorizing each operation. Each of these methods is expandable, and once it is expanded, a full list of parameters with their corresponding examples can be provided.

  Figure 5-10 provides an example of the Swagger UI from Cisco SD-WAN.

Figure 5-10 *Swagger UI from Cisco SD-WAN*

- **Swagger Codegen:** You can find this open-source tool on GitHub. Codegen helps with the build process for both software development kits (SDKs) and APIs. It can do this by generating server stubs (stubs can be used for quick prototyping and mocking). For example, if you want to provide an SDK along with your API, Swagger Codegen would be great tool to help implement it.

Network API Styles

The two most-used network APIs today are HTTP-based APIs and NETCONF-based APIs. To be considered a RESTful API, the API must adhere to six architectural constraints:

- Client/server
- Stateless
- Cacheable
- Uniform interface
- Layer system
- Code on demand (optional)

Here, we look at client/server, stateless, and uniform interfaces.

RESTful APIs can support network programming. This is a type of software development for applications that can connect and communicate over networks, such as the Internet or via software-defined controllers, network management software, and network analytics engines. A network API provides a means to access protocols and reusable software libraries. The API is able to support web databases, web browsers, and mobile applications. They are widely supported across many programming languages and operating systems, which can be leveraged to provide the details or state of devices and make configuration changes. This architecture is often referred to as a distributed application structure client/server model. The client communicates over the network, but there are two separate systems. They might be connected on the same network (LAN) or be physically separate; for example, the client might be in a remote office and the server in a data center or cloud. The client initiates the communication, and the server is in a state of waiting for the client to request the information. When it does, the server shares its resources with the client.

Figure 5-11 illustrates how RESTful APIs operate in a client/server architecture.

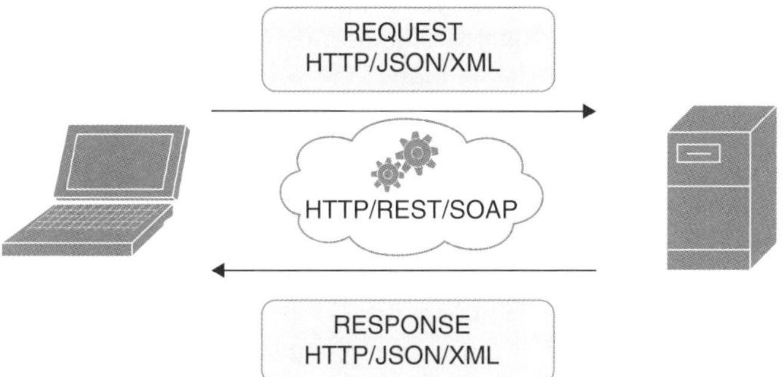

Figure 5-11 *RESTful APIs Operate in a Client/Server Architecture*

If a RESTful API communication between the client and the server is stateless or nonpersistent, this means that when the client sends the data to the server, all the data should be sent for the server to process the request. For example, if the required data is not sent or is incorrect, the server returns an error to the client. When the session is closed out, the server does not retain the session or any information about the request that was made to it.

NOTE HTTP can also use a persistent connection, referred to as HTTP keep-alive. Persistent connections improve network performance because a new connection does not have to be established for each request.

To separate the client and server, RESTful APIs use a uniform interface. The uniform interface provides a mapping to resources. For example, network APIs could be hostnames, routing information, or interface details/state.

There are four main guidelines for uniform interfaces:

- **Resource-based:** Individual resources are identified in requests using URIs as resource identifiers; these are separate from the responses that are returned to the client.
- **Manipulation of resources through representations:** A client has representations of resources (including any metadata attached), and it contains enough information to customize, modify, or delete the resource on the server, provided it has the correct permission to do so.
- **Self-descriptive messages:** Every message includes detailed information to describe how to process the message so that the server can analyze the request. The responses also clearly indicate their cacheability.
- **Hypermedia as the Engine of Application State (HATEOAS):** Clients deliver the state via the body content, query-string parameters, request headers, and the request URI. Services deliver state, which also needs to include links for each response so that clients can discover other resources easily.

NETCONF APIs

For many years, network devices such as routers, switches, and firewalls were configured using the CLI, but this model did not scale and was subject to human error. The NETCONF protocol was developed and standardized by the Internet Engineering Task Force (IETF). It was developed in the NETCONF working group and published in December 2006 as RFC 4741 and later revised in June 2011 and published as RFC 6241. Looking to make network devices more programmable, NETCONF was created to address configuration management, gathering configuration and operation details from network devices.

Operational data is read-only. In this use case, NETCONF could be used to gather the same information that would be gathered from issuing **show** commands. For example, say an engineer is looking to gather all the information from a number of devices as part of an audit of the access lists to ensure the network devices meet the security compliance. Configuration data requires a change to be made on the network devices. Again, to compare this to the

CLI, this would be when the engineer uses the configuration terminal to enter **configuration** commands to make changes to the network devices. For example, after the engineer has completed the audit of the access lists, several updates and new requirements are needed on the network devices to prevent a breach in security.

The NETCONF API can use two types of YANG models—open and native. The NETCONF protocol uses (typically) XML-encoded YANG-modeled data.

- *Open models* allow commonality across devices and platforms. An open configuration promotes a vendor-neutral model for network management that uses YANG, a data modeling language for data sent over via the NETCONF protocol. Open YANG models are developed by vendors and standards bodies. Open is further broken down into open standard and open source.
- *Native models* are developed and maintained by each vendor. They are designed to integrate to features or configuration relevant only to that vendor's platform.

NETCONF works in a client/server model. A common example of this seen today is via Python or Ansible being the client and a router being the server. NETCONF supports JSON and XML as the data encoding methods, but Cisco does not support JSON. A NETCONF message is based on an RPC-based communication; this allows the XML message to be transport independent. The most-often-used transport is Secure Shell version 2 (SSHv2).

5

Table 5-4 shows the main differences between RESTful and NETCONF APIs.

Table 5-4 Differences Between RESTful and NETCONF APIs

	RESTful API	NETCONF
Transport	HTTP	SSHv2, TLS
Message	HTTP/1.1	RCP, RCP REPLY
Content	JSON/XML	XML
Operations	HTTP GET, HTTP POST, HTTP PUT, HTTP DELETE	get-config, get, copy-config, lock, unlock, edit-config, delete-config, kill-session, close-session
State	Stateless	Stateful

NETCONF also can use different device datastores: they are running, startup, and candidate. If you utilize the candidate configuration datastore, you can load device changes into the candidate datastore without impacting the running or startup configuration/datastore. Only until the configuration is pushed via a commit will the changes be applied to the devices and written to the running configuration. This capability can also be very useful to roll back changes because the device keeps past candidate configurations. (Cisco IOS XE and IOS XR keep 10 candidate configuration files; this number can be expanded to more if required and is platform specific.)

Figure 5-12 shows the operational workflows and datastore when using NETCONF.

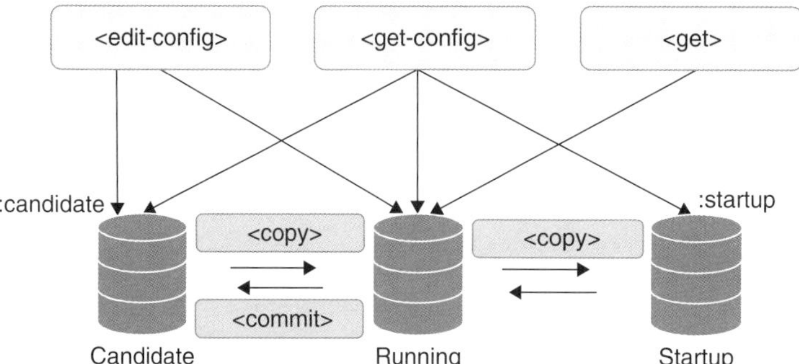

Figure 5-12 *The Operational Workflows and Datastore When Using NETCONF*

Exam Preparation Tasks

As mentioned in the section "How to Use This Book" in the Introduction, you have a couple of choices for exam preparation: the exercises here, Chapter 17, "Final Preparation," and the exam simulation questions in the Pearson Test Prep Software Online.

Review All Key Topics

Review the most important topics in this chapter, noted with the Key Topic icon in the outer margin of the page. Table 5-5 lists a reference of these key topics and the page numbers on which each is found.

Table 5-5 Key Topics for Chapter 5

Key Topic Element	Description	Page Number
Section	Methods	133
Section	Formats	134
Section	What Is API Development?	144
Section	REST vs. RPC	152
Section	Network API Styles	157

Complete Tables and Lists from Memory

There are no memory tables or lists in this chapter.

Define Key Terms

Define the following key terms from this chapter and check your answers in the glossary:

method, objects, formats, web scraping

References

URL	QR Code
https://apiconsole.cisco.com/	
https://github.com/public-apis/public-apis	
https://imdb-api.com/Identity/Account/Register	
https://www.postman.com/ciscodevnet	
https://www.ics.uci.edu/~fielding/pubs/dissertation/top.html	

5

CHAPTER 6

API Development

This chapter covers the following topics:

- **Creating API Clients:** This section provides guidance around best practices for building an API client/software development kit. The focus is the value gained by saving developers time by not having to do all the coding, helping to standardize application development.
- **API Design Considerations:** This section identifies the challenges that need to be addressed when designing an API and considers what functionality is required by consumers or customers of the API.

This chapter maps to the *Developing Applications Using Cisco Core Platforms and APIs v1.0* (350-901) Exam Blueprint Section 2.0, "Using APIs."

Application programming interface (API) development covers both API design and API architecture. Whereas API design focuses on the API itself, API architecture is the entire solution, which includes the back end or infrastructure that the API provides access to. APIs are designed for developers; end users do not often see the API itself. When creating an API, developers should ensure that the API is clean and reusable. Being consistent in both use for consumption and in documentation ensures that developers will continue to use and consume an API. Providing an API client/**software development kit (SDK)** assists developers by speeding up adoption and integration into other applications and services, no matter the language that the developers have chosen to use.

There are two main methods of building APIs: inside-out and outside-in. Both methods have advantages and disadvantages. This design selection depends on what stage a company or team is in its API development. All APIs should be built with security at the forefront of the design. One of the first steps is API authentication; this process ensures the security of the company's API, prevents attacks and data breaches, and safeguards critical services by identifying and authorizing clients.

There are several API authorization methods, and as part of the API development process, the first step in securing an API is to accept only queries sent over a secure channel, such as **Transport Layer Security (TLS)**, the successor to the now-deprecated Secure Sockets Layer (SSL). Security methods on top of this include basic authentication, API keys or tokens, and OAuth. Some APIs also use rate limiting and error handling. This additional layer of protection helps by throttling API requests, using algorithmic-based rate limiting, and preventing an API from distributed denial-of-service (DDoS) attacks and other malicious abuse. When an API is secure, consumption and performance of the API will keep developers happy and their connections, applications, and experience better too.

Pagination and caching can help the performance of an API. Pagination can help break down the data and resources into small chunks. Depending on the API being developed, the two most popular types of API pagination are cursor-based and offset-based. Cursor-based pagination is more resource heavy to implement properly and can be slightly slower compared to offset-based pagination, which provides a better experience and API behavior.

API performance can also be enhanced with API caching. Caching an API's data either from the client side or API side and storing data frequently can vastly improve API performance and reduce the number of calls made to the API endpoints.

There are many ways to achieve a good API design and development. A lot is defined by the company and requirements of the API. Throughout the design and development phase, a lot of these details are ironed out.

"Do I Know This Already?" Quiz

The "Do I Know This Already?" quiz allows you to assess whether you should read this entire chapter thoroughly or jump to the "Exam Preparation Tasks" section. If you are in doubt about your answers to these questions or your own assessment of your knowledge of the topics, read the entire chapter. Table 6-1 lists the major headings in this chapter and their corresponding "Do I Know This Already?" quiz questions. You can find the answers in Appendix A, "Answers to the 'Do I Know This Already?' Quizzes."

Table 6-1 "Do I Know This Already?" Section-to-Question Mapping

Foundation Topics Section	Questions
Creating API Clients	1–5
API Design Considerations	6–10

1. What does a software development kit (SDK) help speed up and improve?
   a. Asynchronous API performance
   b. Adoption and developer experience of an API
   c. Adoption and modification of an API
   d. Adoption of API documentation
2. What is the OpenAPI Specification (OAS)?
   a. OAS defines a standard, programming language–agnostic interface description for all APIs.
   b. OAS defines a standard, programming language–agnostic interface description for GraphQL.
   c. OAS defines a standard, programming language–agnostic interface description for REST APIs.
   d. OAS defines a standard, programming language–agnostic interface description for REST and RPC API.
3. An API client allows the client to abstract which of the following? (Choose two.)
   a. Authentication
   b. Resources
   c. Headers
   d. Parameters

4. An OAuth2.0 bearer token is an opaque string that is ____________.
   a. A multiple string, which acts as the authentication of the API request
   b. Intended to have meaning to clients using it
   c. A fixed or defined length
   d. Not intended to have any meaning to clients using it
5. A WebSocket uses a bidirectional protocol, in which there are no predefined message patterns such as request/response. The client and the server can send messages to each other. True or False?
   a. True
   b. False
6. In an inside-out API design approach, which of the following is correct?
   a. The back-end infrastructure already exists within an organization and is used as a foundation for defining the API.
   b. The back-end infrastructure does not exist within an organization.
   c. The back-end infrastructure is built in tandem and will be used as a foundation for defining the API.
   d. The back-end infrastructure is a mock server and is used as a foundation for defining the API.
7. Outside-in API design allows for a lot more elasticity than inside-out API design. Which of the following are advantages of this approach? (Choose all that apply.)
   a. Decrease in API calls
   b. Faster adoption rate
   c. Reduction in API bandwidth
   d. The UI is last to be built
8. HTTP methods should not be included in endpoints. True or False?
   a. True
   b. False
9. What does page-based pagination allow the developer of the API to do? (Choose two.)
   a. Choose to view the required number of pages
   b. Choose to view the required range of pages
   c. Use the previous or next feature when requesting pages
   d. Return a pointer to a specific item in the dataset
10. Which of the following are API rate-limiter techniques and algorithms for measuring and limiting rates?
   a. Leaky bucket
   b. Fixed window
   c. Sliding window
   d. Token bucket
   e. All of these answers are correct.

Foundation Topics

Creating API Clients

An API client or API software development kit (SDK) can help speed up and improve the adoption and developer experience of an API. (The term *devkit* is also used when referring to an API or SDK.) API clients are not limited to being created by API owners or companies. Consumers who frequently use APIs as part of their daily workflow often create API clients if there isn't an official API client library available or the ones that are available do not meet their requirements. Because most REST APIs use HTTP request methods, using an API client allows a client to abstract the API methods, such as authentication, resources, and error handling, from the end developer no matter which programming language is used. The use of multiple programming languages lowers the requirement for developers to write custom implementation of an API based on the programming language being used.

When creating an API client, teams should adhere to several best practices. Following best practices ensures adoption of an API client if it is to be shared with other teams or outside the team, perhaps to customers. The API client should be automatically generated from an API definition such as the **OpenAPI Specification (OAS)**. This specification helps define but is not limited to the API endpoints and authentication processes. It helps any updates to the API client and removes the burden of updating API endpoints manually. The automation of this process can also provide a changelog, providing a documentation path when a new API version is released. An out-of-date API client can lead to frustration, broken pipelines, and in the worst case, outages or loss of service.

Code Generation Client API Libraries for IMDb

When you want to start building an SDK using OAS, Swagger provides a number of tools implementing the OpenAPI specification. One of these tools is SwaggerHub. **SwaggerHub** provides all the tools to be able to generate client SDKs for APIs in many languages. Once built, the SDK contains wrapper classes that can used to call the API from code, such as Python or an application, without having to use HTTP requests and responses.

To start, open a web browser and navigate to https://swagger.io/tools/swaggerhub/. There, you can create a free 14-day trial account. (You can create a free personal account in SwaggerHub using an email address or a GitHub ID, as shown in Figure 6-1.) When creating an account, enter the required developer name and password account details. You can skip the organization sections. After you complete this step and set up the account, go to My Hub to start using SwaggerHub.

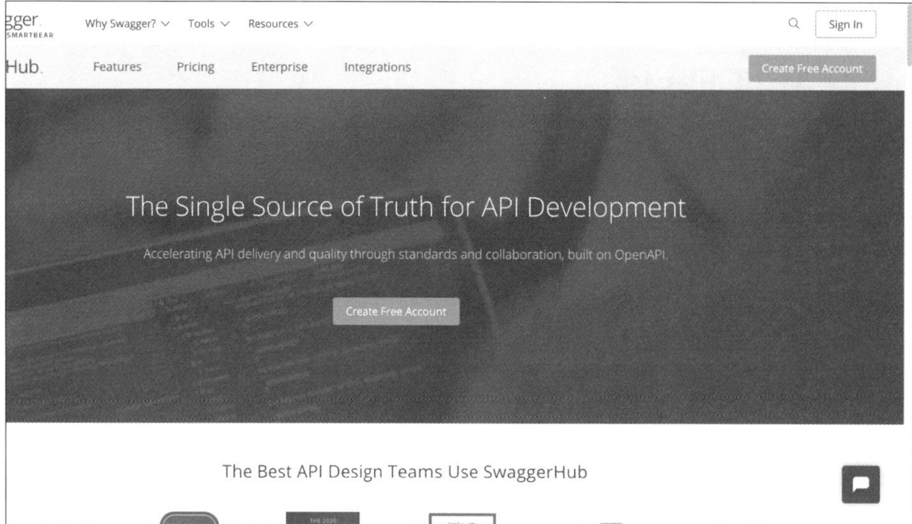

Figure 6-1 *Creating a Free Personal Account in SwaggerHub*

When you're in My Hub, you can start to create the API client. To do so, click the Create API button, as shown in Figure 6-2.

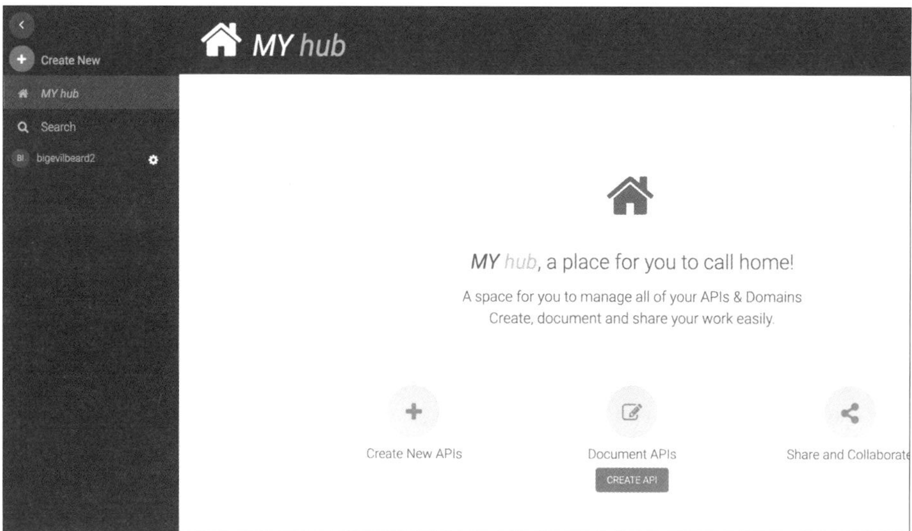

Figure 6-2 *Creating an API Client by Clicking the Create API Button*

The Import API box then appears (see Figure 6-3). In this box, fill in the fields, starting with the IMDb-API URL in the Path field; in this case, use https://imdb-api.com/swagger/IMDb-API/swagger.json. Then enter the owner name (this is your account and should be prepopulated; if it is not, select your owner name from the list). For this example, you do not need to publish the API client. Leave the Visibility field set as Private. When these fields are complete, click the Import button.

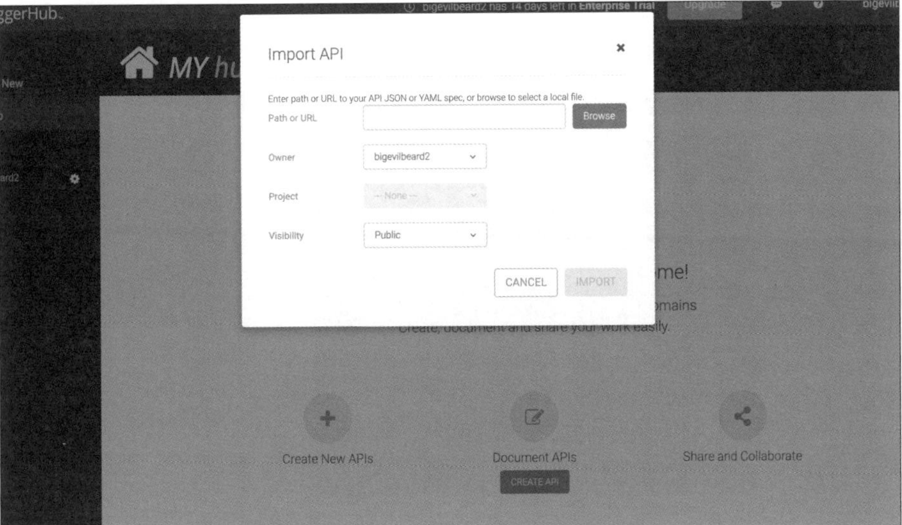

Figure 6-3 *Inserting the IMDb-API URL to Begin Creating the SDK*

SwaggerHub checks the imported URL file to ensure it is a valid JSON file and can be converted into the YAML format. The name and version can be left as the defaults; leaving them ensures any future versions from the IMDb-API are shown and displayed as separate versions. Providing a self-describing file such as JSON helps create a CHANGELOG for the API client, which is easy to parse.

To import the new API, click the Import OpenAPI button, as shown in Figure 6-4.

Figure 6-4 *Importing a New API JSON File into OpenAPI*

After the JSON file is imported and converted to YAML, the IMDb API is loaded into your personal SwaggerHub. There are a lot of features, which allow you, as developer, to view the API, and the API version (this capability is very useful because you can create API content per version of the API). Features include autogeneration of HTML/HTML2 documentation and server stub, which allows developers to download and test their API locally before it is deployed into a production environment. The API can be downloaded in both JSON and YAML, whether resolved or unresolved. SwaggerHub has many features to build API content, from clients to documentation (see Figure 6-5).

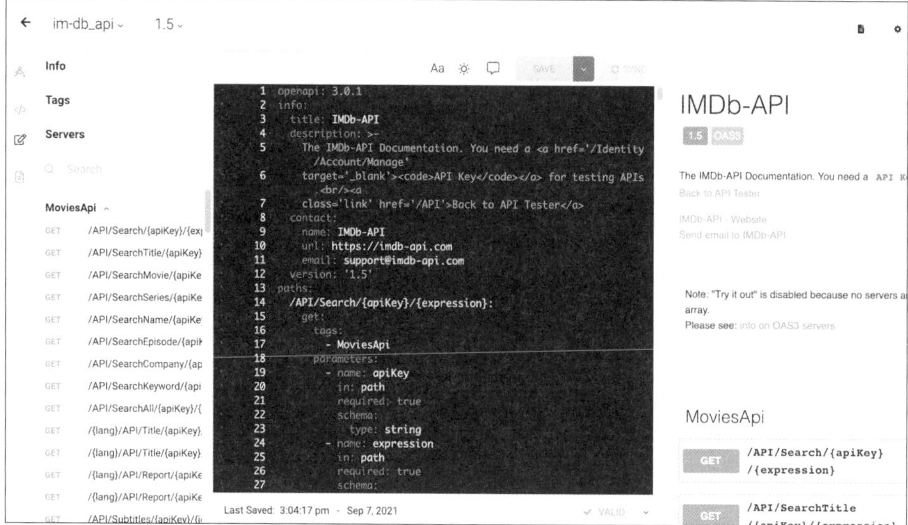

Figure 6-5 *SwaggerHub's Features for Building API Content*

To create an SDK from the newly created IMDb API documentation, select Export, and from the drop-down, select Client SDK. Here, the IMDb-API can be generated into client SDKs for APIs in many languages. Select Python as the desired language from the menu (see Figure 6-6) and download the zipped SDK file.

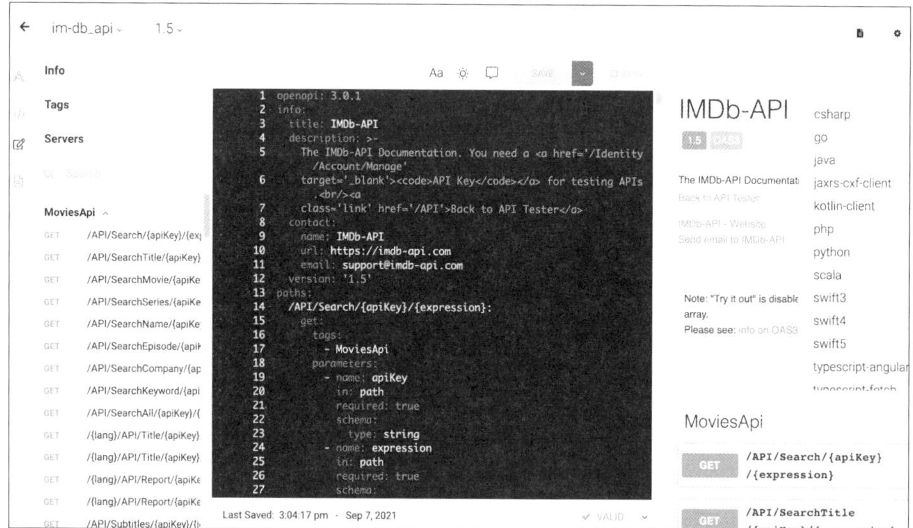

Figure 6-6 *SwaggerHub Features Used to Build API Content into Client SDKs for APIs in Many Languages*

After you open the zipped file, there are several options to use the new IMDb SDK. For the sample API client, treat this as a published SDK for a test developer to be able to install and use. Start by creating a new GitHub repository. In this example (see Figure 6-7 and Figure 6-8), a private repository called python-client-generated is created, but feel free to give the repository a suitable name of your choice.

```
46      def __init__(self):
47          """Constructor"""
48          # Default Base url
49          self.host = "https://imdb-api.com/en"
50          # Temp file folder for downloading files
51          self.temp_folder_path = None
```

Figure 6-7 *Creating a New Public or Private GitHub Repository for the IMDb SDK CLI*

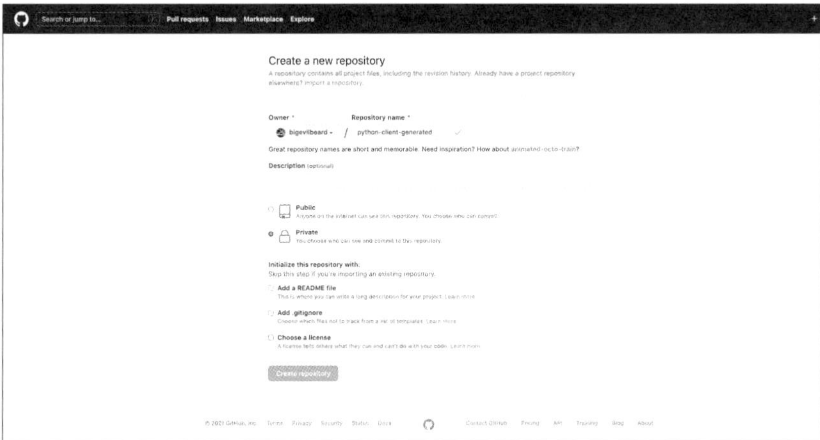

Figure 6-8 *Creating a New Public or Private GitHub Repository for the IMDb SDK*

No URL or endpoint is defined in the newly built SDK; therefore, the default base URL in the SDK code needs to be updated to https://imdb.com/en before the SDK will work with the IMDb API database. Because this SDK has been designed to work with the IMDb API, you can hard-code the IMDB API URL into the back-end code. Not all SDKs have hard-coded endpoints; some SDKs allow the use of environment files or the importing of environment details, so the SDK can be used on different systems. For example, the Cisco DNAC SDK at https://github.com/CiscoDevNet/DNAC-Python-SDK allows you to specify the IP/FQDN, username, and password at the command line.

To change the endpoint of the SDK, open the SDK folder that was downloaded. Within the SDK folder, open the swagger_client folder and navigate to the configuration.py file. Next, open the configuration.py file in your code editor (such as VSCode/Atom); then update line 49 with the URL https://imdb.com/en. When this is done, save and close this file.

Next, initialize the new repository. Then add, commit, and push the IMDb SDK files as shown in Example 6-1.

Example 6-1 *Initializing the New Repository, and Adding, Committing, and Pushing the IMDb SDK Files*

```
git init
git add *
git commit -m 'first push'
git remote add origin git@github.com:[username]/python-client-generated.git
git branch -M main
git push -u origin main
```

If you head back to the newly created GitHub repository (see Figure 6-9), you will find a fully documented guide for using the new IMDb SDK with complete README, Installation, and Getting Started documentation for API endpoints.

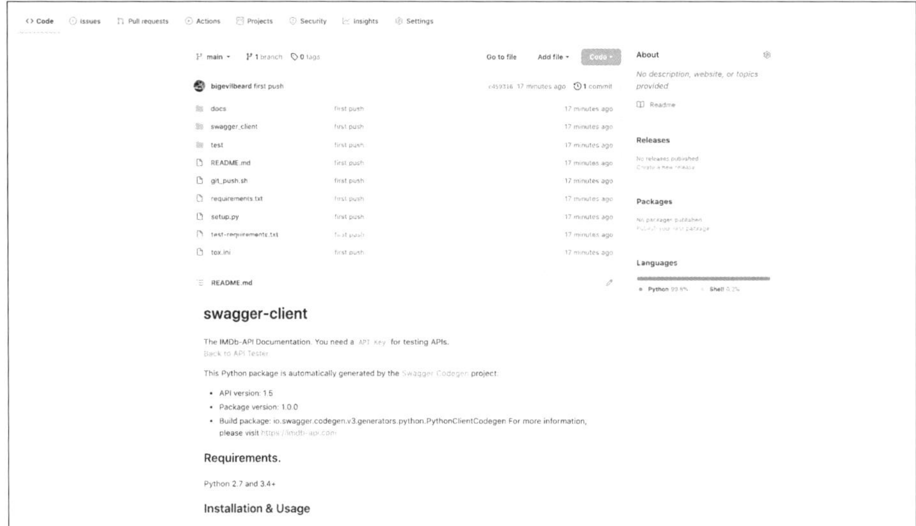

Figure 6-9 *A Fully Documented Guide for Using the New IMDb SDK*

Now that you've cloned the IMDb Python SDK from GitHub to a local machine, you can test it out within the Python REPL. (REPL stands for Read Evaluate Print Loop, which is the name given to the interactive MicroPython prompt that is accessible on Pycom devices.)

At this point, you need to install the newly created IMDb SDK. The first step is installing the requirements.txt file via PIP (see Example 6-2). The requirements.txt file includes the following five Python libraries, which are used by the SDK:

- Certifi provides Mozilla's carefully curated collection of root certificates for validating the trustworthiness of SSL certificates while verifying the identity of TLS hosts. (It has been extracted from the Requests project.)
- Six is a Python 2 and 3 compatibility library. It provides utility functions for smoothing over the differences between the Python versions with the goal of writing Python code that is compatible on both Python versions.
- The dateutil module provides powerful extensions to the standard datetime module, available in Python.
- Setuptools is a fully featured, actively maintained, and stable library designed to facilitate packaging Python projects.
- urllib3 is a powerful, user-friendly HTTP client for Python.

Example 6-2 *Installing Five Python Libraries in the IMDb SDK*

```
(venv)root/DEVCORE$ cat requirements.txt
certifi >= 14.05.14
six >= 1.10
python_dateutil >= 2.5.3
setuptools >= 21.0.0
urllib3 >= 1.15.1
```

After you install the requirements file and run setup.py, you can import the swagger client and run it. The **dir()** method returns a list of valid attributes of the object, as shown in Example 6-3.

Example 6-3 *Installing the IMDb SDK in a Python Environment*

```
(venv)root/DEVCORE$ pip install -r requirements.txt
(venv)root/DEVCORE$ python setup.py install
(venv)root/DEVCORE$ python
>>> import swagger_client
>>> dir(swagger_client)
['ActorShort', 'ApiClient', 'BoxOfficeAllTimeData', 'BoxOfficeAllTimeDataDetail',
'BoxOfficeShort', 'BoxOfficeWeekendData', 'BoxOfficeWeekendDataDetail', 'CastMovie',
'CastShort', 'CastShortItem', 'CompanyData', 'CompanyShort', 'Configuration', 'Epi-
sodeShortDetail', 'ExternalSiteData', 'ExternalSiteItem', 'FAQData', 'FAQDetail',
'FullCastData', 'IMDbListData', 'IMDbListDataDetail', 'ImageData', 'ImageDataDe-
tail', 'KeyValueItem', 'KeywordData', 'KnownFor', 'LanguageUrl', 'MetacriticRe-
viewData', 'MetacriticReviewDetail', 'MostPopularData', 'MostPopularDataDetail',
'MovieShort', 'MoviesApiApi', 'NameData', 'NewMovieData', 'NewMovieDataDetail',
'PosterData', 'PosterDataItem', 'RatingData', 'ReviewData', 'ReviewDetail', 'Search-
Data', 'SearchResult', 'SeasonEpisodeData', 'SimilarShort', 'StarShort', 'Sub-
titleData', 'SubtitleDataDetail', 'TitleData', 'Top250Data', 'Top250DataDetail',
'TrailerData', 'TvEpisodeInfo', 'TvSeriesInfo', 'UserRatingData', 'UserRatingDataDe-
tail', 'WikipediaData', 'WikipediaDataPlot', 'YouTubeData', 'YouTubeDataItem', 'You-
TubePlaylistData', 'YouTubePlaylistDataItem', 'YouTubeTrailerData', '__builtins__',
'__cached__', '__doc__', '__file__', '__loader__', '__name__', '__package__', '__
path__', '__spec__', 'absolute_import', 'api', 'api_client', 'configuration', 'mod-
els', 'rest']
```

The SDK also provides examples in Python; they were prebuilt when the SDK was created within SwaggerHub. You can use the example to test the SDK and provide results from the IMDb API without having to write a lot of code. This capability is very useful and important for an SDK; when this SDK is shared, the developer who wishes to use the SDK can look at the examples and quickly start to build code to consume the API resources.

For example, to test this newly built SDK, in the GitHub README file for the SDK, navigate to the API **a_pi_top250_movies_api_key_get** (see Figure 6-10).

README.md

MoviesApiApi	a_pi_search_episode_api_key_expression_get	GET /API/SearchEpisode/{apiKey}/{
MoviesApiApi	a_pi_search_keyword_api_key_expression_get	GET /API/SearchKeyword/{apiKey}/{
MoviesApiApi	a_pi_search_movie_api_key_expression_get	GET /API/SearchMovie/{apiKey}/{ex
MoviesApiApi	a_pi_search_name_api_key_expression_get	GET /API/SearchName/{apiKey}/{ex
MoviesApiApi	a_pi_search_series_api_key_expression_get	GET /API/SearchSeries/{apiKey}/{ex
MoviesApiApi	a_pi_search_title_api_key_expression_get	GET /API/SearchTitle/{apiKey}/{expr
MoviesApiApi	a_pi_season_episodes_api_key_id_season_number_get	GET /API/SeasonEpisodes/{apiKey}/{id}/
MoviesApiApi	a_pi_subtitles_api_key_id_get	GET /API/Subtitles/{apiKey}/{id}
MoviesApiApi	a_pi_subtitles_api_key_id_season_number_get	GET /API/Subtitles/{apiKey}/{id}/{se
MoviesApiApi	a_pi_top250_movies_api_key_get	GET /API/Top250Movies/{apiKey}
MoviesApiApi	a_pi_top250_t_vs_api_key_get	GET /API/Top250TVs/{apiKey}
MoviesApiApi	a_pi_trailer_api_key_id_get	GET /API/Trailer/{apiKey}/{id}
MoviesApiApi	a_pi_user_ratings_api_key_id_get	GET /API/UserRatings/{apiKey}/{id}
MoviesApiApi	a_pi_you_tube_api_key_v_get	GET /API/YouTube/{apiKey}/{v}
MoviesApiApi	a_pi_you_tube_playlist_api_key_list_get	GET /API/YouTubePlaylist/{apiKey}/{
MoviesApiApi	a_pi_you_tube_trailer_api_key_id_get	GET /API/YouTubeTrailer/{apiKey}/{i
MoviesApiApi	a_pifaq_api_key_id_get	GET /API/FAQ/{apiKey}/{id}
MoviesApiApi	a_piim_db_list_api_key_id_get	GET /API/IMDbList/{apiKey}/{id}
MoviesApiApi	lang_api_report_api_key_id_get	GET /{lang}/API/Report/{apiKey}/{id
MoviesApiApi	lang_api_report_api_key_id_options_get	GET /{lang}/API/Report/{apiKey}/{id
MoviesApiApi	lang_api_title_api_key_id_get	GET /{lang}/API/Title/{apiKey}/{id}
MoviesApiApi	lang_api_title_api_key_id_options_get	GET /{lang}/API/Title/{apiKey}/{id}/{
MoviesApiApi	lang_api_wikipedia_api_key_id_get	GET /{lang}/API/Wikipedia/{apiKey}/

Figure 6-10 *How to Use the Python IMDb SDK in the IMDb SDK README Documentation*

The README has a complete list of all the API endpoints and how a developer can use this SDK. By clicking the selected API, you can open and use a code example and use case of the API endpoint (see Figure 6-11).

Figure 6-11 *URL Links to Each API from the IMDb Swagger Documentation*

You can copy the code for the API endpoint API/Top250Movies in Example 6-4 into the Python REPL or into a code editor. The API client documentation shows that a developer IMDB API key is required in a string format. If the SDK and code are run without an IMDB API key, an error log is shown:

```
{'error_message': 'Invalid API Key', 'items': []}
```

Example 6-4 *Python Code Using the IMDb Endpoint API/Top250Movies*

```
from __future__ import print_function
import time
import swagger_client
from swagger_client.rest import ApiException
from pprint import pprint
# create an instance of the API class
api_instance = swagger_client.MoviesApiApi()
api_key = '[add user key]' # str |
try:
    api_response = api_instance.a_pi_top250_movies_api_key_get(api_key)
    pprint(api_response)
except ApiException as e:
    print("Exception when calling MoviesApiApi->a_pi_top250_movies_api_key_get: %s\n"
% e)
```

After the Python script is executed, it retrieves the API endpoint data and prints out the top 250 movies of all time from the IMDb endpoint in JSON format (see Example 6-5). When the code runs, it checks for any errors being returned from the API. In this example, the code completed without error. Because the output is quite verbose, you can save the file locally to review or look for errors. You can do this quickly using output redirection on the command line. The > symbol creates a new file if one is not present, or it overwrites the file if one already exists. This file can then be opened in a text file via a code or text file editor.

You can use the redirect feature by providing the following path:

```
python imdb.sdk.py > ~/Desktop/imdb_sdk.txt
```

Example 6-5 *Python Code Output from IMDb Endpoint Top250Movies*


```
{'error_message': '',
 'items': [{'crew': 'Frank Darabont (dir.), Tim Robbins, Morgan Freeman',
            'full_title': 'The Shawshank Redemption (1994)',
            'id': 'tt0111161',
            'im_db_rating': '9.2',
            'im_db_rating_count': '2465589',
            'image': 'https://m.media-amazon.com/images/M/MV5BMDFkYTc0MGEtZmNhMC00Z-
DIzLWFmNTEtODM1ZmRlYWMwMWFmXkEyXkFqcGdeQXVyMTMxODk2OTU@._V1_UX128_CR0,3,128,176_AL_.
jpg',
            'rank': '1',
            'title': 'The Shawshank Redemption',
            'year': '1994'},
```

Adding CLI Wrapper Code

Adding a CLI wrapper can take all published functions in an SDK library and make them available to the developer as a standard command-line tool. A CLI tool can build its own arguments directly from an SDK. These can be features such as help options, optional commands, and switches. Building a CLI wrapper from an SDK improves its capabilities because they exactly match those of the SDK and are updated automatically when or if an API adds new capabilities and resources.

NOTE Per Wikipedia: "A command-line interface (CLI) processes commands to a computer program in the form of lines of text. The program which handles the interface is called a command-line interpreter or command-line processor. Operating systems implement a command-line interface in a shell for interactive access to operating system functions or services. Such access was primarily provided to developers by computer terminals starting in the mid-1960s and continued to be used throughout the 1970s and 1980s on VAX/VMS, Unix systems and personal computer systems including DOS, CP/M and Apple DOS."

(See https://en.wikipedia.org/wiki/Command-line_interface.)

Two of the most popular Python libraries for creating a CLI wrapper are argparse and Click. Argparse is part of the standard Python library (from Python 2.7; argparse was the replacement for outparse). Arguments can generate different actions; for example, **add_argument()** can be used to create an argument. The default action, though, is to store the argument value. Additional supported actions of argparse include storing the argument as a single argument or as part of a list, and storing a constant value when the argument is encountered, such as handling true/false values for Booleans.

The Python Click module is used to create CLI wrappers also. Click is an alternative to the standard optparse and argparse modules. Click allows arbitrary nesting of commands and automatic help page generation; it can also support the loading of subcommands at runtime. Click uses a slightly different approach than argparse because it uses the notion of decorators. These commands need to be functions that can be wrapped using decorators. The creator of the Click library wrote the "why of click" at https://click.palletsprojects.com/en/8.0.x/why/.

Making Calls to IMDb Using a CLI Program

Adding a CLI program into the SDK Python code can help make the functionality of developer code simpler and reusable. The same piece of code can be transformed into multiple-use code, thus removing the need for single pieces of Python code per API call or request. The CLI can add a helper function to call IMDb endpoints via the SDK library using command-line parameters, allowing command selection and built-in documents.

To add the Python Click library to the IMDb code, the first steps are installing the library via PIP and importing the Python library into the code.

Using PIP, install the Python Click library into a local Python environment:

```
pip install click
```

In Example 6-6, you can add three IMDb endpoints from the SDK code: **top250**, **box_office**, and **in_theaters.** Click provides a command-line parameter to call each of these API endpoints using the IMDb SDK. The beginning of the code is the same as the previous example for the **top250** code. Here, you add the **import click** statement so that this module is accessible for the code to run. Next, under the **api_key**, you create a **click.group** with the function of CLI, which ends with **pass.** The pass statement allows for multiple subcommands to be attached later in the code for additional functionality.

Example 6-6 *Importing the Click Library and Creating a Click Group*

```
from __future__ import print_function
import time
import swagger_client
from swagger_client.rest import ApiException
from pprint import pprint
import click

# create an instance of the API class
api_instance = swagger_client.MoviesApiApi()
api_key = '' # str |

@click.group()
def cli():
    pass
```


Each API call is created as a function and adds the **@click.command()** decorator to it. In Click, commands are the basic building blocks of command-line interfaces. Example 6-7 shows how to create a new command and use the decorated function as a callback. The function, named **get_250**, is passed to the command. In most examples of CLI helpers, the command is often named after the function or API call to help describe the action being performed.

Example 6-7 *Creating a New Command for the Function Using Click*

```
@click.command()
def get_250():
    try:
        api_response = api_instance.a_pi_top250_movies_api_key_get(api_key)
        pprint(api_response)
    except ApiException as e:
        print("Exception when calling MoviesApiApi->a_pi_top250_movies_api_key_get:
%s\n" % e)
```

To make this command callable from the CLI, you attach commands to other commands of a type group; this process is referred to as arbitrary nesting of scripts. For this example, the function name **get_250** is used:

```
cli.add_command(get_250)
```

The great part about Click is being able to add additional API endpoints or functions without refactoring a lot of code. In this case, it is simple to add additional functions and Click commands to extend the flexibility of code. To complete this and add additional features, you add the next two API endpoints: **box_office** and **in_theaters**. In any command that has a hyphen (-) in it, the hyphen is automatically converted to an underscore (_) when referring to the API endpoints (see Example 6-8).

Example 6-8 *Converting Hyphens Automatically to Underscores*

```
def in_theaters():
    """
    Show those movies still in theaters.
    """
in-theaters         Show those movies still in theaters
```

Before running the code, you can look at the optional arguments now built into the code. Click has a great built-in feature that automatically builds a help function into the commands (see Example 6-9). This feature provides details to which argument can be run at the command line. Additional information can also be added for each command as an overview of what each argument does or the expected results (see Example 6-10).

Example 6-9 *Click's Built-In Help Function*

```
python imdb.sdk.click.py --help
Usage: imdb.sdk.click.py [OPTIONS] COMMAND [ARGS]...
Options:
  --help  Show this message and exit.
Commands:
  get-250
  get-box-office
  get-theaters
```

Example 6-10 *Complete Code with Three API Endpoints*

```
from __future__ import print_function
import time
import swagger_client
from swagger_client.rest import ApiException
from pprint import pprint
import click

# create an instance of the API class
api_instance = swagger_client.MoviesApiApi()
api_key = ' ' # str |

@click.group()
def cli():
    pass

@click.command()
def get_250():
```

```
    try:
        api_response = api_instance.a_pi_top250_movies_api_key_get(api_key)
        pprint(api_response)
    except ApiException as e:
        print("Exception when calling MoviesApiApi->a_pi_top250_movies_api_key_get:
%s\n" % e)

@click.command()
def get_box_office():
    try:
        api_response = api_instance.a_pi_box_office_api_key_get(api_key)
        pprint(api_response)
    except ApiException as e:
        print("Exception when calling MoviesApiApi->a_pi_box_office_api_key_get:
%s\n" % e)

@click.command()
def get_theaters():
    try:
        api_response = api_instance.a_pi_in_theaters_api_key_get(api_key)
        pprint(api_response)
    except ApiException as e:
        print("Exception when calling MoviesApiApi->a_pi_in_theaters_api_key_get:
%s\n" % e)

cli.add_command(get_250)
cli.add_command(get_box_office)
cli.add_command(get_theaters)

if __name__ == "__main__":
    cli()
```

When running the complete code, you can pass an argument after the filename from the command list. Passing no argument shows the help page. Each argument runs only the API endpoint call linked to the **click** command.

Adding the **get-theaters** argument to the command line calls the IMDb API endpoint for **in_theaters** and returns the results in JSON format:

```
python imdb.sdk.click.py get-theaters
```

API Design Considerations

When designing and building an API, a team or company undertakes a number of steps to plan and evaluate its architecture. The design of the API will influence how well developers are able to consume it, integrate it, and even if use it. All API designs should start out with defining the goals of the API. Typically, APIs are built to help expose a service or data for customers or partners, who can be either internal or external to a company. If, for example, your team provides an API to another team to provision, update a service within the infrastructure your team owns, and manage, these are still your API customers. Likewise, if you build an API for external-use customers, your company is providing an API service that will create their experience. Often the best API design comes from asking the customers or consumers what they want from the API, such as workflow integrations, alerting/monitoring, and what applications will be accessing the API.

A lot of enterprise services are already up and running, and an API is often built on top of this fully functioning infrastructure. This method is called **API inside-out design**. This type of design has number of advantages because it allows the design to be modeled on the current infrastructure and services. The API resembles normal operations, but many of the interactions are shifted and then performed via an API. This method allows API developers to select the most common workflows and request and work on them first. This approach shows problems such as security flaws or performance factors. Some of the downsides to this approach are that you do not have access to customer/developer feedback. The downsides of this lead to wasted code cycles and trying to over-replicate the functionality of back-end systems. Often, in an inside-out approach, if the API is designed or built during an ongoing project, the API is thought of as being bolted on. This results in a bad developer experience and low standard in API design in most cases. Having a good developer experience and a high standard is the main reward of using an API-first design, or **API outside-in/ user interface (API first approach)**. This design considers what functionality is required by the consumers or customers of the API and what they will be asking for. Also, this design covers what is important to the end developers—for example, which features they need and how easily the developers or consumers can integrate their applications and workflows. An outside-in API design allows for a lot more elasticity, covering more use cases in single API calls, thus leading to fewer API requests and calls being made by consumers and less traffic on the wire and back-end infrastructure for the provider. Outside-in API design leads to a more elegant API and one that a developer or consumer can use.

Good API REST architecture and design follow the HTTP methods GET, PUT, PATCH, POST, and DELETE, as described in Chapter 5, "Network APIs." Most APIs operate over HTTP, which allows a solid base for these APIs to be designed over. When you're naming resources, either singular or plural is acceptable if resource names are maintained and consistent on all APIs. The same goes for the use of capitalization.

Singular API naming resource:

```
/data/device
```

Plural API naming resource:

```
/data/devices
```

HTTP methods such as GET and PUT should not be included in endpoints. The endpoint should contain only nouns because the API call is transferring state, not processing instructions. For example:

```
/data/getDevice
```

For further reading on API design, consider Roy Fielding's 2000 dissertation, "Architectural Styles and the Design of Network-based Software Architectures," which introduced REST (https://www.ics.uci.edu/~fielding/pubs/dissertation/fielding_dissertation_2up.pdf). Also, see RFC 3986, "Uniform Resource Identifier (URI): Generic Syntax," by Tim Berners-Lee, Roy T. Fielding, and L. Masinter (http://www.rfc-editor.org/rfc/rfc3986.txt).

API Authentication Models

When you're designing and building APIs, security should always be your first thought within the design. Poorly designed authentication models can result in attackers being able to access or gain control over accounts or personal data. Attackers can even make financial transactions such as money transfers and credit card fraud. API developer authentication should be administered individually from standard API endpoints.

The type of authentication depends on the type of API being built and the developer base that will be consuming the API resources. For example, if the API is designed for internal or external use or for private, partner, or public use, a different authentication model might be chosen. When you're using an API, authentication is sort of like going on holiday to another country and being asked to show your passport upon entry to that country. Your passport confirms who you are and is evidence or proof that you are who you say you are. Authentication is different from authorization, however, in that authorization refers to the level of access. For example, authorization is like the level of security clearance your company allows your ID badge to have. Your ID badge might allow you in the office, break room, meeting rooms, and stationery or storeroom, but not the server or data room within the office.

Here, we look at the primary API authentication models. Basic authentication (or basic auth) requires that the application have a previous developer name (ID) and password set up on the service or a response back from the server asking for a developer name and password before access to resources is given. Basic authorization can be set up to allow both authentication and authorization, because after the developer's ID has been entered, a level of security and access can be defined for the service. For example, developer A could have read-only access (GET method) to an SDN controller, such as a Cisco DNA Center.

6

Basic authentication is considered the lowest form of authentication. Base64 is easy to decrypt because it is an encoding algorithm that merely presents data in an alternative format. It does not in any way attempt to hide data; it merely expresses the same data in an alternative syntax.

Developer credentials are passed as a Base64-encoded header (as in Example 6-11) or as parameters in an HTTP client. The header contains the word **Basic** followed by a space and the Base64-encoded string *developername:password*. Base64 converts the developer name and password into a set of 64 characters to ensure safe transmission. Because this type of authentication uses the HTTP header, there is no requirement for additional or further complex responses.

Example 6-11 *Base64-Encoded Authentication*

```
headers = {
  'Content-Type': 'application/yang-data+json',
  'Accept': 'application/yang-data+json',
  'Authorization': 'Basic YWRtaW46Q2lzY28xMjM='
}
```

If you were to copy and paste the Base64 details into a decoder tool, you would see that the *developername:password* is **admin:Cisco123**. When you're using Base64 as the authentication method, it is highly recommended that you employ additional security mechanisms such as HTTPS/TLS.

Bearer authentication (token authentication) depends on how the API is defined. For example, basic authentication requires the request to send a developer name and password or identifying credentials to the requester; again, the developer account is set up on the server. This is often why bearer authentication is considered an extension of basic authentication. After the initial request is made via the credentials (typically, an HTTP POST request), the request asks for a token to be returned. Further API calls will leverage the token; there is no further requirement to send the developer credentials for subsequent API calls, only the token itself. Hence, the word *bearer* implies the developer has a ticket (token), and if it is valid, access is permitted. Tokens can be short-lived and last a few hours, or they can be long-lived. Some tokens can be refreshed and might last a week, or they can be nonrefresh and nonexpiring. There is no fixed design when it comes to a token's lifetime or expiry when designing an API. Companies choose the option or mixture of options that best meets their API design requirements.

A bearer token is an opaque string that is generated by the server in response to a developer login request and not intended to have any meaning to clients using it. The client must send this token in to the authorization header when making requests to protected resources. The bearer token can have a lifetime too; for example, Cisco DNA Center's API uses token-based authentication and HTTPS basic authentication to generate an authentication cookie and security token that are used to authorize subsequent requests. By issuing an HTTP POST request API call, Cisco DNAC returns a token in the response body:

```
{"Token":"<token>"}
```

As with the basic authentication method, additional security mechanisms such as HTTPS/SSL should be employed.

As you saw with the IMDb API example, API keys are another method of API security. Developers can request an API key. However, the API keys don't identify developers; they identify projects.

The key is sent in the query string, in the request header, or as a cookie. Like a password, the key is meant to be a secret that is known only between the client and server. API keys are not considered secure; they are accessible to clients, making it easy for someone to steal. When an API key is stolen, it generally does not expire, making the API key reusable indefinitely, unless the API key is revoked or a new key is regenerated.

Best practice suggests that API keys are least secure when sent in a query string, and it is strongly suggested that API keys should be used in the authorization header instead of a query.

API keys should be considered for use in authentication if an API needs to block unidentified traffic or to limit or rate limit the number of calls made to an API. This method allows filtering by logging the key to the API. The IMDb API does this, limiting the free account to 100 calls per day. However, this limit could be as short as per hour or per minute. As with the basic authentication method, additional security mechanisms such as HTTPS/TLS should be employed when using API keys.

Cookie authentication uses the HTTP cookies to authenticate the client requests and maintain session information on the server over the stateless HTTP protocol. The client sends a developer name and password, as you saw with basic and bearer authentication. The developer account is set up on the server to establish a session. When it is successful, the server response includes the Set-Cookie header that contains the cookie name, value, and expiry time. With every subsequent client request to the server, the client sends back all previously stored cookies to the server using the cookie header.

Cookie authentication is vulnerable to cross-site request forgery (CSRF) attacks, so using CSRF tokens for protection is recommended. This feature adds protection against CSRFs that occur when using REST APIs. This protection is provided by including a CSRF token with API requests. You can put requests on an allowed list so that they do not require protection if needed.

The last authentication method to discuss is OAuth 2.0, which is the industry standard. OAuth 2.0 provides limited access to a client. The OAuth protocol for getting an access token or refresh token is called flows (or grant types). The flows allow the resource owner to share the protected content from the resource server without having to share credentials. Several popular flows are suitable for different types of API clients when using OAuth2.0:

- **Client:** The client is the application requesting access to a protected resource on behalf of the resource owner. This access must be authorized by the developer, and the authorization must be validated by the API.
- **Resource owner:** Typically, the resource owner is the developer who authorizes an application to access their account.
- **Resource server:** The resource server hosts the protected resources. This is the API you want to access.
- **Authorization server:** The authorization server verifies, identifies, and authenticates the resource owner and then issues access tokens to the application.

6

The most-used implementations of OAuth are access tokens or refresh tokens. A designer might choose to use one or both methods:

- **Access token:** The server issues a token to clients, much like an API key, and then it allows the client to access resources. However, unlike an API key, an access token can expire. After the token expires, the client has to request a new one.
- **Refresh token:** OAuth 2.0 introduced an artifact called a refresh token, which is an optional part of an OAuth flow. When a new access token is required, an application can make a POST request back to the token endpoint using the grant type **'refresh_token'**. This request allows an application to obtain a new access token without having to prompt the developer.

Flow Control (Pagination vs. Streaming)

Why use pagination in your API? RESTful API pagination is the process of splitting data sets into discrete pages with a set of paginated endpoints. An API call to a paginated endpoint is called a paginated request. API endpoints paginate their responses to make the result set easier to handle. Here, we look at two of the most common pagination techniques:

- Page-based pagination (offset pagination)
- Cursor pagination

If a developer is working with smaller subsets of data, pagination improves the API response time. It enables the developer to not return everything in a single response when returning data with multiple replies. This also prevents huge volumes of data traveling over a network, and for this reason, pagination can help conserve bandwidth and memory. Overall, pagination in API design helps with the end developer experience. When developers are designing an API to support pagination, the most-often-used method is to have predetermined page size. Defining the right size of data to be returned per page is normally based on several factors, such as use, capacity, and end developer experience. By using page size, a developer can limit how much data or item per page is returned. Default limits are often built in, but when dealing with unknown limits, the recommendation is to allow developers to set a limit themselves. If an API response does not contain a link to the next page of results, this would mean the developer has reached the final page. For example, the default limit request might return 20 pages, and due to the size, this request is slow and hard to parse. With pagination, the developer can choose to view the required number of pages and items on the page. This could be a single page or a preset range of pages—say, pages 5 and 6. An API could allow the developer to select a starting page—for example, page 10 through page 15; this is referred to as offset pagination.

The GitHub API supports page-based pagination. By using cURL and the GitHub stargazer tool, you can list the people who have starred the repository at ciscodevnet/yang explorer (see Example 6-12). To fetch all the stargazers for ciscodevnet/yang explorer, you would have to make two requests.

Example 6-12 *GitHub Stargazer Tool Listing the People Who Have Starred the Repository at ciscodevnet/yang explorer*

```
curl -I https://api.github.com/repos/ciscodevnet/yang-explorer/stargazers
HTTP/2 200
server: GitHub.com
date: Mon, 23 Aug 2021 10:00:51 GMT
content-type: application/json; charset=utf-8
cache-control: public, max-age=60, s-maxage=60
vary: Accept, Accept-Encoding, Accept, X-Requested-With
etag: W/"8e407f3e6d12cb560d3e01b0f42804a29724a5a4894174e4e87301b99ec4532e"
x-github-media-type: github.v3; format=json
link: <https://api.github.com/repositories/42690240/stargazers?page=2>; rel="next",
<https://api.github.com/repositories/42690240/stargazers?page=13>; rel="last"
[output removed for brevity]
```

When making a REST API call to a Meraki Dashboard API, after you make a GET request to an endpoint, the results that are returned could contain a huge amount of data. Using pagination on the results ensures responses are easier to handle because only a subset of the results is returned in the first response. If you need to get more data, you can execute subsequent requests to the endpoint with slightly different parameters to get the rest of the data.

The Meraki Dashboard API allows developers to sort data. The developer also can determine the data before it is sent back. An example is timestamps. Developers can use the timestamp values **startingAfter** and **endingBefore** if they want to paginate based on time. Using a timestamp on data can be very effective when using real-time data. However, offset pagination does not care that the data has been modified; it just gets the same data at the offset (in this example, page 5). If real-time pagination is required, cursor-based pagination should be used. APIs on social media sites such as Facebook and Twitter use cursor-based pagination. Cursor-based pagination does not use the concept of pages; because the data changes quickly, results are considered either "previous" or "next." If there is no concept of pages, this means developers cannot skip to a certain page, as you saw with offset pagination; cursor-based pagination works by returning a pointer to an exact item in the dataset. Some APIs (Facebook being one) do support both methods of pagination. If page selection is required, offset-based pagination tends to be used. If the API is to provide performance and real-time data, cursor-based pagination is used.

In both offset-based pagination and cursor-based pagination, developers poll or call the API, which is the most typical use of APIs where a developer or application is making a request every 30 seconds—for example, in the client/server architecture. This means that if the client or application is sending a request every 30 seconds to the server, new data could be available for 19.9 seconds with the client or application.

Another drawback could be that the API is rate limiting calls per hour or per day. This is similar to the concept of SNMP polling versus event-based model-driven telemetry, where most SNMP polling was done every 5 to 10 minutes; this left enough of a gap for customers to notice their router interfaces were down before their provider (the one they were paying to monitor) noticed!

Figure 6-12 shows stateless versus stateful connection differences between RESTful APIs and streaming APIs.

Key Topic

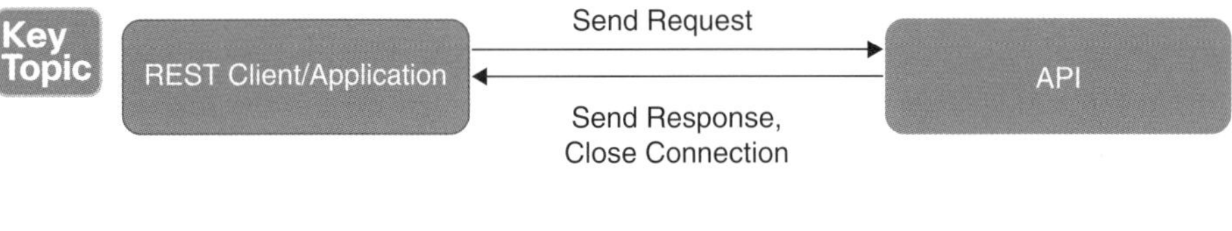

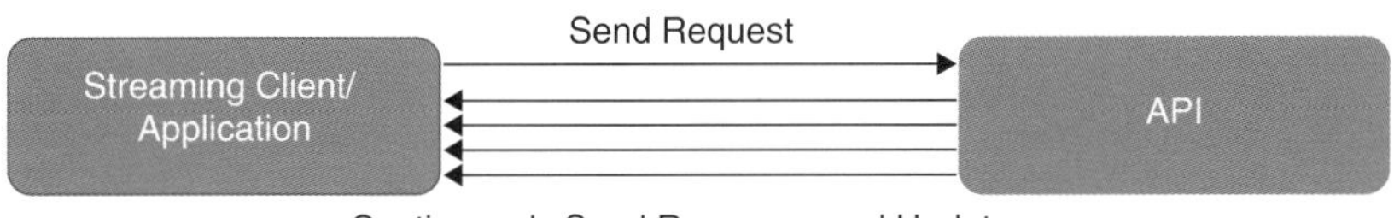

Figure 6-12 *Stateless versus Stateful Connection Differences Between RESTful APIs and Streaming APIs*

Push/streaming APIs can help solve the problem of experiencing lag or delay and are perfect for examining data in real time. For developers looking to get information accurately and quickly, push/streaming APIs provide the best results. Because push/streaming APIs are stateful, after they are opened, they are persistent in connection; this is unlike RESTful APIs, which are stateless.

In the push method the client/application subscribe to some information, and that information is initiated from a server to the client. A great example of this is webhooks, which is often referred to as reverse API or HTTP callback. Webhooks enable the push-model mechanism to send notifications such as alarms or events in real time. When an event happens, the

API provider (which could be an SDN controller such as Cisco SD-WAN or Webex Teams) can send an HTTP POST request to an external system in real time after an alarm or event is received. When you create a webhook for a particular event or alarm, the notification data is sent as an HTTP POST (often in a JSON format). The streaming method still operates over the same HTTP methods as RESTful API, but this is still a unidirectional method. Even if the client sends the initial connection, HTTP and HTTPS are unidirectional protocols where the client always initiates the request.

The Streaming API methods commonly utilize the WebSocket protocol, which is standardized by the IETF as RFC 6455 (https://datatracker.ietf.org/doc/html/rfc6455). A WebSocket uses a bidirectional protocol, and there are no predefined message patterns such as request/response. The client and the server can send messages to each other. Unlike the request/response method seen with REST API, using a WebSocket allows the client or server to talk independently of one another; this is referred to as full-duplex. A WebSocket does not require a new connection to be set up for each message to be sent between the client and server. As soon as an initial connection is set up, the messages can be sent and received continuously without any interruption. The trade-off here is that having a communication open all the time does increase the overhead of resources because the client and the server communicate over the same TCP connection for the duration of the WebSocket connection lifetime.

Error Handling, Timeouts, and Rate Limiting

When creating an API, all teams should stick to the mandate of good error handling. No engineer has ever jumped with joy at the sight of an error, but they might have if the information provided in response to the error was helpful and informative. Understanding error messages can be very helpful when debugging or troubleshooting an issue. Errors can fall into two categories: there is either an issue with a request, or the server/API could not understand what it was being sent. For example, if the JSON is incorrectly formatted or the API has an issue itself, the error could be due to the server being overloaded, which is a network issue (reachability).

Most REST APIs follow the approach of using appropriate HTTP response status codes to indicate whether a specific HTTP request has been successfully completed or has failed. This response is provided in two parts: the status code and reason phrase. The status code element is a three-digit integer result code made in the attempt to understand and satisfy the request, and the reason phrase is a brief overview to help the user understand the output (also known as status text) and to summarize the meaning of the code. The first digit in the status code is the class of the response, but the last two digits do not have a categorized role.

Table 6-2 provides a summary of HTTP status codes and reason phrases.

Table 6-2 HTTP Status Codes and Reason Phrases

Status Code	Reason Phrase	Additional Information (Not Supplied in the Response)
1xx	Informational	The request was received; the process continues.
2xx	Success	The action was successfully received, understood, and accepted.
3xx	Redirection	Further action must be taken to complete the request.
4xx	Client Error	The request contains bad syntax or cannot be fulfilled.
5xx	Server Error	The server failed to fulfill an apparently valid request.

Next, we focus on the 4XX and 5XX status codes.

For a simple example of an error code format, let's look at how Cisco DNA Center responds to an API HTTP POST request when the wrong developer name is provided in the authentication method. This request should yield the 401 error code because the error has come from the client side. The sample output for this request is shown in Example 6-13.

Example 6-13 *Sample Output of HTTP Error Code 401*

```
HTTP/1.1 401 Unauthorized
Server: nginx/1.13.12
Date: Tue, 17 Aug 2021 10:03:19 GMT
Content-Type: application/json
Content-Length: 72
Connection: keep-alive
Via: api-gateway
Cache-Control: no-store
Pragma: no-cache
Content-Security-Policy: default-src 'self' 'unsafe-inline' 'unsafe-eval' blob:
data:
X-Content-Type-Options: nosniff
X-XSS-Protection: 1
Strict-Transport-Security: max-age=31536000; includeSubDomains
X-Frame-Options: SAMEORIGIN

{"error":"Authentication has failed. Please provide valid credentials."}
```

6

From this information, you can see the details. The 401 error code field is an integer coding the error type. Next to this is a string giving the unauthorized message. Both the code and message are mandatory. The last line is the description; this is an optional field in the error response. If it is used in the error format, it can provide detailed information about which parameter is missing or what the acceptable values are. The Cisco DNA Center API does provide this information, and from the output, you can see that this is a string. In this case, the error denotes that the incorrect credentials were provided in the request.

The only other optional information not shown in the example is the infoURL field. When used in the error response, it would provide a URL linking to documentation.

API timeouts should be handled by the following error codes: 408, 504, and 599. If a 408 error code is returned when consuming, the client or application did not produce a request within the time that the server was prepared to wait and thus shut down the connection. In the RESTful client/server architecture, a client consuming an API does not send the complete HTTP request within three minutes. In this case, the connection is closed straightaway, and the server should issue a 408 error code within the header field back to the client in the response. In some cases, the client might have a remaining request that has been delayed on the wire. In this case, the client could repeat the request but only by creating a new connection.

The following output shows HTTP error code 408 received by the client:

```
HTTP/1.1 408 REQUEST_TIMEOUT

Content-Length:0

Connection: Close
```

The 504 status error is a timeout error. It denotes that a web server attempting to load a page for you did not get a response within a given timeframe from another server from which it requested the information. It's called a 504 error because this is the HTTP status code that the web server uses to define this type of error. Typically, the error can happen for a few reasons, but the two most common are that the server is overloaded with requests or is under some form of attack (DDoS), or some maintenance is being performed at the time the request was sent. Other possible issues could be DNS or firewall rules. From an API design side, you should ensure that the API Gateway sends an HTTP response to the client and set a maximum integration timeout, such as 30 seconds.

Nginx (https://www.nginx.com/) is good choice as an API gateway because it has advanced HTTP processing capabilities needed for handling API traffic. It also can add higher timeouts such as **connect_timeout**, **send_timeout**, or **read_timeout** if there are known or expected network latency issues to the API destination (see Example 6-14).

Example 6-14 *A 504 Error Code Generated by an Nginx API Gateway*

```
<html>
<head><title>504 Gateway Time-out</title></head>
<body bgcolor="white">
<center><h1>504 Gateway Time-out</h1></center>
<hr><center>nginx/1.13.12</center>
</body>
</html>
```

Also like error code 504 is error code 599. This status code is not specified in any RFCs but is used by some HTTP proxies to signal a network connect timeout behind the proxy to a client in front of the proxy. This error handling code is issued if a server takes too long to respond (most people have encountered this typical error when requesting information over the Internet). The server should generate this error code to prevent the developer or application from waiting in an endless state for a reply. The error should be triggered by the server being overloaded; thus, the response back to the client or application notifies them that the server is taking too long to respond. When a client makes an API call to a server, the server only begins the countdown timer when the server receives the request and begins counting how long it takes to respond. In most cases, this error is caused by network latency.

The common element of error codes 408, 504, and 599 is that they are seen and used in cases that can be linked to limiting—whether the issue is limited resources on the server, the network, or timing. Rate limiting in an API is an important design concept because it prevents an API from being overwhelmed by too many requests. Consequently, API rate limiting is put in place as a method of defense. No matter whether the request is genuine or malicious, rating limiting should be implemented in an API design to ensure service availability and performance.

As you saw with the IMDb API, rate limiting is applied based on the developer's account. As you can see in the example shown in Figure 6-13, even the top tier account does not permit unlimited use. This method used by IMDb and other API providers is referred to as a *developer rate limiter* in which the number of API requests is tied into the developer's account or API key. Another type of rate limiter is a *concurrent rate limiter*. This method tracks or limits the number of parallel sessions. They could be limited based on developer, IP address,

API key, or any other type of identifier—even developer location, such as country. Concurrency is used to help prevent intentional attacks such as DDoS attacks.

NOTE When limits are reached, the APIs return a limiting signal or a 429 HTTP response.

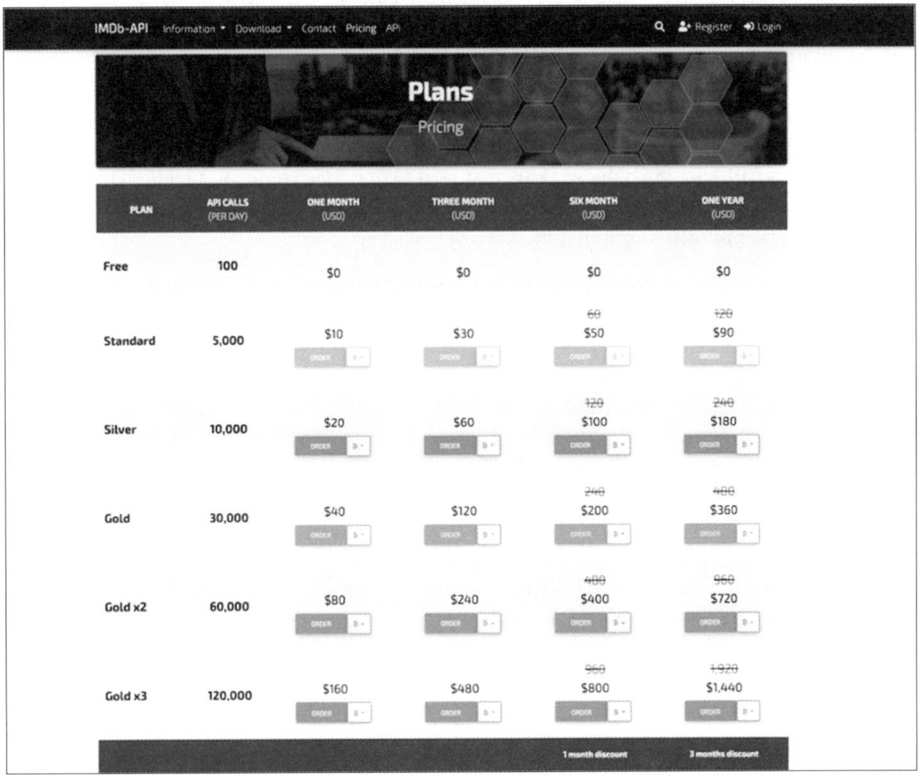

IMDb-API Information Download Contact Pricing API Register Login

Plans

Pricing

PLAN	API CALLS (PER DAY)	ONE MONTH (USD)	THREE MONTH (USD)	SIX MONTH (USD)	ONE YEAR (USD)
Free	100	$0	$0	$0	$0
Standard	5,000	$10	$30	~~60~~ $50	~~120~~ $90
Silver	10,000	$20	$60	~~120~~ $100	~~240~~ $180
Gold	30,000	$40	$120	~~240~~ $200	~~480~~ $360
Gold x2	60,000	$80	$240	~~480~~ $400	~~960~~ $720
Gold x3	120,000	$160	$480	~~960~~ $800	~~1,920~~ $1,440
				1 month discount	3 months discount

Figure 6-13 *API Rate Limiting in IMDb Based on Developer Accounts*

There are several rate limiting techniques and algorithms for measuring and limiting rates. Depending on the developer case, each has its own implications and caveats.

Token bucket is like an allowance. Before the API call is allowed to continue, the token bucket is checked to see whether there are any tokens in it. If there is a token in the bucket, the request is able to continue. If, however, the token bucket is empty, the request is denied. Tokens are added in a fixed rate, depending on the agreement and contract, such as per day, per hour, or even per minute.

Leaky bucket is similar to token bucket: the rate is limited by the amount that can drip or leak out of the bucket. The leaky bucket algorithm allows a client or application to make an unlimited number of requests in sporadic bursts of time. This technique helps shape or smooth out traffic if it is expecting the traffic will burst instead of discarding the request when a threshold or limit is reached.

There is also the fixed window (also known as simple window). As the term *fixed* implies, a fixed rate tracks the number of requests being made with a counter. This rate is then administered via a time interval. This permits only the fixed number of requests in the time allowed. For example, if a client or application is allowed to make 1000 calls per day, they could make these calls within 30 minutes and saturate the API resources.

Sliding window addresses the issues that can occur with the fixed window algorithm. The sliding window algorithm, like the leaky bucket, helps smooth out traffic. It can do this by setting a counter, but it considers the previous window to shape the traffic, estimating the size of the current request rate for the current window. This creates a rolling window smoothing out the traffic.

Caching

Caching can improve the performance of an API and lower the number of requests being sent to the server. API caching achieves this result by using an expiration mechanism. On the server, caching reduces the need to send a full response back to the client. In both cases, it reduces network bandwidth requirements.

There are two main types of cache headers: expires and cache-control. The expires header sets a timer for a date/time in the future, and after it expires, the client needs to send a new request to the API. Cache-control is a preferred expiration mechanism (or a failsafe for expiration caching). The cache-control header states how long the cache will be available. Cache-control has several options, referred to as directives. The directives, described here, determine whether a response is cacheable and can be set to specifically determine how cache requests are handled.

- **no-cache:** The content can be cached but must be revalidated for every request until the server provides the content. This directive checks to see if there is an updated version. The no-cache directive uses the ETag header (a response header uses a token that identifies the version or state of a resource if a resource changes, as does the ETag).
- **no-store:** This directive is normally used for sensitive data (such as credit card or bank details). This means the cache cannot be stored.
- **public:** This directive means the resource can be stored by any cache and by any intermediate caches.
- **private:** Unlike public, this directive can be cached only by a client and not by an intermediate cache.
- **max-age:** This directive indicates the maximum time that a cached response should be used (seconds). The maximum value is 1 year (31,536,000 seconds).

Figure 6-14 shows the three types of API cache models. The first is a client, or private, cache model; it lives on a client machine. Typically, this type of cache is used by an individual developer or application. A proxy cache resides between the client and the API server. Some **content delivery networks/content distribution networks (CDNs)** and ISPs (Internet service providers) use a proxy cache because the API is meant to be used by many developers or applications. The final example is an API server, or gateway, cache; it is configured on the API server itself. An API gateway responds to a client or application request by looking up the endpoint response from the cache instead of making a new request.

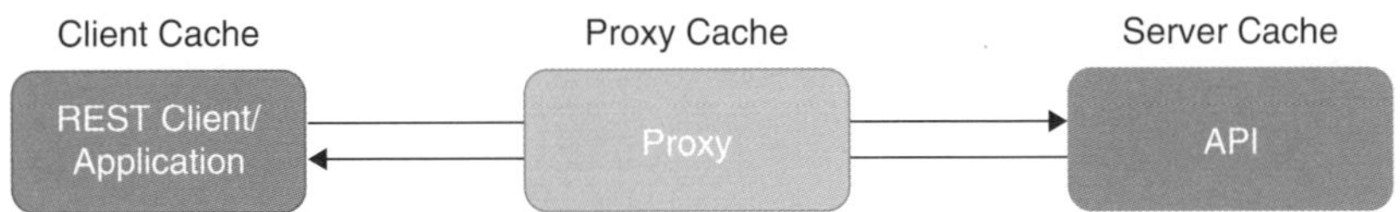

Figure 6-14 *Three Types of API Cache Models*

Exam Preparation Tasks

As mentioned in the section "How to Use This Book" in the Introduction, you have a couple of choices for exam preparation: the exercises here, Chapter 17, "Final Preparation," and the exam simulation questions in the Pearson Test Prep Software Online.

Review All Key Topics

Review the most important topics in this chapter, noted with the Key Topic icon in the outer margin of the page. Table 6-3 lists a reference of these key topics and the page numbers on which each is found.

Table 6-3 Key Topics for Chapter 6

Key Topic Element	Description	Page Number
Paragraph	Add a CLI wrapper	174
Section	API Design Considerations	177
Section	API Authentication Models	179
Section	Flow Control (Pagination vs. Streaming)	181
Figure 6-12	Stateless versus Stateful Connection Differences Between RESTful APIs and Streaming APIs	183
Section	Caching	188

Complete Tables and Lists from Memory

There are no memory tables or lists for this chapter.

Define Key Terms

Define the following key terms from this chapter and check your answers in the glossary:

Transport Layer Security (TLS), software development kit (SDK), OpenAPI Specification (OAS), content delivery network/content distribution network (CDN), SwaggerHub, API inside-out design, API outside-in/user interface (API first approach), pagination

References

URL	QR Code
https://swagger.io/tools/swaggerhub/	

URL	QR Code
https://imdb-api.com/swagger/IMDb-API/swagger.json	
https://github.com/CiscoDevNet/DNAC-Python-SDK	
https://en.wikipedia.org/wiki/Command-line_interface	
https://click.palletsprojects.com/en/8.0.x/why/	
http://www.rfc-editor.org/rfc/rfc3986.txt	
https://datatracker.ietf.org/doc/html/rfc6455	
https://www.nginx.com	

CHAPTER 7

Application Deployment

This chapter covers the following topics:

- **The Evolution of Application Responsibilities:** This section covers the background and the transition from monolithic silos to cross-functional teams.
- **CI/CD Pipeline Implementation:** This section helps you understand CI, CD, and GitOps principles and functionality and how application deployment has changed over time.
- **Application Deployment Methods over Time:** This section investigates different cloud deployments, the steps required, and proper app design for cloud portability.
- **Software Practices for Operability: The 12-Factor App:** This section explores key components that make for scalable, available, and observable applications in both on-premises and cloud-based data centers.

This chapter maps to the *Developing Applications Using Cisco Core Platforms and APIs v1.0 (350-901)* Exam Blueprint Section 4.0, "Application Deployment and Security," specifically subsections 4.2, 4.5, and 4.6.

Traditionally, after an application was ideated, created, and developed, the responsibility of the development team ended, and the resulting work product was given to the operations teams to deploy and maintain for the end users. However, over the past decade, the demarcation that once existed between the two teams has blurred, especially as software development methodologies became iterative and agile, rather than releases at specific points in time when features obtained critical mass. The resulting change in approach has created not only many new ways that applications can move from code to production but also changes in the ongoing maintenance and improvement of the application, as well as where that application resides in relation to both the application owner and the users.

To this end, several organization structures and philosophies have been borne that enable organizations to make such a drastic shift, including the hybridization of development and operations (DevOps) and teams focused on maintaining and ensuring the stability of the application and its underlying infrastructure using automated processes and enhanced visibility enabled through new application design approaches. These teams work in tandem, leveraging automated code test, build, and deployment methodologies for both infrastructure as well as applications to ensure that applications are delivered reliably and consistently to everyone, regardless of whether those applications are hosted in a private or public cloud.

This chapter provides context around this foundational shift in application development and delivery, starting with the early days of developers and system administrators, through modern-day agile teams delivering microservices-based applications to a cloud provider with the click of a mouse or a commit to the main branch of code. Although the focus of this chapter is on applications, methodologies appropriate and required for the underlying infrastructure of the application are covered also, because this is a foundational requirement for reliable delivery. Finally, concepts and ideas for designing an application for this new paradigm are covered and intertwined throughout the discussion as key points for any development teams.

"Do I Know This Already?" Quiz

The "Do I Know This Already?" quiz allows you to assess whether you should read this entire chapter thoroughly or jump to the "Exam Preparation Tasks" section. If you are in doubt about your answers to these questions or your own assessment of your knowledge of the topics, read the entire chapter. Table 7-1 lists the major headings in this chapter and their corresponding "Do I Know This Already?" quiz questions. You can find the answers in Appendix A, "Answers to the 'Do I Know This Already?' Quizzes."

Table 7-1 "Do I Know This Already?" Section-to-Question Mapping

Foundation Topics Section	Questions
The Evolution of Application Responsibilities	1–2
CI/CD Pipeline Implementation	3–5
Application Deployment Methods over Time	6–7
Software Practices for Operability: The 12-Factor App	8

1. What is the core tenet of DevOps?
   a. A spreading of work to limit failure domains
   b. Training operations teams to write code
   c. A cultural shift focused on empathy and understanding
   d. Automating infrastructure and application deployments
2. Where do DevOps and SRE principles overlap?
   a. They bring in new people to institute process changes.
   b. Adoption in changes of process ensures uptime, availability, and understanding of the many-faceted nature of application deployment.
   c. They don't overlap; they are two conceptually different concepts.
   d. Change is enforced from a cultural shift at the top of an organization with no new personnel.
3. What is the purpose of continuous integration?
   a. To integrate new code into production
   b. To add new features to an existing application
   c. To integrate user feedback into the code development process
   d. To build/compile, test, and secure code
4. What data format or language is typically used to build CI/CD pipeline definitions?
   a. JSON
   b. YAML
   c. XML
   d. Python

5. Which of the following is *not* a valid application CD release strategy?
   a. Blue-green
   b. Canary
   c. Pilot
   d. Rolling
6. What does a serverless infrastructure provide to an end user?
   a. Code runs without servers.
   b. Operations and management of the server platform and its underlying dependencies are removed.
   c. Code runs anywhere, automatically.
   d. All of these answers are correct.
7. Which statements about cloud abstraction are true? (Choose two.)
   a. More abstraction requires less management of the underlying compute for the application.
   b. More abstraction provides more flexibility in how the code is deployed and run.
   c. More abstraction requires more management of the underlying compute for the application.
   d. More abstraction provides less flexibility in how the code is deployed and run.
8. What is a 12-factor app?
   a. Twelve areas of unit testing that an application undergoes before being moved to production
   b. Twelve aspects of the user experience that every app should adhere to
   c. Twelve tests of security and application functionality to be performed during a CI/CD pipeline build
   d. Twelve best-practice recommendations on designing and delivering a web-based application

Foundation Topics

The Evolution of Application Responsibilities

Application development and delivery have gone through a drastic shift in the past several decades, creating new roles, methodologies, and processes along the way. Prior to any discussion of how things have evolved, it is important to set a baseline of terminology and tools because the evolution of these processes, methodologies, and mindsets has created a bit of confusion and blurring of lines, even for the most experienced individuals. After the definitions have been established, it becomes much easier to see where tooling, processes, or both are required to achieve the end result of application deployment.

The Hybridization of Development and Operations

On the surface, development and operations are tasked with different responsibilities (sometimes in conflict with one another) for the apps and infrastructure that support the end customers of a business. In the traditional software development lifecycle (SDLC), developers are responsible for adding new features, bug fixes, or product enhancements for the applications that directly impact anyone who uses those applications or services. These developers would work within their defined teams to prioritize the tasks that were to be accomplished within the window of time in which the work was slated. When the work was completed and tested, the resulting work product was shipped to the operations team to deploy and run.

Where development left off, operations picked up. This team (or set of teams, depending on the application and infrastructure) was responsible for keeping the application or system functional and responsive for the end customers. This team was also thought of as the front-line support for any issues that manifested, either through the deployment or through operation of the application/system at scale (both in network and in load) that wasn't feasible during testing in the development lifecycle.

You can easily see how these two teams could quickly come in conflict with one another: operations teams blaming developers as being "lazy" in their code by making assumptions or not testing the full suite of features/options/functionality and developers blaming operations for being resistant to change and always saying "no" to updates or new deployments to support the application/system. This conflict, which is very unproductive for cohesive culture within an organization, also creates problems for end users of the application or system because features are slow to be rolled out and adopted against the codebase, resulting in a less than satisfactory experience.

While the root causes for the distrust vary by organization and team, much of the friction is caused by the seemingly opposing ideas of the two teams: development is supposed to add new features, whereas operations is tasked with keeping the application or system running at all times. New features or bug fixes merged into the production codebase could have unintended knock-on effects that could require operations to troubleshoot an issue beyond their control, while development must respond to the needs of the end users to ensure a quality experience, attract new users, or prevent users from abandoning the service for something else.

You could additionally make an argument that some of the issue stems from trust between the teams. Neither team believes that the other is operating in good faith and is only focused on the metrics that they are judged on, rather than working in tandem to ensure that the ultimate metric is achieved, supporting end users throughout their journey within the application or service.

The Journey to DevOps

In 2009, the term **DevOps** was first coined by Patrick Debois. The portmanteau of *development* and *operations* was followed by the term *days* as the name of the conference that he arranged in October that year. The use of the term rocketed from there and has been used in a variety of contexts ever since. However, over the years the term has been conflated to mean a variety of things, some of which are encompassed in DevOps, some of which are tangential to, and some that are simply used incorrectly (whether intentional or not).

DevOps is rooted in the principle that while both development and operations have different roles to fill within the delivery of applications and services to end users, they are both there to enable a business to perform its end function for those customers and that the conflict that arises between these two functions creates a friction point that hinders the end goal. To efficiently create and deliver an application or service, the two teams must ensure a strong working relationship and have empathy for the critical roles that each plays in enabling the business; in short, "developers that have operational mindsets and operations teams that think like developers."

In addition to the cross-functional nature of the teams, there are several generally accepted practices for DevOps teams to implement within their environment.

- An ability to automate the infrastructure lifecycle process
- A version control system (VCS) or some other source code management (SCM) platform
- An automated build process, including testing and security scanning
- An automated delivery or deployment process, with an agreed-upon methodology for deploying the code into production prior to full rollout
- Observability and instrumentation to provide required metrics back to measure against key performance indicators
- A real-time communications system that can link human interactions with feedback from observability instrumentation

A Cultural Shift

What often gets lost in any discussion of DevOps is that an organization does not simply "buy DevOps." It is not the tools, the process, or even a job role at its core; it's a cultural change and standard method of operation that needs to be adopted within an organization. This requires an organization that embraces change and failure, is open and transparent in communication (and systems, code, and metrics), and most importantly, creates and fosters trust between organizations. Only through embracing this culture can an organization decide on the actual implementation of how DevOps will look internally, from roles and responsibilities, tooling, and operational processes. These processes work toward these goals of embracing a culture of change and agility, ensuring sources of truth for all code that all have visibility to, providing testing and validation of code prior to release, and enabling automated infrastructure changes, allowing teams to reduce errors and focus on higher-level problems associated with enabling the business. However, the tooling, team organizational and reporting structures, and even the methodologies used to release the software vary drastically from organization to organization (and sometimes between business entities within an organization). This is the flexibility (and some would say challenge) with implementing DevOps; there's no single way to perform these functions, and it can take many small changes or iterations to settle on the exact tooling and procedures for an organization or entity. As DevOps has roots in agile software development methodology, some would say this is a feature rather than a bug.

The Emergence of the Site Reliability Engineer(ing)

The concept of **site reliability engineering (SRE)** predates the creation of the term *DevOps*. Originally a concept of the Google engineering teams, the idea of the SRE was to ensure the reliability and uptime of the systems used within Google. This original team of SREs was tasked with spending approximately 50 percent of their time on operations tasks, with the other half of their time focused on product development and management duties. This approach provided a natural visibility into both the creation and design of the applications, as well as the view of the requirements of running code on large-scale production systems.

Modern-day SREs generally have backgrounds in software design and engineering, systems engineering, system administration, and network design and engineering (or some permutation of the listed competencies). These individuals act as a conduit, assisting in bridging the gaps between operations and development, while also providing leadership and vision beyond the sprint, anticipating and remediating potential issues before they appear to ensure utmost reliability. In its purest form, SRE can be practiced and performed by anyone; it needn't be a specific job title.

The distinction here, while somewhat pedantic, is important when referring to the differences in organizational concepts and processes. DevOps principles work on breaking down the walls that exist between development and operations through culture and a blending of teams and responsibilities (though everyone has their own unique strengths and weaknesses), whereas SRE looks to solve the silo problem through adding additional people with the responsibility of translation to the process. Neither solution is right or wrong, but is a by-product of the organization and business unit to which these principles are applied, the current talent of the contributing teams, and the ability to upskill and learn new processes. To use the common answer within IT, "it depends."

SRE Responsibilities and Tenets

Much like DevOps, there is no firm consensus on what exactly is in and out of scope for an SRE. The responsibilities often vary in scale and scope depending on the organization and the product or service they deliver. Additionally, SREs may be scope-limited based on their underlying knowledge or the needs of the business, creating specific SREs focused on infrastructure or networks, observability and monitoring, or focused on a specific product or service offered by the organization. These classifications and delineations can be mixed and matched to ensure the most positive outcome to the services and products being delivered to the business.

Despite there being no written rules about SRE, some generally accepted practices are mentioned most often within the definition of SRE:

- The lifecycle of the infrastructure is automated, especially anything that introduces "toil" into the build-and-deploy process.
- A rigid focus is placed on reliability above and beyond what would be considered acceptable through definition of SLAs/SLOs. This could be achieved through systems, network, or application design, or a combination of the three to achieve the desired reliability, latency, or efficiency specs that exceed objectives.
- Anything implemented as part of the infrastructure lifecycle process should include instrumentation and observability. This also should follow the same principle as reliability, in that the observability should provide information that isn't known to be needed ahead of time (that is, being ahead of the curve).

Out of these practices, you could create principles that SRE should strive for that are tangential to these tenets. Again, there is no common standard for these principles, but by combing through SRE requirements docs posted to job boards, you can see the varying responsibilities that these individuals can have, but you can draw a parallel with these responsibilities against these core tenets. Some SREs specifically focus on things like capacity planning and infrastructure design, which align with the second and third points, because planning and design can't occur without proper understanding of the current environment's load, latency, and growth in usage over time (which requires observability tooling). Other SREs may be focused on the operational efficiencies gained through creation of CI/CD pipelines, which focuses on the energy, time, and frustration spent in moving apps from development to production in a secure manner (the "toil" mentioned previously) but doing so in a fashion that ensures reliability and uptime of the application and system. This function touches on all three principles because automated infrastructure and deployments are beneficial only when uptime is compromised and any resulting issue with the application/system is identified through detailed observability at all layers.

SRE vs. DevOps

As you look over the practices and principles of SRE, you can easily see the alignment and overlap that they have with DevOps and some of the responsibilities that fall out of that culture. This overlap is not accidental because both ideas came from similar lineage within the evolutionary path of the SDLC. However, the ways in which they achieve the overall goals differ in their approach.

Recall that DevOps is a change in culture, breaking down the traditional walls that existed between development and operations through empathy and cross-functional teams that span both sides of the application/system experience. The idea is that through cross-pollination of all members of the team, everyone views all aspects of delivering the outcome to the business with a similar lens, leading to better outcomes for all. The tooling and process that follow this organizational shift are ancillary to the overall shift.

SRE, on the other hand, does not require the outright blending of development and operations. Rather, it achieves this goal through specific individuals or teams that are tasked with overseeing the integration work needed to achieve (and exceed) the outcomes required by the business for the service or application. While culture must shift in support and recognition of the work that SRE is tasked with performing, it may not necessarily be as drastic a shift as that within DevOps.

Finally, to put a simplistic point on this, Google engineers, in their popular SRE books, state that "SRE implements DevOps," further confusing everything and providing the perspective that everything is made up and nothing really matters (at least in title). The important takeaway is that empathy and understanding between development and operations are critical to being able to deploy and maintain services at scale while ensuring changes and updates are added in a timely fashion to the codebase.

Continuous Integration/Continuous Delivery (Deployment)

In this chapter alone, **continuous integration/continuous delivery** (or deployment), also known as CI/CD, has been mentioned on several occasions and is a key piece to implement regardless of whether SRE or DevOps methodology is being followed. While *CI* and *CD* are often used together, *CI/CD* is a combination of two concepts, driven together to create an automated outcome for both development and operations teams. The "pipeline," the process that software goes through as it is put through the CI/CD process, is also only a function or sidecar to a larger **version control system (VCS)**. This VCS provides some integration with the "runner" that will perform the actual integration delivery/deployment process based on the configuration applied to a specific repository. This process runs whenever an update is added to the repository (either in the "main" or a feature branch), and the process can be completely customized to fit the requirements of the repository of code that is being worked on.

The choice of VCS and CI/CD provider is driven mostly by the organization, collaboration and security requirements, and third-party integrations with other functions (such as security and vulnerability scanning). Typical VCS include git, svn, hg, or p4 (though git is most prevalent), any of which could be hosted on-premises or through an SaaS offering. After the VCS system is selected, the desired CI/CD platform can be chosen. Some of them, such as Jenkins, are external applications that require integration into the chosen repositories, whereas others, such as GitLab-CI, integrate directly with GitLab to provide a single portal for both source code and pipelines. For the scope of this section, the choice of VCS and CI provider is largely inconsequential to the overall understanding of the functions they provide, and this section focuses on those functions.

NOTE Specific implementations of a VCS and technology (such as a git-based implementation with GitHub, GitLab, or BitBucket) are referred to as a **source code manager (SCM)**. Although *VCS* and *SCM* are sometimes used interchangeably, these two terms refer to two separate concepts.

As mentioned earlier, the full pipeline provided by a CI/CD system is two discrete functions, integration and delivery/deployment, which are interrelated but serve two purposes and divisions in labor. The following sections describe this division and the functions that occur within the two subsystems in more detail.

Continuous Integration (CI)

Continuous integration is the cornerstone of a pipeline and generally the first item to be implemented when organizations need to accelerate the speed at which code moves into production, because without the integration of code, it cannot be delivered or deployed to the end systems. As with most concepts addressed so far, what comprises the act of integration depends on the organization and the level at which different stages can be successfully automated as part of the pipeline.

The need for CI arises with the nature of distributed development teams working across a variety of segments of the code concurrently, using the tools within the VCS (such as support for "git") to commit, branch, and merge the respective features and fixes into the mainline codebase. Rather than a single individual writing code and compiling it against "their machine" (which could have specific dependencies or one-off configurations applied to it that make the software compile and run as expected), the CI platform creates a single platform against which all code is linted (validated for proper syntax), tested against a variety of units or other tests (testing within the code itself, rather than at the application/functionality level), scanned against security vulnerabilities, and published as a complete software package (also known as an "artifact" of the CI process). These artifacts can be packaged as releases, ready to be shipped off to a staging or production environment through manual interaction with the finished package and the end systems on which it will be deployed.

The flexibility of the CI pipeline allows for complete customization of what tests are performed where and to what level. For example, as developers work on adding new features, they may create a branch within the repository to separate this work from the main branch. At each commit to the branch, the code could be put through a series of unit tests to ensure that the code itself works at a functional level based on desired inputs and outputs. These tests provide feedback at every commit being made and may be sufficient for work within a specific feature. However, once the code is merged from the feature branch into the main code, it may undergo additional testing from vulnerability or security scans to ensure that the entire package as written does not contain a known vulnerability, which may not have been tested adequately in performing the same security analysis against the code for a single feature. This level of customization is entirely possible within the pipeline.

Continuous Delivery: One of the CDs

The latter half of the CI/CD pipeline is the method in which the resulting integration artifact makes it from the VCS release system out to the end users. Most sources online reference CD as a monolithic item that is always the same, but subtle differences exist, depending on whether the resultant pipeline uses continuous *delivery* or continuous *deployment*. Although the two have a similar outcome, the resulting integrated software from the VCS is deployed to end users; both ideas are covered in this section for completeness. In a real-world environment, only one method would be used per code repository, though both methods could be used within a single organization or business unit, depending on release methodologies in place.

The idea behind continuous delivery is that after the resultant software is tested and built, it is "shipped," or placed in a location in which it can be manually placed on the infrastructure, often in a Q/A or test environment. This allows for some level of human control over the environment, ensuring that the supporting infrastructure and required set of test users are ready prior to allowing the application or service to "go live." This ensures focused testing across the desired range of users and situations, allowing staggered or segmented release of the resultant product in a controlled manner, as defined by the organization's methodologies or processes. When the testing phase is completed and the key results, metrics, and performance indicators are reviewed and found to be satisfactory, the code is pushed to the production environment.

Continuous Deployment: The Other CD

Continuous deployment takes the concept of continuous delivery one step further. Rather than relying on manual intervention to move the software into test and then to production, continuous deployment automates the movement into production. While the process doesn't move every node/system to the new version of the application/service at once, it assumes that end users, rather than designated test or Q/A groups, are responsible for testing the service. As you can imagine, this testing requires an understanding and readiness of the supporting infrastructure, as well as levels of observability and instrumentation to be able to identify issues with the rollout as they appear (sometimes users are not aware of or are more tolerant of less than expected performance and may not report issues or be aware of how to report them). Teams responsible for monitoring the application, infrastructure, and overall performance must also be aware of how the new version is released into production.

Like both CI and continuous *delivery*, the way in which the deployment of the committed code occurs is entirely up to the way the pipeline is constructed. In general terms, only the "main" code branch is deployed directly to production because it includes all the different components that make up the full application/service. Feature branches are still worked on independently and validated through the defined CI process for nonmain branches. When the code from the feature branch is merged into the main branch, a separate CI process, followed by the deployment process, is executed, and the new code moves into production. If code is inadvertently committed to the main branch, the pipeline should be written well enough to ensure that it catches and prevents broken code from being automatically moved into production, but it is entirely within the realm of possibility that it may pass the required tests but not function correctly in production. Because of this, strong adherence to the branch/merge discipline, a focus on unit and functional testing, and a continuous improvement cycle for the pipeline should all be implemented to adhere to the rigorous uptimes required by production systems, applications, and services.

CI/CD Pipeline Implementation

Conceptually, *continuous integration* and *continuous deployment* create a simple process to move code from a VCS repository into a deployment environment. However, within the overall pipeline are several stages to the process, ensuring that the code is verified and tested before implementing in an environment (with potential user impact). While every pipeline is different based on the VCS, development language, application, system requirements, and so on, some general assumptions can be made to apply broadly across most pipelines and are covered in the following sections. The important point to remember is that the process is flexible and that the end-state pipeline should reflect the requirements of the code and organization.

Example 7-1 illustrates a sample CI/CD pipeline for network automation using Ansible. This pipeline has several stages that will validate the syntax of the committed files, deploy to a given environment (test, prod), and then verify that the changes deployed did not affect the reachability of services within the network.

Example 7-1 *Sample CI/CD Pipeline*

```
stages:
  - validate
  - deploy_to_prod
  - deploy_to_test
  - verify_deploy_to_prod
  - verify_deploy_to_test
  - verify_website_reachability

lint:
  stage: validate
  image: geerlingguy/docker-centos8-ansible:latest
  variables:
  script:
    - ansible-playbook --syntax-check -i inventory/prod.yaml site.yaml
    - ansible-playbook --syntax-check -i inventory/test.yaml site.yaml

deploy_to_prod:
  image: geerlingguy/docker-centos8-ansible:latest
  stage: deploy_to_prod
  script:
    - echo "Deploy to prod env"
    - ansible-playbook -i inventory/prod.yaml site.yaml
  environment:
    name: production
  only:
  - master
```

7

```
deploy_to_test:
  image: geerlingguy/docker-centos8-ansible:latest
  stage: deploy_to_test
  script:
    - echo "Deploy to test env"
    - ansible-playbook -i inventory/test.yaml site.yaml
  environment:
    name: test
  only:
  - test

verify_test_environment:
  image: ciscotestautomation/pyats:latest-robot
  stage: verify_deploy_to_test
  environment:
    name: test
  script:
    - pwd
    - cd tests
    # important: need to add our current directory to PYTHONPATH
    - export PYTHONPATH=$PYTHONPATH:$(pwd)
    - robot test.robot

  artifacts:
      name: "TEST_${CI_JOB_NAME}_${CI_COMMIT_REF_NAME}"
      when: always
      paths:
        - ./tests/log.html
        - ./tests/report.html
        - ./tests/output.xml
  only:
  - test

verify_prod_environment:
  image: ciscotestautomation/pyats:latest-robot
  stage: verify_deploy_to_prod
  environment:
    name: test
  script:
    - pwd
    - cd tests
    # important: need to add our current directory to PYTHONPATH
    - export PYTHONPATH=$PYTHONPATH:$(pwd)
    - robot prod.robot
```

```
  artifacts:
     name: "PROD_${CI_JOB_NAME}_${CI_COMMIT_REF_NAME}"
      when: always
      paths:

        - ./tests/log.html
        - ./tests/report.html
        - ./tests/output.xml
  only:
  - master

internet_sites:
  image: ciscotestautomation/pyats:latest-robot
  stage: verify_website_reachability
  environment:
    name: test
  script:
    - pwd
    - cd tests/websites/
    - make test
  only:
  - master
```

Pipeline Components

A CI/CD pipeline is composed of several stages, each of which has a defined action or set of actions defined within it. These stages are declared at the top of a CI/CD definition file (usually written in YAML, but varies based on CI/CD provider) and define the process in moving the code from source to finished product. Figure 7-1 shows the process for a simple CI/CD pipeline in which the code progresses serially through each of the defined stages of the process.

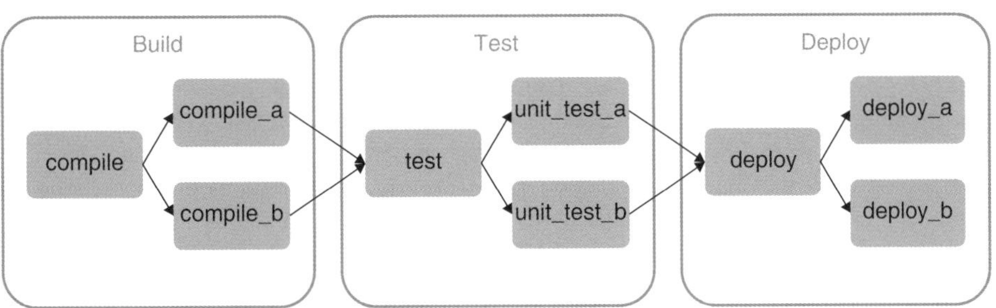

Figure 7-1 *Serial CI/CD Pipeline*

The flow illustrates that the code moves serially between stages, which can be sufficient depending on the end requirements, but it is possible to create pipelines that work in parallel, building different components with independent serial pipelines, as shown in Figure 7-2.

7

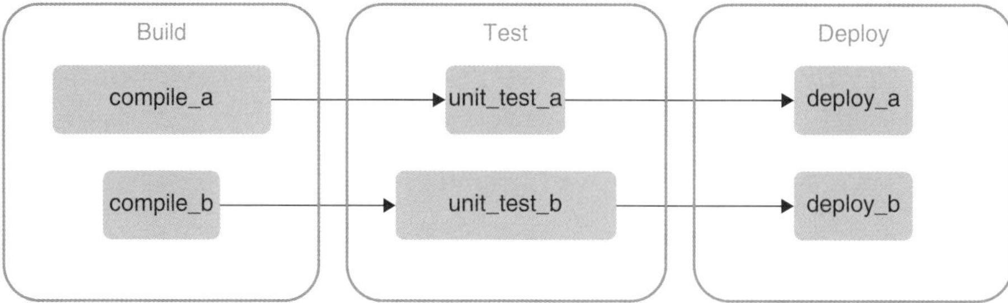

Figure 7-2 *Directed Acyclic Pipeline*

The pipeline is also flexible in how the stages are defined and what is included in each stage. A well-designed pipeline (especially one deploying the finished product to the infrastructure) should be created in such a way that adequate testing, both at the code and app level, prevents catastrophic failure when the app is deployed. This may also include security analysis of code dependencies, or vulnerability scans after the app has been packaged, to ensure that any application moving into production is safe and secure.

Another flexibility of the pipeline is that the same CI and CD process does not need to be followed for every branch created within the VCS being used. It is possible to define requirements for feature or bugfix pipelines that may include the integration and testing but not create the full package (or create but not deploy to an environment). This approach ensures that any new commits are checked at the code level but not fully packaged (or deployed), eliminating the need to ensure code will run at every commit (and possibly saving resources/cost if running in a cloud environment). However, when the feature/fix is determined to be complete and the code is moved to the "main" branch, a more complete or comprehensive pipeline can be invoked that includes the security and vulnerability scanning, as well as the delivery and deployment of the application to a running environment.

The final decision (and flexibility) within the pipeline is the choice of execution method (often called executor). These executors are the method in which the "work" being done by the pipeline is performed and can be performed through direct shell access, virtual machine instantiation, or container-based methods like Docker and Kubernetes (often abbreviated *K8s* due to there being eight letters between the *k* and *s* in the name). Because of their prevalence and ease of use, most pipelines call on one or more container images to perform the desired actions. These containers can provide a sanitized build environment with all required dependencies included and can be pulled from either a public (such as Docker Hub) or private (hosted internally using JFrog Artifactory or similar) container registry. When run, the CI/CD pipeline passes the repository into the container, performs any linting, compiles (or equivalent in interpreted languages) the code, performs unit or external testing, passes the completed artifact to an external location, and then deploys the finalized application to an environment, whether testing, staging, or production.

Build

The build stage is responsible for moving the code from its source to a verified and final product. The resultant product differs depending on source code, because languages like C, C++, Java, Python, and Go create binary files (or bytecode), whereas languages like Ruby do not. However, the result is that the code has been linted (checked for syntactical errors/omissions), compiled, and (optionally) built into a Docker container.

Test

After the image is built (regardless of binary file, Docker container, or otherwise), automated testing helps validate that the code is functional at a base level. This may include performing unit tests of individual components of the functions of the code, performing load or performance testing, or validating interoperability with resources required by the application. By automating these tests, developers ensure their apps deploy correctly to the environment and behave as anticipated or expected. Thorough testing and validation are required to ensure that the application is functional as expected; untested functions or integrations are not caught in this stage and can be a blind spot for developers. Tools like Codecov exist to provide an understanding of how much of the written code is covered by tests within the pipeline, ensuring that as new features are incorporated into the application, testing and coverage can evolve to ensure the automation doesn't provide a false sense of security.

Testing also needn't be a singular phase within the pipeline. Although things like unit tests should be done at the front end of the pipeline, integration and interoperability tests may not occur until the release is deployed within an environment (because there may be no way to perform this test within the pipeline without a deployment). The idea, however, should always be to catch any issues, exceptions, or errors as early as possible within the pipeline as is feasible to prevent those problems from leaking into a production environment.

Release/Deliver

If everything succeeds during the testing phase, the software is moved to the release (or delivery, if keeping with the *continuous delivery* convention) phase. In this stage, the compiled and tested software is moved to an artifact repository so that it is ready to be deployed, whether in manual or automatic fashion. This artifact repository is kept separate from the source code repository because they serve different functions, and it is impractical to include compiled binaries that developers do not need within the main repository.

The artifact repository varies depending on the tooling and privacy required for the finished application. For internal applications leveraging an on-premises CI/CD pipeline, the artifact could be internal file storage accessible via HTTP/FTP, JFrog Artifactory, or an internal Docker registry. If the application is deployed via SaaS applications (such as GitHub), the registry could simply be the "Releases" section of the repository or a container pushed to Docker Hub. Regardless of the location of the repository, the CI/CD pipeline supports the passing of credentials through environment variables or through a secret keystore (such as Vault) to ensure that the credentials can be changed as needed and to ensure that they are not exposed within the pipeline definition file (because it is committed as part of the source code repository). The resulting release can signify the end of the pipeline if the goal is only to deliver the application (for example, delivering an application within a container to be consumed by other users within their environments), or if moving the application is required to be a manual process due to a business process.

Deploy

After the application has been released and stored within the artifact repository, it can then be deployed to one or more environments. To deploy the resultant application to the infrastructure, the pipeline must be made aware of the systems on which it is to deploy the application. While the deployment methodology varies based on the organization or development team, it is common practice to use some sort of automated configuration management platform, such as Puppet, Ansible, or SaltStack. If the infrastructure supporting the application needs to be reprovisioned, any configuration changes could be provided by Puppet, Ansible, or SaltStack, but also could be done using Terraform to scaffold in preparation for the app's deployment.

Much like testing, deployment can occur at multiple stages of the pipeline. Deploying directly to production may not be in everyone's plans, so a deployment stage could be added when a feature branch is added to a testing branch, which will deploy the code to a test environment, wherein a limited set of users or testers will validate the function of the app under conditions that simulate the real world. When this manual testing is deemed sufficient, a merge can be performed between the testing and main branch, resulting in a deployment to production of the tested code.

Deployment also offers several different options in rolling the finished product out to the desired environment. While the product could be deployed to tests all at once, given the small subset of users, production deployment is done in such a way that the "blast radius" or number of users affected during any issue encountered during a rollout is minimized. Because the deployment phase is aware of the infrastructure, the finished application can be deployed using one of several common methods:

- **Rolling:** The application is updated on all nodes in a serial fashion, resulting in users potentially hitting different versions of the application, depending on how the ingress traffic is directed, the number of nodes requiring the new release, and the time required to move the node to the new release.
- **Blue-green:** Parallel segments of production are deployed within an environment, allowing for a complete update of one side (for example, blue) while users are still directed to the previous version (for example, green). When the blue nodes are fully updated, the ingress traffic is flipped to direct users to the "blue" rollout. This method enables quick rollbacks of a deployment, at the expense of having duplicate sets of infrastructure to maintain parity.

  When the deployment is deemed to be a success, the green side can be updated to the current version of the code/application and used as the environment for which the next release is deployed to first.
- **Canary:** This release is similar to the rolling release, in that nodes are gradually updated to the new version of the application. However, thresholds define the stages of the rollout, limiting the scope of impact in a failure. For example, a rollout may start with 15 percent of the nodes being rolled out initially. When this segment's rollout is successful, the deployment would then deploy to another 35 percent (making 50 percent of the nodes) and then finally deploy to the remaining 50 percent.

  The canary rollout offers a failsafe above the rolling release without the need for parallel infrastructure required for a blue-green deployment. However, ensuring a successful canary rollout is nontrivial due to the instrumentation and feedback loops required to determine "successful" rollouts. Some CI/CD providers offer integrations to enable a canary rollout, but they require both nondefault configuration to be enabled and infrastructure that supports the required metrics to be returned to determine the success (such as K8s).

Adding Deployment to Integration

While nontrivial, the process taken to perform the integration to software tends to mimic the procedures used to compile software locally on a developer's machine. Although developers need to worry about the abstraction of the executor of the pipeline (such as a container performing the action), they understand these methods and requirements because the process of building or compiling software is part of their usual set of tasks. Because developers are already using VCS tools within their organizations, integration testing generally becomes the first component of the pipeline. This complexity is only modestly increased when using security and vulnerability management utilities. These tools, such as Synk, can be integrated within the pipeline with a few simple commands. Others, such as Dependabot, which analyzes code within a GitHub repository and automatically "bumps" required dependencies to secure and updated versions, or GitGuardian, which scans repositories for leaked secrets, credentials, and API keys, don't even need to be integrated into a pipeline; these tools are enabled within a repo and will scan after a commit and over time as dependency modules are updated.

Moving the integrated result into production is another matter, however. Although DevOps and SRE have broken down the walls that separate developers and operations, developers may still not have a full picture of the infrastructure to which the application will be deployed. Even if the target of the deployment is within public cloud infrastructure, developers within a single application or service may not have the full perspective of the enterprise's cloud.

Integration deployment into a pipeline requires knowledge of state, which is in contrast from the ephemeral actions that are built into integration pipelines. Ensuring that this state is kept up to date as the infrastructure or environments change is critical and can be overlooked if maintainers of the code repository do not adhere to rigor and discipline. Finally, moving the resulting product to the infrastructure requires tooling perform the actual deployment. These tools vary depending on whether the pipeline is focused on infrastructure or applications, but generally leverage products such as Ansible, Terraform, or some other automated configuration management tool (whether it's open source or vendor specific).

7

It is also possible to create delivery pipelines without crafting a full CI/CD pipeline file, but rather using GitOps tooling and integration with a VCS. These delivery tools use various methods (webhooks, APIs) to connect to the VCS and allow for nondeveloper-focused teams to leverage the power of traceability/history, version control, feature branching, source code review, and centralized management of configuration without the (possibly foreign) requirements of full CI/CD integration.

Deploying to Infrastructure (Terraform + Atlantis)

Terraform is a popular tool used for infrastructure provisioning. Terraform uses individually created providers, which contain the possible endpoint APIs that Terraform can use to either retrieve information from or apply configuration to one or more targets. The configuration that Terraform follows or applies is defined in a flat text file using HashiCorp Configuration Language (HCL), which has a similar look and feel to JSON, though the two are not directly interchangeable.

Terraform has several key differences in the way that it works when compared to some of the other utilities in this space, such as Ansible, Salt, and Puppet. The first is that Terraform captures the current state of the target prior to configuration application and then creates a delta between the current and desired state. The previous state is saved such that even after the configuration is applied, the previous state can be restored through a rollback action. Second, Terraform functions on the concept of immutable infrastructure, devices, and targets that are meant to be unchanged, and if any change to the infrastructure is required, it generally destroys and re-creates with the new configuration (rather than updates in place) though there are exceptions to this. Finally, Terraform is written in Go and does not include a mechanism for accessing devices over SSH. The only way that Terraform can interface with a device, controller, or cloud is via REST API. However, Terraform, using its redundancy graph, ensures that regardless of how the configuration is written within the HCL file, it is applied in the correct order against the REST APIs; stepwise or ordered configuration is not required for Terraform to interact with the target's APIs.

Because Terraform defines the end state of the infrastructure in a codified fashion **(Infrastructure as Code, IaC)**, it lends itself to being included as part of a CI/CD pipeline to effect change on the devices or cloud on which applications will be deployed. In an infrastructure pipeline, the HCL configuration files are committed to a branch within a VCS repository, and the pipeline runs the required init, plan, and apply functions against the branch's environment (for example, test). After the configuration is applied, automated testing, such as reachability or verification of the infrastructure control plane, can be performed to ensure the desired outcome is achieved through the configuration. When these tests are completed, the branch can be merged into the main branch, kicking off a deployment to the production infrastructure (and subsequent testing, if desired).

Using Terraform is not without its challenges, however. To assist with this effort, applications such as Atlantis were created, providing an interactive experience between the VCS and the application of the HCL configuration. Atlantis works by listening for webhooks from the VCS, which cause it to perform a Terraform action, such as "plan." When Atlantis performs the action, it returns the results of the action to the VCS via API. These results are displayed within the VCS pull request management menu. A workflow would look like the following:

1. An infrastructure developer creates a Terraform HCL file based on the desired end state.
2. The HCL file is pushed to VCS with a branch.
3. A pull request is initiated within the VCS.
4. Atlantis is mentioned within the VCS PR comment tool to run a "plan" against the HCL.
5. Atlantis runs the desired plan against the target infrastructure using Terraform. Results are then returned to the VCS PR window for review.
6. If all checks out, Atlantis can be invoked again using the **apply** command to deploy the change to the infrastructure, and the PR can be merged into the main code branch.
7. If someone else attempts to create a PR within the same directory before the previous one has been applied, Atlantis prevents the second change from occurring until the first change is either applied or discarded.

It is possible to test Atlantis using a local machine, a GitHub account, and a port-forwarding tool such as ngrok. The host running the Atlantis server binary needs access to the VCS and to the target infrastructure, though if using a developer workstation for testing, the port-forwarding tool can easily expose a URL for the webhooks to be relayed to the workstation without worrying about firewalls and NAT. The device can also utilize VPN connections to the infrastructure, allowing Atlantis to be tested using sandboxes or other infrastructure in remote locations.

Although the Atlantis documentation walks you through the required setup based on VCS, the example uses a Terraform "null-resource." Extending this concept, it is possible to provision some network infrastructure, assuming a Terraform provider exists for that infrastructure. In Examples 7-2 and 7-3, a set of Terraform configurations containing a "variable" file, as well as the desired end state of the fabric, is provided.

Example 7-2 *Atlantis variable.tf File*

```
internet_sites:
variable "user" {
  description = "Login information"
  type        = map
  default     = {
    username = "admin"
    password = "C1sco12345"
    url      = "https://10.10.20.14"
  }
```

Example 7-3 *Atlantis main.tf file*

```
terraform {
  required_providers {
    aci = {
      source = "CiscoDevNet/aci"
    }
  }
}
# Configure the provider with your Cisco APIC credentials.
provider "aci" {
  username = var.user.username
  password = var.user.password
  url      = var.user.url
  insecure = true
}
# Define an ACI Tenant Resource
resource "aci_tenant" "atlantis-testing" {
    name        = "atlantis-testing"
    description = "This tenant is created by terraform using atlantis"
}
```

After this configuration is committed to a branch within a repository and a pull request (PR) created, Atlantis receives the webhook; it processes a workflow like using Terraform on a local workstation (specific Terraform commands are seen in Example 7-4).

Example 7-4 *Atlantis Receiving the Webhook from GitHub and Performing Terraform Actions*

```
{"level":"info","ts":"2021-11-29T16:34:15.437-0700","caller":"events/events_control-
ler.go:318","msg":"identified event as type \"opened\"","json":{}}
{"level":"info","ts":"2021-11-29T16:34:15.437-0700","caller":"events/events_control-
ler.go:346","msg":"executing autoplan","json":{}}
{"level":"info","ts":"2021-11-29T16:34:20.841-0700","caller":"events/work-
ing_dir.go:202","msg":"creating dir \"/Users/qsnyder/.atlantis/repos/qsnyder/
devcor-atlantis/1/default\"","json":{"repo":"qsnyder/devcor-atlantis","pull":"1"}}
{"level":"info","ts":"2021-11-29T16:34:21.757-0700","caller":"events/project_com-
mand_builder.go:266","msg":"found no atlantis.yaml file","json":{"repo":"qsnyder/
devcor-atlantis","pull":"1"}}
{"level":"info","ts":"2021-11-29T16:34:21.757-0700","caller":"events/project_finder.
go:57","msg":"filtered modified files to 2 .tf or terragrunt.hcl files: [main.tf
variable.tf]","json":{"repo":"qsnyder/devcor-atlantis","pull":"1"}}
{"level":"info","ts":"2021-11-29T16:34:21.757-0700","caller":"events/
project_finder.go:78","msg":"there are 1 modified project(s) at path(s):
.","json":{"repo":"qsnyder/devcor-atlantis","pull":"1"}}
{"level":"info","ts":"2021-11-29T16:34:21.757-0700","caller":"events/project_
command_builder.go:271","msg":"automatically determined that there were 1 projects
modified in this pull request: [repofullname=qsnyder/devcor-atlantis path=.]","json"
:{"repo":"qsnyder/devcor-atlantis","pull":"1"}}
{"level":"info","ts":"2021-11-29T16:34:21.758-0700","caller":"events/project_
command_context_builder.go:240","msg":"cannot determine which version to use from
terraform configuration, detected 0 possibilities.","json":{"repo":"qsnyder/
devcor-atlantis","pull":"1"}}
{"level":"info","ts":"2021-11-29T16:34:22.059-0700","caller":"events/project_locker.
go:80","msg":"acquired lock with id \"qsnyder/devcor-atlantis/./default\"","json":
{"repo":"qsnyder/devcor-atlantis","pull":"1"}}
{"level":"info","ts":"2021-11-29T16:34:25.066-0700","caller":"terraform/terraform_
client.go:279","msg":"successfully ran \"/usr/local/bin/terraform init -input=false
-no-color -upgrade\" in \"/Users/qsnyder/.atlantis/repos/qsnyder/devcor-atlantis/1/
default\"","json":{"repo":"qsnyder/devcor-atlantis","pull":"1"}}
{"level":"info","ts":"2021-11-29T16:34:26.319-0700","caller":"terraform/terraform_
client.go:279","msg":"successfully ran \"/usr/local/bin/terraform workspace show\"
in \"/Users/qsnyder/.atlantis/repos/qsnyder/devcor-atlantis/1/default\"","json":
{"repo":"qsnyder/devcor-atlantis","pull":"1"}}
{"level":"info","ts":"2021-11-29T16:34:28.251-0700","caller":"terraform/terraform_
client.go:279","msg":"successfully ran \"/usr/local/bin/terraform plan -input=false
-refresh -no-color -out \\\"/Users/qsnyder/.atlantis/repos/qsnyder/devcor-atlantis/
1/default/default.tfplan\\\"\" in \"/Users/qsnyder/.atlantis/repos/qsnyder/
devcor-atlantis/1/default\"","json":{"repo":"qsnyder/devcor-atlantis","pull":"1"}}
```

This example creates a local artifact (the outfile from Terraform) that can then be applied via communication in the pull request window, as shown in Figure 7-3.

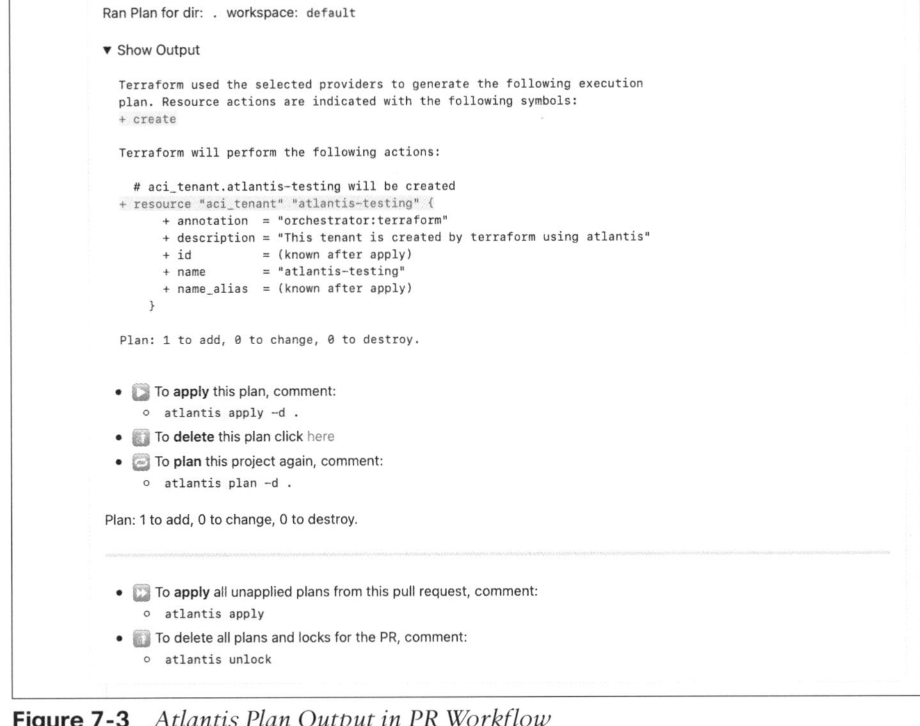

Figure 7-3 *Atlantis Plan Output in PR Workflow*

Applying the plan yields more webhooks to the Atlantis application. This is done through the comment section of the PR workflow, illustrated by Figure 7-4. Example 7-5 shows the output indicating that when the **apply** command is issued, Atlantis issues a **terraform apply**.

Figure 7-4 *Applying a Terraform Plan Within the PR Workflow Using Atlantis*

Example 7-5 *Atlantis Performing an Apply Action Using Terraform*

```
{"level":"info","ts":"2021-11-29T16:37:58.469-0700","caller":"events/events_control-
ler.go:417","msg":"parsed comment as command=\"apply\" verbose=false dir=\"\" work-
space=\"\" project=\"\" flags=\"\"","json":{}}
{"level":"info","ts":"2021-11-29T16:38:04.360-0700","caller":"events/apply_command_
runner.go:110","msg":"pull request mergeable status: true","json":{"repo":"qsnyder/
devcor-atlantis","pull":"1"}}
{"level":"info","ts":"2021-11-29T16:38:04.373-0700","caller":"events/project_com-
mand_context_builder.go:240","msg":"cannot determine which version to use from
terraform configuration, detected 0 possibilities.","json":{"repo":"qsnyder/
devcor-atlantis","pull":"1"}}
{"level":"info","ts":"2021-11-29T16:38:04.373-0700","caller":"runtime/
apply_step_runner.go:37","msg":"starting apply","json":{"repo":"qsnyder/
devcor-atlantis","pull":"1"}}
{"level":"info","ts":"2021-11-29T16:38:06.490-0700","caller":"terraform/terraform_
client.go:279","msg":"successfully ran \"/usr/local/bin/terraform apply -input=false
-no-color \\\"/Users/qsnyder/.atlantis/repos/qsnyder/devcor-atlantis/1/default/
default.tfplan\\\"\" in \"/Users/qsnyder/.atlantis/repos/qsnyder/devcor-atlantis/1/
default\"","json":{"repo":"qsnyder/devcor-atlantis","pull":"1"}}
{"level":"info","ts":"2021-11-29T16:38:06.490-0700","caller":"runtime/apply_step_
runner.go:56","msg":"apply successful, deleting planfile","json":{"repo":"qsnyder/
devcor-atlantis","pull":"1"}}
```

The result is a successful application within the PR window, as well as within the fabric, indicating that a new tenant has been created per the Terraform configuration, with the resulting creation similar to what is seen in Figures 7-5 and 7-6.

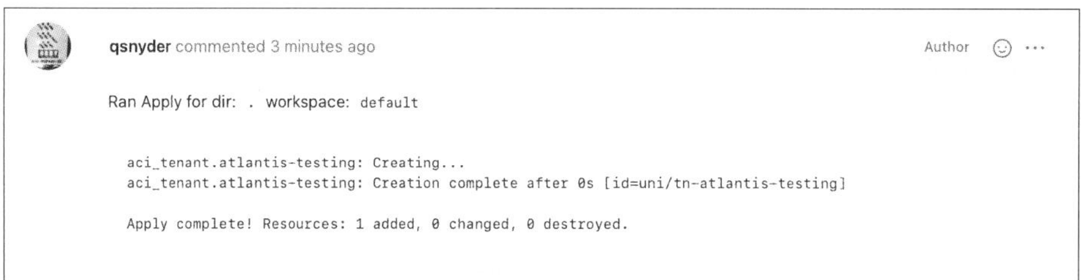

Figure 7-5 *Successful Output from Atlantis Applying Terraform Configuration*

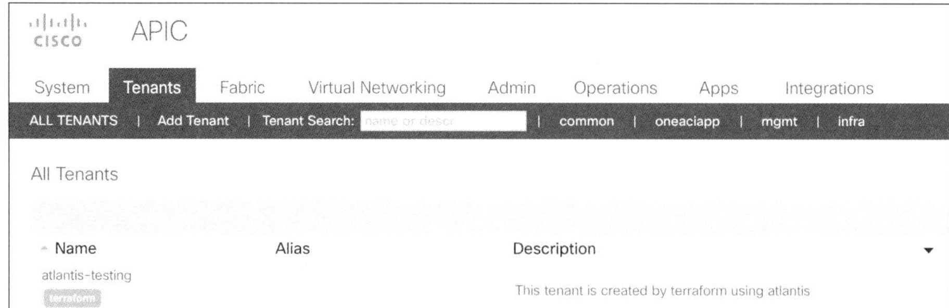

Figure 7-6 *Verification of Tenant Creation Within ACI*

The PR can now be merged inside the repository. This is important because Terraform has locked the workspace from making any changes within the directory, ensuring that only a single PR is effecting change on the infrastructure at any one time. When the PR is merged, this lock is removed and the directory can now have additional changes made to it through the GitOps workflow. This is reflected in the final webhook output, shown in Example 7-6.

Example 7-6 *Atlantis Removing the Configuration Lock Within the Repository*

```
{"level":"info","ts":"2021-11-29T16:38:06.490-0700","caller":"runtime/apply_step_
runner.go:56","msg":"apply successful, deleting planfile","json":{"repo":"qsnyder/
devcor-atlantis","pull":"1"}}
{"level":"info","ts":"2021-11-29T16:43:17.865-0700","caller":"events/events_
controller.go:318","msg":"identified event as type \"closed\"","json":{}}
{"level":"info","ts":"2021-11-29T16:43:23.720-0700","caller":"events/events_
controller.go:360","msg":"deleted locks and workspace for repo qsnyder/devcor-
atlantis, pull 1","json":{}}
```

Deploying Applications (Flux + Kubernetes)

Kubernetes ("K8s") is a distributed platform that supports the deployment, operations, and management of containerized, "cloud native" applications. After K8s is deployed, the entire application management lifecycle is handled through interactions with APIs; even if an operator is leveraging a CLI interface, the commands invoked through the CLI are translated to API actions on the control node. Because K8s is entirely API-centric, a multitude of tools and applications exists to abstract varying levels of complexity away from the operator when deploying or managing applications. This illustrates the positive aspects of API-driven development, as well as the negatives: the availability of choices leads to a variety of different opinions on which method, tool, or process leads to the best outcomes. Tools like Helm, kustomize, and Kapitan provide different ways of deploying apps on the underlying K8s infrastructure, and each can be integrated within a CI/CD pipeline to deploy the resultant containerized applications to K8s. However, each requires a unique deployment configuration file to be followed and a different set of commands to be included within the CI/CD definition file. As a project grows larger, encompassing a greater number of developers or teams, this may create technical debt that slows down the development team to implement changes in an agile manner.

Application deployments within K8s also expose an interesting paradigm: end packages may be an amalgamation of both readily available packages entirely (composed in novel ways), or one or more bespoke applications coupled with other preexisting applications. In both examples, it may be entirely possible (and reasonable) for a repository to be created that exists solely for the act of deployment of the application, creating a traceable history of the applications and versions deployed to the infrastructure over time. This repository would exist solely to track and deploy the applications, either third-party or delivered through a continuous integration/continuous delivery pipeline to allow operations-focused personnel to leverage the benefits of GitOps in a way that doesn't rely on the inclusion of raw code.

Flux is a pure CD platform focused on the deployment of applications to K8s. When the Flux agent is installed, along with the credentials/keys required to integrate an application with a VCS account, Flux can manage the application deployments residing on a cluster through a single push to a VCS repo. Unlike other pipelines leveraging branching and merging, Flux leverages only the main branch for all configuration files, with locations and state for deployments delineated within folders for different environments, rather than having different actions within the CI/CD definition file and state for each deployment location.

Flux works by watching a VCS repository for application deployment manifests to be created, modified, or removed. When a manifest is added, Flux deploys the application to the cluster based on the configuration within the manifest file. If any changes are made to the manifest (or through the **kubectl** CLI), Flux replicates those changes within the deployment of that application (and if a change is made through **kubectl**, Flux reflects that change by modifying the manifest and storing it within the VCS). This workflow not only allows for a source of truth for all applications deployed within a cluster but also ensures that the VCS remains the source of truth even through changes outside of the repository.

Flux also handles two challenges that arise as a consequence of continuous deployment: handling application version upgrades and providing a staged rollout of applications to production. Flux can be configured to periodically scan container registries for updated versions of applications deployed to the cluster. When a version is incremented in the registry, Flux can automatically update the tracked deployment manifest within the VCS and then perform a redeploy action of that app using the updated version. Flux can also interact with Flagger to provide a staggered rollout of any new or updated applications to the cluster.

A typical workflow using Flux would follow (assuming Flux is installed and bootstrapped):

1. The cluster administrator configures Flux to watch a VCS repository. This becomes the single source of truth repository for all applications deployed by Flux.
2. The cluster administrator creates a source manifest within the tracked repository. This manifest provides information to Flux about the application's source repository, which branch the application should be pulled from, and some other K8s-specific information (like namespaces).
3. The source manifest is then committed to the VCS repository.
4. Flux is then used to create a Kustomize deployment manifest, referencing the source manifest created in the previous step.
5. The deployment manifest is then committed to the VCS repository.
6. Flux detects the changes within the VCS repository and initiates the installation of the apps based on the deployment manifest, by pulling the source from the repository indicated in the source manifest.

Flux has a guide to quickly get started deploying a simple application written in Go on top of an existing Kubernetes cluster by using an application manifest (Kustomization). However, this assumes that the user has an existing cluster. Additionally, if an application is deployed using a Helm chart, some changes are required to recognize the alternative application description.

It is possible to create a small Kubernetes cluster on a development workstation using KIND (Kubernetes in Docker). Using KIND, you are able to test Flux without needing a production Kubernetes cluster.

NOTE KIND is bound by the same limitations as Docker within the host workstation. As such, for this example, the target system may have insufficient memory to fully deploy the "sock shop" app. If there is a resource or other contention, the containers are staged for deployment and the application is partially functional, but the deployment is functionally the same as one in a production cluster.

After the binaries for KIND and Docker are installed on the target host, you can create a KIND cluster. To expose the NodePort from the sock shop app, you need to use a custom KIND configuration at runtime. Example 7-7 should be saved as config.yml.

Example 7-7 *Custom KIND Configuration*

```
apiVersion: kind.x-k8s.io/v1alpha4
kind: Cluster
nodes:
- role: control-plane
  extraPortMappings:
  - containerPort: 30001
    hostPort: 30001
    listenAddress: "0.0.0.0"
    protocol: tcp
- role: worker
- role: worker
```

The cluster can then be created. This command downloads the KIND containers and initializes them such that the cluster will be functional:

```
kind create cluster --config=config.yaml
```

When the cluster is functional, Flux can be bootstrapped on the cluster. This assumes that a GitHub token is assigned as an environment variable ($GITHUB_TOKEN), as well as the GitHub user ($GITHUB_USER) and the repository that will hold the Flux configuration ($GITHUB_REPO). The repository needn't be created within the user's account, and it will be created as a private repository, ensuring limited visibility to the applications running on the infrastructure.

7

```
flux bootstrap github \
  --owner=$GITHUB_USER \
  --repository=$GITHUB_REPO \
  --path=clusters/my-cluster \
  --personal
```

After Flux has been bootstrapped, clone the resulting directory to the local system. This clone needn't happen on the system in which Flux is running because the bootstrap process adds an SSH key to the VCS account to ensure communication. After it is cloned, navigate to the $GITHUB_REPO/clusters/my-cluster/ directory. Additionally, because the sock shop app should be deployed within its own namespace, you need to create this on the cluster by using **kubectl**:

```
kubectl create namespace sock-shop
```

The last step is to create the source files within the repository and commit them. Flux requires two files to be created: one that declares the source of the files that will be deployed to the cluster (in this case, a git repository) and a second that declares that a Helm chart will be used to deploy the application to the cluster. These specific files reference the location of the repository as well as the path within the repository to find the required Helm chart to deploy the application. They can be given any arbitrary names, but, for ease of management, use the names **sock-source.yml** and **sock-release.yml**. Examples 7-8 and 7-9 provide examples for the source and release files, including the mapping of the sock shop app Helm chart to a Flux release.

Example 7-8 *sock-source.yml*

```
apiVersion: source.toolkit.fluxcd.io/v1beta1
kind: GitRepository
metadata:
  name: sock-shop
  namespace: flux-system
spec:
  interval: 1m
  url: https://github.com/microservices-demo/microservices-demo
  ref:
    branch: master
```

Example 7-9 *sock-release.yml*

```
apiVersion: helm.toolkit.fluxcd.io/v2beta1
kind: HelmRelease
metadata:
  name: sock-shop
  namespace: sock-shop
spec:
  interval: 4m
  chart:
    spec:
      chart: ./deploy/kubernetes/helm-chart/
      sourceRef:
        kind: GitRepository
        name: sock-shop
        namespace: flux-system
      interval: 1m
  values:
    replicaCount: 1
```

After these files have been created, they can be committed and pushed to the repository tracked by Flux. When you push them to the remote repository, Flux reads the configuration and begins to reconcile the resources and then begins the deployment of the application to the cluster:

```
git add -A && git commit -m "Pushing sock-shop config" && git push
```

After the files have been committed, the logs for Flux can be examined to ensure the application will be deployed. By invoking flux logs, you can see the stages that Flux goes through to deploy the application, the reconciliation of which is shown in Example 7-10.

Example 7-10 *Flux Reconciling the Configuration Files Within the Repository*

```
2021-11-30T17:27:26.954Z error HelmChart/sock-shop-sock-shop.flux-system - Reconciler
error no artifact found for source `sock-shop` kind &#39;GitRepository&#39;
2021-11-30T17:27:26.975Z error HelmChart/sock-shop-sock-shop.flux-system - Reconciler
error no artifact found for source `sock-shop` kind &#39;GitRepository&#39;
2021-11-30T17:27:27.006Z error HelmChart/sock-shop-sock-shop.flux-system - Reconciler
error no artifact found for source `sock-shop` kind &#39;GitRepository&#39;
2021-11-30T17:27:27.045Z error HelmChart/sock-shop-sock-shop.flux-system - Reconciler
error no artifact found for source `sock-shop` kind &#39;GitRepository&#39;
2021-11-30T17:27:27.134Z error HelmChart/sock-shop-sock-shop.flux-system - Reconciler
error no artifact found for source `sock-shop` kind &#39;GitRepository&#39;
2021-11-30T17:27:27.233Z error HelmChart/sock-shop-sock-shop.flux-system - Reconciler
error no artifact found for source `sock-shop` kind &#39;GitRepository&#39;
2021-11-30T17:27:27.418Z error HelmChart/sock-shop-sock-shop.flux-system - Reconciler
error no artifact found for source `sock-shop` kind &#39;GitRepository&#39;
2021-11-30T17:27:27.758Z error HelmChart/sock-shop-sock-shop.flux-system - Reconciler
error no artifact found for source `sock-shop` kind &#39;GitRepository&#39;
2021-11-30T17:27:27.783Z info GitRepository/sock-shop.flux-system - Reconciliation
finished in 899.751555ms, next run in 1m0s
2021-11-30T17:27:28.210Z info GitRepository/sock-shop.flux-system - Reconciliation
finished in 427.223286ms, next run in 1m0s
2021-11-30T17:27:28.309Z info HelmChart/sock-shop-sock-shop.flux-system -
Reconciliation finished in 527.686846ms, next run in 1m0s
2021-11-30T17:27:28.583Z info HelmChart/sock-shop-sock-shop.flux-system -
Reconciliation finished in 184.304943ms, next run in 1m0s
```

When the reconciliation is complete, the containers begin to deploy on the cluster. You can examine the status using standard **kubectl** commands, and when the deployment is complete (or as complete as possible given potential resource constraints on the end system), you can access the sock shop app by opening a web browser to the KIND host on port 30001, seen in Figure 7-7.

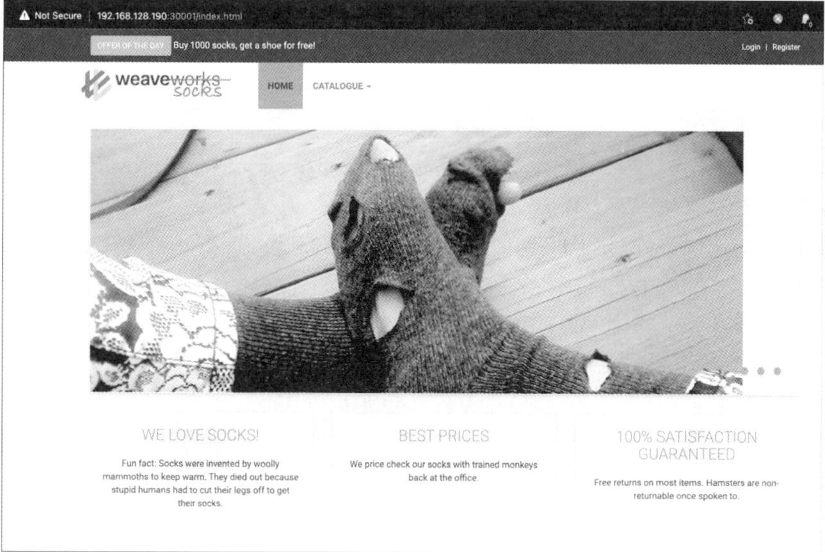

Figure 7-7 *The Sock Shop App Running on KIND Deployed via FluxCD*

Application Deployment Methods over Time

Any discussion of application deployment would be incomplete without a review of the different options available over time. The purpose is to gain an understanding about the amount of change that has transpired over the years and empathy for the amount of work and operational and system change required to support the new models of deployment. These changes did not happen overnight, nor did they happen in a vacuum, because prevailing conditions around speed, agility, and locations of end users have caused the entire industry to shift. While we've broken out this review of the application deployment methods into rough decades of time, we are in no way saying that one method is better than the other. Rather, we used this approach to show the progress and evolution over time and how deployment-related tooling has had to shift with the needs and wants of the end users. Within a single organization, it may be possible to find all the methods discussed, regardless of the adoption of SRE or DevOps principles.

The 2000s: Sysadmins, Terminals, and SSH

As applications moved from centralized mainframes to being distributed among multiple servers (either for load sharing or geographic resiliency), system administrators and operations staff had a much larger task on their hands because most software had to be compiled from source code. As anyone who worked on an *NIX-based workstation during this timeframe can tell you, deploying applications by building from source can be a daunting task, even under ideal conditions, and operations teams lived this life on a regular basis.

A standard workflow for operations to deploy software would be similar to the following:

1. Clone source code from VCS using Concurrent Version System (CVS) or Subversion (SVN).

   In the mid-2000s, options like Mercurial and Git appeared.

2. Through documentation or by working with developers, understand any required headers, libraries, or packages for the software to be compiled.
   - Most applications were written in C or C++ and were required to be compiled before execution.
   - Java code came with its own dependencies, often requiring both compilation as well as a JVM to process the runtime.
3. Compile the code on the machine, either using the language toolchain or using a Makefile within the project repository.
   - This process may be iterative, depending on how exacting the dependencies are.
   - Resolving conflicting versions of a dependency may take multiple attempts, additional install/uninstall of software, and troubleshooting if the offending conflict is needed by another piece of software.
4. Execute the resulting binary executable file, ensuring runtime errors do not occur.
5. Validate the application function through manual testing, especially if required services/connections exist on other servers.
6. Repeat for all devices that require this application.

A sample Makefile is shown in Example 7-11. This example builds an application called edit, which depends on several other source files to be built prior to the main application build. When you invoke the top-level item, it subsequently builds all of the other dependent items as required.

Example 7-11 *GNU Makefile*

```
edit : main.o kbd.o command.o display.o \
       insert.o search.o files.o utils.o
        cc -o edit main.o kbd.o command.o display.o \
                   insert.o search.o files.o utils.o
main.o : main.c defs.h
        cc -c main.c
kbd.o : kbd.c defs.h command.h
        cc -c kbd.c
command.o : command.c defs.h command.h
        cc -c command.c
display.o : display.c defs.h buffer.h
        cc -c display.c
insert.o : insert.c defs.h buffer.h
        cc -c insert.c
search.o : search.c defs.h buffer.h
        cc -c search.c
files.o : files.c defs.h buffer.h command.h
        cc -c files.c
utils.o : utils.c defs.h
        cc -c utils.c
clean :
        rm edit main.o kbd.o command.o display.o \
           insert.o search.o files.o utils.o
```

You start the build process by invoking **make**. This step compiles the required output objects from source using the C code and header files. After each of the dependent output files has been compiled, the main application (edit) can be built. The final target (**clean**) is just a "phony" target that, when invoked, performs an action defined by the bash script following the target name.

You can easily see how fragile this process *could* be, especially given the differences in installed headers and compilers, requiring system administrators to keep close track of each system. When the sysadmin team grew beyond a few people, this logging and tracking of information became nearly impossible, because the time and effort required to document and share information were not available given the demands of keeping the servers and software functional for the end users.

This process was made marginally easier with Linux packages (.deb, .rpm, etc.) and package management front ends (such as Debian's apt and Yellow Dog's yum) for packaged software and dependencies (though circular-dependency references can make for a nightmarish experience). Any software needing to be compiled on the system still went through the same progression.

It's not difficult to see the burden this process placed on operations teams, who were responsible for moving code into production, ensuring the proper function of the overall system/application stack, and ensuring uptime and reliability during patching/bugfix/maintenance events. Often, operations and systems personnel would create shell scripts to help automate the process. Although this effort helped speed the time to deployment, these scripts could be fragile, depending on configuration standardization across server fleets, both in base operating system and installed packages. This fragility eventually became less and less of a problem because many enterprises moved to Linux on x86 platforms, ultimately enabling the next leap in application deployment automation.

The 2010s: Automated Configuration Management

With the standardization on platforms, operating systems, and package management utilities, the conditions were right for something beyond shell (generally bash) scripting to assist with configuration management and deployment. Apps needed to scale faster, and infrastructure was treated as a commodity rather than something that needed constant care and feeding (the analogy of treating something like cattle, rather than a pet). The combination of these two shifts drove a need for stronger distributed configuration management among systems (and therefore apps). These tools allowed system administrators and operations teams to define the desired end state of a system in a flat text file written in a domain-specific language (DSL). A typical workflow would look like the following:

1. A flat file is written in tooling DSL, defining the end state of the device.
   - Includes dependencies and versions
   - Contains edits to any configuration files (either edited or pulled from remote locations into proper directories)
   - Performs application package installation
2. The tool is executed using the configuration from the flat file.
3. Results of individual steps are reported back to the control station.
4. When complete, the server and application end in a valid state.

While this process does not detail the time that is spent to create the DSL flat file, the process is much simpler to execute (and to repeat across tens or even hundreds of servers). There are several added benefits to this approach as well, some of which align to DevOps (or SRE) principles:

1. Automation removes tedious, manual labor ("toil").
2. The same tooling used to deploy to a test or staging area can be used to deploy into production (changing end device targets, of course), allowing for a standard platform from which to test and observe behavior.
3. Because the tooling defines the end state, if any server is lost, unresponsive, or fails, the tooling can deploy an exact copy of what is required directly to that machine, reducing mean time to recovery and increasing reliability and uptime.

A full discussion of each of the different tools is beyond the scope of this section, but some of the popular configuration management tools of the time, as well as some high-level details, are given in Table 7-2.

Table 7-2 Popular Configuration Management Utilities

Tool Name	Year Released	Language	Agent?	Notes
Puppet	2005	Ruby	Sometimes	Initially agent based, now supports network devices without an agent. Ruby-based DSL for "manifests."
Chef	2009	Ruby	Yes	Used for server infrastructure, very limited network device capabilities. Ruby-based DSL for "recipes."
SaltStack	2011	Python	Sometimes	Leverages YAML definition files with Jinja2 templating, supports both network and server, can pull configuration files from master servers.
Ansible	2012	Python	No	Large community support, network device support through paramiko. Supports third-party collections. YAML playbook syntax.
Terraform	2014	Go	No	No support for SSH; limited individual network device support (more supported in network controller platforms); API driven, primary focus on cloud providers. HCL syntax.

Most of these tool names should sound familiar, though adoption and use of some have waned over the years. One tool, Ansible, has grown in popularity over time, not just as a configuration management tool for servers and systems, but for network devices and cloud automations as well.

Ansible (arguably the most popular configuration management and automation tool today) is written in Python and allows for device management in a completely agentless fashion. Playbooks written in YAML define tasks that perform a small unit of work on the target device. These tasks reference modules, written in Python, which are copied to the end system and executed as Python code, using parameters defined in the playbook as input variables where appropriate. These tasks can manipulate system parameters (users, groups, and so on), modify configuration files (either through edits or by copying from remote sources), manage installed packages with full CRUD operations, or any perform combination thereof. Ansible is declarative rather than procedural, allowing for human-readable configuration playbooks instead of a script composed of chained shell commands. Ansible supports external files as variable sources for information in the playbooks, allowing the same tasks to be run across different systems (such as dev, Q/A, and production) by importing the appropriate set of variables files. Finally, Ansible playbooks are not only well supported through SCM applications (GitHub, GitLab) but also can be used to drive automation inside of CI/CD pipelines, due to Ansible's declarative, agentless operating model.

A sample playbook that performs an installation of Python through the operating system's package management system (yum), clones code from several SCM repositories, creates a Python virtual environment, and then installs the Python packages within the virtual environment is shown in Example 7-12.

Example 7-12 *Ansible Playbook Driving Device Automation*

```
---
- hosts: localhost
  gather_facts: no
  vars:
    packages:
      - python36
      - python36-devel
      - vim
    repositories:
      - { org: 'qsnyder', repo: 'arya' }
      - { org: 'qsnyder', repo: 'webarya' }
      - { org: 'datacenter', repo: 'acitoolkit' }
      - { org: 'CiscoDevNet', repo: 'pydme' }
    cobra_eggs:
      - { url: 'https://d1nmyq4gcgsfi5.cloudfront.net/fileMedia/1f3d41ce-d154-44e3-
74c1-d6cf3b525eaa/', file: 'acicobra-4.2_3h-py2.py3-none-any.whl' }
      - { url: 'https://d1nmyq4gcgsfi5.cloudfront.net/fileMedia/b3b69aa3-891b-41ff-
46db-a73b4b215860/', file: 'acimodel-4.2_3h-py2.py3-none-any.whl' }
    virtualenv: py3venv
    dev_folder: ~/aci

  tasks:
    - name: Create ACI code repository
      file:
        path: "{{ dev_folder }}"
        state: directory
        mode: '0755'

    - name: Install packages via YUM
      yum:
        name: "{{ packages }}"
        state: latest

    - name: Install virtualenv module for Python3
      pip:
        name: virtualenv
        executable: pip3.6

    - name: Make virtualenv inside of development folder; install requirements
      pip:
       requirements: ~/requirements.txt
       virtualenv: "{{ dev_folder }}/{{ virtualenv }}"
```

```
        virtualenv_command: /usr/bin/python3.6 -m venv

    - name: Clone code into directory
      git:
        repo: "https://github.com/{{ item.org }}/{{ item.repo }}.git"
        dest: "{{ dev_folder }}/{{ item.repo }}"
      with_items: "{{ repositories }}"

    - name: Download the Cobra modules for ACI 4.2(3h)
      get_url:
        url: "{{ item.url }}{{item.file}}"
        dest: /tmp/
      with_items: "{{ cobra_eggs }}"

    - name: Install Cobra modules into virtualenv
      pip:
        name: file:///tmp/{{ item.file }}
        virtualenv: "{{ dev_folder }}/{{ virtualenv }}"
      with_items: "{{ cobra_eggs }}"

    - name: Install ACI toolkit, Arya, pyDME
      shell: source {{ dev_folder }}/{{ virtualenv }}/bin/activate && python setup.
py install
      args:
        chdir: "{{ dev_folder }}/{{ item }}"
      with_items:
        - acitoolkit
        - arya
        - pydme

    - name: Install WebArya requirements
      pip:
        requirements: "{{ dev_folder }}/webarya/requirements.txt"
        virtualenv: "{{ dev_folder }}/{{ virtualenv }}
```

Configuration management applications helped drive the speed and agility that the business drivers demanded from the infrastructure, but there was a finite limit on how elastic the infrastructure could be. Even with infrastructure provisioning and application rollout automated, if there were more applications required than servers that could host them, purchasing cycles would remove whatever time and energy savings were realized.

As the latter half of the 2010s arrived, elasticity was no longer a "nice to have," but a requirement for many organizations, both startups looking for capital-light ways to scale and large enterprises finding ways to burst periods of high demand without having to have idle infrastructure. The problem of elasticity was solved through cloud computing, but this meant that as cloud resources spun up to meet demand (which could be only a short duration), provisioning routines would need to be run, causing delays in ability to use the new resources.

7

Elasticity was not the only concept to experience a renaissance; the concept of ephemeral infrastructure also experienced a significant shift. As ideas like containerization became popular, along with management and orchestration platforms like Kubernetes, the idea of deployments requiring specific requirements of the infrastructure started to disappear. With containers, the entire app and its dependencies could be packaged in a single file that could be shipped to any host, which could run the container if it had the runtime installed. This model greatly simplified individual host management because all requirements would be packaged in the container at build (inside of the CI/CD pipeline) automatically. However, this new model of application required new models of deployment options for utmost speed and elasticity.

The 2020s: The Clouds Never Looked So Bright

The promise of the cloud was ultimate flexibility and scale to support whatever infrastructure need the business had (for a cost, of course). Public cloud providers, such as Amazon, Microsoft, and Google, have absolutely delivered on this promise. However, with great flexibility comes the potential for confusion, especially as many services offered by a single cloud provider seem to overlap or have only subtle differences. It would be impossible to cover every cloud service available for running applications in this new paradigm; however, the concepts within each option should be generally applicable enough to understand the broad differences between the varying layers of abstraction offered and the requirements to successfully deploy an application on the specific service "type." Each cloud provider also has similar offerings to the ones detailed in the following subsections, but you should take the time to understand any idiosyncratic differences due to architectural designs within each cloud.

Managed Kubernetes (e.g., GKE)

Kubernetes was released as an open-source project in 2014. Originally created by Google, it provides an API-driven platform on which to run, manage, operate, and schedule containerized workloads within an enterprise. With add-on packages, it is possible to provide for overlay networking between nodes, enable distributed storage, and create full-featured "network-centric" services like firewalls and load balancers. However, with the flexibility of being able to shape the cluster as an organization saw fit came the challenge of managing the cluster, software versions, and underlying physical network and server infrastructure. In much the same way the system administrators and operations teams struggled with dependencies in the 2000s compiling software from source, the K8s platform administrators of the mid-2010s often struggled with managing updates and changes to K8s and its required (and third-party) software packages.

By moving the underlying K8s platform into the cloud, enterprises can focus on higher-level problems, rather than the nitty-gritty of platform administration. In this shift, the cloud provider ensures that the cluster is up to date and functional at the sacrifice of complete flexibility (for example, some services may be provided only by the provider, rather than having full support of every third-party tool), but the overall gain in agility and speed to deployment outweighs the loss of (a potentially unused) flexibility.

It only makes sense then that Google's cloud product (Google Cloud Platform, GCP) offers managed K8s within its suite of offers and tools. Google Kubernetes Engine (GKE) allows organizations to leverage Google's cloud and automation to manage and provision clusters to deploy apps, while removing the need to worry about things like

- Load balancing across compute instances
- Node failure and repair

- Scaling of the cluster as load increases
- Logging and observability of the cluster
- Software and package upgrades to the underlying K8s infrastructure

GKE provides two different levels of administration requirements to the end user, standard and autopilot, providing an additional layer of abstraction to the end resources. In autopilot, everything from the size and number of compute nodes to the underlying node operating system, all the way down to the security measures at boot time, is handled by Google. This comes at a cost of support for things like GPUs, Calico network overlays, or Istio service-mesh, and even support for some of GCP's other products, but serves as a way for administrators to focus strictly on the K8s API and the outcomes delivered through their microservices applications.

Access to GKE (and GCP in general) is provided either through a web UI, a web-based console, or locally installed console tools. API access is also supported, allowing for the use of automation and orchestration tools (like Ansible or Terraform) to provision and manage cloud infrastructure. As an example of using GKE, you can deploy the microservice demo sock shop app to GKE using the cloud console.

Deploying an application to GKE is similar to any Kubernetes application deployment. The majority of the configuration steps required are GCP-specific, ensuring that the specific region and zone are set, as well as scaling the cluster size. To deploy the sock-shop application, you need to create the GKE cluster:

```
gcloud config set compute/zone us-west1-a

gcloud config set compute/region us-west1

gcloud container clusters create sock-shop --num-nodes=3
```

These commands create a cluster in US-West-1 within GCP but can be modified to suit the desired region and zone close to another location. After the cluster is created, a functional Kubernetes cluster is presented (this may take several minutes). When the cluster is functional, the next steps are the same as if you were deploying the application to on-premises Kubernetes:

```
kubectl create namespace sock-shop

kubectl apply -f https://raw.githubusercontent.com/microservices-
demo/microservices-demo/master/deploy/kubernetes/complete-demo.yaml
```

These commands apply the manifest on the Kubernetes cluster and deploy the application to a fully functional state within a few minutes. The final step to accessing the application requires the default GCP firewall to allow connections to the sock-shop app and find the IP address of one of the nodes running the app:

```
gcloud compute firewall-rules create sock-shop --allow tcp:30001

kubectl get nodes -o wide
```

The output provides the external IP addresses of the three nodes provisioned within the cluster. Each one of these nodes has the sock-shop app port exposed (tcp/30001). Sample output is shown in Example 7-13.

Example 7-13 *Determining External IP Addresses of GKE Cluster Running the Sock-shop Application*

```
snyderq@cloudshell:~ (devcor-studies)$ kubectl get nodes -o wide
NAME                                       STATUS   ROLES    AGE     VERSION
INTERNAL-IP   EXTERNAL-IP     OS-IMAGE                             KERNEL-VERSION
CONTAINER-RUNTIME
gke-sock-shop-default-pool-30c3b3ad-n844   Ready    <none>   5m37s
v1.21.5-gke.1302   10.138.0.6   34.145.72.58     Container-Optimized OS from Google
5.4.144+         containerd://1.4.8
gke-sock-shop-default-pool-30c3b3ad-v31p   Ready    <none>   5m36s
v1.21.5-gke.1302   10.138.0.5   35.185.195.99    Container-Optimized OS from Google
5.4.144+         containerd://1.4.8
gke-sock-shop-default-pool-30c3b3ad-v6tf   Ready    <none>   5m36s
v1.21.5-gke.1302   10.138.0.7   104.198.107.29   Container-Optimized OS from Google
5.4.144+         containerd://1.4.8w
```

Navigating to one of the external IP addresses on port 30001 brings up the sock-shop sample application, shown in Figure 7-8, using one of the IP addresses shown in Example 7-13.

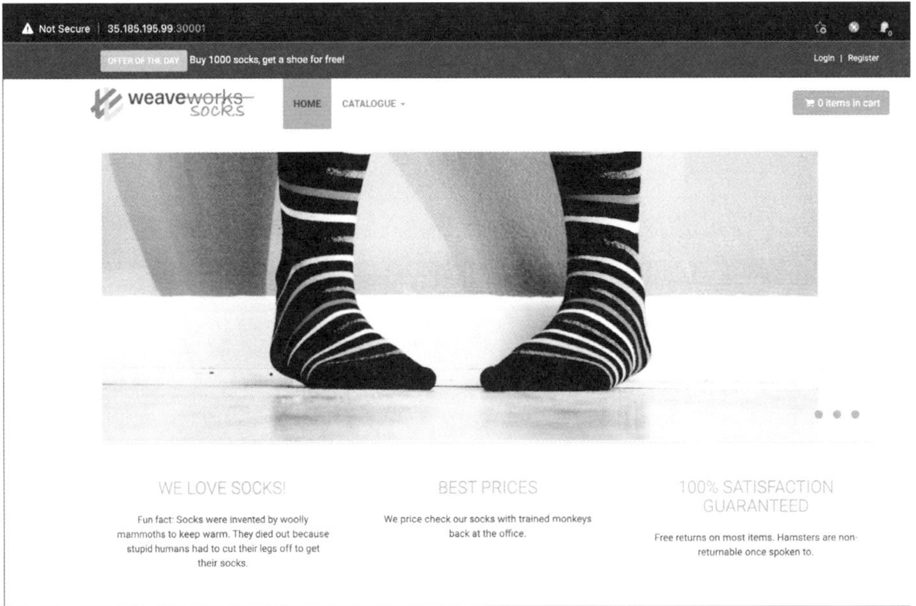

Figure 7-8 *The Sock-shop Application Running on GKE*

After the application is verified to be working, ensure that the cluster is destroyed to ensure that no additional charges are incurred:

```
gcloud container clusters delete sock-shop
```

Containers on Serverless Clouds (e.g., AWS ECS on Fargate)

The goal of any cloud provider is to remove the barriers to entry that present themselves through infrastructure and abstract them away, such that the administrator can focus on the tasks that are relevant to the business. Despite the levels of abstraction afforded by managed Kubernetes offerings, the underlying infrastructure is still Kubernetes and carries with it the management responsibilities of that platform. Even in autopilot mode, you must be cognizant of what can and cannot be done within the platform and (some would say more importantly) the cost implications of running a heavyweight container platform in the cloud (because everything comes with a price).

Amazon Web Service's (AWS) Elastic Container Service (ECS) has existed for many years, even before Amazon's own managed Kubernetes offering, to run Docker-packaged containers on AWS's cloud. ECS can either be run using the Elastic Compute Cloud (EC2) launch type, which is similar in spirit to running Docker on cloud hosts, or using a Fargate launch type, which abstracts the underlying compute instances away from the end user. If running ECS in EC2 mode, the user must first create the underlying systems and clusters capable of supporting the containerized workloads and then register them with ECS. However, that overhead can be removed if leveraging Fargate launch types within ECS.

Fargate itself is not an AWS offering; it is a deployment methodology that exists within the AWS cloud that abstracts the underlying infrastructure supporting containerized workloads away from the end user. The net result is that for a user to run an arbitrary workload on ECS, that user simply needs to define the compute requirements for the container and deploy the app to the cloud using AWS's tooling, which is like GCP's tooling in that a web UI, a web-based console, and locally installable CLI tools are available. This tooling creates a **serverless** feel to running containers, in that the system and administration duties that are normally required with running enterprise applications are removed; the only focus is on the end application being deployed.

7

Although products like Google Cloud Run and Azure Container Instances also provide a similar experience (albeit through their own interfaces) to ECS on Fargate, we focus on the latter in deploying a sample application to review the process using the AWS CloudShell, which you access by logging in to an AWS account and clicking the terminal icon on the top bar, as seen in Figure 7-9.

Figure 7-9 *Accessing the AWS CloudShell*

When the CloudShell is active and connected to an instance, there are some prerequisites to ensure proper permissions and settings are instantiated within the cluster. First, you need to create an IAM role by creating a JSON file (task-execution.json) with the payload described in Example 7-14.

Example 7-14 *Task Execution IAM Role File Payload*

```
{
  "Version": "2012-10-17",
  "Statement": [
    {
      "Sid": "",
      "Effect": "Allow",
      "Principal": {
        "Service": "ecs-tasks.amazonaws.com"
      },
      "Action": "sts:AssumeRole"
    }
  ]
}
```

NOTE Be sure not to change the version value; this is not a date value but references a specific revision of IAM policy that can be applied within the AWS IAM universe.

You then can create the IAM policy and attach it to the account:

```
aws iam --region us-west-2 create-role --role-name
ecsTaskExecutionRole --assume-role-policy-document file://task-
execution.json
```

```
aws iam --region us-west-2 attach-role-policy --role-name
ecsTaskExecutionRole --policy-arn arn:aws:iam::aws:policy/service-
role/AmazonECSTaskExecutionRolePolicy
```

NOTE You need to perform this task only once—the first time you bring up the ECS cluster. After this is done the first time, the IAM policy is persistent and tied to the account in use.

NOTE The example references the use of us-west-2 as the compute region for the ECS cluster. You might need to change this depending on the desired AWS compute region.

After the IAM role has been attached, the ECS parameters can be defined. You can do this through the CloudShell using **ecs-cli** (as shown in the following output) but can also define it within the ~/.ecs/ directory of the CloudShell instance using YAML definitions:

```
ecs-cli configure --cluster DEVCOR --default-launch-type FARGATE
--config-name DEVCOR --region us-west-2
```

```
ecs-cli configure profile --access-key AWS_ACCESS_KEY_ID --secret-
key AWS_SECRET_ACCESS_KEY --profile-name DEVCOR-Profile
```

This code creates a configuration profile for the ECS cluster. ECS supports multiple profiles, which can be referenced at cluster launch time. However, because only a single profile is defined, this profile is used by default. You can create the AWS_ACCESS_KEY_ID and AWS_SECRET_ACCESS_KEY by navigating to the IAM settings window, clicking Users, the desired username, and then the Security Credentials tab.

NOTE You need to apply this configuration only once. After it is applied, the ecs-cli parameters are translated to a YAML file in ~/.ecs/. The credentials file is translated to another YAML file in the same directory.

Now that the cluster parameters and keys are stored, the cluster can be created and an application deployed to the cluster. In this example, a Jupyter notebook container is deployed and exposed to the public Internet. The following output shows the result of bringing up the ECS cluster using the **ecs-cli** command. As the command runs, information about the created VPC and subnets is displayed on the CLI.

```
ecs-cli up

    ....

    VPC created: vpc-0f87e8258f2e01577

    Subnet created: subnet-077625f74808df789

    Subnet created: subnet-03cf7318516bb08d6
```

The displayed values will become important. In Example 7-15, the VPC_ID value referenced in the command string is the value displayed after bringing up the cluster. The important value to record is the value for the GroupId, which is the security group value that controls network policy for the cluster.

Example 7-15 *Gathering the Security Group Information for the Deployed Cluster*

```
aws ec2 describe-security-groups --filters Name=vpc-id,Values=VPC_ID --region
us-west-2
...
{
    "SecurityGroups": [
        {
            "Description": "default VPC security group",
            "GroupName": "default",
            "IpPermissions": [],
            "OwnerId": "860261725131",
            "GroupId": "sg-0e7357356e89b1c31",
            "IpPermissionsEgress": [
                {
                    "IpProtocol": "-1",
                    "IpRanges": [
                        {
```

```
                                "CidrIp": "0.0.0.0/0"
                            }
                        ],
                        "Ipv6Ranges": [],
                        "PrefixListIds": [],
                        "UserIdGroupPairs": []
                    }
                ],
                "VpcId": "vpc-0f87e8258f2e01577"
            }
        ]
}
```

Now that the security group ID value is known, the policy to allow ingress traffic to the ECS cluster can be permitted. By default, the Jupyter notebook container has TCP/8888 exposed, which needs to be allowed through the ACL applied. Ensure that the value of GroupId is placed in the appropriate location within the command illustrated in Example 7-16.

Example 7-16 *Allowing Inbound Traffic to the ECS Container*

```
aws ec2 authorize-security-group-ingress --group-id SECURITY_GROUP_ID --protocol tcp
--port 8888 --cidr 0.0.0.0/0 --region us-west-2
{
    "Return": true,
    "SecurityGroupRules": [
        {
            "SecurityGroupRuleId": "sgr-002ff2137fc89825a",
            "GroupId": "sg-0e7357356e89b1c31",
            "GroupOwnerId": "860261725131",
            "IsEgress": false,
            "IpProtocol": "tcp",
            "FromPort": 8888,
            "ToPort": 8888,
            "CidrIpv4": "0.0.0.0/0"
        }
    ]
}
```

The infrastructure has been prepared to allow connections and traffic to the cluster. All that remains is to deploy the application. Deployment requires two files to be created: one defines the parameters for the task execution on ECS, and the other is the docker-compose.yml file (shown in Example 7-18), which defines the application to be deployed. You need to create them using CloudShell. Additionally, within the ecs-params.yml file (an example of which is shown in Example 7-17), the subnets and security groups need to be filled in with the values obtained when the cluster is created.

NOTE Filenames should follow the exact naming of ecs-params.yml and docker-compose.yml because ECS looks to these files by default when instantiating an application. It is possible to reference others using command-line switches, but they are omitted for simplicity. Ensure the files end in .yml.

Within the docker-compose.yml file, note the volume mapping. As ECS abstracts the underlying infrastructure from the end user, a host mapping is not required. Defining the volume is sufficient for ECS to map a data storage volume to the container.

Example 7-17 *ecs-params.yml*

```
version: 1
task_definition:
  task_execution_role: ecsTaskExecutionRole
  ecs_network_mode: awsvpc
  os_family: Linux
  task_size:
    mem_limit: 8192
    cpu_limit: 2048
run_params:
  network_configuration:
    awsvpc_configuration:
      subnets:
        - "SUBNET_1"
        - "SUBNET_2"
      security_groups:
        - "SECURITY_GROUP_ID"
      assign_public_ip: ENABLED
```

Example 7-18 *docker-compose.yml*

```
version: "3"
services:
  minimal-notebook:
    image: jupyter/minimal-notebook
    environment:
      - NB_USER=USERNAME
      - PASSWORD=cisco12345
      - JUPYTER_TOKEN=cisco12345
    volumes:
      - work
    ports:
      - "8888:8888"
    container_name: minimal-notebook-container
```

7

After creating the two files, you can now deploy the application by using **ecs-cli**. The output of running the **ecs-cli** command should look similar to the output shown in Example 7-19.

Example 7-19 *Instantiating the Application on the ECS Cluster*

```
ecs-cli compose service up
...
WARN[0000] Skipping unsupported YAML option for service... option name=container_
name service name=minimal-notebook
INFO[0000] Using ECS task definition                      TaskDefinition="cloudshell-
user:8"
INFO[0000] Auto-enabling ECS Managed Tags
INFO[0010] (service cloudshell-user) has started 1 tasks: (task 60ab7a0ad7ee-
4a69a95d3caef79b409f). timestamp="2021-12-02 00:13:37 +0000 UTC"
INFO[0106] Service status                                 desiredCount=1 running-
Count=1 serviceName=cloudshell-user
INFO[0106] (service cloudshell-user) has reached a steady state. time-
stamp="2021-12-02 00:15:15 +0000 UTC"
INFO[0106] (service cloudshell-user) (deployment ecs-svc/9087318749417985970)
deployment completed. timestamp="2021-12-02 00:15:15 +0000 UTC"
INFO[0106] ECS Service has reached a stable state        desiredCount=1 running-
Count=1 serviceName=cloudshell-user
INFO[0106] Created an ECS service                         service=cloudshell-user
taskDefinition="cloudshell-user:8"
```

After the service has been created in ECS, you are able to gather the exposed IP address of the application on the cluster:

```
ecs-cli compose service ps

...

WARN[0000] Skipping unsupported YAML option for service... option
name=container_name service name=minimal-notebook

Name
State    Ports                              TaskDefinition     Health

DEVCOR/60ab7a0ad7ee4a69a95d3caef79b409f/minimal-notebook  RUNNING
54.190.18.166:8888->8888/tcp  cloudshell-user:8  UNKNOWN
```

Finally, after you open a web browser and enter the IP address and port information, a window appears with the Jupyter notebook login. This password is what was defined within the docker-compose.yml file. A Jupyter notebook is now running on serverless containers within AWS. Figure 7-10 shows the login for the notebook, password protected using credentials in the docker-compose.yml file, and Figure 7-11 illustrates the mapped data folder for generated notebook files.

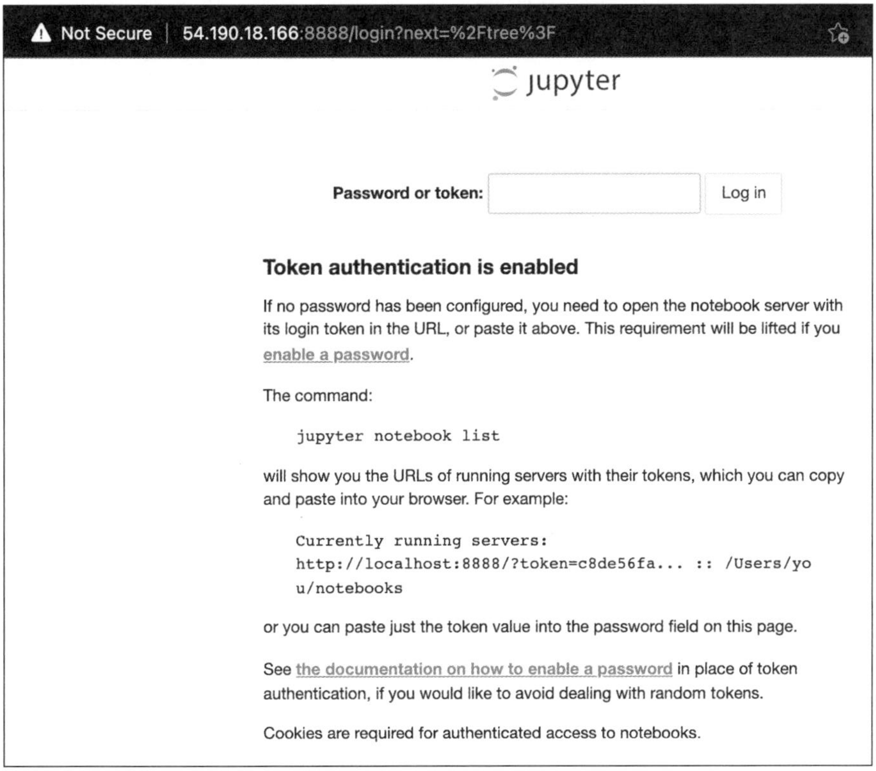

Not Secure | 54.190.18.166:8888/login?next=%2Ftree%3F

jupyter

Password or token: Log in

Token authentication is enabled

If no password has been configured, you need to open the notebook server with its login token in the URL, or paste it above. This requirement will be lifted if you enable a password.

The command:

```
jupyter notebook list
```

will show you the URLs of running servers with their tokens, which you can copy and paste into your browser. For example:

```
Currently running servers:
http://localhost:8888/?token=c8de56fa... :: /Users/yo
u/notebooks
```

or you can paste just the token value into the password field on this page.

See the documentation on how to enable a password in place of token authentication, if you would like to avoid dealing with random tokens.

Cookies are required for authenticated access to notebooks.

Figure 7-10 *Jupyter Notebook Login*

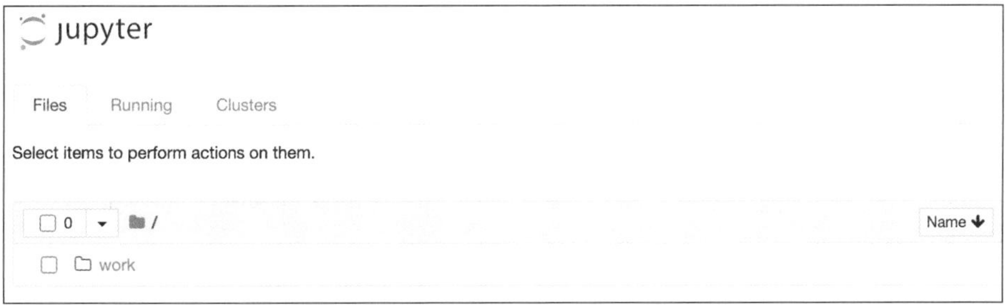

jupyter

Files Running Clusters

Select items to perform actions on them.

0 / Name

work

Figure 7-11 *Jupyter Notebook Running on ECS*

Finally, when the application has served its purpose, you should shut it down to avoid incurring unnecessary costs. This two-step process requires draining the application service from the cluster, followed by shutting down the cluster itself, both of which are shown in Example 7-20.

Example 7-20 *Stopping the Service and Destroying the ECS Cluster*

```
ecs-cli compose service down
...
WARN[0000] Skipping unsupported YAML option for service... option name=container_
name service name=minimal-notebook
INFO[0000] Deleted ECS service                          service=cloudshell-user
INFO[0000] Service status                               desiredCount=0 running-
Count=1 serviceName=cloudshell-user
INFO[0020] Service status                               desiredCount=0 running-
Count=0 serviceName=cloudshell-user
INFO[0020] (service cloudshell-user) has stopped 1 running tasks: (task
12999444a1f9488dbe73536d53d59610). timestamp="2021-12-02 00:29:09 +0000 UTC"
INFO[0020] ECS Service has reached a stable state       desiredCount=0 running-
Count=0 serviceName=cloudshell-user


ecs-cli down
...
Are you sure you want to delete your cluster? [y/N]
y
INFO[0002] Waiting for your cluster resources to be deleted...
INFO[0002] Cloudformation stack status                  stackStatus=DELETE_IN_PROG-
RESS
INFO[0063] Cloudformation stack status                  stackStatus=DELETE_IN_PROG-
RESS
INFO[0093] Deleted cluster                              cluster=DEVCOR
```

Serverless Functions (e.g., AWS Lambda)

If ECS removes the underlying infrastructure from running containerized workloads, you can assume without any prior knowledge, based on the trajectory of this section, that serverless functions serve to provide another layer of abstraction and packaging removal from the end user. Whereas products like ECS remove the necessity of managing the server infrastructure from running container workloads, products like AWS Lambda remove the requirement of packaging and shipping a container from running a single application within the cloud.

On its surface, the move from packaging containers to running cloud functions may seem trivial, or even a step backward. In a container workflow, the application can be packaged and deployed on any number of local or cloud providers; you know the application can be ported because the application and dependencies are included within the container package file, which can be executed by the container runtime. However, if this is stripped back, given a consistent environment (that is, one that consists of a given set of prerequisites, dependencies, and language versions), the container packaging creates an unnecessary layer of "stuff" that hides the code from the end user. Sure, there is portability in the container, but if the need arises, that code *can* be placed in a container and shipped elsewhere, whether that be cloud or on-premises hosts.

AWS Lambda enables you to run pure code (Python, Go, Node, C#, Java, Ruby, or PowerShell) within a predefined environment. Compute resources, such as RAM and CPU, are allocated to the function, and any requirements for the code are uploaded as a custom environment for the runtime execution. When the environment is in place, you can add code to the function using a variety of methods, including copy/paste, API, or some pipeline within AWS that adds the code from a VCS code repository. This code can then be invoked through a timed-based setting, through an API gateway provided by AWS, or through a larger chain of events triggered through a messaging bus or service (such as Kafka).

Both ECS on Fargate and Lambda are referred to as serverless. The common question "if it's serverless, how does it run?" refers to the idea that there must be a server underneath the abstraction that is performing the desired action. This misses the point because serverless is not a technology that is devoid of servers themselves but references the removal of the management aspect of the compute infrastructure and applications/packages required to support running the desired application. These application operating models enable developers to focus on the code and application (and the intended outcomes of it) rather than the operations and maintenance aspects that were required in decades past.

All the abstraction and removal of infrastructure comes at a cost, however. By removing the requirement for management of the servers, operating systems, and supporting applications, cloud providers also remove the level of customization and flexibility afforded to the end user. Although many common use cases are covered, if an application or enterprise has requirements outside of what is supported, then it must be deployed on products that provide a similar look and feel to on-premises infrastructure, as well as similar overhead of management, patching, and dependencies. As a result, organizations sometimes standardize on what is possible within their development process in order to ensure they comply with the requirements of the serverless platform to which they deploy.

Deploying a function to Lambda is slightly different from the other methods discussed thus far; while other methods rely on external packages, manifests, or charts to run the application, Lambda is completely bespoke and requires the end user to build the environment that can be run on the Lambda platform. This means that if a developer builds a Python function (making Lambda a Function as a Service [FaaS] platform), the developer would build and test their code locally and then deploy that exact environment as a layer within the Lambda platform.

This effort can easily be accomplished by packaging up the Python virtualenv in use as a ZIP file. This requires navigation to the site-packages folder of the virtualenv and invoking the **zip** command:

```
sounding-data » cd venv/lib/python3.8/site-packages/

site-packages » zip -r ../../../../python-bot.zip .
```

After the ZIP archive is created, the source code for the Lambda function must be added. This code must be named lambda_function.py so that it can be executed by the Lambda environment. If this file is not named appropriately, the function cannot be invoked by a Lambda trigger.

After the virtualenv has been added to the ZIP archive, it can be uploaded to AWS as a Lambda layer. You do this in the Lambda console under the Layers menu. Within the Create Layer menu, you upload the ZIP archive, along with the desired application runtime environment, license, and a layer name. Figure 7-12 shows how to create a sample layer within the AWS console.

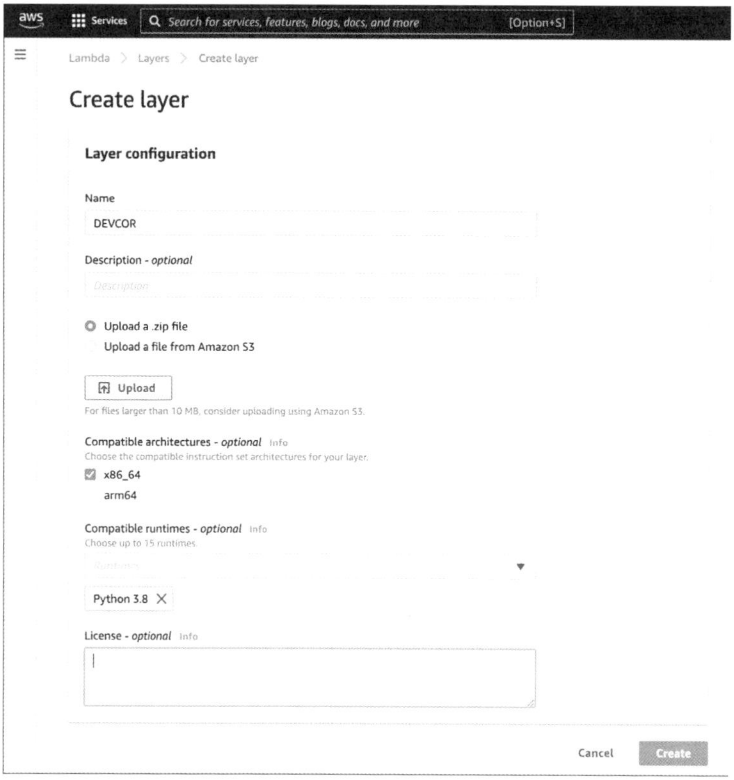

Figure 7-12 *Uploading a Layer to Lambda*

Next, a function needs to be created to tie the code and the layer together. You do this under the Functions menu. This function needs to be given a name and runtime environment. The default setting of Author from Scratch will suffice because the code has already been written and tested on a local machine, which is shown in Figure 7-13.

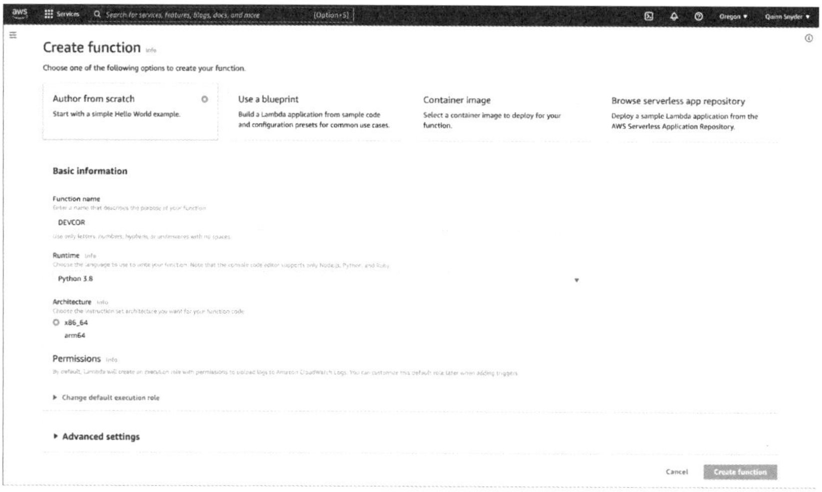

Figure 7-13 *Creating New Lambda Function*

After the function is created, a new window appears with a code editor. First, the code needs to be added to the function. You can do this by creating a ZIP archive of the code, which replaces what is currently within the editor:

```
site-packages » cd ../../../../

sounding-data » zip lambda_function.zip lambda_function.py
```

After the code is added to a ZIP archive on the local machine, you can upload it to Lambda by selecting Upload From at the top right of the code editor. This allows a ZIP archive to be uploaded and adds the desired code to the function. Figure 7-14 shows the location of the ZIP upload menu item, but alternatively, an S3 bucket location can be specified if the code resides there.

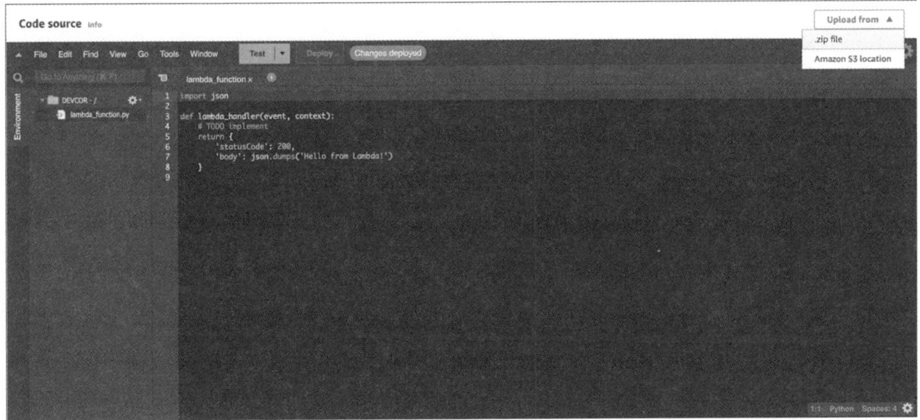

Figure 7-14 *Selecting a ZIP Upload Method for Code*

When the upload is complete, the code editor reflects the code tested locally on the workstation.

The next step is to add the runtime layer to the function, because without it, any custom module or library (even those that exist by default within a given language) will not work. You create the layer association at the bottom of the console by selecting the Add a Layer button, shown in Figure 7-15. Figure 7-16 illustrates the association of the layer to the function within the AWS console.

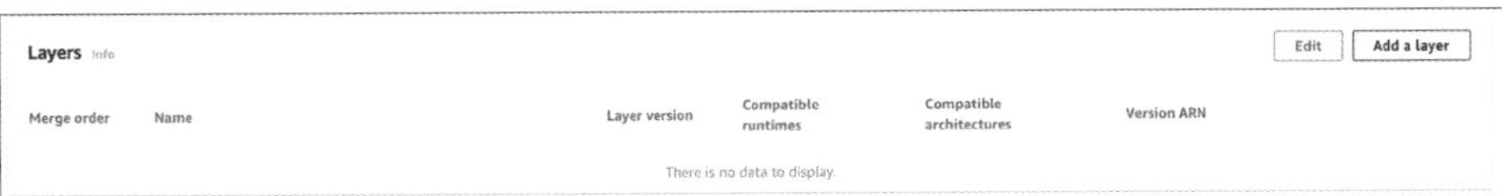

Figure 7-15 *Adding a Layer to the Lambda Function*

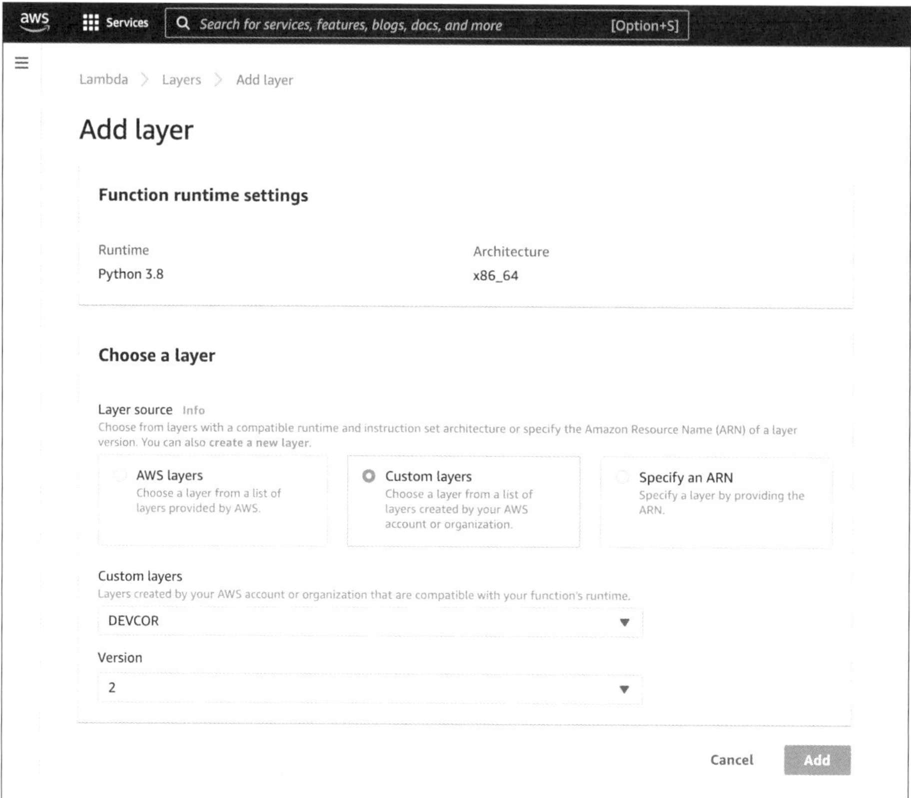

Figure 7-16 *Associating the Custom Layer to the Lambda Function*

The function is now deployed and can be tested using the console. However, after the code is written, it needs to be triggered by some event. These triggers are configured using the Add Trigger button under Function Overview. Supported triggers include simple cron timings to API gateways to database or Alexa events. A full discussion of these triggers is outside the scope of this chapter, but a common use is to tie the function to an API Gateway, which will receive an HTTP verb via an exposed REST URI. The verb used in interrogating this API endpoint, along with any payload (if required), can be passed to the function for processing.

Software Practices for Operability: The 12-Factor App

Much of this chapter has focused on the act of deploying an app and the infrastructure on which it can be deployed. By using tools for automation and ways to abstract the need for continuous maintenance on infrastructure, teams that adopt SRE or DevOps principles can drastically reduce the amount of time focused on responsibilities that are ancillary to the applications and their uptime. This ensures that time is left for "higher-order" problems, process improvements, and innovate thinking, key aspects for any agile team.

However, just as the tooling and supporting infrastructure must be ready to handle the speed of rapid deployment, the application and its development process must also adhere to certain guidelines in order to be deployed in such a manner. If an application is not tracked in a VCS, does not declare specific dependencies, lacks an ability to scale out, or does not handle logging in a graceful manner, the ability for any team (no matter how DevOps-y) to operate, maintain, and upgrade the application under the demands of the app economy is significantly hampered.

To create a baseline of application development best practices, a team at Heroku (a Platform as a Service, or PaaS, that supports application development and serverless hosting) created the notion of a 12-factor application design and development methodology and released it to the public around 2011. Although not entirely canonical across every development team or platform, the 12 factors create a baseline to ensure an application is not the weakest link in DevOps or SRE principles—namely, resilience, uptime, and an ability to run anywhere to meet those needs. It is also important to realize that, although some of these factors are self-evident today, in the era of development in which these factors were released, practices and methodologies were much less rigid and prescriptive. For a deeper dive into the 12-factor app, refer to *The 12-Factor App* (see the "References" section at the end of this chapter).

Factor 1: Codebase

Factor 1 is self-explanatory: everything must be in a VCS code repository (the original book mentions others, but the de facto standard is Git-based). In addition, that codebase should be the single source of truth for *all* deployments, whether in development, test, or production. This is not to say that feature or bugfix branches within the codebase can't occur or that development, test, and production can't be running at different points within the branches, but that all branching, edits, and deployments should be done from the same repository.

Factor 2: Dependencies

Within the codebase, every application should explicitly define the required supporting packages to be able to run. In fact, if you have downloaded a Python application recently, you may find that it includes a requirements.txt file that can install all required dependencies using pip (Ruby, Perl, and others also have similar mechanisms). In addition, these dependencies must be able to be installed in a self-contained environment, like a Python virtualenv, to ensure that any required system dependencies do not interfere with what is required for the application to run. Both aspects make up the second factor and should be considered basic hygiene for all written applications.

Additionally, all required dependencies should be explicitly declared as part of the codebase to the point where there are no requirements of any system-installed applications; the code should be able to be self-contained and functional through the explicit dependencies and the language isolation mechanism.

Factor 3: Config

Limits of duplicate infrastructure exist within every organization. Under ideal circumstances, it would be very beneficial for app developers to have the identical sets of IP addresses, credentials, or resources existing in development, test, and production environments. In the real world, this is highly impractical, especially because limitations on the duplicity are placed on the app from externalities, like the network, compute resources, cloud applications, and the like.

To overcome this, external constants (also known as the apps "config") should be abstracted away from the code itself and either imported at runtime through environment variables or through a secret store with an external API, like HashiCorp Vault. This has a two-factor side effect in that (a) the code can be released (either intentionally or not) to the public without compromise of sensitive information and (b) the same code can be used across development, test, and production environments with a simple change of the configuration, while the code is still the same.

Factor 4: Backing Services

Just as the applications configuration should be abstracted from the application itself, services that support the application should be coded into the application in such a way that the idiosyncrasies of an individual package or deployment of the service are inconsequential to the application's function. Supporting services, such as databases or messaging queues, should be defined as resources, irrespective of whether the service resides within the same data center or resides in the cloud. This abstraction allows for the portability between backing services, for cost or supportability reasons, in pursuit of utmost uptime principles. The credentials or locations of these backing services can be defined within the application's configuration and can differ between environments in which the app is run such as development, test, or production.

Factor 5: Build, Release, Run

For any code to be moved into production, it must be transformed into some sort of executable process that can be invoked by the system on which it is installed. When separate stages are defined for the build, release, and run stages, the code is provided isolation and immutability at runtime. When the codebase is moved to a binary file through compilation, it is moved to a defined packaged release based on the procedures within the releasing organization. This release creates a "line in the sand" definition that is unique from both prior and future releases in its features and support. When this release is moved into production, it is run, but the running release does not have the ability to move, modify, or edit the code on which it is running. The only process for moving changes into production is through a modification of the codebase and a repetition of the cycle.

This idea does become slightly blurred when discussing or developing with applications that are compiled at runtime (such as Python) when compared to compiled languages (such as C/C++ or Go). In runtime-compiled languages, there is no concept of a compiled binary because this is done at the invocation of the file containing the code. However, when you are developing with such languages, the release strategy should still be adopted to create a clear demarcation of the application and its features, and, most importantly, the running code should not be able to change the code on which it was originally invoked, creating unique outcomes depending on the run.

Factor 6: Processes

Applications designed within the 12-factor process are meant to be stateless in nature. This (loosely) means that any transaction that occurs between one or more parts of the application is completely independent from another transaction. More importantly, this transaction is not shared between different components of the app unless there is a specific request that is invoked between components, which in and of itself is stateless. If any transaction or record is required, it must be stored in a database or object store, because any other component is not designed to store this state.

If you are familiar with microservices, or even have read the example provided by nginx, this concept should be familiar. Because you should be able to be restart, upgrade, or scale each component of the application independently of the other components, nothing should be contained within an individual invocation of the application or service. Treating different components of the application in this way ensures that as demands require it, reliability and scalability are present.

Factor 7: Port Binding

Port binding combines the concepts of several different factors. At its core, any application defining an external service should declare the service and start it from its invocation, rather than leveraging a preinstalled service running on the target host. Any code defining that service (for example, a web server) should be compiled at runtime and be immutable unless another build, release, or run cycle is performed. Finally, because the methods in which the application may be accessed (locally in development versus a cloud server in production), the use of an environment configuration based on the deployment location may be necessary.

The most important takeaway from factor 7 is that any service that exposes a service northbound should be explicitly declared and exposed on the individual host. That service should be listening for any request from any other component or resource within the application stack.

Factor 8: Concurrency

In much the same way that port binding combines multiple aspects, concurrency is enabled through the adherence of other previous factors. By ensuring that applications handle externalities as resources rather than built-in components, referenced by individual configuration files, the applications become stateless in nature. This stateless nature enables the individual components of a larger application (web, application, and database to use a common three-tier app) to be scaled independently according to need at the time. These different components should be able to be scaled in a nondaemonized fashion (that is, separate processes for each invocation, rather than using a global parent process with unique children), leveraging tools like systemd for process management, which is responsible for the lifecycle of the process itself (restarts, crashes, and so on). The concurrent management of disparate numbers of the application's process should be transparent to both the operations team supporting the application, as well as the end user.

Factor 9: Disposability

Disposability is a concept extended from the stateless nature of the application itself. If the components that make up the application have no data or state, it becomes trivial if those components scale upward (due to load) or are removed (due to a lull). The application should gracefully handle the removal of the scaled services, through a standard SIGTERM on the process managed by the process manager, assuming no work is destined for that scaled component. Disposability also states that if some scaled worker process no longer responds or times out, it should be removed from the worker queue (and ideally some queueing process should requeue the work for a node that is alive).

Factor 10: Dev/Prod Parity

On its surface, you may look at parity to mean that the *environment* that exists between development and production should be the same. This means that if the application is meant to run in production with a given set of applications as resources (for example, using nginx as a web server), then that web server should be used when code is being developed and run in a test environment. This might seem self-evident; however, if a single developer's laptop is being used to mock and mimic the application, resource, time, or knowledge constraints may cause the developer to look for lightweight applications to use in substitution. While completely well intentioned, the use of a single system to mock entire environments not only exposes production to issues due to different application behavior but also makes troubleshooting an issue harder because there is no replicated environment to understand the code's steady-state operation.

Parity should also exist in two other areas that will seem familiar to principles within DevOps methodology. The first is that there should be as little a gap as possible between code being committed to the main repository and it being moved into a deployed state (which could be a test environment; the code needn't move directly into production). The complete code parity aligns directly with the automated integration, build, and deploy process advocated by DevOps and SREs. The second parity involves the folks tasked with supporting the application as it has moved into a deployment stage; namely, those who built the application should be the same people tasked with supporting the deployment when it is live. While the 12-factor app is neither DevOps nor SRE, the concepts in this factor strongly overlap.

Factor 11: Logs

Visibility into applications is critical for the support of the running application. This visibility is required both at an application's steady state, as well as when certain aspects of the app are not performing as desired due to some issue. Visibility is gained through access and correlation to the logs of the application as it is running; however, an application designed to the 12-factor principles should not directly handle the logs or the logging process. Within *NIX-based operating systems, output from an application is passed to a stream, generally either stdout or stderr. These operating systems have robust utilities and output redirection abilities to move this output to purpose-built applications to handle logging, especially the centralized logging required for high-visibility observability. These tools allow for streamed application output to be passed to tools such as syslog, Logstash, Splunk, or other log collection utilities. The use of log streams coupled with purpose built logging applications frees the developer from having to rewrite implementations of these tools (such as sending data to syslog) within the application or from having to design a mechanism to pass locally created flat logfiles to the centralized process (incurring delays in visibility and having to design logfile rotation mechanisms).

The important distinction is that factor 11 focuses on the concept of the logs streamed from the app. It is important to design proper logging within the application to ensure that proper information is relayed to the stream process after the application is executed on the server. If no information is being captured and sent to the logging stream, you have no ability to monitor and ensure the proper function or performance of the application.

Factor 12: Admin Processes

Admin processes within an application are ancillary functions that perform maintenance, administration, or other duties that are not invoked within the application's execution. These could be situations in which the module needs to be installed, internal databases need to be migrated or reset to a clean state, or the consistency of the environment from which the application is being run needs to be ensured.

In keeping with the first factor, these admin processes should be included within the single codebase, the same one that includes the application code. They should explicitly declare any dependencies required and should be able to be executed from the same environment in which the application runs. Finally, any external or required configuration should be explicitly defined and stored outside of the administrative process functions to ensure consistency and function across environments. In short, you should treat any administration processes with the same discipline and rigor that you would when designing and developing the main application.

Summary

This chapter focuses on the guiding principles, cultures, and methodologies of modern application development teams. It provides some insight into how applications move from repositories of code to compiled applications and binaries to being deployed on infrastructure and examples of leveraging the capabilities of such pipelines for both infrastructure and applications. These pipelines are contrasted with some of the challenges that operations staff faced in the early days of application deployment and support as well as how modern operations staff can be removed from supporting the infrastructure. Finally, the chapter discusses the design principles that can serve as a baseline for the development of a modern web-based or SaaS application.

Exam Preparation Tasks

As mentioned in the section "How to Use This Book" in the Introduction, you have a couple of choices for exam preparation: the exercises here, Chapter 17, "Final Preparation," and the exam simulation questions in the Pearson Test Prep Software Online.

Review All Key Topics

Review the most important topics in this chapter, noted with the Key Topic icon in the outer margin of the page. Table 7-3 lists a reference of these key topics and the page numbers on which each is found.

Table 7-3 Key Topics for Chapter 7

Key Topic Element	Description	Page Number
Section	SRE vs. DevOps	198
Paragraph	Need and purpose of continuous integration (CI) pipelines	199
List	Automated deployment methodologies of applications	206
Paragraph	Ways in which CI/CD pipelines (or outcomes) can be built	207
Table 7-2	Popular Configuration Management Utilities	221
Paragraph	Explanation of value of managed Kubernetes offerings	224
Paragraph	Definition and operation of serverless container platforms	227
Paragraph	What are serverless functions?	234

Complete Tables and Lists from Memory

There are no memory tables or lists in this chapter.

Define Key Terms

Define the following key terms from this chapter and check your answers in the glossary:

DevOps, site reliability engineering (SRE), continuous integration (CI), continuous delivery (CD), continuous deployment (CD), version control system (VCS), source code manager (SCM), Infrastructure as Code (IaC), serverless, Kubernetes

References

URL	QR Code
https://cloud.google.com/blog/products/devops-sre/how-sre-teams-are-organized-and-how-to-get-started	
https://sre.google/sre-book/introduction/	
https://www.runatlantis.io/guide/testing-locally.html	
https://kind.sigs.k8s.io/docs/user/quick-start/	
https://www.tiobe.com/tiobe-index/	
https://www.gnu.org/software/make/manual/html_node/Simple-Makefile.html	

URL	QR Code
https://microservices-demo.github.io/docs/	
https://12factor.net	

CHAPTER 8

Security in Application Design

This chapter covers the following topics:

- **Protecting Privacy:** This section covers what constitutes personally identifiable information (PII), data states (in motion or at rest), and how the state affects the security architecture and process. Laws and regulations governing privacy and security are also discussed.
- **Storing IT Secrets:** In this section, you learn about the various types of "secrets" or credentials used to authenticate and authorize any communication or transaction. Passwords are a common example, but others also are described in this section.
- **Public Key Infrastructure (PKI):** This section covers PKI, which is a type of asymmetric cryptography algorithm that requires the generation of two keys. One key is secure and known only to its owner; it's the private key. The other key, called the public key, is available and known to anyone or anything that wishes to communicate with the private key owner.
- **Securing Web and Mobile Applications:** This section provides a detailed look at the Open Web Application Security Project (OWASP) application security verification system and discusses a few common attacks and how to prevent them.
- **OAuth Authorization Framework:** This section discusses how OAuth 2.0 works and the most common flows for authorization.

This chapter maps to the first part of the *Developing Applications Using Cisco Core Platforms and APIs v1.0 (350-901)* Exam Blueprint Section 4.0, "Application Deployment and Security," specifically subsections 4.9, 4.10, and 4.11.

This chapter focuses on various security aspects in application design and execution. As applications become more distributed, business data is forced to cross multiple boundaries outside the control of enterprise security systems. Throughout the chapter, we cover a few issues and scenarios related to designing and building applications with security in mind. In addition to security needed to protect assets and your business reputation, it has also become an important focus area for regulations and compliance. There has been a rise in multiple regulations and frameworks related to data privacy and sovereignty, such as the General Data Protection Regulation (GDPR) in the European Union and the California Consumer Protection Act (CCPA), a US-based state regulation example.

In the following sections, we run through a number of examples about security design in application development.

“Do I Know This Already?” Quiz

The “Do I Know This Already?” quiz allows you to assess whether you should read this entire chapter thoroughly or jump to the “Exam Preparation Tasks” section. If you are in doubt about your answers to these questions or your own assessment of your knowledge of the topics, read the entire chapter. Table 8-1 lists the major headings in this chapter and their corresponding “Do I Know This Already?” quiz questions. You can find the answers in Appendix A, “Answers to the ‘Do I Know This Already?’ Quizzes.”

Table 8-1 “Do I Know This Already?” Section-to-Question Mapping

Foundation Topics Section	Questions
Protecting Privacy	1–3
Storing IT Secrets	4, 5
Public Key Infrastructure (PKI)	6, 7
Securing Web and Mobile Applications	8, 9
OAuth Authorization Framework	10

1. What does the information security CIA triad stand for?
   a. Central Intelligence Agency
   b. Confidentiality, integrity, and availability
   c. Certificate Improvement Administration
   d. None of these answers are correct.
2. The term *data states* refers to data being ________. (Choose all that apply.)
   a. In motion or at rest
   b. Encrypted or decrypted
   c. Clear text or encrypted
   d. In a relational or nonrelational database
3. What does data at rest mean?
   a. Data is not in transit
   b. On a hard drive
   c. Stored in a database
   d. All of these answers are correct.
4. What does PII refer to?
   a. Personally identifiable information
   b. Personal and interested identity
   c. Professionally identifiable information
   d. None of these answers are correct.

5. GDPR is a data protection law in the EU; what does it stand for?
   a. General Data Public Relations
   b. General Data Protection Regulation
   c. Generic Decision Probability Router
   d. None of these answers are correct.
6. IT secrets are all the following except ________.
   a. Passwords
   b. API keys
   c. Account credentials
   d. Vehicle identification number (VIN)
7. What is a certificate authority's main function?
   a. Certifying authorities in data communication
   b. Issuing and signing certificates
   c. Certifying account security
   d. Storing personal passwords
8. Which of the following is considered to be an injection attack? (Choose all that apply.)
   a. SQL injection
   b. LDAP
   c. Operating system commands
   d. All of these answers are correct.
9. Which of the following is *not* a cryptographic attack?
   a. Brute-force attack
   b. Implementation attack
   c. Statistical attack
   d. PoH attack
10. What is the difference between a two-legged authorization flow and a four-legged one?
   a. The two-legged one utilizes an authorization server.
   b. The four-legged one takes longer to execute.
   c. There is no such thing as a four-legged authorization.
   d. They are identical.

Foundation Topics

Information system security can be summed up in three fundamental components: confidentiality, integrity, and availability. This is sometimes referred to as the *CIA triad*, as shown in Figure 8-1.

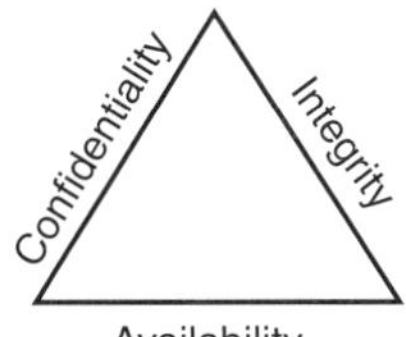

Figure 8-1 *Information System Security Triad*

Simply put:

- **Confidentiality:** The capability to protect data from unauthorized access.
- **Integrity:** The capability to protect data from modification (authorized or unauthorized modification). Any interception of data that affects the content is considered a violation of the integrity of the data.
- **Availability:** The capability of an authorized entity or process to access data anytime it needs to reliably.

Included within or adjacent to CIA are a number of supporting security elements:

- Authentication
- Authorization
- Identity and identity management
- Auditing
- Anomaly detection

In some scenarios, security used to be external to the software development process. In other words, applications had functions to perform, and they were protected by perimeter-type security devices like firewalls enabled with the appropriate access polices or intrusion detection or prevention systems watching for specific signatures and stopping them. You can think of security as a negative goal. It cannot be achieved and guaranteed; therefore, these methods focused on the "don'ts" (things that cannot happen). When you look at security from a nonfunctional requirement perspective, you immediately realize that you're facing a difficult task, and trade-offs must apply. A simple trade-off would be: If you want a highly secure system, then be prepared to give up some performance.

8

The next best alternative was to standardize a checklist-type process like the **Open Web Application Security Project (OWASP)** application security verification system. The OWASP website at https://owasp.org/ lists the Top 10 Web Application Security Risks for 2021:

1. Broken access control
2. Cryptographic failures
3. Injection
4. Insecure design
5. Security misconfiguration

6. Vulnerable and outdated components
7. Identification and authentication failures
8. Software and data integrity failures
9. Security logging and monitoring failures
10. Server-side request forgery

With the emergence of DevOps, a shift toward integration of security began early in the design and development lifecycles. You may see this movement of security referred to as the "shift left." In the following sections, we work on concepts for designing security into the application and its data at rest or in motion.

Protecting Privacy

Privacy is one of the hottest issues in security today. The emergence of the digital economy, e-commerce, and social media continues to put privacy issues at the forefront. Eventually, local (or global) governments and standard bodies had to step in and bring awareness and regulations to protect individuals. But first they had to define what constitutes private information.

Personally Identifiable Information

Personally identifiable information (PII) is any information that can be used to identify a person. Various standard and regulatory bodies define PII in their own ways and in various contexts, and using generic language; however, the following examples are common to most definitions:

- Name(s)
- Social Security number or tax identification number
- Driver's license number
- Credit card number
- Address
- Personal biometric data: fingerprints, retina scan, voice
- Photographs
- The list goes on and could possibly depend on the context in which the data is being used.

PII data is everywhere and is used in almost every transaction and must be protected. The applications you're writing must protect PII data and must pass periodic audits.

Data States

To protect data, you must first know the state it is in. Data is either in motion, at rest, or in use:

- **Data in motion:** The data is in transit or traveling between two nodes or across the network. Data needs to move between nodes and applications to create transactions. For example, data needs to move between a point-of-sale (POS) system and a credit card processing application. It must be protected. You would commonly think of encryption to protect that data while in transit. Encryption can be applied at different stages of the data journey: at the link level, network level, or application level.

Transport Layer Security (TLS) is the most common encryption protocol and is considered to be strong enough for web traffic. Commonly, web data is transmitted over the Secure Sockets Layer (SSL) using TLS 1.1 or 1.2. TLS is used for ensuring integrity and confidentiality over a network. It uses symmetric cryptography using a shared key negotiated at the initialization of a session. It is also possible to use TLS for authentication using public key–based authentication involving digital certificates.

- **Data at rest:** When data is not being transmitted, then it is considered at rest. When data is stored on a hard drive, tape, or any other media type, then it is at rest. A great deal of sensitive data is at rest. Examples include password files, databases, and backup data. In today's distributed system web applications, the definition is widened to include data within personal hard drives, network-attached storage (NAS), storage-area networks (SANs), and cloud-based storage. Similar to data in motion, encryption plays a big role in protecting data at rest. Encryption can be applied to the entire disk or to individual files. Encrypting the entire disk may tax performance, but it's a small price to pay to secure sensitive data.
- **Data in use:** Some security and privacy standards define this third state. When data is being processed, updated, or generated, then it is considered to be in use. You could argue that when data is the in the in-use state, it is actually sitting in memory or "swap" space somewhere and could be considered "at rest." You would not be wrong.

Whether data is at rest or in motion, protecting the data with access control, encryption, or other means is what we discuss in the next few sections.

Laws, Regulations, and Standards for Protecting Privacy

A number of US, European, and global standards and regulations continue to evolve to keep up with the speed of change in how business is conducted and information is shared.

In addition, these regulations specify and make a clear distinction among the following:

- **Data privacy:** Addresses confidentiality of data and preventing unauthorized access.
- **Data sovereignty:** Identifies who has power over the data. If data resides in the US, it does not matter what entity or government owns it, the data is subject to US laws.
- **Data localization:** Specifies where the data should be located. For example, all data related to EU citizens must be located in the EU, even if the entity in possession of the data is a US-based company.

The following are laws or regulations that you may see or hear about:

- **General Data Protection Regulation (GDPR):** This regulation gives European Union (EU) citizens control over their own personal data. In addition, it is built with the digital economy in mind. GDPR is increasing new personal data rights to EU citizens, including the right to withdraw consent, have easier access to their data, understand where their data is stored, and know if their data has been compromised by a cyberattack within 72 hours, depending on the relevance of the attack. In a nutshell, GPDR helps people gain more control over their personal data and, in turn, mandates companies to be transparent, accountable, and fair when using personal data.

- **Health Insurance Portability and Accountability Act (HIPAA):** This US federal law creates national standards for protecting patient data. It controls the use and disclosure of people's health information. HIPAA not only is for all US health-care businesses that have access to protected health information (that is, hospitals, private doctors, health insurance companies) but also covers business associates that provide services to those covered entities that process protected health information (PHI) on their behalf (including cloud service providers hosting health-care applications).
- **Sarbanes-Oxley Act of 2002 (SOX):** SOX might not seem to be a "privacy" law initially, but it does include some privacy clauses in it. It's designed to protect investors by improving the accuracy and reliability of corporate reporting.
- **Payment Card Industry Data Security Standard (PCI DSS):** This standard aims to secure credit card data and transactions against theft or fraud.

GDPR is the toughest of these examples and is much broader in scope than the other three; it includes security, privacy, and data localization elements.

Storing IT Secrets

To move at the speed of business, today's enterprises utilize commercial off-the-shelf (COTS), home-grown, and open-source software to build applications that automate their business and serve their customers. There are no magic applications; applications need to interact with other applications and do so using credentials. These credentials are called *secrets*; in an IT context, they're called *IT secrets*, and are used as "keys" to unlock protected applications or application data.

The following examples are secrets exchanged between applications:

- Passwords
- API keys
- Account credentials
- Encryption keys
- Credentials for connecting to databases
- Credentials used for API calls

Secrets can be used by the application for

- Securing CI/CD pipelines and tools (for example, Jenkins, Ansible, Puppet)
- Securing containers
- Improving portability

- Providing direct code storage or through environment variables
- Providing database storage
- Enabling API calling and synchronization
- Furnishing encrypted code storage
- Presenting cloud-based secret services

Managing and storing secrets can be easy or can be difficult. That ease or difficulty depends on the scope of the applications and the boundaries that the application interaction must cross. You can store secrets in the source code, and it can be seen by everyone who reviews your code (this approach is not recommended). Secrets can also be stored directly in the code but encrypted. You can also use an external secret management service.

When planning to protect application secrets, you should consider the following:

- Make this a design decision. Take all applications (centralized or distributed), networks, and cloud interactions into consideration.
- Update secrets before moving the application into production. Do not use the same set of secrets for development, QA, and production.
- Use multifactor authentication when possible and for critical information retrieval.
- Using single sign-on is recommended whenever possible and whenever the capabilities are available and simple to apply.

The following are common secrets-storing strategies:

- **Embedded into the code:** This strategy is not the best because anyone with access to the code will have access to the secrets. You can change secrets after code reviews and audits, if possible, but again, this is not a safe way. This approach is not recommended and is shown in the following example:

  ```
  # MyApp_example.py
  MyApp_API_KEY = 'lkajdfuishglkjg' # Hello World, look at my
  password
  ```

  On the other hand, it can be used with encryption if you manage to store and use the key safely.

- **In the environment:** This strategy is safer than the method before it. It has more control as to who has access to secrets. However, it is also prone to user misconfigurations because you have to update environments on every server. Automated orchestration of passwords may not be a bad idea here:

  ```
  # MyApp_example.py
  MyApp_API_KEY = os.environ["MyApp_API_Key"]
  ```

- **In a database:** In this strategy, a single infrastructure is used to manage passwords and secrets:

  ```
  # MyApp_example.py
  db = MySQLdb.connect ("192.168.100.2","username","mypassword",
  "MYDB")
  ```

- **At a syncing service:** This strategy provides a centralized way for managing secrets. You manage a single password to manage a service that manages all your secrets; however, all passwords and API keys need to be hosted with that service. Understanding your application's landscape and dependencies is essential at this stage.

  The syncing service can also be hosted in the cloud as SaaS—for example, Amazon's AWS Key Management Service (KMS). Similarly, Microsoft Azure offers Vault as an alternative. The advantages are clear:

  - Centralized key management
  - Fully managed service
  - Low cost, depending on your organization
  - Support for auditing
  - Help with your compliance efforts

  HashiCorp Vault is widely used; it is a free and open-source product that can also come with an enterprise offer.

Public Key Infrastructure (PKI)

A **public key infrastructure (PKI)** is a type of asymmetric (a.k.a. public key) cryptography algorithm that requires the generation of two keys. One key is secure and known only to its owner; it is called the *private* key. The other key, called the *public* key, is available and known to anyone or anything that wishes to communicate with the private key owner. PKI has multiple components that coordinate the trust and the generation and destruction (revocation) of keys, so let's look at a quick summary of the main ones.

A **certificate authority (CA)** is the main component that brings together the full cycle that starts with a "trusted" certificate authority issuing and signing a certificate. Certificate authorities are third-party or neutral organizations that certify that the other entities communicating with each are in fact who they say they are. The communicating entities (such as the server/client) can be users, machines, servers, or databases.

When a CA certifies an entity, the CA verifies that entity's identity and grants it a certificate, signing it with the CA's private key. The CA has its public key, available to everyone. It also has a private key, which is securely stored. Servers and clients use the CA's root certificate to verify signatures that the certificate authority has issued.

A simple search for the top certification authorities revealed multiple "top 10" results. The following names are common to the majority of the lists:

1. Symantec
2. GeoTrust
3. Comodo
4. DigiCert
5. Thawte
6. GoDaddy
7. Network Solutions
8. RapidSSLonline
9. SSL.com
10. Entrust Datacard

As you build your security architecture, it is important to know your CA landscape. In the majority of cases, your organization has probably made the choice for you, so you don't have to know much above and beyond which CA you should direct your traffic to initially. It is also worth mentioning that it is not uncommon to see private (organization-specific) implementations of PKI.

Figure 8-2 demonstrates what's referred to as the enrollment and verification process and how a user requests and receives a CA's identity certificate.

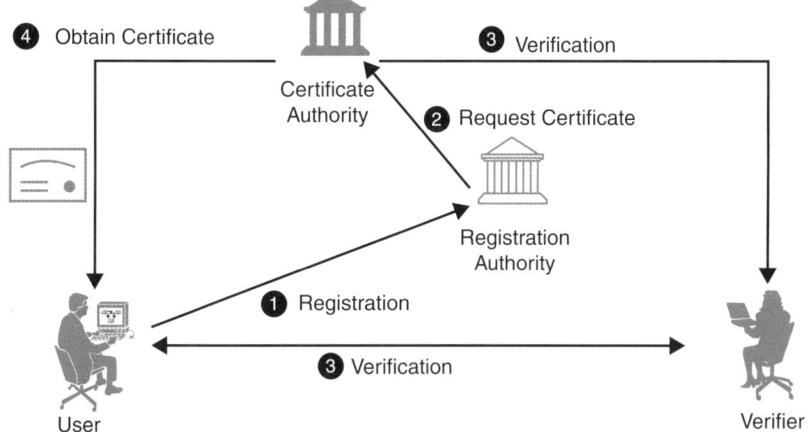

Figure 8-2 *User Request and Verification*

The steps are as follows:

1. Register with the CA or the registration authority (RA) (this can be a physical meeting or other means of identity verification).
2. Request a certificate from the CA admin.

3. Independently verify the identity of the user and that the certificate planned for issue is not on the certificate revocation list.
4. The CA admin issues and signs a certificate.

Digital certificates (or simply *certificates*) are identities verified and issued by the CA. The format of the certificates is defined by the International Telecommunication Union (ITU) in their X.509 standard, and it includes:

- Version
- Serial number
- Signature (algorithm ID used to sign the certificate)
- Name of issuer
- Validity (dates, durations)
- Subject (owner's name, also called distinguished name)
- Subject's public key information
- Issuer's unique ID (CA's ID)
- Subject's unique ID
- Optional extensions for specific implementations

Certificate Revocation

As you saw in the preceding section, certificates have a "validity" period or an expiration date. When certificates expire, they become in doubt, or some foul play is expected, they get revoked. Revoked certificates and their serial numbers are added to a certificate revocation list (CRL). Figure 8-3 shows a high-level illustration of the revocation process and the storing of the CRL at the CA server.

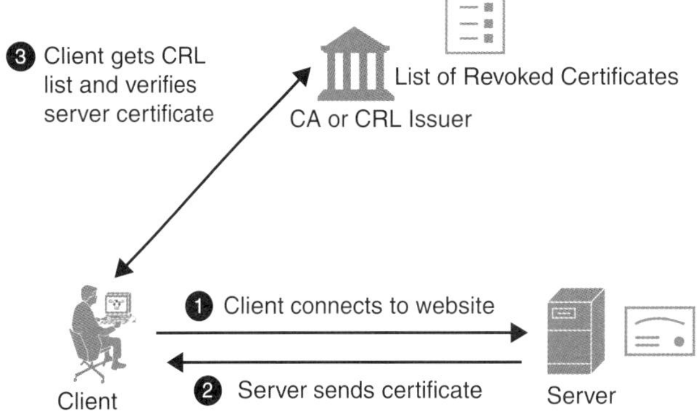

Figure 8-3 *Certificate Revocation*

Certificate revocation is a centralized function, providing push and pull methods to obtain a list of revoked certificates periodically or on demand.

Hierarchical Multiple CA Infrastructure

PKI has a hierarchical structure where it has a root CA and subordinate CAs. The subordinate CAs are used for offloading the root CA or for flexibility to support various use cases. The hierarchy can also help with reliability and availability because CAs can validate one another or for one another. Figure 8-4 shows an example of hierarchical CA implementation.

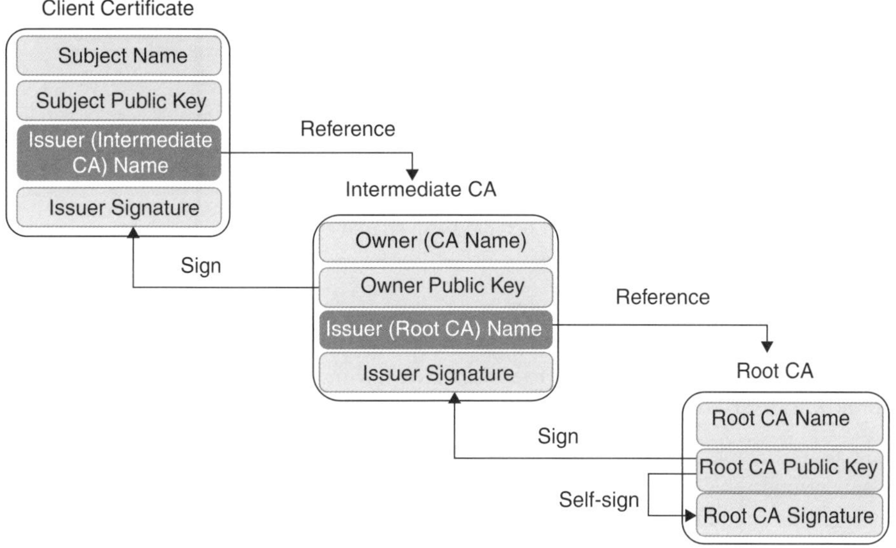

Figure 8-4 *Hierarchical CA Implementation*

The root CA has a self-assigned certificate. The trust within the hierarchy is derived from the Rivest-Shamir-Adleman (RSA) algorithm. RSA is an asymmetric key cryptography system that provides both encryption and digital signatures used for nonrepudiation and authentication.

TLS, PKI, and Web Applications Security

As business moves more and more into the digital or e-commerce economy, web applications are used to conduct most of that business. Encryption is an essential facilitator of communication with web applications. SSL/TLS have become the standard security protocols for authentication and integrity for protecting HTTP traffic.

Figure 8-5 shows the client/server exchange for negotiating and establishing a new TLS connection.

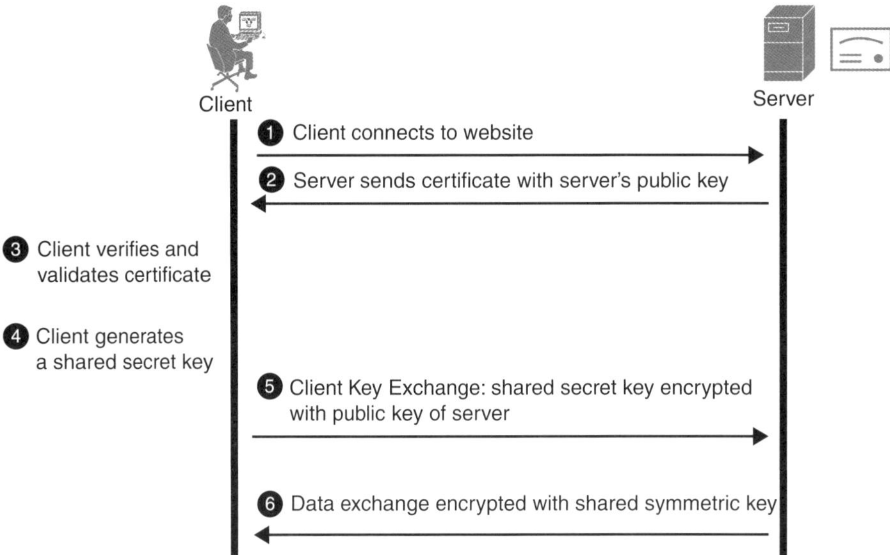

Figure 8-5 *TLS New Connection Exchange*

In practice, the certificates are stored and hidden from the user within the browser. The TLS validation is also hidden unless the user wants to view the details. Here's an example of where or how to verify the exchange:

1. The user attempts to connect to a security training site (see Figure 8-6). When the connection to the server is first initialized, the server provides its PKI certificate to the client. This contains the public key of the server and is signed with the private key of the CA that the owner of the server has used.

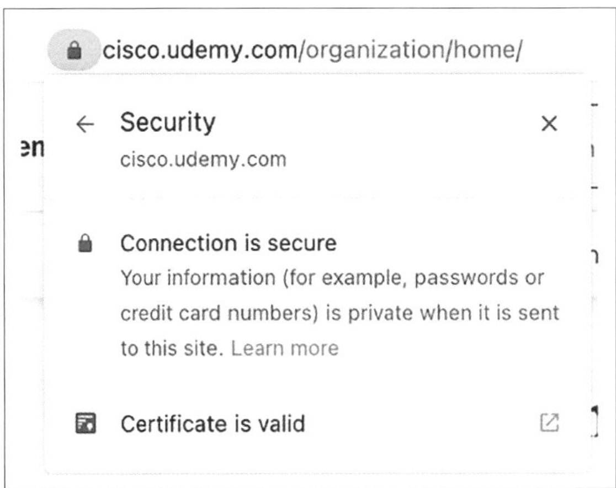

Figure 8-6 *User Connects to a Web App*

2. The signature is subsequently verified to confirm that the PKI certificate is trustworthy. If the signature can be traced back to a public key that already is known to the client, the connection is considered trusted. Figures 8-7 and 8-8 show an example that was executed on a macOS and may look a little different than one executed on a Windows or Linux operating system.

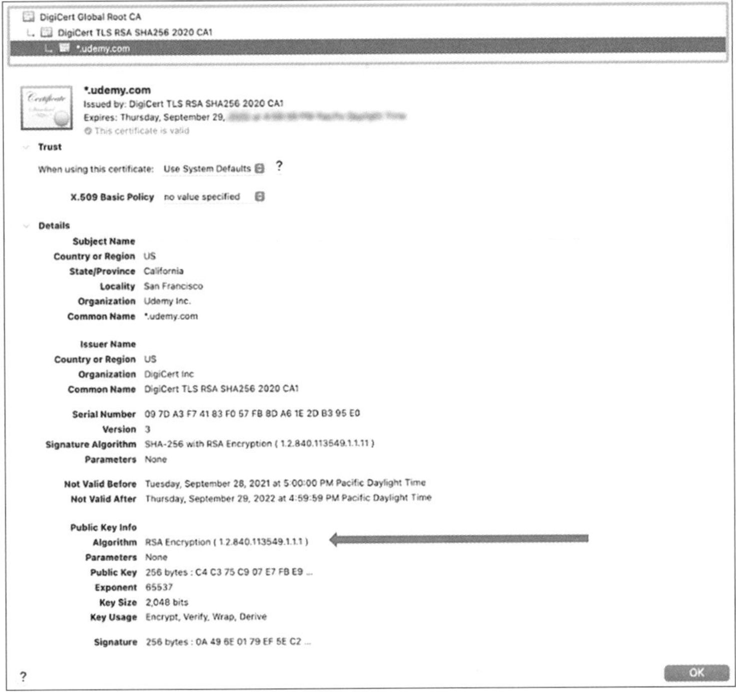

Figure 8-7 *Valid and Trusted Certificate*

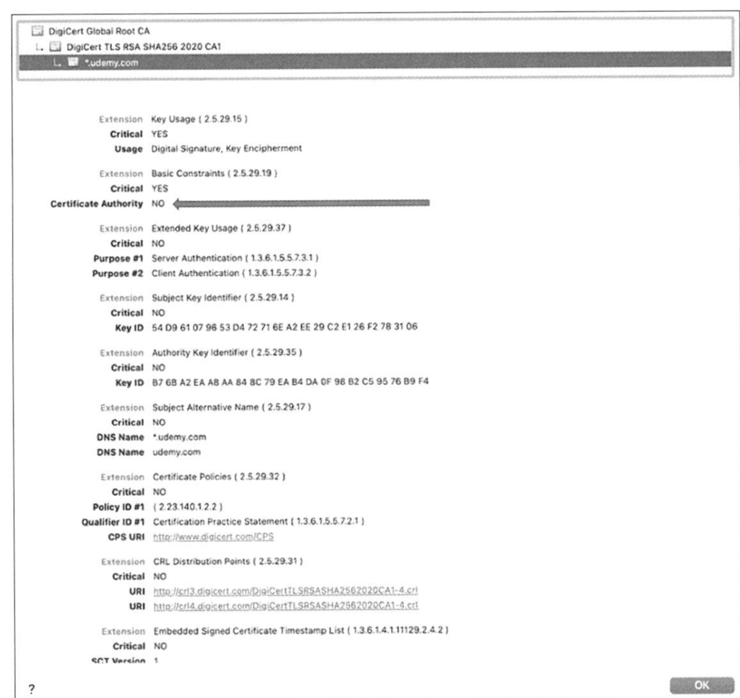

Figure 8-8 *Continuation from the Data Viewed in Figure 8-7*

3. Now that the connection is trusted, the client can send encrypted packets to the server. Figure 8-9 shows that after verification, the connection is trusted, and encrypted traffic can be exchanged with the server.

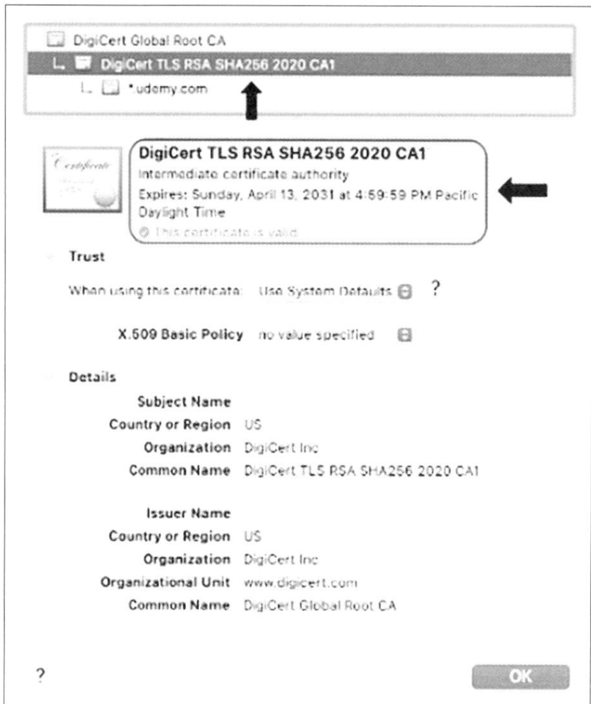

Figure 8-9 *Highlighting the Validity, Trust, and Encryption (Highlighted and Boxed)*

4. Because public/private key encryption is one-way encryption, only the server can decrypt the traffic by using its private key. Figure 8-10 displays further verification that only the shown server can decrypt the traffic.

In Figure 8-10, it is possible to view the path to the issuing CA. Before a certificate is trusted, the system (the client OS) must verify that the certificate comes from a trusted source. This process is called *certificate path validation (CPV)*, which says that every certificate's path from the root CA to the client (or host system) is legitimate or valid. CPV can also help ensure that the session between two nodes remains trusted. If there is a problem with one of the certificates in the path, or if the host OS cannot find a certificate, the path is considered "untrusted." Typically, the certification path includes a root certificate and one or more intermediate certificates.

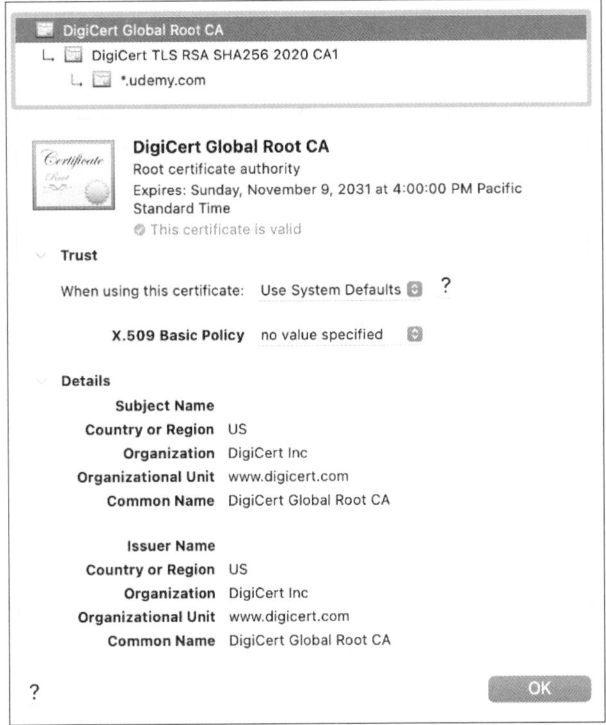

Figure 8-10 *Root CA Path Validation*

Browser Security Issues

As a web app developer, you must be able to handle and absorb warning messages related to certificate validation. Clear messages are usually displayed at the event of any issue, regardless of the severity. Don't ignore the warnings; they may turn out to be easy-to-fix issues or may actually be cryptographic attacks. The most common issues associated with security warnings are as follows:

- **Hostname/identity mismatch:** URLs specify a web server name. If the name specified in the URL does not match the name specified in the server's identity certificate, the browser displays a security warning. Hence, DNS is critical to support the use of PKI in web browsing.
- **Validity date range:** X.509v3 certificates specify two dates: not before and not after. If the current date is within those two values, there is no warning. If it is outside the range, the web browser displays a message. The validity date range specifies the amount of time that the PKI will provide certificate revocation information for the certificate.

- **Signature validation error:** If the browser cannot validate the signature on the certificate, there is no assurance that the public key in the certificate is authentic. Signature validation will fail if the root certificate of the CA hierarchy is not available in the browser's certificate store. A common reason may be that the server uses a self-signed certificate.
- **Cryptographic attacks:** There are many types of cryptographic attacks; they may or may not look any different than other security-type attacks, which include
  - **Brute-force attacks:** These attacks utilize highly capable computational systems to try every combination of keys or passwords.
  - **Statistical attacks:** These attacks exploit statistical weaknesses in the crypto system or algorithm.
  - **Implementation attacks:** These attacks exploit weaknesses in the implementation of the crypto system. As mentioned earlier, anyone can implement the system with or without adherence to X.509v3.
  - **Others:** Other types of attacks may be related to specific implementations or customizations, such as meet-in-the-middle, side-channel, birthday, or social engineering attacks.

Securing Web and Mobile Applications

We introduced OWASP at the beginning of the chapter and briefly discussed a few vulnerabilities or common security scenarios affecting web applications. We also briefly described the Top 10 web application security risks. OWASP published a list in 2017 and recently published the list shown in 2021. The items on the list are ranked based on a score presented and justified by OWASP and the community of security professionals it surveys. The scores are based on factors like exploitability, detectability, likelihood, and impact. Here's the list with details as published on https://owasp.org/www-project-top-ten/. We highly recommend that you visit the site and learn about the security issues and possible techniques for mitigating them.

- **A01:2021-Broken Access Control:** Access control enforces policy such that users cannot act outside of their intended permissions. Failures typically lead to unauthorized information disclosure, modification, or destruction of all data or performing a business function outside the user's limits.
- **A02:2021-Cryptographic Failures:** Cryptography failures or attacks often lead to sensitive data exposure or system compromise.
- **A03:2021-Injection:** When user data is not frequently validated, then injection or extraction of sensitive records is possible.
- **A04:2021-Insecure Design:** This broad category represents different weaknesses, expressed as "missing or ineffective control design." This category was not listed in the 2017 list.

- **A05:2021-Security Misconfiguration:** This is an important category, and it comes in many forms: missing information, password management issues, error handling, and so on.
- **A06:2021-Vulnerable and Outdated Components:** This is also a broad category that we mention in this book multiple times. You should have a good handle on all versions, vulnerabilities, and the recommended versions.
- **A07:2021-Identification and Authentication Failures:** Confirmation of the user's identity, authentication, and session management is critical to protect against authentication-related attacks.
- **A08:2021-Software and Data Integrity Failures:** This new category for 2021 focuses on making assumptions related to software updates, critical data, and CI/CD pipelines without verifying integrity.
- **A09:2021-Security Logging and Monitoring Failures:** This one is self-explanatory. Without logging and monitoring, your ability to detect breaches or attacks is diminished.
- **A10:2021-Server-Side Request Forgery:** This category is also self-explanatory and is considered to be high on the list of issues needing attention.

In the next few sections, we provide a practical approach to dealing with a few of the items on the list.

Injection Attacks

Injection attacks affect a wide range of attack vectors. In the 2017 OWASP Top 10 list, injection attacks were classified as the top web application security risk. On the 2021 list, it dropped to third place, possibly because of advanced tooling and monitoring allowing you to detect injections or because the top risks have been observed more frequently. Regardless of the ranking, injection remain a serious issue.

The most common injection attacks are related to SQL and common databases; however, the following list will possibly grow:

- SQL, NoSQL injection
- Object relational mapping
- LDAP injection
- Operating system commands
- Code injection
- CRLF injection
- Email header injection
- Host header injection
- Operating system command injection
- XPath injection

SQL attacks are the most common type of attack, partly due to the nature of the language and the ability to build dynamic queries. SQL injection attacks happen when an application is not able to differentiate trusted from untrusted.

```
string query = 'SELECT * FROM users_data WHERE user = ' + user_name
```

If the user gives the input as **user_name = "' OR 1=1"**, the query returns all users in the database because **1=1** always evaluates as true and all user data is displayed.

To protect your code and database against injection, we recommend following these leading practices:

- Use prepared statements with variable binding (parameterize queries). Prepared statements are specific. Using **1=1** does not have specificity and in essence means nothing. These statements are also simple to write and easier to read than dynamic queries.
- Allow lists are the next best alternative when you're unable to use variable binding because it is not always allowed or legal in SQL. Creating allow lists increases the difficulty for an attacker to inject queries. Allow lists match every user input to a list of "allowed" or "acceptable" characters.
- OWASP.org mentions stored procedures as another defense option. In a way, they're like prepared statements where prepared (or canned) SQL is built, saved, and used frequently and as needed.

NOTE The OWASP website offers great information for understanding the attacks and provides you with various ways to protect your code and applications. We found the "SQL Injection Prevention Cheat Sheet" to be of great value:

https://cheatsheetseries.owasp.org/cheatsheets/SQL_Injection_Prevention_Cheat_Sheet.html

Cross-Site Scripting

Cross-site scripting (XSS) comes in various forms and outcomes and is also considered a type of an injection attack. With XSS, attackers inject malicious scripts into a web application to obtain information about the application or its users. The three main types of XSS are

- **Stored XSS:** In Figure 8-11, the attacker injects a script (a.k.a. a Payload) into a web server, and the script is triggered every time a user visits the website.

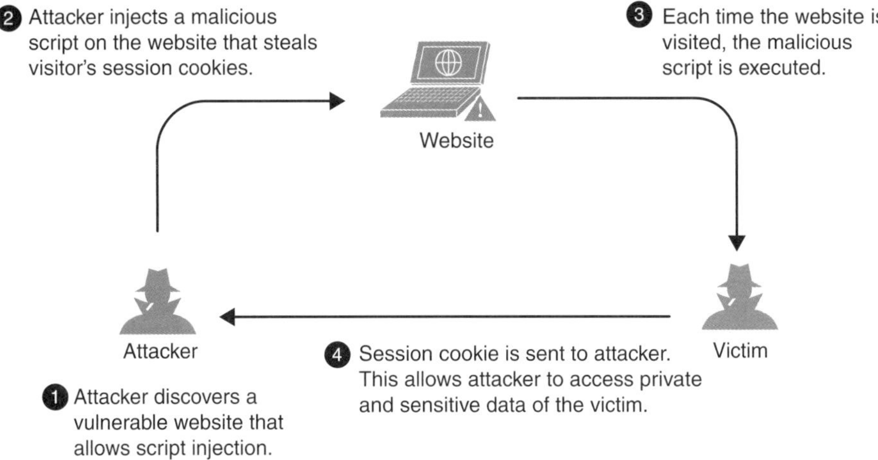
2 Attacker injects a malicious script on the website that steals visitor's session cookies.
3 Each time the website is visited, the malicious script is executed.
Website
Attacker
Victim
4 Session cookie is sent to attacker. This allows attacker to access private and sensitive data of the victim.
1 Attacker discovers a vulnerable website that allows script injection.

Figure 8-11 *Stored XSS Attack*

- **Reflected XSS:** This attack or injection, detailed in Figure 8-12, is delivered to the "victim" using a trusted email or URL. The injection can also be reflected off a website like an error message or query result. The victim is then tricked into clicking or responding, leading to the execution of the code.

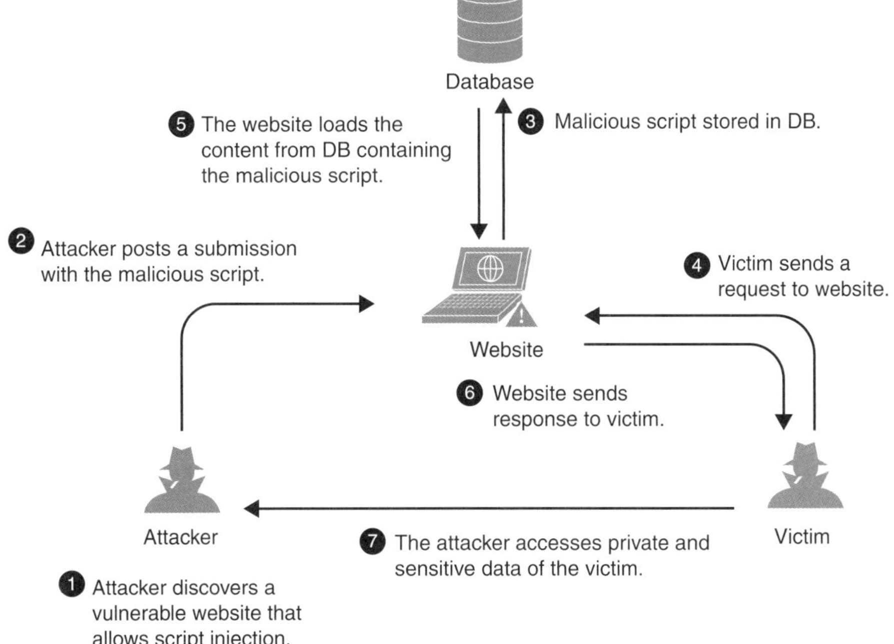
Database
5 The website loads the content from DB containing the malicious script.
3 Malicious script stored in DB.
2 Attacker posts a submission with the malicious script.
Website
4 Victim sends a request to website.
6 Website sends response to victim.
Attacker
Victim
7 The attacker accesses private and sensitive data of the victim.
1 Attacker discovers a vulnerable website that allows script injection.

Figure 8-12 *Reflected XSS Attack*

- **DOM-based XSS:** The attacker injects a script or payload into the Document Object Model (DOM), and the script is triggered through the console. The steps are clearly detailed in Figure 8-13. Unlike the stored and reflected attacks, a DOM-based attack is a client-based attack instead of a server-side attack.

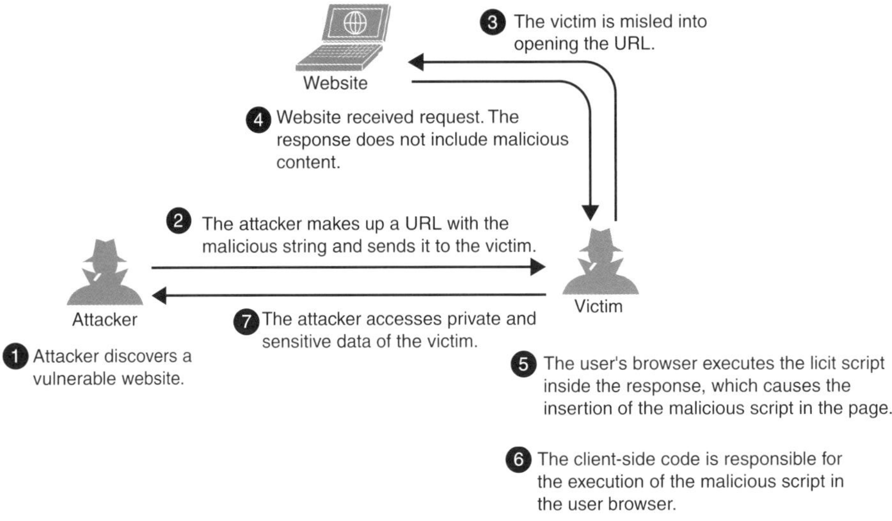

Figure 8-13 *DOM-Based XSS Attack*

OAuth Authorization Framework

Open Authentication (OAuth) is an open standard defined by IETF RFC 6749. Two versions are in use today: OAuth 1.0 and 2.0. OAuth 2.0 is not backward compatible with OAuth 1.0 (RFC 5849). OAuth 2.0 is widely used and is briefly covered in this chapter.

OAuth is designed with HTTP in mind and allows users to log in to multiple sites or applications with one account.

NOTE RFC 6749 is a good read, and we highly recommend that you get familiar with the main concepts if your work responsibilities include building application security components: https://datatracker.ietf.org/doc/html/rfc6749.

How Does OAuth Work?

If you've ever logged in to your Google account and used the same account to log in to Facebook and Twitter, then there is a high probability that single sign-on (SSO) was involved and OAuth was at work. To grant access to a Facebook service, you in essence authorized an OAuth server via authentication to issue an OAuth token to Facebook. By allowing the sharing of tokens with the third party (Facebook in this example), you're allowing Google to grant Facebook a token without sharing your credentials.

OAuth defines these four roles:

- **Resource owner (end user or thing):** Normally, the end user but can also be any compute entity.
- **Resource server:** The host of the secured accounts. The server responds to the client.
- **Client (client application):** The application making a resource request.
- **Authorization server:** The server issuing access tokens to the client after it verifies identity.

OAuth also defines four grant type flows. A *grant* is a credential representing the end user's authorization used by the client application to obtain an access token. The four grant types are as follows:

- **Authorization code:** The authorization code is obtained by an authorization server as intermediary between the client and the end user.
- **Implicit flow:** This simplified authorization code flow is optimized for client applications implemented in a browser using a scripting language. Instead of issuing the client and authorization code, the client is issued an access token directly.
- **Resource owner password credentials:** Simply put, this one is more like a name and password for the end user.
- **Client credentials:** Client application credentials can be used when the client is acting on its own behalf. This means when the client application is acting as a resource owner (or end user) requesting access to protected resources with the authorization server.

Figure 8-14 details the exchange among the four defined roles.

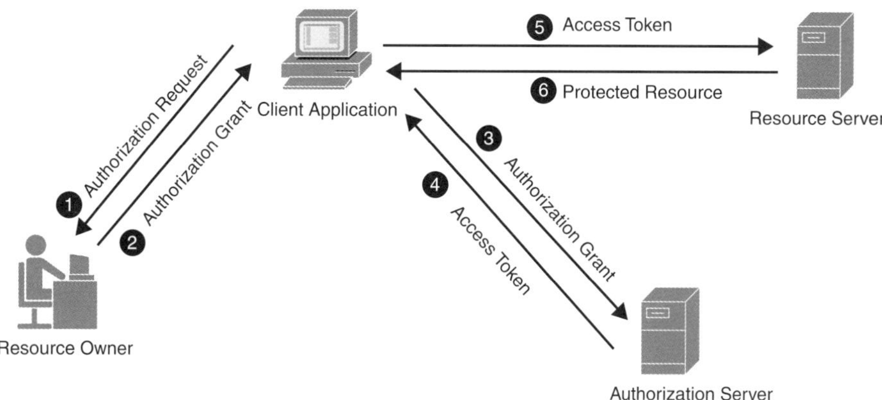

Figure 8-14 *OAuth 2.0 Protocol Flow*

The flow steps illustrated in Figure 8-14 are as follows:

1. The client requests *authorization* from the resource owner (end user). The authorization request can be made directly to the resource owner (as shown), or preferably indirectly via the authorization server as an intermediary.

2. The client receives an *authorization grant*, which is a credential representing the resource owner's authorization, expressed using one of four grant types defined in this specification or using an extension grant type. The authorization grant type depends on the method used by the client to request authorization and the types supported by the authorization server.
3. The client requests an access token by authenticating with the *authorization server* and presenting the authorization grant.
4. The authorization server authenticates the client and validates the authorization grant, and if valid, issues an *access token*.
5. The client requests the protected resource from the resource server and authenticates by presenting the access token.
6. The resource server validates the access token, and if valid, serves the request.

OAuth 2.0 has two authorization flows: two-legged and three-legged.

OAuth 2.0 Two-Legged Authorization

The two-legged flow authorization has two exchanges (flows) among three components. It involves three parties: the authorization server, client application, and resource server. It is a simple and straightforward flow. As seen in Figure 8-15, the two-legged authorization flow does not require the presence of an end user.

Key Topic

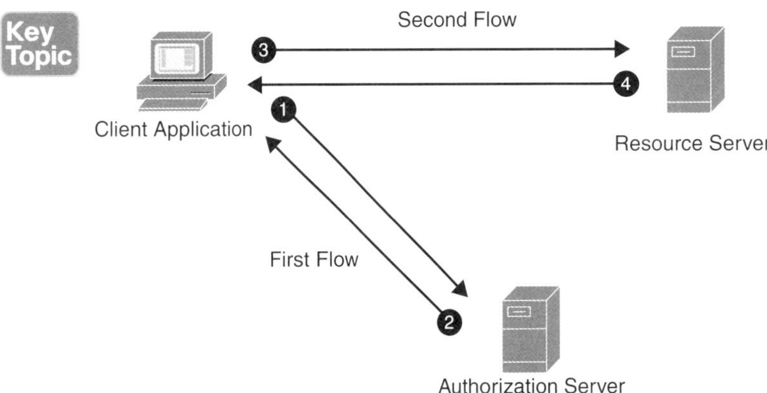

Figure 8-15 *Two-Legged OAuth Flow*

Initially, the client application authenticates with the authorization server and requests an access token. This action is done by making the request with **grant_type = client_credentials** and providing the **client_id** and **client_secret**. The following code example illustrates the point:

```
POST /oauth/oauth20/token HTTP/1.1

Host: server.devcor.com

Content-Type: application/x-www-form-urlencoded

Accept: application/json


grant_type=client_credentials
```

```
client_id=pwmdisdz78fs9dujtn35wps67

client_secret=45kj86985utjfk98u389o658ogwti
```

The authorization server then authenticates the request and, if valid, issues an access token including any additional parameters:

```
HTTP/1.1 200 OK

Date: Wed, 15 Dec 2021 14:32:12 GMT

Content-Type: application/json


{

 "access_token":"2YotnFZFEjr1zCsicMWpAA",

 "token_type":"bearer",

 "expires_in":3600,

 "example_parameter":"example_value"

 }
```

OAuth 2.0 Three-Legged Authorization

The three-legged OAuth flow requires four parties: the authorization server, client application, resource server, and resource owner (end user). The three flows or exchanges among the four parties are why the authorization is called *three-legged*. By looking at the difference in interaction between the two-legged and the three-legged authorization, you can probably guess that the two-legged one is used for API authorization versus end-user authorization with the three-legged flow.

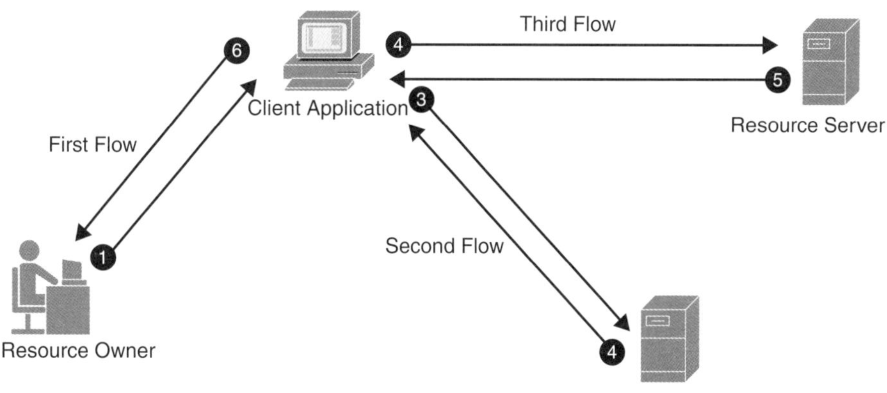

Figure 8-16 *Conceptual Diagram of the Three-Legged Authorization*

Figure 8-16 provides a general representation of the three-legged authorization. The first step is to retrieve the authorization code. The second step is to exchange the authorization code for an access token. The third exchange is to use the token. The flows or exchanges represented in Figures 8-16 and 8-17 assume that the authorization server uses two authentication protocols: OAuth and OpenID. The two protocols work well together to ensure a seamless authorization process.

Key Topic

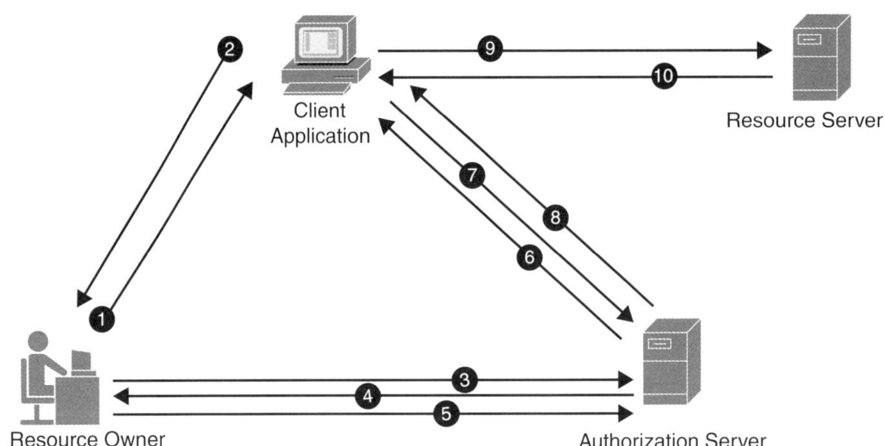

Figure 8-17 *Detailed Workflow of the Three-Legged Authorization*

Figure 8-17 illustrates the detailed exchange of the three-legged OAuth 2.0 authorization:

1. The end user (resource owner) sends a request to the OAuth client application.
2. The client application sends the resource owner a "redirect" to the authorization server.
3. The resource owner connects directly with the authorization server and authenticates.
4. The authorization server presents a form to the resource owner to grant access.
5. The resource owner submits the form to allow or to deny access.
6. Based on the response from the resource owner, the following processing occurs:
   - If the resource owner allows access, the authorization server sends the OAuth client a redirection with the authorization grant code or the access token.
   - If the resource owner denies access, then the request is redirected to the client without a grant.
7. The OAuth client sends the authorization grant code, client ID, and the certificate to the authorization server.
8. When the information is verified, the authorization server sends the client an access token and a refresh token (refresh tokens are optional).
9. The client sends the access token to the resource server to request protected resources.
10. If the access token is valid for the requested protected resources, then the OAuth client can access the protected resources.

Additional OAuth Authorization Code Grant Types

In the following sections, we briefly describe additional OAuth authorization grant types and illustrate their flows.

OAuth 2.0 Client Credentials

The client credentials grant type is used by clients (applications) to obtain an access token for their own resources, not on behalf of a user. Figure 8-18 illustrates the flows.

Key Topic

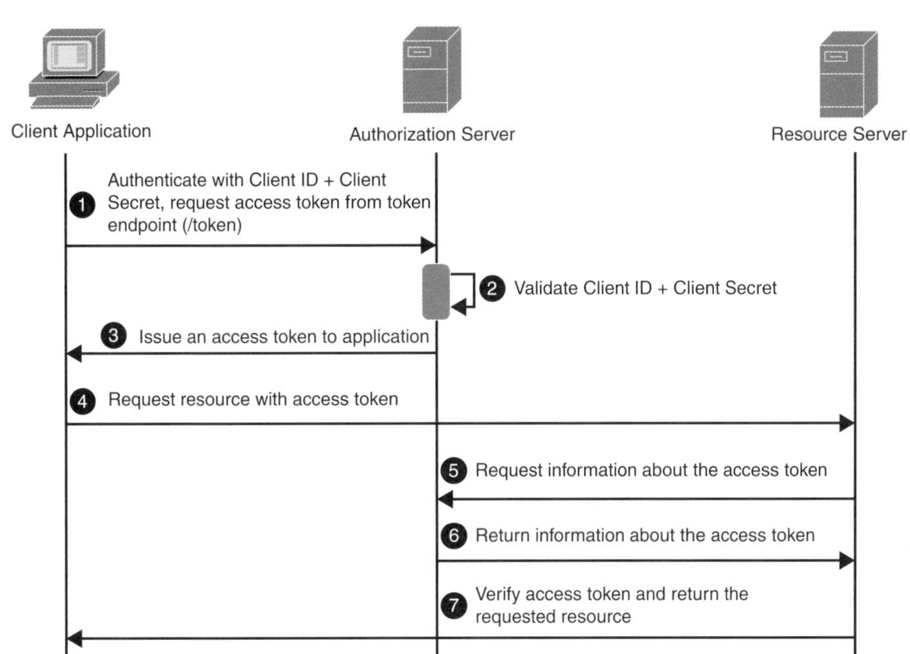

Figure 8-18 *Client Credential Flow*

The steps are as follows:

1. The client application requests an access token from the authorization server using the token endpoint and passing the client ID and client secret parameters. The following request call is made to the /token endpoint:

```
POST /token HTTP/1.1

Host: authorization-server.example.com

Content-Type: application/x-www-form-urlecoded

grant_type=client_credentials  // - Required

&scope={Scopes}                // - Optional
```

```
client_id= -kUr9VhvB_tWvv2orfPsKHGz
client_secret= LSidh2foCzJngCJqLSElXIl5TchjvL9_217OzbRpEFW6RlNf
```

2. The authorization server validates the client ID and client secret.
3. The authorization server issues an access token to the application. The following is an example of the authorization server response:

```
HTTP/1.1 200 OK
Content-Type: application/json;charset=UTF-8
Cache-Control: no-store
Pragma: no-cache
{
  "access_token": "{Access Token}",     // - Always included
  "token_type": "{Token Type}",         // - Always included
  "expires_in": {Lifetime In Seconds}, // - Optional
  "scope": "{Scopes}"                   // - Mandatory if the
                                              granted
                                        //    scopes differ from the
                                        //    requested ones.
}
```

4. The client application retrieves the access token and requests the resource from the resource server.
5. The resource server requests information about the access token from the authorization server, for verification purposes.
6. The authorization server returns the requested information to the resource server.
7. The resource server verifies the access token, and if valid, it returns the resource to the client application.

Resource Owner Password Credential Flow

Figure 8-19 illustrates the resource owner password credential flows.

Key Topic

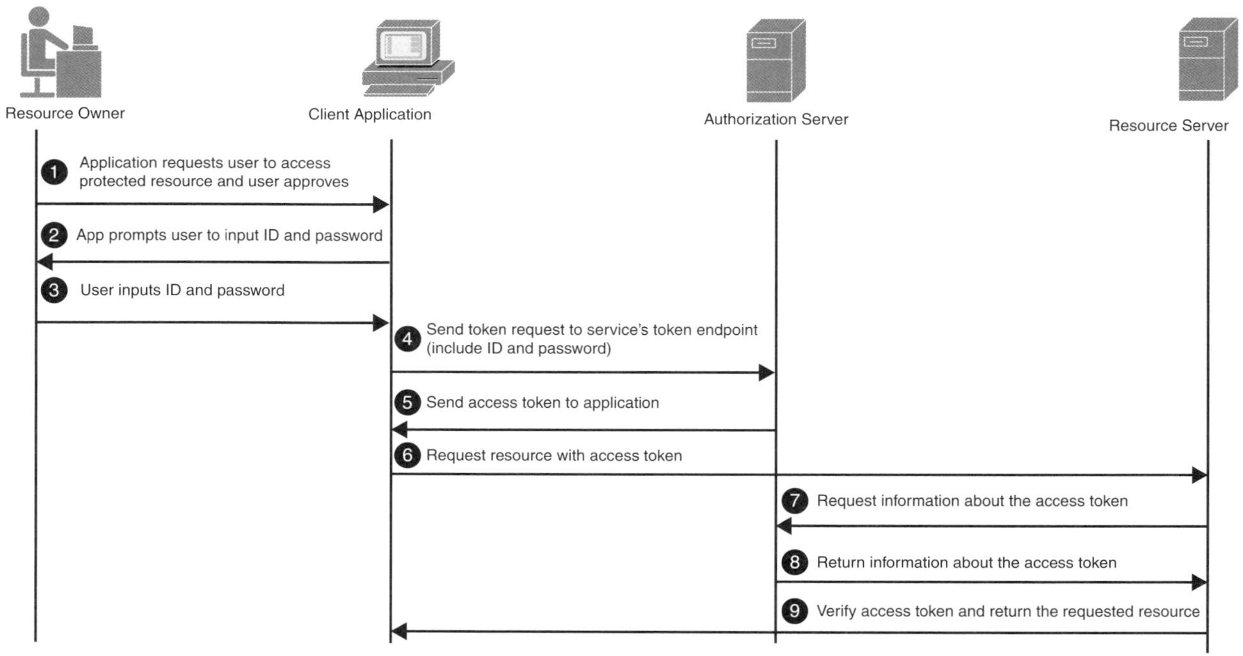

Resource Owner

Client Application

Authorization Server

Resource Server

1 Application requests user to access protected resource and user approves

2 App prompts user to input ID and password

3 User inputs ID and password

4 Send token request to service's token endpoint (include ID and password)

5 Send access token to application

6 Request resource with access token

7 Request information about the access token

8 Return information about the access token

9 Verify access token and return the requested resource

Figure 8-19 *Resource Owner Password Credential Flow*

The steps are as follows:

1. The client application requests access to a protected resource, and the resource owner approves.
2. The client application prompts the resource owner to input credentials: ID and password.
3. The resource owner inputs their ID and password.
4. The client application sends a token request to the authorization server token endpoint, including the ID and password. The following request is made to the token endpoint:

```
POST /token HTTP/1.1

Host: https://authorization-server.example.com

Content-Type: application/x-www-form-urlecoded

grant_type=password

&username={User ID}

&password={Password}

&scope={Scopes}
```

5. The authorization server sends an access token to the client application. The following is an example of a response from the token endpoint:

```
HTTP/1.1 200 OK

Content-Type: application/json;charset=UTF-8

Cache-Control: no-store

Pragma: no-cache{

  "access_token": "{Access Token}",

  "token_type": "{Token Type}",

  "expires_in": {Lifetime In Seconds},

  "refresh_token": "{Refresh Token}",

  "scope": "{Scopes}"

}
```

6. The client application requests the resource from the resource server using the access token.
7. The resource server requests information about the access token from the authorization server, for verification purposes.
8. The authorization server returns the requested information to the resource server.
9. The resource server verifies the access token, and if valid, it returns the resource to the client application.

OAuth 2.0 Implicit Flow

Figure 8-20 illustrates the OAuth 2.0 implicit flow.

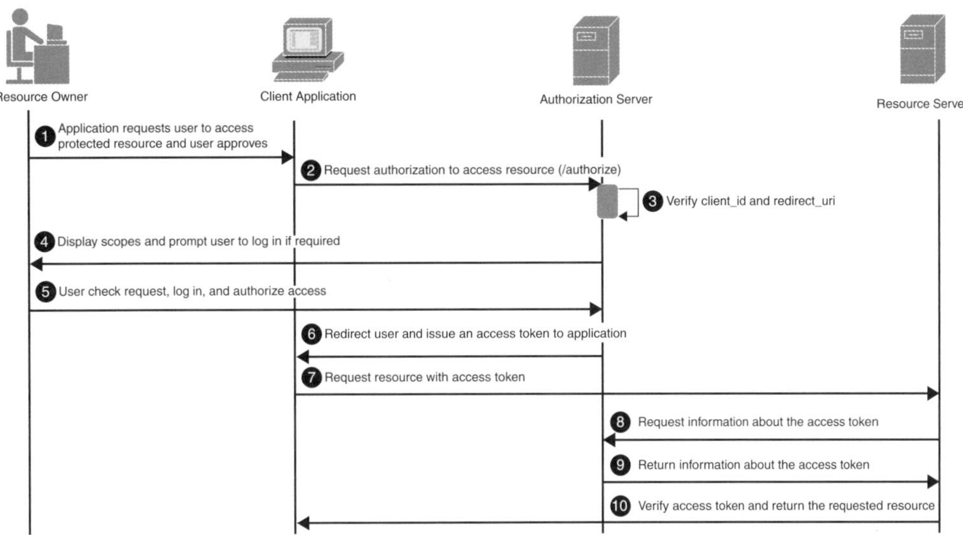

Figure 8-20 *OAuth 2.0 Implicit Flow*

The steps are as follows:

1. The application requests the user to access protected resources, and the user approves.
2. Build the authorization URL and redirect the user to the authorization server:

```
https://authorization-server.example.com/authorize?
 response_type=token
  &client_id=-kUr9VhvB_tWvv2orfPsKHGz
  &redirect_uri=https://example-app.com/implicit.html
  &scope=photo
  &state=RqQ-hXJYv3seO6Mp
```

3. Verify client_id and redirect_uri.
4. Display scopes and prompt the user to log in if required.
5. The user logs in and authorizes access.
6. Redirect the user and issue an access token to the application.
   - Verify the state matches:

```
access_token=V2tY2H9NSV3nlDIRUSN2CHUsbkH9Hn3Hx1jcvZ6N6v2
OYFWUoKhAqEHUxqc7r76FqVIDQHWE&token_type=Bearer&expires_
in=86400&scope=photos&state=RqQ-hXJYv3seO6Mp
```

NOTE The implicit flow is being deprecated in the Security BCP because there is no solution in OAuth for protecting the implicit flow, and it will not stop a malicious actor from injecting an access token into your client.

- Extract the access token from the URL fragment:

```
access_token: c1CqK7fBYqg7XEno4H82wpw4P_
  Pn3p7mUk4No05xOJ81x8kqgcq4B3HghETCBx3PizwZHLPF

token_type:    Bearer

expires_in:    86400

scope:          photos
```

7. Request a resource with the access token.
8. The resource server requests information about the access token.
9. The authorization server returns information about the access token.
10. The resource owner verifies the access token and, if valid, then it returns the requested resource.

OAuth 2.0 Authorization Code Flow

Figure 8-21 illustrates the authorization code flow of OAuth 2.0.

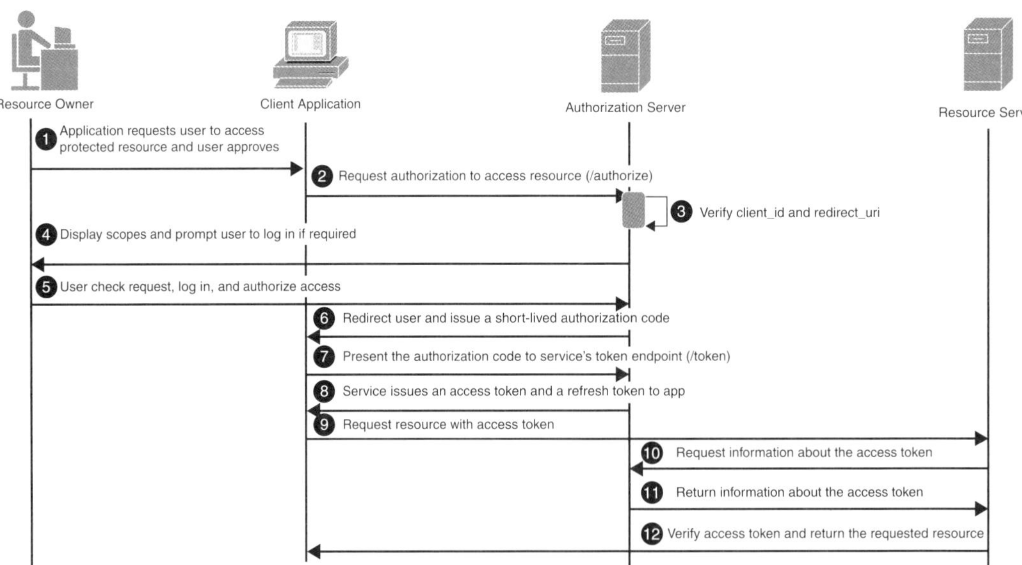

Figure 8-21 *OAuth 2.0 Authorization Code Flow*

The steps are as follows:

1. The application requests the user to access protected resources, and the user approves.
2. Build the authorization URL and redirect the user to the authorization server:

```
https://authorization-server.example.com/authorize?
  response_type=code
  &client_id=-kUr9VhvB_tWvv2orfPsKHGz
  &redirect_uri=https://www.example-app.com/authorization-code.html
  &scope=photo+offline_access
  &state=SzbChK9KrCGa8Gnp
```

3. Verification.
4. Display scope and prompt the user to log in if required.
5. The user authorizes access.
6. Redirect the user and issue a short-lived authorization code:
   - Verify the state parameter:

```
?state=SzbChK9KrCGa8Gnp&code=sescvu5DJd568Xso8z2RxgonSk9Ucl0MIe8JD5
  sJ8Z_dojc
```

7. Exchange the authorization code for an access token:

```
POST https://authorization-server.example.com/token
grant_type=authorization_code
&client_id=-kUr9VhvB_tWvv2orfPsKHGz
&client_secret=LSidh2foCzJngCJqLSElXIl5TchjvL9_2l7OzbRpEFW6RlNf
&redirect_uri=https://www.example-app.com/authorization-code.html
&code=sescvu5DJd56-8Xso8z2RxgonSk9Ucl0MIe8JD5sJ8Z_dojc
```

8. The token endpoint response is as follows:

```
{
  "token_type": "Bearer",
  "expires_in": 86400,
  "access_token": "kzTq84yQvIhjEgNlg7Jb3tOrbuydA0mpO4fSuDA-
    xMzzhPOf-a4x9iF8wQF2PzSxCgIBkGVW",
  "scope": "photo offline_access",
  "refresh_token": "a0fbHhsmcrV1VBNeimrJdNk8"
}
```

9. Extract the access token and request a resource with the access token.
10. The resource server requests information about the access token.
11. The authorization server returns information about the access token.
12. The resource owner verifies the access token and, if valid, it returns the requested resource.

OAuth 2.0 PKCE Flow

Figure 8-22 illustrates the PKCE flow of OAuth 2.0.

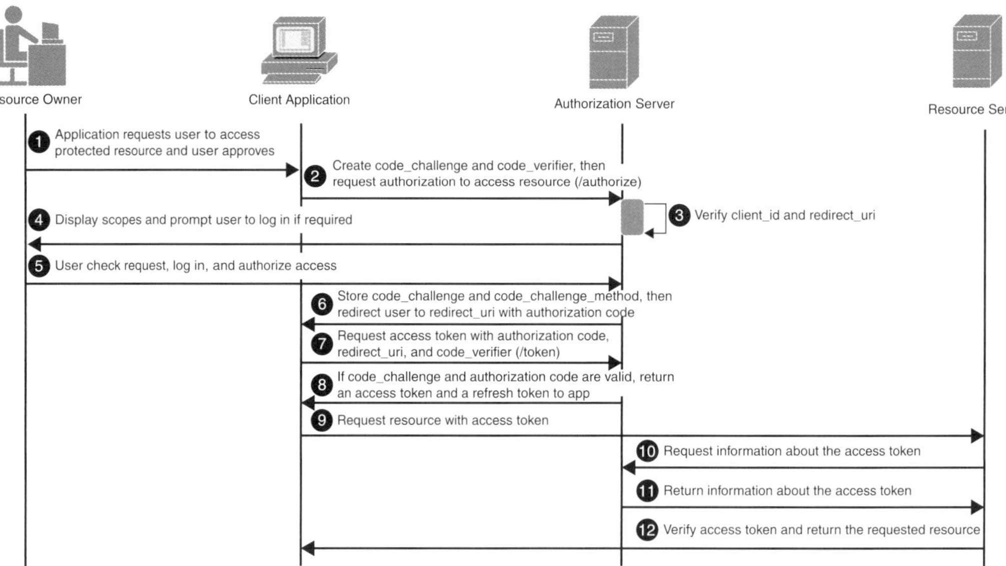

Figure 8-22 *OAuth 2.0 PKCE Flow*

The steps are as follows:

1. The application requests the user to access protected resources, and the user approves.
2. Create a code verifier and challenge; then build the authorization URL:

```
Code verifier: Jrl0qZuBNMuA9vpwg49DgwcQaP4tMBKVgZUlOE__kbGAlAm3

Code Challenge: base64url(sha256(code_verifier)) =
  QesOP7mDGTTFDzZgFTZAYMWIXv17SRE9G4i601mwE4M

The client needs to store the code_verifier for later use.

https://authorization-server.example.com/authorize?

  response_type=code

  &client_id=-kUr9VhvB_tWvv2orfPsKHGz
```

```
&redirect_uri=https://www.example.com/authorization-code-with-
  pkce.html
&scope=photo+offline_access
&state=nb3l0xXX4MlHR3k_
&code_challenge=QesOP7mDGTTFDzZgFTZAYMWIXv17SRE9G4i601mwE4M
&code_challenge_method=S256
```

The client includes the **code_challenge** parameter in this request, which the authorization server stores and compares later during the code exchange step.

3. Verify the client_id and redirect_uri.
4. Display the scope and prompt the user to log in if required.
5. The user logs in and authorizes access.
6. The authorization server stores code_challenge and code_challenge_method and then redirects the user and issues an authorization code:
   - Verify the state parameter.

   The user is redirected back to the client with a few additional query parameters in the URL:

```
?state=nb3l0xXX4MlHR3k_&code=70diP-rT46VdBFb2SSf_hrFxczgyO1QbH
  pQmQQTdqoLPMY7_
```

The state value isn't strictly necessary here because the PKCE parameters provide CSRF protection themselves.

7. Exchange the authorization code for an access token.

   The client builds a POST request to the token endpoint with the following parameters:

```
POST https://authorization-server.example.com/token
grant_type=authorization_code
&client_id=-kUr9VhvB_tWvv2orfPsKHGz
&client_secret=LSidh2foCzJngCJqLSElXIl5TchjvL9_217OzbRpEFW6RlNf
&redirect_uri=https://www.example.com/authorization-code-with-
  pkce.html
&code=70diP-rT46VdBFb2SSf_hrFxczgyO1QbHpQmQQTdqoLPMY7_
&code_verifier=Jrl0qZuBNMuA9vpwg49DgwcQaP4tMBKVgZUl0E__kbGAlAm3
```

The code_verifier is sent along with the token request. The authorization server checks whether the verifier matches the challenge that was used in the authorization request. This ensures that a malicious party that intercepted the authorization code is not able to use it.

8

8. The token endpoint response follows.

The response includes the access token and refresh token:

```
{
  "token_type": "Bearer",
  "expires_in": 86400,
  "access_token": "8K63E0hHj_NdQokyP-1_awC8_pSwnJxnPKbmJEw98DHssRg
    W7NU1XEAC2M2ZGF1pQJD4Ak2P",
  "scope": "photo offline_access",
  "refresh_token": "Ni8yoGKqWT9gfjeREMn5Rkol"
}
```

9. Extract the access token and request a resource with the access token.

10. The resource server requests information about the access token.

11. The authorization server returns information about the access token.

12. The resource owner verifies the access token and, if valid, it returns the requested resource.

Refresh Token Flow

Figure 8-23 illustrates the refresh token flow. Here, assume that the application has a refresh token that was issued previously with an access token during an authorization request in the past.

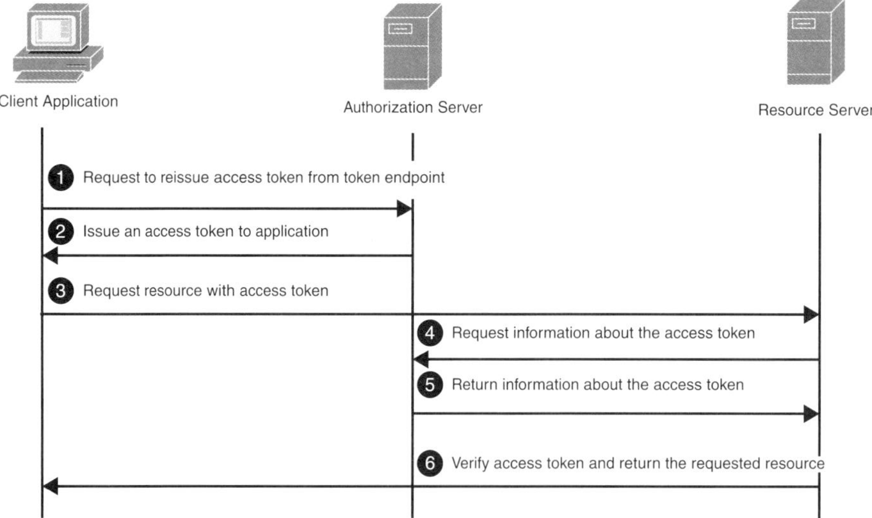

Figure 8-23 *Refresh Token Flow*

The steps are as follows:

1. The client application sends a request to the authorization server token endpoint to reissue the access token. The following request is made to the token endpoint:

```
POST {Token Endpoint} HTTP/1.1
Host: {Authorization Server}
Content-Type: application/x-www-form-urlecoded
grant_type=refresh_token
&refresh_token={Refresh Token}
&scope={Scopes}
```

2. The authorization server provides the access token to the client application. The following is an example of the response from the authorization server token endpoint:

```
HTTP/1.1 200 OK
Content-Type: application/json;charset=UTF-8
Cache-Control: no-store
Pragma: no-cache{
  "access_token": "{Access Token}",
  "token_type": "{Token Type}",
  "expires_in": {Lifetime In Seconds},
  "refresh_token": "{Refresh Token}",
  "scope": "{Scopes}"
}
```

3. The client application requests the resource from the resource server using the access token.
4. The resource server requests information about the access token from the authorization server, for verification purposes.
5. The authorization server returns the requested information to the resource server.
6. The resource server verifies the access token, and if valid, it returns the resource to the client application.

8

OAuth 2.0 Device Code Flow

Figure 8-24 illustrates the device code flow of OAuth 2.0.

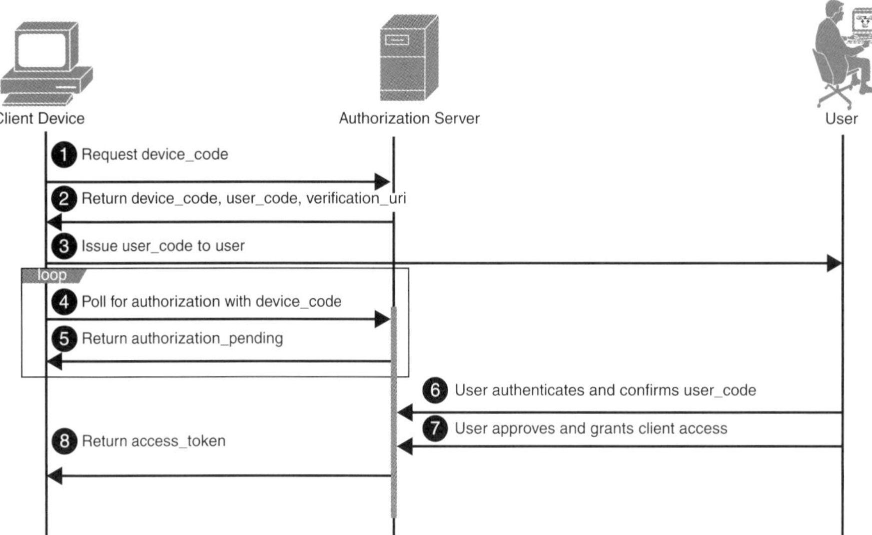

Figure 8-24 *OAuth 2.0 Device Code Flow*

The steps are as follows:

1. Request a device code from the authorization server:

```
POST https://example.com/device

client_id=https://www.oauth.com/example/
```

2. The authorization server returns a response that includes the device code, a code to display to the user, and the URL the user should visit to enter the code.

```
{

  "device_code": "NGU5OWFiNjQ5YmQwNGY3YTdmZTEyNzQ3YzQ1YSA",

  "user_code": "BDWD-HQPK",

  "verification_uri": "https://example.com/device",

  "interval": 5,

  "expires_in": 1800

}
```

3. Present the verification_uri and user_code to the user and instruct the user to enter the code at the URL.

4. Poll the token endpoint.

   While you wait for the user to visit the URL, sign in to their account, and approve the request, you need to poll the token endpoint with the device code until an access token or error is returned:

```
POST https://example.com/token

grant_type=urn:ietf:params:oauth:grant-type:device_code
```

```
&client_id=https://www.oauth.com/example/
&device_code=NGU5OWFiNjQ5YmQwNGY3YTdmZTEyNzQ3YzQ1YSA
```

5. Poll: Before the user has finished signing in and approving the request, the authorization server returns a status indicating the authorization is still pending.

```
HTTP/1.1 400 Bad Request
{
  "error": "authorization_pending"
}
```

6. The user authenticates and confirms user_code.
7. The user approves client access.
8. Poll the authorization server periodically until the code has been successfully entered.

   When the user approves the request, the token endpoint responds with the access token:

```
HTTP/1.1 200 OK
{
  "token_type": "Bearer",
  "access_token": "RsT5OjbzRn430zqMLgV3Ia",
  "expires_in": 3600,
  "refresh_token": "b7a3fac6b10e13bb3a276c2aab35e97298a060e0ed
    e5b43ed1f720a8"
}
```

Now the device can use this access token to make API requests on behalf of the user.

Exam Preparation Tasks

As mentioned in the section "How to Use This Book" in the Introduction, you have a couple of choices for exam preparation: the exercises here, Chapter 17, "Final Preparation," and the exam simulation questions on the companion website.

Review All Key Topics

Review the most important topics in this chapter, noted with the Key Topic icon in the outer margin of the page. Table 8-2 lists a reference of these key topics and the page numbers on which each is found.

Table 8-2 Key Topics for Chapter 8

Key Topic Element	Description	Page Number
Section	Personally Identifiable Information	250
Section	Storing IT Secrets	252
Section	TLS, PKI, and Web Applications Security	257
Section	Injection Attacks	263
Section	Cross-Site Scripting	264
Figure 8-15	Two-Legged OAuth Flow	268
Figure 8-16	Conceptual Diagram of the Three-Legged Authorization	269
Figure 8-17	Detailed Workflow of the Three-Legged Authorization	270
Figure 8-18	Client Credential Flow	271
Figure 8-19	Resource Owner Password Credential Flow	273

Complete Tables and Lists from Memory

There are no memory tables or lists in this chapter.

Define Key Terms

Define the following key terms from this chapter and check your answers in the glossary:

certificate authority (CA), data at rest, data in motion, digital certificate, General Data Protection Regulation (GDPR), injection attack, Open Authentication (OAuth), Open Web Application Security Project (OWASP), personally identifiable information (PII), public key infrastructure (PKI), Transport Layer Security (TLS), cross-site scripting (XSS)

References

URL	QR Code
RFC 6749: https://datatracker.ietf.org/doc/html/rfc6749	
Open Web Application Security Project (OWASP): https://owasp.org/	

URL	QR Code
ITU X.509: https://www.itu.int/rec/T-REC-X.509	
GDPR: https://gdpr.eu/	

CHAPTER 9

Infrastructure

This chapter covers the following topics:

- **Network Management:** This section covers the purpose of network management through concept, engineering, provisioning, monitoring/operations, and decommissioning.
- **Methods of Network Provisioning:** This section reveals different methods in the process of network provisioning, such as CLI/console, SNMP, file transfer, embedded management, and the use of management systems.
- **Zero-Touch Provisioning (ZTP):** This section covers the concept of zero-touch provisioning or bootstrap configuring a device without physical access and manual effort.
- **Atomic or SDN-Like/Controller-Based Networking:** This section covers the concept of software-defined networking and its impact on network engineering and management.
- **Advanced Concepts—Intent-Based Networking:** This section covers intent-based networking and the advanced concepts that propel networks into the next generation of functionality.

This chapter maps to the first part of the *Developing Applications Using Cisco Core Platforms and APIs v1.0 (350-901)* Exam Blueprint Section 5.0, "Infrastructure and Automation."

We cover historical capabilities in infrastructure provisioning for context but move on to recommended methods and protocols for modern, automated environments. If you've been doing network infrastructure for a while, some of these references may bring back fond memories. If you're new to the industry or have a cloud-native focus, some of this content may make you laugh, but hopefully you appreciate the progress. We all start from somewhere.

"Do I Know This Already?" Quiz

The "Do I Know This Already?" quiz allows you to assess whether you should read this entire chapter thoroughly or jump to the "Exam Preparation Tasks" section. If you are in doubt about your answers to these questions or your own assessment of your knowledge of the topics, read the entire chapter. Table 9-1 lists the major headings in this chapter and their corresponding "Do I Know This Already?" quiz questions. You can find the answers in Appendix A, "Answers to the 'Do I Know This Already?' Quizzes."

Table 9-1 "Do I Know This Already?" Section-to-Question Mapping

Foundation Topics Section	Questions
Network Management	1, 3
Methods of Network Provisioning	2, 4, 7, 8
Element Management Systems	9
Zero-Touch Provisioning (ZTP)	5
Atomic or SDN-Like/Controller-Based Networking	7
Advanced Concepts—Intent-Based Networking	6

1. What does the acronym PDIOO stand for?
   a. Prep, do, inform, organize, operate
   b. Python, define, integrate, own, observe
   c. Plan, design, implement, operate, optimize
   d. Plan, do, integrate, organize, operate
2. SNMPv3 uses
   a. The MD5 and SHA authentication methods.
   b. Community string-based authentication.
   c. Key-based authentication.
   d. The AES-128 authentication method.
3. What does SRE stand for?
   a. Source route engineering
   b. Site reliability engineering
   c. Self-regulating entity
   d. Source route entity
4. What type of network is used for highly partitioned administrative traffic?
   a. FWM (firewall management)
   b. SR (segment routing)
   c. OOB (out-of-band network)
   d. VLAN (virtual local-area network)
5. What is an example of zero-touch deployment functionality?
   a. Powered-on provisioning
   b. Plug-and-play (PNP)
   c. Auto SmartPorts
   d. Papoose

6. Intent-based networking transforms a hardware-centric network of manually provisioned devices into a controller-centric network that uses ____________ translated into policies that are automated and applied consistently across the network.
   a. Business requirements
   b. Software definitions
   c. Routing protocols
   d. Artificial intelligence
7. What is NETCONF?
   a. A collaboration protocol for audio conferencing.
   b. A JSON-based schema for configuration management.
   c. A network controller function using Python.
   d. A protocol standardized by the IETF to normalize configuration management across multiple vendors using XML-based schemas and YANG models.
8. What is a 2FA or MFA function used to do?
   a. Develop resilient Python functions for device auditing.
   b. Provide a user-access accounting service.
   c. Validate something a user knows with proof of who they are to provide access.
   d. Programmatically initiate a Webex meeting.
9. An embedded management function is all that is needed for comprehensive IT Service Management.
   a. True
   b. False

Foundation Topics

Network Management

Ahh, network management. The oft-maligned discipline of network IT. If you ever worked in an environment where you were given marching orders, you might have cringed at the boss's directive: "I need you to work on network management." If you were in an environment where you were able to pick your own priorities, you probably did not select network management as a first choice. However, much has changed; there have been great strides and improvements in network management and operations that can be attributed to advancements with software-defined networks (SDN), DevOps, continuous integration/continuous deployment (CI/CD), and site reliability engineering (SRE).

You can't deal with network infrastructure without using proper planning, design, implementation, operation, and optimization (PDIOO) methodologies. The PDIOO model has been used for many years to provide structure in the networking discipline. Implementation, operations, and optimization have been most impacted by network programmability and automation over the years. The other planning and design components have also seen benefits from frameworks such as the Information Technology Information Library (ITIL), The Open Group Architecture Framework (TOGAF), and Control Objectives for Information and Related Technologies (COBIT). Whichever IT service management model is used, it is important that automation be a prime consideration in order to reduce human effort and errors, to increase speed of service delivery, and to gain operational efficiencies and repeatability of services against the network infrastructure.

However, you might wonder why network management and operations were given short shrift. Many times, it was the last consideration on the proposal/budget and the first to get cut. It's true that a well-engineered network could operate for a time without network management focus and still perform well. Over time that well-engineered network would undergo changes. A few configuration changes here. A decommissioned syslog event server there. An additional branch network here or 20 everywhere, and before you know it, serious problems need to be addressed! How many times have you heard about someone walking through the data center to see a red or amber light on a module, fan, or power supply, and then look at the logs and see the alert was first registered months ago (something like Figure 9-1)? Surely that has never happened to you!

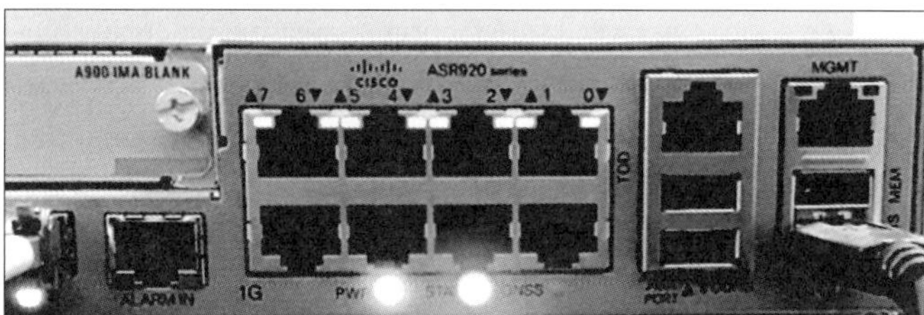

Figure 9-1 *Alarming Device*

Network has always been important. Depending on an organization's complexity, level of sophistication, and operational needs, using common commercial offerings from Cisco, such as DNA Center, Prime Infrastructure, Crosswork Network Automation, or Network Services Orchestrator (NSO), may be well suited to the situation. There are also well-equipped solutions from other vendors. However, as complexity increases and as scope of services expands, then automation, orchestration, and integration—among many other management tools and controllers—must occur.

A company that has multiple networking domains and dependent services will have many management tools and controllers to consider. Additionally, other IT systems, both commercial and open source, would be common. Popular open-source solutions, such as Grafana, Zabbix, Nagios, and OpenNMS, are often seen. Figure 9-2 shows an example.

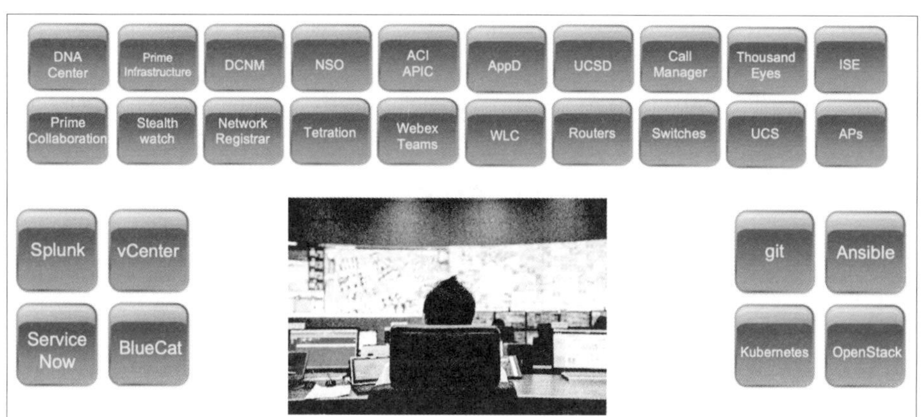

Figure 9-2 *A Broad IT Service Management Ecosystem*

Network management concepts provided strong roots for current alignments to automation, orchestration, **software-defined networking (SDN)**, DevOps, CI/CD, and site reliability engineering (SRE). SDN is a mature technology by now, whereas DevOps, CI/CD, and SRE may be new concepts to traditional network engineers. The collaboration among developers and network operations personnel to achieve highly automated solutions in a quick fashion is the foundation of **DevOps**. **Continuous integration/continuous deployment (CI/CD)** refers to a combined practice in software development of continuous integration and either continuous delivery or continuous deployment. **Site reliability engineering** is a practice that brings together facets of software engineering and development, applying them to infrastructure and operations. SRE seeks to create functional, scalable, and highly reliable software systems. It is good to have foundational networking skills, but it is even better when you can complement them with programming skills that can make monitoring and provisioning more automated and scalable.

As an engineer, like you, I experience a lot of personal satisfaction in creating practical solutions that impact my company and the world.

So, network management is not the career-limiting role it was once considered. Those in that discipline benefited by augmenting their skills with network programmability because it felt like a logical extension of the work already being done. And it served as the foundation for the skills professionals are aspiring to today. Don't lose heart if you're just joining us on your own network programmability journey; you're not too late! When you break free from continuous fire-fighting mode and enjoy the benefits of automation and network programmability, there is a lot of satisfaction. Ideally, the network management, operations, or SRE teams are doing their best work when network IT is transparent and accountable to the user and customer.

Indeed, the automation of network management, including service provisioning, has been a key differentiator for several large, successful companies. As an example, consider how Netflix moved from private data centers to the public cloud between 2008 and 2016. The company focused on automating its processes and tooling to give it a sense of assurance, even though its service operated over physical infrastructure it did not control. The company recognized that while it didn't own the infrastructure, it still owned the customer experience. Automation reduces effort for you and your customers. A customer-experience-focused business is a differentiator. Remember Henry Ford's 1909 comment about his Model T that you could "have any color so long as it's black"? That was not a customer-inclusive concept then and remains so now. Obviously, the company has since transformed its business to appeal to broader customer preferences.

Many companies differentiate themselves from competitors through automation. When they automate more services, they save money and meet customer expectations faster.

Methods of Network Provisioning

Network provisioning has taken many forms over the years. To be sure, the industry had to start somewhere. All the way back to the earliest Cisco products of AGS, AGS+, and IGS in the late 1980s and early 1990s, network engineers would interact with their network devices through serial console cables directly connected to their terminal. Who can forget the ubiquitous blue serial console cable that came in the box with a router or switch (see Figure 9-3)? How many have a dozen or so squirreled away in the lab or at home?

Figure 9-3 *The Ubiquitous Serial Console Cable*

In a worst-case scenario of needing to do a password reset, you might even have used dual in-line package (DIP) switches that needed to be flipped in sequence.

Fortunately, the industry has come a *long* way. Ideally, you don't even need to see a device physically or know where it exists to influence its operation. In some environments, the networking functions are not even physical devices. Consider the Cisco Cloud Services Router (CSR) 1000V. It is a wholly software virtualized router running Cisco IOS XE software, commonly deployed in cloud environments. Virtualization of network functions and services means no more physical console cables and no need to "touch" something to affect its function or operation.

As the device (or node) count increases, it is unrealistic to expect individuals to interact with them physically or manually. There are just too many devices and too many changes. Some resource or feature requirements can be very short-lived. If human effort, which can be error-prone from time to time, is regularly used, then your deployments and customer experience will suffer. Customers expect speedy delivery in a consistent fashion. Waiting for an engineer to read an email, process a request, and implement it takes too long.

CLI/Console

The original serial console connection methods morphed into solutions using terminal servers that could aggregate 8, 16, 32, or more terminal connections into one device that would fan out to many other devices in the same or nearby racks. Figure 9-4 shows a logical network representation illustrating where a multiplexing terminal server might reside.

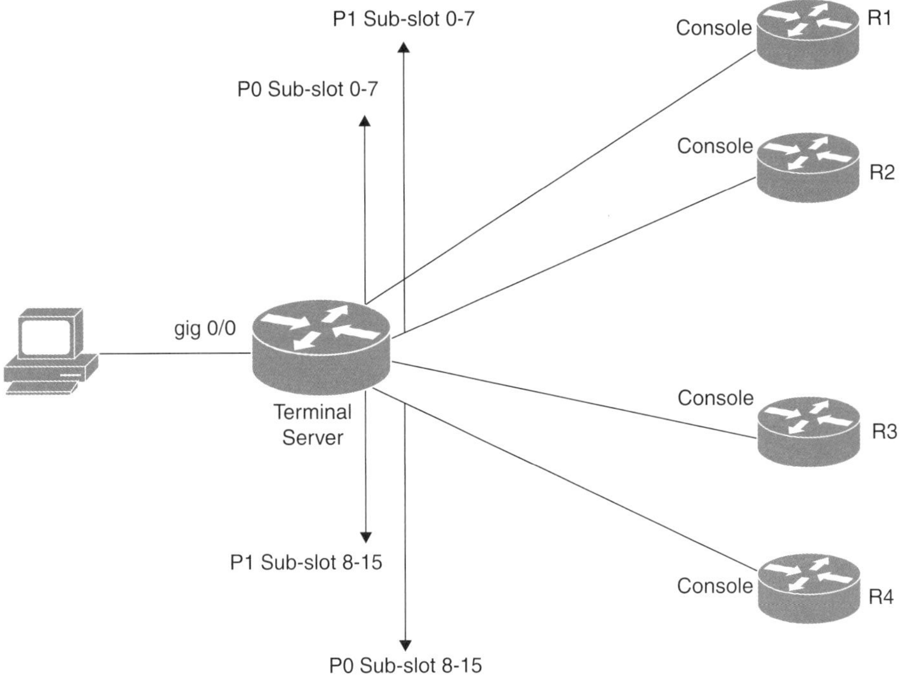

Figure 9-4 *A Typical Terminal Server Deployment*

This out-of-band (OOB) management model separates a dedicated management network from production traffic. OOB models persist in highly available or remotely accessible environments today. In-band management models intermingle the administrative and management traffic with the regular user and production traffic.

In-band management became de rigueur with insecure Telnet persisting for many years. Eventually, slowly, Secure Shell (SSH) took over as the preferred mode to connect to a device for configuration management or other interaction. The initial methods of configuration management would entail typing entire configuration syntax. Only slightly more advanced was using terminal cut-and-paste operations, if you had a well-equipped terminal emulator! However, this method does not scale, nor is it efficient.

Let's look at a classic "what not to do" user example from many years ago. In this situation, the network team used a service request management (SRM) system to document, request, review, and gain approvals for change requests. However, the SRM was not integrated with their change management processes, which were PuTTY and HyperTerminal. The change one Friday night was to implement an almost 10,000-line access control list (ACL). The network engineer dutifully accepted the approved change, took a copy of the 10K-line ACL from the pages of a Microsoft Word document detailing the change request, and then started PuTTY. The engineer SSH'd into the device, entered configuration mode, and pasted the ACL. Because a command-line interface (and paste) is a flow-control-based method, it took more than 10 minutes to get the ACL into the system. When the engineer saw the device prompt, they copied the running configuration to the startup configuration and went home at the end of their shift. Four hours later, the engineer was called back in because network traffic was acting unexpectedly. Some desirable traffic was being blocked, and other, undesirable traffic was being passed! Eventually, the root cause was determined. The engineer had a 10K-line access control list, but the terminal emulator was configured for a maximum of 5K lines. They pasted only half the total ACL!

Despite examples like this, the CLI model of managing a device has persisted for many years. I often refer to it as finger-defined networking (FDN) in a snarky accommodation against the preferred software-defined networking (SDN) model everyone aspires to, as you can see in Figure 9-5.

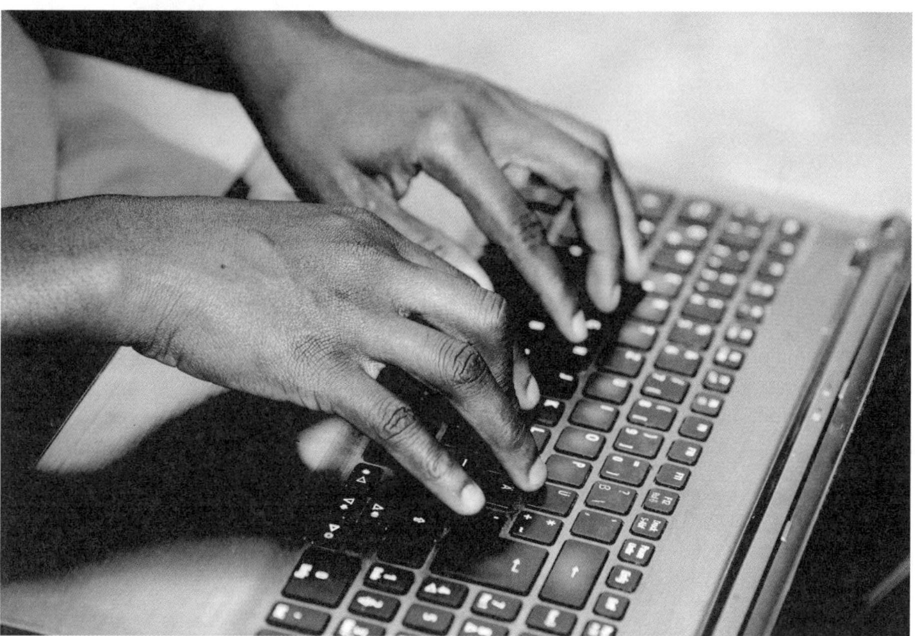

Figure 9-5 *Finger-Defined Networking*

Why has this model persisted so long? The reality of ease of use with command arguments and syntax that suit users' readability explains the "death grip" among many network engineers. If you want to see an FDN-centric engineer squirm, disable or delete their terminal emulator.

If you're going to be using FDN, you should at least do so securely. Thankfully, SSH is ubiquitous today. It is used in foundational interactions with device CLIs, but also as the Secure Copy Protocol (SCP) subsystem to move files. The growth of git and the use of SSH to synchronize code and files in repositories only increase the need for security. The interactive username/password model has been common for authentication. Key-based authentication has been available for many years, but some organizations are resistant to use it, despite it being well suited to automation and unattended device interaction. Two-factor authentication (2FA) and multifactor authentication (MFA) are some of the most impactful innovations in securing user access. Combining something you know, like a username and password, with something that proves who you are, like the possession of a smartphone with an authentication app or a hardware token generator or even a biometric reader, has significant impact on authorized access.

The Cisco acquisition of Duo in 2018 provides MFA that enables varied and flexible alternative factor authentication methods, such as smartphone app, callback, SMS, and hardware token generator, as shown in Figure 9-6.

Figure 9-6 *A Cisco Duo Hardware Token Generator*

Although some 2FA token generators are physical devices, recognize that alternative solutions are necessary to generate tokens for automated and programmatic purposes.

Some environments implement 2FA for human user interaction and have alternative key-based authentication for automated service accounts. Thankfully, the staunch dependency to continue FDN and yet increase the security posture influenced the industry to create programmatic token generators for Python scripts and other automated and unattended uses.

The most desirable methods for interacting with a physical or virtual device, in order of security posture, are

- SSHv2 with two-factor authentication
- SSHv2 with key-based authentication
- SSHv2 with username/password authentication
- Terminal server/console (physical)
- Telnet (not suggested)

The use of insecure Trivial File Transfer Protocol (TFTP) transfer of a configuration with a TFTP server is still popular. However, the better-intentioned Secure Copy Protocol is where most discerning network operators focus.

SNMP

Simple Network Management Protocol (SNMP) continues to exist, seemingly off to the side.

NOTE SNMP is not part of the DEVCOR exam, so the information provided here is for historical context.

Many network engineers repeat the joke that SNMP is *not* simple. Can you configure a device with it? In some cases, many more MIB objects are readable versus those that are writable. SNMP has been the standard method for collecting performance, configuration, inventory, and fault information. It did not take off as well for provisioning. Indeed, the closest that SNMP got to network provisioning for most situations was using an SNMP Set operation against the CISCO-CONFIG-MAN-MIB to specify a TFTP server and a file to transfer representing text of the configuration. A second SNMP Set operation triggered the merge with a device's running configuration.

Thankfully, the industry pushes toward streaming telemetry, a more efficient and programmatic method that we cover later. It's notable that Google talked of its push away from SNMP at the North American Network Operators' Group (NANOG) 73 conference in the summer of 2018. Reference the video at https://youtu.be/McNm_WfQTHw and presentation at https://pc.nanog.org/static/published/meetings/NANOG73/1677/20180625_Shakir_Snmp_Is_Dead_v1.pdf.

Then Google shared experiences with its three-year project to remove SNMP usage. Because SNMP is still widely used in many environments and the core collection mechanism of most performance management tools, we continue our review of it, limited to the more secure SNMPv3, which you should be using if doing SNMP at all.

SNMPv3 brought new excitement to the network management space in the early 2000s. SNMPv3 brought authentication and encryption along with other security features like anti-replay protections. The criticisms about SNMPv1 and v2c being insecure finally could be addressed. The use of MIB objects did not change, only the transport and packaging of the SNMP packets. Figure 9-7 alludes to the promise of securing the sensitive management traffic.

Figure 9-7 *The Promise of Encryption for Sensitive Management Data*

The Internet Engineering Task Force (IETF) defined SNMPv3 in RFCs 3410 to 3418, while RFC 3826 brought advanced encryption. SNMPv3 provides secure access to devices through a combination of authenticating and encrypting packets. The security features provided in SNMPv3 are

- **Message integrity:** Ensuring that a packet has not been tampered with in transit
- **Authentication:** Determining the message is from a valid source
- **Encryption (optional):** Obscuring the contents of an SNMP payload, preventing it from being seen by an unauthorized source

Whereas SNMPv1/2c required *community strings* to read/write a device's MIB variables, in SNMPv3 *user/group assignments* with an authentication password permit authentication. A separate privacy passphrase enables encryption, if desired.

Every SNMPv3 sender/receiver has a snmpEngineID that uniquely identifies it. Even back to legacy Cisco IOS 12.0 in 2000, if you looked at a device config, an **snmp-server engineID local 000** statement existed. This was the foundation for SNMPv3 on the device.

Any read/write done with an invalid snmpEngineID is rejected, and a REPORT packet, a new type of notification, is generated.

Each device can have multiple identities called a context, which is essentially a separate MIB environment or partitioned space, used with situations like BRIDGE-MIB/VLAN polling or VRFs.

Figure 9-8 shows the new SNMPv3 category levels and capabilities.

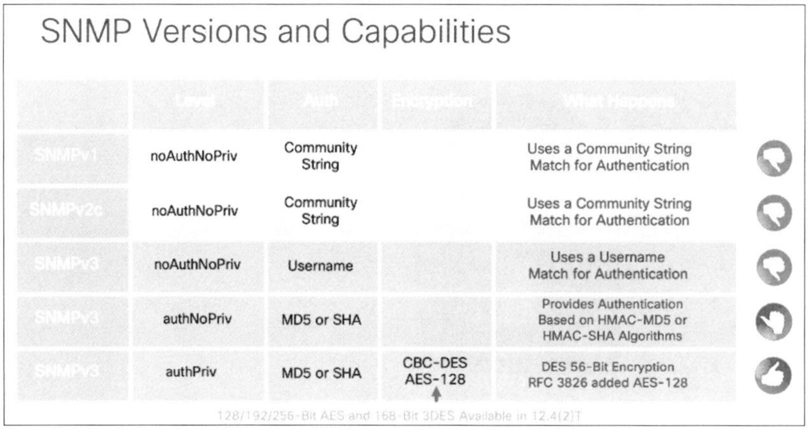

SNMP Versions and Capabilities

	Level	Auth	Encryption	What Happens
SNMPv1	noAuthNoPriv	Community String		Uses a Community String Match for Authentication
SNMPv2c	noAuthNoPriv	Community String		Uses a Community String Match for Authentication
SNMPv3	noAuthNoPriv	Username		Uses a Username Match for Authentication
SNMPv3	authNoPriv	MD5 or SHA		Provides Authentication Based on HMAC-MD5 or HMAC-SHA Algorithms
SNMPv3	authPriv	MD5 or SHA	CBC-DES AES-128	DES 56-Bit Encryption RFC 3826 added AES-128

128/192/256-Bit AES and 168-Bit 3DES Available in 12.4(2)T

Figure 9-8 *SNMPv3 Versions and Capabilities*

Many organizations and network management tools initially test the waters by supporting authNoPriv—Authentication with No Privacy (encryption). This can be a reasonable first step; SNMP interactions are authenticated, and if encryption isn't a goal, such as with internal networks or labs, then the model is sufficient. For organizations needing more security, such as financial, government, and health-care industries, then authPriv—Authentication with Privacy—is more desirable.

The initial IETF specification for SNMPv3 called for 56-bit DES encryption. For some environments, this is enough. However, there was pressure from the financial industry to embrace more sophisticated encryption models. The IETF complied through RFC 3826 by adding AES-128; many devices and management tools likewise added support for the additional specification. Cisco went a step further with even more enhanced encryption models to include 168-bit triple-DES: 128-, 168-, and even 256-bit AES. It is important to map the device authentication and encryption capabilities with those of the management tools; otherwise, the security will not be as desired.

File Transfer Methods

For network provisioning, TFTP is common in lower-risk areas, such as development and testing environments. Traditional methods of archiving a device configuration or changing it through TFTP would be logging in to the device with a terminal emulator through an out-of-band console or in-band SSH session and issuing a **copy tftp running-config** (or similar) command. This method is also used for file transfer of device software images. Some of the CLI and UI representations in Figure 9-9 should be familiar.

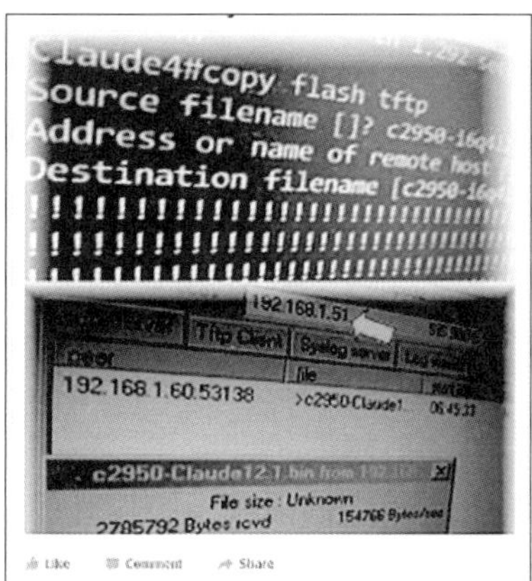

Figure 9-9 *A TFTP Process and Application*

Regular File Transfer Protocol (FTP) and the more secure method, Secure File Transfer Protocol (SFTP), are options with devices to a varying level of adoption. When it comes to secure transfer of configurations or software images, the Secure Copy Protocol has been more widely used because it depends on a subsystem of SSH for its secure transport, which is already, hopefully, being used for command-line access.

9

Element Management Systems

While progress was being made to help device manageability, most service providers and large enterprise environments were looking for more efficiencies. In the late 1990s and early 2000s, the story on the network management application side was not much better. The applications, or element management systems (EMSs), as they became known, were focused on their individual functionality. The notion of even sharing device lists—hostnames, IP addresses, and credentials—was largely an unrealized concept. The EMSs acted as isolated islands of functionality and information. Eventually, attempts were made to integrate, first among product suites of individual vendors, then across popular EMSs. The integration adapters were the first pair-wise data sharing systems. A network management operator in the early 2000s might remember hearing about the integration adapters between CiscoWorks 2000 and HP OpenView Network Node Manager. Other adapters became available with popular EMSs like Concord eHealth, Tivoli OMNIbus Netcool, and Infovista. However, these were still one-to-one pairings, as depicted in Figure 9-10.

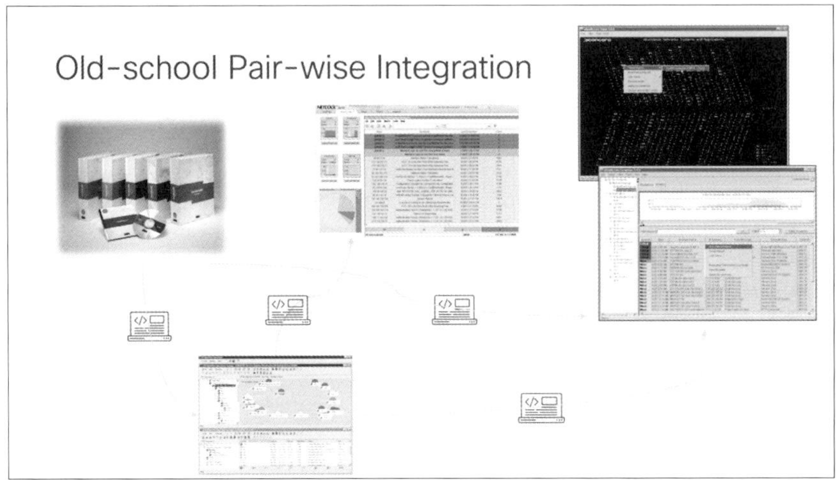

Figure 9-10 *Legacy, Pair-wise Integration*

Web interfaces on routers and switches became possible but underutilized for making changes. People just loved the CLI and FDN!

The device-by-device web method lacked efficiencies that large-scale environments sought even though the browser-based model appeared intriguing.

Some attempts at vendor- and product-specific interactions with remote-procedure calls (RPCs) were also developed. Eventually, around 2006, the industry recognized that having different configuration syntax for different device types, models, and vendors was inefficient. The IETF working group for NETCONF (network configuration) was born to normalize configuration management through the use of common Extensible Markup Language (XML) schemas. The operator or management tool would perform a terminal connection to a specific port, and the device's NETCONF agent would respond. The XML-rendered configuration would be pushed, and the NETCONF agent would translate it to the device's native syntax. The hope was there would be no further need for the Cisco IOS BGP configlet, the Cisco IOS-XR BGP configlet, the Juniper JUNOS BGP configlet, the HP BGP configlet, and so on. If you had multiple device models, operating systems, and/or vendors, you could have *one* representation of that BGP configuration standard. It could be pushed to any NETCONF-supporting device with equal effect.

It wasn't until the advent of SDN starting in 2008 that there was a push to include network programmability in earnest with control plane and data plane separation and network virtualization. The IT industry experienced a proliferation of mechanisms to change network devices. Some methods came from the compute/application IT discipline because they had similar needs to perform rapid and scalable configuration changes. Users first saw Puppet and Chef, and the now-popular Ansible and Terraform. Sophisticated and cloud-native environments use Kubernetes and Terraform-based solutions to achieve orchestrated provisioning. Some of these systems required agents on the managed devices, as the early Puppet and Chef implementations did, but others were agentless and would leverage the near-ubiquitous SSH interface on devices to automate the same commands and configuration directives a person would perform manually. The agentless model is largely used now. It was the primary method for Ansible and was later picked up by Puppet and Chef.

An interesting artifact of the drive to network programmability was the growing community of programmers and coders who were joining the network IT discipline. These innovators brought with them the notions of DevOps, CI/CD, and Infrastructure as Code (IaC). When the coders were onboard with IaC, new solutions that abstracted the network device configuration into intent-based models became relevant, such as HashiCorp's Terraform.

Embedded Management

As centralized EMSs increased in prominence, the notion of a device's "self-monitoring" was considered. The benefits of distributing the management work or dealing with a network isolation issue were found through embedded management techniques. Cisco's Embedded Event Manager (EEM) has been a popular and mature feature for many years in distributing management functions to the devices themselves.

Some use cases with EEM have been

- Monitoring an interface error counter and administratively disabling when a threshold is reached
- Sending an email or syslog event message when a CPU or memory threshold is reached
- Changing a routing metric when a specific condition is met
- Clearing a terminal line that has been running over a defined time length

Often, having the device self-monitor with EEM could be more frequent than a centralized monitoring solution that may be managing hundreds, thousands, or more devices. This is especially true if the condition being monitored is not something that needs to be collected and graphed for long-term reporting. Consider monitoring an interface or module health state every 30 seconds. This rate may be unachievable with a centralized system that has tens of thousands of devices to manage. However, a device may be able to use embedded management functions to self-monitor at this rate with little impact. It could then send notifications back to a centralized fault management system as necessary.

9

In IT, service management performance and fault management often have similar goals. Performance management usually entails periodic polling or reception of streaming telemetry in a periodic fashion. The performance information may be below thresholds of concern, and the information is not especially useful. However, retaining the periodically gathered data can be useful for trending and long-term analysis.

Conversely, the fault management function may collect data to compare against a threshold or status and not retain it if the data doesn't map to the condition. This function becomes very ad hoc and may not align to standard polling frequencies. Fault management also benefits from asynchronous alerts and notifications, usually through Syslog event messaging or SNMP traps.

For CiscoLive events, the network operations center (NOC) has used advanced EEM scripts to monitor CDP neighbor adjacency events; identify the device type; and configure the connected port for the appropriate VLAN, security, QoS, and interface description settings.

Using Embedded Event Manager is beneficial for device-centric management; however, it should not be relied on solely for health and availability management. If you didn't get an email or syslog event message from the device, does that mean all is healthy? Or does it mean the device went offline and can't report? It is wise to supplement embedded management solutions with a robust availability monitoring process to ensure device reachability.

Zero-Touch Provisioning (ZTP)

A **zero-touch provisioning (ZTP)** function enables you to provision and configure devices automatically. It is useful primarily during the initial setup of an unconfigured, or virgin state, device. ZTP has been achieved by different feature names on varying platforms, such as AutoInstall, **Power-On Auto Provisioning (POAP)**, Network Plug and Play (PnP), and SmartInstall. AutoInstall is the most ubiquitous and historical of these options.

The general process is similar, however; an unconfigured device starts up, seeking its IP address from a DHCP server, and kicks off a process to download a base configuration file from a file server identified in DHCP options. The secure and recommended approach would be via HTTPS, whereas the TFTP service was initially offered in the feature. Even older variations rely on BOOTP processes that will not be covered.

It's notable that the Meraki and Cisco SD-WAN platforms fundamentally use ZTP as their core means of provisioning via cloud or centralized controller means. Essentially, these classes of devices organically have enough network intelligence and process/workflow embedded to make connections through the Internet to their cloud-based provisioning systems. The network administrator uses the Meraki or SD-WAN portal to "claim" the device and proceed with specific customizations.

ZTP is an alternative method for configuration on many other platforms using IOS-XE, NX-OS, IOS-XR, and so on, when there is no base configuration. It is also intriguing to network programmers because it allows mass provisioning in a programmatic sense.

A ZTP process has several common functions that mimic some familiar staging tasks:

- Obtaining base network connectivity (DHCP, DNS, default routing)
- Performing software/firmware upgrades
- Obtaining and incorporating "Day-0" base config (core services such as NTP, SSH, SNMP, Syslog; generating/importing certificates, or using Trusted Platform Module or International Organization for Standardization and the International Electrotechnical Commission (ISO/IEC) Standard 11889, and so on)
- Obtaining and incorporating "Day-0" device/function-specific configuration (interfaces, routing protocols, VLANs/VRFs, and so on)

The ZTP process has most of its notable magic in the Obtaining Base Network Connectivity task. Consider the standard flow of ZTP for NX-OS, IOS-XR, and IOS-XE devices from Figure 9-11.

Key Topic

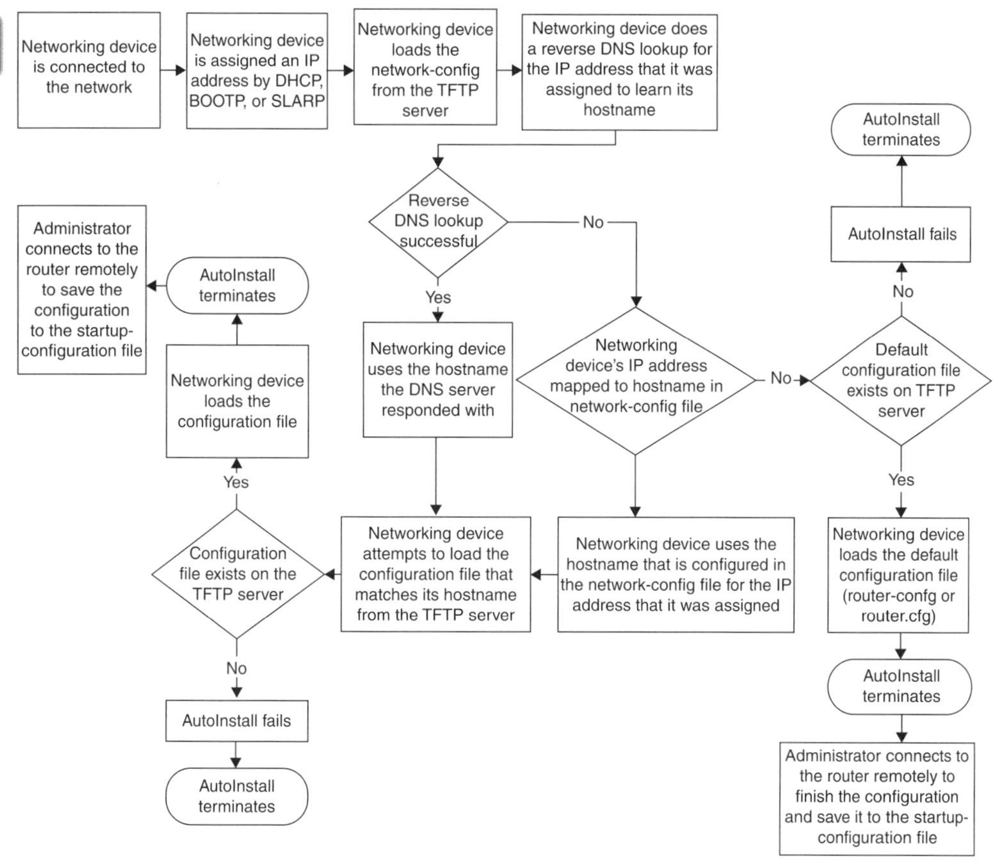

Figure 9-11 *A Typical AutoInstall Process Flow*

NOTE Check your platform support with the Cisco Feature Navigator (https://cfnng.cisco.com/).

Of interest to network programmers is the enhanced AutoInstall Support for TCL Script feature. It enhances AutoInstall by providing more flexibility in the installation process. The administrator can program the device with TCL scripts to get information about what to download and to choose the type of file server and the required file transfer protocol.

Of special interest to network programmers is the even more advanced option to ZTP using Python scripts, as found in the IOS-XE 16.6+ platforms. In this case, DHCP option 67 settings are used to identify a Python script to download. The device executes the Python script locally using Guest Shell on-box functionality, as depicted in Figure 9-12.

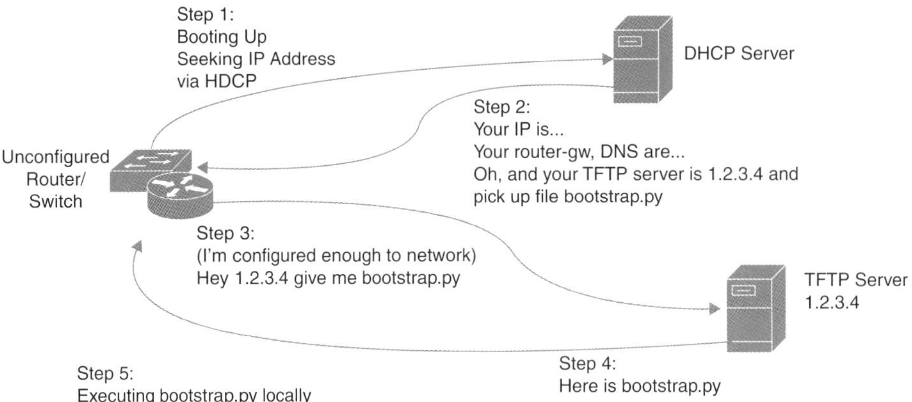

Figure 9-12 *ZTP with Python Script Enhancements*

With a script-based deployment, you can program and execute a dynamic installation process on the device itself instead of relying on a configuration management function driven by a centralized server.

As an example, consider the Python ZTP script in Example 9-1.

Example 9-1 *Python ZTP Script*

```
# Importing cli module
import cli

print('\n## Bootstrap ZTP Python Script\n')
cli.execute('configure replace flash:base-config force')

print('## Executing show version\n\n')
cli.executep('show version')
print('## Configuring Loopback Interface\n\n')
cli.configurep(["interface loop 10", "ip address 10.1.1.1 255.255.255.255", "end"])

print('## Executing show ip interface brief\n')
cli.executep('show ip int brief')

print('## Bootstrap ZTP Python Script Execution Complete\n\n')
```

NOTE If you are using a platform with legacy Python 2.x support, the print statements need to be modified as follows:

print "Example"

This simplistic Python script merely echoes the **show version** command (to the console, when booting up), configures a Loopback 10 interface, and then echoes the **show ip interface brief** command. Obviously, in its current form, the script is not portable, but with some basic Python skills, you can easily enhance it to have conditional logic or even off-box, alternate server interactions performing basic GET/POST operations to a REST API. This is when the magic happens: the device could provide a unique identifier, such as serial number or first interface MAC address, which could be used for more sophisticated and purposeful device provisioning.

Atomic or SDN-Like/Controller-Based Networking

The traditional element management system (EMS) approach to network management is very atomic and becoming untenable. In atomic-based EMSs, devices are managed one by one with little or no consideration to interdependencies and relationships across devices. The EMS might expect *you* to provide the intelligence and discernment that upgrading both devices in service-pairs, such as HSRP, primary/backup DHCP, or route reflectors, at the same time is unwise. The EMS may dutifully take both out of service, without warning you of the implication to service availability.

With atomic EMSs, the notion of *service* is largely foreign because it involves characteristics and relationships spanning multiple devices.

In traditional networking, there is the notion of the **control plane** and **data plane** residing on the same device. These logical concepts functionally separate the forwarding determinations and decisions, as a brain would, from the actual processing of the packets for forwarding, as muscles would. There is also a provisioning distinction known as the **management plane** that deals with protocols and methods to configure the control plane, such as SNMP, NETCONF/RESTCONF, and REST. Table 9-2 shows this distinction.

Table 9-2 Logical Plane Models

Model	Function	Example
Control plane	Determines/calculates packet or frame-forwarding decisions	Software processes, such as OSPF, EIGRP, BGP, IS-IS, LDP, and ARP
Data plane	Executes on packet or frame forwarding	Interfaces
Management plane	Protocols/methods for provisioning the control plane	CLI/SSH, SNMP, NETCONF/ RESTCONF

Figure 9-13 depicts this model graphically.

9

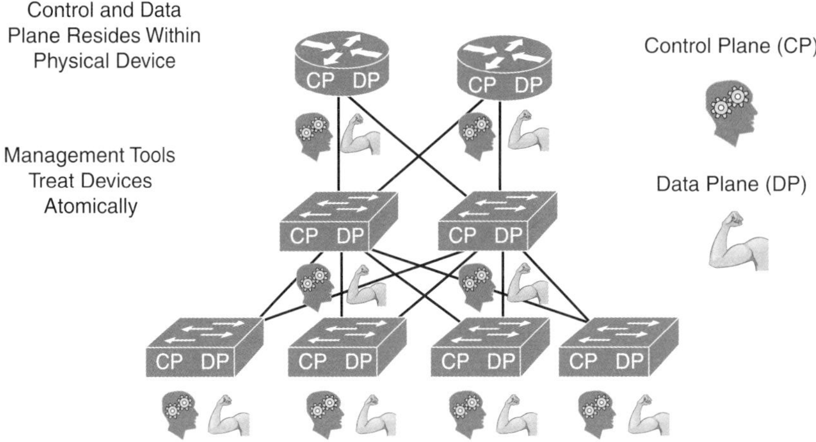
Control and Data
Plane Resides Within
Physical Device
Management Tools
Treat Devices
Atomically
Control Plane (CP)
Data Plane (DP)
CP DP
Control Plane Learns/Computes Forwarding Decisions
Data Plane Acts on the Forwarding Decisions
Each Device Operates Autonomously Without Regard for Others

Figure 9-13 *Traditional Networking: Converged Control and Data Plane Functions*

If you find yourself running network discovery or entering device management addresses and credentials with a network management tool, you are probably dealing with a traditional EMS system. Systems like Prime Infrastructure, Data Center Network Manager (DCNM), Prime Collaboration, Statseeker, and others are examples of atomic EMSs.

The advent of software-defined networking catalyzed the centralized controller management model. In most cases, the managed devices seek out the *controller* that manages it. Minimal, if any, initial configuration is necessary on the device. The controller identification may occur by expected IP address or hostname, broadcast/multicast address, a DHCP option, DNS resource record (SRV), or a Layer-2/3 discovery process.

After the device registers with the controller, it shows up in the inventory. Additional authorization may have been performed with the device and/or controller. In the Meraki or Cisco SD-WAN models, the devices register with a central, cloud-based controller, and administrators must "claim" the device. Additional examples of SDN and controller-like management systems are DNA Center and the ACI APIC controller.

You can look to the wireless industry for some examples of both atomic EMS and SDN controller models. Initially, wireless access points (WAPs) operated autonomously and required individual configuration. A centralized management tool, like Cisco Prime Network Control System (NCS), which eventually converged with Prime Infrastructure, was used to manage autonomous WAPs. Later, centralized controller-based WAPs, or lightweight WAPs (LWAPs), were developed that used the wireless LAN controller (WLC) appliance for central management. Yet another iteration of manageability occurred with a distributed model using wiring closet-based controllers in the Catalyst 3850. The multiple options existed to suit customer deployment preference and need.

In a more SDN literal model, the control plane function is separated from the device and is provided by a centralized controller. The data plane function still resides on the device, as seen in Figure 9-14.

The Network As It Could Be...to an SDN "Purist"

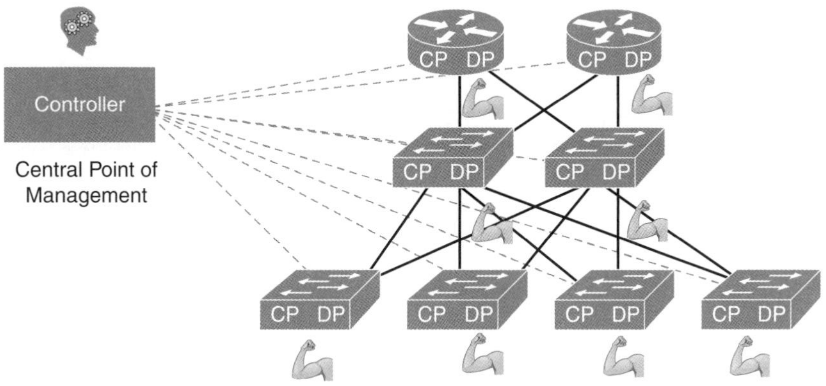

Figure 9-14 *SDN Networking: Separate Control and Data Plane Functions*

Advanced Concepts—Intent-Based Networking

Intent-based networking (IBN) is one of the newest principles to transform the networking industry. Users, devices, and distributed applications have exploded in number, greatly outstripping legacy frameworks such as IPv4 and complicating security frameworks.

The Cisco Annual Internet Report (www.cisco.com/c/en/us/solutions/collateral/executive-perspectives/annual-internet-report/white-paper-c11-741490.html) describes a healthy growth of Internet-connected users and devices. Figure 9-15 shows how growth appears over several years.

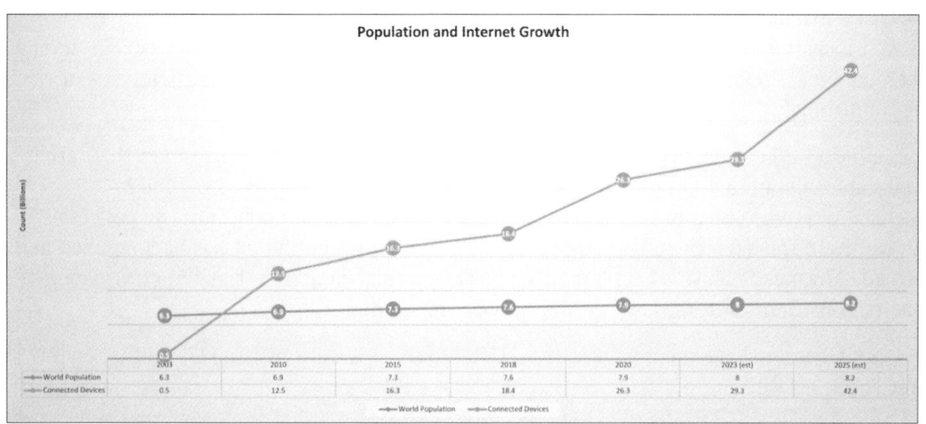

Figure 9-15 *Population and Internet Growth (Source: Cisco IBSG 2011, Cisco VNI results and forecasts 2010, 2015, 2018, 2020)*

When you consider the growth of underpinning network devices necessary to accommodate the mobile user, servers, and virtual machines, you can quickly understand how atomic EMS-based management is truly untenable. To address the diversity of endpoints and functions, the networking environment has become exponentially more complex. IBN transforms a hardware-centric network of manually provisioned devices into a controller-centric network that uses business intent translated into policies that are automated and applied consistently across the network. The network continuously monitors and adjusts network configuration and performance to achieve the specified business outcomes. Operational efficiencies are realized when IBN models allow for natural language directions to be translated to native controller-centric directives as conceptualized in Figure 9-16.

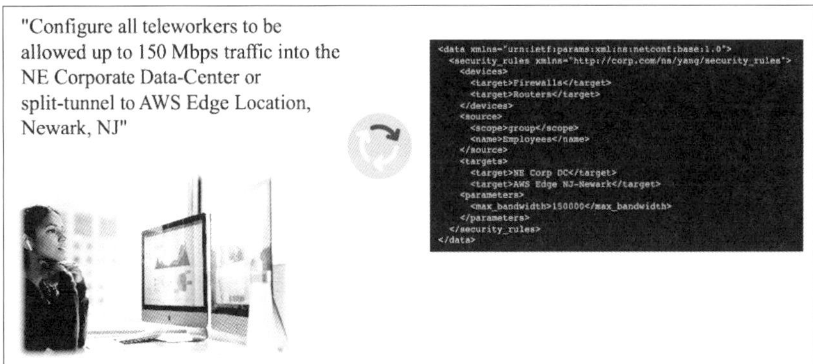

Figure 9-16 *Natural Language to Native Controller Directives*

IBN augments the network controller model of software-defined networking. The network controller is the central, authoritative control point for network provisioning, monitoring, and management. Controllers empower network abstraction by treating the network as an integrated whole. This is different from legacy element management systems where devices are managed atomically, without functional or relational consideration. Cross-domain orchestration is enabled when controllers span multiple domains (access, WAN, data center, compute, cloud, security, and so on) or when they provide greater efficiencies in programmability.

A closed-loop function of IBN ensures practical feedback of provisioning intent that reflects actual implementation and operations. The activation function translates the intent into policies that are provisioning into the network. An assurance function continuously collects analytics from the devices and services to assess whether proper intent has been applied and achieved. Advanced solutions apply machine learning to accurately estimate performance or capacity constraints before they become service impacting.

The DNA Center management solution and CX Cloud are solutions from Cisco that enable intent-based networking.

Summary

This chapter focuses on capabilities in network management, infrastructure provisioning, element management systems, zero-touch provisioning (ZTP), atomic or SDN-like/controller-based networking, and intent-based networking. It depicts the growth and transformation in the network industry over the past 30 years. As technological problems were identified, solutions were made and transformation occurred. Each step of the way, refined principles have improved the state of networking. If you find yourself implementing or sustaining the legacy methods first described, you are highly encouraged to adopt the newer methods defined later in the chapter.

Exam Preparation Tasks

As mentioned in the section "How to Use This Book" in the Introduction, you have a couple of choices for exam preparation: the exercises here, Chapter 17, "Final Preparation," and the exam simulation questions in the Pearson Test Prep Software Online.

Review All Key Topics

Review the most important topics in this chapter, noted with the Key Topic icon in the outer margin of the page. Table 9-3 lists a reference of these key topics and the page numbers on which each is found.

Table 9-3 Key Topics for Chapter 9

Key Topic Element	Description	Page Number
Paragraph	Network management concepts	290
Paragraph	Embedded management concepts	299
Figure 9-11	A Typical AutoInstall Process Flow	301
Table 9-2	Logical Plane Models	303
Paragraph	Intent-based network concepts	306

Complete Tables and Lists from Memory

Print a copy of Appendix C, "Memory Tables" (found on the companion website), or at least the section for this chapter, and complete the tables and lists from memory. Appendix D, "Memory Tables Answer Key," also on the companion website, includes completed tables and lists to check your work.

Define Key Terms

Define the following key terms from this chapter and check your answers in the glossary:

continuous integration/continuous deployment (CI/CD), control plane, data plane, DevOps, intent-based networking (IBN), management plane, Power-On Auto-Provisioning (POAP), software-defined networking (SDN), site reliability engineering (SRE), zero-touch provisioning (ZTP)

References

URL	QR Code
https://youtu.be/McNm_WfQTHw	
https://pc.nanog.org/static/published/meetings/NANOG73/1677/20180625_Shakir_Snmp_Is_Dead_v1.pdf	
https://cfnng.cisco.com/	
https://www.cisco.com/c/en/us/solutions/collateral/executive-perspectives/annual-internet-report/white-paper-c11-741490.html	

CHAPTER 10

Automation

This chapter covers the following topics:

- **Challenges Being Addressed:** This section identifies the challenges that need to be addressed with the advent of software-defined networking, DevOps, and network programmability.
- **Software-Defined Networking (SDN):** This section covers the genesis of software-defined networking, its purpose, and the value gained.
- **Application Programming Interfaces (APIs):** This section provides guidance around application programming interfaces. Network engineering and operations were very different before APIs; some environments are still resistant to change, but the benefits outweigh the risks of not embracing them.
- **REST APIs:** This section provides insights to the functionality and benefit of REST APIs and how they are used.
- **Cross-Domain, Technology-Agnostic Orchestration:** This section contains material that is not covered in the DEVCOR certification test. However, as network IT continues to transform, it provides an important consideration for the transformation of environments.
- **Impact to IT Service Management and Security:** This section acknowledges the influence of IT service management and security to network programmability. With so many companies investing in ITIL and TOGAF methodologies in the early 2010s, understanding the alignments is helpful.

This chapter maps to the second part of the *Developing Applications Using Cisco Core Platforms and APIs v1.0 (350-901)* Exam Blueprint Section 5.0, "Infrastructure and Automation."

As we've learned about the infrastructure involved in network IT and see the continued expansion, we also recognize that static, manual processes can no longer sustain us. When we were managing dozens or hundreds of devices using manual methods of logging in to terminal servers, through a device's console interface, or through inband connectivity via SSH, it may have been sufficient. However, now we are dealing with thousands, tens of thousands, and in a few projects I've been on, *hundreds* of thousands of devices. It is simply untenable to continue manual efforts driven by personal interaction. At some point, these valuable engineering, operations, and management resources must be refocused on more impactful activities that differentiate the business. So, automation must be embraced. This chapter covers some key concepts related to automation: what challenges need to be addressed, how SDN and APIs enable us, and the impact to IT service management and security.

"Do I Know This Already?" Quiz

The "Do I Know This Already?" quiz allows you to assess whether you should read this entire chapter thoroughly or jump to the "Exam Preparation Tasks" section. If you are in doubt about your answers to these questions or your own assessment of your knowledge of the topics, read the entire chapter. Table 10-1 lists the major headings in this chapter and their corresponding "Do I Know This Already?" quiz questions. You can find the answers in Appendix A, "Answers to the 'Do I Know This Already?' Quizzes."

Table 10-1 "Do I Know This Already?" Section-to-Question Mapping

Foundation Topics Section	Questions
Challenges Being Addressed	1–5
Software-Defined Networking (SDN)	6
Application Programming Interfaces (APIs)	11
REST APIs	7–10

1. When you are considering differences in device types and function, which technology provides the most efficiencies?
   a. Template-driven management
   b. Model-driven management
   c. Atomic-driven management
   d. Distributed EMSs
2. The SRE discipline combines aspects of _______ engineering with _______ and _______.
   a. Hardware, software, firmware
   b. Software, infrastructure, operations
   c. Network, software, DevOps
   d. Traffic, DevOps, SecOps
3. What do the Agile software development practices focus on?
   a. Following defined processes of requirements gathering, development, testing, QA, and release.
   b. Giving development teams free rein to engineer without accountability.
   c. Pivoting from development sprint to sprint based on testing results.
   d. Requirements gathering, adaptive planning, quick delivery, and continuous improvement.
4. Of the software development methodologies provided, which uses a more visual approach to the what-when-how of development?
   a. Kanban
   b. Agile
   c. Waterfall
   d. Illustrative

5. Concurrency focuses on _______ lots of tasks at once. Parallelism focuses on _______ lots of tasks at once.
   a. Doing; working with
   b. Exchanging; switching
   c. Threading; sequencing
   d. Working with; doing
6. The _______ specification, originally the _______ specification, defines a model for machine-readable interface files for describing, producing, consuming, and visualizing RESTful web services.
   a. OpenAPI; Swagger
   b. REST; CLI
   c. SDN; Clean Slate
   d. OpenWeb; CORBA
7. What would be the correct method to generate a basic authentication string on a macOS/Linux CLI?
   a. **echo -n 'username:password' | openssl md5**
   b. **echo -n 'username:password' | openssl**
   c. **echo -n 'username:password' | openssl base64**
   d. **echo -n 'username&password' | openssl base64**
8. What does XML stand for?
   a. Extendable machine language
   b. Extensible markup language
   c. Extreme machine learning
   d. Extraneous modeling language
9. In JSON, what are records or objects denoted with?
   a. Angle braces < >
   b. Square brackets [ ]
   c. Simple quotes " "
   d. Curly braces { }
10. Which REST API HTTP methods are *both* idempotent?
    a. PATCH, POST
    b. HEAD, GET
    c. POST, OPTIONS
    d. PATCH, HEAD
11. Which are APIs? (Choose two.)
    a. REST
    b. RMON
    c. JDBC
    d. SSH

Foundation Topics

Challenges Being Addressed

As described in the chapter introduction, automation is a necessity for growing sophisticated IT environments today. Allow me to share a personal example: if you've been to a CiscoLive conference in the US, it is common to deploy a couple thousand wireless access points in the large conference venues in Las Vegas, San Diego, and Orlando. I'm talking a million square feet plus event spaces.

Given that the network operations center (NOC) team is allowed onsite only four to five days before the event starts, that's not enough time to manually provision everything with a couple dozen event staff volunteers. The thousands of wireless APs are just one aspect of the event infrastructure (see Figure 10-1). There are still the 600+ small form-factor switches that must be spread across the venue to connect breakout rooms, keynote areas, World of Solutions, testing facilities and labs, the DevNet pavilion, and other spaces (see Figure 10-2).

Figure 10-1 *Moving a Few Wireless APs*

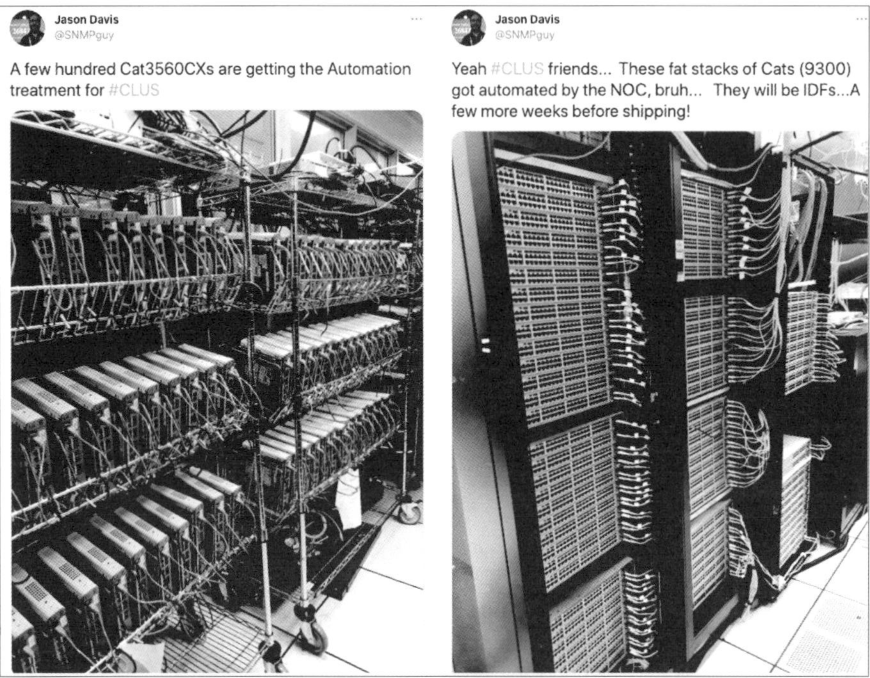

Figure 10-2 *Lots of Equipment to Stage*

Automation is a "do or die" activity for our businesses: without it, we overwork individuals and that impacts the broader organization. Automation must also extend beyond provisioning into the wide-scale collection of performance, health, and fault information.

Discerning companies are investigating how artificial intelligence and machine learning (AI/ML) can benefit them in obtaining new operational insights and reducing human effort even more.

We might even acknowledge "change is hard and slow." If you started networking after prior experience with a more programmatic environment or dealt with other industries where mass quantities of devices were managed effectively, you might wonder why network IT lags. This is a fair question, but also to be fair, enormous strides have been made in the last 10 years with an industry that found its start in ARPANET at the end of the 1960s. Cisco incorporated in 1984, and the industry has been growing in scale and functionality ever since.

Being involved in the latter part of the first wave of network evolution has been a constant career of learning and advancing skills development. The change and expansion of scope and function with networking have been very interesting and fulfilling for me.

Differences of Equipment and Functionality

Some of the challenges with networking deal with the diversity of equipment and functionality. In the last part of the 1960s and early 1970s, the aforementioned ARPANET included few network protocols and functions. A router's purpose was to move traffic across different, isolated network segments of specialized endpoints. The industry grew with shared media technologies (hubs), then to switches. Businesses started acquiring their own servers; they weren't limited to government agencies and the development labs of colleges and universities. Slowly, home PCs contributed to a burgeoning technology space.

Connectivity technology morphed from more local-based technologies like token ring and FDDI to faster and faster Ethernet-based solutions, hundred megabit and gigabit local interfaces, also influencing the speed of WAN technologies to keep up.

Switches gave advent to more intelligent routing and forwarding switches. IP-based telephony was developed. Who remembers that Cisco's original IP telephony solution, Call Manager, was originally delivered as a compact disc (CD), as much software was?

Storage was originally directly connected but then became networked, usually with different standards and protocols. The industry then accepted the efficiencies of a common, IP-based network. The rise of business computing being interconnected started influencing home networking. Networks became more interconnected and persistent. Dial-up technologies and ISDN peaked and started a downward trend in light of always-on cable-based technologies to the home. Different routing protocols needed to be created. Multiple-link aggregation requirements needed to be standardized to help with resiliency.

Wireless technologies came on the scene. Servers, which had previously been mere endpoints to the network, now became more integrated. IPv6. Mobile technologies. A lot of hardware innovations but also a lot of protocols and software developments came in parallel. So why the history lesson? Take them as cases in point of why networking IT was slow in automation. The field was changing rapidly and growing in functionality. The scope and pace of change in network IT were unlike those in any other IT disciplines.

Unfortunately, much of the early development relied on consoles and the expectation of a human administrator always creating the service initially and doing the sustaining changes. The Information Technology Information Library (ITIL) and The Open Group Architecture Framework (TOGAF) service management frameworks helped the industry define structure and operational rigor. Some of the concepts seen in Table 10-2 reflect a common vocabulary being established.

Table 10-2 Operational Lifecycle

Operational Perspective	Function
Day-0	Initial installation
Day-1	Configuration for production purpose
Day-2	Compliance and optimization
Day-X	Migration/decommissioning

The full lifecycle of a network device or service must be considered. All too often the "spin-up" of a service is the sole focus. Many IT managers have stories about finding orphaned recurring charges from decommissioned systems. Migrating and decommissioning a service are just as important as the initial provisioning. We must follow up on reclaiming precious consumable resources like disk space, IP addresses, and even power.

In the early days of compute virtualization, Cisco had an environment called CITEIS—Cisco IT Elastic Infrastructure Services, which were referred to as "cities." CITEIS was built to promote learning, speed development, and customer demos, and to prove the impact of automation. A policy was enacted that any engineer could spin up two virtual machines of any kind as long as they conformed to predefined sizing guidelines. If you needed something different, you could get it, but it would be handled on an exception basis. Now imagine the number of people excited to learn a new technology all piling on the system. VMs were spun up;

CPU, RAM, disk space, and IP addresses consumed; used once or twice, then never accessed again. A lot of resources were allocated. In the journey of developing the network programmability discipline, network engineers also needed to apply operational best practices. New functions were added to email (and later send chat messages to) the requester to ensure the resources were still needed. If a response was not received in a timely fashion, the resources were archived and decommissioned. If no acknowledgment came after many attempts over a longer period, the archive may be deleted. These kinds of basic functions formed the basis of standard IT operations to ensure proper use and lifecycle management of consumable resources.

With so many different opportunities among routing, switching, storage, compute, collaboration, wireless, and such, it's also understandable that there was an amount of specialization in these areas. This focused specialization contributed to a lack of convergence because each technology was growing in its own right; the consolidation of staff and budgets was not pressuring IT to solve the issue by building collaborative solutions. But that would change. As addressed later in the topics covering SDN, the industry was primed for transformation.

In today's world of modern networks, a difference of equipment and functionality is to be expected. Certainly, there are benefits recognized with standardizing device models to provide efficiencies in management and device/module sparing strategies. However, as network functions are separated, as seen later with SDN, or virtualized, as seen with Network Function Virtualization (NFV), a greater operational complexity is experienced. To that end, the industry has responded with model-driven concepts, which we cover in Chapter 11, "NETCONF and RESTCONF." The ability to move from device-by-device, atomic management considerations to more service and function-oriented models that comprehend the relationships and dependencies among many devices is the basis for model-driven management.

Proximity of Management Tools and Support Staff

Another situation that needed to be addressed was the proximity of management tools and support staff. Early networks were not as interconnected, persistent, or ingrained to as many aspects of our lives as they are now. It was common to deploy multiple copies of management tools across an environment because the connectivity or basic interface link speed among sites often precluded using a central management tool. Those were the days of "Hey, can you drive from Detroit down to Dayton to install another copy of XYZ?"

Support staff existed at many large sites, sometimes with little collaboration among them or consistency of service delivery across states or countries.

Because early networks often metered and charged on traffic volume across a wide area, they were almost disincentivized to consolidate monitoring and management. "Why would I want to run more monitoring traffic and increase my cost? I only want 'business-critical traffic' across those WAN links now." However, fortunately, even this way of thinking changed.

Today networks are more meshed, persistent, highly available, and faster connected. There is little need to deploy multiple management tools, unless it is purposeful for scale or functional segmentation. The support teams today may include a "follow the sun" model where three or four different support centers are spread across the globe to allow personnel to serve others in their proximate time zone. As businesses experience higher degrees of automation and orchestration, there is reduced need for on-shift personnel. Consolidation of support teams is possible. This pivot to a more on-call or exception-based support model is desired. The implementation of self-healing networks that require fewer and fewer support personnel is even more desirable. Google's concept of site reliability engineering (SRE) is an example of addressing the industry's shortcomings with infrastructure and operations support. The SRE discipline combines aspects of software engineering with infrastructure and operations. SRE aims to enable highly scalable and reliable systems. Another way of thinking about SRE is what happens when you tell a software engineer to do an operations role.

Speed of Service Provisioning

With early networks being "small" and "specialized," there was a certain acceptance to how long it took to provision new services. The network engineer of the late 1990s and early 2000s might have experienced lead times of many *months* to get new circuits from their WAN service provider. However, this was an area of transformation in network IT also. Networks became more critical to businesses. Soon, having a web presence, in addition to any brick-and-mortar location, was a necessity. This would drive a need for faster service provisioning and delivery. Previous manual efforts that included a "truck roll," or someone driving to another location, put too much latency into the process.

Businesses that could provide a service in weeks were driving a competitive differentiator to those that took months. Then this model progressed to those that could provide services in days versus weeks, and now you see the expectation of minutes, or "while I watch from my browser."

Business models have greatly changed. The aforementioned brick-and-mortar model was the norm. As the Internet flourished, having a web presence became a differentiator, then a requirement. To that end, so many years later, it is very difficult to find impactful domain names to register. Or it may cost a lot to negotiate a transfer from another owner!

Today, the physical presence is not required and is sometimes undesirable. More agile business models mean companies can be operated out of the owner's home. Fulfillment can be handled by others, and the store or marketplace is handled through a larger e-commerce entity like Amazon, Alibaba, or eBay.

It is impossible to provide services in such a rapid fashion without automation. The customer sitting at a browser expects to see an order confirmation or expected service access right then. Indeed, some customers give up and look for alternative offers if their request is not met as they wait.

This expectation of *now* forces businesses to consolidate their offers into more consistent or templatized offers. The more consistent a service can be delivered, the better suited it is for automation. It's the exceptions that tend to break the efficiencies of automation and cause longer service delivery cycles.

This rapid pace of service delivery influenced IT service management and development with DevOps and models like Agile and Lean. Figure 10-3 depicts the Agile methodology.

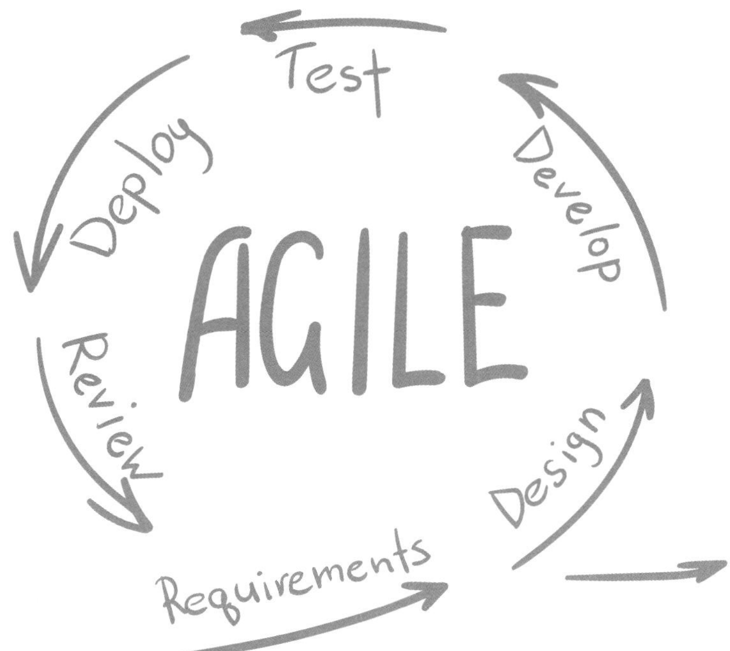

Figure 10-3 *Agile Methodology*

Agile, as a software development practice, focuses on extracting requirements and developing solutions with collaborative teams and their users. Planning with an adaptive approach to quick delivery and continuous improvement sets Agile apart from other, less flexible models. Agile is just one software development methodology, but it has a large following and is suggested for consideration in your network programmability journey. Several more of the broad spectrum of methodologies and project management frameworks are described in Table 10-3.

Table 10-3 Software Development Methodologies and Frameworks

Method Name	Description
Agile	Flexible and incremental design process focused on collaboration
Kanban	Visual framework promoting what, when, and how to develop in small, incremental changes; complements Agile
Lean	Process to create efficiencies and remove waste to produce more with less
Scrum	Process with fixed-length iterations (sprints); follows roles, responsibilities, and meetings for well-defined structure; derivative of Agile
Waterfall	Sequential design process; fully planned; execution through phases

Whatever model you choose, take time to understand the pros and cons and evaluate against your organization's capabilities, culture, motivations, and business drivers. Ultimately, the right software development methodology for you is the one that is embraced by the most people in the organization.

Accuracy of Service Provisioning

Walt Disney is known for sharing this admirable quote, "Whatever you do, do it well." That has been the aspiration of any product or service provider. The same thinking can be drawn to network service provisioning: nobody truly intends to partially deploy a service or to deploy something that will fail. One reason accuracy of service provisioning struggled before network programmability hit its stride was due to the lack of programmatic interfaces.

As we mentioned before, much of the genesis of network IT, and dare we say even IT more broadly, was founded on manual command-line interface interactions. Provisioning a device meant someone was logging into it and typing or pasting a set of configuration directives. The task wasn't quite as bad as that in Figure 10-4, but it sure felt that way!

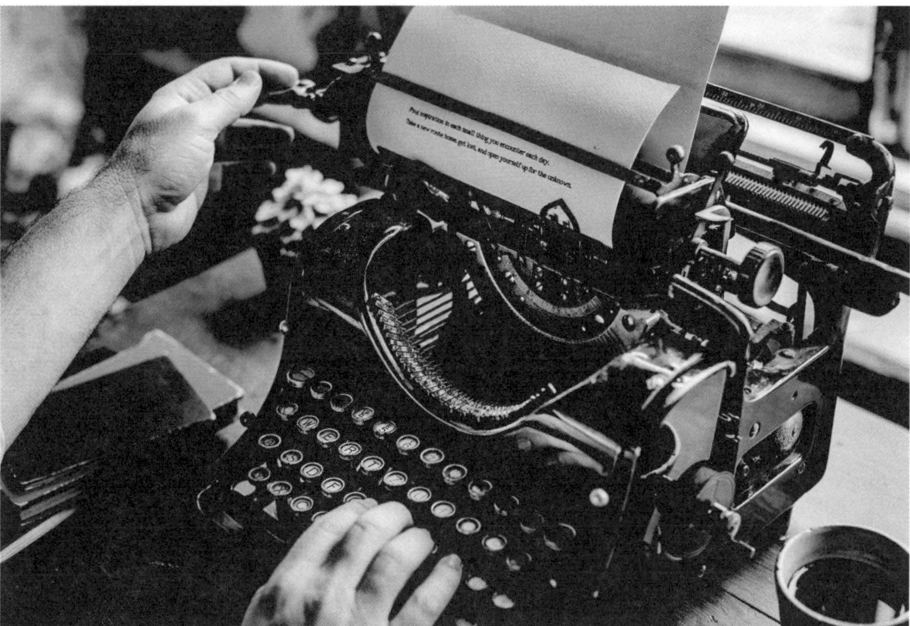

Figure 10-4 *Not Quite This Painful*

A slightly more advanced method might be typing or pasting those directives and putting them into a file to be transferred to the device and incorporated into its running configuration state. However, these manual efforts still required human interaction and an ability to translate intent to a set of configuration statements.

Some automations were, and sometimes still are, simply the collection and push of those same CLI commands (see Figure 10-5), but in an unattended fashion by a script or management application.

Figure 10-5 *Automating the CLI*

The fact that the foundation has been based on CLI automation seems to imply that the industry was conceding the "best" way to interact with a device was through the CLI. A lot of provisioning automation occurs through CLI with many management applications and open-source solutions.

Yet the CLI, while suited for human consumption, is not optimal for programmatic use. If the command syntax or output varies between releases or among products, the CLI-based solutions need to account for the differences. Consider the command output for **show interface** in Example 10-1.

Example 10-1 *Show Interface Output*

```
Switch# show interface te1/0/2
TenGigabitEthernet1/0/2 is up, line protocol is up (connected)
  Hardware is Ten Gigabit Ethernet, address is 0023.ebdd.4006 (bia 0023.ebdd.4006)
  MTU 1500 bytes, BW 10000000 Kbit, DLY 10 usec,
     reliability 255/255, txload 1/255, rxload 1/255
  Encapsulation ARPA, loopback not set
  Keepalive not set
  Full-duplex, 10Gb/s, link type is auto, media type is 10GBase-SR
  input flow-control is off, output flow-control is unsupported
  ARP type: ARPA, ARP Timeout 04:00:00
  Last input 00:00:04, output 00:00:00, output hang never
 Last clearing of "show interface" counters never
  Input queue: 0/75/0/0 (size/max/drops/flushes); Total output drops: 0
  Queueing strategy: fifo
 Output queue: 0/40 (size/max)
```

```
  5 minute input rate 5000 bits/sec, 9 packets/sec
  5 minute output rate 0 bits/sec, 0 packets/sec
     200689496 packets input, 14996333682 bytes, 0 no buffer
     Received 195962135 broadcasts (127323238 multicasts)
     0 runts, 0 giants, 0 throttles
     0 input errors, 0 CRC, 0 frame, 0 overrun, 0 ignored
     0 watchdog, 127323238 multicast, 0 pause input
     0 input packets with dribble condition detected
     7642905 packets output, 1360729535 bytes, 0 underruns
     0 output errors, 0 collisions, 0 interface resets
     0 babbles, 0 late collision, 0 deferred
     0 lost carrier, 0 no carrier, 0 PAUSE output
     0 output buffer failures, 0 output buffers swapped out
```

What are the options for extracting information like number of multicast packets output?

The use of Python scripts is in vogue, so let's consider that with Example 10-2, which requires a minimum of Python 3.6.

Example 10-2 *Python Script to Extract Multicast Packets*

```
import paramiko
import time
import getpass
import re

username = input('Enter Username: ')
userpassword = getpass.getpass('Enter Password: ')
devip = input('Enter Device IP: ')
devint = input('Enter Device Interface: ')

try:
    devconn = paramiko.SSHClient()
    devconn.set_missing_host_key_policy(paramiko.AutoAddPolicy())
    devconn.connect(devip, username=username, password=userpassword,timeout=60)
    chan = devconn.invoke_shell()
    chan.send("terminal length 0\n")
    time.sleep(1)
    chan.send(f'show interface {devint}')
    time.sleep(2)
    cmd_output = chan.recv(9999).decode(encoding='utf-8')
    devconn.close()
    result = re.search('(\d+) multicast,', cmd_output)
    if result:
        print(f'Multicast packet count on {devip} interface {devint} is {result.
group(1)}')
    else:
       print(f'No match found for {devip} interface {devint} - incorrect
interface?')
```

10

```
except paramiko.AuthenticationException:
    print("User or password incorrect - try again")
except Exception as e:
    err = str(e)
    print(f'ERROR: {err}')
```

There's a common theme in methodologies that automate against CLI output which requires some level of string manipulation. Being able to use regular expressions, commonly called regex, or the **re** module in Python, is a good skill to have for CLI and string manipulation operations. While effective, using regex can be difficult skill to master. Let's call it an acquired taste. The optimal approach is to leverage even higher degrees of abstraction through model-driven and structure interfaces, which relieve you of the string manipulation activities. You can find these in solutions like pyATS (https://developer.cisco.com/pyats/) and other Infrastructure-as-Code (IaC) solutions, such as Ansible and Terraform.

Product engineers intend to maintain consistency across releases, but the rapid rate of change and the intent to bring new innovation to the industry often result in changes to the command-line interface, either in provisioning syntax and arguments or in command-line output. These differences often break scripts and applications that depend on CLI; this affects accuracy in service provisioning. Fortunately, the industry recognizes the inefficiencies and results of varying CLI syntax and output. Apart from SNMP, which generally lacked a strong provisioning capability, one of the first innovations to enable programmatic interactions with network devices was the IETF's **NETCONF (network configuration)** protocol.

We cover NETCONF and the follow-on RESTCONF protocol in more detail later in this book. However, we can briefly describe NETCONF as an XML representation of a device's native configuration parameters. It is much more suited to programmatic use. Consider now a device configuration shown in an XML format with Figure 10-6.

```
<?xml version="1.0" encoding="UTF-8"?>
<rpc-reply message-id="11" xmlns="urn:ietf:params:netconf:base:1.0">
  <data>
    <xml-config-data>
      <Device-Configuration xmlns="urn:cisco:xml-pi">
        <version>
          <Param>15.2</Param>
        </version>
        <service>
          <timestamps>
            <debug>
              <datetime>
                <msec/>
              </datetime>
            </debug>
          </timestamps>
        </service>
...
</rpc-reply>
```

Figure 10-6 *Partial NETCONF Device Configuration*

Although the format may be somewhat unfamiliar, you can see patterns and understand the basic structure. It is the consistent structure that allows NETCONF/RESTCONF and an XML-formatted configuration to be addressed more programmatically. By referring to tags or paths through the data, you can cleanly extract the value of a parameter without depending on the existence (or lack of existence) of text before and after the specific parameter(s) you need. This capability sets NETCONF/RESTCONF apart from CLI-based methods that rely on regex or other string-parsing methods.

A more modern skillset would include understanding XML formatting and schemas, along with XPath queries, which provide data filtering and extraction functions.

Many APIs output their data as XML- or JSON-formatted results. Having skills with XPath or JSONPath queries complements NETCONF/RESTCONF. Again, we cover these topics later in Chapter 11.

Another way the industry has responded to the shifting sands of CLI is through abstracting the integration with the device with solutions like Puppet, Chef, Ansible, and Terraform. Scripts and applications can now refer to the abstract intent or API method rather than a potentially changing command-line argument or syntax. These also are covered later in this book.

Scale

Another challenge that needs to be addressed with evolving and growing network is scale. Although early and even some smaller networks today can get by with manual efforts of a few staff members, as the network increases in size, user count, and criticality, those models break. Refer back to Figure 9-19 to see the growth of the Internet over the years.

Scalable deployments are definitely constrained when using CLI-based methodologies, especially when using paste methodologies because of flow control in terminal emulators and adapters. Slightly more efficiencies are gained when using CLI to initiate a configuration file transfer and merge process.

Let me share a personal example from a customer engagement. The customer was dealing with security access list changes that totaled thousands of lines of configuration text and was frustrated with the time it took to deploy the change. One easy fix was procedural: create a new access list and then flip over to it after it was created. The other advice was showing the customer the inefficiency of CLI flow-control based methods. Because the customer was copying/pasting the access list, they were restricted by the flow control between the device CLI and the terminal emulator.

Strike one: CLI/terminal.

Strike two: Size of access list.

Strike three: Time to import.

Pasting the customer's access list into the device's configuration took more than 10 minutes. I showed them the alternative of putting the configuration parameters into a file that could be transferred and merged with the device and the resulting seconds that this approach took instead. Needless to say, the customer started using a new process.

Using NETCONF/RESTCONF protocols to programmatically collect information and inject provisioning intent is efficient. In this case, it is necessary to evaluate the extent of deployment to gauge the next level of automation for scale. Here are some questions to ask yourself:

- How many devices, nodes, and services do I need to deploy?
- Do I have dependencies among them that require staggering the change for optimal availability? Any primary or secondary service relationships?
- How much time is permitted for the change window, if applicable?
- How quickly can I revert a change if unexpected errors occur?

Increasingly, many environments have no maintenance windows; there is no time that they are not doing mission-critical work. They implement changes during all hours of the day or night because their network architectures support high degrees of resiliency and availability. However, even in these environments, it is important to verify that the changes being deployed do not negatively affect the resiliency.

One more important question left off the preceding list for special mention is "How much risk am I willing to take?" I remember working with a customer who asked, "How many devices can we software upgrade over a weekend? What is that maximum number?" Together, we created a project and arranged the equipment to mimic their environment as closely as possible—device types, code versions, link speeds, device counts. The lab was massive—hundreds of racks of equipment with thousands of devices. In the final analysis, I reported, "You can effectively upgrade your entire network over a weekend." In this case, it was 4000 devices, which at the time was a decent-sized network. I followed by saying, "However, I wouldn't do it. Based on what I know of your risk tolerance level, I would suggest staging changes. The network you knew Friday afternoon could be very different from the one Monday morning if you run into an unexpected issue." We obviously pressed for extensive change testing, but even with the leading test methodologies of the time, we had to concede something unexpected could happen. We saved the truly large-scale changes for those that were routine and low impact. For changes that were somewhat new, such as new software releases or new features and protocols, we established a phased approach to gain confidence and limit negative exposure.

- Lab testing of single device(s) representing each model/function
- Lab testing of multiple devices, including primary/backup peers
- Lab testing of multiple devices, including primary/backup peers to maximum scale possible in lab
- Production deployment of limited device counts in low-priority environments (10 percent of total)
    - Change observation for one to two weeks (depending on criticality of change)

- Production deployment of devices in standard priority environments (25 percent of total)
  - Change observation for two to four weeks (depending on criticality of change)
- Second batch deployment in standard priority environments (25 percent of total)
  - Change observation for two to four weeks (depending on criticality of change)
- Production deployment of devices in high-priority environments (10 percent of total)
  - Change observation for two to four weeks (depending on criticality of change)
- Second batch deployment of high-priority environments (10 percent of total)
  - Change observation for two to four weeks (depending on criticality of change)
- Third batch deployment of high-priority environments (20 percent of total)

As you contemplate scale, if you're programming your own solutions using Python scripts or similar, it is worthwhile to understand multithreading and multiprocessing. A few definitions of concurrency and parallelism also are in order.

An application completing more than one task at the same time is considered concurrent. *Concurrency* is working on multiple tasks at the same time but not necessarily simultaneously. Consider a situation with four tasks executing concurrently (see Figure 10-7). If you had a virtual machine or physical system with a one-core CPU, it would decide the switching involved to run the tasks. Task 1 might go first, then task 3, then some of task 2, then all of task 4, and then a return to complete task 2. Tasks can start, execute their work, and complete in overlapping time periods. The process is effectively to start, complete some (or all) of the work, and then return to incomplete work where necessary—all the while maintaining state and awareness of completion status. One issue to observe is that concurrency may involve tasks that have no dependency among them. In the world of IT, an overall workflow to enable a new web server may not be efficient for concurrency. Consider the following activities:

1. Create the virtual network.
2. Create the virtual storage volume.
3. Create the virtual machine vCPUs and vMemory.
4. Associate the VM vNet and vStorage.
5. Install the operating system to the VM.
6. Configure the operating system settings.
7. Update the operating system.
8. Install the Apache service.
9. Configure the Apache service.

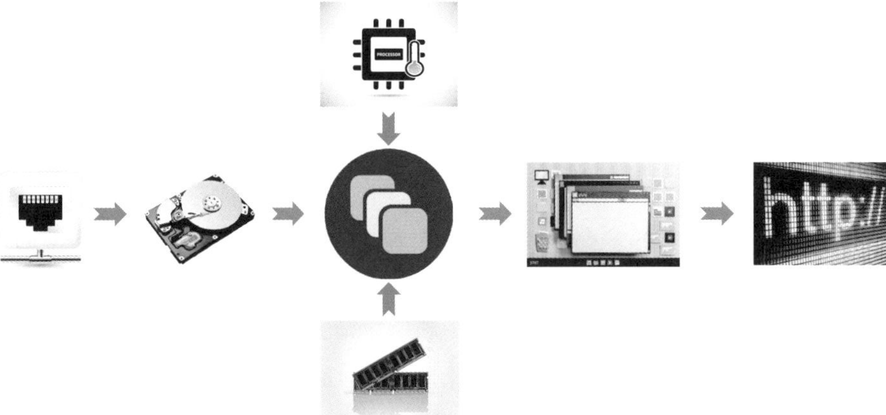

Figure 10-7 *Workflow Creating a Web Server*

Several of these steps depend on a previous step being completed. So, this workflow is not well suited to concurrency. However, deploying software images to many devices across the network would be well suited. Consider these actions on a multidevice upgrade process (see Figure 10-8):

1. Configure Router-A to download new software update (wait for it to process, flag it to return to later, move on to next router), then . . .
2. Configure Router-B to download new software update (wait for it to process, flag it to return to later, move on to next router), then . . .
3. Configure Router-C to download new software update (wait for it to process, flag it to return to later, move on to next router), then . . .
4. Check Router-A status—still going—move on to next router.
5. Configure Router-D to download new software update (wait for it to process, flag it to return to later, move on to next router).
6. Check Router-B status—complete—remove flag to check status; move to next router.
7. Configure Router-E to download new software update (wait for it to process, flag it to return to later, move on to next router).
8. Check Router-A status—complete—remove flag to check status; move to next router.
9. Check Router-C status—complete—remove flag to check status; move to next router.
10. Check Router-D status—complete—remove flag to check status; move to next router.
11. Check Router-E status—complete—remove flag to check status; move to next router.

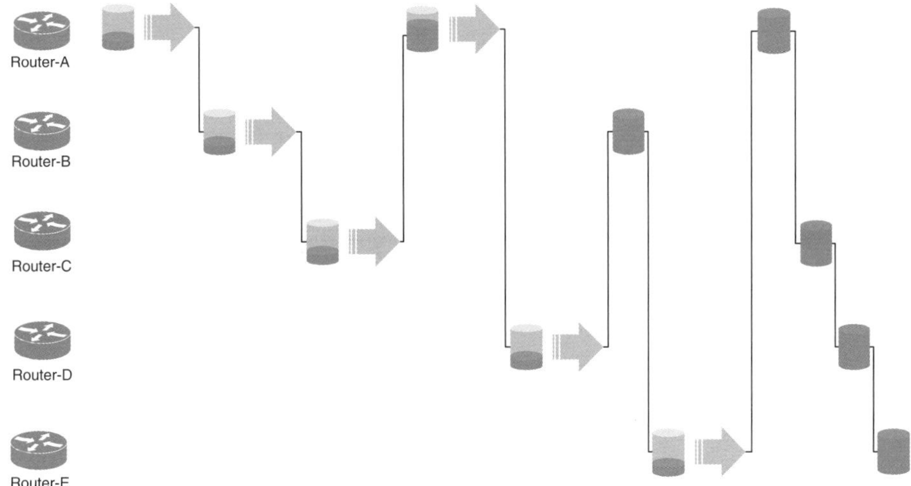

Figure 10-8 *Concurrency Example*

Parallelism is different in that an application separates tasks into smaller activities to process in parallel on multiple CPUs simultaneously. Parallelism doesn't require multiple tasks to exist. It runs parts of the tasks or multiple tasks at the same time using multicore functions of a CPU. The CPU handles the allocation of each task or subtask to a core.

Returning to the previous software example, consider it with a two-core CPU. The following actions would be involved in this multidevice upgrade (see Figure 10-9):

1. Core-1: Configure Router-A to download new software update (wait for it to process, flag it to return to later, move on to next router), while at the same time on another CPU . . .
2. Core-2: Configure Router-B to download new software update (wait for it to process, flag it to return to later, move on to next router).
3. Core-1: Configure Router-C to download new software update (wait for it to process, flag it to return to later, move on to next router).
4. Core-1: Check Router-A status—still going—move on to next router.
5. Core-2: Configure Router-D to download new software update (wait for it to process, flag it to return to later, move on to next router).
6. Core-2: Check Router-B status—complete—remove flag to check status; move to next router.
7. Core-2: Configure Router-E to download new software update (wait for it to process, flag it to return to later, move on to next router).
8. Core-1: Check Router-A status—complete—remove flag to check status; move to next router.
9. Core-1: Check Router-C status—complete—remove flag to check status; move to next router.
10. Core-1: Check Router-D status—complete—remove flag to check status; move to next router.
11. Core-2: Check Router-E status—complete—remove flag to check status; move to next router.

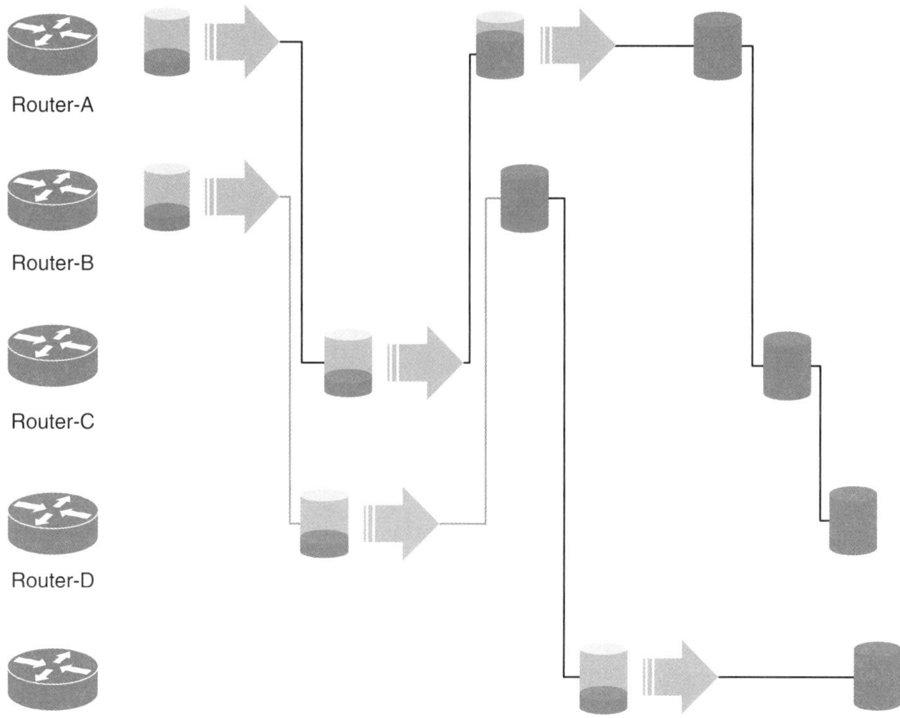

Figure 10-9 *Parallelism Example*

Because two tasks are executed simultaneously, this scenario is identified as parallelism. Parallelism requires hardware with multiple processing units, cores, or threads.

To recap, a system is concurrent if it can support two or more tasks in progress at the same time. A system is parallel if it can support two or more tasks executing simultaneously. Concurrency focuses on *working with* lots of tasks at once. Parallelism focuses on *doing* lots of tasks at once.

So, what is the practical application of these concepts? In this case, I was dealing with the Meraki Dashboard API; it allows for up to five API calls per second. Some API resources like Get Organization (**GET /organizations/{organizationId}**) have few key-values to return, so they are very fast. Other API resources like Get Device Clients (**GET /devices/{serial}/clients**) potentially return many results, so they may take more time. Using a model of parallelism to send multiple requests across multiple cores—allowing for some short-running tasks to return more quickly than others and allocating other work—provides a quicker experience over doing the entire process sequentially.

To achieve this outcome, I worked with the Python asyncio library and the semaphores feature to allocate work. I understood each activity of work had no relationship or dependency on the running of other activities; no information sharing was needed, and no interference across threads was in scope, also known as thread safe. The notion of tokens to perform work was easy to comprehend. The volume of work was created with a loop building a list of tasks; then the script would allocate as many tokens as were available in the semaphore bucket. When the script first kicked off, it had immediate access to do parallel processing of the four tokens I had allocated. As short-running tasks completed, tokens were returned to the bucket and made available for the next task. Some tasks ran longer than others, and that was fine because the overall model was not blocking other tasks from running as tokens became available.

Doing More with Less

Continuing in the theme of challenges being addressed, we must acknowledge the business pressures of gaining efficiencies to reduce operation expenses (OpEx) and potentially improve margins, if applicable. Network IT varies between a necessary cost center and a competitive differentiating profit center for many businesses. It is not uncommon for the cost center–focused businesses to manage budgets by reducing resources and attempting to get more productivity from those remaining. The profit center–focused businesses may do the same, but mostly for margin improvement.

Automation, orchestration, and network programmability provide the tools to get more done with less. If tasks are repetitive, automation reduces the burden—and burnout—on staff. Team members are able to focus on more strategic and fulfilling endeavors.

In reflection with the previous section on scale, if you have a lot of tasks that would benefit from parallel execution, if they are not dependent on each other, then it makes sense to allocate more threads/cores to the overall work. Efficient use of existing resources is desirable. It is a waste of resources if a system with many cores is often idle.

When building automated solutions, observe the tasks and time the original manual process from end to end. After you have automated the process, measure the runtime of the newly automated process and provide reporting that shows time and cost savings with the automation. Having practical examples of return on investment (ROI) helps decision makers understand the benefits of automation and encourage its implementation. You're building the automation; you can create your own telemetry and instrumentation!

Software-Defined Networking (SDN)

The catalyst for software-defined networking is largely attributed to Stanford University's Clean Slate Program in 2008. Cisco was a sponsor of this project, which reimagined what a new Internet would look like if we set aside conventional norms of traditional networks and worked from a clean slate. It was difficult to develop next-generation routing or connectivity protocols if the equipment available was purposely programmed to follow the original conventions. Programmable logic arrays (PLAs) were pretty expensive to test theories, so a more software-based approach was proposed.

What Is SDN and Network Programmability?

Definitions of SDN and network programmability varied among network IT vendors, but some points were generally agreed upon. As illustrated in Figure 10-10, SDN is

- An approach and architecture in networking where control and data planes are decoupled, and intelligence and state are logically centralized
- An enabling technology where the underlying network infrastructure is abstracted from the applications (network virtualization)
- A concept that leverages programmatic interfaces to enable external systems to influence network provisioning, control, and operations

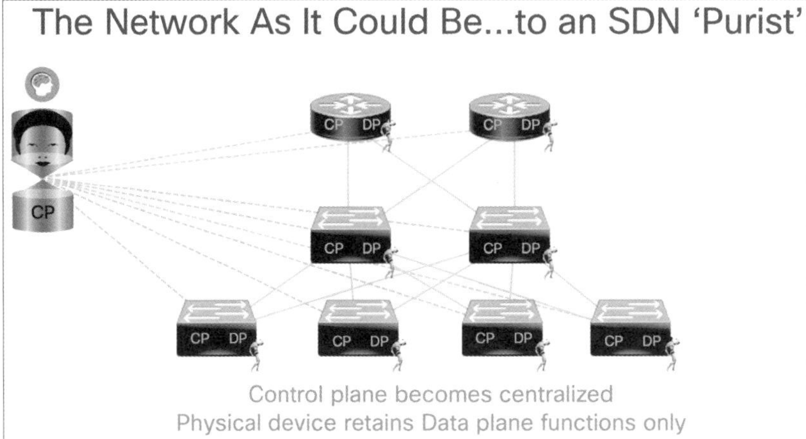
The Network As It Could Be...to an SDN 'Purist'
CP
CP DP
Control plane becomes centralized
Physical device retains Data plane functions only

Figure 10-10 *The SDN Concept*

Although all of these definitions were exciting and transformative, the last item of leveraging programmatic interfaces appeals mostly to the network programming crowd. The last item also enables us to influence the first two through provisioning and monitoring network assets.

In my talks at CiscoLive, I would share that SDN was

- An approach to network transformation*
- Empowering alternative, nontraditional entities to influence network design and operations
- Impacting the networking industry, challenging the way we think about engineering, implementing, and managing networks
- Providing new methods to interact with equipment and services via controllers and APIs
- Normalizing the interface with equipment and services
- Enabling high-scale, rapid network and service provisioning and management
- Providing a catalyst for traditional route/switch engineers to branch out

Approach

So, why the asterisk next to an approach to network transformation? Well, it wasn't the first attempt at network transformation. If we consider separation of the control plane and data plane, we can look no further than earlier technologies, such as SS7, ATM LANE, the wireless LAN controller, and GMPLS. If we were considering network overlays/underlays and encapsulation, the earlier examples were MPLS, VPLS, VPN, GRE Tunnels, and LISP. Finally, if our consideration was management and programmatic interfaces, we had SNMP, NETCONF and EEM. Nonetheless, SDN was a transformative pursuit.

Nontraditional Entities

What about those nontraditional entities influencing the network? As new programmatic interfaces were purposely engineered into the devices and controllers, a new wave of network programmers joined the environment. Although traditional network engineers skilled up to learn programming (and that may be you, reading this book!), some programmers who had little prior networking experience decided to try their hand at programming a network. Or the programmers decided it was in their best interests to configure an underpinning network for their application themselves, rather than parsing the work out to a network provisioning team.

Regardless of the source of interaction with the network, it is imperative that the new interfaces, telemetry, and instrumentation be secured with the same, if not more, scrutiny as the legacy functions. The security policies can serve to protect the network from unintentional harm by people who don't have deep experience with the technology *and* from the intentional harm of bad actors.

Industry Impact

The impact to the network industry with operations and engineering was greatly influenced by control plane and data plane separation and the development of centralized controllers. The network management teams would no longer work as hard to treat each network asset as an atomic unit but could manage a network en masse through the controller. One touchpoint for provisioning and monitoring of all these devices! The ACI APIC controller is acknowledged as one of the first examples of an SDN controller, as seen in Figure 10-11. It was able to automatically detect, register, and configure Cisco Nexus 9000 series switches in a data center fabric.

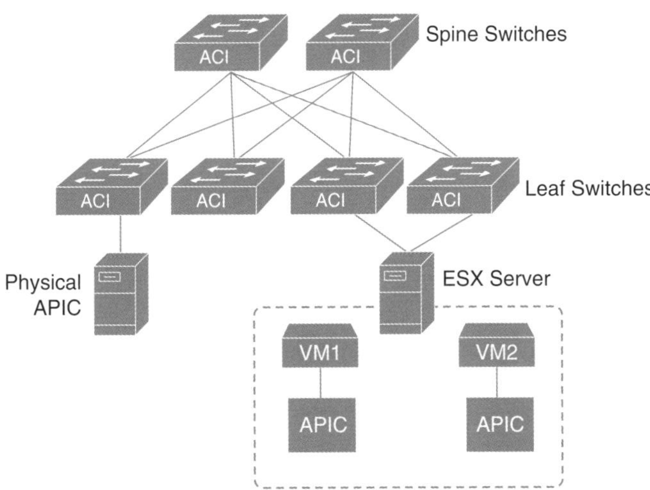

Figure 10-11 *Cisco ACI Architecture with APIC Controllers*

New Methods

With respect to new methods, protocols, and interfaces to managed assets, APIs became more prolific with the SDN approach. Early supporting devices extended a style of REST-like interface and then more fully adopted the model. First NETCONF and then RESTCONF became the desired norm. Centralized controllers, like the wireless LAN controller, ACI's

APIC controller, Meraki, and others, prove the operational efficiency of aggregating the monitoring and provisioning of fabrics of devices. This model has coaxed the question "What else can we centralize?"

Normalization

SDN's impact on network normalization is reflected in the increasingly standardized interfaces. While SNMP had some utility, SDN provided a fresh opportunity to build and use newer management technologies that had security at their core, not just a "bolt-on" consideration. Although the first API experiences felt a bit like the Wild Wild West, the Swagger project started to define a common interface description language to **REST** APIs. Swagger has since morphed into the OpenAPI initiative, and specification greatly simplifies API development and documentation tasks.

Enabling Operations

Network operations, service provisioning, and management were influenced with SDN through the new interfaces, their standardization, and programmatic fundamentals. Instead of relying on manual CLI methods, operators began to rely on their growing knowledge base of REST API methods and sample scripts in growing their operational awareness and ability to respond and influence network functions.

Besides the REST API, other influences include gRPC Network Management Interface (gNMI), OpenConfig, NETCONF, RESTCONF, YANG, time-series databases, AMQP pub-sub architectures, and many others.

Enabling Career Options

Finally, SDN provided traditional network engineers an opportunity to extend their skills with new network programming expertise. The traditional network engineer with years of domain experience could apply that knowledge in an impactful way with these programmatic interfaces. They could deploy more services at scale, with fewer errors and more quickly.

How impactful could SDN be? Let's consider the early days of IP telephony: it didn't ramp up as quickly as desired. On one side there were the traditional "tip-ring telco" team members; on the other side was the new "packet-switch" team. IP telephony technology was slow to gain momentum because few individuals crossed the aisle to learn the other side and become change and translation agents for the greater good. When people started to understand and share the nuanced discipline of the other side, then SDN started to make strides.

Network programmability is in that same transition: there are *strong* network engineers who understand their tradition route/switch technology. Likewise, there are very strong software developers who understand how to build apps and interact with systems; they just don't have the network domain expertise. As network engineers skill up with the automation and network programming discipline, they bring their experience of networks with them. So, let's do IT!

Use Cases and Problems Solved with SDN

SDN aimed to address several use cases. The research and academic communities were looking for ways to create experimental network algorithms and technologies. The hope was to turn these into new protocols, standards, and products. Because existing products closely adhered to well-defined routing protocol specifications, SDN was to help separate the current norms from new, experimental concepts.

The massively scalable data center community appreciated SDN for the ability to separate the control plane from the data plane and use APIs to provide deep insight into network traffic. Cloud providers drew upon SDN for automated provisioning and programmable network overlays. Service providers aligned to policy-based control and analytics to optimize and monetize service delivery. Enterprise networks latched onto SDN's capability to virtualize workloads, provide network segmentation, and orchestrate security profiles.

Nearly all segments realized the benefits of automation and programmability with SDN:

- Centralized configuration, management control, and monitoring of network devices (physical or virtual)
- The capability to override traditional forwarding algorithms to suit unique business or technical needs
- The capability of external applications or systems to influence network provisioning and operation
- Rapid and scalable deployment of network services with lifecycle management

Several protocols and solutions contributed to the rise of SDN. See Table 10-4 for examples.

Table 10-4 Contributing Protocols and Solutions to SDN

Protocol/Solution	Definition	Function
OpenFlow		Layer-2 programmable forwarding protocol and specification for switch manufacturing
I2RS	Interface to Routing System	Layer-3 programmable protocol to the routing information base (RIB); allowed manipulation and creation of new routing metrics
PCEP	Path Computation Element Protocol	L3 protocol capable of computing a network path or route based on a network graph and applying computational constraints
BGP-LS/FS	BGP Link-State / Flow Spec	The ability to gather IGP topology of the network and export to a central SDN controller or alternative method to remotely triggered black hole filtering useful for DDoS mitigation

Protocol/Solution	Definition	Function
OpenStack		Hypervisor technology for virtualization of workloads
OMI	Open Management Infrastructure	Open-source Common Information Model with intent to normalize management
Puppet		Agent-based configuration management solution embedded in devices (later updated to agentless)
Ansible		Agentless configuration management solution
NETCONF	Network Configuration standard	IETF working group specification normalizing configuration across vendors using XML schemas (later updated with YANG)
YANG	Data Modeling Language	Data modeling language for defining IT technologies and services

Overview of Network Controllers

One of the main benefits of SDN was the notion of control plane and data plane separation. You can think of the control plane as the brains of the network: it makes forwarding decisions based on interactions with adjacent devices and their forwarding protocols. The data plane is the muscle, acting on the forwarding decisions programmed into it. Routing protocols like OSPF and BGP operate in the control plane. A link aggregation protocol like LACP or the MAC address table would be representative of the data plane.

The first traditional networks combined the functionality of the control plane/data plane into the same device. Each device acted autonomously, creating and executing its own forwarding decisions. With the advent of SDN, the notion of centralizing that brain function into one control unit yet keeping the data plane function at the managed device was the new architectural goal. These centralized controllers aggregated the monitoring and management function. They oftentimes also provided that centralized forwarding path determination and programming function.

The separation of functional planes also resulted in the definition of new overlay and underlay functionality. Network overlays defined that tunnel endpoints terminated on routers and switches. The physical devices executed the protocols to handle resiliency and loops. Some examples are OTV, VXLAN, VPLS, and LISP.

Host overlays defined that tunnel endpoints terminated on virtual nodes. Examples of host overlays are VXLAN, NVGRE, and STT. Finally, integrated overlays allowed for physical or virtual endpoints in tunnel termination. The Cisco ACI fabric with Nexus 9000 series switches are examples of integrated overlays.

The Cisco Solutions

Cisco has many offerings in the SDN space, the most prominent being the Cisco ACI fabric with Nexus 9000 series switches. Software-defined access (SDA) is enabled by Cisco DNA Center on enterprise fabric-enabled devices. Software-defined wide-area networks (SD-WANs) can be seen in the acquired technologies of Viptela, resulting in the vManage solution for central cloud management, authentication, and licensing.

Network Function Virtualization (NFV) enables cloud technology to support network functions, such as the Cisco Integrated Services Virtual Router (ISRv), ASAv, and vWLC. The Cisco Managed Services Accelerator (MSX) provides automated end-to-end SD-WAN services managed from the service provider cloud.

Application Programming Interfaces (APIs)

Application programming interfaces are the foundational method for interacting with devices, applications, controllers, and other networked entities. Although the command-line interface has reigned supreme for years, we must admit, if an entity has an API, it is the desirable method for interacting with it.

APIs are common in many fashions: some are application to application, whereas others are application to hardware entity. Consider some of the following interactions as examples:

- DNAC software controller API call to Cisco Support API endpoint for opening cases: software to software
- Cisco Intersight with UCS IMC for device registration, monitoring, and provisioning from the cloud: software to hardware
- Network Services Orchestrator (NSO) to ASR1000 for provisioning and monitoring: software to hardware

To use an API, you must know the way to make requests, how to authenticate to the service, how to handle the return results (data encoding), and other conventions it may use, such as cookies. Public APIs often involve denial-of-service protections beyond authentication, such as rate limiting the number of requests per time period, the number of requests from an IP endpoint, and pagination or volume of data returned.

For the purposes of network IT, we mostly focus on web APIs, as we discuss in the next section on REST APIs, but other common APIs you may experience are the Java Database Connectivity (JDBC) and Microsoft Open Database Connectivity (ODBC) APIs. JDBC and ODBC permit connections to different types of databases, such as Oracle, MySQL, and Microsoft SQL Server, with standard interfaces that ease application development.

The Simple Object Access Protocol (SOAP) is also a well-known design model for web services. It uses XML and schemas with a strongly typed messaging framework. A web service definition (WSDL) defines the interaction between a service provider and the consumer. In Cisco Unified Communications, the Administrative XML Web Service (AXL) is a SOAP-based interface enabling insertion, retrieval, updates, and removal of data from the Unified Communication configuration database.

Because a SOAP message has the XML element of an "envelope" and further contains a "body," many people draw the parallel of SOAP being like a postal envelope, with the necessary container and the message within, to REST being like a postcard that has none of the "wrapper" and still contains information. Figure 10-12 illustrates this architecture.

Figure 10-12 *Cisco ACI Architecture with APIC Controllers*

APIs are used in many Internet interactions—logins, data collection, performance reporting, analytics. Microservices are associated with APIs as self-contained, lightweight endpoints that you can interact with to gather data or effect change. They are usually specific to a function, such as validate login, and are engineered with resiliency in mind, so continuous integration/continuous deployment (CI/CD) processes allow for routine maintenance without service impact to users.

REST APIs

RESTful APIs (or representational state transfer APIs) use Web/HTTP services for read and modification functions. This stateless protocol has several predefined operations, as seen in Table 10-5. Because it's a stateless protocol, the server does not maintain the state of a request. The client's request must contain all information needed to complete a request, such as session state.

Table 10-5 REST API Operation Types

Method	Function	Idempotency	Safety/Read-only Function
GET	Reads resource data, settings	YES	YES
HEAD	Tests the API endpoint for validity, accessibility, and recent modifications; similar to GET without response payload	YES	YES
POST	Creates a new resource	NO	NO
PUT	Updates or replaces a resource	YES	NO
PATCH	Modifies changes to a resource (not complete replacement)	NO	NO
DELETE	Deletes a resource	YES	NO
CONNECT	Starts communications with the resource; opens a tunnel	YES	YES
OPTIONS	Provides information about the capabilities of a resource, without initiating a resource retrieval function	YES	YES

API Methods

Another important aspect of a RESTful API is the API method's *idempotency*, or capability to produce the same result when invoked, regardless of the number of times. The same request repeated to an idempotent endpoint should return an identical result regardless of two executions or hundreds.

API Authentication

Authentication to a RESTful API can take any number of forms: basic authentication, API key, bearer token, OAuth, or digest authentication, to name a few. Basic authentication is common, where the username is concatenated with a colon and the user's password. The combined string is then Base64-encoded. You can easily generate the authentication string on macOS or other Linux derivatives using the built-in **openssl** utility. Windows platforms can achieve the same result by installing OpenSSL or obtaining a Base64-encoding utility.

NOTE Do *not* use an online website to generate Base64-encoded authentication strings. You do not know whether the site is logging user input, and security may be undermined.

Example 10-3 shows an example of generating a basic authentication string with **openssl** on macOS.

Example 10-3 *Generating Base64 Basic Authentication String on MacOS*

```
Mac ~ % echo -n 'myusername:DevNet4U!' | openssl base64
bXl1c2VybmFtZTpEZXZOZXQ0VSE=
Mac ~ %
```

This method is not considered secure due to the encoding; at a minimum, the connection should be TLS-enabled so that the weak security model is at least wrapped in a layer of transport encryption.

Either API key or bearer token is more preferable from a security perspective. These models require you to generate a one-time key, usually from an administrative portal or user profile page. For example, you can enable the Meraki Dashboard API by first enabling the API for your organization: **Organization > Settings > Dashboard API access**. Then the associated Dashboard Administrator user can access the My Profile page to generate an API key. The key can also be revoked and a new key generated at any time, if needed.

API Pagination

API pagination serves as a method to protect API servers from overload due to large data retrieval requests. An API may limit return results, commonly rows or records, to a specific count. For example, the DNA Center REST API v2.1.2.x limits device results to 500 records at a time. To poll inventory beyond that, you would use pagination:

```
GET /dna/intent/api/v1/network-device/{index}/{count}
```

For example, if you had 1433 devices in inventory, you would use these successive polls:

```
GET /dna/intent/api/v1/network-device/1/500
```

```
GET /dna/intent/api/v1/network-device/501/500
```

```
GET /dna/intent/api/v1/network-device/1000/433
```

Other APIs may provide different cues that pagination was in effect. The API return results may include the following parameters:

```
Records: 2034

First: 0

Last: 999

Next: 1000
```

Payload Data Formats JSON XML

When dealing with REST APIs, you often need to provide a request payload containing parameters. The parameters could be anything—username to provision, interface name to poll, operating system template for a virtual machine. The API response payload body likewise has information to be consumed. In either case, it is common to work with XML- or JSON-formatted data, although others are possible and less common. These two data encoding models are conducive to programmatic use.

XML

The **Extensible Markup Language (XML)** is a markup language and data encoding model that has similarities to HTML. It is used to describe and share information in a programmatic but still humanly readable way.

XML documents have structure and can represent records and lists. Many people look at XML as information and data wrapped in tags. See Example 10-4 for context.

Example 10-4 *XML Document*

```
<Document>
   <Nodes>
      <Node>
         <Name>Router-A</Name>
         <Location>San Jose, CA</Location>
         <Interfaces>
            <Interface>
               <Name>GigabitEthernet0/0/0</Name>
               <IPv4Address>10.1.2.3</IPv4Address>
               <IPv4NetMask>255.255.255.0</IPv4NetMask>
               <Description>Uplink to Switch-BB</Description>
            </Interface>
            <Interface>
               <Name>GigabitEthernet0/0/1</Name>
               <IPv4Address>10.2.2.1</IPv4Address>
               <IPv4NetMask>255.255.255.128</IPv4NetMask>
               <Description />
            </Interface>
         </Interfaces>
      </Node>
   </Nodes>
</Document>
```

In this example, the structure of this XML document represents a router record. <Document>, <Nodes>, <Node>, <Name>, and <Location> are some of the tags created by the document author. They also define the structure. Router-A, San Jose, CA, and GigabitEthernet0/0/0 are values associated with the tags. Generally, when an XML document or schema is written, the XML tags should provide context for the value(s) supplied. The values associated with the tags are plaintext and do not convey data type. As a plaintext document, XML lends well to data exchange and compression, where needed.

XML has a history associated with document publishing. Its functional similarity with HTML provides value: XML defines and stores data, focusing on content; HTML defines format, focusing on how the content looks. The Extensible Stylesheet Language (XSL) provides a data transformation function, XSL Transformations (XSLT), for converting XML documents from one format into another, such as XML into HTML. When you consider that many APIs output results in XML, using XSLTs to convert that output into HTML is an enabling feature. This is the basis for simple "API to Dashboard" automation.

Referring to Example 10-4, you can see that XML documents contain starting tags, such as <Node>, and ending (or closing) tags, such as </Node>. There is also the convention of an empty element tag; note the <Description /> example. All elements must have an end tag or be described with the empty element tag for well-formed XML documents. Tags are case sensitive, and the start and end tags must match case. If you're a document author, you are able to use any naming style you wish: lowercase, uppercase, underscore, Pascal case, Camel case, and so on. It is suggested that you do not use dashes (-) or periods (.) in tags to prevent misinterpretation by some processors.

All elements must be balanced in nesting, but the spacing is not prescribed. A convention of three spaces aids the reader. It is acceptable for no spacing in a highly compressed document, but the elements must still be nested among start and end tags.

XML can have attributes, similar to HTML. In the HTML example <img src="devnet_logo.png" alt="DevNet Logo" />, you can recognize attributes of src and alt with values of "devnet_logo.png" and "DevNet Logo". Similarly, in XML, data can have attributes—for example, <interface type="GigabitEthernet">0/0/0</interface>.

Attribute values, such as "GigabitEthernet", must be surrounded by double quotes. Values between tags, such as 0/0/0, do not require quotes.

XML documents usually start with an XML declaration or prolog to describe the version and encoding being used, but it is optional:

```
<?xml version="1.0" encoding="UTF-8"?>
```

XML documents are often described as trees composed of elements. The root element starts the document. Branches and child elements define the structure with elements potentially having subelements, or children. In Example 10-4, the root element is <Document>. Because XML does not predefine tags, you may see other root element tags. Some common ones are <Root>, <DocumentRoot>, <Parent>, and <rootElement>. It is up to the document author to define the tags and structure.

10

The <Nodes> element is a child. The <Node> elements are also children. The <Node> elements are also siblings to each other, as a list of records. The <Name>, <IPv4Address>, <IPv4NetMask>, and <Description> elements are children to <Node>, siblings to each other and form a record. Because there are multiple <Node> elements, a list is formed.

XML documents can be viewed in browsers, typically through an Open File function. The browser may render the XML with easy-to-understand hierarchy and expand or collapse functions using + and -or ^ and > gadgets. See Figure 10-13 for another example of ACI XML data, rendered in a browser.

This XML file does not appear to have any style information associated with it. The document tree is shown below.


```
▾<polUni>
  ▾<fvTenant name="tenant1">
    ▾<vnsAbsGraph name="WebGraph">
      ▾<vnsAbsTermNodeCon name="Input1">
          <vnsAbsTermConn name="C1"/>
        </vnsAbsTermNodeCon>
        <!-- FW1 Provides FW functionality -->
      ▾<vnsAbsNode name="FW1" funcType="GoThrough">
          <vnsRsDefaultScopeToTerm tDn="uni/tn-tenant1/AbsGraph-WebGraph/AbsTermNodeProv-Output1/outtmnl"/>
        ▾<vnsAbsFuncConn name="external" attNotify="yes">
            <vnsRsMConnAtt tDn="uni/infra/mDev-CISCO-ASA-{dp_version}/mFunc-Firewall/mConn-external"/>
          </vnsAbsFuncConn>
        ▾<vnsAbsFuncConn name="internal" attNotify="yes">
            <vnsRsMConnAtt tDn="uni/infra/mDev-CISCO-ASA-{dp_version}/mFunc-Firewall/mConn-internal"/>
          </vnsAbsFuncConn>
        ▸<vnsAbsDevCfg>
          ...
          </vnsAbsDevCfg>
        ▸<vnsAbsFuncCfg>
          ...
          </vnsAbsFuncCfg>
          <vnsRsNodeToMFunc tDn="uni/infra/mDev-CISCO-ASA-{dp_version}/mFunc-Firewall"/>
        </vnsAbsNode>
      ▸<vnsAbsTermNodeProv name="Output1">
        ...
        </vnsAbsTermNodeProv>
      ▸<vnsAbsConnection name="CON1">
        ...
        </vnsAbsConnection>
      ▸<vnsAbsConnection name="CON2" unicastRoute="no">
        ...
        </vnsAbsConnection>
      </vnsAbsGraph>
    </fvTenant>
  </polUni>
```


Figure 10-13 *ACI XML Data Rendered in Browser*

JSON

JavaScript Object Notation (JSON) is a newer data encoding model than XML and is growing in popularity and use with its more compact notation, ease of understanding, and closer integration with Python programming. It is lightweight, self-describing, and programming language independent. If your development includes JavaScript, then JSON is an easy choice for data encoding with its natural alignment to JavaScript syntax.

The JSON syntax provides data being written as name-value pairs. Data is separated by commas. Records or objects are defined by curly braces { }. Arrays and lists are contained within square brackets [ ].

The name of a name-value pair should be surrounded by double quotes. The value should have double quotes if representing a string. It should not have quotes if representing a numeric, Boolean (true/false), or null value. See Example 10-5 for a sample JSON record.

Example 10-5 *REST API Payload as JSON*

```
{
   "Document": {
      "Nodes": {
         "Node": {
            "Name": "Router-A",
            "Location": "San Jose, CA",
            "InterfaceCount": 2,
            "Interfaces": {
               "Interface": [
                  {
                     "Name": "GigabitEthernet0/0/0",
                     "IPv4Address": "10.1.2.3",
                     "IPv4NetMask": "255.255.255.0",
                     "Description": "Uplink to Switch-BB",
                     "isConnected": true
                  },
                  {
                     "Name": "GigabitEthernet0/0/1",
                     "IPv4Address": "10.2.2.1",
                     "IPv4NetMask": "255.255.255.128",
                     "Description": null,
                     "isConnected": false
                  }
               ]
            }
         }
      }
   }
}
```

Using this example, you can compare the structure with the previous XML representation. There is a list of interfaces; each interface is a record or object.

With APIs, the system may not give you a choice of data formatting; either XML or JSON may be the default. However, content negotiation is supported by many APIs. If the server drives the output representation, a Content-Type header shows "application/xml" or "application/json" as the response body payload type.

If the requesting client can request what's desired, then an Accept header specifies similar values for preference. With some APIs, appending .xml or .json to the request URI returns the data with the preferred format.

Cross-Domain, Technology-Agnostic Orchestration (CDTAO)

This section is not part of the official DEVCOR certification; however, in the spirit of growing network programmability skills, it does seem appropriate to discuss. You may skip this section if you prefer.

Most work in network IT tends to be very domain-specific. It's not unusual to see engineers and operators focus on specific technologies—enterprise networking, route/switch, wireless, storage networks, compute, wide-area networking, MPLS, security, and so on. However, many do embrace multidomain expertise.

Often the management applications follow a similar segmentation. It is easy to appreciate, then, when management apps bring a multidomain perspective to monitoring, provisioning, and management. However, consider *why* you're doing IT: there's *a lot* to support a business and the apps it depends on for the services it provides. Some typical supporting technologies include DNS, server connectivity, link aggregation, routing, switching, storage, compute, virtualized workloads, authentication, databases, firewall security, content filtering security, threat mitigation security, and application hosting. I'm sure you can think of many more!

So, is your operational perspective keeping up with the scope of your IT services? If you end up using multiple tools for different domains or scale or geographical segments or security segmentation, do you have an aggregate view of the health of your IT services, or do you switch back and forth between multiple tools? Doesn't this issue get exacerbated when you pull in other IT vendors and open-source solutions? Is this something you accept as "the way it is" or do you try to "glue" together these systems for more unified operational insight?

How do you glue these systems together?

APIs are the unifying capability that enable you to achieve that glue. Most partner-vendors, Cisco included, strive to provide the best customer experience possible with their product and service offers. However, there are many customer segments, different sizes, different areas of concentration, and constraints. I have been asked, "Why isn't there just one management tool?" Can you imagine the size in server requirements, cost, and maintenance necessary to provide such a solution? Would the broad functions, some of which don't apply to your circumstances, distract your focus or enable it? In a friendly recognition to Hasbro, the movie series, and the legacy Cisco management suite, we would have to call it "Cisco Optimus Prime"! Most would agree that's a bit unrealistic. Even building an uber-modular framework to allow the specific selection of desired functions and device support would increase complexity.

So is there an answer? Most providers enable their tools with APIs. If you pick the tools and apps you need based on function, need, cost, and preference, then you can obtain a converged operational perspective by using orchestration to collect the key health indicators from the individual tools and controllers. The orchestrator's workflow would also include activities to create dashboards and portals unifying the information into converged operational portals that direct your attention to the domain-specific management tools, as necessary.

Is this possible? It's not provided out of the box, again due to the variety of device types and functions, but it is doable. Consider the portal developed for the CiscoLive NOC in Figure

10-14. This example represents, essentially, a mashup of key health metrics from several tools: Prime Infrastructure, DNA Center, vCenter, Prime Network Registrar, Hyperflex, and so on.

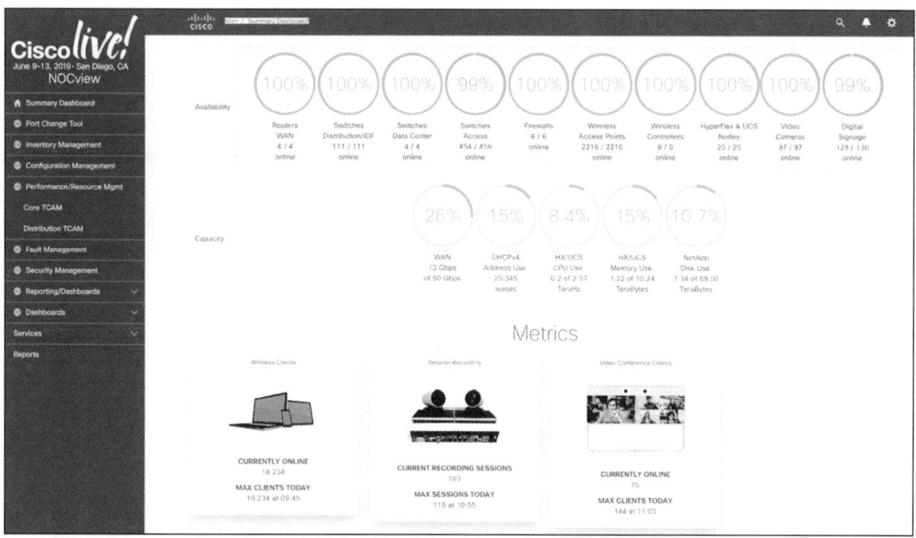

Figure 10-14 *NOC Dashboard*

So what does the technology-agnostic part of Cross-Domain, Technology-Agnostic Orchestration (CDTAO) entail? It's a wonderful concept to glue together network IT services in a cross-domain perspective. What about some out-of-the-box thinking that also brings in non-networking IT? From Figure 10-14, you can observe collaboration, digital signage, and NetApp storage. What other network-connected technology (think IoT) can be accessed and operational insight retrieved?

What industry do you work in?

- **Healthcare:** Pull in network-connected systems, such as blood-pressure cuffs, pulse ox monitors, and crash carts.
- **Financial:** Pull in ATM (cash, not legacy networking!), vault/deposit box status.
- **Retail:** Fork lifts, credit card and point-of-sale terminals.
- **Education:** Digital projector status, teacher location/availability, bus/parking lot, camera status.

If you add "business care-abouts" to the network IT perspectives, does that allow you to see contribution and impact of the supporting infrastructure to the broader company? Sure, it does!

Impact to IT Service Management and Security

This section is a continuation and amplification of the earlier "Software-Defined Networking (SDN)" section mentioning the impact of other nontraditional entities influencing the network. In a traditional networking case, you probably wrapped security around your change management and provisioning of the network devices, even if performed manually. SSH was enabled; access lists permitting only NOC or other specific personnel and network ranges were configured; logging and accounting were enabled; possibly two-factor or multifactor authentication was provisioned. In any case, security was given a strong consideration.

So now that network devices, management applications, and controllers have programmatic interfaces to extract and change functions of networks, are you continuing the same scrutiny? Are you the main source of API integration, or were other people with strong programming experience brought in to beef up automation? Do they have strong networking experience in concert with their programming skills? Are they keeping in touch with you about changes? Oh no! Did that network segment go down?

Okay, enough of the histrionic "what if" scenario. You just need to make sure the same rigor applied to traditional network engineering and operations is also being applied to newer, SDN, and programmatic environments.

What are the leading practices related to programmable networks? First, consider your risk. What devices and services are managed through controllers? They should be secured first because they have the broadest scope of impact with multiple devices in a fabric. Enable all the security features the controller provides with the least amount of privileges necessary to the fewest number of individuals (and other automated systems). If the controller has limited security options, consider front-ending it with access lists or firewall services to limit access and content. Remember to implement logging and accounting; then *review* it periodically.

The next order of business should be high-priority equipment where the loss of availability has direct service, revenue, or brand recognition impact. It's the same activity: tighten up access controls to the newer programmatic interfaces and telemetry.

Finally, go after the regular and low-priority equipment to shore up their direct device management interfaces in a similar fashion.

Exam Preparation Tasks

As mentioned in the section "How to Use This Book" in the Introduction, you have a couple of choices for exam preparation: the exercises here, Chapter 17, "Final Preparation," and the exam simulation questions in the Pearson Test Prep Software Online.

Review All Key Topics

Review the most important topics in this chapter, noted with the Key Topic icon in the outer margin of the page. Table 10-6 lists a reference of these key topics and the page numbers on which each is found.

Table 10-6 Key Topics for Chapter 10

Key Topic Element	Description	Page Number
Figure 10-3	Agile Methodology	318
Paragraph	SDN concepts	329
Table 10-4	Contributing Protocols and Solutions to SDN	333
Table 10-5	REST API Operation Types	336
Paragraph	XML description	338
Paragraph	JSON description	340

Complete Tables and Lists from Memory

Print a copy of Appendix C, "Memory Tables" (found on the companion website), or at least the section for this chapter, and complete the tables and lists from memory. Appendix D, "Memory Tables Answer Key," also on the companion website, includes completed tables and lists to check your work.

Define Key Terms

Define the following key terms from this chapter and check your answers in the glossary:

JavaScript Object Notation (JSON), Network Configuration Protocol (NETCONF), REST, Extensible Markup Language (XML), YANG

References

URL	QR Code
https://developer.cisco.com/pyats/	

CHAPTER 11

NETCONF and RESTCONF

This chapter covers the following topics:

- **Catalyst for NETCONF:** This section covers the reasons and benefits for NETCONF.
- **Atomic and Model-Driven Configuration Management:** This section covers the differences between atomic, templatized, and model-driven configuration management.
- **How to Implement NETCONF:** This section covers the methods for implementing NETCONF, the skills needed, and sample configuration guidelines.
- **YANG Models:** This section covers the reasons and benefits for YANG models.
- **The Evolution with RESTCONF:** This section covers the additional benefits beyond NETCONF provided with RESTCONF.
- **Management Solutions Using NETCONF and RESTCONF:** This section provides insights into the current management tool offerings that leverage NETCONF and/or RESTCONF. Both commercial and open-source examples are shared.

This chapter maps to the *Developing Applications Using Cisco Core Platforms and APIs v1.0 (350-901)* Exam Blueprint Section 5.2, "Utilize RESTCONF to configure a network device including interfaces, static routes, and VLANs (IOS XE only)."

NETCONF and RESTCONF are relatively new but mature management protocols that are well suited for network programmability. This chapter covers the basic theory behind NETCONF and RESTCONF. It shows examples of how to use them so that you can apply them in your Cisco network environment.

"Do I Know This Already?" Quiz

The "Do I Know This Already?" quiz allows you to assess if you should read this entire chapter. If you miss no more than one of these self-assessment questions, you might want to move ahead to the "Exam Preparation Tasks" section. Table 11-1 lists the major headings in this chapter and the "Do I Know This Already?" quiz questions covering the material in those headings so you can assess your knowledge of these specific areas. You can find the answers in Appendix A, "Answers to the 'Do I Know This Already?' Quizzes."

Table 11-1 "Do I Know This Already?" Section-to-Question Mapping

Foundation Topics Section	Questions
Catalyst for NETCONF	1–2
Atomic and Model-Driven Configuration Management	3
How to Implement NETCONF	4–6
YANG Models	7–8
The Evolution with RESTCONF	9–10

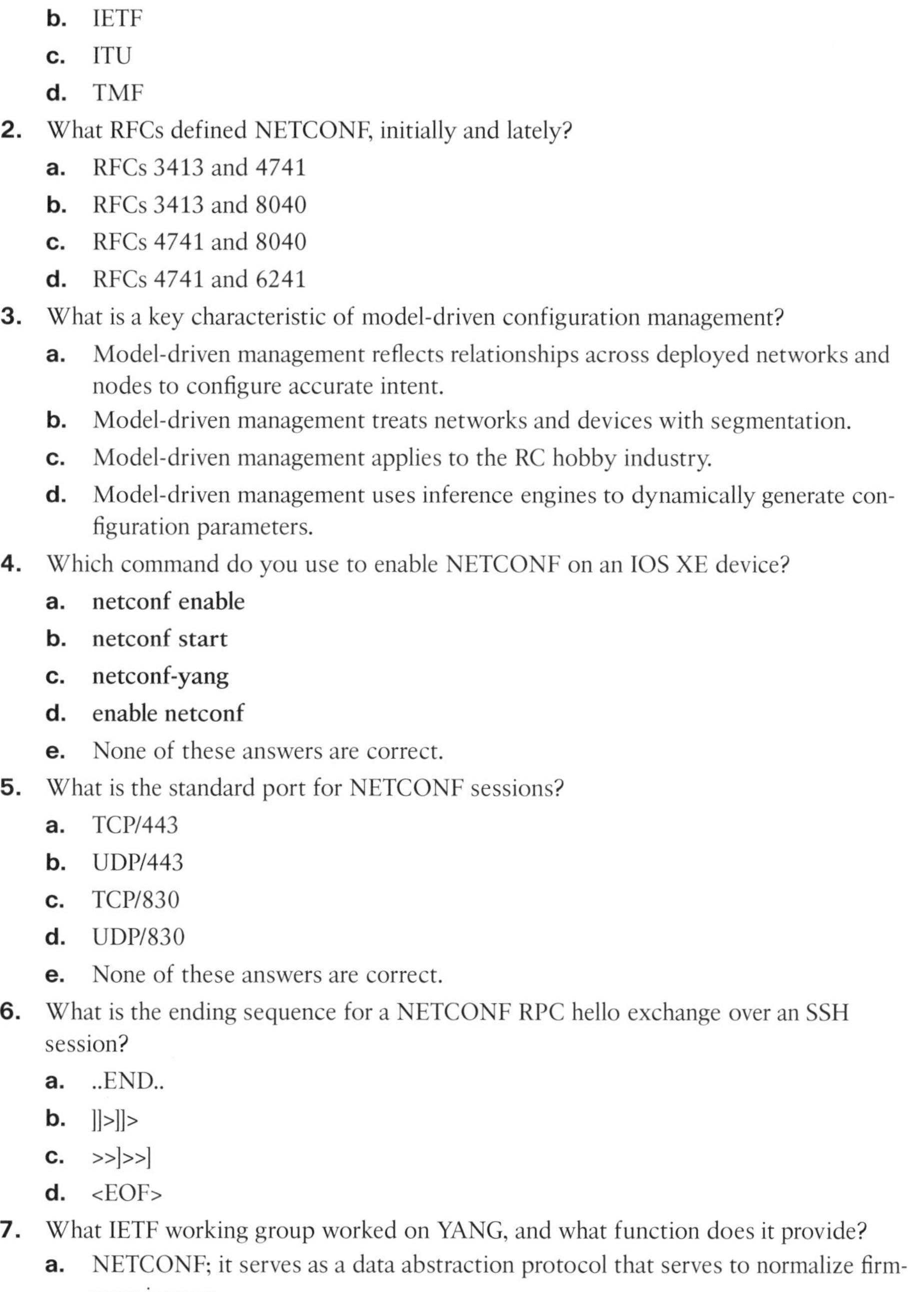

1. Which standards body started the work on NETCONF?
   a. ANSI
   b. IETF
   c. ITU
   d. TMF
2. What RFCs defined NETCONF, initially and lately?
   a. RFCs 3413 and 4741
   b. RFCs 3413 and 8040
   c. RFCs 4741 and 8040
   d. RFCs 4741 and 6241
3. What is a key characteristic of model-driven configuration management?
   a. Model-driven management reflects relationships across deployed networks and nodes to configure accurate intent.
   b. Model-driven management treats networks and devices with segmentation.
   c. Model-driven management applies to the RC hobby industry.
   d. Model-driven management uses inference engines to dynamically generate configuration parameters.
4. Which command do you use to enable NETCONF on an IOS XE device?
   a. **netconf enable**
   b. **netconf start**
   c. **netconf-yang**
   d. **enable netconf**
   e. None of these answers are correct.
5. What is the standard port for NETCONF sessions?
   a. TCP/443
   b. UDP/443
   c. TCP/830
   d. UDP/830
   e. None of these answers are correct.
6. What is the ending sequence for a NETCONF RPC hello exchange over an SSH session?
   a. ..END..
   b.]]>]]>
   c. >>]>>]
   d. <EOF>
7. What IETF working group worked on YANG, and what function does it provide?
   a. NETCONF; it serves as a data abstraction protocol that serves to normalize firmware images.
   b. NETCONF; it provides a complementary encoding method to YIN.

   c. NETMOD; it serves as a data modeling language to characterize configuration, state, and administrative functions.
   d. NETMOD; it is the next-generation availability monitoring protocol that extends ICMP ping.
8. What are common YANG objects?
   a. Module, container, list, leaf
   b. Container, spine, leaf
   c. spine, leaf, interconnect
   d. None of these answers are correct.
9. What header and value should be provided in a RESTCONF operation to identify an intent to receive results in JSON format?
   a. Content-Type: application/json
   b. Content-Type: application/yang-data+json
   c. Accept: application/json
   d. Accept: application/yang-data+json
10. Suppose you want to update an existing configuration setting via RESTCONF. What would be the most appropriate operation type?
   a. GET
   b. POST
   c. PUT
   d. DELETE

Foundation Topics

Catalyst for NETCONF

As the number of network equipment manufacturers increased, so did the variety of configuration syntaxes and parameters to provision and monitor those systems. Sometimes, as it was for Cisco, network equipment suppliers had multiple product lines that used different software—essentially network operating systems. These different operating systems often meant different command syntax and provisioning arguments. Even considering a fundamental feature like Border Gateway Protocol (BGP) meant different "golden configs" or templates across operating systems for Cisco IOS, Cisco IOS XE, Cisco NX-OS, Cisco IOS-XR, Juniper Junos OS, HPE Comware, Arista EOS, and so on. This difference in configuring the same function across different device vendors, models, and operating systems led to many network engineers maintaining multiple configuration standards. Having multiple configuration standards meant a higher probability of variance, especially when periodic review and synchronization were not part of a standard process. The industry, most notably the service provider segment, sought a way to have "one configuration to rule them all." We're sure this would make Frodo the network engineer happy!

In May 2003, the Internet Engineering Task Force (IETF) formed the **NETCONF (network configuration)** working group. Their work was first published as RFC 4741 in December

2006. Cisco provided initial support all the way back in IOS 12.4(9)T and presented the NETCONF topic at the CiscoLive 2009 event in San Diego. Several updates and enhancements have been developed over the years; the foundational protocol was updated as RFC 6241 in June 2011.

Figure 11-1 shows the layered model for NETCONF, which includes a bottoms-up transport layer, messaging container, operational directives, and content payload.

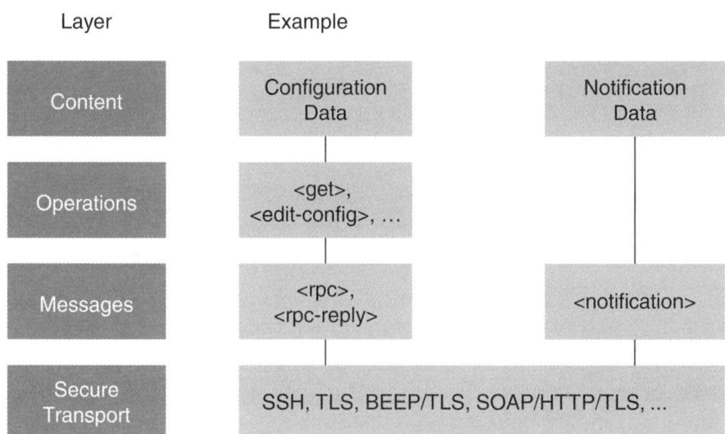

Figure 11-1 *NETCONF Conceptual Layers*

Content

Originally, the content of NETCONF operations was founded on the Extensible Markup Language (XML). XML provided structure and syntax for encoding data in a format that is both human-readable and machine-readable. This provision served the needs of both traditional network engineers who wanted more control over the provisioning and monitoring of their network and devices with those who wanted more programmatic options. The NETCONF protocol has also been enhanced to support JavaScript Object Notation (JSON) (note RFC 7951), but it remains common to see XML in implementations.

Later in this chapter, you learn how the NETMOD (network modeling) working group aimed to define a modeling language that was also easy to use for humans. It would define semantics of operational data, configuration data, notifications, and operations in a standard called **YANG**.

XML has its origins in Standard Generalized Markup Language (SGML) and has similarities to Hypertext Markup Language (HTML). Markup is a type of artificial language used to annotate a document's content to give instructions regarding structure or how it is to be displayed (rendered). XML is used to describe data, whereas HTML is used to display or render the data.

XML provides many benefits: it promotes the capability to use data or text in many ways from one original input source. This capability promotes data exchange and enables cross-platform data sharing. XML provides a software- and hardware-independent markup language for structuring and transmitting data. So the early days of NETCONF drove market trends leaning to it for configuration management and provisioning, verification, fault, and operational state monitoring. Later and more currently, JSON is being used more prominently for data encoding in the network IT discipline.

Operations

To effectively manage device configurations, different tasks and operation types have to be accommodated. The standard editing and deleting of a configuration are nearly universal across vendors and products. The support of more sophisticated methods, such as locking a configuration, varies in device implementation.

The base NETCONF protocol defines several operation types, as seen in Table 11-2.

Table 11-2 NETCONF Protocol Operations

Operation	Description
get	Retrieves running configuration and device state information
get-config	Retrieves all or part of a specified configuration
edit-config	Loads all or part of a specified configuration to the specified target configuration
copy-config	Creates or replaces an entire configuration datastore with the contents of another complete configuration datastore
delete-config	Deletes a configuration datastore
lock	Locks an entire configuration datastore of a device
unlock	Releases a configuration lock previously obtained with the <lock> operation
close-session	Requests graceful termination of a NETCONF session
kill-session	Forces the termination of a NETCONF session

Messages

The NETCONF messages layer is a simple, transport-independent framing mechanism for encoding directives. Remote-procedure calls (RPCs) are declared with <rpc> messages. The RPC results are handled with <rpc-reply> messages, and asynchronous notifications or alerts are defined by <notification> message types.

Every NETCONF message is a well-formed XML document. An original <rpc> message provides an association to <rpc-reply> with a message-id attribute. Multiple NETCONF messages can be sent without waiting for sequential RPC result messages. Figure 11-2 shows a simple XML-encoded NETCONF message. Note the structure and message-id linkage. We cover more specifics in the "How to Implement NETCONF" section.

```
<?xml version="1.0" encoding="UTF-8"?>
<rpc message-id="4" xmlns="urn:ietf:params:xml:ns:netconf:base:1.0">
  <get-config>
    <source>
      <running/>
    </source>
    <filter type="cli">
      <config-format-xml options="all"></config-format-xml>
    </filter>
  </get-config>
</rpc>
]]>]]>
```

Request
Manager
to
Device

```
<?xml version="1.0" encoding="UTF-8"?>
<rpc-reply message-id="4" xmlns="urn:ietf:params:netconf:base:1.0">
  <data>
    <xml-config-data> Building configuration...
        <Device-Configuration>
        <version>
          <Param>15.2</Param>
        </version>
        <service>
          <timestamps>
            <log>
              <datetime>
                <msec/>
              </datetime>
            </log>
          </timestamps>
        </service>
        <service>
          <password-encryption/>
        </service>
        <hostname><SystemNetworkName>NetConfRouter</SystemNetworkName></hostname>
...
```

Response
Device
to
Manager

Figure 11-2 *NETCONF Request and Reply*

Transport

When you are dealing with the transfer of critical infrastructure configurations, it is mandatory to keep the information private and secure. This was a shortcoming in version 1 and 2c of the Simple Network Management Protocol (SNMP). SNMP did not have inherent security for the authentication of management systems or the encryption of the data being transferred. SNMPv3 transformed the protocol by bringing both authentication and encryption. The IETF NETCONF working group planned security as a foundational requirement for NETCONF. The initial RFC 4741 stipulated that NETCONF connections must provide authentication, data integrity, and confidentiality. It further provided that connections may be encrypted in Transport Layer Security (TLS) or Secure Shell (SSH). The most widely used implementations were the transport layer for NETCONF using SSHv2. An additional option was the Blocks Extensible Exchange Protocol (BEEP); however, it was not widely supported and is not suggested for future implementations.

RFC 7589 has brought additional functionality in TLS with Mutual X.509 Authentication.

Atomic and Model-Driven Configuration Management

Using atomic configuration management techniques is common and familiar. Most engineers are comfortable with the model of creating a configuration template and noting the variable parameters that must be reconciled among deployments. Maybe you're deploying a standard interface configuration for an access layer switch and its downstream connection to a server, as in Figure 11-3.

11

```
interface GigabitEthernet##INT_NUM##
 description ##DESCRIPTION##
 switchport access vlan ##VLAN_NUM##
 switchport mode access
 switchport port-security maximum 10
 switchport port-security
 switchport port-security aging time 10
 switchport port-security aging type inactivity
 no logging event link-status
 load-interval 30
 storm-control broadcast level pps 100
 storm-control multicast level pps 2k
 storm-control action trap
 spanning-tree portfast
```

Figure 11-3 *Sample Configuration Template*

Or maybe you've deployed configurations using Configuration Management functions in a templatized sense that were part of commercial tools, like Prime Infrastructure, as in Figure 11-4.

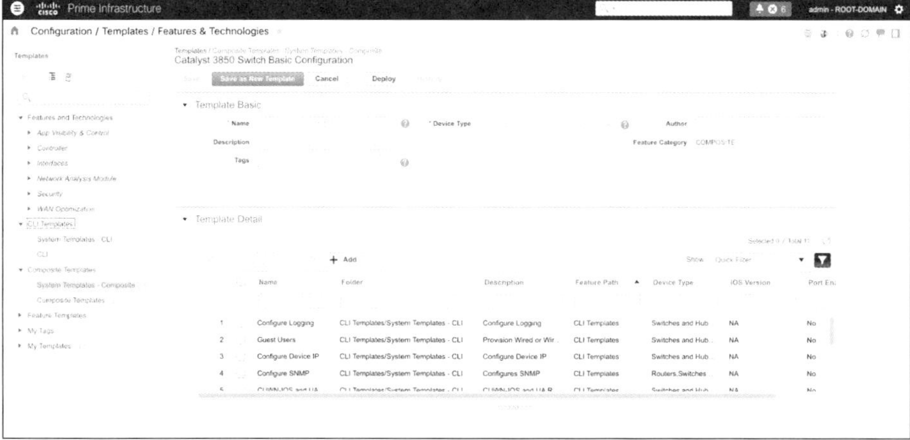

Figure 11-4 *Configuration Management with Templates in Prime Infrastructure*

There's even the next level of sophistication, where you've deployed configurations by answering questions in provisioning wizards that generated the configurations, as with DNA Center.

In any case, these systems depended on a known set of conventions with the command syntax and arguments where the network engineer provided answers to the variables. Additionally, this atomic model generally referred to specific devices and did not maintain an awareness or understanding of interdependencies *among* the devices. The configuration management function was unintelligent; it merely pushed what it was told without consideration of peering relationships and dependencies.

If you consider a well-known feature such as Hot Standby Router Protocol (HSRP), you can recognize there's a configuration template for the primary router and a similar but slightly different configuration template for the standby router(s). An atomic configuration management solution would not recognize the interdependencies and would allow you to push the changes in a way that may not function or could cause a larger service outage.

Conversely, model-driven configuration management strives to abstract the individual device configurations in favor of the deployment of a *service* or *feature*. The resulting configuration(s) generated may involve multiple devices as they form the basis for deploying the service/feature. The model is either fully deployed successfully, or it is rolled back or removed entirely so that no partial configuration fragments are left on any devices.

Another well-known but more advanced example would be deploying Multiprotocol Label Switching (MPLS). Figure 11-5 depicts a standard architecture for MPLS.

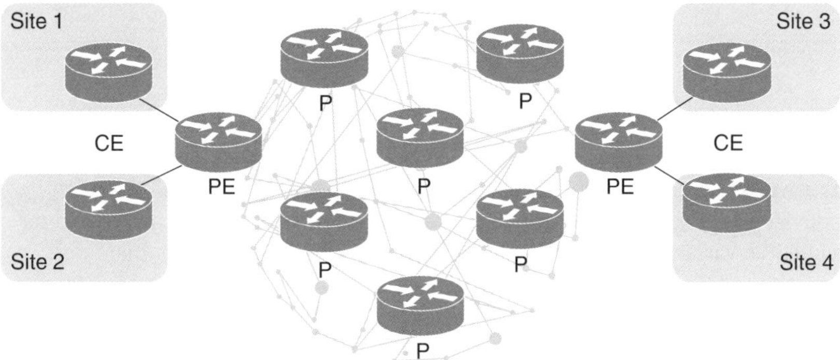

Figure 11-5 *Standard MPLS Architecture*

Consider how a virtual routing and forwarding (VRF) feature is deployed. It involves several device types and functions. In a typical MPLS deployment, a customer edge (CE) router performs local routing and shares routing information with the provider edge (PE) where routing tables are virtualized. PE routers encapsulate traffic, marking it to identify the VRF instance, and transmit it across the service provider backbone network over provider devices to the destination PE router. The destination PE router then decapsulates the traffic and forwards it to the CE router at the destination. The backbone network is completely transparent to the customer equipment, allowing multiple customers or user communities to use the common backbone network while maintaining end-to-end traffic separation.

Now consider the previous architecture with a bit more configuration definition. In Figure 11-6 note the commonalities across the highlighted devices.

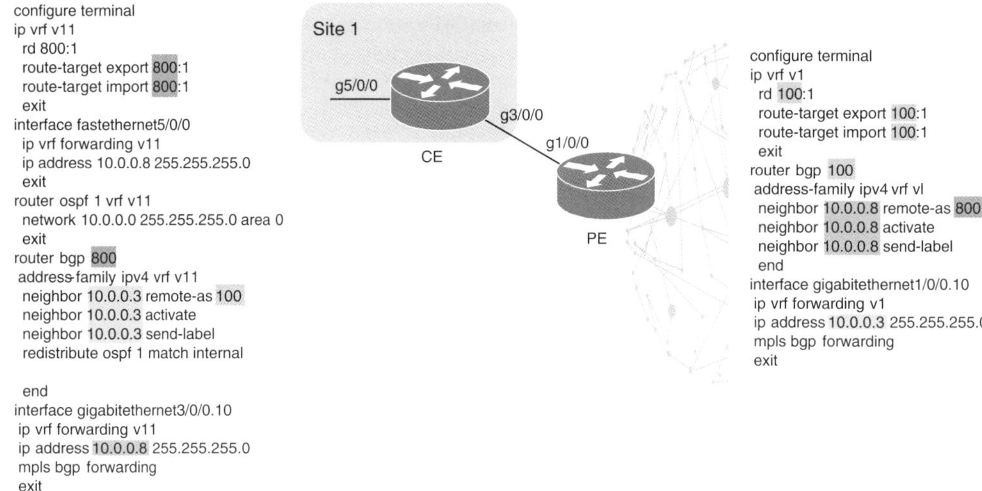

configure terminal
ip vrf v11
rd 800:1
route-target export 800:1
route-target import 800:1
exit
interface fastethernet5/0/0
ip vrf forwarding v11
ip address 10.0.0.8 255.255.255.0
exit
router ospf 1 vrf v11
network 10.0.0.0 255.255.255.0 area 0
exit
router bgp 800
address-family ipv4 vrf v11
neighbor 10.0.0.3 remote-as 100
neighbor 10.0.0.3 activate
neighbor 10.0.0.3 send-label
redistribute ospf 1 match internal
end
interface gigabitethernet3/0/0.10
ip vrf forwarding v11
ip address 10.0.0.8 255.255.255.0
mpls bgp forwarding
exit
Site 1
g5/0/0
g3/0/0
g1/0/0
CE
PE
configure terminal
ip vrf v1
rd 100:1
route-target export 100:1
route-target import 100:1
exit
router bgp 100
address-family ipv4 vrf vl
neighbor 10.0.0.8 remote-as 800
neighbor 10.0.0.8 activate
neighbor 10.0.0.8 send-label
end
interface gigabitethernet1/0/0.10
ip vrf forwarding v1
ip address 10.0.0.3 255.255.255.0
mpls bgp forwarding
exit

Figure 11-6 *MPLS CE-PE Configlets*

In a traditional, atomic configuration model, those configlets would be templates, and the highlighted parts would be parameters that need to be reconciled across the deployment to two (or more) devices. It would be up to the network engineer and operations personnel to correctly reconcile the variables and deploy them device by device. The deployment personnel would be responsible for each device implementation and have to gauge its correct deployment or remove all associated configurations from all the devices, again device by device. Can you see the possibility for user-induced error?

In a model-driven configuration management approach, those templates would be merged into a common model that would deploy the rendered configlets appropriately to the devices involved in the service. The configurations would deploy accurately, or they would be rolled back from each associated device so that no partially deployed configurations would remain. The network administrator would still need to identify the device(s), their role(s), and the required parameters to deploy the *service*, but they wouldn't need to treat each device individually.

How to Implement NETCONF

As mentioned earlier, NETCONF interactions are typically done via an SSH transport and the NETCONF subsystem; the default port is TCP/830. A specifically formed XML document is transmitted to share a hello and capabilities exchange. The hello and capabilities exchange is typically followed by the NETCONF directives and response. Most Cisco devices running IOS XR, IOS XE, or NX-OS, and recent software versions support NETCONF/YANG because it is a mature feature. Initial support for NETCONF was released all the way back to traditional IOS 12.4(9)T and later, and IOS XE 2.1.

TIP If you want to get some hands-on experience with the feature but would rather not use your own equipment (or don't have dev-test equipment), then check out the DevNet Always On Labs and Sandbox environments at https://developer.cisco.com/site/sandbox/. There are shared Always On environments for IOS XE, IOS XR, and NX-OS to use.

Let's get started by enabling the feature and work from there.

Enabling NETCONF on IOS XE

If you wish to have a separate NETCONF user account (which is recommended), then ensure it is enabled in your AAA (or local) configuration with level 15 access.

Enable the NETCONF (and YANG) feature from the configuration mode with

```
Device (config)# netconf-yang
```

That's it!

Candidate datastores (essentially "work in progress" or "scratch config" spaces) can be enabled with

```
Device (config)# netconf-yang feature candidate-datastore
```

You can validate the NETCONF feature with the following command:

```
Device# show netconf-yang datastores

Datastore Name                 : running
```

The command output shows any configuration locks, if they exist, by session identifier and date-time.

If there are current sessions, they can be identified with the command shown in Example 11-1.

Example 11-1 *Identifying Current Sessions with* **show netconf-yang sessions**

```
Device# show netconf-yang sessions

R: Global-lock on running datastore
C: Global-lock on candidate datastore
S: Global-lock on startup datastore
Number of sessions : 4
session-id transport   username source-host global-lock
-----------------------------------------------------------
10         netconf-ssh admin    10.15.1.110 None
12         netconf-ssh admin    10.15.1.110 None
14         netconf-ssh admin    10.15.1.110 None
16         netconf-ssh admin    10.15.1.110 None
```

You can obtain detailed NETCONF session data with the command shown in Example 11-2.

Example 11-2 *Using* **show netconfig-yang** *to Get Detailed Session Data*

```
Device# show netconf-yang sessions detail

R: Global-lock on running datastore
C: Global-lock on candidate datastore
S: Global-lock on startup datastore

Number of sessions     : 1

session-id             : 10
transport              : netconf-ssh
username               : netconf-admin
source-host            : 2001:db8::110
login-time             : 2021-04-15T10:22:13+00:00
in-rpcs                : 0
in-bad-rpcs            : 0
out-rpc-errors         : 0
out-notifications      : 0
global-lock            : None
```

Finally, if you're interested in the amount of NETCONF feature use, you can use the command shown in Example 11-3.

Example 11-3 *Using* **show netconf-yang** *to Get Feature Statistics*

```
Device# show netconf-yang statistics
netconf-start-time : 2021-04-15T10:25:33+00: 00

in-rpcs : 0
in-bad-rpcs : 0
out-rpc-errors : 0
out-notifications : 15
in-sessions : 124
dropped-sessions : 0
in-bad-hellos : 0
```

Enabling NETCONF on IOS XR

If you wish to have a separate NETCONF user account (which is recommended), then ensure it is enabled in your AAA (or local) configuration.

Enable the NETCONF (and YANG) feature from the configuration mode with

```
RP/0/RSP0/CPU0:router (config)# netconf agent ssh
```

```
RP/0/RSP0/CPU0:router (config)# ssh server netconf vrf NETCONF_VRF
ipv4 access-list IPV4_NETOPS ipv6 access-list IPV6_NETOPS
```

```
RP/0/RSP0/CPU0:router (config)# ssh server netconf port 830
```

The VRF and access-list definition should be defined to suit your environment. The last command, **ssh server netconf port**, can be omitted if you use the default port 830; otherwise, include the custom port desired.

To view the NETCONF (and YANG) statistics, you can use the command shown in Example 11-4.

Example 11-4 *Using* **show netconfig-yang** *to Extract Statistics*

```
RP/0/RSP0/CPU0:router# show netconf-yang statistics
Summary statistics    reqs|         total time|    min time / req|    max time / req|
  avg time / req|
other                    0|  0h  0m  0s   0ms| 0h  0m  0s   0ms| 0h  0m  0s   0ms|
  0h  0m  0s   0ms|
close-session            4|  0h  0m  0s   3ms| 0h  0m  0s   0ms| 0h  0m  0s   1ms|
  0h  0m  0s   0ms|
kill-session             0|  0h  0m  0s   0ms| 0h  0m  0s   0ms| 0h  0m  0s   0ms|
  0h  0m  0s   0ms|
get-schema               0|  0h  0m  0s   0ms| 0h  0m  0s   0ms| 0h  0m  0s   0ms|
  0h  0m  0s   0ms|
get                      0|  0h  0m  0s   0ms| 0h  0m  0s   0ms| 0h  0m  0s   0ms|
  0h  0m  0s
get-config               1|  0h  0m  0s   1ms| 0h  0m  0s   1ms| 0h  0m  0s   1ms|
  0h  0m  0s   1ms|
edit-config              3|  0h  0m  0s   2ms| 0h  0m  0s   0ms| 0h  0m  0s   1ms|
  0h  0m  0s   0ms|
commit                   0|  0h  0m  0s   0ms| 0h  0m  0s   0ms| 0h  0m  0s   0ms|
  0h  0m  0s   0ms|
cancel-commit            0|  0h  0m  0s   0ms| 0h  0m  0s   0ms| 0h  0m  0s   0ms|
  0h  0m  0s   0ms|
lock                     0|  0h  0m  0s   0ms| 0h  0m  0s   0ms| 0h  0m  0s   0ms|
  0h  0m  0s   0ms|
unlock                   0|  0h  0m  0s   0ms| 0h  0m  0s   0ms| 0h  0m  0s   0ms|
  0h  0m  0s   0ms|
discard-changes          0|  0h  0m  0s   0ms| 0h  0m  0s   0ms| 0h  0m  0s   0ms|
  0h  0m  0s   0ms|
validate                 0|  0h  0m  0s   0ms| 0h  0m  0s   0ms| 0h  0m  0s   0ms|
  0h  0m  0s   0ms|
```

Additionally, you can obtain detailed session and client information with the following command:

```
RP/0/RSP0/CPU0:router# show netconf-yang clients

client session ID| NC version| client connect time|    last OP
   time|    last OP type|   <lock>|

                 423|          1.1|      0d   1h 13m 33s|
14:36:24|   close-session|         No|

                 424           1.1|      0d   1h 35m  1s|
14:57:25|       get-config|        No|
```

Enabling NETCONF on NX-OS

If you wish to have a separate NETCONF user account (which is recommended), then ensure it is enabled in your AAA (or local) configuration and has level 15 privilege.

11

Ensure the SSHv2 feature is enabled.

Enable the NETCONF (and YANG) feature from the configuration mode with

```
switch(config)# feature netconf
switch(config)# netconf idle-timeout 10
switch(config)# netconf sessions 5
```

Basic Manual Use of NETCONF

Now that the NETCONF agent is enabled on the device, you can start to interact with it. For the sake of learning, you can use manual SSH sessions to show the exchanges between the manager (the SSH terminal emulator) and the NETCONF device. These interactions would be done behind the scenes by NETCONF-enabled management tools, such as Cisco Network Services Orchestrator (NSO) and others.

First, connect to the device's NETCONF subsystem using your preferred SSH terminal emulator (connecting to default port 830) or with a common SSH command-line tool, as seen in any common Linux or macOS distribution in the next example:

```
client-host$ ssh -s admin@192.168.1.110 -p 830 netconf
```

The device responds with a capabilities exchange, which could be hundreds of lines long reflecting all the features and YANG models that are supported and installed, like that shown in Example 11-5.

Example 11-5 *NETCONF Capabilities Exchange/Hello*

```
<?xml version="1.0" encoding="UTF-8"?>
<hello xmlns="urn:ietf:params:xml:ns:netconf:base:1.0">
<capabilities>
<capability>urn:ietf:params:netconf:base:1.0</capability>
<capability>urn:ietf:params:netconf:base:1.1</capability>
<capability>urn:ietf:params:netconf:capability:writable-running:1.0</capability>
<capability>urn:ietf:params:netconf:capability:xpath:1.0</capability>
<capability>urn:ietf:params:netconf:capability:validate:1.0</capability>
<capability>urn:ietf:params:netconf:capability:validate:1.1</capability>
<capability>urn:ietf:params:netconf:capability:rollback-on-error:1.0</capability>
<capability>urn:ietf:params:netconf:capability:notification:1.0</capability>
<capability>urn:ietf:params:netconf:capability:interleave:1.0</capability>
<capability>urn:ietf:params:netconf:capability:with-defaults:1.0?basic-
mode=explicit&amp;also-supported=report-all-tagged</
capability>
<capability>urn:ietf:params:netconf:capability:yang-library:1.0?revision=2016-
06-21&amp;module-set-id=7294e20b121b24ac71a8fb609b7d3afd</
capability>
<capability>http://tail-f.com/ns/netconf/actions/1.0</capability>
<capability>http://tail-f.com/ns/netconf/extensions</capability>
```

```
<capability>http://cisco.com/ns/cisco-xe-ietf-ip-
deviation?module=cisco-xe-ietf-ip-deviation&amp;revision=2016-08-10</
capability>
<capability>http://cisco.com/ns/cisco-xe-ietf-ipv4-unicast-routing-
deviation?module=cisco-xe-ietf-ipv4-unicast-routing-deviation&amp;revis
ion=2015-09-11</capability>
<capability>http://cisco.com/ns/cisco-xe-ietf-ipv6-unicast-routing-
deviation?module=cisco-xe-ietf-ipv6-unicast-routing-deviation&amp;revis
ion=2015-09-11</capability>
. . . (MANY lines omitted) . . .
<capability>urn:ietf:params:xml:ns:yang:ietf-netconf-with-
defaults?module=ietf-netconf-with-defaults&amp;revision=2011-06-01</
capability>
<capability>
        urn:ietf:params:netconf:capability:notification:1.1
      </capability>
</capabilities>
<session-id>21</session-id></hello>]]>]]>
```

Some items of note: the usual XML declaration line is followed by a <hello> element, followed by a <capabilities> list element of many <capability> child elements. Finally, there's a session identifier (21 in this case), some closing tags, and a unique session ending sequence:

```
]]>]]>
```

This sequence is important for both manager and managed device to recognize the end of an exchange.

To (manually) interact with the NETCONF agent, you must send your capabilities also, or the agent will not respond to any other input. For example, you can send into the SSH terminal the text (pasted) shown in Example 11-6.

Example 11-6 *NETCONF Hello from Management Station*

```
<?xml version="1.0" encoding="UTF-8"?>
<hello xmlns="urn:ietf:params:xml:ns:netconf:base:1.0">
    <capabilities>
        <capability>urn:ietf:params:netconf:base:1.0</capability>
    </capabilities>
</hello>]]>]]>
```

You do not see any results from the device, but it registers your capabilities (NETCONF base 1.0) and awaits your next directives.

NETCONF uses RPCs to wrap the directives. Let's assume the next thing you want to do is obtain the running configuration from the device. Using this method is a good way to understand the structure and syntax of an XML-encoded configuration. You would send the code shown in Example 11-7 in your SSH session.

11

NOTE The device may time out after a few minutes of nonactivity. If so, reconnect and resend the capabilities exchange.

Example 11-7 *NETCONF XML Payload to Get Configuration*

```
<?xml version="1.0" encoding="UTF-8" ?>
<rpc message-id="200" xmlns="urn:ietf:params:xml:ns:netconf:base:1.0">
    <get-config>
        <source>
            <running/>
        </source>
    </get-config>
</rpc>]]>]]>
```

In this case, the device immediately responds with the running configuration in a compact XML form, as shown in Example 11-8.

Example 11-8 *NETCONF Response from Device*

```
<?xml version="1.0" encoding="UTF-8"?>
<rpc-reply xmlns="urn:ietf:params:xml:ns:netconf:base:1.0" mes-
sage-id="200"><data><native xmlns="http://cisco.com/ns/yang/
Cisco-IOS-XE-native"><version>16.9</version><boot-start-marker/><boot-end-
marker/><banner><motd><banner>^C</banner></motd></banner><service><timestamps><debug
><datetime><msec></msec></datetime></debug><log><datetime><msec/></datetime></log></
timestamps></service><platform><console xmlns="http://cisco.com/ns/yang/Cisco-IOS-
XE-platform"><output>virtual</output></console></platform><hostname>csr1000v-1</host
name><enable><secret><type>5</type>
. . . (A LOT OF CONFIG OMITTED . . .
</routing-instance></routing></data></rpc-reply>]]>]]>
```

Running this response through an XML formatting utility may be useful to discern the structure.

NOTE Don't copy and paste the XML-formatted configuration of one of your devices into an online XML utility. It is hard to say whether those free online services are retaining your data input. One of the easiest ways to view this without an external or a third-party resource is to save the output, minus the]]>]]> closing sequence, to a text file with an .xml file extension and then load that text file into your browser. The browser renders it formatted and enables you to expand or close branches of configurations. Figure 11-7 shows the results of a browser processing the compact XML output from Example 11-8.

```
This XML file does not appear to have any style information associated with it. The document tree is shown below.

▼<rpc-reply xmlns="urn:ietf:params:xml:ns:netconf:base:1.0" message-id="200">
  ▼<data>
    ▼<native xmlns="http://cisco.com/ns/yang/Cisco-IOS-XE-native">
        <version>16.9</version>
        <boot-start-marker/>
        <boot-end-marker/>
      ▶<banner>
        ...
        </banner>
      ▼<service>
        ▼<timestamps>
          ▶<debug>
            ...
            </debug>
          ▼<log>
            ▼<datetime>
                <msec/>
              </datetime>
            </log>
          </timestamps>
        </service>
      ▼<platform>
        ▼<console xmlns="http://cisco.com/ns/yang/Cisco-IOS-XE-platform">
            <output>virtual</output>
          </console>
        </platform>
        <hostname>csr1000v-1</hostname>
      ▶<enable>
        ...
        </enable>
      ▶<username>
        ...
        </username>
      ▶<username>
        ...
        </username>
      ▶<username>
        ...
        </username>
      ▼<ip>
        ▼<domain>
            <name>abc.inc</name>
          </domain>
        ▼<forward-protocol>
            <protocol>nd</protocol>
          </forward-protocol>
        ▼<route>
          ▼<ip-route-interface-forwarding-list>
              <prefix>0.0.0.0</prefix>
              <mask>0.0.0.0</mask>
            ▼<fwd-list>
                <fwd>GigabitEthernet1</fwd>
              ▼<interface-next-hop>
                  <ip-address>10.10.20.254</ip-address>
                </interface-next-hop>
              </fwd-list>
            </ip-route-interface-forwarding-list>
          </route>
```


Figure 11-7 *NETCONF Configuration as XML Rendered in a Browser*

Now let's do a simple NETCONF configuration editing operation. In this example, you change an interface description, so what you learn does not impact the service. If you collapse much of the XML structure from the configuration shown in Figure 11-7 in your browser, you can see some structure that is helpful. Focus on GigabitEthernet2 in this example (see Figure 11-8).

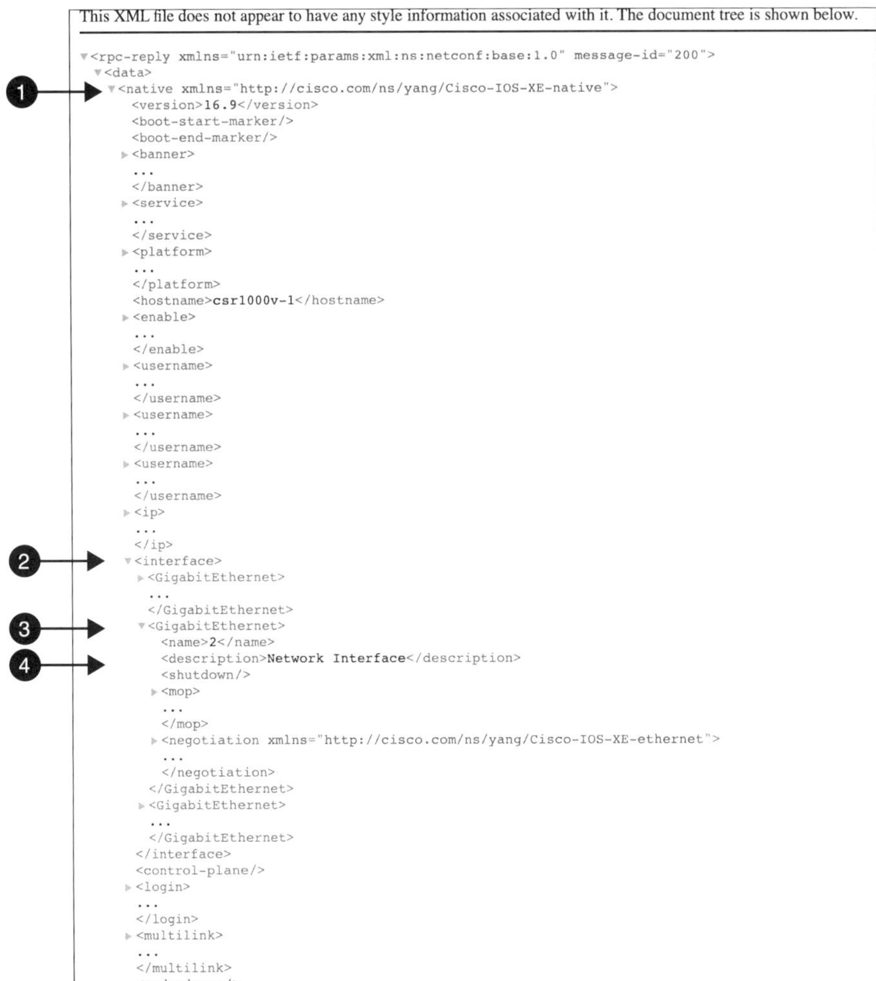

Figure 11-8 *NETCONF Configuration of Gig2 Interface as XML Rendered in a Browser*

To (manually) create the XML RPC to do a configuration change, you need to retain the XML hierarchy after the <data> element, down to the specific interface and the <description> element you wish to change. Example 11-9 shows the partial XML of interest.

Example 11-9 *XML Fragment for RPC Building*

```
<native xmlns="http://cisco.com/ns/yang/Cisco-IOS-XE-native">
<interface>
 <GigabitEthernet>
   <name>2</name>
 <description>
```

The intermediary parts are nonessential and can be omitted. You only need to send in the hierarchy and the element being changed. Example 11-10 shows how to change GigabitEthernet2's port description.

Example 11-10 *NETCONF XML Payload to Edit the Configuration*

```
<?xml version="1.0" encoding="UTF-8"?>
<rpc xmlns="urn:ietf:params:xml:ns:netconf:base:1.0" message-id="300">
    <edit-config>
        <target>
            <running/>
        </target>
        <config>
            <native xmlns="http://cisco.com/ns/yang/Cisco-IOS-XE-native">
                <interface>
                    <GigabitEthernet>
                        <name>2</name>
                        <description>My Description from NETCONF message-id 300</
                          description>
                    </GigabitEthernet>
                </interface>
            </native>
        </config>
    </edit-config>
</rpc>]]>]]>
```

When you push that into an active NETCONF session (with the capabilities exchange already being complete), you get the following result from the device:

```
<rpc-reply xmlns="urn:ietf:params:xml:ns:netconf:base:1.0" message-
id="300"><ok/></rpc-reply>]]>]]>
```

The highlighted <ok/> element signifies a good result from the device. You can confirm that in several ways. You can log in to the device and look at the interface descriptions, such as that shown in Example 11-11.

Example 11-11 *Device Interface Descriptions*

```
csr1000v-1# show int description
Interface           Status         Protocol Description
Gi1                 up             up       MANAGEMENT INTERFACE - DON'T TOUCH ME
Gi2                 admin down     down     My Description from NETCONF message-id 300
Gi3                 admin down     down     Network Interface
csr1000v-1#
```

Or, more appropriately to your network programmability interest, you could execute the same <get-config> operation as before and get the configuration back in XML form, as seen in Figure 11-9, rendered in an XML editor.

11

```
<?xml version="1.0" encoding="utf-8"?>
<rpc-reply xmlns="urn:ietf:params:xml:ns:netconf:base:1.0" message-id="400">
    <data>
        <native xmlns="http://cisco.com/ns/yang/Cisco-IOS-XE-native">
            <version>16.9</version>
            <boot-start-marker/>
            <boot-end-marker/>
            <banner> ... </banner>
            <service> ... </service>
            <platform> ... </platform>
            <hostname>csr1000v-1</hostname>
            <enable> ... </enable>
            <username> ... </username>
            <username> ... </username>
            <username> ... </username>
            <ip> ... </ip>
            <interface>
                <GigabitEthernet> ... </GigabitEthernet>
                <GigabitEthernet>
                    <name>2</name>
                    <description>My Description from NETCONF message-id 300</description>
                    <shutdown/>
                    <mop>
                        <enabled>false</enabled>
                        <sysid>false</sysid>
                    </mop>
                    <negotiation xmlns="http://cisco.com/ns/yang/Cisco-IOS-XE-ethernet">
                        <auto>true</auto>
                    </negotiation>
                </GigabitEthernet>
                <GigabitEthernet> ... </GigabitEthernet>
            </interface>
            <control-plane/>
            <login> ... </login>
            <multilink> ... </multilink>
            <redundancy/>
            <spanning-tree> ... </spanning-tree>
            <subscriber> ... </subscriber>
            <crypto> ... </crypto>
            <license> ... </license>
            <line> ... </line>
            <diagnostic xmlns="http://cisco.com/ns/yang/Cisco-IOS-XE-diagnostics"> ... </diagnostic>
        </native>
        <licensing xmlns="http://cisco.com/ns/yang/cisco-smart-license"> ... </licensing>
        <interfaces xmlns="http://openconfig.net/yang/interfaces"> ... </interfaces>
        <network-instances xmlns="http://openconfig.net/yang/network-instance"> ... </network-instances>
        <interfaces xmlns="urn:ietf:params:xml:ns:yang:ietf-interfaces"> ... </interfaces>
        <nacm xmlns="urn:ietf:params:xml:ns:yang:ietf-netconf-acm"> ... </nacm>
        <routing xmlns="urn:ietf:params:xml:ns:yang:ietf-routing"> ... </routing>
    </data>
</rpc-reply>
```

Figure 11-9 *NETCONF Configuration Updated as XML Rendered in a Browser*

Note that the GigabitEthernet2 port description in the boxed area reflects the change you pushed with the <edit-config> operation.

If you're an astute observer of the XML structure, you may have also noticed the use of the <native xmlns="http://cisco.com/ns/yang/Cisco-IOS-XE-native"> hierarchy to edit the configuration. However, there is also an element reference of <interfaces xmlns="urn:ietf:params:xml:ns:yang:ietf-interfaces">.

The first reference managed the device using its native syntax and model. This may not be especially portable. The second reference mentioning YANG and IETF provides a more cross-platform approach to referencing device configurations and represents the spirit of NETCONF's focus: cross-platform configuration management. We cover that in the next section. The device could have been configured in either native or YANG model methods; both models also show the same results when getting the configuration.

It is helpful that the device and operating system supported *both* models, so you have options in how you want to manage the device—familiar, native syntax or cross-platform, device-abstracted syntax. Get familiar with both methods; you will find, however, the YANG model approach provides the closest option to that single "golden configuration standard" that can be applied across multiple devices.

YANG Models

NETCONF provides the protocol layer for managing device configurations in a programmatic and consistent way, but to be more effective, a data modeling language needed to be paired with NETCONF. The Yet Another Next Generation, or YANG, data modeling language provides a standardized way to represent operational and configuration data of a network device. YANG is protocol independent and can be converted into any encoding format, such as XML or JSON. You may also hear YANG referred to as a data model or even device data.

Similar to NETCONF, YANG was born from an IETF working group. The NETMOD working group was charged with creating a "human-friendly" modeling language to define semantics of operational data, configuration data, notifications, and operations. The original version of YANG was defined in RFC 6020 with an update (version 1.1) in RFC 7950. RFC 6991 defined "Common YANG Data Types," such as seen in Table 11-3. Although SNMP is not a foundational component of the DEVCOR exam, the SMIv2 types are shown for comparison for those with SNMP background.

Table 11-3 IETF YANG Types Compared to SMIv2 Types

YANG Type	Equivalent SMIv2 type (module)
counter32	Counter32 (SNMPv2-SMI)
zero-based-counter32	ZeroBasedCounter32 (RMON2-MIB)
counter64	Counter64 (SNMPv2-SMI)
zero-based-counter64	ZeroBasedCounter64 (HCNUM-TC)
gauge32	Gauge32 (SNMPv2-SMI)
gauge64	CounterBasedGauge64 (HCNUM-TC)
object-identifier	—
object-identifier-128	OBJECT IDENTIFIER
yang-identifier	—
date-and-time	—
timeticks	TimeTicks (SNMPv2-SMI)
timestamp	TimeStamp (SNMPv2-TC)
phys-address	PhysAddress (SNMPv2-TC)
mac-address	MacAddress (SNMPv2-TC)
xpath1.0	—
hex-string	—
uuid	—
dotted-quad	—

Separate Internet types, ietf-inet-types, were also defined and can be seen in Table 11-4.

Table 11-4 IETF INET Types Compared to SMIv2 Types

YANG Type	Equivalent SMIv2 type (module)
ip-version	InetVersion (INET-ADDRESS-MIB)
dscp	Dscp (DIFFSERV-DSCP-TC)
ipv6-flow-label	IPv6FlowLabl (IPV6-FLOW-LABEL-MIB)
port-number	InetPortNumber (INET-ADDRESS-MIB)
ip-address	—
ipv4-address	—
ipv6-address	—
ip-prefix	—
ipv4-prefix	—
ipv6-prefix	—
domain-name	—
host	—
uri	Uri (URI-TC-MIB)

NETMOD also worked on foundational configuration models such as system, interface, and routing. These models are part of a class of *open models* that are meant to be independent from the platform. The intent is also to normalize configuration syntax across vendors. Open YANG models are developed by the IETF, the ITU agency, the OpenConfig consortium, and other standards bodies. Conversely, *native models* are developed by equipment manufacturers. The models may be specialized to features or syntax specific to that device type, model, or platform.

Besides being the data modeling language for NETCONF, YANG also became associated with RESTCONF and gRPC, which is covered in Chapter 12, "Model-Driven Telemetry," for streaming telemetry.

Let's look at some of the structure of YANG modules by using a familiar construct such as device interfaces. Review the IETF's implementation of the interface's YANG model at https://github.com/YangModels/yang/blob/master/standard/ietf/RFC/ietf-interfaces.yang.

As we review Figure 11-10, you'll see some easy-to-understand constructs.

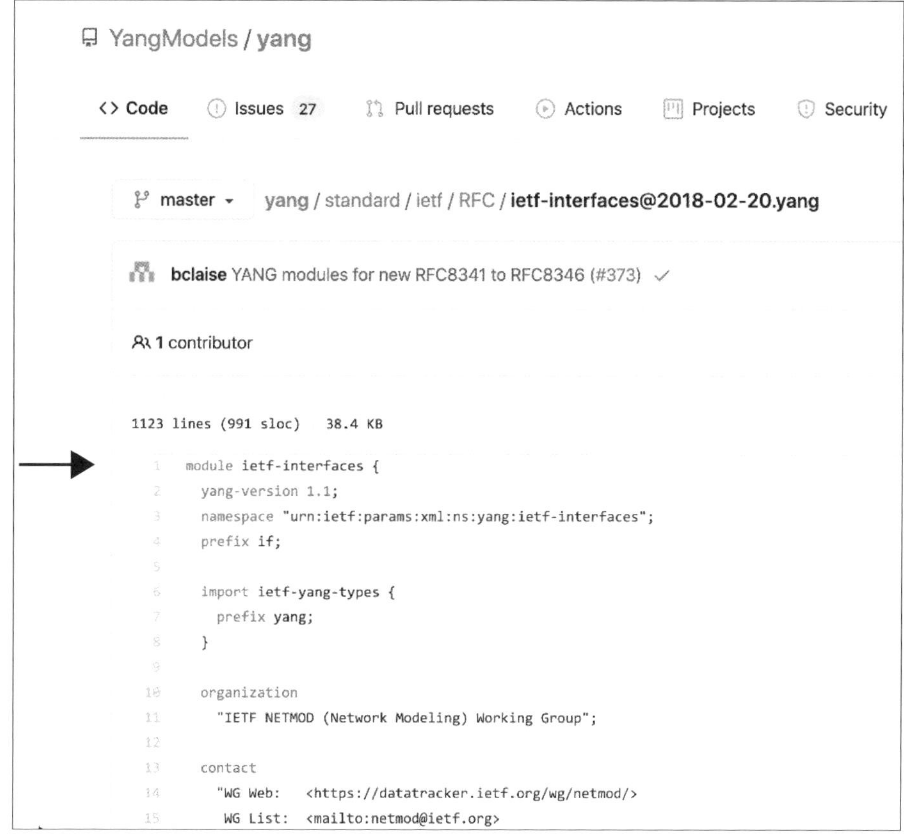

Figure 11-10 *ietf-interfaces YANG Model*

In this figure, you can see a module name, ietf-interfaces, with version, namespace, and prefix. The standard ietf-yang-types, mentioned earlier, are imported for use in this model, so data types are recognized. If you navigate down to the **interfaces** section as in Figure 11-11, you see more familiar structure.

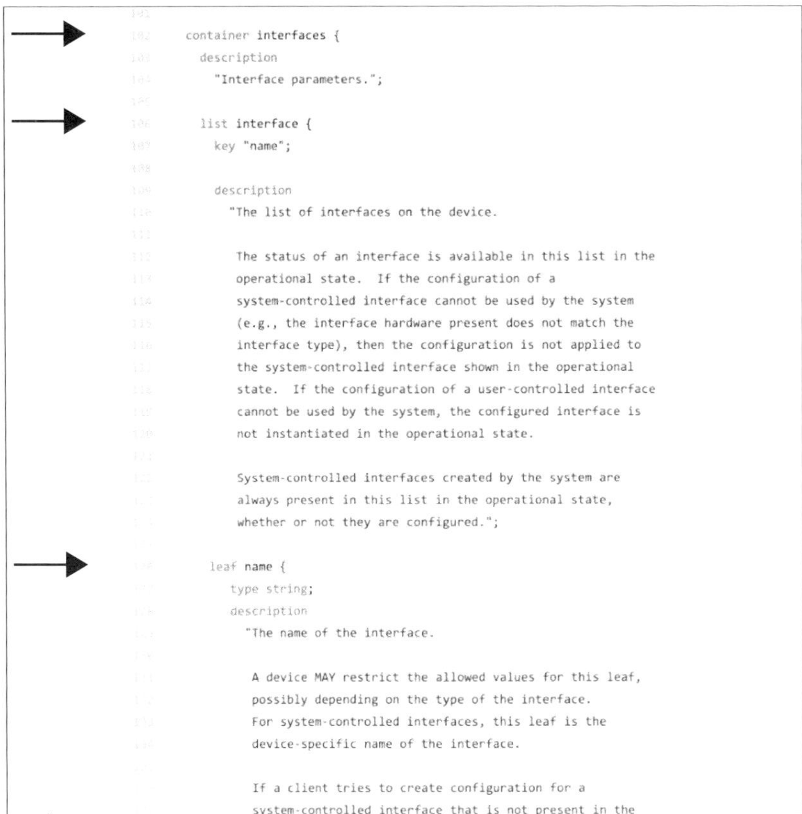

Figure 11-11 *ETF-interfaces YANG Model—Interfaces Section*

Specifically, note the container component called interfaces, which has hierarchy over a of list of individual interface items, keyed by name. Then below that in the hierarchy is the name as a leaf component.

At this point, the verbosity of the YANG model may make comprehension a bit difficult. Using a tool like **pyang** from Github at https://github.com/mbj4668/pyang can be more helpful in familiarizing yourself with the model.

The **pyang** tool is used to validate and transform YANG models. It also has a code generator function, which is helpful when you get more in depth with YANG. It can easily be installed to a Python development environment, such as a virtual environment, with the **pip** command shown in Example 11-12.

Example 11-12 *Pip Installing* pyang

```
(pyang) [yanguser@pthon-vm pyang]$ pip install pyang
Collecting pyang
  Downloading https://files.pythonhosted.org/packages/12/22/16c98564086f4f5901b7e8d8
86ad928ce6eceb577b3504edc333762df92f/pyang-2.4.0-py2.py3-none-any.whl (591kB)
     |████████████████████████████████| 593kB 1.8MB/s
Collecting lxml (from pyang)
  Downloading
https://files.pythonhosted.org/packages/e5/d7/2d8b9e1d4fe05b8b72b3d2345d5a741b005640
681482502b5ce3d8f020d4/lxml-4.6.3-cp38-cp38-manylinux1_x86_64.whl (5.4MB)
     |████████████████████████████████| 5.4MB 29.2MB/s
Installing collected packages: lxml, pyang
Successfully installed lxml-4.6.3 pyang-2.4.0
(pyang) [yanguser@pthon-vm pyang]$
```

After installing the **pyang** utility, you can use it to review the ietf-interfaces.yang module. First, you need to download the YANG module; then you use the utility to read it in a tree format. Because you're looking at the GitHub ietf-interfaces YANG model, note that the official reference of https://github.com/YangModels/yang/blob/master/standard/ietf/RFC/ietf-interfaces.yang is actually a symbolic link to a date-referenced version that aligns to RFC updates. As of this writing, the latest correct reference is https://raw.githubusercontent.com/YangModels/yang/master/standard/ietf/RFC/ietf-interfaces%402018-02-20.yang; this is what you should reference to download with **wget**, as shown in Example 11-13.

Key Topic

Example 11-13 *Using the* wget *Utility to Download the YANG Model*

```
(pyang) [yanguser@python-vm pyang]$ wget https://raw.githubusercontent.com/
YangModels/yang/master/standard/ietf/RFC/ietf-interfaces%402018-02-20.yang
--2021-04-18 16:59:41--  https://raw.githubusercontent.com/YangModels/yang/master/
standard/ietf/RFC/ietf-interfaces%402018-02-20.yang
Resolving raw.githubusercontent.com (raw.githubusercontent.com)... 185.199.108.133,
185.199.110.133, 185.199.109.133, ...
Connecting to raw.githubusercontent.com (raw.githubusercontent.
com)|185.199.108.133|:443... connected.
HTTP request sent, awaiting response... 200 OK
Length: 39365 (38K) [text/plain]
Saving to: 'ietf-interfaces@2018-02-20.yang'


ietf-interfaces@2018-02-20.yang 100%[==============================================
=======>]  38.44K  --.-KB/s    in 0.008s


2021-04-18 16:59:41 (4.67 MB/s) - 'ietf-interfaces@2018-02-20.yang' saved
[39365/39365]


(pyang) [yanguser@python-vm pyang]$ pyang -f tree ietf-interfaces\@2018-02-20.yang
module: ietf-interfaces
  +--rw interfaces
  |  +--rw interface* [name]
  |     +--rw name                        string
  |     +--rw description?               string
```

```
|     +--rw type                        identityref
|     +--rw enabled?                    boolean
|     +--rw link-up-down-trap-enable?   enumeration {if-mib}?
|     +--ro admin-status                enumeration {if-mib}?
|     +--ro oper-status                 enumeration
|     +--ro last-change?                yang:date-and-time
|     +--ro if-index                    int32 {if-mib}?
|     +--ro phys-address?               yang:phys-address
|     +--ro higher-layer-if*            interface-ref
|     +--ro lower-layer-if*             interface-ref
|     +--ro speed?                      yang:gauge64
|     +--ro statistics
|        +--ro discontinuity-time     yang:date-and-time
|        +--ro in-octets?             yang:counter64
|        +--ro in-unicast-pkts?       yang:counter64
|        +--ro in-broadcast-pkts?     yang:counter64
|        +--ro in-multicast-pkts?     yang:counter64
|        +--ro in-discards?           yang:counter32
|        +--ro in-errors?             yang:counter32
|        +--ro in-unknown-protos?     yang:counter32
|        +--ro out-octets?            yang:counter64
|        +--ro out-unicast-pkts?      yang:counter64
|        +--ro out-broadcast-pkts?    yang:counter64
|        +--ro out-multicast-pkts?    yang:counter64
|        +--ro out-discards?          yang:counter32
|        +--ro out-errors?            yang:counter32
x--ro interfaces-state
   x--ro interface* [name]
      x--ro name                  string
      x--ro type                  identityref
      x--ro admin-status          enumeration {if-mib}?
      x--ro oper-status           enumeration
      x--ro last-change?          yang:date-and-time
      x--ro if-index              int32 {if-mib}?
      x--ro phys-address?         yang:phys-address
      x--ro higher-layer-if*      interface-state-ref
      x--ro lower-layer-if*       interface-state-ref
      x--ro speed?                yang:gauge64
      x--ro statistics
         x--ro discontinuity-time     yang:date-and-time
         x--ro in-octets?             yang:counter64
         x--ro in-unicast-pkts?       yang:counter64
         x--ro in-broadcast-pkts?     yang:counter64
         x--ro in-multicast-pkts?     yang:counter64
```

```
            x--ro in-discards?          yang:counter32
            x--ro in-errors?            yang:counter32
            x--ro in-unknown-protos?    yang:counter32
            x--ro out-octets?           yang:counter64
            x--ro out-unicast-pkts?     yang:counter64
            x--ro out-broadcast-pkts?   yang:counter64
            x--ro out-multicast-pkts?   yang:counter64
            x--ro out-discards?         yang:counter32
            x--ro out-errors?           yang:counter32
(pyang) [yanguser@python-vm pyang]$
```

Looking at Figure 11-12 with annotations, you can more easily understand the structure, syntax, and data-type representations.

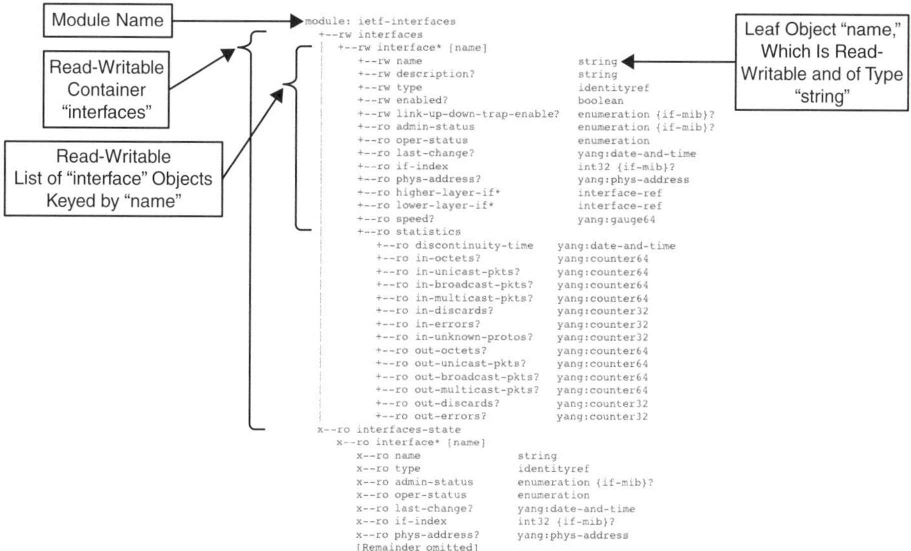

Figure 11-12 *ietf-interfaces YANG Model Processed Through* ***pyang***

The Evolution with RESTCONF

Although NETCONF was a lot of fun to start with in 2007, YANG brought better structure to the use of the protocol in 2010. However, the notion of software-defined networking (SDN) lit a fire under vendors to enable their management products and devices with APIs. RESTful APIs were useful for many use cases. The question became, "Can we make NETCONF a bit more RESTful API like?" Thus, **RESTCONF** came into being with the publication of the IETF's RFC 8040 in 2017. There, it is defined as

> *an HTTP-based protocol that provides a programmatic interface for accessing data defined in YANG, using the datastore concepts defined in the Network Configuration Protocol (NETCONF).*

While RESTCONF provides an API-like functionality using familiar HTTP-based techniques, some feature-parity still must be addressed. You may find yourself using hybrid management tasks that include both NETCONF and RESTCONF until that time comes.

The RESTCONF Protocol Stack

As defined in RFC 8040, RESTCONF is an HTTP-based protocol, but HTTPS is the only supported transport. For obvious security reasons, HTTPS was defined as the secure extension to HTTP. Installing and configuring an SSL/TLS certificate enable the use of the HTTPS protocol to establish a secure connection with the network device.

RESTCONF continues the alignment to YANG data model definitions that you learned with NETCONF. It also facilitates the use of XML or JSON data encoding. When you look at Figure 11-13, the RESTCONF protocol stack becomes more clear.

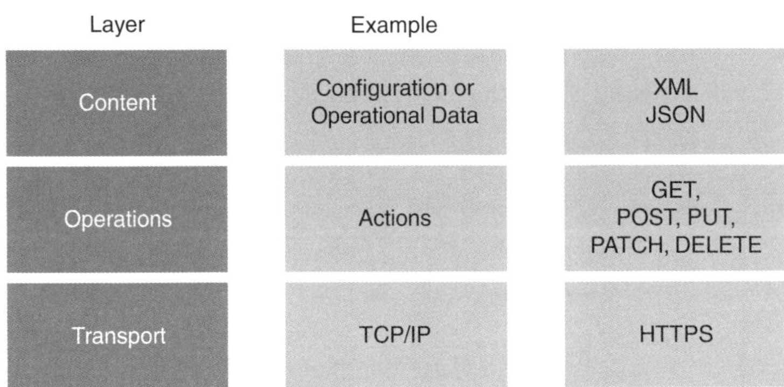

Figure 11-13 *RESTCONF Protocol Stack*

RESTCONF Operations

Similar to RESTful APIs, RESTCONF uses a familiar request/response model where the management tool or application makes a request to the network device that provides the response. Ideally, you get a familiar HTTP 200 OK response!

The use of REST APIs also parallels create, retrieve, update, delete (CRUD)–style operations. Table 11-5 shows a mapping of NETCONF operations to HTTP operation and RESTCONF equivalents.

Table 11-5 Mapping of NETCONF to HTTP/RESTCONF Operations

NETCONF	RESTCONF (HTTP)
<get>, <get-config>	GET
<edit-config> (operation="create")	POST
<edit-config> (operation="create/replace")	PUT
<edit-config> (operation="merge")	PATCH
<edit-config> (operation="delete")	DELETE

Content-Type and Accept headers are often used to define the data type being sent from the requester and the desired type to be returned. Here are the options to define the data being sent from the requester:

```
Content-Type: application/yang-data+json
```

```
Content-Type: application/yang-data+xml
```

And here are the options to define the desired data type to be returned:

```
Accept: application/yang-data+json

Accept: application/yang-data+xml
```

RESTCONF and Authentication

RESTCONF operates much like other RESTful APIs and requires authentication. It uses basic authentication, as defined in RFC 7617, where a request contains a header field in the form of Authorization: Basic <credentials>. In this form, *credentials* is the Base64 encoding of username and password joined by a single colon (:).

It is simple to generate the authentication string on macOS or other Linux derivatives using the built-in **openssl** binary. Windows platforms can achieve the same by installing OpenSSL or obtaining a Base64 encoding utility.

NOTE Do *not* use an online website to generate Base64-encoded authentication strings. It is not known whether the site is logging the user input, and security may be undermined.

Example 11-14 shows an example of generating a basic authentication string with **openssl** on macOS. Try it on your system.

Example 11-14 *Generating Base64 Basic Authentication String on a Mac*

```
Mac ~ % echo -n 'myusername:DevNet4U!' | openssl base64
bXl1c2VybmFtZTpEZXZOZXQ0VSE=
```

The basic authentication mechanism does not provide confidentiality of the transmitted credentials. Base64 is only encoding data; it is not equivalent to encryption or hashing. So, basic authentication must be used in conjunction with HTTPS to provide confidentiality through an encrypted transport session, as is required in RESTCONF.

RESTCONF URIs

All RESTCONF URIs follow this format:

```
https://<DeviceNameOrIP>/<ROOT>/data/<[YANGMODULE:]CONTAINER>/
    <LEAF>[?<OPTIONS>]
```

The components are explained in Table 11-6.

Table 11-6 RESTCONF URI Components

Component	Explanation
https://	The default, secure HTTP transport, as specified by RFC 8040.
DeviceNameOrIP	The DNS name or IP address for the RESTCONF agent; also provides the port (such as 8443) if using a nonstandard port other than 443.
<ROOT>	The main branch for RESTCONF requests. The de facto convention is **restconf**, but it should be verified to ensure proper operation.
data	The RESTCONF API resource type for data. An operations resource type accesses RPC operations.

11

Component	Explanation
[YANG MODULE:] CONTAINER	The base model container being used; inclusion of the module name is optional.
LEAF	An individual element from within the container.
[?<OPTIONS>]	Query parameters that modify or filter returned results; see Table 11-7.

Optional query parameters or options are explained in Table 11-7.

Table 11-7 Optional RESTCONF Query Parameters

Query Parameter	Explanation
depth=unbounded	Follow nested models to end [Integer value] = only to specified hierarchical depth
depth=N	Follow nested model to hierarchical depth of N level(s)
content=all	Show all types of returned data (default)
content=config	Show only configuration-related data
content=nonconfig	Show only non-configuration-related data, essentially operational data
fields=<expr>	Limit what leaves are returned to the expression, <expr>

Before connecting to a RESTCONF server, you must determine the root, or the main branch, for NETCONF requests. Per the RESTCONF standard and RFC 6415, devices expose a resource called **/.well-known/host-meta** to enable discovery of the root programmatically.

Example 11-15 shows how to obtain this information via cURL, but you can use well-known tools like Postman that are shown in the next section. You access the DevNet Sandbox environment and the IOS XE on CSR Recommended Code Always On lab. For the latest DevNet Sandbox information, go to https://devnetsandbox.cisco.com.

Example 11-15 *Determining Main Branch for NETCONF Requests*

```
[restconfuser@python-vm ~]$ curl --insecure -u developer:C1sco12345 https://sandbox-
iosxe-latest-1.cisco.com:443/.well-known/host-meta
<XRD xmlns='http://docs.oasis-open.org/ns/xri/xrd-1.0'>
    <Link rel='restconf' href='/restconf'/>
</XRD>
```

In your situation, use the **--insecure** option if using a self-signed certificate on the managed device, or remove it if using registered certificates. For the DevNet Sandbox environment, the NETCONF agent is purposely registered on port 9443, which is different than yours if using defaults. Also, your specific username-password combination for basic authentication will be different.

Note that the device returns XML-formatted data with an XRD element. There also may be multiple Link child elements; if so, the one of note is the entry with the **rel** attribute of **restconf**. In this case, the **href** attribute value of **/restconf/** is the information you need, matching the normal convention.

Performing a RESTCONF GET Operation with cURL

For the next example, let's continue the focus on device interfaces in the IETF-INTERFACES YANG model, as we discussed earlier. In Example 11-16, you can continue to use cURL, but now access the NETCONF URI at https://sandbox-iosxe-latest-1.cisco.com:443/restconf/data/ietf-interfaces:interfaces.

Example 11-16 *Using RESTCONF to Get Interface Information with cURL*

```
[restconfuser@python-vm ~]$ curl --insecure -u developer:C1sco12345 https:// sand-
box-iosxe-latest-1.cisco.com:443/restconf/data/ietf-interfaces:interfaces


<interfaces xmlns="urn:ietf:params:xml:ns:yang:ietf-interfaces"  xmlns:if="urn:ietf:
params:xml:ns:yang:ietf-interfaces">
  <interface>
    <name>GigabitEthernet1</name>
    <description>MANAGEMENT INTERFACE - DON'T TOUCH ME</description>
    <type xmlns:ianaift="urn:ietf:params:xml:ns:yang:i
ana-if-type">ianaift:ethernetCsmacd</type>
    <enabled>true</enabled>
    <ipv4 xmlns="urn:ietf:params:xml:ns:yang:ietf-ip">
      <address>
        <ip>10.10.20.48</ip>
        <netmask>255.255.255.0</netmask>
      </address>
    </ipv4>
    <ipv6 xmlns="urn:ietf:params:xml:ns:yang:ietf-ip">
    </ipv6>
  </interface>
  <interface>
    <name>GigabitEthernet2</name>
    <description>Configured by RESTCONF</description>
    <type xmlns:ianaift="urn:ietf:params:xml:ns:yang:i
ana-if-type">ianaift:ethernetCsmacd</type>
    <enabled>true</enabled>
    <ipv4 xmlns="urn:ietf:params:xml:ns:yang:ietf-ip">
      <address>
        <ip>10.255.255.1</ip>
       <netmask>255.255.255.0</netmask>
      </address>
      <address>
        <ip>10.255.255.1</ip>
        <netmask>255.255.255.0</netmask>
      </address>
    </ipv4>
    <ipv6 xmlns="urn:ietf:params:xml:ns:yang:ietf-ip">
    </ipv6>
  </interface>
```

```
  <interface>
    <name>GigabitEthernet3</name>
    <description>Configured by RSTconf</description>
    <type xmlns:ianaift="urn:ietf:params:xml:ns:yang:i
ana-if-type">ianaift:ethernetCsmacd</type>
    <enabled>true</enabled>
    <ipv4 xmlns="urn:ietf:params:xml:ns:yang:ietf-ip">
      <address>
        <ip>10.255.244.14</ip>
        <netmask>255.255.255.0</netmask>
      </address>
    </ipv4>
    <ipv6 xmlns="urn:ietf:params:xml:ns:yang:ietf-ip">
    </ipv6>
  </interface>
  <interface>
    <name>Loopback1000</name>
    <description>Added with Restconf</description>
    <type xmlns:ianaift="urn:ietf:params:xml:ns:yang:i
ana-if-type">ianaift:softwareLoopback</type>
    <enabled>true</enabled>
    <ipv4 xmlns="urn:ietf:params:xml:ns:yang:ietf-ip">
      <address>
        <ip>1.1.5.5</ip>
        <netmask>255.255.255.255</netmask>
      </address>
    </ipv4>
    <ipv6 xmlns="urn:ietf:params:xml:ns:yang:ietf-ip">
    </ipv6>
  </interface>
  <interface>
    <name>Loopback1313</name>
    <description>'test interface'</description>
    <type xmlns:ianaift="urn:ietf:params:xml:ns:yang:i
ana-if-type">ianaift:softwareLoopback</type>
    <enabled>false</enabled>
    <ipv4 xmlns="urn:ietf:params:xml:ns:yang:ietf-ip">
      <address>
        <ip>13.13.13.13</ip>
        <netmask>255.255.255.255</netmask>
      </address>
    </ipv4>
    <ipv6 xmlns="urn:ietf:params:xml:ns:yang:ietf-ip">
    </ipv6>
  </interface>
</interfaces>
```

How many interfaces do you see in the DevNet Sandbox IOS XE on CSR Recommended Code Always On lab device? How many interfaces are enabled?

If you had another device with many interfaces, this could be a much larger result! You can get a subset of this information by specifying a desired leaf, as with Example 11-17, using the following URI: https://sandbox-iosxe-latest-1.cisco.com:443/restconf/data/ietf-interfaces:interfaces/interface=GigabitEthernet2.

Example 11-17 *Querying for Interface-Specific Results with RESTCONF and cURL*

```
[restconfuser@python-vm ~]$ curl --insecure -u developer:C1sco12345 https://
sandbox-iosxe-latest-1.cisco.com:443/restconf/data/ietf-interfaces:interfaces/
interface=GigabitEthernet2


<interface xmlns="urn:ietf:params:xml:ns:yang:ietf-interfaces"  xmlns:if="urn:ietf:p
arams:xml:ns:yang:ietf-interfaces">
  <name>GigabitEthernet2</name>
  <description>Configured by RESTCONF</description>
  <type xmlns:ianaift="urn:ietf:params:xml:ns:yang:i
ana-if-type">ianaift:ethernetCsmacd</type>
  <enabled>true</enabled>
  <ipv4 xmlns="urn:ietf:params:xml:ns:yang:ietf-ip">
    <address>
      <ip>10.255.255.1</ip>
      <netmask>255.255.255.0</netmask>
    </address>
    <address>
      <ip>10.255.255.1</ip>
      <netmask>255.255.255.0</netmask>
    </address>
  </ipv4>
  <ipv6 xmlns="urn:ietf:params:xml:ns:yang:ietf-ip">
  </ipv6>
</interface>
```

Excellent! Now you can try your hand at modifying a configuration using RESTCONF.

Performing RESTCONF GET Operations with the Postman Utility

Because we're going to eventually pivot to performing a REST PUT operation, you can also switch to using the Postman utility. Postman is a multiplatform utility that is helpful in doing API testing. It also has a helpful code generator that can be the starting point for scripting work. You can obtain Postman free from https://www.postman.com. You may also be interested in the DevNet Postman collection at https://www.postman.com/ciscodevnet.

For this example, create a new collection called RESTCONF, as seen in Figure 11-14.

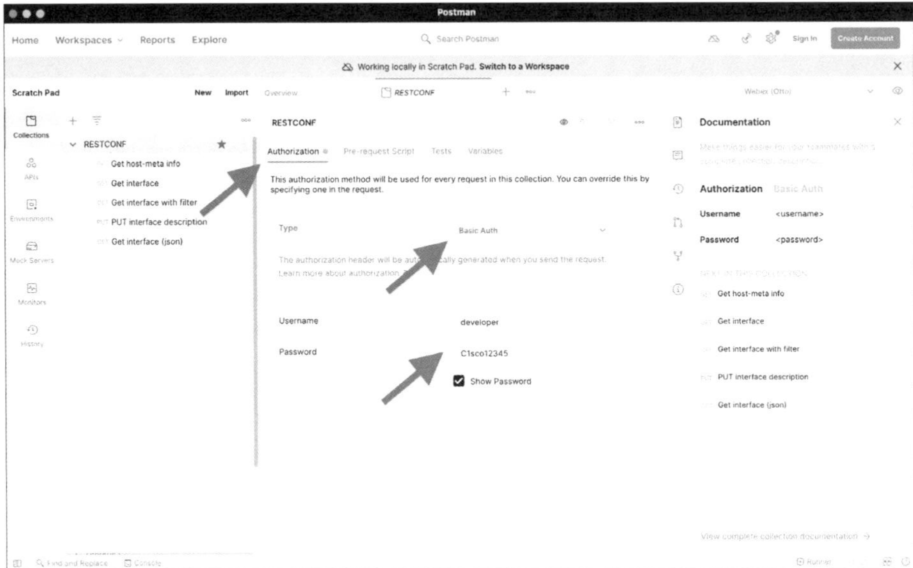

Figure 11-14 *Creating a Postman Collection*

Also, for ease of use, on the collection-level Authorization tab, set Type to Basic Auth and the username and password to their appropriate values. Setting the values at the collection-level allows you to inherit these authorization sessions for all other requests in the containing collection or folder.

To reinforce the previous experience with cURL, build a Postman equivalent of pulling the same IETF-INTERFACES YANG model data. Yours should look similar to Figure 11-15.

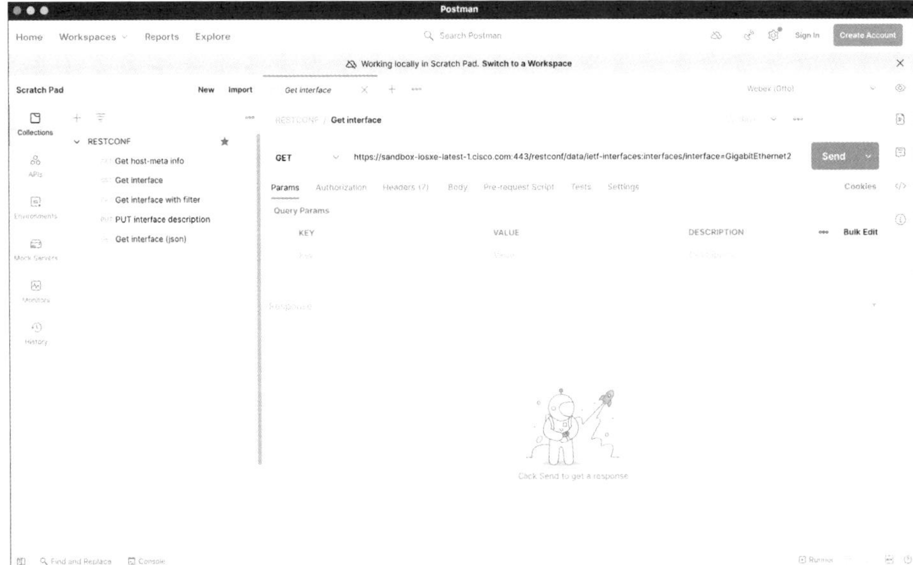

Figure 11-15 *Creating a Postman Request to a GET Interface*

On the Authorization tab, you should see Inherit Auth from Parent. The operation should be GET, and the request URL should be https://sandbox-iosxe-latest-1.cisco.com:443/restconf/data/ietf-interfaces:interfaces/interface=GigabitEthernet2.

Now, if you execute the request by clicking the Send button, you get results similar to Figure 11-16.

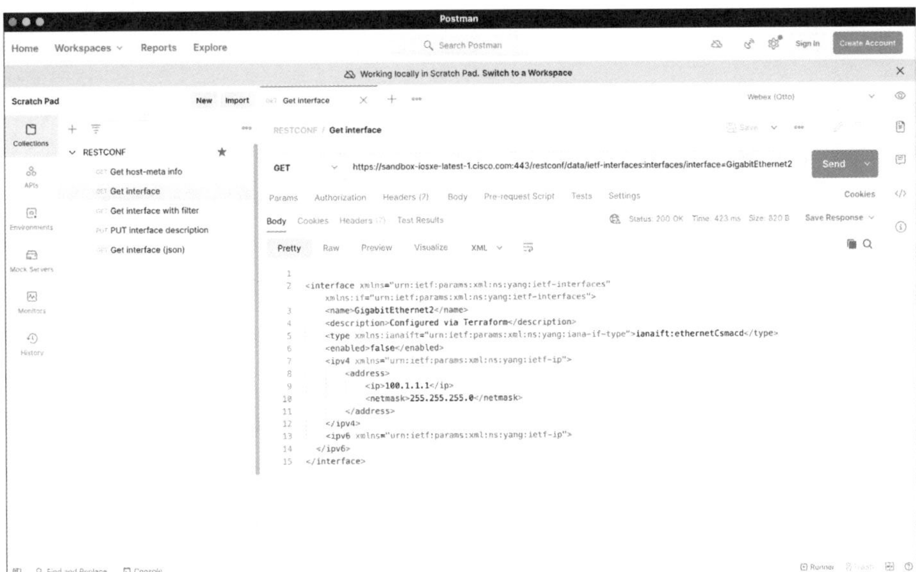

Figure 11-16 *Executing a Postman Request to a GET Interface*

If you click the Code button, which appears as the </> icon, on the right side and select **Python > Requests**, then you get the helpful code snippet shown in Example 11-18.

Example 11-18 *Postman Code Snippet*

```
import requests

url = "https://sandbox-iosxe-latest-1.cisco.com:443/restconf/data/
ietf-interfaces:interfaces/interface=GigabitEthernet2"

payload={}
headers = {
  'Authorization': 'Basic ZGV2ZWxvcGVyOkMxc2NvMTIzNDU='
}

response = requests.request("GET", url, headers=headers, data=payload)

print(response.text)
```

How cool is that!? This code can serve to seed a more sophisticated Python script. Of course, you should do some appropriate security cleanup, such as removing the credentials from being fixed in your script, but it's a start!

Let's do one more GET operation to exercise your understanding of using query options (parameters). Now create a copy of the earlier Postman request, but this time onto the end of the URI, add **?fields=name;description;enabled.** Your entry (and execution) should be similar to Figure 11-17.

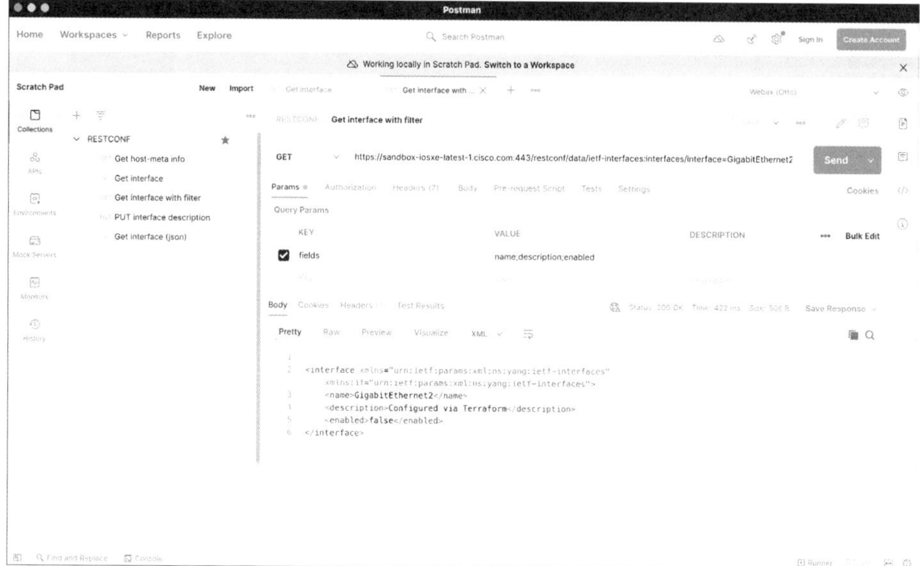

Figure 11-17 *Executing a Postman Request to GET Interface with Query Option*

Now that you've rebuilt the GET method in Postman, you can pivot to doing a PUT operation and pushing an updated interface description into the device, as you did earlier with NETCONF means.

Create a copy of the GET Interface request, but save it as PUT Interface Description. In the new request, change the request type from GET to PUT. Select the Headers tab and create or modify the Content-Type header to a value of **application/yang-data+xml.** On the Body tab, select the Raw option and paste the following:

```
<interface xmlns="urn:ietf:params:xml:ns:yang:ietf-interfaces" xml
ns:if="urn:ietf:params:xml:ns:yang:ietf-interfaces">

    <name>GigabitEthernet2</name>

    <description>Configured by RESTCONF again</description>

    <type xmlns:ianaift="urn:ietf:params:xml:ns:yang:iana-if-
type">ianaift:ethernetCsmacd</type>

</interface>
```

You can make the description anything you like. After you click Send, the results should appear similar to Figure 11-18.

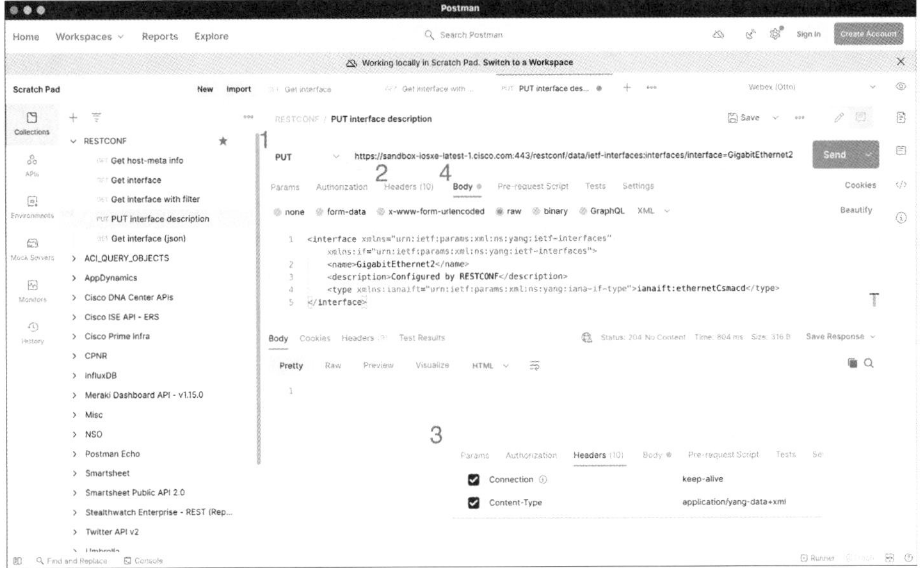

Figure 11-18 *Creating and Executing a Postman Request to PUT Interface Description*

Again, you can use the Postman Code feature to generate a Python-Requests code snippet, allowing you to create more robust scripts that would programmatically change the device configuration with RESTCONF via Python.

Try your hand at getting information in JSON format. Remember that you'll need to change the Accept header for a GET operation to **application/yang-data+json**. See Figure 11-19 as the JSON equivalent to the operation performed in Figure 11-16.

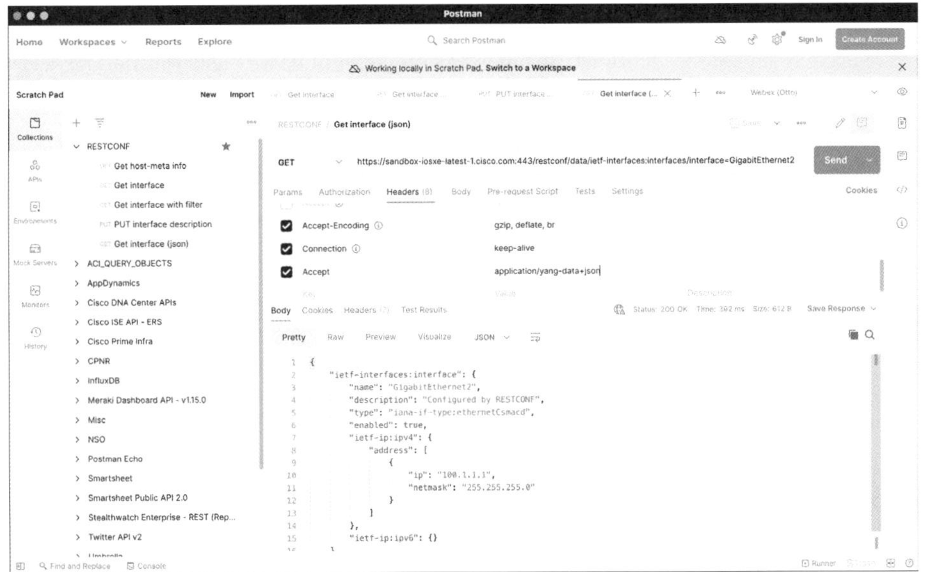

Figure 11-19 *Executing a Postman Request to GET Interface Information as JSON*

11

Hopefully, you're seeing the prospects of using RESTCONF to programmatically obtain and change device settings.

Management Solutions Using NETCONF and RESTCONF

By now, you've seen a few manual methods to interact with NETCONF using an SSH terminal emulator. You've also seen manual methods to interact with RESTCONF using cURL, Postman, and the Python code snippets it generates. Some commercial management products that leverage NETCONF and RESTCONF methods may be appealing in your situation.

Tail-f Systems was one of the first companies to release a commercial application that embraced NETCONF. The company's Network Control System (NCS) product was created by several industry shapers of the NETCONF protocol. Cisco acquired Tail-f Systems in 2014, with the product evolving into Cisco's Network Services Orchestrator (NSO). NSO is a multivendor configuration management platform that provides a north-bound abstraction layer to managed devices using network element drivers (NEDs), which may involve NETCONF, SNMP, SSH, or REST methods to interact with the managed devices.

NSO is widely used by large service providers and enterprise companies to solve their multivendor and model-driven configuration management challenges. More information is available on NSO at https://www.cisco.com/c/en/us/products/cloud-systems-management/network-services-orchestrator/index.html.

A DevNet-specific portal for NSO can be found at https://developer.cisco.com/site/nso/.

Increasingly more and more management tools are pivoting from SNMP-initiated TFTPing of configurations as text files or SSH-driven pasting of the same to NETCONF- and RESTCONF-style management. Be on the lookout for NETCONF/RESTCONF setting requirements with your next set of tools, and ask your vendors when they'll support the newer style management methods!

If you're using open-source solutions, **pyang** is an excellent utility for validating and inspecting YANG models without the verbosity of the YANG model file. Cisco has provided another graphical tool, YANG Suite, available at https://developer.cisco.com/yangsuite/.

Ansible supports the following modules that are helpful with NETCONF:

- community.yang.fetch
- community.yang.get
- community.yang.configure
- community.yang.generate_spec

In the summer of 2020, work was started on the ansible.netcommon.restconf HttpApi plug-in for devices supporting RESTCONF API.

If you are a Puppet user, check out this DevNet Code Exchange entry that uses Puppet and NETCONF to manage IOS XR-based devices: https://developer.cisco.com/codeexchange/github/repo/cisco/cisco-yang-puppet-module/.

The previous examples of using Postman and the Code generator, especially for Python-Requests code snippets, should be helpful to get you started with RESTCONF options. Consider the next time you have a need to change all Syslog and SNMP trap receivers in your environment. In the past, have you simply jammed the new ones in the configurations and held off on removing the old ones? Were you sure you got all decommissioned options out of the configuration? By using the newer manageability protocols and some simple Python scripting, you will be able to execute mass configuration updates and do it quickly and effectively!

Exam Preparation Tasks

As mentioned in the section "How to Use This Book" in the Introduction, you have a couple of choices for exam preparation: the exercises here, Chapter 17, "Final Preparation," and the exam simulation questions in the Pearson Test Prep Software Online.

Review All Key Topics

Review the most important topics in this chapter, noted with the Key Topic icon in the outer margin of the page. Table 11-8 lists a reference of these key topics and the page numbers on which each is found.

Table 11-8 Key Topics for Chapter 11

Key Topic Element	Description	Page Number
Paragraph	NETCONF definition	348
Figure 11-1	NETCONF Conceptual Layers	349
Table 11-2	NETCONF Protocol Operations	350
Paragraph	Enabling NETCONF on IOS-XE	355
Paragraph	Enabling NETCONF on NX-OS	358
Paragraph	YANG definition	365
Example 11-13	Using the **wget** Utility to Download the YANG Model	369
Figure 11-13	RESTCONF Protocol Stack	372
Paragraph	NETCONF/YANG IETF interfaces	375

Complete Tables and Lists from Memory

Print a copy of Appendix C, "Memory Tables" (found on the companion website), or at least the section for this chapter, and complete the tables and lists from memory. Appendix D, "Memory Tables Answer Key," also on the companion website, includes completed tables and lists to check your work.

Define Key Terms

Define the following key terms from this chapter and check your answers in the glossary:

NETCONF (network configuration), RESTCONF, YANG

References

URL	QR Code
https://developer.cisco.com/site/sandbox/	
https://github.com/YangModels/yang/blob/master/standard/ietf/RFC/ietf-interfaces.yang	
https://github.com/mbj4668/pyang	
https://devnetsandbox.cisco.com	
https://www.postman.com	
https://www.postman.com/ciscodevnet	
https://www.cisco.com/c/en/us/products/cloud-systems-management/network-services-orchestrator/index.html	

URL	QR Code
https://developer.cisco.com/site/nso/	
https://developer.cisco.com/yangsuite/	
https://developer.cisco.com/codeexchange/github/repo/cisco/cisco-yang-puppet-module/	

CHAPTER 12

Model-Driven Telemetry

This chapter covers the following topics:

- **Transformation of Inventory, Status, Performance, and Fault Monitoring:** This section covers the challenges and necessary transformation of the network engineering, management, and operations disciplines toward inventory, status, performance, and fault monitoring.
- **Scaling with the Push Model:** This section covers the intentions of model-driven telemetry (MDT).
- **How to Implement Model-Driven Telemetry:** This section covers how MDT is configured and used on various Cisco platforms.
- **Picking Sensor Paths and Metrics:** This section covers the methodology in determining sensor paths and metrics used to monitor an MDT-enabled environment.
- **Practical Application of Streaming Telemetry:** This section covers a practical application of streaming telemetry and shows how sensor paths are determined, configured, and implemented in Telegraf, InfluxDB, and Grafana stacks.
- **Beyond MDT—Event-Driven Telemetry:** This section covers the progression to event-driven telemetry (EDT).

This chapter maps to the *Developing Applications Using Cisco Core Platforms and APIs v1.0 (350-901)* Exam Blueprint Section 5.1, "Explain considerations of model-driven telemetry (including data consumption and data storage)."

Network engineering and operations have seen many changes over the years. Despite the standardization and adoption of the Simple Network Management Protocol (SNMP), which was often mocked as being anything but simple, change needed to happen. Even as early as mid-2002, the IETF recognized that the current protocols were insufficient for future growth and innovation. The concerns were documented in Informational RFC 3535 (https://tools.ietf.org/html/rfc3535). To that end, innovation *has* happened in this space, which can be seen in the development and adoption of model-driven telemetry (MDT). MDT provides a fresh perspective at obtaining network inventory, performance, and fault information using an efficient push model over the traditional request-response methods seen in SNMP. Indeed, some innovators in the cloud space largely bypassed SNMP in lieu of MDT approaches. At NANOG 73 (June 2018), Google shared its experience moving away from SNMP to MDT, as seen in its presentation link (https://pc.nanog.org/static/published/meetings//NANOG73/daily/day_2.html#talk_1677).

NOTE URLs in this book are also shared in the chapter-ending "References" section with QR codes to ease use.

In this chapter, first we review the benefits of adopting model-driven telemetry and then weigh options for our purposes.

"Do I Know This Already?" Quiz

The "Do I Know This Already?" quiz allows you to assess whether you should read this entire chapter thoroughly or jump to the "Exam Preparation Tasks" section. If you are in doubt about your answers to these questions or your own assessment of your knowledge of the topics, read the entire chapter. Table 12-1 lists the major headings in this chapter and their corresponding "Do I Know This Already?" quiz questions. You can find the answers in Appendix A, "Answers to the 'Do I Know This Already?' Quizzes."

Table 12-1 "Do I Know This Already?" Section-to-Question Mapping

Foundation Topics Section	Questions
Transformation of Inventory, Status, Performance, and Fault Monitoring	1, 8
Scaling with the Push Model	2
How to Implement Model-Driven Telemetry	3, 4, 5
Picking Sensor Paths and Metrics	6
Practical Application of Streaming Telemetry	7
Beyond MDT—Event-Driven Telemetry	9, 10

1. When you are comparing the different capabilities of SNMP with model-driven telemetry, which is true?
   a. SNMPv1 data security is similar to MDT data security.
   b. SNMPv2c data security is similar to MDT data security.
   c. SNMPv1 and 2c data security is similar to MDT data security.
   d. SNMPv3 data security is similar to MDT data security.
2. MDT gRPC uses which application protocol?
   a. HTTP
   b. HTTP/2
   c. SPDY
   d. SCP
   e. sFTP
3. Considering MDT dial-out mode, which statement is true?
   a. The device is the client and source pushing data; the telemetry receiver is the server.
   b. The device is passive; the telemetry receiver initiates the connection, requesting the data.
   c. The device is active; the telemetry receiver initiates the connection, requesting the data.

   d. The device is the server; the telemetry receiver is the client.
   e. The device maintains no configuration; the telemetry receiver updates the subscriptions to the device.

4. Which one of the following is *not* a major task needed to configure telemetry dial-out?
   a. Create a destination group.
   b. Create a sensor group.
   c. Create a flow spec.
   d. Create a subscription.
5. What is GPB encoding an acronym for?
   a. General Port Buffers
   b. Giant Port Buffers
   c. Google Protocol Buffers
   d. Good Protocol Borders
   e. Gopher Protocol Bandwidth
6. What is a sensor path?
   a. A combination of SNMP MIB object and interface
   b. A hierarchy to chassis/module/interface
   c. The pathway from managed element to receiving telemetry collector
   d. A combination of YANG data model and metric node
7. Where are YANG data models published for most vendors and standards bodies? (Choose two.)
   a. https://stackoverflow.com/YangModels
   b. https://github.com/YangModels/yang
   c. https://yang.org
   d. https:/yangcatalog.org
   e. https://www.ietf.org/yang-data-models
8. The TIG stack refers to which open-source project components?
   a. Telemetry, Ingestion, and Graphing
   b. Telemetry, Injection, and Graphing
   c. Telegraphy, Importation, and Generation
   d. Telegraf, InfluxDB, and Grafana
9. Which MDT policy is most frugal with disk space and overhead processing?
   a. periodic
   b. data-pump
   c. on-change
   d. gzip
10. What is an optimal way to evaluate disk usage with model-driven telemetry?
   a. Add the number of network elements and multiply by 1480 bytes.
   b. Baseline the telemetry consumption for a time period and extrapolate.
   c. (# of devices) * (sensor paths) * (frequency/min)
   d. Use the IEFT Telemetry calculator from RFC 2795.

Foundation Topics

Transformation of Inventory, Status, Performance, and Fault Monitoring

As discussed earlier, the stone age of network IT involved manual effort by logging in to a device through a serial console cable and using Telnet or (eventually) SSH. The process of executing **show** commands worked fine for checking device inventory, status, and performance and for fault monitoring in smaller environments. However, as network device counts increased, the need for automation and network programmability became clear. Would you want to manage a network of 230,000 devices using command-line methods of SSH and **show** commands? Of course not!

Some improvements were gained over using the CLI with management tools; a progression was to use SNMP to access similar instrumentation. For example, the ENTITY-MIB could identify much of a device's inventory. The IF-MIB could show interface statistics. But a more effective approach for fault monitoring was needed—ideally, in a "push me a notification" model.

SNMP notifications (traps) and syslog event messages were useful for fault monitoring. Unfortunately, their scope and information depth were different. Let's consider a popular legacy platform: the Catalyst 6500. It supported about 100 SNMP notifications, but over 8,000 syslog event messages. Environments that were focused on just SNMP notifications missed a lot of event visibility. Additionally, SNMP notifications did not have severity identifiers unless the Management Information Base (MIB) developer intentionally put a varbind (variable binding) into a notification type that included a severity declaration.

Syslog event messages were great; they had severity identifiers and were written with generally readable facility, severity, mnemonic, and message text, as in this example:

```
*Mar  9 13:41:34.452 UTC: %LINEPROTO-5-UPDOWN: Line protocol on
Interface GigabitEthernet0, changed state to up
```

However, their human-readable form wasn't optimized for programmatic use.

Using SNMP for data gathering was effective, and many network management tools still use this approach today. There was structure to the instrumentation, but using this method also remained more of an art than a science for many users. SNMP did not gain a strong adoption for configuration management and service provisioning. There was not a large number of read-write-capable MIB objects. Indeed, when SNMP was used to effect configuration changes, it was largely done by writing parameters to the CISCO-CONFIG-MAN-MIB, defining a text file that needed to be pushed via TFTP to a network element's flash location. The device would replace or merge the configuration, as directed. Other configuration tasks might have been affected by automating CLI methods using **copy tftp flash**, which performed a similar function. Worst-case scenarios were systems that automated CLI sessions and pasted the configuration through flow-control-based Telnet/SSH sessions. I remember several customer engagements where pushing multi-thousand-line access lists would take minutes or longer.

All of these issues were unacceptable to growing networks that needed automation and network programmability. Addressing the need for network monitoring, streaming telemetry provided an alternative to SNMP. The generic term *streaming telemetry* is used when referring to **model-driven telemetry (MDT)** or **event-driven telemetry (EDT)**. With streaming telemetry, the network element pushes, or "streams," the instrumentation or data measurement to a streaming telemetry collector (or controller). Model-driven telemetry uses **YANG** models that define the structure and instrumentation of a device or service model. MDT is commonly sample-interval-based, also known as cadence-based. EDT also depends on YANG models, but rather than sample-interval-based, its data is pushed upon change of an object or data measurement. Both employ the concept of **sensor path**, which defines the object, instrumentation, or data measurement of concern. This is an analog to SNMP's MIB object.

Telemetry applications can subscribe to specific data items they need, by using standards-based YANG data models. The transport can be based on NETCONF, RESTCONF, gRPC, or gRPC Network Management Interface protocols. **Subscriptions** can also be created by using CLIs if they are configured subscriptions.

Google Remote Procedure Call (gRPC) is a **remote-procedure call (RPC)** system developed by Google in 2015. gRPC uses HTTP/2 for transport with TLS and token-based authentication. The HTTP/2 support provides low latency and scalability beyond SNMP implementations. With support of the OpenConfig community in 2017, Google also introduced **Google Remote Procedure Call (gRPC) Network Management Interface (gNMI)**. gNMI focuses on configuration management and state retrieval. It complements telemetry in that regard. The expectation is that gNMI will take more prominence as more platforms adopt support.

Within telemetry, structured data is published at a defined cadence, or on-change, based on the subscription criteria and data type. Streaming telemetry has several benefits, as seen in Table 12-2.

Table 12-2 SNMP and Streaming Telemetry Comparison

Function	SNMP	Streaming Telemetry
Model	Request-response	Push
Security	SNMPv1 and 2c—none SNMPv3 authentication and privacy	TLS default
Encoding	ASN.1	GPB, JSON, XML
Programmatic Use	Medium	High
Transport	UDP	TCP, NETCONF, gRPC, gNMI
Instrumentation model	MIB	YANG Model

When you have a high-level understanding of streaming telemetry being pushed from a network element, the next question is "What is the telemetry receiver or controller it is pushing to?" Several options are available. On the commercial software side, the Cisco Crosswork solution provides a telemetry receiver (https://www.cisco.com/c/en/us/products/collateral/cloud-systems-management/crosswork-network-automation/datasheet-c78-743287.html).

A fine open-source solution for consuming streaming telemetry is the TIG stack—Telegraf, InfluxDB, and Grafana. We cover the TIG stack in a later section with practical examples. Other options are Apache Kafka and the Cloud Native Computing Foundation's hosted project named Prometheus.

Scaling with the Push Model

One of the largest benefits from streaming telemetry has been the use of its push model. Comparatively, SNMP is a poll-request model. An SNMP agent on the managed device (network element) responds to every CPU, interface, or memory (or other) data collection initiated from an SNMP manager (management application) as a request. Because SNMP is also a UDP-based protocol, the initial request is not guaranteed to be delivered. It is possible to have missed polls and data responses in a congested or lossy network.

Let's consider the smallest SNMP request of one managed object. RFCs stipulate a minimum size of 484 bytes. SNMP supports packing the payload with multiple requests; think CPU, multiple interfaces, and memory counters. These are considered variable bindings, or varbinds—the combination of an object identifier (OID) and a value. Traditional SNMP packet size would be limited to the MTU size of the network, such as 1500 or 9500 bytes. If you're going with nondefault or jumbo frames, it's also good to question whether the network management system has a limit of what it can receive, such as 8192-byte PDUs. It's common to see payloads of up to 10 SNMP varbinds and stay within the default of 1500-byte MTUs.

On the minimum side, you would have a 484-byte request and a similar response. On the maximum side, you would have a 1500-byte request and a 1500- to 9000-byte response.

Streaming telemetry can use a few different transport options, which we cover in the next section. However, for now, let's consider streaming telemetry with gRPC. On the minimum side, you would have a 1286-byte exchange for the first RPC. gRPC is intended for multiple RPCs and gains efficiency in that model, much like packing SNMP payloads. Additional RPCs would be 564 bytes. On the maximum side, gRPC benefits from TCP sessions and windowing, but it also has a default maximum message size set arbitrarily at 4 MB.

So right off, you can see an advantage of gRPC's HTTP/2 and TCP pedigree against SNMP's UDP. You can also acknowledge the difference in maximum payload. Cisco engineer Shelly Cadora has used this wonderful graphic, shown in Figure 12-1, for years at CiscoLive and IETF events; it aptly shows the processing contention that manifests in SNMP as the number of pollers or polled objects increases.

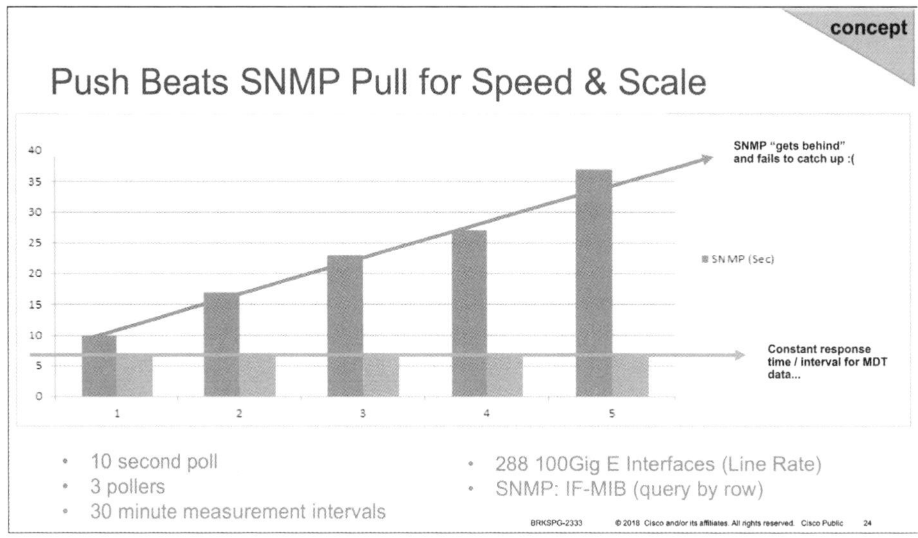

Figure 12-1 *gRPC Versus SNMP in Speed and Scale Comparison*

SNMP is just not able to keep up with its legacy protocol, data encoding, and processing models against gRPC from 2015 using the latest technology. That's okay, SNMP; you were there at the beginning when we needed you, and we thank you for it! Now it's appropriate for our evolving requirements to focus on gRPC and more enhanced functionality.

Beyond gRPC is another Google innovation: the gRPC Network Management Interface, or gNMI. Initially, the industry focused on configuration management aspects, as seen with NETCONF. Although NETCONF was capable of obtaining operational data, it was not oriented to streaming data as seen with the innovations it preceded. Initial telemetry development happened later, and soon management interfaces for configuration management, operational state, and telemetry needed to be consolidated. gNMI provides the mechanism to install, change, and delete the configuration of network devices, and also to view operational data. The content provided through gNMI can be modeled using YANG. gRPC carries gNMI and provides the means to define and transmit data and operation requests.

Another aspect of scaling optimization touches the configuration management function. In the next section, we cover the dial-in/dial-out modes of streaming telemetry, but for now let's consider where the configuration change must happen. In a **dial-out** mode, the managed device, or source of telemetry data, has a static or configured subscription that is part of the device's running configuration. Some configuration management systems must provide a mechanism to create those telemetry subscription configurations *and* do the configuration management actions necessary to implement them. These configurations get pushed across many devices and must be maintained, archived, and change controlled. In an absolute worst-case scenario, some engineer needs to do the work manually—logging in to each device and installing the configuration. In either case, the authoritative definition of the telemetry subscriptions is peppered across devices in the network.

In a **dial-in** mode, the telemetry receiver creates the subscription and becomes the initiator. No configuration change is made to the running configuration of the device, even as the operational configuration and state can be shown, if needed. The telemetry subscriptions are created and managed in a central location, characteristic of one of the foundational principles of software-defined networking—centralized controllers. This centralization of the configuration management function serves to benefit scale and reduce operational burden.

How to Implement Model-Driven Telemetry

To appreciate the functionality of model-driven telemetry, you should first understand the basic concept of telemetry. In its most basic form, telemetry is a data point or measurement representing health, performance, or fault status of a device component or service. Does SNMP provide telemetry? Generally, yes, but most network operators reserve the use of telemetry for methods that use an automated communications process where measurements are collected at the device and transmitted to a receiving collector. A model-driven telemetry approach uses this mechanism but augments it through the use of device and/or service models that represent features and functionality to be configured or monitored.

Model-driven telemetry replaces the periodic polling of network elements as seen with the SNMP request-response method. Instead, a subscription defines what information, or sensor path, is created with the network element where a subscriber, or telemetry controller (receiver), can obtain continuous streams of updates. The updates can be sent periodically or as the objects, data, or status changes. This is why it is sometimes referred to as streaming telemetry.

In some MDT implementations, a subscription is defined on the publisher (network element) with a target of the subscriber (telemetry controller or receiver), as seen in Figure 12-2. This type of implementation requires a higher degree of configuration management discipline.

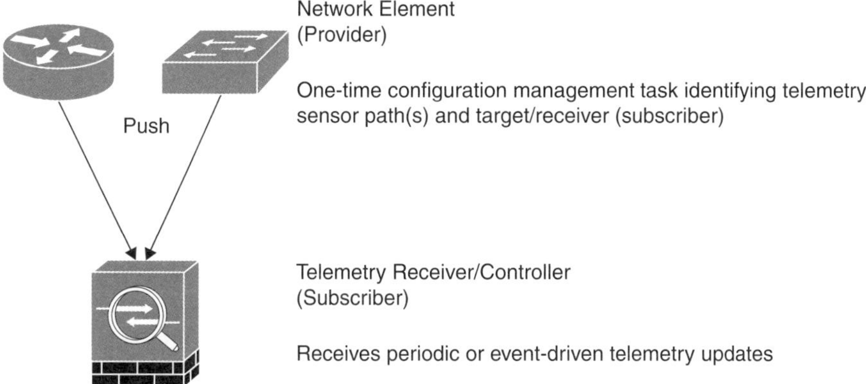

Figure 12-2 *Network Element and Telemetry Receiver Concept*

In other implementations, the subscriber pushes the telemetry subscription of desired sensor paths to the publisher (managed device) as a one-time configuration task, or subscription configuration, as depicted in Figure 12-3. The network element, acting as the publisher, honors the subscription parameters of sensor paths and frequency. This implementation type follows a more SDN controller-like model.

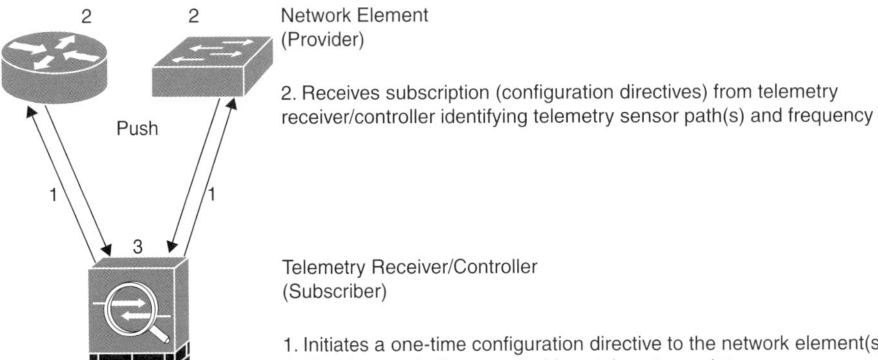

Figure 12-3 *Detailed Push Model Exchange*

Key concepts used in streaming model-driven telemetry data are

- **Session:** One or more telemetry receivers collect the streamed data using a dial-in or dial-out mode.

- **Dial-in mode:** The receiver "dials in" to the network element and subscribes dynamically to one or more sensor paths. This process effectively creates a configuration change on the network element (although it may not be rendered in the device's running configuration). The network element acts as the provider, and the receiver is the subscriber (client). The network element streams telemetry data through the same session. The dial-in mode of subscriptions is dynamic. This dynamic subscription terminates when the receiver-subscriber cancels the subscription or when the session terminates. Figure 12-4 depicts a dial-in mode, compared with a dial-out mode.

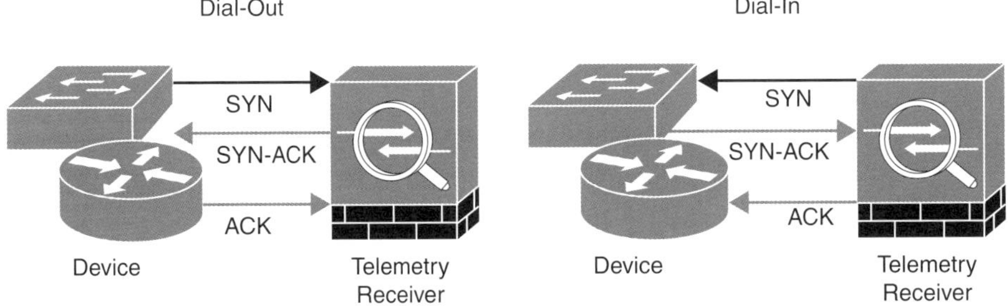

Figure 12-4 *Dial-In and Dial-Out Mode Comparison*

- **Dial-out mode:** The network element "dials out" to the receiver. This is the default mode of operation. The network element acts as a client, and the receiver acts as a server. In this mode, sensor paths and destinations are configured and bound together into one or more subscriptions. The network element establishes a session with each destination in the subscription and streams data to the receiver. The dial-out mode of subscriptions is persistent. When a session terminates, the network element continually attempts to re-establish a new session with the receiver every 30 seconds. As mentioned, Figure 12-4 depicts a dial-in mode, compared with a dial-out mode.

- **Sensor path:** The sensor path describes a YANG path or a subset of data definitions in a YANG model with a container. In a YANG model, the sensor path can be specified to end at any level in the container hierarchy (for example, Cisco-IOS-XR-infra-statsd-oper:infra-statistics/interfaces/interface/latest/generic-counters).
- **Subscription:** A configuration session that binds one or more sensor paths to destinations and specifies the criteria to stream data. In time- or cadence-based telemetry, data is streamed continuously at a configured frequency.
- **Transport and encoding:** The network element streams telemetry data using a transport mechanism. The generated data is encapsulated into the desired format using encoders.

Dial-In and Dial-Out Mode

The distinction between dial-in and dial-out modes bears even more consideration because it has implications on where configurations are generated and stored, along with session maintenance. Figure 12-4 shows these two modes graphically.

Essentially, dial-out mode provides for the telemetry source device initiating a session with the telemetry receiver defined in the subscription configuration. The subscription configuration is defined and provisioned on the device's running configuration and shows the parameters of the subscription—destination, sensor path(s), and subscription. Dial-in mode has the telemetry subscriber-receiver initiating the session and pushing the subscription parameters to the telemetry source device, which streams it back to the subscriber-receiver.

Table 12-3 describes other dial-in/dial-out considerations of note.

Table 12-3 Dial-In and Dial-Out Comparison

Dial-In Mode	Dial-Out Mode
Subscription configuration is dynamically provisioned.	Subscription configuration is statically (purposely) provisioned on the device.
Telemetry data is sent to the initiator/subscriber requesting it.	Telemetry data is sent to the specified receiver/collector(s).
Lifetime of the subscription is associated with the session that created it (and sends the data).	Lifetime of the subscription is associated with the existence of the device configuration defining it.
No change to the telemetry source's running configuration is seen.	Telemetry source's running configuration reflects the subscription settings.
Subscriptions must be reinitiated after a reload or stateful switchover (established sessions are killed).	Subscriptions automatically connect to the receiver/collector after reload/stateful switchover.
Subscription identifier is dynamically generated when successfully established.	Subscription identifier is defined as part of the subscription configuration.

Encoding (Serialization)

Several encoding, or data serialization, mechanisms are used in telemetry. XML is a legacy and has inefficient encoding due to its verbosity with open and close tags. It has a strong history in dynamic content management, especially with web publishing because of its alignments with HTML and CSS.

JSON is widely adopted in software development projects because of its ease of human readability, coupled with excellent programmatic use. It is an efficient encoding method that is seen across many aspects of IT for configuration, inventory, and other basic data encoding.

Google Protocol Buffer (GPB), sometimes colloquially called *protobufs*, is another data encoding method to serialize structured data. Google created it with a design intended for simplicity and performance. Its encoding and efficiency beat XML in all regards and do well against JSON. However, the efficiency brings operational complexity because it is not very human-readable. Interpreting GPB-encoded structured data requires a type of "secret decoder ring" in the form of a .proto file that defines the mappings and data types. Compact GPB was the original format seen with Cisco IOS XR 6.0.0. kvGPB is a derivative—a self-describing key-value pair Google Protocol Buffer. kvGPB is trending to be the de facto encoding of choice. It is easier to interpret because the key-value pairings are typically human-readable.

Figure 12-5 shows these data encodings side by side for comparison.

XML

```
<data>
  <interface_name>GigabitEthernet0/0</interface_name>
  <packets_sent>5938501</packets_sent>
  <bytes_sent>69286077</bytes_sent>
  <packets_received>492884</packets_received>
  <bytes_received>48829336</bytes_received>
</data>
```

Compact GPB

```
1: GigabitEthernet0/0
50: 5938501
51: 69286077
52: 492884
53: 48829336
<...>
```

JSON

```
{ "keys":{
  "interface-name":"GigabitEthernet0/0"
},
"content":{
"packets-sent": 5938501,
"bytes-sent": 69286077,
"packets-received": 492884,
"bytes-received": 48829336,
<. . . >
```

Key–Value GPB

```
{InterfaceName: GigabitEthernet0/0
 GenericCounters {
    PacketsSent: 5938501
    BytesSent: 69286077
    PacketsReceived: 492884
    BytesReceived: 48829336
 <...>
```

Figure 12-5 *Data Encoding Comparisons*

Protocols

The next topic of consideration is the type of protocol used. The protocol that is used for the connection between a telemetry publishing device and the telemetry receiver decides how the data is sent. This protocol is referred to as the transport protocol and is independent of the management protocol for configured subscriptions. The transport protocol also impacts the encoding used. Telemetry implementations can span several options, depending on platform support—NETCONF, RESTCONF, HTTP, TCP, UDP, secure UDP (DTLS), gRPC, and gNMI.

NETCONF and RESTCONF are typically associated with configuration management functions, but they can also be used to extract operational data. The NETCONF protocol is available on IOS XE platforms for the transport of dynamic subscriptions and can be used with yang-push and yang-notif-native streams using XML encoding.

HTTP is observed as an option since NX-OS 7.0 with JSON encoding. HTTPS is also supported if a certificate is configured.

TCP is supported for dial-out only on Cisco IOS-XR platforms since Release 6.1.1 on the 64-bit Linux-based platforms, such as NCS5500, NCS5000, and ASR9000, and the 32-bit IOS XR platforms, such as CRS and legacy ASR9000.

UDP is supported also for dial-out only on IOS-XR platforms since Release 6.1.1 on the 64-bit Linux-based platforms, such as NCS5500, NCS5000, and ASR9000. Starting with Cisco NX-OS Release 7.0(3)I7(1), UDP and secure UDP (DTLS) are supported as telemetry transport protocols. You can add destinations that receive UDP. The encoding for UDP and secure UDP can be GPB or JSON.

gRPC is a preferred transport protocol and is supported on IOS-XR platforms since Release 6.1.1 on the 64-bit Linux-based platforms, such as NCS5500, NCS5000, and ASR9000. It is also broadly supported on the common IOS XE-based platforms, such as the Catalyst 9000 Series.

Because of the variety of support and dependencies, Table 12-4 represents a matrix of mode, encoding, and telemetry protocols.

Table 12-4 Matrix of Telemetry Modes, Encoding, and Protocols

Transport Protocol	NETCONF		gRPC		gNMI		HTTP	TCP	UDP
Mode	Dial-in	Dial-out	Dial-in	Dial-out	Dial-in	Dial-out	Dial-out	Dial-out	Dial-out
Stream									
yang-push	Yes	No	NA	Yes	Yes	No			
yang-notif-native	Yes	No	NA	No	No	No			
Encodings	XML	NA	NA	kvGPB, JSON	JSON_IETF	NA	JSON	GPB, JSON	GPB, JSON
Platforms	IOS XE	IOS XE	IOS XR	IOS XE, NX-OS, IOS XR	NX-OS 9.3(5)	NX-OS 9.3(5)	NX-OS	IOS XR	IOS XR

NOTE The yang streaming table row references are specific to IOS XE platforms.

Configuring MDT in IOS-XR

The following YANG models are used to configure and monitor MDT:

- Cisco-IOS-XR-telemetry-model-driven-cfg.yang and openconfig-telemetry.yang—Configure MDT using NETCONF or merge-config over gRPC.
- Cisco-IOS-XR-telemetry-model-driven-oper.yang—Get operational information about MDT.

As previously mentioned, the sensor path, transport, and encoding are key considerations in enabling MDT. The mode, whether dial-out or dial-in, must also be determined.

NOTE From IOS-XR Release 6.1.1, Cisco introduced support for the 64-bit Linux-based IOS XR operating system. The 64-bit platforms, such as NCS5500, NCS5000, and ASR9000, support gRPC, UDP, and TCP protocols. All 32-bit IOS XR platforms, such as CRS and legacy ASR9000, support only the TCP protocol. TCP, in this sense, uses the familiar three-way handshaking without the benefits of gRPC, which also uses TCP, but with HTTP/2 for advanced traffic forwarding.

Configuring Dial-Out Mode

With dial-out mode, the network element initiates a session to the telemetry receiver(s) based on the subscription.

The process to configure a dial-out mode involves these steps:

- Create a destination group.
- Create a sensor group.
- Create a subscription.
- Verify the dial-out configuration.

Step 1: Create a Destination Group

A destination group specifies the destination address, port, encoding, and transport that the network element uses to send out telemetry data. Example 12-1 shows the configuration template.

Example 12-1 *Configuration Template for Creating a Destination Group*

```
telemetry model-driven
  destination-group <group-name>
  vrf <vrf-name>
  address family ipv4 <IP-address> port <port-number>
    encoding <encoding-format>
    protocol <transport>
    commit
```

NOTE Your implementation may not require virtual routing and forwarding (VRF), so the next command may not apply in your implementation.

Example 12-2 shows the destination group DestGroup1 created for TCP dial-out configuration with encoding of self-describing-gpb (reflecting key-value Google Protocol Buffers).

Example 12-2 *Destination Group for TCP Dial-Out*

```
Router(config)# telemetry model-driven
Router(config-model-driven)# destination-group DestGroup1
Router(config-model-driven-dest)# address family ipv4 192.168.1.10 port 5432
Router(config-model-driven-dest-addr)# encoding self-describing-gpb
Router(config-model-driven-dest-addr)# protocol tcp
Router(config-model-driven-dest-addr)# commit
```

To use UDP dial-out, replace **protocol tcp** with **protocol udp**.

Note that model-driven telemetry with UDP is not suitable for critical production networks. There is no retry if a message is dropped before it reaches the collector. TCP dial-out is suggested for critical product networks because a retry is possible in potentially lossy environments.

To use gRPC dial-out, you need to address a few more considerations. First, ensure that the network element is a 64-bit platform. The gRPC protocol supports TLS; model-driven telemetry uses TLS to dial out by default. The certificate for the receiver-server must be copied to the network element's /misc/config/grpc/dialout/ flash storage directory. Example 12-3 depicts the certificate store.

Example 12-3 *Certificate Store on a Device*

```
RP/0/RP0/CPU0:ios# run
Mon Feb 24 13:10:13.713 UTC
[xr-vm_node0_RP0_CPU0:~]$ls -l /misc/config/grpc/dialout/
total 4
-rw-r--r-- 1 root root 4017 Feb 19 14:22 dialout.pem
[xr-vm_node0_RP0_CPU0:~]$
```

The CommonName (CN) used in the certificate must be configured similarly to the previous example with an additional protocol parameter defined as **protocol grpc tls-hostname** ***<CommonName>***.

For dev-test environments or where you want to bypass the TLS option, modify the protocol parameter to use **protocol grpc no-tls**.

Step 2: Create a Sensor Group

A sensor group specifies one or more YANG models to be streamed. Example 12-4 shows the configuration template.

Example 12-4 *Configuration Template for Creating a Sensor Group*

```
telemetry model-driven
   sensor-group <group-name>
      sensor-path <XR YANG model>
      commit
```

Example 12-5 depicts a more complete representation of a sample configuration.

Example 12-5 *Sensor Group for Dial-Out with the YANG Model for Interface Statistics*

```
Router(config)# telemetry model-driven
Router(config-model-driven)# sensor-group SensorGroup1
Router(config-model-driven-snsr-grp)# sensor-path Cisco-IOS-XR-
infra-statsd-oper:infra-statistics/interfaces/interface/latest/
generic-counters
Router(config-model-driven-snsr-grp)# commit
```

NOTE See "Picking Sensor Paths and Metrics" later in this chapter for additional guidance on identifying YANG models and sensor paths.

Step 3: Create a Subscription

A subscription associates a destination group with a sensor group and sets the streaming frequency—sample-interval-based or event-based telemetry. Example 12-6 shows a configuration template for deploying a subscription.

Example 12-6 *Configuration Template for Creating a Subscription*

```
telemetry model-driven
   subscription <subscription-name>
      sensor-group-id <sensor-group> sample-interval <interval>
      destination-id <destination-group>
      source-interface <source-interface>
   commit
```

NOTE The source-interface configuration syntax may not be required in your implementation.

Example 12-7 shows the subscription Subscription1 that is created to associate the sensor group and destination group and to configure an interval of 20 seconds to stream data.

Example 12-7 *Subscription for Sample-Interval-Based Dial-Out Configuration*

```
Router(config)# telemetry model-driven
Router(config-model-driven)# subscription Subscription1
Router(config-model-driven-subs)# sensor-group-id SensorGroup1 sample-interval 20000
Router(config-model-driven-subs)# destination-id DestGroup1
Router(config-mdt-subscription)# commit
```

If a sample-interval is set to 0, then event-based telemetry is provisioned. The network element streams updates to the destination-receiver when measurements change. This method is more efficient when you're monitoring items such as interface or module state. In a periodic sample-interval configuration, the same value may be returned over and over.

Time-0 Interface: Up

Time+1 Interface: Up

Time+2 Interface: Up

Time+3 Interface: Up

Consider Example 12-8, where event-based dial-out configuration is used for more efficiency in monitoring the interface state.

Example 12-8 *Configuration Template for Event-Based Dial-Out*

```
telemetry model-driven
 destination-group DestGroup1
  address family ipv4 192.168.1.10 port 5432
   encoding self-describing-gpb
   protocol grpc tls-hostname telem-receiver.example.com
  !
 !
 sensor-group SensorGroup1
  sensor-path Cisco-IOS-XR-pfi-im-cmd-oper:interfaces/interface-xr/interface/state
!
 subscription Subscription2
  sensor-group-id SensorGroup1 sample-interval 0
  destination-id DestGroup1
!
```

Step 4: Verify the Dial-Out Configuration

Use the following command to verify that you have correctly configured the network element for dial-out:

```
Router# show telemetry model-driven subscription <subscription-group-name>
```

Example 12-9 shows the results of this command output for reference.

Example 12-9 *Validation for TCP Dial-Out*

```
Router# show telemetry model-driven subscription Subscription1
Tue Feb 25 16:22:31.320 UTC
Subscription: Subscription1                    State: ACTIVE
-------------
  Sensor groups:
  Id                 Interval(ms)        State
  SensorGroup1            30000               Resolved
  Destination Groups:
  Id                 Encoding            Transport   State    Port     IP
  DestGroup1            self-describing-gpb tcp         Active  5432     192.168.1.10
```

If you use gRPC dial-out, the results would be slightly different, as seen in Example 12-10.

Example 12-10 *Validation for gRPC Dial-Out*

```
Router# show telemetry model-driven subscription Subscription2
Tue Feb 25 16:27:44.635 UTC
Subscription: Subscription2                    State: ACTIVE
-------------
  Sensor groups:
  Id                 Interval(ms)        State
  SensorGroup2            30000               Resolved
  Destination Groups:
  Id                 Encoding            Transport   State    Port     IP
  DestGroup2            self-describing-gpb grpc        ACTIVE       57500
192.168.1.10
```

Configuring Dial-In Mode

In a dial-in mode, the destination (telemetry receiver) initiates a session to the network element and subscribes to data to be streamed.

The process to configure a dial-in mode involves these tasks:

- Enable gRPC.
- Create a sensor group.
- Create a subscription.
- Validate the configuration.

Step 1: Enable gRPC

Configure the gRPC server on the network element to accept incoming connections from the collector (telemetry receiver). This will be an HTTP/2 connection:

```
Router# configure
Router (config)# grpc
```

Enable access to a specified port number:

```
Router (config-grpc)# port <port-number>
```

The <*port-number*> range is from 57344 to 57999. If the port number is already in use, an error is displayed.

In the configuration mode, set the session parameters:

```
Router (config)# grpc{ address-family | dscp | max-request-per-
user | max-request-total | max-streams | max-streams-per-user |
no-tls | service-layer | tls-cipher | tls-mutual | tls-trustpoint
| vrf }
```

Table 12-5 shows gRPC options.

Table 12-5 gRPC Options and Functionality

grpc Option	Function
address-family	Sets the address family identifier type.
dscp	Sets QoS marking DSCP on the transmitted gRPC.
max-request-per-user	Sets the maximum concurrent requests per user.
max-request-total	Sets the maximum concurrent requests in total.
max-streams	Sets the maximum number of concurrent gRPC requests. The maximum subscription limit is 128 requests. The default is 32 requests.
max-streams-per-user	Sets the maximum concurrent gRPC requests for each user. The maximum subscription limit is 128 requests. The default is 32 requests.
no-tls	Disables Transport Layer Security (TLS). TLS is enabled by default. Using this option is not advised unless security impact is well understood.
service-layer	Enables the gRPC service layer configuration.
tls-cipher	Enables the gRPC TLS cipher suites.
tls-mutual	Sets the mutual authentication.
tls-trustpoint	Configures trustpoint.
server-vrf	Enables server vrf.

Commit the configuration:

```
Router(config-grpc)# commit
```

Example 12-11 shows the output of the **show grpc** command. The sample output displays the gRPC configuration when TLS is enabled on the network element.

Example 12-11 grpc *Command Output*

```
Router# show grpc

Address family               : ipv4
Port                         : 57300
VRF                          : global-vrf
TLS                          : enabled
TLS mutual                   : disabled
Trustpoint                   : none
Maximum requests             : 128
Maximum requests per user    : 10
Maximum streams              : 32
Maximum streams per user     : 32

TLS cipher suites
  Default                    : none
  Enable                     : none
  Disable                    : none

  Operational enable         : ecdhe-rsa-chacha20-poly1305
                             : ecdhe-ecdsa-chacha20-poly1305
                             : ecdhe-rsa-aes128-gcm-sha256
                             : ecdhe-ecdsa-aes128-gcm-sha256
                             : ecdhe-rsa-aes256-gcm-sha384
                             : ecdhe-ecdsa-aes256-gcm-sha384
                             : ecdhe-rsa-aes128-sha
                             : ecdhe-ecdsa-aes128-sha
                             : ecdhe-rsa-aes256-sha
                             : ecdhe-ecdsa-aes256-sha
                             : aes128-gcm-sha256
                             : aes256-gcm-sha384
                             : aes128-sha
                             : aes256-sha
  Operational disable        : none
```

Step 2: Create a Sensor Group

A sensor-group specifies one or more YANG models to be streamed. Example 12-12 shows a configuration template for creating a sensor group.

Example 12-12 *Configuration Template for Creating a Sensor Group*

```
telemetry model-driven
   sensor-group <group-name>
      sensor-path <XR YANG model>
      commit
```

Example 12-13 shows the sensor group SensorGroup3 created for gRPC dial-in configuration with the OpenConfig YANG model for interfaces.

Example 12-13 *Sample Configuration of a Sensor Group for gRPC Dial-In*

```
Router(config)# telemetry model-driven
Router(config-model-driven)# sensor-group SensorGroup3
Router(config-model-driven-snsr-grp)# sensor-path openconfig-interfaces:interfaces/
interface
Router(config-model-driven-snsr-grp)# commit
```

Step 3: Create a Subscription

A subscription associates a sensor group with a streaming frequency—sample-interval-based or event-based telemetry. Example 12-14 depicts a configuration template for creating a subscription.

Example 12-14 *Configuration Template for Creating a Subscription*

```
telemetry model-driven
   subscription <subscription-name>
      sensor-group-id <sensor-group> sample-interval <interval>
      destination-id <destination-group>
   commit
```

Example 12-15 shows the subscription Subscription3 that is created to associate the sensor group with an interval of 20 seconds to stream data.

Example 12-15 *Subscription for gRPC Dial-In*

```
Router(config)# telemetry model-driven
Router(config-model-driven)# subscription Subscription3
Router(config-model-driven-subs)# sensor-group-id SensorGroup3 sample-interval 20000
Router(config-mdt-subscription)# commit
```

Step 4: Validate the Configuration

Use the command shown in Example 12-16 to verify that you have correctly configured the router for gRPC dial-in.

Example 12-16 *Validating Telemetry Subscription*

```
Router# show telemetry model-driven subscription

Example: Validation for gRPC Dial-in
Router# show telemetry model-driven subscription Subscription3
Wed Feb 26 14:31:12.473 UTC
Subscription: Subscription3
-------------
  State:      ACTIVE
  Sensor groups:
  Id: SensorGroup3
    Sample Interval:     20000 ms
    Sensor Path:         openconfig-interfaces:interfaces/interface
    Sensor Path State:   Resolved

  Destination Groups:
  Group Id: DialIn_1005
    Destination IP:      192.168.1.10
    Destination Port:    44841
    Encoding:            self-describing-gpb
    Transport:           dialin
    State:               Active
    Total bytes sent:    13909
    Total packets sent:  14
    Last Sent time:      2020-02-26 14:29:25.131464901 +0000

  Collection Groups:
  ------------------
    Id: 2
    Sample Interval:     30000 ms
    Encoding:            self-describing-gpb
    Num of collection:   5
    Collection time:     Min:   24 ms Max:   41 ms
    Total time:          Min:   24 ms Avg:   41 ms Max:   54 ms
    Total Deferred:      0
    Total Send Errors:   0
    Total Send Drops:    0
    Total Other Errors:  0
    Last Collection Start: 2020-02-26 14:20:25.134464823 +0000
    Last Collection End: 2020-02-26 14:29:24.032887433 +0000
    Sensor Path:         openconfig-interfaces:interfaces/interface
```

Picking Sensor Paths and Metrics

As you saw in a previous section, one of the common activities to set up streaming telemetry is to define a sensor group. The sensor group would contain one or more sensor paths. It might be helpful to think of it like SNMP MIB objects that are being polled (or pushed, as in the desirable case with streaming telemetry). So how do you pick sensor paths? Fortunately, there are several methods to do this. Sensor paths come from the YANG models that are most commonly defined by feature or functionality. Take, for example, some of the sensor paths used in the previous configuration examples:

```
openconfig-interfaces:interfaces/interface

Cisco-IOS-XR-pfi-im-cmd-oper:interfaces/interface-xr/interface/
state
```

Researching Public Documentation

One method to find sensor paths is to review public documentation. Cisco publishes its vendor-specific YANG models on GitHub and Yang Catalog. The following URLs provide access to many vendors' hardware-specific YANG models, along with standards bodies' models for services:

https://github.com/YangModels/yang/tree/master/vendor/cisco

https://yangcatalog.org

Figure 12-6 shows the Cisco YANG model repository on GitHub.

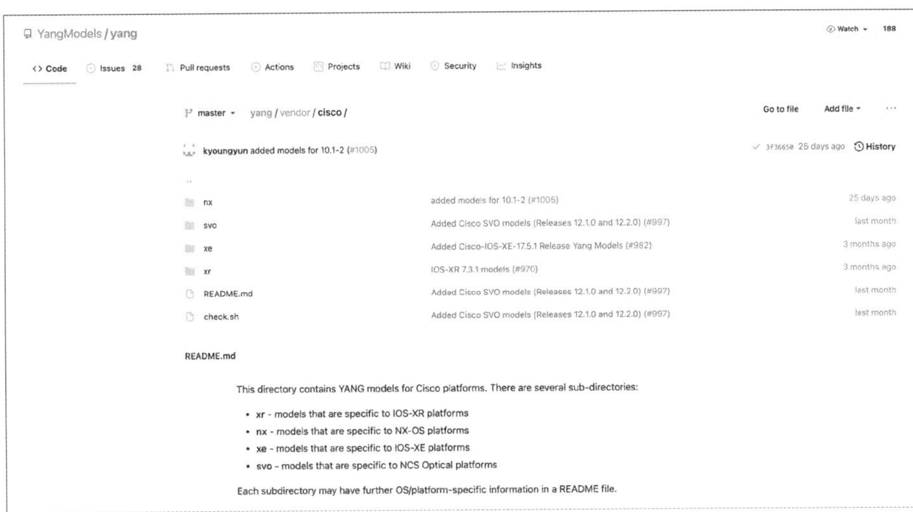

Figure 12-6 *Cisco YANG Model Repository on GitHub*

Additionally, you should be aware that there is increasing support for the OpenConfig data models. You can find them at https://github.com/openconfig/public/tree/master/release/models.

Although the documentation method provides visibility into the entire complement of YANG models, it doesn't guarantee device support. Testing the support or finding other documentation that verifies the support is important. For this point, getting the model support declarations from the device itself is more effective.

Extracting Model Support from the Device—NETCONF Manually

In Chapter 11, "NETCONF and RESTCONF," we reviewed NETCONF capabilities. You can use that information to extract the YANG models a device supports. Refer to that chapter to refresh your memory on how to enable NETCONF/YANG in your environment. For this next example, let's use the DevNet *IOS XE on CSR Latest Code Always On* sandbox lab environment. It is described more fully at https://devnetsandbox.cisco.com/RM/Diagram/Index/7b4d4209-a17c-4bc3-9b38-f15184e53a94?diagramType=Topology.

Because this sandbox lab environment is already online and enabled, you just need to use the target reference and credentials described in the preceding link to manually obtain the NETCONF capabilities. You can do this through a simple SSH connection:

```
client-host$ ssh -s USER@DEVICE -p 830 netconf
```

The device responds with a capabilities exchange, which could be hundreds of lines long, reflecting all the features and YANG models that are supported and installed. You can see a NETCONF capabilities exchange in Example 12-17.

Example 12-17 *NETCONF Capabilities Exchange Dialogue*

```
client-host$ ssh -s developer@sandbox-iosxe-latest-1.cisco.com -p 830 netconf
developer@sandbox-iosxe-latest-1.cisco.com's password: ********
<?xml version="1.0" encoding="UTF-8"?>
<hello xmlns="urn:ietf:params:xml:ns:netconf:base:1.0">
<capabilities>
<capability>urn:ietf:params:netconf:base:1.0</capability>
<capability>urn:ietf:params:netconf:base:1.1</capability>
<capability>urn:ietf:params:netconf:capability:writable-running:1.0</capability>
<capability>urn:ietf:params:netconf:capability:rollback-on-error:1.0</capability>
<capability>urn:ietf:params:netconf:capability:validate:1.0</capability>
<capability>urn:ietf:params:netconf:capability:validate:1.1</capability>
<capability>urn:ietf:params:netconf:capability:xpath:1.0</capability>
[ . . . TRIMMED . . .]
<capability>http://cisco.com/ns/yang/Cisco-IOS-XE-aaa?module=Cisco-IOS-XE-aaa&amp;
revision=2020-07-01</capability>
<capability>http://cisco.com/ns/yang/Cisco-IOS-XE-aaa-oper?module=Cisco-IOS-XE-aaa-
oper&amp;revision=2019-05-01</capability>
<capability>http://cisco.com/ns/yang/Cisco-IOS-XE-acl?module=Cisco-IOS-XE-acl&amp;
revision=2020-03-01</capability>
<capability>http://cisco.com/ns/yang/Cisco-IOS-XE-acl-oper?module=Cisco-IOS-XE-acl-
oper&amp;revision=2020-03-01</capability>
<capability>http://cisco.com/ns/yang/Cisco-IOS-XE-app-hosting-cfg?module=Cisco-
IOS-XE-app-hosting-cfg&amp;revision=2020-03-01</capability>
<capability>http://cisco.com/ns/yang/Cisco-IOS-XE-app-hosting-oper?module=Cisco-
IOS-XE-app-hosting-oper&amp;revision=2019-05-01</capability>
<capability>http://cisco.com/ns/yang/Cisco-IOS-XE-arp?module=Cisco-IOS-XE-arp&amp;
revision=2019-07-01</capability>
<capability>http://cisco.com/ns/yang/Cisco-IOS-XE-arp-oper?module=Cisco-IOS-XE-
arp-oper&amp;revision=2019-05-01</capability>
<capability>http://cisco.com/ns/yang/Cisco-IOS-XE-atm?module=Cisco-IOS-XE-atm&amp;
revision=2020-07-01</capability>
```

```
<capability>http://cisco.com/ns/yang/Cisco-IOS-XE-bba-group?module=Cisco-IOS-XE-
bba-group&amp;revision=2019-07-01</capability>
<capability>http://cisco.com/ns/yang/Cisco-IOS-XE-bfd?module=Cisco-IOS-XE-bfd&amp;
revision=2020-07-01</capability>
<capability>http://cisco.com/ns/yang/Cisco-IOS-XE-bfd-oper?module=Cisco-IOS-XE-
bfd-oper&amp;revision=2019-05-01</capability>
<capability>http://cisco.com/ns/yang/Cisco-IOS-XE-bgp?module=Cisco-IOS-XE-bgp&amp;
revision=2020-07-01</capability>
<capability>http://cisco.com/ns/yang/Cisco-IOS-XE-bgp-common-oper?module=Cisco-
IOS-XE-bgp-common-oper&amp;revision=2019-05-01</capability>
<capability>http://cisco.com/ns/yang/Cisco-IOS-XE-bgp-oper?module=Cisco-IOS-XE-bgp-
oper&amp;revision=2019-11-01</capability>
<capability>http://cisco.com/ns/yang/Cisco-IOS-XE-bgp-route-oper?module=Cisco-IOS-
XE-bgp-route-oper&amp;revision=2019-05-01</capability>
<capability>http://cisco.com/ns/yang/Cisco-IOS-XE-bridge-domain?module=Cisco-IOS-XE-
bridge-domain&amp;revision=2020-03-01</capability>
[ . . . TRIMMED . . .]
<capability>http://openconfig.net/yang/bgp-policy?module=openconfig-bgp-policy
&amp;revision=2016-06-21&amp;deviations=cisco-xe-openconfig-bgp-policy-deviation</
capability>
<capability>http://openconfig.net/yang/bgp-types?module=openconfig-bgp-types&amp;
revision=2016-06-21</capability>
<capability>http://openconfig.net/yang/cisco-xe-openconfig-if-ip-deviation?module=
cisco-xe-openconfig-if-ip-deviation&amp;revision=2017-03-04</capability>
<capability>http://openconfig.net/yang/cisco-xe-openconfig-interfaces-deviation?
module=cisco-xe-openconfig-interfaces-deviation&amp;revision=2018-08-21</capability>
<capability>http://openconfig.net/yang/cisco-xe-routing-csr-openconfig-platform-
deviation?module=cisco-xe-routing-csr-openconfig-platform-deviation&amp;revis
ion=2010-10-09</capability>
<capability>http://openconfig.net/yang/cisco-xe-routing-openconfig-system-deviation?
module=cisco-xe-routing-openconfig-system-deviation&amp;revision=2017-11-27</
capability>
<capability>http://openconfig.net/yang/fib-types?module=openconfig-aft-types&amp;
revision=2017-01-13</capability>
[ . . . TRIMMED . . . ]
<capability>
        urn:ietf:params:netconf:capability:notification:1.1
      </capability>
</capabilities>
<session-id>201</session-id></hello>]]>]]>
```

In the highlights in Example 12-17, you can see that many Cisco vendor-specific YANG models are supported—more than 100. The highlighted samples should be familiar networking functions. The search criteria to filter more could be as simple as

```
<capability>http://cisco.com/ns/yang/Cisco-*
```

Many OpenConfig YANG models also are supported—almost 60. You can find them with the following search criteria:

```
<capability>http://openconfig.net/yang/*
```

Extracting Model Support from the Device—Python and NETCONF

This book about network programmability and DevNet concerns wouldn't be complete without Python scripts. You can also use the following handy Python method to connect to the device via NETCONF and extract the capabilities that you saw from the manual SSH method just described.

You can start by making a Python virtual environment to contain your project-specific modules and Python script, as seen in Example 12-18. Make sure you have a Python3 environment on your laptop or virtual machine. After you create the virtual environment, you can import the ncclient module, which is a useful Python library for client-side scripting and application development with the NETCONF protocol.

Example 12-18 *Installing ncclient*

```
devnetuser@mylaptop Python % python3 -m venv pynetconf
devnetuser@mylaptop Python % cd pynetconf
devnetuser@mylaptop pynetconf % source bin/activate
(pynetconf) devnetuser@mylaptop pynetconf % pip install ncclient
Collecting ncclient
  Downloading ncclient-0.6.12.tar.gz (106 kB)
     |████████████████████████████████| 106 kB 2.9 MB/s
Requirement already satisfied: setuptools>0.6 in ./lib/python3.9/site-packages (from
ncclient) (56.0.0)
Collecting paramiko>=1.15.0
  Downloading paramiko-2.7.2-py2.py3-none-any.whl (206 kB)
     |████████████████████████████████| 206 kB 3.9 MB/s
Collecting lxml>=3.3.0
  Downloading lxml-4.6.3-cp39-cp39-macosx_10_9_x86_64.whl (4.6 MB)
     |████████████████████████████████| 4.6 MB 4.2 MB/s
Collecting six
  Downloading six-1.16.0-py2.py3-none-any.whl (11 kB)
Collecting cryptography>=2.5
  Downloading cryptography-3.4.7-cp36-abi3-macosx_10_10_x86_64.whl (2.0 MB)
     |████████████████████████████████| 2.0 MB 12.4 MB/s
Collecting bcrypt>=3.1.3
  Downloading bcrypt-3.2.0-cp36-abi3-macosx_10_9_x86_64.whl (31 kB)
Collecting pynacl>=1.0.1
  Downloading PyNaCl-1.4.0-cp35-abi3-macosx_10_10_x86_64.whl (380 kB)
     |████████████████████████████████| 380 kB 10.7 MB/s
Collecting cffi>=1.1
  Downloading cffi-1.14.5-cp39-cp39-macosx_10_9_x86_64.whl (177 kB)
     |████████████████████████████████| 177 kB 8.5 MB/s
Collecting pycparser
  Downloading pycparser-2.20-py2.py3-none-any.whl (112 kB)
     |████████████████████████████████| 112 kB 9.8 MB/s
Using legacy 'setup.py install' for ncclient, since package 'wheel' is not
installed.
```

```
Installing collected packages: pycparser, six, cffi, pynacl, cryptography, bcrypt,
paramiko, lxml, ncclient
    Running setup.py install for ncclient ... done
Successfully installed bcrypt-3.2.0 cffi-1.14.5 cryptography-3.4.7 lxml-4.6.3 nccli-
ent-0.6.12 paramiko-2.7.2 pycparser-2.20 pynacl-1.4.0 six-1.16.0
(pynetconf) devnetuser@mylaptop pynetconf %
```

Next, the Python script in Example 12-19 helps extract the YANG module capabilities from a device. Here, you can use the DevNet *IOS XE on CSR Latest Code Always On* sandbox lab environment again.

Example 12-19 *Simple Python Script to Extract NETCONF Capabilities*

```
from ncclient import manager
with manager.connect(
    host='sandbox-iosxe-latest-1.cisco.com',
    port=830,
    username='developer',
    password='C1sco12345',
    device_params={'name': 'csr'}
) as session:
    for capability in session.server_capabilities:
        print(capability)
```

Now, execute this Python script, using the process shown in Example 12-20.

Example 12-20 *Executing pynetconf.py Script*

```
(pynetconf) devnetuser@mylaptop pynetconf % python3 pynetconf.py
urn:ietf:params:netconf:base:1.0
urn:ietf:params:netconf:base:1.1
urn:ietf:params:netconf:capability:writable-running:1.0
urn:ietf:params:netconf:capability:rollback-on-error:1.0
[ . . . TRIMMED . . . ]
http://cisco.com/ns/yang/Cisco-IOS-XE-aaa?module=Cisco-IOS-XE-aaa&revision=2020-07-01
http://cisco.com/ns/yang/Cisco-IOS-XE-aaa-oper?module=Cisco-IOS-XE-aaa-
oper&revision=2019-05-01
http://cisco.com/ns/yang/Cisco-IOS-XE-acl?module=Cisco-IOS-XE-acl&revision=2020-03-01
http://cisco.com/ns/yang/Cisco-IOS-XE-acl-oper?module=Cisco-IOS-XE-acl-
oper&revision=2020-03-01
http://cisco.com/ns/yang/Cisco-IOS-XE-app-hosting-cfg?module=Cisco-IOS-XE-app-host-
ing-cfg&revision=2020-03-01
http://cisco.com/ns/yang/Cisco-IOS-XE-app-hosting-oper?module=Cisco-IOS-XE-app-hos-
ting-oper&revision=2019-05-01
http://cisco.com/ns/yang/Cisco-IOS-XE-arp?module=Cisco-IOS-XE-arp&revision=2019-07-01
http://cisco.com/ns/yang/Cisco-IOS-XE-arp-oper?module=Cisco-IOS-XE-arp-
oper&revision=2019-05-01
http://cisco.com/ns/yang/Cisco-IOS-XE-atm?module=Cisco-IOS-XE-atm&revision=2020-07-01
[ . . . TRIMMED . . . ]
```

```
http://openconfig.net/yang/bgp?module=openconfig-bgp&revision=2016-06-21
http://openconfig.net/yang/bgp-policy?module=openconfig-bgp-policy&revision=2016-
06-21&deviations=cisco-xe-openconfig-bgp-policy-deviation
http://openconfig.net/yang/bgp-types?module=openconfig-bgp-types&revision=2016-06-21
[ . . . TRIMMED . . . ]
http://openconfig.net/yang/interfaces?module=openconfig-interfaces&revision=2018-
01-05&deviations=cisco-xe-openconfig-if-ip-deviation,cisco-xe-openconfig-interfaces-
deviation,cisco-xe-routing-openconfig-vlan-deviation
http://openconfig.net/yang/interfaces/aggregate?module=openconfig-if-
aggregate&revision=2018-01-05
http://openconfig.net/yang/interfaces/ethernet?module=openconfig-if-
ethernet&revision=2018-01-05
http://openconfig.net/yang/interfaces/ip?module=openconfig-if-ip&revision=2018-
01-05&deviations=cisco-xe-openconfig-if-ip-deviation,cisco-xe-openconfig-interfaces-
deviation
http://openconfig.net/yang/interfaces/ip-ext?module=openconfig-if-ip-
ext&revision=2018-01-05
[ . . . TRIMMED . . . ]

        urn:ietf:params:netconf:capability:notification:1.1

(pynetconf) devnetuser@mylaptop pynetconf %
```

In this example, you can again see the Cisco vendor-specific and OpenConfig models. To obtain telemetry, you map the function—BGP, interfaces, AAA, ARP, and so on—to the YANG model name as a reference. The *-oper YANG models are focused on operational statistics, so you can start there when looking for metrics you might associate with dashboards when showing volume, consumption, performance, and so on.

The following list provides some popular YANG models you might be interested in trying out when getting started. A mixture of IOS-XR and IOS-XE models is listed. First, note the model name before the colon (:) and the subtree path afterward. This combination is supplied in the sensor path (or filter path) definition when creating a telemetry configuration. The preceding section includes references on configuration templates.

- Health
  - Cisco-IOS-XR-wdsysmon-fd-oper:system-monitoring/cpu-utilization
  - Cisco-IOS-XR-nto-misc-oper:memory-summary/nodes/node/summary
  - Cisco-IOS-XR-shellutil-oper:system-time/uptime
  - Cisco-IOS-XR-telemetry-model-driven-oper:telemetry-model-driven
  - Cisco-IOS-XE-process-cpu-oper: cpu-usage/cpu-utilization/five-seconds
  - Cisco-IOS-XE-environment-oper
  - Cisco-IOS-XE-memory-oper: memory-statistics
  - Cisco-IOS-XE-platform-software-oper
  - Cisco-IOS-XE-process-memory-oper

- **Interfaces**
  - Cisco-IOS-XR-infra-statsd-oper:infra-statistics/interfaces/interface/latest/generic-counters
  - Cisco-IOS-XR-ipv6-ma-oper:ipv6-network/nodes/node/interface-data/vrfs/vrf/global-briefs/global-brief
  - Cisco-IOS-XR-pfi-im-cmd-oper:interfaces/interface-summary
  - Cisco-IOS-XR-pfi-im-cmd-oper:interfaces/interface-xr/interface
  - Cisco-IOS-XR-ethernet-lldp-oper:lldp/global-lldp/lldp-info
  - Cisco-IOS-XR-ethernet-lldp-oper:lldp/nodes/node/interfaces/interface
  - Cisco-IOS-XR-ethernet-lldp-oper:lldp/nodes/node/neighbors/details/detail
  - ietf-interfaces
  - Openconfig-interfaces
  - Openconfig-network-instance
- **Inventory**
  - Cisco-IOS-XR-plat-chas-invmgr-oper:platform-inventory/racks/rack
- **Optics**
  - Cisco-IOS-XR-controller-optics-oper:optics-oper/optics-ports/optics-port/optics-info
- **Routing**
  - Cisco-IOS-XR-clns-isis-oper:isis/instances/instance/levels/level/adjacencies/adjacency
  - Cisco-IOS-XR-clns-isis-oper:isis/instances/instance/statistics-global
  - Cisco-IOS-XR-ip-rib-ipv4-oper:rib/vrfs/vrf/afs/af/safs/saf/ip-rib-route-table-names/ip-rib-route-table-name/protocol/isis/as/information
  - Cisco-IOS-XR-ipv4-bgp-oper:bgp/instances/instance/instance-active/default-vrf/process-info
  - ietf-ospf
  - ietf-routing
  - Openconfig-routing-policy
- **MPLS Traffic Engineering**
  - Cisco-IOS-XR-mpls-te-oper:mpls-te/tunnels/summary
  - Cisco-IOS-XR-ip-rsvp-oper:rsvp/interface-briefs/interface-brief
  - Cisco-IOS-XR-ip-rsvp-oper:rsvp/counters/interface-messages/interface-message

Digging into the YANG Models

Researching and navigating the YANG models to understand hierarchy, containers, leaves, and available functionality is important. You can glean some information by reviewing the YANG models as documented in the GitHub links mentioned earlier, but the manual method may be a case of last resort. How many times did you revert to reading SNMP MIB files? Fortunately, there are some helpful, graphical tools to help you investigate the YANG models. One such tool is YANG Suite. It replaces a mature Yang Explorer open-source project that needed to be updated due to its dependency on Flash technology.

The next steps are to install Docker on a Linux VM, obtain the YANG Suite docker container, run it, and then use YANG Suite.

Installing Docker to the Linux VM

For this step, start with a virgin Linux virtual machine (RedHat, CentOS, Ubuntu, and so on). You need Docker installed. If it's not there, install it.

To start, you add the repository to the system:

```
mylinuxvm$ sudo dnf config-manager --add-repo=https://
download.docker.com/linux/centos/docker-ce.repo
```

Then install the Docker package:

```
mylinuxvm$ sudo dnf install docker-ce docker-ce-cli containerd.io
```

Next, start the Docker service and add it to autorun:

```
mylinuxvm$ sudo systemctl enable --now docker
```

Some Linux operating systems have client firewalls enabled by default. If so, find out how to enable a masquerade rule. Masquerading is a type of NAT used to link a private network with the Internet. In the CentOS 8 system, you can use these commands to add a masquerade rule:

```
mylinuxvm$ sudo firewall-cmd --zone=public --add-masquerade
-permanent
```

```
mylinuxvm$ sudo firewall-cmd --reload
```

Docker is often installed along with the docker-compose utility, which enables you to deploy a project to another machine simply. To download it, run the following command:

```
mylinuxvm$ sudo curl -L "https://github.com/docker/compose/
releases/download/1.29.2/docker-compose-$(uname -s)-$(uname -m)"
-o /usr/local/bin/docker-compose
```

Make the newly downloaded docker-compose binary executable:

```
mylinuxvm$ sudo chmod +x /usr/local/bin/docker-compose
```

You want to be able to use Docker as a nonroot user, so you must add that user to the docker group. Replace *username* with the desired account in the following command:

```
mylinuxvm$ sudo usermod -aG docker username
```

To pick up all privileges, log out from the system and log in again.

Verify Docker is working properly by pulling down and running a test container, as shown in Example 12-21.

Example 12-21 *Verifying Docker Operation with Hello World*

```
mylinuxvm$ docker run hello-world
Unable to find image 'hello-world:latest' locally
latest: Pulling from library/hello-world
b8dfde127a29: Pull complete
Digest: sha256:9f6ad537c5132bcce57f7a0a20e317228d382c3cd61edae14650eec68b2b345c
Status: Downloaded newer image for hello-world:latest

Hello from Docker!
This message shows that your installation appears to be working correctly.

To generate this message, Docker took the following steps:
 1. The Docker client contacted the Docker daemon.
 2. The Docker daemon pulled the "hello-world" image from the Docker Hub.
    (amd64)
 3. The Docker daemon created a new container from that image which runs the
    executable that produces the output you are currently reading.
 4. The Docker daemon streamed that output to the Docker client, which sent it
    to your terminal.

To try something more ambitious, you can run an Ubuntu container with:
 $ docker run -it ubuntu bash

Share images, automate workflows, and more with a free Docker ID:
 https://hub.docker.com/

For more examples and ideas, visit:
 https://docs.docker.com/get-started/
```

Installing the YANG Suite Docker Image to the Linux VM

Now that you're confident Docker is installed and working, it's time to get the YANG Suite docker container image, shown in Example 12-22.

Example 12-22 *Obtaining YANG Suite from GitHub*

```
mylinuxvm$ git clone https://github.com/CiscoDevNet/yangsuite
Cloning into 'yangsuite'...
remote: Enumerating objects: 727, done.
remote: Counting objects: 100% (727/727), done.
remote: Compressing objects: 100% (495/495), done.
remote: Total 727 (delta 283), reused 610 (delta 215), pack-reused 0
Receiving objects: 100% (727/727), 24.96 MiB | 30.36 MiB/s, done.
Resolving deltas: 100% (283/283), done.
```

Next, you generate self-signed certificates by running a supplied shell script, as described in Example 12-23.

Example 12-23 *Generating Self-Signed Certificates in YANG Suite*

```
mylinuxvm$ cd yangsuite/docker/
mylinuxvm$ ./gen_test_certs.sh
################################################################
## Generating self-signed certificates...                     ##
##                                                             ##
## WARNING: Obtain certificates from a trusted authority!     ##
##                                                             ##
## NOTE: Some browsers may still reject these certificates!! ##
################################################################


Generating a RSA private key
..+++++
.......................+++++
writing new private key to 'nginx/nginx-self-signed.key'
-----
```

Finally, you bring up the docker container by using docker-compose, with Example 12-24 providing the guidance.

Example 12-24 *Starting YANG Suite from the Docker Container*

```
mylinuxvm$ docker-compose up
Creating network "docker_default" with the default driver
Creating volume "docker_static-content" with default driver
Creating volume "docker_uwsgi" with default driver
Building yangsuite
Sending build context to Docker daemon  12.29kB
Step 1/19 : FROM ubuntu:18.04
18.04: Pulling from library/ubuntu
4bbfd2c87b75: Pull complete
d2e110be24e1: Pull complete
889a7173dcfe: Pull complete
Digest: sha256:67b730ece0d34429b455c08124ffd444f021b81e06fa2d9cd0adaf0d0b875182
Status: Downloaded newer image for ubuntu:18.04
[ . . . TRUNCATED . . .]
```

Downloading the container's operating system (Ubuntu 18.04) and other dependencies, such as Python3.6 and nginx, may take several minutes.

After all the downloads are finished and activated, leave the terminal session running and access the console/desktop of the VM to run a browser. Access YANG Suite via the locally running nginx web server at http://127.0.0.1.

You are prompted to accept the End User License Agreement and Privacy Policy, as seen in Figure 12-7.

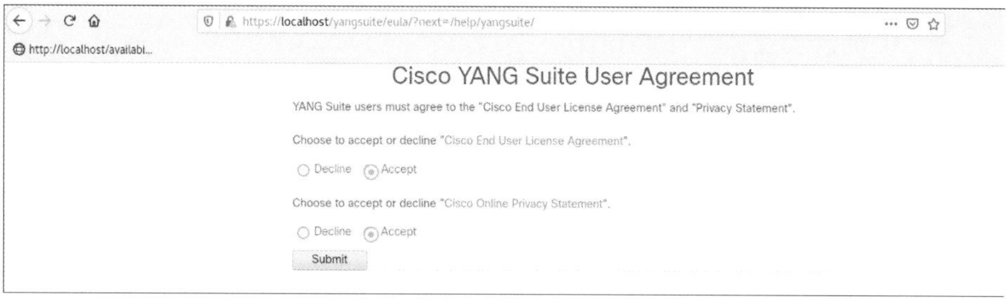

https://localhost/yangsuite/eula/?next=/help/yangsuite/

http://localhost/availabi...

Cisco YANG Suite User Agreement

YANG Suite users must agree to the "Cisco End User License Agreement" and "Privacy Statement".

Choose to accept or decline "Cisco End User License Agreement".

Decline Accept

Choose to accept or decline "Cisco Online Privacy Statement".

Decline Accept

Submit

Figure 12-7 *Cisco YANG Suite Web Portal and User Agreement*

After you accept the agreement and policy, you are presented with a login screen, as shown in Figure 12-8.

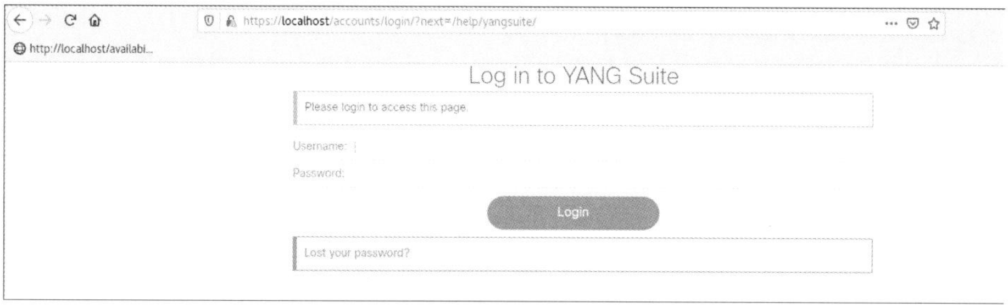

https://localhost/accounts/login/?next=/help/yangsuite/

http://localhost/availabi...

Log in to YANG Suite

Please login to access this page.

Username:

Password:

Login

Lost your password?

Figure 12-8 *Cisco YANG Suite Login Portal*

The default username and password are **admin** and **superuser**. Note that you can change them in the *<installation directory>*/yangsuite/docker/docker-compose.yml file as the services:yangsuite:environment: YS_ADMIN_USER and YS_ADMIN_PASS variables. See Figure 12-9 for an example.

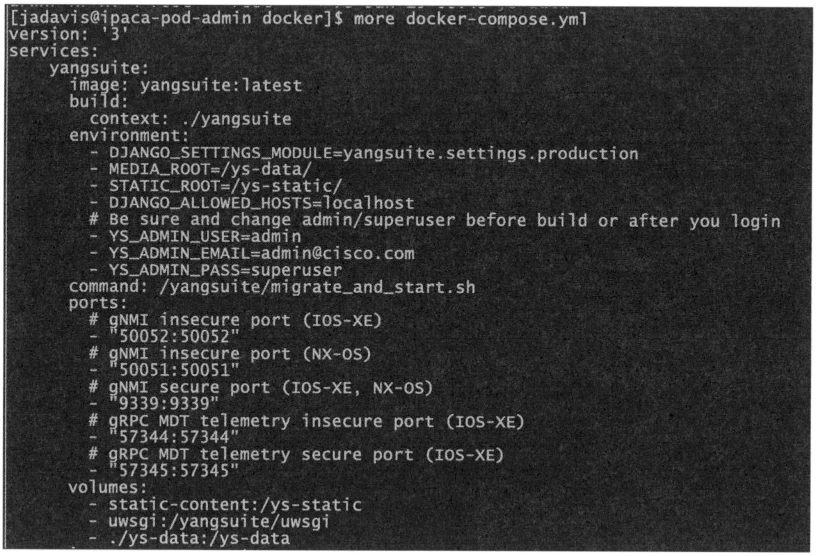

```
[jadavis@ipaca-pod-admin docker]$ more docker-compose.yml
version: '3'
services:
  yangsuite:
    image: yangsuite:latest
    build:
      context: ./yangsuite
    environment:
      - DJANGO_SETTINGS_MODULE=yangsuite.settings.production
      - MEDIA_ROOT=/ys-data/
      - STATIC_ROOT=/ys-static/
      - DJANGO_ALLOWED_HOSTS=localhost
      # Be sure and change admin/superuser before build or after you login
      - YS_ADMIN_USER=admin
      - YS_ADMIN_EMAIL=admin@cisco.com
      - YS_ADMIN_PASS=superuser
    command: /yangsuite/migrate_and_start.sh
    ports:
      # gNMI insecure port (IOS-XE)
      - "50052:50052"
      # gNMI insecure port (NX-OS)
      - "50051:50051"
      # gNMI secure port (IOS-XE, NX-OS)
      - "9339:9339"
      # gRPC MDT telemetry insecure port (IOS-XE)
      - "57344:57344"
      # gRPC MDT telemetry secure port (IOS-XE)
      - "57345:57345"
    volumes:
      - static-content:/ys-static
      - uwsgi:/yangsuite/uwsgi
      - ./ys-data:/ys-data
```

Figure 12-9 *Cisco YANG Suite docker-compose.yml File*

Upon successful login, you see the YANG Suite portal, as shown in Figure 12-10.

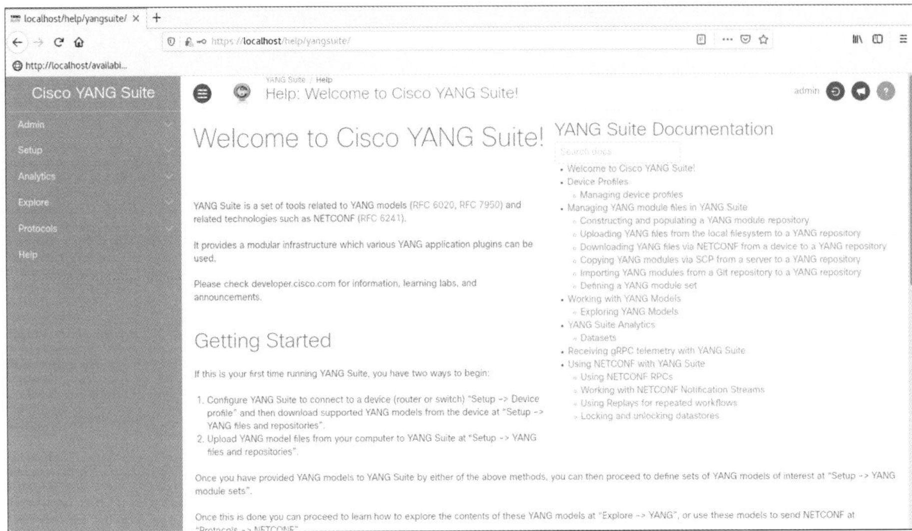

Figure 12-10 *Cisco YANG Suite Initial Portal*

As you can see, the portal suggests the first way to use YANG Suite is to connect to a device and obtain YANG models from it. The second is to load or install them yourself.

For this example, go with the first method. Click the Setup option on the left navigation panel and then Device Profiles. The menu shown in Figure 12-11 then appears.

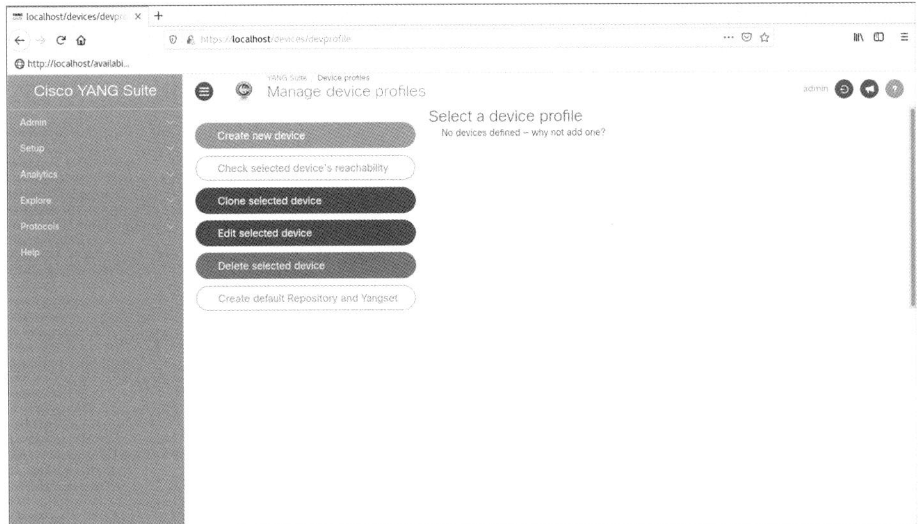

Figure 12-11 *Cisco YANG Suite Device Profile Options*

Click the Create New Device button. You can use the DevNet *IOS XE on CSR Latest Code Always On* sandbox lab environment. It is described more fully at https://devnetsandbox.cisco.com/RM/Diagram/Index/7b4d4209-a17c-4bc3-9b38-f15184e53a94?diagramType=Topology.

You should fill in the New Device Profile fields as shown in Table 12-6.

Table 12-6 Device Profile Field Settings

Field	Value	Notes
Profile Name	DevNet IOS XE	
Description	Always On Sandbox Device	
Address	sandbox-iosxe-latest-1.cisco.com	
Username	developer	
Password	C1sco12345	
Device supports NETCONF	(selected)	
Skip SSH key validation for this device	(selected)	

Your entries should look like those shown in Figure 12-12.

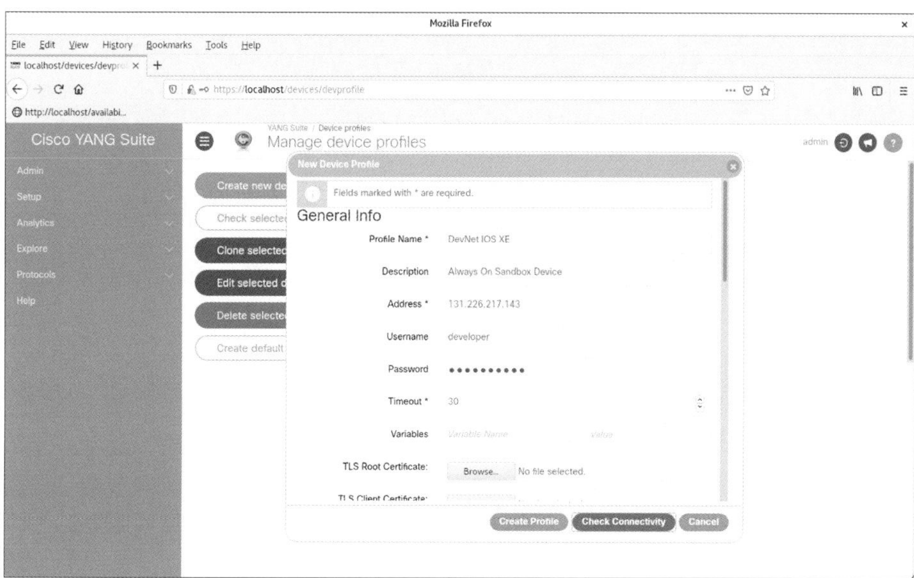

Figure 12-12 *Cisco YANG Suite Device Profile Entry for DevNet Always On Sandbox Device*

Additionally, you can select the Check Connectivity button and get a result, as shown in Figure 12-13.

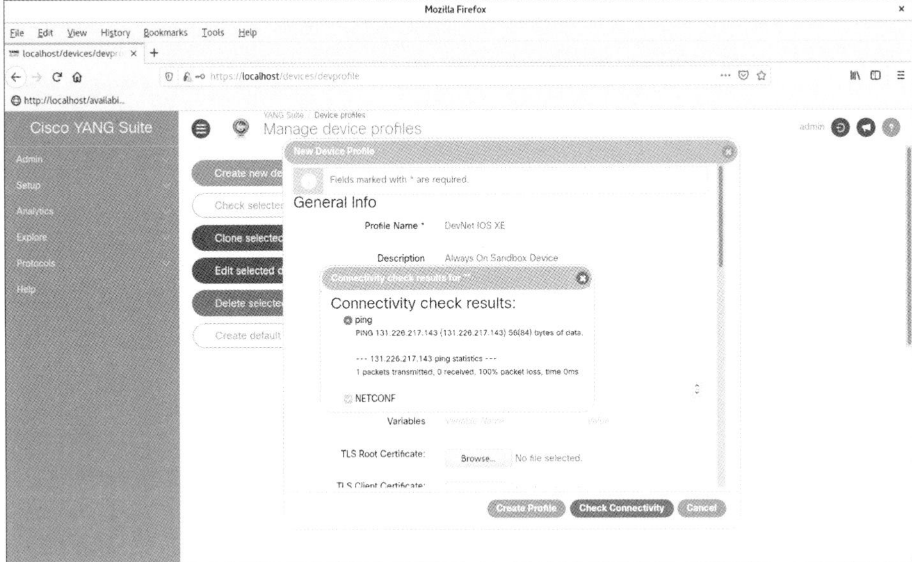

Figure 12-13 *Cisco YANG Suite Device Connectivity Check*

Note that it's fine to have the pings fail because they are blocked in the Sandbox environment. You should see a successful, green NETCONF connection.

Close the connectivity check pop-up window and select the Create Profile button.

Next, select the new DevNet IOS XE device profile in the middle column and select the Create Default Repository and Yangset button (see Figure 12-14) to connect to the device and pull down its YANG models.

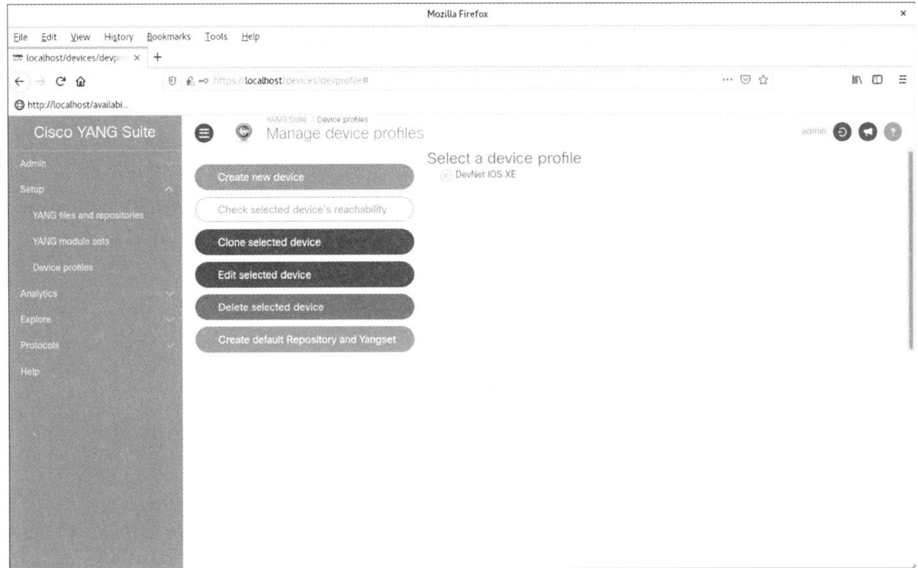

Figure 12-14 *Cisco YANG Suite Option to Create a Default Repository*

The system then retrieves the YANG model information. This process may take several minutes and show a progress bar along the top, as seen in Figure 12-15.

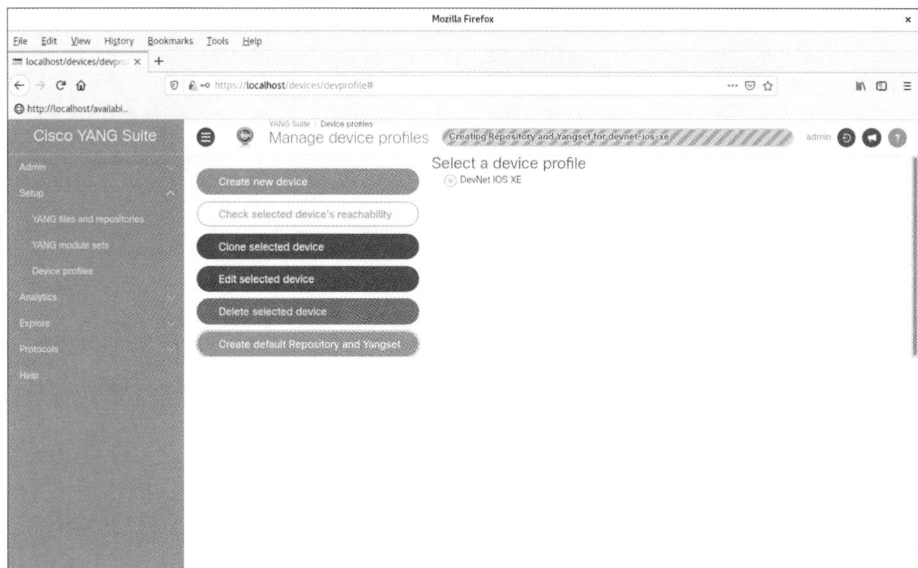

Figure 12-15 *Cisco YANG Suite Progressing Through Device Information Capture*

Eventually, when the process is complete, you see a screen with a success pop-up similar to that shown in Figure 12-16.

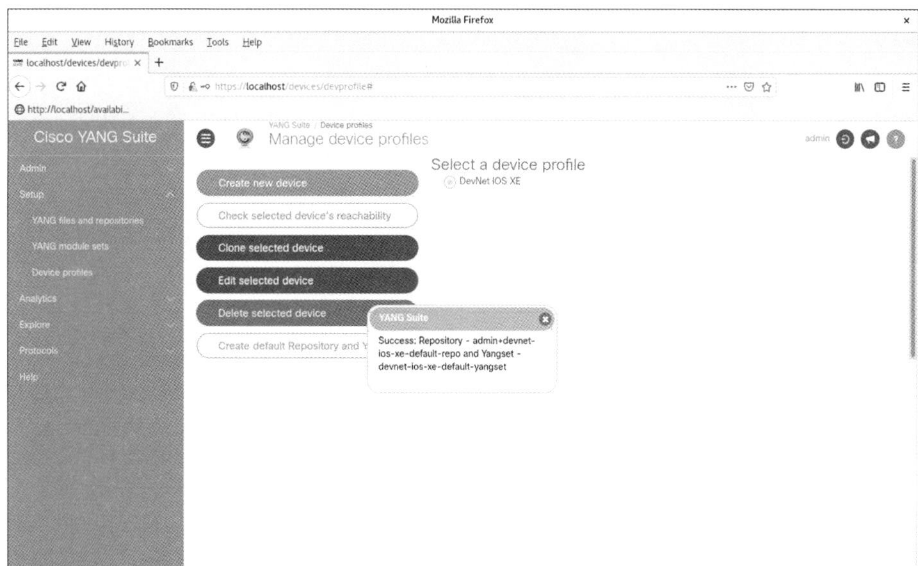

Figure 12-16 *Cisco YANG Suite Success in Connectivity*

Close the pop-up window. On the left-hand navigation panel, select Explore and the YANG option. From the main frame, select the drop-down menu option that reflects the YANG set you just created, probably named devnet-ios-xe-default-yangset. In the Select a YANG Module(s) menu, pick something like the Cisco-IOS-XE-bgp-oper model. Then click the Load Module(s) button on the right side, as shown in Figure 12-17.

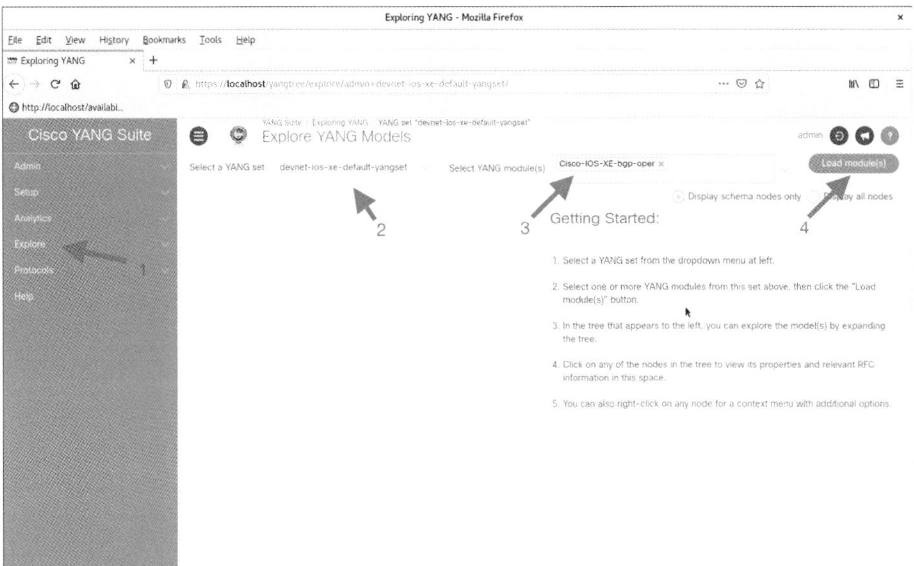

Figure 12-17 *Loading a Module in Cisco YANG Suite*

Feel free to navigate around the web UI and see how YANG models are represented (see Figure 12-18).

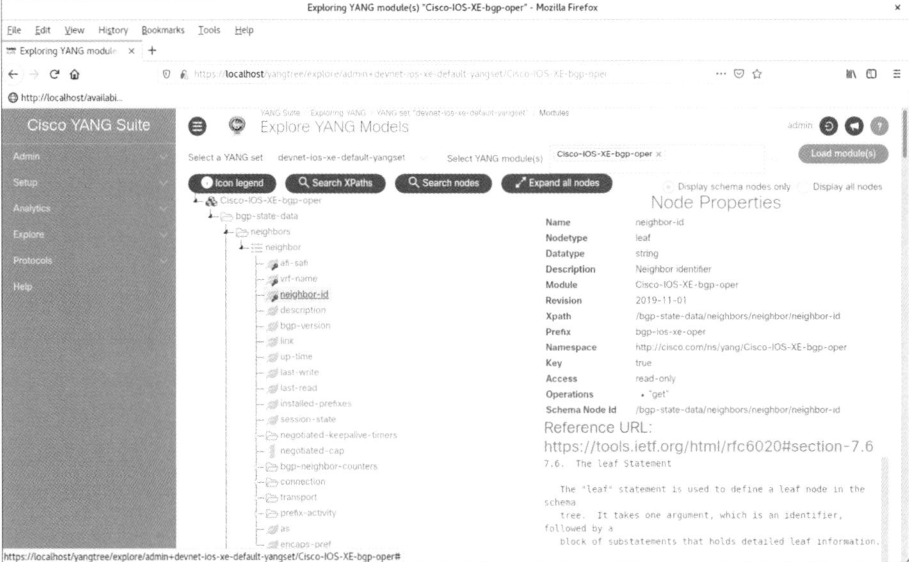

Figure 12-18 *Exploring a YANG Model in Cisco YANG Suite*

Note that when individual leaves are selected, the Node Properties are populated on the right-hand side. The Xpath and Prefix properties are very helpful in forming the streaming telemetry sensor paths for the device or collector configurations.

You now have a solid tool and process for exploring YANG models and developing your desired sensor paths.

Practical Application of Streaming Telemetry

Now let's consider again the cadence-based model-driven telemetry model. Assume you're using a push model of interface statistics on an IOS XE-based platform. IOS XE runs on the Catalyst 9000 series network switches; Catalyst 9800 wireless LAN controllers; routers like the ASR 1000, CSR1000v, and ISR 1000 and 4000s; and other devices in IoT and cable product lines. For this case, target IOS XE 16.6 or newer for MDT support.

For convenience, you can use the preceding section's instructions about using YANG Suite and accessing the DevNet Sandbox Always On IOS XR device. Returning to the YANG Suite and pulling down the models as previously described, you can search for interface type models. Figure 12-19 shows that example.

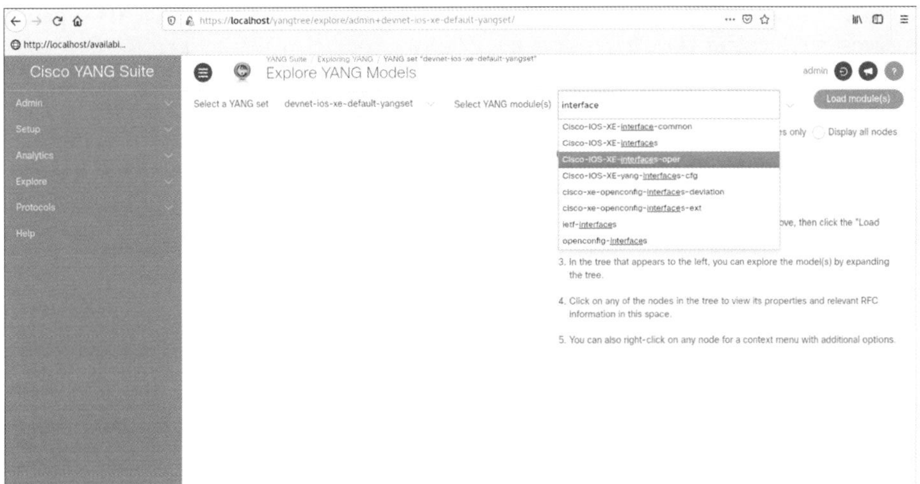

Figure 12-19 *Searching for YANG Models with Interface Names*

You should select the Cisco-IOS-XE-interface-oper model because the oper models have the operational statistics leaves you generally want. Selecting that option and selecting the Load Module(s) button shows the data model in a tree hierarchy. If you expand the main branch of the model, you can see a hierarchy navigating down through *interfaces* and *interface*. Some of the leaf and leaf-list type names should be familiar and self-explanatory. Expanding the *statistics* container, which looks like a folder in YANG Suite, reveals other leaf nodes that should have familiar names, such as *in-octets*, *out-octets*, and *in-unicast-pkts*. For this example, you can settle on selecting the statistics container and viewing the node properties, as seen in Figure 12-20.

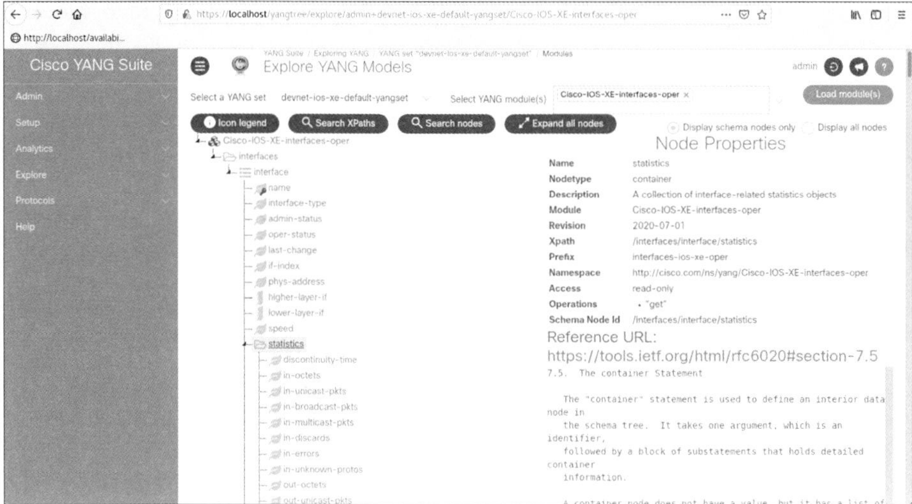

Figure 12-20 *Navigating the Statistics Container in the Interfaces YANG Model*

To build the sensor path reference, you take the prefix, interface-ios-xe-oper, and the Xpath, /interfaces/interface/statistics, to result in the following combined XPath filter:

```
/interface-ios-xe-oper:interfaces/interface/statistics
```

This path would provide telemetry of all nodes below the *statistics* container, which includes the in-octets and out-octets counters you're interested in.

To build a cadence-based configuration in an IOS XE-based device, such as a Cisco CSR1000v, you can enter a configuration similar to that shown in Example 12-25.

Example 12-25 *Configuration Template for Interface Statistics Telemetry*

```
telemetry ietf subscription 100
 encoding encode-kvgpb
 filter xpath /interfaces-ios-xe-oper:interfaces/interface/statistics
 source-address 10.1.1.20
 stream yang-push
 update-policy periodic 1000
 receiver ip address 10.1.1.100 57000 protocol grpc-tcp
```

Example 12-25 uses Google protobufs (GPBs) as key-value pairs, noted as **encoding encode-kvgpb**. It has the **filter xpath** you extracted earlier and uses a **yang-push** streaming model. You define the frequency in centiseconds; for this example, 1000 would be every 10 seconds. Finally, the streaming telemetry receiver IP address and protocol are defined using TCP-based Google RPCs.

If you don't like the preceding configuration template approach, you can push the following XML payload shown in Example 12-26 in a NETCONF session, achieving the same effect.

Example 12-26 *XML Payload for NETCONF Session Creating Interface Statistics Telemetry*


```
<mdt-config-data xmlns="http://cisco.com/ns/yang/Cisco-IOS-XE-mdt-cfg">
    <mdt-subscription>
        <subscription-id>100</subscription-id>
        <base>
            <stream>yang-push</stream>
            <encoding>encode-kvgpb</encoding>
            <source-address>10.1.1.20</source-address>
            <period>1000</period>
            <xpath>/interface-ios-xe-oper:interfaces/interface/statistics</xpath>
        </base>
        <mdt-receivers>
            <address>10.1.1.100</address>
            <port>57000</port>
            <protocol>grpc-tcp</protocol>
        </mdt-receivers>
    </mdt-subscription>
</mdt-config-data>
```


You can check the status of the streaming telemetry with the **show telemetry ietf subscription all detail** command, as seen in Example 12-27.

Example 12-27 *Validating Streaming Telemetry Subscriptions*

```
CSR100V# show telemetry ietf subscription all detail
Telemetry subscription detail:

  Subscription ID: 100
  Type: Configured
  State: Valid
  Stream: yang-push
  Filter:
    Filter type: xpath
    XPath: /interfaces-ios-xe-oper:interfaces/interface/statistics
  Update policy:
    Update Trigger: periodic
    Period: 1000
  Encoding: encode-kvgpb
  Source VRF:
  Source Address: 10.1.1.20
  Notes:

  Receivers:
    Address                                Port     Protocol         Protocol Profile
    -------------------------------------------------------------------------------
    10.1.1.100                             57000    grpc-tcp

CSR100V#
```

Using Telegraph, InfluxDB, and Grafana

An excellent open-source option for a streaming telemetry receiver is the TIG Stack, which includes Telegraf, InfluxDB, and Grafana.

Telegraf is the agent for collecting and reporting metrics and data. It is the receiver or collector of streaming telemetry data. Telegraf uses plug-ins for collecting and reporting metrics. It has integrations to extract metrics, events, and logs from systems it's running on. It can pull metrics from APIs and listen for metrics sourced from StatsD and Kafka. On the output side, it can send metrics to files, message queues, and other endpoints, including InfluxDB, Graphite, OpenTSDB, Kafka, and MQTT.

InfluxDB is the time series database (TSDB) of the stack. InfluxDB is an open-source project written in Go. It is optimized for fast, high-availability storage and retrieval of time series data.

Grafana is also an open-source project. It extracts data from databases like InfluxDB, performs basic or advanced data analytics, and creates dashboards.

Installing InfluxDB

Start by installing InfluxDB. This example uses Ubuntu, specifically Ubuntu Server 20.04.2 LTS, but any Linux distribution should have similar install methods.

First, import the influxdata key to the Ubuntu registry:

```
mdtuser@tig-stack:~$ sudo curl -sL https://repos.influxdata.com/
influxdb.key | sudo apt-key add -
```

Next, add the influxdata repository to the apt sources:

```
mdtuser@tig-stack:~$ source /etc/lsb-release

mdtuser@tig-stack:~$ echo "deb https://repos.influxdata.
com/${DISTRIB_ID,,} ${DISTRIB_CODENAME} stable" | sudo tee /etc/
apt/sources.list.d/influxdb.list
```

Update the local repository and install the influxdb package:

```
mdtuser@tig-stack:~$ sudo apt update

mdtuser@tig-stack:~$ sudo apt install influxdb -y
```

After installation is complete, start the influxdb service. Configure it to launch at every boot:

```
mdtuser@tig-stack:~$ sudo systemctl start influxdb

mdtuser@tig-stack:~$ sudo systemctl enable influxdb
```

Then check to see the service is running with port listeners active by using the process shown in Example 12-28.

Example 12-28 *Verifying Active Port Listeners*

```
mdtuser@tig-stack:~$ ss -plntu
Netid    State     Recv-Q    Send-Q     Local Address:Port          Peer Address:Port
      Process
udp      UNCONN    0         0          127.0.0.53%lo:53                    0.0.0.0:*
tcp      LISTEN    0         4096       127.0.0.53%lo:53                    0.0.0.0:*
tcp      LISTEN    0         128              0.0.0.0:22                    0.0.0.0:*
tcp      LISTEN    0         4096          127.0.0.1:8088                   0.0.0.0:*
tcp      LISTEN    0         4096                *:8086                         *:*
tcp      LISTEN    0         128                [::]:22                       [::]:*
```

You're specifically looking for the port listeners on ports 8086 and 8088.

Next, create an InfluxDB database and database user. Use the **influx** command to access the InfluxDB console:

```
mdtuser@tig-stack:~$ influx
Connected to http://localhost:8086 version 1.8.6
InfluxDB shell version: 1.8.6
>
```

Issue the following commands in the influx shell to create a database and user:

```
create database telegraf
create user telegrafuser with password '<YourPreference>'
```

You can double-check the creation with the following:

```
> show databases
name: databases
name
----
_internal
telegraf
> show users
user          admin
----          -----
telegrafuser false
>
```

Use **exit** to leave the influx shell.

Installing Telegraf

Telegraf comes from the same organization as InfluxDB. Earlier, you imported the influxdata key and repository definitions, so you can reuse them now for Telegraf. Install the Telegraf package:

```
mdtuser@tig-stack:~$ sudo apt install telegraf -y
```

Start Telegraf and enable it to start on boot, as you did earlier with InfluxDB:

```
mdtuser@tig-stack:~$ sudo systemctl start telegraf
mdtuser@tig-stack:~$ sudo systemctl enable telegraf
```

It also makes sense to double-check the service has started. Example 12-29 provides the steps and expected output.

Example 12-29 *Validating Telegraf Process Status*

```
mdtuser@tig-stack:~$ sudo systemctl status telegraf
• telegraf.service - The plugin-driven server agent for reporting metrics into
InfluxDB
     Loaded: loaded (/lib/systemd/system/telegraf.service; enabled; vendor preset:
enabled)
     Active: active (running) since Sun 2021-06-20 23:20:42 UTC; 1min 45s ago
       Docs: https://github.com/influxdata/telegraf
   Main PID: 20504 (telegraf)
      Tasks: 8 (limit: 9448)
     Memory: 32.4M
     CGroup: /system.slice/telegraf.service
             20504 /usr/bin/telegraf -config /etc/telegraf/telegraf.conf -config-
directory /etc/telegraf/telegraf.d


Jun 20 23:20:42 tig-stack systemd[1]: Started The plugin-driven server agent for
reporting metrics into InfluxDB.
Jun 20 23:20:42 tig-stack telegraf[20504]: time="2021-06-20T23:20:42Z" level=error
msg="failed to create cache directory. />
Jun 20 23:20:42 tig-stack telegraf[20504]: time="2021-06-20T23:20:42Z" level=error
msg="failed to open. Ignored. open /etc/>
Jun 20 23:20:42 tig-stack telegraf[20504]: 2021-06-20T23:20:42Z I! Starting Telegraf
1.19.0
Jun 20 23:20:42 tig-stack telegraf[20504]: 2021-06-20T23:20:42Z I! Loaded inputs:
cpu disk diskio kernel mem processes swap>
Jun 20 23:20:42 tig-stack telegraf[20504]: 2021-06-20T23:20:42Z I! Loaded
aggregators:
Jun 20 23:20:42 tig-stack telegraf[20504]: 2021-06-20T23:20:42Z I! Loaded
processors:
Jun 20 23:20:42 tig-stack telegraf[20504]: 2021-06-20T23:20:42Z I! Loaded outputs:
influxdb
Jun 20 23:20:42 tig-stack telegraf[20504]: 2021-06-20T23:20:42Z I! Tags enabled:
host=tig-stack
Jun 20 23:20:42 tig-stack telegraf[20504]: 2021-06-20T23:20:42Z I! [agent] Config:
Interval:10s, Quiet:false, Hostname:"tig>
mdtuser@tig-stack:~$
```

Next, you need to configure Telegraf. First, you can configure it for standard functionality; then you can enhance for handling streaming telemetry functions:

```
mdtuser@tig-stack:~$ cd /etc/telegraf/
```

```
mdtuser@tig-stack:/etc/telegraf$ sudo mv telegraf.conf
telegraf.conf.default
```

Edit telegraf.conf with your favorite editor, such as vi or vim. Then paste the contents of Example 12-30.

Example 12-30 *telegraf.conf File with Sample Settings*

```
# Global Agent Configuration
[agent]
  hostname = "tig-stack"
  flush_interval = "15s"
  interval = "15s"


# Input Plugins
[[inputs.cpu]]
    percpu = true
    totalcpu = true
    collect_cpu_time = false
    report_active = false
[[inputs.disk]]
    ignore_fs = ["tmpfs", "devtmpfs", "devfs"]
[[inputs.io]]
[[inputs.mem]]
[[inputs.net]]
[[inputs.system]]
[[inputs.swap]]
[[inputs.netstat]]
[[inputs.processes]]
[[inputs.kernel]]

# Output Plugin InfluxDB
[[outputs.influxdb]]
  database = "telegraf"
  urls = [ "http://127.0.0.1:8086" ]
  username = "telegrafuser"
  password = "<PasswordFromEarlier>"
```

Add the following to the telegraf.conf file to enable gRPC Dial-Out Telemetry and enable a listener port:

```
# gRPC Dial-Out Telemetry Listener
[[inputs.cisco_telemetry_mdt]]
transport = "grpc-dialout"
service_address = ":57000"
```

Save the file and then restart the Telegraf service:

```
mdtuser@tig-stack:~$ sudo systemctl start telegraf
```

The next task is to install Grafana. Install the grafana snap package:

```
mdtuser@tig-stack:~$ sudo snap install grafana
```

The Grafana app should be installed. Check for a TCP port 3000 listener with the command shown in Example 12-31.

Example 12-31 *Reviewing Listener Ports for the Grafana Service*

```
mdtuser@tig-stack:~$ ss -plntu
Netid   State    Recv-Q  Send-Q   Local Address:Port        Peer Address:Port
Process
udp     UNCONN   0       0        127.0.0.53%lo:53                 0.0.0.0:*
tcp     LISTEN   0       4096     127.0.0.53%lo:53                 0.0.0.0:*
tcp     LISTEN   0       128            0.0.0.0:22                 0.0.0.0:*
tcp     LISTEN   0       4096        127.0.0.1:8088                0.0.0.0:*
tcp     LISTEN   0       4096               *:57000                    *:*
tcp     LISTEN   0       4096                *:8086                    *:*
tcp     LISTEN   0       128               [::]:22                  [::]:*
tcp     LISTEN   0       4096                *:3000                    *:*
```

The last entry in this list shows the port listener, so you can be confident the app is running. Access Grafana through the Ubuntu console and a local web browser at http://localhost. It can also be accessed through another local system with the Ubuntu system's IP address or registered DNS hostname.

The Grafana login portal appears in the browser, as shown in Figure 12-21; use **admin /admin** for the initial login.

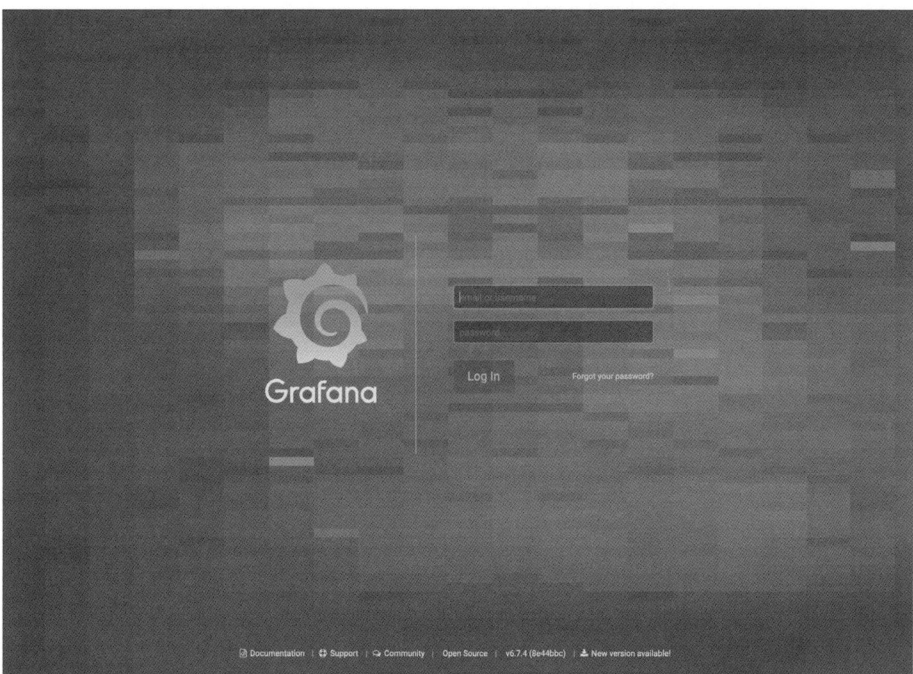

Figure 12-21 *Grafana Login Portal*

The system prompts you to reset the password as a security measure. Select (and record) a new password.

The first action in Grafana is to associate the local InfluxDB as a data source for Grafana. From the left-side navigation panel, select the gear icon and the Data Sources option. Fill out the HTTP URL; enable Basic Auth; define User and Password under Basic Auth Details; and define Database, User, and Password under InfluxDB Details. Finally, click the Save & Test button at the bottom. A screen like the one shown in Figure 12-22 should appear.

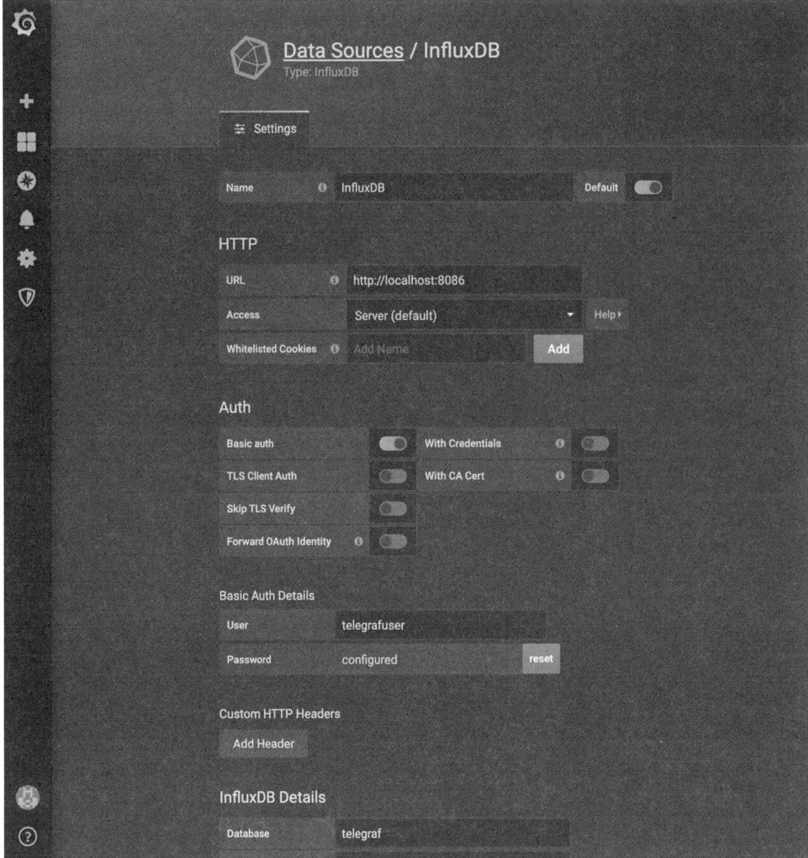

Figure 12-22 *Grafana Data Sources Panel*

Creating a new dashboard is also fairly easy because of the graphical user interface. From the left-side navigation panel, select the plus (+) icon. Then select the Create Dashboard option. Click the Add Query option within the New Panel. Fill out the query parameters as shown in Figure 12-23.

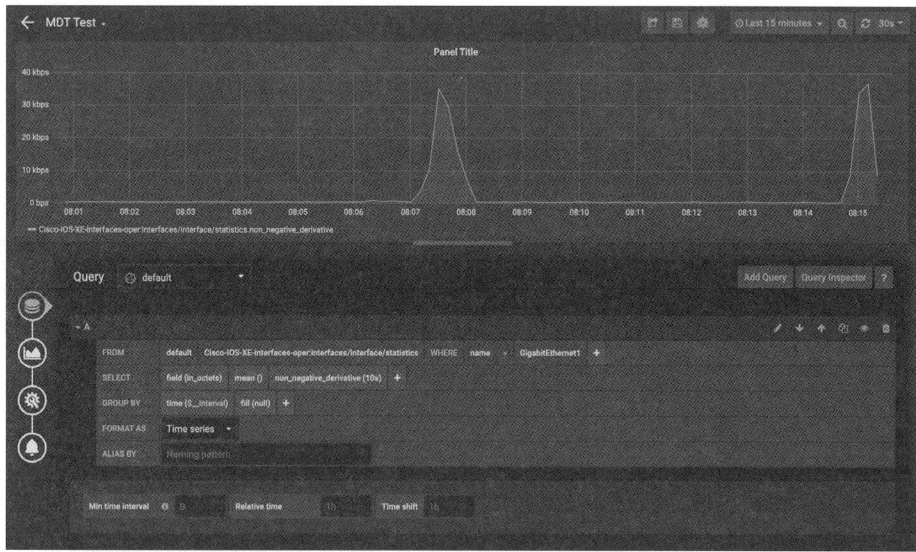

Figure 12-23 *Grafana Create Dashboard and Query Panel*

For the Visualization icon on the left-side navigation panel, you can set Left Y Unit to bits/sec to match the data type. The full dashboard resulting from these settings appears as in Figure 12-24.

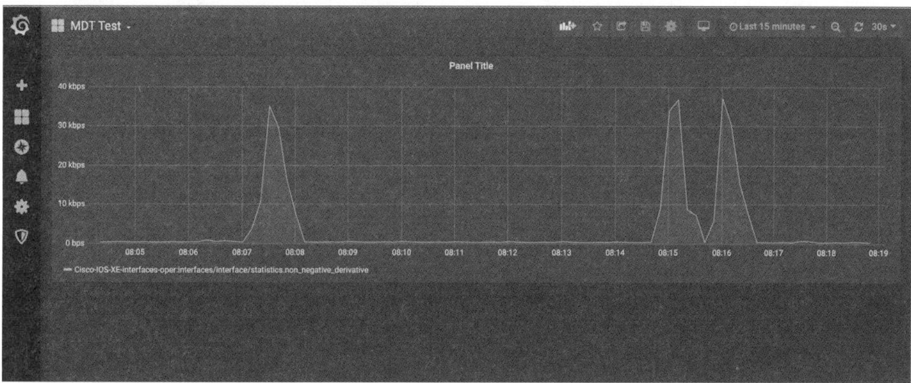

Figure 12-24 *Grafana Panel of a Graph on a Dashboard*

Additional dashboards are easily created and left to your imagination. More advanced functions, such as templates, are available in Grafana to simplify your effort in adding mass numbers of dashboards indexed on interface, module, and so on.

Grafana also supports other visualizations such as data panel, table, heat map, and several others. Take, for example, one of the popular CiscoLive event dashboards from the NOC where WAN traffic stats are merged with IPv4 and IPv6 information (see Figure 12-25).

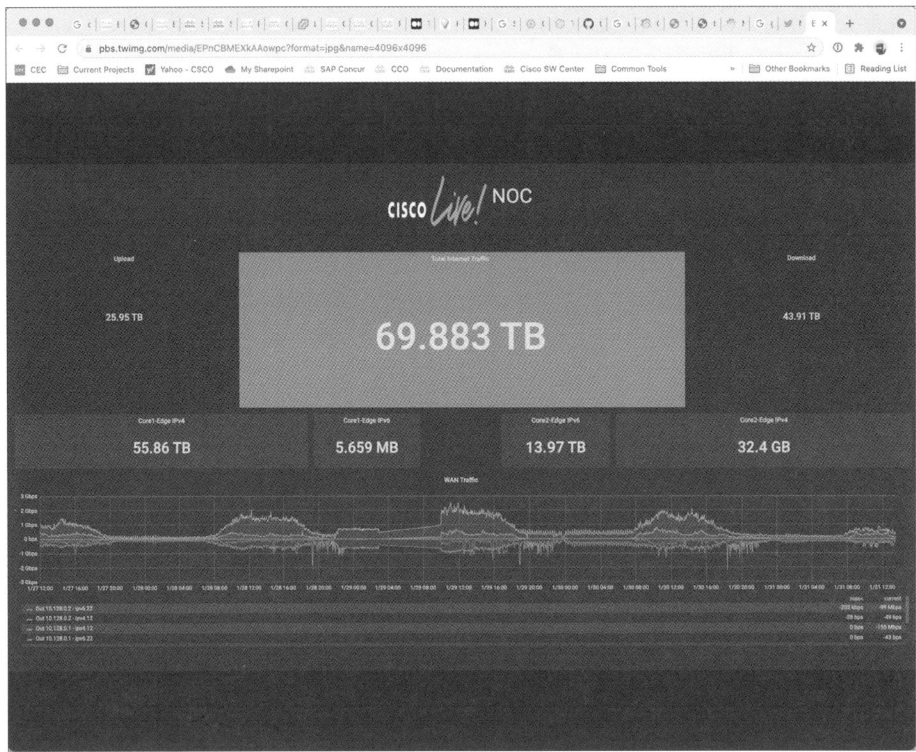

Figure 12-25 *A Grafana Dashboard of the CiscoLive NOC*

So now your opportunities are limitless! Determine what metrics are important to you; research and extract their sensor paths with YANG Suite; build the device configuration; export to a TIG stack VM; and create your dashboard.

Beyond MDT—Event-Driven Telemetry

The earlier examples in the "How to Implement Model-Driven Telemetry" and "Practical Application of Streaming Telemetry" sections focused on time- or cadence-based telemetry with a quick mention of event-driven telemetry. Let's double-click more deeply on EDT now by comparing the two.

In the "Practical Application" section, you learned how to extract interface statistics. Specifically, you graphed in-octets, or the number of bytes coming into an interface. This counter metric should always be increasing as long as the interface is up and receiving traffic. This kind of metric makes a lot of sense for cadence-based telemetry monitoring.

However, what if your sensor path is something other than a counter? What if it is **oper-status**, as seen in Figure 12-26?

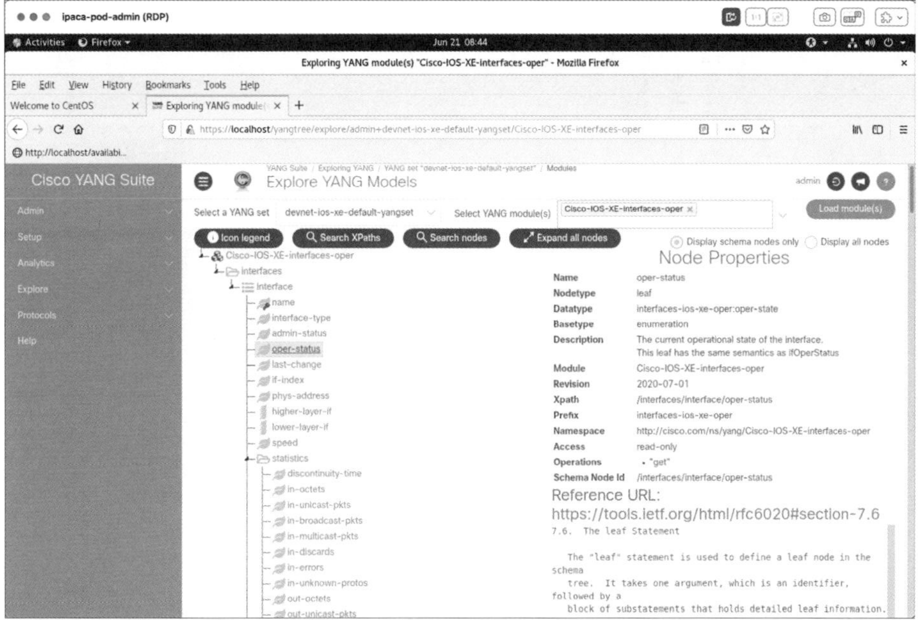

Figure 12-26 *YANG Model of Interfaces Oper(ational) Statistics*

You know operational status of an interface is an important metric. You want to know when a link goes down. The YANG Suite perspective of the interfaces YANG model shows the oper-status node to be an enumeration basetype. This type represents values from a set of assigned names. YANG Suite doesn't extract the set of assigned names, but if you're interested, you can look more closely at the YANG data model. Go to the GitHub source of the Cisco-IOS-XE-interfaces-oper YANG data model at https://github.com/YangModels/yang/blob/master/vendor/cisco/xe/1681/Cisco-IOS-XE-interfaces-oper.yang.

Within that text file, use the browser search function for **oper-status**. You should see the information shown in Figure 12-27.

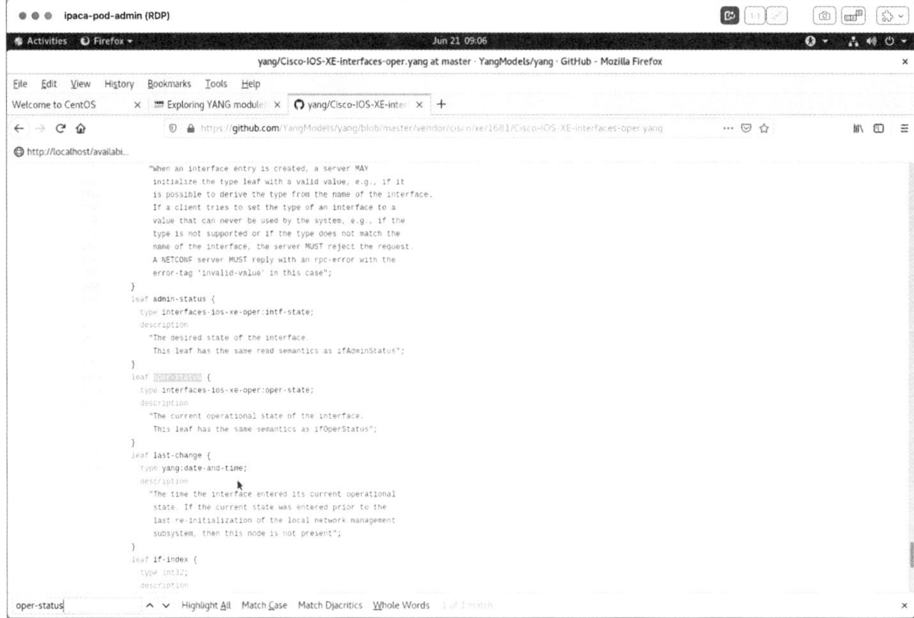

Figure 12-27 *YANG Interfaces Oper-Status Leaf Summary*

Looking more closely at the oper-status leaf, note the type, which is interface-ios-xe-oper:oper-state. Use the browser search function again for **oper-state.** This time you should see results like those shown in Figure 12-28.

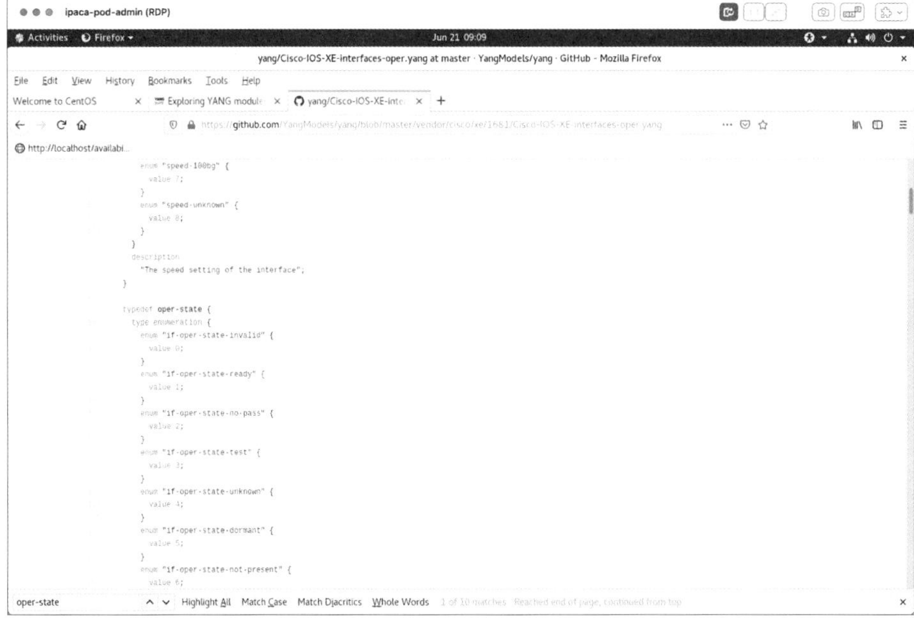

Figure 12-28 *YANG Interfaces Oper-State Details*

In this figure, you see the oper-status enumeration resolves to several predefined enum types, such as if-oper-state-invalid, if-oper-state-ready, if-oper-state-dormant, and if-oper-state-ready.

Indeed, you can update the CSR1000v configuration with a new subscription that captures this oper-status node and exports to the Telegraf instance. The following configuration should be pushed to the device:

```
telemetry ietf subscription 101
 encoding encode-kvgpb
 filter xpath /interfaces-ios-xe-oper:interfaces/interface/oper-
status
 source-address 10.1.1.10
 stream yang-push
 update-policy periodic 1000
 receiver ip address 10.1.1.100 57000 protocol grpc-tc
```

After a few minutes of exporting metrics, you can see the results injected into the Influx database. Use the Ubuntu VM's **influx** command as seen in Example 12-32.

Example 12-32 *Reviewing InfluxDB-Received Telemetry Data*

```
mdtuser@tig-stack:~$ influx
Connected to http://localhost:8086 version 1.8.6
InfluxDB shell version: 1.8.6
> use telegraf
Using database telegraf
> SELECT "name", "oper_status" from "Cisco-IOS-XE-interfaces-oper:interfaces/inter-
face" where "name" = 'GigabitEthernet1'
name: Cisco-IOS-XE-interfaces-oper:interfaces/interface
time                name             oper_status
----                ----             -----------
1624280416736000000 GigabitEthernet1 if-oper-state-ready
1624280426736000000 GigabitEthernet1 if-oper-state-ready
1624280436736000000 GigabitEthernet1 if-oper-state-ready
1624280446736000000 GigabitEthernet1 if-oper-state-ready
1624280456736000000 GigabitEthernet1 if-oper-state-ready
1624280466736000000 GigabitEthernet1 if-oper-state-ready
1624280476736000000 GigabitEthernet1 if-oper-state-ready
1624280486736000000 GigabitEthernet1 if-oper-state-ready
[ . . . a lot more info trimmed . . . ]
```

As you can see in the output in this example, the GigabitEthernet1 interface has a status of if-oper-state-ready, and it repeats over and over. Because you configured the subscription for a push every 10 seconds, you get a *lot* of the same information repeating with little gain. As a matter of fact, you're being inefficient because of so many repeat values. It makes sense to preserve disk usage. So, how do you do that?

Event-driven telemetry.

Although cadence-driven telemetry is the de facto usage of model-driven telemetry, you can pivot to an event-driven method where you receive a push only when the value changes. This way, you preserve disk space and unnecessary processing overhead.

With the Cisco IOS XE platform, you can display the list of YANG models that support on-change subscriptions, using the **show platform software ndbman switch {switch-number | active | standby} models** command.

With Cisco IOS XR platforms, you can determine the YANG models that support event-driven telemetry where the model is annotated with **xr:event-telemetry**. For example, Cisco-IOS-XR-ip-rib-ipv6-oper has this for IPv6 RIB operational monitoring:

```
leaf v6-nexthop {
        type inet:ipv6-address;
        description
          "V6 nexthop";
        xr:event-telemetry "Subscribe Telemetry Event";
      }
```

To configure event-driven telemetry on a subscription, set the update policy definition to update policy on-change. See the full configuration below. You can also remove the previous cadence-based example with a new sensor path that targets the Cisco-IOS-XE-ios-events-oper YANG model and specifically the /ios-events-ios-xe-oper:interface-state-change xpath.

For good measure, Figure 12-29 shows the YANG Suite representation of that node.

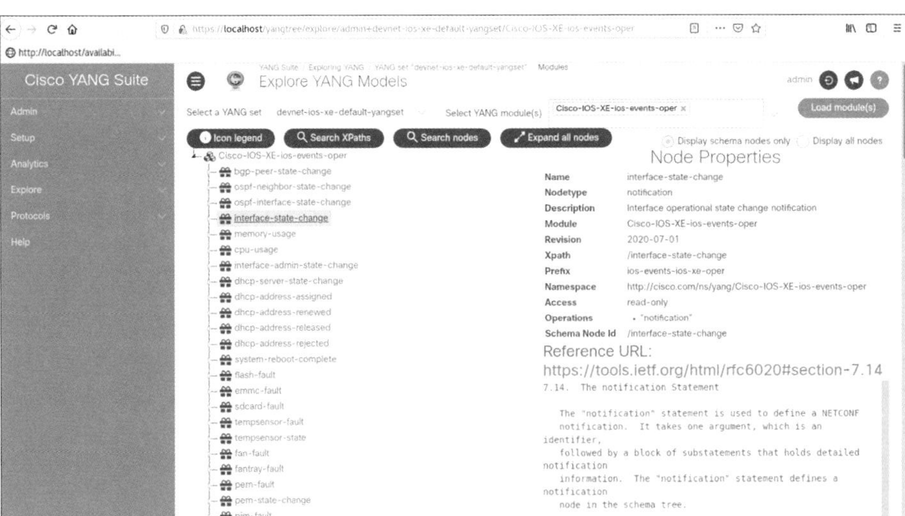

Figure 12-29 *Interfaces YANG Model with interface-state-change leaf*

And now the configuration:

```
no telemetry ietf subscription 102
telemetry ietf subscription 102
 encoding encode-kvgpb
 filter xpath /ios-events-ios-xe-oper:interface-state-change
 source-address 10.1.1.20
 stream yang-notif-native
 update-policy on-change
 receiver ip address 10.1.1.100 57000 protocol grpc-tcp
```

After waiting for a bit, you can go into that CSR1000v and use **no shut** on one of the currently down interfaces, as shown in Example 12-33.

Example 12-33 *Triggering an Interface Status Change*

```
CSR100V# show ip inter brief
Interface              IP-Address      OK? Method Status                Protocol
GigabitEthernet1       10.1.1.20       YES manual up                    up
GigabitEthernet2       unassigned      YES unset  administratively down down
GigabitEthernet3       unassigned      YES unset  administratively down down
CSR100V# conf term
Enter configuration commands, one per line. End with CNTL/Z.
CSR100V(config)# int GigabitEthernet2
CSR100V(config-if)# no shut
CSR100V(config-if)# exit
CSR100V(config)# exit
CSR100V# show ip inter brief
Interface              IP-Address      OK? Method Status                Protocol
GigabitEthernet1       10.1.1.20       YES manual up                    up
GigabitEthernet2       unassigned      YES DHCP   up                  up
GigabitEthernet3       unassigned      YES unset  administratively down down
CSR100V#
```

Now if you return to the Ubuntu VM and the InfluxDB shell, you can see the event change recorded without the cadence-driven pushes. Example 12-34 shows the process.

Example 12-34 *InfluxDB Query Searching for Interface Changes*

```
> select "if_name", "new_state" from "Cisco-IOS-XE-ios-events-oper:interface-state-
change"
name: Cisco-IOS-XE-ios-events-oper:interface-state-change
time                     if_name          new_state
----                     -------          ---------
2021-06-21T17:28:06.005Z GigabitEthernet2 interface-notif-state-down
2021-06-21T17:28:12.386Z GigabitEthernet2 interface-notif-state-up
2021-06-21T17:29:41.559Z GigabitEthernet2 interface-notif-state-down
2021-06-21T17:31:32.389Z GigabitEthernet2 interface-notif-state-up
2021-06-21T17:43:57.63Z  GigabitEthernet2 interface-notif-state-down
2021-06-21T17:44:12.396Z GigabitEthernet2 interface-notif-state-up
>
```

Notice the timing isn't spaced 10 seconds (other otherwise) between state transitions. The times correspond to the instance of enabling or disabling the port.

The next option would be to create a new Grafana dashboard as a panel that would show the last value of **new_state**. You might even alias the **interface-notif-state-down** and **-up** values to toggle to more friendly versions.

Other Considerations—Disk Usage

Clearly, the on-change model with event-driven telemetry is optimal for saving space and processing overhead. But it doesn't make sense for always changing metrics like interface statistics, which grow in value with time. Generally, any consumption-based counter or metric is a good candidate for cadence-based policy. When thinking about features and which policy to use, consider the suggestions listed in Table 12-7 for the two policies.

Table 12-7 Comparing Cadence and Event-Based Policies for Metrics/Sensor Selection

Cadence-Based (Policy Periodic)	Event-Based (Policy On-change)
Interface statistics (octets, packets)	Interface state (admin/oper)
Routing table size	Routing adjacencies/peer count
CPU percentage	
Memory percentage	
	CDP/LLDP neighbor adjacencies
Temperature	Fan status (running, failure)
Optics power (dbm)	Optics status (on, off)
MAC Address / CAM table size	
	Last config change date/time

A common question when using the cadence-driven method (policy) is "How much disk space will I use?" This is not an easy question to answer because several levers are at play:

- Number of devices
- Number of interfaces (per device and in total)
- Number of sensor paths

Frequency of Telemetry Push

Trying to build a spreadsheet with macros to gauge all the permutations would be chasing levels of minutiae.

If disk space on the telemetry receiver (TIG stack or other) is a concern, the best option is to baseline the environment and extrapolate. Start by using **tcpdump** or Wireshark on the incoming interface of the telemetry receiver and filtering traffic for the receiver port—TCP 57000 in these examples. Measure the traffic volume for at least a day; one week, if possible. Knowing how many devices, subscriptions, and sensor paths are configured, you can extrapolate that information to disk consumption for a month, quarter, and year. This information should help with planning any need to extend storage volumes or to prune existing collected data.

Baselining provides a much more accurate representation of your circumstances over trying to build mathematical models.

Exam Preparation Tasks

As mentioned in the section "How to Use This Book" in the Introduction, you have a couple of choices for exam preparation: the exercises here, Chapter 17, "Final Preparation," and the exam simulation questions in the Pearson Test Prep Software Online.

Review All Key Topics

Review the most important topics in this chapter, noted with the Key Topic icon in the outer margin of the page. Table 12-8 lists a reference of these key topics and the page numbers on which each is found.

Table 12-8 Key Topics for Chapter 12

Key Topic Element	Description	Page Number
Paragraph	Streaming telemetry concept	390
Table 12-2	SNMP and Streaming Telemetry Comparison	390
Paragraph	gRPC and gNMI concepts	392
List	Key concepts of MDT	394
Table 12-3	Dial-In and Dial-Out Comparison	395
Paragraph	GPB concept	396
Paragraph	gRPC concept	397
List	Configuring dial-out mode	398

Key Topic Element	Description	Page Number
List	Configuring dial-in mode	402
Figure 12-18	Exploring a YANG Model in Cisco YANG Suite	422
Section	Configuring Telegraf for MDT	429
Section	Configuring Cisco CSR1000v for telemetry	437
Section	Configuring event-driven/on-change telemetry	438
Section	Considering storage impact of MDT	440

Complete Tables and Lists from Memory

Print a copy of Appendix C, "Memory Tables" (found on the companion website), or at least the section for this chapter, and complete the tables and lists from memory. Appendix D, "Memory Tables Answer Key," also on the companion website, includes completed tables and lists to check your work.

Define Key Terms

Define the following key terms from this chapter and check your answers in the glossary:

dial-in, dial-out, event-driven telemetry (EDT), Google Network Management Interface (gNMI), Google Remote Procedure Call (gRPC), model-driven telemetry (MDT), remote-procedure call (RPC), sensor-path, subscription, YANG

References

URL	QR Code
https://tools.ietf.org/html/rfc3535	
https://pc.nanog.org/static/published/meetings//NANOG73/daily/day_2.html#talk_1677	
https://www.cisco.com/c/en/us/products/collateral/cloud-systems-management/crosswork-network-automation/datasheet-c78-743287.html	

URL	QR Code
https://github.com/YangModels/yang/tree/master/vendor/cisco	
https://yangcatalog.org/	
https://github.com/openconfig/public/tree/master/release/models	
https://devnetsandbox.cisco.com/RM/Diagram/Index/7b4d4209-a17c-4bc3-9b38-f15184e53a94?diagramType=Topology	
https://github.com/YangModels/yang/blob/master/vendor/cisco/xe/1681/Cisco-IOS-XE-interfaces-oper.yang	

CHAPTER 13

Open-Source Solutions

This chapter covers the following topics:

- **Infrastructure-as-Code (IaC) Concepts:** This section covers the concepts defining Infrastructure as Code and its benefits.
- **Provisioning or Configuration Management:** This section covers the provisioning and configuration management models, plus their similarities and differences.
- **Differences Between Agent and Agentless Solutions:** This section discusses the differences between agent and agentless solutions and includes benefits and resource requirements.
- **Agent-Based Solutions—Puppet and Chef:** This section provides commentary on Puppet and Chef with detailed guidance on how to install Puppet and build a manifest, including examples.
- **Agentless Solutions—Ansible and Terraform:** This section provides an overview of Ansible and Terraform as agentless solutions. Detailed examples of building both are provided, along with examples of Ansible playbooks and Terraform configurations.
- **Cisco Solutions Enabled for IaC:** Finally, this section provides some closing thoughts on Cisco's solutions that are enabled for Infrastructure-as-Code projects.

This chapter maps to the *Developing Applications Using Cisco Core Platforms and APIs v1.0 (350-901)* Exam Blueprint Section 5.3, "Construct a workflow to configure network parameters with: Ansible playbook and Puppet manifest."

Open-source solutions are a popular option for network programmability projects. Although commercial network management applications and controllers offer an "all batteries included" approach that may be specialized to a specific vendor or technology, open-source solutions often provide broad device-type capabilities and function extensibility through code modification. Open-source solutions that have extensive community support may also reduce the risk associated with supportability. This chapter addresses several open-source concepts and solutions. We encourage you to approach open-source projects with discernment and a critical view. Although the notion of "free" is appealing, there are always costs to any project, even if the source code is freely available. Ideally, before implementing such projects, you are fully apprised of all functionality and are comfortable with reviewing code to ensure "fit for purpose" and security intents are followed. Open source works best when you contribute back to the community. If you are new to open source, even helping to write documentation and test is appreciated.

"Do I Know This Already?" Quiz

The "Do I Know This Already?" quiz allows you to assess whether you should read this entire chapter thoroughly or jump to the "Exam Preparation Tasks" section. If you are in doubt about your answers to these questions or your own assessment of your knowledge of the topics, read the entire chapter. Table 13-1 lists the major headings in this chapter and their corresponding "Do I Know This Already?" quiz questions. You can find the answers in Appendix A, "Answers to the 'Do I Know This Already?' Quizzes."

Table 13-1 "Do I Know This Already?" Section-to-Question Mapping

Foundation Topics Section	Questions
Infrastructure-as-Code (IaC) Concepts	1–3
Provisioning or Configuration Management	4
Differences Between Agent and Agentless Solutions	5
Agent-Based Solutions—Puppet and Chef	6–7
Agentless Solutions—Ansible and Terraform	8–10

1. How are Infrastructure-as-Code solutions offered?
   a. Only as declarative modeled solutions
   b. Only as imperative modeled solutions
   c. As both declarative and imperative modeled solutions
   d. As neither declarative nor imperative modeled solutions
2. What functionality does an imperative model solution provide?
   a. It provides a programming paradigm.
   b. It expresses the logic of programming without describing control flow.
   c. It expresses the logic of programming by describing control flow and state.
   d. A and B
   e. A and C
3. What functionality does a declarative model solution provide?
   a. It provides a programming paradigm.
   b. It expresses the logic of programming without describing control flow.
   c. It expresses the logic of programming by describing control flow and state.
   d. A and B
   e. A and C
4. Which statement is true about provisioning and configuration management?
   a. Provisioning is a zero task deployment (ZTD) function.
   b. Provisioning generally refers to the action of performing device changes, whereas configuration management refers to the function or concept.
   c. ZTD methods involve XModem file transfer.
   d. Configuration management functions require GLBP services.

5. Which is true about open-source solutions using agent or agentless models? (Choose three.)
   a. Chef is agent-based.
   b. Chef is agentless.
   c. Puppet supports both agent and agentless modes.
   d. Ansible is agent-based.
   e. Ansible is agentless.
6. The Puppet Facter tool outputs data in which default data exchange method?
   a. ANSI
   b. JSON
   c. XML
   d. YAML
7. What is the configuration file for a Puppet operation called?
   a. Configuration file
   b. Data Definition Language (DDL)
   c. Manifest
   d. Playbook
8. With which data exchange format can an Ansible inventory source file be written? (Choose two.)
   a. INI
   b. JSON
   c. YAML
   d. zsh
9. Which Ansible inventory format allows for inline references of Ansible Vault definitions?
   a. INI
   b. JSON
   c. YAML
   d. XML
10. What sequence of commands is used to deploy a Terraform configuration from start to finish?
    a. **terraform add config_file.tf, terraform deploy config_file.tf**
    b. **terraform create, terraform deploy config_file.tf**
    c. **terraform init, terraform plan, terraform apply**
    d. **terraform add ., terraform build ., terraform deploy**

Foundation Topics

Infrastructure-as-Code (IaC) Concepts

When networks were small, services few, and users more limited, the notion of manual, interactive provisioning was not resource demanding. Operational expenses (OpEx) were not regularly considered. However, organizations have all experienced the immense growth of an ever-growing, ever-evolving network that provides more services that ebb and flow on a regular basis. Users are no longer constrained to an office or specific geography. Equipment can exist in any location, even in the most inaccessible places where there are no users.

Most network engineers have IT war stories of supporting a device that required hours of travel to access. How many have needed specialized training to even access the device? There have been times at CiscoLive conferences when accessing a wireless access point in a ceiling space 30 feet above the event floor required specialized lift training and certification. Figure 13-1 suggests only those without a fear of heights should apply.

Figure 13-1 *Those with Fear of Heights Need Not Apply*

Could you imagine having to support equipment in space? Figure 13-2 shows the Cisco Space Router from 2010.

Figure 13-2 *Routers in Space*

Obviously, the use of a console cable is nontrivial. As the industry evolved in scale and breadth of deployment, so did the management interfaces and processes.

Infrastructure as Code (IaC) relates to the process of configuring (or provisioning) and monitoring IT systems, such as compute, storage, and networking components. Whereas legacy processes involved manual efforts and direct engineer involvement, IaC provides an alternative that is automated through machine-readable definition files that are also administrator-friendly. IaC has a strong following in cloud and data center deployments. However, it can be used broadly across many domains and is equally impactful for bare-metal and virtualized components.

With a focus in coding and software development disciplines and the use of machine-readable definition files, IaC is also well suited to version control, so the concepts and disciplines learned previously around git will be well used. IaC is often described in terms of using declarative or imperative functions.

Imperative and Declarative Models

Configuration changes to network infrastructure have traditionally been made atomically, on a per-device basis. The specific command syntax and arguments needed to be specified. On the one hand is the **imperative model**: the exact steps to achieve an end-state are specified. If a new task must be performed, a new workflow (or script) must be created. The workflows can be quite large as the number of devices and functions increases. Because syntax and arguments can vary across device operating systems, the infrastructure engineer must have extensive training and knowledge of the equipment.

On the other hand is the **declarative model**. An infrastructure engineer describes the layout and architecture of the environment, and the network elements and management tools (controllers) determine the implementation specifics. The network infrastructure and management tools essentially translate the generic directives to native, device-specific configurations.

Declarative or model-based configuration management techniques allow architects and managers to model an entire infrastructure beyond the data center. The benefits are large when considering the diversity of equipment types, models, and software versions.

Provisioning or Configuration Management

Provisioning and *configuration management* are terms that have been used interchangeably. One distinction is using the term *provisioning* to denote an action and *configuration management* to describe a function or concept.

Regardless of the differences between these terms, a basic activity is required to make a device useful: changing the operational state or function of it. If a device is in a virgin state upon startup, it may perform an initial configuration process that requests its operational parameters from an authoritative source. This is sometimes called zero-touch deployment (ZTD). A common method for ZTD involves the mature Dynamic Host Configuration Protocol (DHCP) regularly used to obtain an IP address for a connected interface. The common scenario for a virgin device startup would be for it to send a DHCP request out its first network-connected interface. The DHCP server would respond with a lease offer of an available IP address, but also include additional options containing a file server address and filename. If the device is operating in ZTD mode, it uses those options to download a set of configuration directives using common file transport protocols, such as TFTP or HTTPS. The device may attempt a specific configuration file that could be based on matching device name, MAC, or IP address. The initial configuration could contain all device parameters, or it may be limited to only enough parameters to allow the device to be accessed completely in a secure fashion. The remaining configuration parameters would be pushed by a configuration management solution or controller.

Some types of equipment, such as Cisco's Meraki products, have embedded processes that determine optimal network connectivity to cloud-based provisioning systems. Once online and connected to the Meraki cloud, the device owner "claims" it through the management portal and then follows with the intended, final state configuration.

We certainly have come a long way from legacy equipment that would pause the startup, waiting for an infrastructure administrator to complete its operational personality, sometimes requiring console-connected means! Certainly, that option still exists, but if this is your primary way of initializing network devices: Just. Say. No!

With the advent of software-defined networking (SDN) and the growth of controller-based architectures, the initial device provisioning and ongoing configuration management are greatly simplified. If you consider a controller-based solution, such as the Cisco Application Centric Infrastructure (ACI) for data center fabric topologies, you can see how access-layer "leaf" switches are discovered by core "spine" switches, which are likewise managed through a cluster of centralized controllers—the Cisco Application Policy Infrastructure Controller (APIC). The APIC becomes the central source of truth, policy, and management for all devices in its domain. Whereas legacy provisioning processes used a device-by-device approach, new controller models are a single-point administrative console that impacts a large amount of equipment.

Differences Between Agent and Agentless Solutions

Agent and agentless configuration management solutions are common in network programmability and IaC. We begin this section with open-source options for DevOps tooling. Although there are many, we cover four: Puppet, Chef, Ansible, and Terraform. We close out the section with some Cisco-specific solutions for your consideration.

The **agent-based** Puppet solution was released in 2005, with Chef coming on the scene in 2009. Both solutions require a software component, an agent, running on the device. In some cases, the agent may be an embedded part of the device's core operating system or a separate, virtualized environment, like a containerized service. This specialized component listens for and translates the provisioning directives to the native syntax of the device. A centralized server component communicates directly to the device agent providing configuration directives. A common requirement with agent-based solutions is that the software component must be in existence or be added to the device before the broader management solution can operate.

In some environments, the installation, administration, and maintenance of these agents are considered an operational burden.

On the other side of the spectrum are **agentless** solutions like Ansible, which was first released in 2012, and Terraform, which was initially released in 2014 but obtained version 1.0.0 status in June 2021. These solutions use functionality that already exists, such as an embedded SSH server, within the networked device. Because SSH is commonly available and may already be configured for terminal access, its reuse for programmatic functions reduces administrative overhead.

Using an embedded SSH server simplifies connectivity requirements, but it doesn't provide for sophisticated device-side processing. Therefore, agentless solutions depend fully on their management server or controller to handle the conversion of provisioning directives into native syntax of the networked device.

In the early days of IaC, the agent-based systems were the ones capable of "call-home" actions triggered at the device targeting the managing server or controller asynchronously. The agents would sense change events local to the device or work from a specific schedule to check in for needed updates. As a software agent, it could operate autonomously and provide more functionality. However, it is possible for both models to achieve a call-home-like function now.

Agent-Based Solutions—Puppet and Chef

When we look at Puppet and Chef, there are a few differences for consideration. Several Cisco and industry surveys imply that Puppet has a larger following than Chef. Both are strong configuration management solutions that started their base in server management and branched out to network management. Both treat the provisioned device as mutable and can change them incrementally as needed. Both solutions were born through server and operating system provisioning and later added network infrastructure functionality. Both operate with a server-to-agent architecture.

Chef is procedural and imperative; an administrator creates "recipes" representing foundational configuration directives written in Ruby, specifying step by step how to reach a desired end state. One or more recipes are included in a "cookbook," which defines a scenario of configuration and policy management. Chef also has a higher licensing cost than Puppet.

To align with the DevNet certification blueprint, we focus on Puppet here. However, if you find that your organization has more resources and investments in Chef, it may be beneficial to assess expanding that investment into the networking domain.

13

Again, considering that **Puppet** is a server-to-agent based solution, the obvious first dependency check is "Does this equipment have an embedded Puppet agent, or can I install it?"

We've talked about Puppet being agent-based. And it was, initially. The great news is that, since 2019, the **ciscopuppet** module enables many NX-OS devices to be supported in agentless mode (see Figure 13-3). Table 13-2 reflects the latest (summer 2021) support matrix from Puppetlabs.

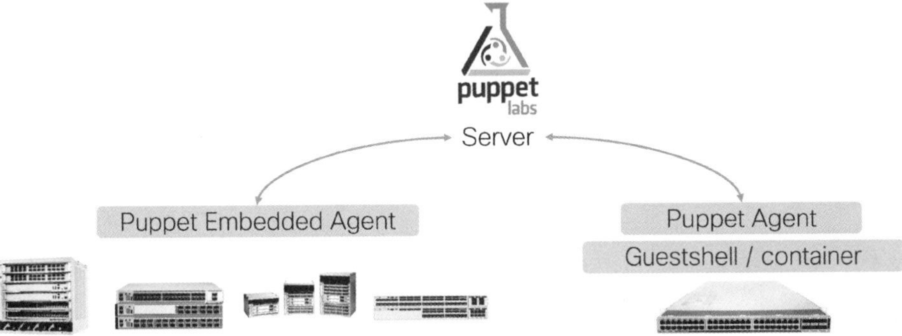

Figure 13-3 *Puppet Server to Client Interaction*

Key Topic

Table 13-2 Puppet Platform Support Matrix

Platform	Environment	Description
N3k	agentless, bash-shell, guestshell	N30xx and N31xx models only N35xx is not supported
N3k-F	agentless, bash-shell, guestshell	All N3xxx models running NX-OS 7.0(3) Fx(x)
N5k	Open Agent Container (OAC)	N56xx models only N50xx and N55xx not supported
N6k	agentless, Open Agent Container	All N6xxx models
N7k	agentless, Open Agent Container	All N7xxx models
N9k	agentless, bash-shell, guestshell	All N9xxx models
N9k-F	agentless, bash-shell, guestshell	All N95xx models running NX-OS 7.0(3) Fx(x)

If you wish to install the Puppet agent on a guestshell or containerized environment, follow this git repository: https://github.com/cisco/cisco-network-puppet-module/blob/develop/docs/README-agent-install.md.

However, going forward, we suggest you use agentless as the preferred mode of interaction. Let's start with some high business-impact, low device-impact actions, such as extracting device information, and then move to an activity that could modify a device configuration. The Puppet framework requires a server; the legacy name was Puppet Master, but now it is known as the Puppet Server.

Puppet enables you to define the desired end state of your infrastructure devices; it does not require you to define the sequence of actions necessary to achieve the end state. This makes it effectively a declarative solution. Puppet supports a variety of devices, servers, and network components across many operating systems. Puppet code is used to write the infrastructure code in Puppet's domain-specific language (DSL). The Puppet primary server then automates the provisioning of the devices to obtain your defined state. In a legacy agent-based mode, the Puppet primary server uses the code to direct the Puppet agent on the device to translate the directives into native commands, arguments, and syntax. Since 2019 the **ciscopuppet** module supports an agentless mode that leverages the NX-OS NX-API feature and does not require a Puppet agent. In this mode, the Puppet primary server talks directly to the switch's NX-API service. In either mode, the execution of the Puppet process is called a Puppet run.

Figure 13-4 shows the simplified server-agent architecture.

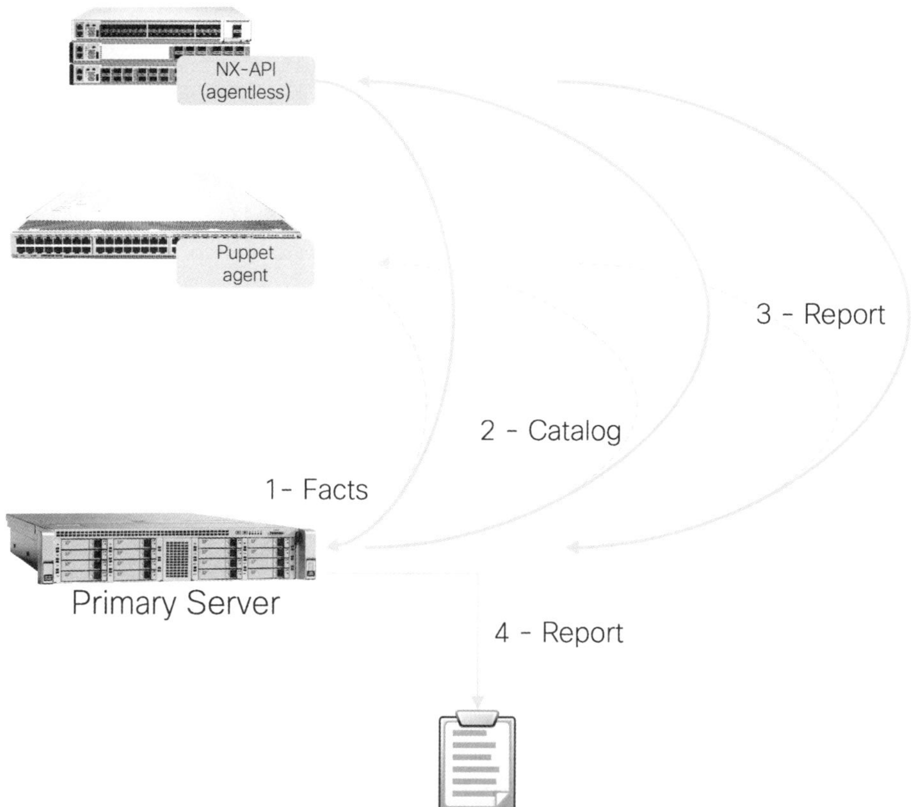

Figure 13-4 *Puppet-to-Device Exchanges*

Let's assume you're starting from scratch. You need a **puppetserver** component installed. **puppetserver** is supported on several Linux distributions. The server install includes a Puppet agent for the local system. It's good to know that agents can be installed on a variety of systems; more than 30 operating systems are supported! We do *not* have you install the agent on a Nexus switch because you'll use agentless mode. But first, you can start with a vanilla Ubuntu Server install. For this exercise, you can install Ubuntu 20.04.

NOTE Currently, the **grpc** module required for agentless NX-API use requires a Ruby version between 2.0 and 2.6. The latest Puppet 7 installs Ruby version 2.7. Please follow the GitHub issue at https://github.com/grpc/grpc/issues/21514 to see when the **grpc** support catches up to Puppet 7 and Ruby 2.7. Workarounds exist to allow Puppet 7, but for purposes of a simpler install in this use case with agentless NX-API, we suggest you install the earlier Puppet 6 release.

Step 1. Download puppet software using **wget** or **curl** (see Example 13-1).

Example 13-1 *Using* **wget** *to Download Puppet Software*

```
puppetadmin@puppetserver:~$ wget https://apt.puppet.com/puppet6-release-focal.deb
--2021-08-28 15:26:35--  https://apt.puppet.com/puppet6-release-focal.deb
Resolving apt.puppet.com (apt.puppet.com)... 13.249.38.122, 13.249.38.117,
13.249.38.64, ...
Connecting to apt.puppet.com (apt.puppet.com)|13.249.38.122|:443... connected.
HTTP request sent, awaiting response... 200 OK
Length: 11752 (11K) [application/x-debian-package]
Saving to: 'puppet6-release-focal.deb'

puppet6-release-focal.deb          100%[============================================
====================>]  11.48K  --.-KB/s    in 0s

2021-08-28 15:26:36 (221 MB/s) - 'puppet6-release-focal.deb' saved [11752/11752]

puppetadmin@puppetserver:~$
```

Step 2. Install the package with **dpkg** (see Example 13-2).

Example 13-2 *Using the* **dpkg** *Utility to Install Puppet*

```
puppetadmin@puppetserver:~$ sudo dpkg -i puppet6-release-focal.deb
Selecting previously unselected package puppet6-release.
(Reading database ... 71474 files and directories currently installed.)
Preparing to unpack puppet6-release-focal.deb ...
Unpacking puppet6-release (6.0.0-14focal) ...
Setting up puppet6-release (6.0.0-14focal) ...
```

Step 3. Update the package information from all configured repositories (see Example 13-3).

Example 13-3 *Performing Repository Updates*

```
puppetadmin@puppetserver:~$ sudo apt-get update
Hit:1 http://us.archive.ubuntu.com/ubuntu focal InRelease
Get:2 http://us.archive.ubuntu.com/ubuntu focal-updates InRelease [114 kB]
Get:3 http://apt.puppetlabs.com focal InRelease [99.1 kB]
Get:4 http://us.archive.ubuntu.com/ubuntu focal-backports InRelease [101 kB]
Get:5 http://us.archive.ubuntu.com/ubuntu focal-security InRelease [114 kB]
Get:6 http://us.archive.ubuntu.com/ubuntu focal-updates/main amd64 Packages [1,169 kB]
Get:7 http://us.archive.ubuntu.com/ubuntu focal-updates/universe amd64 Packages [848 kB]
Get:8 http://apt.puppetlabs.com focal/puppet6 all Packages [5,927 B]
Get:9 http://apt.puppetlabs.com focal/puppet6 amd64 Packages [22.5 kB]
Fetched 2,473 kB in 1s (3,078 kB/s)
Reading package lists... Done
```

Note the apt-get update retrieval of multiple packages from puppetlabs.com.

Step 4. Use the package manager to install the Puppet server software (see Example 13-4).

Example 13-4 *Using the Package Manager to Install the Puppet Server*

```
puppetadmin@puppetserver:~$ sudo apt-get install puppetserver
Reading package lists... Done
Building dependency tree
Reading state information... Done
The following additional packages will be installed:
  ca-certificates-java fontconfig-config fonts-dejavu-core java-common libavahi-cli-
ent3 libavahi-common-data libavahi-common3 libcups2
  libfontconfig1 libjpeg-turbo8 libjpeg8 liblcms2-2 libpcsclite1 libxi6 libxrender1
libxtst6 net-tools openjdk-8-jre-headless puppet-agent
  x11-common
Suggested packages:
  default-jre cups-common liblcms2-utils pcscd libnss-mdns fonts-dejavu-extra fonts-
ipafont-gothic fonts-ipafont-mincho fonts-wqy-microhei
 fonts-wqy-zenhei fonts-indic
The following NEW packages will be installed:
  ca-certificates-java fontconfig-config fonts-dejavu-core java-common libavahi-cli-
ent3 libavahi-common-data libavahi-common3 libcups2
 libfontconfig1 libjpeg-turbo8 libjpeg8 liblcms2-2 libpcsclite1 libxi6 libxrender1
libxtst6 net-tools openjdk-8-jre-headless puppet-agent
  puppetserver x11-common
0 upgraded, 21 newly installed, 0 to remove and 0 not upgraded.
Need to get 118 MB of archives.
After this operation, 330 MB of additional disk space will be used.
Do you want to continue? [Y/n] y
```

```
Get:1 http://apt.puppetlabs.com focal/puppet6 amd64 puppet-agent amd64 6.24.0-1focal
[22.3 MB]
Get:2 http://us.archive.ubuntu.com/ubuntu focal/main amd64 java-common all 0.72
[6,816 B]
[ . . . SOME OUTPUT TRIMMED . . . ]
done.
Setting up puppetserver (6.16.1-1focal) ...
usermod: no changes
Processing triggers for libc-bin (2.31-0ubuntu9.2) ...
Processing triggers for systemd (245.4-4ubuntu3.11) ...
Processing triggers for man-db (2.9.1-1) ...
Processing triggers for ca-certificates (20210119~20.04.1) ...
Updating certificates in /etc/ssl/certs...
0 added, 0 removed; done.
Running hooks in /etc/ca-certificates/update.d...

done.
done.
```

Step 5. Start and enable the Puppet Server service for restart and check its status (see Example 13-5).

Example 13-5 *Starting and Enabling the Puppet Server Service*

```
puppetadmin@puppetserver:~$ sudo systemctl start puppetserver
puppetadmin@puppetserver:~$ sudo systemctl enable puppetserver
Synchronizing state of puppetserver.service with SysV service script with /lib/
systemd/systemd-sysv-install.
Executing: /lib/systemd/systemd-sysv-install enable puppetserver
Created symlink /etc/systemd/system/multi-user.target.wants/puppetserver.service → /
lib/systemd/system/puppetserver.service.
puppetadmin@puppetserver:~$ sudo systemctl status puppetserver
● puppetserver.service - puppetserver Service
     Loaded: loaded (/lib/systemd/system/puppetserver.service; enabled; vendor pre-
set: enabled)
    Active: active (running) since Sat 2021-08-28 15:36:06 UTC; 16s ago
   Main PID: 31249 (java)
     Tasks: 42 (limit: 4915)
     Memory: 974.1M
     CGroup: /system.slice/puppetserver.service
             └─31249 /usr/bin/java -Xms2g -Xmx2g -Djruby.logger.class=com.puppetlabs.
jruby_utils.jruby.Slf4jLogger -XX:OnOutOfMemoryError=">

Aug 28 15:35:43 puppetserver systemd[1]: Starting puppetserver Service...
Aug 28 15:36:06 puppetserver systemd[1]: Started puppetserver Service.
puppetadmin@puppetserver:~$
```

Installing **puppetserver** also installs the puppet-agent locally for the server. However, if you need to install the agent separately (or on another server), the package manager can perform this task, as shown in Example 13-6.

Example 13-6 *Using Package Manager to Install the Puppet Agent*

```
puppetadmin@puppetserver:~$ sudo apt-get install puppet-agent
Reading package lists... Done
Building dependency tree
Reading state information... Done
[...package install process trimmed...]
done.
puppetadmin@puppetserver:~$
```

In the Ubuntu environment, the package installer puts the contents into /opt/puppetlabs. The puppet-agent installer also provides a useful shell script to add the package binaries to the executable path. Run the following command and consider adding it to the user's startup shell script: **$HOME/.bashrc**.

Step 6. Execute the puppet agent profile script (see Example 13-7).

Example 13-7 *Enabling the Puppet Environment Variables*

```
puppetadmin@puppetserver:~$ source /etc/profile.d/puppet-agent.sh
```

Now you can verify the executable path, as shown in Example 13-8.

Example 13-8 *Reviewing the Executable Path*

```
puppetadmin@puppetserver:~$ echo $PATH
/usr/local/sbin:/usr/local/bin:/usr/sbin:/usr/bin:/sbin:/bin:/usr/games:/usr/local/
games:/snap/bin:/opt/puppetlabs/bin
puppetadmin@puppetserver:~$
```

Consider also adding the /opt/puppetlabs/bin directory to sudo's **secure_path** so that using **sudo** with Puppet commands will result in the correct path being used:

```
puppetadmin@puppetserver:~$ sudo visudo
```

Edit the **Defaults secure_path** setting to appear like the following.

```
Defaults        secure_path="/usr/local/sbin:/usr/
local/bin:/usr/sbin:/usr/bin:/sbin:/bin:/snap/bin:/opt/
puppetlabs/bin"
```

Next, you can verify the installation with version checks, as in Example 13-9.

Example 13-9 *Reviewing the Puppet Server and Agent Versions*

```
puppetadmin@puppetserver:~$ puppetserver -v
puppetserver version: 6.16.1
puppetadmin@puppetserver:~$ puppet -V
6.24.0
puppetadmin@puppetserver:~$ puppet agent -V
6.24.0
```

The next activity is to configure the server setting that defines which Puppet server the Puppet client accesses. It is the only mandatory setting. You can set this option by editing the /etc/puppetlabs/puppet/puppet.conf file directory or by using the **puppet config set** command-line interface, as shown in Example 13-10. Because you are configuring the local agent to the local server, you define the server as the puppet server's DNS name.

Step 7. Configure the Puppet server location on the local agent (see Example 13-10).

Example 13-10 *Configuring the Puppet Server Setting*

```
puppetadmin@puppetserver:~$ sudo puppet config set server puppetserver.cisco.com
--section main
puppetadmin@puppetserver:~$
```

Then you can verify the setting by looking at the puppet.conf file, as shown in Example 13-11.

Example 13-11 *Reviewing the puppet.conf Configuration File*

```
puppetadmin@puppetserver:~$ cat /etc/puppetlabs/puppet/puppet.conf
[main]
server = puppetserver.cisco.com
# This file can be used to override the default puppet settings.
# See the following links for more details on what settings are available:
# - https://puppet.com/docs/puppet/latest/config_important_settings.html
# - https://puppet.com/docs/puppet/latest/config_about_settings.html
# - https://puppet.com/docs/puppet/latest/config_file_main.html
# - https://puppet.com/docs/puppet/latest/configuration.html
[server]
vardir = /opt/puppetlabs/server/data/puppetserver
logdir = /var/log/puppetlabs/puppetserver
rundir = /var/run/puppetlabs/puppetserver
pidfile = /var/run/puppetlabs/puppetserver/puppetserver.pid
codedir = /etc/puppetlabs/code
puppetadmin@puppetserver:~$
```

Step 8. Start and enable the Puppet agent service (see Example 13-12).

Example 13-12 *Starting and Enabling the Puppet Agent Service*

```
puppetadmin@puppetserver:~$ sudo puppet resource service puppet ensure=running
enable=true
[sudo] password for puppetadmin:
Notice: /Service[puppet]/ensure: ensure changed 'stopped' to 'running'
service { 'puppet':
  ensure   => 'running',
  enable   => 'true',
  provider => 'systemd',
}
```

An optional task is to install PuppetDB. For the purposes of this chapter, you can use the embedded database, but you should consider PuppetDB and PostgresQL integration for a large, production implementation.

Because Puppet uses certificates and TLS, check and sign for any outstanding certificates, as shown in Example 13-13.

Example 13-13 *Reviewing Puppet Certificates*

```
puppetadmin@puppetserver:~$ sudo puppetserver ca list --all
Signed Certificates:
    puppetserver.cisco.com       (SHA256)  C4:FD:EA:3E:E4:5E:1A:25:28:72:A9:64:4B:E8
:C8:AF:1C:B2:A4:2D:65:76:C5:31:22:6F:6B:58:FC:5D:76:D5     alt names: ["DNS:puppet",
"DNS:puppetserver.cisco.com"] authorization extensions: [pp_cli_auth: true]
puppetadmin@puppetserver:~$ sudo puppetserver ca sign --all
Error:
    No waiting certificate requests to sign
puppetadmin@puppetserver:~$
```

Next, test the agent connectivity, as shown in Example 13-14; because you're running the server and agent on the same system, this test is trivial.

Example 13-14 *Testing Puppet Agent Connectivity*

```
puppetadmin@puppetserver:~$ sudo puppet agent --test
Info: Using configured environment 'production'
Info: Retrieving pluginfacts
Info: Retrieving plugin
Info: Retrieving locales
Info: Caching catalog for puppetserver.cisco.com
Info: Applying configuration version '1630170859'
Notice: Applied catalog in 0.01 seconds
puppetadmin@puppetserver:~$
```

Now that you have the Puppet server and agent on the same system, you can do a low-risk, medium-impact activity: extract information from the environment. Because only the local agent is registered, you get only the Puppet server's "facts." You will expand to a network device later.

Puppet has a module called **facter** that deals with collecting facts about the managed devices, servers, network elements, and so on. So one of the first IoC actions can be to extract this information for review and reuse. You can start at the command line for familiarity and branch out from there.

13

The **facter** command with the **p** flag loads Puppet libraries, providing Puppet-specific facts. These facts may or may not be useful in your implementation, so you can assess and decide. The **j** flag is suggested because it produces the output in JSON (see Example 13-15). Without the **j** flag, the output appears in a key-value pair form.

Example 13-15 *Getting Puppet Node Inventory Information Via* facter

```
puppetadmin@puppetserver:~$ facter -p -j
{
  "aio_agent_version": "7.10.0",
  "augeas": {
    "version": "1.12.0"
  },
  "disks": {
    "sda": {
      "model": "Virtual disk",
      "size": "40.00 GiB",
      "size_bytes": 42949672960,
      "type": "hdd",
      "vendor": "VMware"
    },
    "sr0": {
      "model": "VMware SATA CD00",
      "size": "1.00 GiB",
      "size_bytes": 1073741312,
      "type": "hdd",
      "vendor": "NECVMWar"
    }
  },
[. . . TRIMMED OUTPUT . . . ]
  },
  "system_uptime": {
    "days": 0,
    "hours": 2,
    "seconds": 9854,
    "uptime": "2:44 hours"
  },
  "timezone": "EDT",
  "virtual": "vmware"
}
puppetadmin@puppetserver:~$
```

There's a *lot* of output to consider. If you have the Linux **jq** utility installed, you can use it to identify the major output categories. If you don't have the **jq** utility on your system, follow Example 13-16 to install it.

Example 13-16 *Installing the* jq *Utility*

```
puppetadmin@puppetserver:~$ sudo apt-get install jq
Reading package lists... Done
Building dependency tree
Reading state information... Done
The following additional packages will be installed:
  libjq1 libonig4
The following NEW packages will be installed:
  jq libjq1 libonig4
0 upgraded, 3 newly installed, 0 to remove and 63 not upgraded.
Need to get 271 kB of archives.
After this operation, 1,090 kB of additional disk space will be used. [...package
install process trimmed...]
done.
puppetadmin@puppetserver:~$
```

Continue on with the extraction of major output categories, as keys, by using the **jq** utility. You can see the results in Example 13-17.

Example 13-17 *Using the* jq *Utility with* facter *to Extract Keys*

```
puppetadmin@puppetserver:~$ facter -p -j | jq '. | keys'
[
  "aio_agent_version",
  "augeas",
  "disks",
  "dmi",
  "facterversion",
  "filesystems",
  "fips_enabled",
  "hypervisors",
  "identity",
  "is_virtual",
  "kernel",
  "kernelmajversion",
  "kernelrelease",
  "kernelversion",
  "load_averages",
  "memory",
  "mountpoints",
 "networking",
  "os",
```

```
  "partitions",
  "path",
  "processors",
  "puppetversion",
  "ruby",
  "ssh",
  "system_uptime",
  "timezone",
  "virtual"
]
```

The Puppetlabs documentation site has some good references on the **facter** core facts; see https://puppet.com/docs/puppet/7/core_facts.html. See also Figure 13-5 for a portion.

Figure 13-5 *Puppet Core Facts Obtained with facter*

Knowing these facts, you can choose ones important to your work. Because you're interested in network connectivity, extracting the networking fact is a good call; the **facter** utility enables you to filter (see Example 13-18).

Example 13-18 *Extracting Puppet Networking Facts with* facter

```
puppetadmin@puppetserver:~$ facter -p -j networking
{
  "networking": {
    "domain": "cisco.com",
    "fqdn": "puppetserver.cisco.com",
    "hostname": "puppetserver",
    "interfaces": {
      "ens160": {
        "bindings": [
          {
            "address": "172.31.0.160",
            "netmask": "255.255.254.0",
            "network": "172.31.0.0"
          }
        ],
        "bindings6": [
          {
            "address": "fe80::250:56ff:feb6:7ea3",
            "netmask": "ffff:ffff:ffff:ffff::",
            "network": "fe80::",
            "scope6": "link",
            "flags": [
              "permanent"
            ]
          }
        ],
        "ip": "172.31.0.160",
        "ip6": "fe80::250:56ff:feb6:7ea3",
        "mac": "00:50:56:b6:7e:a3",
        "mtu": 1500,
        "netmask": "255.255.254.0",
        "netmask6": "ffff:ffff:ffff:ffff::",
        "network": "172.31.0.0",
        "network6": "fe80::",
        "scope6": "link"
      }
    },
    "ip": "172.31.0.160",
    "ip6": "fe80::250:56ff:feb6:7ea3",
    "mac": "00:50:56:b6:7e:a3",
    "mtu": 1500,
    "netmask": "255.255.254.0",
    "netmask6": "ffff:ffff:ffff:ffff::",
    "network": "172.31.0.0",
```

```
    "network6": "fe80::",
    "primary": "ens160",
    "scope6": "link"
  }
}
puppetadmin@puppetserver:~$
```


Likewise, being comfortable using the **jq** utility and JSON path queries affords benefits across many programming activities.

So what other ways might be interesting to use Puppet and read-only access to facts? How about as an availability monitor backup? For instance, you can show the uptime on a device to be alerted to a reboot, whether planned or unplanned, as in Example 13-19.

Key Topic

Example 13-19 *Using Puppet* **facter** *to Extract* **system_uptime**

```
puppetadmin@puppetserver:~$ facter -p -j system_uptime
{
  "system_uptime": {
    "days": 0,
    "hours": 6,
    "seconds": 24356,
    "uptime": "6:45 hours"
  }
}
puppetadmin@puppetserver:~$
```

By extracting that **seconds** key and its value, you can check for devices that have less than 120 seconds of uptime.

Now let's approach integration from a Python script perspective. Moving forward, let's use Puppet against a Cisco Nexus switch. To continue, first install the **ciscopuppet** module. You can do it from within Puppet, as in Example 13-20.

Example 13-20 *Installing the* **ciscopuppet** *Module*

```
puppetadmin@puppetserver:~$ sudo puppet module install puppetlabs-ciscopuppet
--version 2.1.0
[sudo] password for puppetadmin:
Notice: Preparing to install into /etc/puppetlabs/code/environments/production/
modules ...
Notice: Downloading from https://forgeapi.puppet.com ...
Notice: Installing -- do not interrupt ...
/etc/puppetlabs/code/environments/production/modules
└─┬ puppetlabs-ciscopuppet (v2.1.0)
  ├── puppetlabs-netdev_stdlib (v0.23.0)
  └─┬ puppetlabs-resource_api (v1.1.0)
    └── puppetlabs-puppetserver_gem (v1.1.1)
puppetadmin@puppetserver:~$
```

Next, edit the Puppet device.conf file to specify device type and configuration file location, as in Example 13-21.

Example 13-21 *Editing the Puppet device.conf File*

```
puppetadmin@puppetserver:~$ sudo vi /etc/puppetlabs/puppet/device.conf
```

Then ensure the file contents appear as Example 13-22 depicts.

Example 13-22 *Puppet device.conf Example*

```
[sandbox-nxos-1.cisco.com]
type cisco_nexus
url file:////etc/puppetlabs/puppet/devices/sandbox-nxos-1.cisco.com.conf
```

The next step is to create a device-specific configuration file in the puppet/devices directory. It is helpful to maintain the device name for quick identification. Call this one **sandbox-nxos-1.cisco.com.conf** to align with the DevNet always-on NX-OS device you're using. Edit the file using Example 13-23 as a guide.

Example 13-23 *Editing the Puppet Device Configuration File*

```
puppetadmin@puppetserver:~$ sudo vi /etc/puppetlabs/puppet/devices/sandbox-nxos-1.
cisco.com.conf
```

At this point, edit the file to appear as shown in Example 13-24. These credentials map to the Sandbox documentation defined at https://devnetsandbox.cisco.com/RM/Diagram/Index/dae38dd8-e8ee-4d7c-a21c-6036bed7a804?diagramType=Topology.

Example 13-24 *Modified Puppet Device Configuration File*

```
host: sandbox-nxos-1.cisco.com
user: admin
password: "Admin_1234!"
port: 443
transport: https
```

Now trigger Puppet to connect to the device by using the **puppet device --target** command, as in Example 13-25.

Example 13-25 *Triggering Puppet to Connect to a Device*

```
puppetadmin@puppetserver:~$ sudo puppet device --verbose --target sandbox-nxos-1.
cisco.com
Info: Creating a new RSA SSL key for sandbox-nxos-1.cisco.com
Info: csr_attributes file loading from /opt/puppetlabs/puppet/cache/devices/sandbox-
nxos-1.cisco.com/csr_attributes.yaml
Info: Creating a new SSL certificate request for sandbox-nxos-1.cisco.com
Info: Certificate Request fingerprint (SHA256): 88:B5:CE:47:0B:06:2F:31:39:B7:55:46:
93:6D:A4:0F:AE:42:86:AC:9A:81:7F:58:90:E2:82:6C:FC:F8:B1:02
```

```
Info: Certificate for sandbox-nxos-1.cisco.com has not been signed yet
Couldn't fetch certificate from CA server; you might still need to sign this agent's
certificate (sandbox-nxos-1.cisco.com).
Info: Will try again in 120 seconds.
^CCancelling startup
```

13

The output in Example 13-25 shows that Puppet has not signed the device agent's pending certificate. You can show Puppet's certificates by using the **puppetserver ca list** command. Example 13-26 depicts the command syntax to list and sign the certificates.

Example 13-26 *Listing and Signing Puppet Certificates*

```
puppetadmin@puppetserver:~$ sudo puppetserver ca list --all
Requested Certificates:
    sandbox-nxos-1.cisco.com       (SHA256)  88:B5:CE:47:0B:06:2F:31:39:B7:55:46:93:
6D:A4:0F:AE:42:86:AC:9A:81:7F:58:90:E2:82:6C:FC:F8:B1:02
Signed Certificates:
    puppetserver.cisco.com       (SHA256)  C4:FD:EA:3E:E4:5E:1A:25:28:72:A9:64:4B:E8
:C8:AF:1C:B2:A4:2D:65:76:C5:31:22:6F:6B:58:FC:5D:76:D5     alt names: ["DNS:puppet",
"DNS:puppetserver.cisco.com"] authorization extensions: [pp_cli_auth: true]
puppetadmin@puppetserver:~$ sudo puppetserver ca sign --all
Successfully signed certificate request for sandbox-nxos-1.cisco.com
```

You might need to install the cisco_node_utils Ruby **gem**. You can use the Puppet-supplied **gem** command to install from public repositories. Example 13-27 shows the process.

Example 13-27 *Installing the cisco_node_utils Ruby* gem

```
puppetadmin@puppetserver:~$ sudo /opt/puppetlabs/puppet/bin/gem install
cisco_node_utils
Fetching: cisco_node_utils-2.1.0.gem (100%)
Building native extensions. This could take a while...
Successfully installed cisco_node_utils-2.1.0
Parsing documentation for cisco_node_utils-2.1.0
Installing ri documentation for cisco_node_utils-2.1.0
Done installing documentation for cisco_node_utils after 4 seconds
1 gem installed
```

Now let's pivot to using Puppet with an NX-OS based device. For this exercise, I used the Nexus 9000v virtual appliance as an OVA image integrated with my VMware environment. After booting the image and providing an IP address for the management interface I enabled the feature nxapi and saved the configuration. I updated the Puppet device.conf and the device-specific credentials file, as seen previously using the device IP and credentials I configured.

To follow along, tell Puppet to attempt a connection to obtain the certificate; then press Ctrl+C when it starts looping. Example 13-28 reflects the process.

Example 13-28 *Connecting Puppet to an NX-OS Device*

```
puppetadmin@puppetserver:~$ sudo puppet device -verbose -target n9kv-nxapi-1.cisco.
com
Info: Creating a new RSA SSL key for n9kv-nxapi-1.cisco.com
Info: csr_attributes file loading from /opt/puppetlabs/puppet/cache/devices/n9kv-
nxapi-1.cisco.com/csr_attributes.yaml
Info: Creating a new SSL certificate request for n9kv-nxapi-1.cisco.com
Info: Certificate Request fingerprint (SHA256): DC:59:ED:D6:1A:2C:68:9B:1E:C2:AF:B3:
9D:C2:E0:7B:C0:7D:A1:8C:52:94:BE:66:97:55:69:41:EC:CC:3A:A1
Info: Certificate for n9kv-nxapi-1.cisco.com has not been signed yet
Couldn't fetch certificate from CA server; you might still need to sign this agent's
certificate (n9kv-nxapi-1.cisco.com).
Info: Will try again in 120 seconds.
^Ccancelling startup
```

Now tell the Puppet server to retrieve the certificates list, as in Example 13-29.

Example 13-29 *Listing Puppet Certificates*

```
puppetadmin@puppetserver:~$ sudo puppetserver ca list --all
Requested Certificates:
    n9kv-nxapi-1.cisco.com       (SHA256)  DC:59:ED:D6:1A:2C:68:9B:1E:C2:AF:B3:9D:C2
:E0:7B:C0:7D:A1:8C:52:94:BE:66:97:55:69:41:EC:CC:3A:A1
Signed Certificates:
    sandbox-nxos-1.cisco.com       (SHA256)  91:0D:3C:B9:2B:90:71:9D:B8:48:6D:76:9F:
72:3A:39:54:22:4F:E0:11:D3:68:3D:2C:6A:29:2C:ED:32:A9:F8
        alt names: ["DNS:sandbox-nxos-1.cisco.com"]
    puppetserver.cisco.com         (SHA256)  C4:FD:EA:3E:E4:5E:1A:25:28:72:A9:64:4B:
E8:C8:AF:1C:B2:A4:2D:65:76:C5:31:22:6F:6B:58:FC:5D:76:D5
        alt names: ["DNS:puppet", "DNS:puppetserver.cisco.com"] authorization exten-
sions: [pp_cli_auth: true]
```

Note the outstanding signing request from the new device, n9kv-nxapi-1.cisco.com.

Now, have the Puppet server use its intermediary certificate authority (CA) to sign them. Signing the certificate is shown in Example 13-30.

Example 13-30 *Signing Certificates with the Puppet Server*

```
puppetadmin@puppetserver:~$ sudo puppetserver ca sign --all
Successfully signed certificate request for n9kv-nxapi-1.cisco.com
```

Next, repeat the connection to the new device and note that a *lot* more output is generated with the successful connection. Example 13-31 should reflect your experience in a similar fashion.

Example 13-31 *Puppet Device Connectivity After Signing Certificates*

```
puppetadmin@puppetserver:~$ sudo puppet device --verbose --target n9kv-nxapi-1.
cisco.com
Info: csr_attributes file loading from /opt/puppetlabs/puppet/cache/devices/n9kv-
nxapi-1.cisco.com/csr_attributes.yaml
Info: Creating a new SSL certificate request for n9kv-nxapi-1.cisco.com
Info: Certificate Request fingerprint (SHA256): DC:59:ED:D6:1A:2C:68:9B:1E:C2:AF:B3:
9D:C2:E0:7B:C0:7D:A1:8C:52:94:BE:66:97:55:69:41:EC:CC:3A:A1
Info: Downloaded certificate for n9kv-nxapi-1.cisco.com from https://puppetserver.
cisco.com:8140/puppet-ca/v1
Info: Retrieving pluginfacts
Info: Retrieving plugin
Notice: /File[/opt/puppetlabs/puppet/cache/devices/n9kv-nxapi-1.cisco.com/lib/
facter]/ensure: created
Notice: /File[/opt/puppetlabs/puppet/cache/devices/n9kv-nxapi-1.cisco.com/lib/
facter/cisco.rb]/ensure: defined content as '{md5}0e4175be403bdfc856fbb0d5104efa36'
Notice: /File[/opt/puppetlabs/puppet/cache/devices/n9kv-nxapi-1.cisco.com/lib/
facter/cisco_nexus.rb]/ensure: defined content as
[ . . . A LOT OF TRIMMED OUTPUT . . . ]
Info: Retrieving locales
Info: starting applying configuration to n9kv-nxapi-1.cisco.com at file:////etc/pup-
petlabs/puppet/devices/n9kv-nxapi-1.cisco.com.conf
Info: Using configured environment 'production'
/opt/puppetlabs/puppet/lib/ruby/gems/2.5.0/gems/cisco_node_utils-2.1.0/lib/cisco_
node_utils/node.rb:153: warning: constant ::Fixnum is deprecated
Info: Caching catalog for n9kv-nxapi-1.cisco.com
Info: Applying configuration version '1630279177'
Info: Creating state file /opt/puppetlabs/puppet/cache/devices/n9kv-nxapi-1.cisco.
com/state/state.yaml
Notice: Applied catalog in 0.03 seconds
puppetadmin@puppetserver:~$
```

Now, collect Puppet facts from this new remote Nexus device, as in Example 13-32.

Example 13-32 *A More Complete Output of Puppet Facts*

```
puppetadmin@puppetserver:~$ sudo puppet device --verbose --facts --target n9kv-
nxapi-1.cisco.com
Info: retrieving facts from n9kv-nxapi-1.cisco.com at file:////etc/puppetlabs/pup-
pet/devices/n9kv-nxapi-1.cisco.com.conf
{
  "name": "n9kv-nxapi-1.cisco.com",
  "values": {
    "operatingsystem": "nexus",
    "cisco_node_utils": "2.1.0",
    "cisco": {
     "images": {
        "system_image": "bootflash:///nxos64.10.2.1.F.bin",
        "full_version": "10.2(1)",
```

```
      "packages": {
      }
    },
    "hardware": {
      "type": "cisco Nexus9000 C9500v Chassis",
      "cpu": "Intel(R) Xeon(R) CPU E5-2699 v4 @ 2.20GHz",
      "board": "9F3I6MFDAW2",
      "last_reset": "",
      "reset_reason": "Unknown",
      "memory": {
        "total": "10211572K",
        "used": "5171128K",
        "free": "5040444K"
      },
      "uptime": "1 days, 4 hours, 37 minutes, 35 seconds"
    },
    "inventory": {
      "chassis": {
        "descr": "Nexus9000 C9500v Chassis",
        "pid": "N9K-C9500v",
        "vid": "",
        "sn": "9WYQFON66B3"
      },
      "Slot 1": {
        "descr": "Nexus 9000v 64 port Ethernet Module",
        "pid": "N9K-X9564v",
        "vid": "",
        "sn": "904TSSBDH5Q"
      },
      "Slot 27": {
        "descr": "Supervisor Module",
        "pid": "N9K-vSUP",
        "vid": "",
        "sn": "9F3I6MFDAW2"
      }
    },
    "interface_count": 65,
    "interface_threshold": 9,
    "virtual_service": {
    },
    "feature_compatible_module_iflist": {
      "fabricpath": [

      ]
    }
  },
```

```
    "hostname": "n9kv-nxapi-1",
    "operatingsystemrelease": "10.2(1)",
    "clientcert": "n9kv-nxapi-1.cisco.com",
    "clientversion": "6.24.0",
    "clientnoop": false
  },
  "timestamp": "2021-08-29T19:40:11.902778717-04:00",
  "expiration": "2021-08-29T20:10:11.902898379-04:00"
}
puppetadmin@puppetserver:~$
```

Using that same process with the **jq** utility, as described previously, you can extract the device uptime. Example 13-33 provides guidance.

Example 13-33 *Using Puppet and the* jq *Utility to Extract Device Uptime*

```
puppetadmin@puppetserver:~$ sudo puppet device --verbose --facts --target n9kv-
nxapi-1.cisco.com 2> /dev/null | sed -n '/{/,/^}/p' - | jq '.values.cisco.hardware.
uptime'
"1 days, 4 hours, 53 minutes, 50 seconds"
```

Unpacking that, you use the **puppet device** command with options, redirecting standard err (STDERR) or file handle #2 to /dev/null, effectively ignoring errors. The output of the command is fed with a pipe (|) into the Linux **sed** (stream editor) utility to capture any output that starts with an opening brace ({) and ends with a closing brace (}). This effectively captures the JSON output of the **puppet** command, ignoring other output. That output is fed into the **jq** utility, which filters for the hierarchy of values, cisco, hardware, and uptime.

Now that you have an idea about how to programmatically access device information or facts, you can move on to more sophisticated examples, such as programmatically changing a device configuration.

To set device parameters or configurations, you still use the **puppet device** command, but this time you use the **--apply** option and specify a Puppet manifest that generally ends with a .pp extension.

What is a Puppet manifest? **Manifests** are a collection of resource definitions (configurable items) and their variables/parameters, collected into a single "Puppet policy" file with the .pp extension. Typically, these files exist on the Puppet server in the /etc/puppetlabs/code/environments/production/manifests directory. Manifests support the use of variables, loops, conditionals, and importing of other files and classes from separate Puppet files. These capabilities allow you to make complex provisioning scenarios, if needed.

In Example 13-34, a manifest completes many actions. It defines a specific Ethernet1/61 port for an access port and labels it to be used for a server. It provisions three different VLANs, also pulling in their configuration parameters from another file. Then it requires a specific NTP server to *not* exist, as if you are unconfiguring a decommissioned server. Then it configures a new one. On the Puppet server, this is the /etc/puppetlabs/code/environments/production/manifests/site.pp file.

Example 13-34 *Puppet Manifest to Change a Device*

```
node 'n9kv-nxapi-1.cisco.com' {
        cisco_interface { 'Ethernet1/61' :
                shutdown        => false,
                switchport_mode => access,
                description     => 'Puppet managed - server port',
                access_vlan     => 100,
        }

        include vlan_data

        $vlan_data::vlans.each |$vlanid,$value|
        {
                $vlanname       = "${value[name]}"
                $intfName       = "Vlan${vlanid}"

                #Create VLAN
                cisco_vlan {"${vlanid}":
                 vlan_name => $vlanname,
                 ensure    => present
                }

                #Create VLAN interface (stage 2)
                cisco_interface { $intfName:
                        description     => $vlanname,
                        shutdown        => false,
                }
        }

        ntp_server { '1.2.3.4':
          ensure => 'absent',
        }

        ntp_server { '64.100.58.75':
          ensure => 'present',
          prefer => true,
          vrf => 'management',
          minpoll => 4,
          maxpoll => 10,
        }
}
```

Example 13-35 contains the associated vlan_data.pp file, which is called with the **include vlan_data** directive seen in Example 13-34.

Example 13-35 *vlan_data.pp File for the Puppet Manifest Reference*

```
class vlan_data {

 $vlans = {
    100 => { name => "Production" },
    200 => { name => "Site_Backup" },
    300 => { name => "Development" },
 }
}
```

Example 13-36 shows how you can trigger Puppet to pull down this policy and reconfigure the device.

Example 13-36 *Triggering Puppet to Connect to a Device and Run a Policy*

```
puppetadmin@puppetserver:/etc/puppetlabs/code/environments/production/manifests$
sudo puppet device --verbose --target n9kv-nxapi-1.cisco.com
[sudo] password for puppetadmin:
Info: Retrieving pluginfacts
Info: Retrieving plugin
Info: Retrieving locales
Info: starting applying configuration to n9kv-nxapi-1.cisco.com at
file:////etc/puppetlabs/puppet/devices/n9kv-nxapi-1.cisco.com.conf
Info: Using configured environment 'production'
Info: Caching catalog for n9kv-nxapi-1.cisco.com
Info: Applying configuration version '1630358256'
Info: Puppet::Type::Cisco_interface::ProviderCisco: [prefetch each interface
independently] (threshold: 9)
Notice: /Stage[main]/Main/Node[n9kv-nxapi-1.cisco.com]/Cisco_
interface[Ethernet1/61]/ensure: created (corrective)
Notice: /Stage[main]/Main/Node[n9kv-nxapi-1.cisco.com]/Cisco_vlan[100]/ensure:
created (corrective)
Notice: /Stage[main]/Main/Node[n9kv-nxapi-1.cisco.com]/Cisco_interface[Vlan100]/
ensure: created (corrective)
Notice: /Stage[main]/Main/Node[n9kv-nxapi-1.cisco.com]/Cisco_vlan[200]/ensure:
created (corrective)
Notice: /Stage[main]/Main/Node[n9kv-nxapi-1.cisco.com]/Cisco_interface[Vlan200]/
ensure: created (corrective)
Notice: /Stage[main]/Main/Node[n9kv-nxapi-1.cisco.com]/Cisco_vlan[300]/ensure:
created (corrective)
Notice: /Stage[main]/Main/Node[n9kv-nxapi-1.cisco.com]/Cisco_interface[Vlan300]/
ensure: created (corrective)
Notice: /Stage[main]/Main/Node[n9kv-nxapi-1.cisco.com]/Ntp_server[64.100.58.75]/
ensure: defined 'ensure' as 'present' (corrective)
Notice: ntp_server[64.100.58.75]: Creating: Setting '64.100.58.75' with
{:name=>"64.100.58.75", :ensure=>"present", :maxpoll=>10, :minpoll=>4,
:prefer=>true, :vrf=>"management"}
Notice: ntp_server[64.100.58.75]: Creating: Finished in 0.146842 seconds
Info: Node[n9kv-nxapi-1.cisco.com]: Unscheduling all events on Node[n9kv-nxapi-1.
cisco.com]
Notice: Applied catalog in 18.20 seconds
puppetadmin@puppetserver:/etc/puppetlabs/code/environments/production/manifests$
```

Now you can look at the configuration changes of the n9kv-nxapi-1.cisco.com node using a method similar to Example 13-37.

Example 13-37 *Puppet-Influenced Configuration Change Results*

```
n9kv-nxapi-1# sh running-config

!Command: show running-config
!Running configuration last done at: Mon Aug 30 21:17:55 2021
!Time: Mon Aug 30 21:19:48 2021

version 10.2(1) Bios:version
switchname n9kv-nxapi-1
vdc n9kv-nxapi-1 id 1
  limit-resource vlan minimum 16 maximum 4094
  limit-resource vrf minimum 2 maximum 4096
  limit-resource port-channel minimum 0 maximum 511
  limit-resource m4route-mem minimum 58 maximum 58
  limit-resource m6route-mem minimum 8 maximum 8

feature nxapi
feature interface-vlan

no password strength-check
username admin password 5 $5$***w2  role network-admin
ip domain-lookup
copp profile strict
snmp-server user admin network-admin auth md5 207E4F*** priv aes-128 205E0B***
localizedV2key
ntp server 64.100.58.75 prefer use-vrf management maxpoll 10
system default switchport

vlan 1,100,200,300
vlan 100
  name Production
vlan 200
  name Site_Backup
vlan 300
  name Development

vrf context management
  ip route 0.0.0.0/0 172.31.0.1

interface Vlan1
```

```
interface Vlan100
  description Production
  no shutdown

interface Vlan200
  description Site_Backup
  no shutdown

interface Vlan300
  description Development
  no shutdown

interface Ethernet1/1

interface Ethernet1/2

[ . . . SOME OUTPUT TRIMMED . . . ]

interface Ethernet1/60

interface Ethernet1/61
  description Puppet managed - server port
  switchport access vlan 100

interface Ethernet1/62

interface Ethernet1/63

interface Ethernet1/64

interface mgmt0
  vrf member management
  ip address 172.31.0.170/20
icam monitor scale

line console
line vty
no system default switchport shutdown

n9kv-nxapi-1#v
```

How cool is that? By programmatically creating the site.pp and device.conf files, you can perform highly automated provisioning. This is Infrastructure as Code, or IaC.

Agentless Solutions—Ansible and Terraform

So far we have discussed IaC solutions like Puppet and a bit of agent and agentless technology solutions. **Ansible** is another IaC solution that commands a large following. It is also an agentless technology, so there is no device-side installation of software bits.

Although you do not need an agent on the managed nodes, you do need SSH for Ansible to communicate with them. When Ansible communicates with many server operating systems, it uses SSH for connectivity and SFTP for transferring Python code and modules. SFTP is not a common transport for network devices, so Ansible uses SSH and secure copy protocol (SCP).

You first need to ensure the SSH server is configured appropriately for Ansible to access your devices with the appropriate user, password, public/private key, routing, and access control lists. Fortunately, those configurations are probably the same ones that were done for terminal access anyway.

Let's start in a similar fashion as done with the Puppet example in the previous section: start with a virgin Ubuntu 20.04 server and build the Ansible server to connect to the managed devices.

NOTE Feel free to use a desktop operating system like macOS or Windows if you have the Linux subsystem enabled.

You can choose a simple package manager install or a more involved installation from a virtualized Python package installer (pip) install. Pick your preference from the next two sections. Note that the package manager install provides a version that lags the latest. The virtualized Python pip environment installs a more recent version without the complexity of doing a source-code-based install.

NOTE As of 2021, the Ansible project is in a transitionary period with version numbering. With Ansible 3.0 and later, the project is separated into two packages:

- ansible-core (previously known as ansible-base in ansible 3.0), the runtime, and a built-in Collection (select core modules, plug-ins, and so on)
- ansible, community-curated Collections

The ansible-core package maintains the existing versioning scheme (like the Linux Kernel), whereas the ansible package is adopting semantic versioning.

The current Ansible 4.0 comprises two packages: ansible-core 2.12 and ansible 4.0.

Installing Ansible from the Package Manager

Installing Ansible from the package manager is straightforward in most Linux distributions. For Ubuntu, you use the basic **sudo apt install ansible** command, as in Example 13-38.

Example 13-38 *Installing Ansible from Ubuntu Server 20.04*

```
ansibleadmin@ansibleserver:~$ sudo apt install ansible
[sudo] password for ansibleadmin:
Reading package lists... Done
Building dependency tree
Reading state information... Done
The following additional packages will be installed:
  ieee-data python3-argcomplete python3-crypto python3-dnspython python3-jmespath
python3-kerberos python3-libcloud python3-lockfile
  python3-netaddr python3-ntlm-auth python3-requests-kerberos python3-requests-ntlm
python3-selinux python3-winrm python3-xmltodict
Suggested packages:
  cowsay sshpass python-lockfile-doc ipython3 python-netaddr-docs
The following NEW packages will be installed:
  ansible ieee-data python3-argcomplete python3-crypto python3-dnspython python3-
jmespath python3-kerberos python3-libcloud
  python3-lockfile python3-netaddr python3-ntlm-auth python3-requests-kerberos
python3-requests-ntlm python3-selinux python3-winrm
  python3-xmltodict
0 upgraded, 16 newly installed, 0 to remove and 0 not upgraded.
Need to get 9,643 kB of archives.
After this operation, 90.2 MB of additional disk space will be used.
Do you want to continue? [Y/n] y
Get:1 http://us.archive.ubuntu.com/ubuntu focal/main amd64 python3-crypto amd64
2.6.1-13ubuntu2 [237 kB]
Get:2 http://us.archive.ubuntu.com/ubuntu focal/main amd64 python3-dnspython all
1.16.0-1build1 [89.1 kB]
Get:3 http://us.archive.ubuntu.com/ubuntu focal/main amd64 ieee-data all 20180805.1
[1,589 kB]
Get:4 http://us.archive.ubuntu.com/ubuntu focal/main amd64 python3-netaddr all
0.7.19-3 [235 kB]
Get:5 http://us.archive.ubuntu.com/ubuntu focal/universe amd64 ansible all
2.9.6+dfsg-1 [5,794 kB]
[ . . . Some output trimmed . . . ]
Selecting previously unselected package ansible.
Preparing to unpack .../04-ansible_2.9.6+dfsg-1_all.deb ...
Unpacking ansible (2.9.6+dfsg-1) ...
[ . . . Some output trimmed . . . ]
Progress: [ 98%] [####################################################################
################################################..]
[ . . . Some output trimmed . . . ]
Setting up ansible (2.9.6+dfsg-1) ...
Processing triggers for man-db (2.9.1-1) ...
ansibleadmin@ansibleserver:~$
```

That installation is painless. You can check the version installed for your information. Observe the operation in Example 13-39.

Example 13-39 *Showing Ansible Version*

```
ansibleadmin@ansibleserver:~$ ansible --version
ansible 2.9.6
  config file = /etc/ansible/ansible.cfg
  configured module search path = ['/home/ansibleadmin/.ansible/plugins/modules', '/
usr/share/ansible/plugins/modules']
  ansible python module location = /usr/lib/python3/dist-packages/ansible
  executable location = /usr/bin/ansible
  python version = 3.8.10 (default, Jun  2 2021, 10:49:15) [GCC 9.4.0]
```

As of summer 2021, Ansible 2.9.6 version is getting a bit dated, so if you want a newer version, you need to forgo the package manager version and install in a different manner. Follow the steps in the next section for the most recent version.

Installing the Latest Ansible from a Virtual Python Environment with pip

The process of installing Ansible from a virtual Python environment with pip gets you the latest functionality and decent separation from other projects on the server. You do have to depend on Python, so ensure you have the latest Python installed first. Example 13-40 depicts how to install Python 3.9.

Example 13-40 *Installing Python 3.9 on Ubuntu Server 20.04*

```
ansibleadmin@ansibleserver:/opt/ansible$ sudo apt-get install python3.9
python3.9-venv
Reading package lists... Done
Building dependency tree
Reading state information... Done
The following additional packages will be installed:
  libpython3.9-minimal libpython3.9-stdlib python-pip-whl python3.9-minimal
Suggested packages:
  python3.9-doc binutils binfmt-support
The following NEW packages will be installed:
  libpython3.9-minimal libpython3.9-stdlib python-pip-whl python3.9 python3.9-mini-
mal python3.9-venv
0 upgraded, 6 newly installed, 0 to remove and 0 not upgraded.
Need to get 1,811 kB/6,788 kB of archives.
After this operation, 22.2 MB of additional disk space will be used.
Do you want to continue? [Y/n] y
Get:1 http://us.archive.ubuntu.com/ubuntu focal-updates/universe amd64 python-pip-
whl all 20.0.2-5ubuntu1.6 [1,805 kB]
Get:2 http://us.archive.ubuntu.com/ubuntu focal-updates/universe amd64 python3.9-
venv amd64 3.9.5-3~20.04.1 [5,444 B]
Fetched 1,811 kB in 0s (4,148 kB/s)
Selecting previously unselected package libpython3.9-minimal:amd64.
(Reading database ... 71637 files and directories currently installed.)
Preparing to unpack .../0-libpython3.9-minimal_3.9.5-3~20.04.1_amd64.deb ...
Unpacking libpython3.9-minimal:amd64 (3.9.5-3~20.04.1) ...
```

```
Selecting previously unselected package python3.9-minimal.
Preparing to unpack .../1-python3.9-minimal_3.9.5-3~20.04.1_amd64.deb ...
Unpacking python3.9-minimal (3.9.5-3~20.04.1) ...
Selecting previously unselected package libpython3.9-stdlib:amd64.
Preparing to unpack .../2-libpython3.9-stdlib_3.9.5-3~20.04.1_amd64.deb ...
Unpacking libpython3.9-stdlib:amd64 (3.9.5-3~20.04.1) ...
Selecting previously unselected package python-pip-whl.
Preparing to unpack .../3-python-pip-whl_20.0.2-5ubuntu1.6_all.deb ...
Unpacking python-pip-whl (20.0.2-5ubuntu1.6) ...
Selecting previously unselected package python3.9.
Preparing to unpack .../4-python3.9_3.9.5-3~20.04.1_amd64.deb ...
Unpacking python3.9 (3.9.5-3~20.04.1) ...
Selecting previously unselected package python3.9-venv.
Preparing to unpack .../5-python3.9-venv_3.9.5-3~20.04.1_amd64.deb ...
Unpacking python3.9-venv (3.9.5-3~20.04.1) ...
Setting up libpython3.9-minimal:amd64 (3.9.5-3~20.04.1) ...
Setting up python-pip-whl (20.0.2-5ubuntu1.6) ...
Setting up python3.9-minimal (3.9.5-3~20.04.1) ...
Setting up libpython3.9-stdlib:amd64 (3.9.5-3~20.04.1) ...
Setting up python3.9 (3.9.5-3~20.04.1) ...
Setting up python3.9-venv (3.9.5-3~20.04.1) ...
Processing triggers for man-db (2.9.1-1) ...
Processing triggers for mime-support (3.64ubuntu1) ...
ansibleadmin@ansibleserver:/opt/ansible$
```

You can check which specific version of Python you have installed, as in Example 13-41.

Example 13-41 *Checking Python Version*

```
ansibleadmin@ansibleserver:~$ python3.9 -V
Python 3.9.5
ansibleadmin@ansibleserver:~$
```

Now prepare for a project directory for Ansible under /opt, where optional software usually is installed. This setup can be found in Example 13-42.

Example 13-42 *Setting Up a Project Directory*

```
ansibleadmin@ansibleserver:~$ sudo chgrp ansibleadmin /opt/ansible/
ansibleadmin@ansibleserver:~$ sudo chmod 775 /opt/ansible/
ansibleadmin@ansibleserver:~$ ls -ld /opt/ansible/
drwxrwxr-x 2 root ansibleadmin 4096 Sep  1 23:18 /opt/ansible/
```

Now create the virtual environment, which Example 13-43 explains.

Example 13-43 *Setting Up a Python Project Virtual Environment*

```
ansibleadmin@ansibleserver:/opt/ansible$ cd /opt/ansible
ansibleadmin@ansibleserver:/opt/ansible$ python3.9 -m venv env
```

Then activate the virtual environment with Example 13-44 as a reference.

Example 13-44 *Activating a Python Virtual Environment*

```
ansibleadmin@ansibleserver:/opt/ansible$ source env/bin/activate
(env) ansibleadmin@ansibleserver:/opt/ansible$
```

Note that the virtual environment is activated by the inclusion of **env** at the command-line prompt.

You can also validate where the Python executable is referenced and which version the environment is running by using the steps in Example 13-45.

Example 13-45 *Validating Python Path and Version*

```
(env) ansibleadmin@ansibleserver:/opt/ansible$ which python
/opt/ansible/env/bin/python
(env) ansibleadmin@ansibleserver:/opt/ansible$ python -V
Python 3.9.5
(env) ansibleadmin@ansibleserver:/opt/ansible$
```

It is a good idea to ensure that the latest version of the pip is available. Example 13-46 identifies the actions to validate and update.

Example 13-46 *Validating and Updating the Python pip Utility*

```
(env) ansibleadmin@ansibleserver:/opt/ansible$ pip --version
pip 20.0.2 from /opt/ansible/env/lib/python3.9/site-packages/pip (python 3.9)
(env) ansibleadmin@ansibleserver:/opt/ansible$ pip install --upgrade pip
Collecting pip
  Downloading pip-21.2.4-py3-none-any.whl (1.6 MB)
    |████████████████████████████████| 1.6 MB 6.5 MB/s
Installing collected packages: pip
  Attempting uninstall: pip
    Found existing installation: pip 20.0.2
    Uninstalling pip-20.0.2:
      Successfully uninstalled pip-20.0.2
Successfully installed pip-21.2.4
(env) ansibleadmin@ansibleserver:/opt/ansible$ pip --version
pip 21.2.4 from /opt/ansible/env/lib/python3.9/site-packages/pip (python 3.9)
(env) ansibleadmin@ansibleserver:/opt/ansible$
```

Now you can install the latest Ansible using Python pip. This process is shown in Example 13-47.

Example 13-47 *Using Python pip to Install Ansible*

```
(env) ansibleadmin@ansibleserver:/opt/ansible$ python -m pip install ansible
Collecting ansible
  Downloading ansible-4.5.0.tar.gz (35.5 MB)
     |████████████████████████████████| 35.5 MB 6.4 MB/s
Collecting ansible-core<2.12,>=2.11.4
  Downloading ansible-core-2.11.4.tar.gz (6.8 MB)
     |████████████████████████████████| 6.8 MB 44.5 MB/s
Collecting PyYAML
  Downloading PyYAML-5.4.1-cp39-cp39-manylinux1_x86_64.whl (630 kB)
     |████████████████████████████████| 630 kB 46.2 MB/s
Collecting cryptography
  Downloading cryptography-3.4.8-cp36-abi3-manylinux_2_24_x86_64.whl (3.0 MB)
     |████████████████████████████████| 3.0 MB 48.8 MB/s
Collecting jinja2
  Downloading Jinja2-3.0.1-py3-none-any.whl (133 kB)
     |████████████████████████████████| 133 kB 62.9 MB/s
Collecting packaging
  Downloading packaging-21.0-py3-none-any.whl (40 kB)
     |████████████████████████████████| 40 kB 13.3 MB/s
Collecting resolvelib<0.6.0,>=0.5.3
  Downloading resolvelib-0.5.4-py2.py3-none-any.whl (12 kB)
Collecting cffi>=1.12
  Downloading cffi-1.14.6-cp39-cp39-manylinux1_x86_64.whl (405 kB)
     |████████████████████████████████| 405 kB 51.7 MB/s
Collecting pycparser
  Downloading pycparser-2.20-py2.py3-none-any.whl (112 kB)
     |████████████████████████████████| 112 kB 62.2 MB/s
Collecting MarkupSafe>=2.0
  Downloading MarkupSafe-2.0.1-cp39-cp39-manylinux_2_5_x86_64.manylinux1_x86_64.
manylinux_2_12_x86_64.manylinux2010_x86_64.whl (30 kB)
Collecting pyparsing>=2.0.2
  Downloading pyparsing-2.4.7-py2.py3-none-any.whl (67 kB)
     |████████████████████████████████| 67 kB 6.7 MB/s
Using legacy 'setup.py install' for ansible, since package 'wheel' is not installed.
Using legacy 'setup.py install' for ansible-core, since package 'wheel' is not
installed.
Installing collected packages: pycparser, pyparsing, MarkupSafe, cffi, resolvelib,
PyYAML, packaging, jinja2, cryptography, ansible-core, ansible
    Running setup.py install for ansible-core ... done
    Running setup.py install for ansible ... done
Successfully installed MarkupSafe-2.0.1 PyYAML-5.4.1 ansible-4.5.0
ansible-core-2.11.4 cffi-1.14.6 cryptography-3.4.8 jinja2-3.0.1 packaging-21.0
pycparser-2.20 pyparsing-2.4.7 resolvelib-0.5.4
(env) ansibleadmin@ansibleserver:/opt/ansible$
```

Looking through the output, you can see that at the time of this installation Ansible 4.5.0 with ansible-core package version 2.11.4 was installed.

Another quick confirmation at the command-line interface is shown in Example 13-48.

Example 13-48 *Reviewing Ansible Version*

```
(env) ansibleadmin@ansibleserver:/opt/ansible$ ansible --version
ansible [core 2.11.4]
  config file = None
  configured module search path = ['/home/ansibleadmin/.ansible/plugins/modules', '/
usr/share/ansible/plugins/modules']
  ansible python module location = /opt/ansible/env/lib/python3.9/site-packages/
ansible
  ansible collection location = /home/ansibleadmin/.ansible/collections:/usr/share/
ansible/collections
  executable location = /opt/ansible/env/bin/ansible
  python version = 3.9.5 (default, May 19 2021, 11:32:47) [GCC 9.3.0]
  jinja version = 3.0.1
  libyaml = True
(env) ansibleadmin@ansibleserver:/opt/ansible$
```

A quick verification on the Ansible release summary website confirms that this release is the latest.

One last thing to do is to install the **paramiko** module, which is useful for SSH-based projects. Example 13-49 depicts the pip install process.

Example 13-49 *Python pip Installing the* **paramiko** *Module*

```
(env) ansibleadmin@ansibleserver:/opt/ansible$ python -m pip install paramiko
Collecting paramiko
  Downloading paramiko-2.7.2-py2.py3-none-any.whl (206 kB)
     |████████████████████████████████| 206 kB 6.2 MB/s
Collecting pynacl>=1.0.1
  Downloading PyNaCl-1.4.0-cp35-abi3-manylinux1_x86_64.whl (961 kB)
     |████████████████████████████████| 961 kB 34.2 MB/s
Requirement already satisfied: cryptography>=2.5 in ./env/lib/python3.9/site-pack-
ages (from paramiko) (3.4.8)
Collecting bcrypt>=3.1.3
  Downloading bcrypt-3.2.0-cp36-abi3-manylinux2010_x86_64.whl (63 kB)
     |████████████████████████████████| 63 kB 5.7 MB/s
Collecting six>=1.4.1
  Downloading six-1.16.0-py2.py3-none-any.whl (11 kB)
Requirement already satisfied: cffi>=1.1 in ./env/lib/python3.9/site-packages (from
bcrypt>=3.1.3->paramiko) (1.14.6)
Requirement already satisfied: pycparser in ./env/lib/python3.9/site-packages (from
cffi>=1.1->bcrypt>=3.1.3->paramiko) (2.20)
Installing collected packages: six, pynacl, bcrypt, paramiko
Successfully installed bcrypt-3.2.0 paramiko-2.7.2 pynacl-1.4.0 six-1.16.0
(env) ansibleadmin@ansibleserver:/opt/ansible$
```

Now that the foundational software is laid, you can start your Ansible IaC journey by creating an inventory file to define devices and their credentials.

Configuring Ansible Inventory

13

Because Ansible uses SSH to connect to the managed devices, you must maintain your credentials somewhere. You *could* put them in your Ansible files—the **playbooks**—but that's a security disaster waiting to happen. So we don't even show how to set your passwords in the playbooks. Instead, we show you how to use a "Secure First" strategy and use the Ansible Vault feature, which provides an encryption model.

To start, you create a vault password in a secure, limited-access vault credentials file. Your vault password can be any string you prefer. Do *not* include this file in shared version control, such as git. Example 13-50 shows these steps.

Example 13-50 *Creating an Ansible Vault Password*

```
(env) ansibleadmin@ansibleserver:/opt/ansible$ echo -n "my_secure_password" >
my_vault_cred
(env) ansibleadmin@ansibleserver:/opt/ansible$ chmod 600 my_vault_cred
(env) ansibleadmin@ansibleserver:/opt/ansible$ ls -l my_vault_cred
-rw------- 1 ansibleadmin ansibleadmin 18 Sep  2 16:07 my_vault_cred
```

Next, assume you have a device password that you want to encrypt, so the encrypted string can be included in a version-controlled Ansible playbook, thus reducing your security exposure. You can choose your own variable name; the standard **ansible_password** variable is used in Example 13-51 to represent the password for infrastructure devices in a DMZ environment.

Example 13-51 *Encrypting Strings for Device Passwords in Ansible*

```
(env) ansibleadmin@ansibleserver:/opt/ansible$ ansible-vault encrypt_string --vault-
id dmz@my_vault --stdin-name 'ansible_password'
Reading plaintext input from stdin. (ctrl-d to end input, twice if your content does
not already have a newline)
************
ansible_password: !vault |
          $ANSIBLE_VAULT;1.2;AES256;dmz
          36343665373737326533646435363164363336353732393135336636386366663434323636
316130
          35353363335646136643338333631353136326661323164630a396330613639346264636531
363931
          33373332653064666134653034343433383636393161353839336566326634653730346464
623234
          62383432353762656 60a396266663339626238346664323562363761666136393337626433
616331
          6364
Encryption successful
```

Now you can take that **ansible_pass** variable with the trailing data to represent the password in the Ansible playbook without exposing the device password(s).

Let's progress further by creating a basic project-level inventory file and validate the connectivity.

Creating a Project-Level Inventory File

If you installed Ansible from a package manager version, note that a new global inventory file exists in /etc/ansible/hosts. However, if you installed using a virtualized Python environment with pip, this file does not exist. You can create your own inventory file in a project-oriented directory. This is considered a leading practice. You can name the inventory file anything you want and define it using YAML data encoding, as seen in Example 13-52. Although Ansible inventory files do support INI format, they do not support the inline vault references, which we prefer for security reasons. So, if you're not comfortable using YAML to build inventory files and other configuration-related data, here are a couple of good references to learn it:

https://www.w3schools.io/file/yaml-introduction/

https://docs.ansible.com/ansible/latest/reference_appendices/YAMLSyntax.html

Now you can create a file called inventory by using YAML syntax as shown in Example 13-52.

Key Topic

Example 13-52 *Ansible Inventory File in YAML Syntax*

```
---

all:
  vars:
    ansible_connection: ansible.netcommon.network_cli

infra:
  hosts:
    n9kv-nxapi-1:
      ansible_host: 172.31.0.170
    n9kv-nxapi-2:
      ansible_host: 172.31.0.171
  vars:
    ansible_become: yes
    ansible_become_method: enable
    ansible_network_os: cisco.ios.ios
    ansible_user: admin
    ansible_password: !vault |
          $ANSIBLE_VAULT;1.2;AES256;dmz
          36343665373737326533646435363164363336353732393135336636386366663434323636
316130
          35353363356461366433383336313531363266613231646 30a396330613639346264636531
363931
          33373332653064666134653034343433383636393161353839336566326634653730346464
623234
          6238343235376265660a396266663339626238346664323562363761666136393337626433
616331
          6364
```

Now that you've defined an inventory file, you can validate connectivity from the Ansible server to the managed devices by using the Ansible **ping** module. Example 13-53 depicts the process and results.

Example 13-53 *Validating Ansible Connectivity with a Vault-Enabled Device*

```
(env) ansibleadmin@ansibleserver:/opt/ansible$ ansible all -i inventory -m ping
--vault-id dmz@my_vault
n9kv-nxapi-1 | SUCCESS => {
    "changed": false,
    "ping": "pong"
}
n9kv-nxapi-2 | SUCCESS => {
    "changed": false,
    "ping": "pong"
}
```

What happens here is that you tell Ansible to run the **ping** module (**-m ping**) against all hosts in the inventory file (**-i inventory**) and to use the DMZ vault ID with the **my_vault** vault password file (**--vault-id dmz@my_vault**). This effectively decrypts the **ansible_password** inline vault reference to obtain the correct device password for connectivity. The command results show each device is sent a **ping**, and the response of the device is **pong**, or reachable.

Let's move on to a nondestructive, read-only type use case and then later do configuration changes.

Creating an Ansible Playbook to Obtain show Command Results

As you saw in the inventory file, you can create IaC directives in YAML syntax. Ansible also allows for INI format, but you would lose the ability to do inline vault references. To keep your security profile high, keep using YAML.

Let's assume a use case in which you would like to execute and capture the output of several **show** commands and archive the device running-config as JSON. This is the backup-info process. You first create the Ansible playbook as a YAML file:

```
(env) ansibleadmin@ansibleserver:/opt/ansible$ vi backup-info.yaml
```

You start to define the YAML file in the text editor. YAML files in Ansible start with three dashes (---). You have to think of the sequence of activities and tasks you must perform. In this case, you create a directory named job-output in the current project directory where the **ansible-playbook** command will be executed and where the inventory and playbook files exist. You indent and provide a name for the play and the hosts that are involved. The tasks for this play are to create a directory. See the partial playbook in Example 13-54.

Example 13-54 *Ansible Playbook Creating a Filesystem Directory*

```
---
 - name: Create output directory
   hosts: localhost

   tasks:
     - name: Create directory
       file:
         path: ./job-output
         state: directory
```

To create a directory, you use the **file** module and specify the path and state. Ansible has many modules; you can find documentation at https://docs.ansible.com/ansible/latest/collections/index_module.html.

The **file** module is specifically defined as a presupplied built-in at https://docs.ansible.com/ansible/latest/collections/ansible/builtin/file_module.html#ansible-collections-ansible-builtin-file-module.

The next play needs to capture some command output and store it in files. You can capture the output of **show version**, **show ip route**, and **show mac address-table**. You also can get the running-config stored in JSON format so that you can use it programmatically later if you wish.

Continuing to append the earlier playbook, you can add additional content, as described in Example 13-55.

Example 13-55 *Additional Ansible Playbook Content*

```
 - name: Capture show output
   hosts: infra
   gather_facts: no
   connection: network_cli

   tasks:
     - name: Execute show commands
       cisco.nxos.nxos_command:
         commands:
         - show version
         - show ip route
         - show mac address-table
       register: showcmds


     - name: Save show commands output to local directory
       copy:
         content: "{{ showcmds.stdout | replace('\\n', '\n') }}"
         dest: "job-output/{{ inventory_hostname }}.out"
```

The name of the play is now **Capture show output.** The hosts for this play are the **infra** device group. If you recall the inventory file, you created an infra group of the two Nexus 9K switches. Next, you can use the **cisco.nxos.nxos_command** module of Ansible to execute a list of commands. The **ios_command** module is documented at https://docs.ansible.com/ansible/latest/collections/cisco/nxos/nxos_command_module.html.

> **NOTE** Ansible v2.9 is still commonly supplied in many Linux distributions. You may see the unqualified module names in older releases, such as **nxos_command:**. Ensure you understand the version you are running and reference the documentation for proper references.

The module requires you to specify the commands, and you do so as a list. In YAML syntax, a list is prepended with a dash (-). Finally, you log the output using the **register** argument, calling the output variable **showcmds**, which is referenced later.

The next task is named **Save show commands output to local directory** and uses the built-in **copy** module. This module is documented at https://docs.ansible.com/ansible/latest/collections/ansible/builtin/copy_module.html#ansible-collections-ansible-builtin-copy-module.

The **content** and **dest** (destination) parameters define the content of the file and where it is saved. This task is a little more tricky. It uses the standard output (stdout) of the **showcmds** variable you previously defined. It passes that output via a pipe (|) to the **replace** function. The **replace** function takes all **'\\n'** strings and replaces them with **'\n'**, effectively giving you real newline breaks instead of one long string output. Likewise, the **dest** parameter defines the file as going into the job-output directory with the filename of the currently processed inventory hostname appended with .out.

The next two tasks are pretty similar—capturing some output and storing in a file—as seen in Example 13-56.

Example 13-56 *Using Ansible to Obtain JSON-Formatted Device Configuration*

```
      - name: Get running-config as JSON
        cisco.nxos.nxos_command:
          commands:
          - show run | json-pretty
        register: config

      - name: Save running-config JSON to local directory
        copy:
          content: "{{ config.stdout | replace('\\n', '\n') }}"
          dest: "job-output/{{ inventory_hostname }}-config.json"
...
```

One notable callout is the **show run | json-pretty** command. The Nexus 9ks in the environment supports NX-OS features of redirecting command output to JSON in a "pretty" format. This is convenient for programmatic use. The output is stored in a device-hostnamed file with -config.json appended.

Now you can execute the playbook, with Example 13-57 as your guide.

Example 13-57 *Running an Ansible Playbook That Archives a Configuration*

```
(env) ansibleadmin@ansibleserver:/opt/ansible$ ansible-playbook -I inventory--vault-
id dmz@my_vault backup-info.yaml


PLAY [Create output directory] ****************************************************
*******************************************************


TASK [Gathering Facts] ************************************************************
*******************************************************
ok: [localhost]

TASK [Create directory] ***********************************************************
*******************************************************
changed: [localhost]

PLAY [Capture show output] ********************************************************
*******************************************************


TASK [Execute show commands] ******************************************************
*******************************************************
ok: [n9kv-nxapi-1]
ok: [n9kv-nxapi-2]

TASK [Save show commands output to local directory] *******************************
*******************************************************
changed: [n9kv-nxapi-1]
changed: [n9kv-nxapi-2]

TASK [Get running-config as JSON] *************************************************
*******************************************************
ok: [n9kv-nxapi-1]
ok: [n9kv-nxapi-2]

TASK [Save running-config JSON to local directory] ********************************
*******************************************************
changed: [n9kv-nxapi-1]
changed: [n9kv-nxapi-2]

PLAY RECAP ************************************************************************
*******************************************************
localhost                  : ok=2    changed=1    unreachable=0    failed=0
skipped=0    rescued=0    ignored=0
n9kv-nxapi-1               : ok=4    changed=2    unreachable=0    failed=0
skipped=0    rescued=0    ignored=0
n9kv-nxapi-2               : ok=4    changed=2    unreachable=0    failed=0
skipped=0    rescued=0    ignored=0
```

You can see the various plays and tasks executing and the recap showing if there were any device configurations changed or if there were reachability issues and so on.

If you navigate on the Ansible server's CLI to the project directory and the job-output subdirectory, you see the files created, as depicted in Example 13-58.

Example 13-58 *Reviewing Ansible Output*

```
(env) ansibleadmin@ansibleserver:/opt/ansible$ ls -l job-output/
total 72
-rw-rw-r-- 1 ansibleadmin ansibleadmin 28770 Sep  2 21:45 n9kv-nxapi-1-config.json
-rw-rw-r-- 1 ansibleadmin ansibleadmin  1868 Sep  2 21:45 n9kv-nxapi-1.out
-rw-rw-r-- 1 ansibleadmin ansibleadmin 28999 Sep  2 21:45 n9kv-nxapi-2-config.json
-rw-rw-r-- 1 ansibleadmin ansibleadmin  1868 Sep  2 21:45 n9kv-nxapi-2.out
(env) ansibleadmin@ansibleserver:/opt/ansible$ more job-output/n9kv-nxapi-1-config.
json
['{
    "nf:source": {
        "nf:running": null
    },
    "nf:filter": {
        "m:configure": {
            "m:terminal": {
                "switchname": {
                    "__XML__PARAM__name": {
                        "__XML__value": "n9kv-nxapi-1"
                    }
                },
                "vdc": {
                    "__XML__PARAM__e-vdc": {
                        "__XML__value": "n9kv-nxapi-1",
                        "id": {
                            "__XML__PARAM__new_id": {
                                "__XML__value": "1",
[ . . . Additional output trimmed . . . ]
```

Filtering, Templating, and Jinja2

The previous examples showed how to create playbooks that use the Ansible task keyword **register** to store the output of a task. The output was then passed to a simple **replace** filter to provide proper newline outputs on lines in an output file. Behind the scenes, Ansible uses Jinja2 filtering following a common form, seen in Example 13-59.

Example 13-59 *Ansible Jinja2 Filter Format*

```
my_new_var: "{{ <input_var> | <filter()> }}"
```

In a simple activity like the ones shown in Examples 13-55 and 13-56, this syntax is easily understood and used. However, often, parsing the output requires more complex logic—potentially loops and conditionals. In these instances, filters using Ansible built-in functionality or Jinja2 are preferred. RedHat suggests these references for Jinja2:

https://docs.ansible.com/ansible/latest/user_guide/playbooks_templating.html

https://jinja.palletsprojects.com/en/3.0.x/templates/#builtin-filters

Let's try an advanced method that uses the built-in Ansible **ansible.netcommon.parse_xml** filter, which is documented at https://docs.ansible.com/ansible/latest/user_guide/playbooks_filters.html#network-xml-filters.

This filter requires a path to a YAML-formatted **spec file** that defines how to parse the XML output. Example 13-60 shows the syntax.

Example 13-60 *ansible.netcommon.parse_xml Syntax*

```
{{ output | ansible.netcommon.parse_xml('path/to/spec') }}
```

After looking at the **show vlan | xml** output from an NX-OS based Nexus 9000 series switch, you can define this nxos-vlan.yml file as shown in Example 13-61.

Example 13-61 *Sample nxos-vlan.yml File*

```
---
keys:
  vlans:
    value: "{{ vlanid }}"
    top: nf:rpc-reply/nf:data/show/vlan/__XML__OPT_Cmd_show_vlan___readonly__/__
readonly__/TABLE_vlanbrief/ROW_vlanbrief/
    items:
      vlanid: vlanid
      name: name
      state: state
      adminstate: adminstate
      intlist: intlist

vars:
  vlan:
    key: "{{ item.vlanshowbr-vlanid }}"
    values:
      vlanid: "{{ item.vlanshowbr-vlanid }}"
      name: "{{ item.vlanshowbr-vlanname }}"
      state: "{{ item.vlanshowbr-vlanstate }}"
      adminstate: "{{ item.vlanshowbr-shutstate }}"
      intlist: "{{ item.vlanshowplist-ifidx }}"
```

Now using an Ansible playbook with a task that registers **show vlan | xml** to an output variable and defines another action as **debug** or **set_fact** with **{{ output | ansible.netcommon.parse_xml('/path/to/nxos-vlan.yml') }}** renders back structured JSON that you can use in other ways.

To wrap a bow on Ansible, let's create a new playbook that changes device configurations. Let's add some VLANs to these two switches.

Using Ansible to Modify Device Configurations

As you saw in the previous section about simple device information extraction, you can use Ansible modules to interact with a device. The modules are supplied by the Ansible project and community members. Many modules are built-ins, or part of the core project—over 700! Even more modules are available from the community repository, called Galaxy, at https://galaxy.ansible.com/.

To create a playbook that creates VLANs, you need to find a Cisco IOS or NX-OS module that interacts with the VLAN feature. At the most simplistic level, you can use a module that pushes commands you provide, but that approach might not provide the level of abstraction you're looking for. Many modules handle the translation of abstract functions into the device native syntax. These kinds of modules are optimal for programmatic use and in diverse device-type environments. You can research them further in the Ansible collections library at https://docs.ansible.com/ansible/latest/collections/ansible/index.html. Searching for **cisco nx-os vlan** reveals that the **cisco.nxos.nxos-vlans** module is the optimal fit. It is documented at https://docs.ansible.com/ansible/latest/collections/cisco/nxos/nxos_vlans_module.html.

Let's create three new VLANs as done for the previous Puppet example, providing the appropriate names. To start, create a new Ansible playbook called create-vlans.yaml:

```
(env) ansibleadmin@ansibleserver:/opt/ansible$ vi create-vlans.yaml
```

The contents should appear as shown in Example 13-62.

Example 13-62 *Creating VLANs in an Ansible Playbook*

```
---
  - name: Create VLANs
    hosts: infra
    gather_facts: no
    vars:
      ansible_connection: network_cli
      ansible_network_os: nxos
      ansible_become: no

    tasks:
      - name: Merge provided configuration with device configuration.
        cisco.nxos.nxos_vlans:
          config:
          - vlan_id: 100
            name: Production
          - vlan_id: 200
            name: Site_Backup
          - vlan_id: 300
            name: Development
          state: merged
...
```

Then you can execute the playbook, as depicted in Example 13-63.

Example 13-63 *Executing the Ansible Playbook to Deploy VLANs*

```
(env) ansibleadmin@ansibleserver:/opt/ansible$ ansible-playbook -i inventory
--vault-id dmz@my_vault create-vlans.yaml

PLAY [Create VLANs] *******************************************************************
*******************************************************

TASK [Merge provided configuration with device configuration.] ********************
*******************************************************
changed: [n9kv-nxapi-2]
changed: [n9kv-nxapi-1]

PLAY RECAP ****************************************************************************
*******************************************************
n9kv-nxapi-1               : ok=1    changed=1    unreachable=0    failed=0
skipped=0    rescued=0    ignored=0
n9kv-nxapi-2               : ok=1    changed=1    unreachable=0    failed=0
skipped=0    rescued=0    ignored=0

(env) ansibleadmin@ansibleserver:/opt/ansible$
```

Inspecting one of the device configurations, you can see the results shown in Example 13-64.

Example 13-64 *Reviewing Ansible Playbook Results*

```
n9kv-nxapi-1# sh vlan

VLAN Name                             Status    Ports
---- -------------------------------- --------- -------------------------------
1    default                          active    Eth1/1, Eth1/2, Eth1/3, Eth1/4
                                                Eth1/5, Eth1/6, Eth1/7, Eth1/8
                                                Eth1/9, Eth1/10, Eth1/11
                                                Eth1/12, Eth1/13, Eth1/14
                                                Eth1/15, Eth1/16, Eth1/17
[ . . . Some output trimmed . . . ]
                                                Eth1/60, Eth1/61, Eth1/62
                                                Eth1/63, Eth1/64
100  Production                       active
200  Site_Backup                      active
300  Development                      active
```

```
VLAN Type         Vlan-mode
---- -----        ----------
1    enet         CE
100  enet         CE
200  enet         CE
300  enet         CE

Remote SPAN VLANs
-----------------------
```

13

Now let's make a more complicated example that includes conditional logic and loops. In this case, create a playbook that creates two new VLANs if VLAN 200 does not exist; deletes NTP server 10.1.1.100 if it exists; and creates a new message of the day, MOTD, login banner. Call this playbook **prep-dev-env.yaml.**

You can look up Ansible documentation for the **cisco ntp** module from the Ansible collections doc URL provided previously at https://docs.ansible.com/ansible/latest/collections/cisco/nxos/nxos_ntp_module.html.

Likewise, you can look for the banner/MOTD functionality and find **cisco nxos banner** with the module documentation at https://docs.ansible.com/ansible/latest/collections/cisco/nxos/nxos_banner_module.html.

Start by creating the Ansible playbook:

```
(env) ansibleadmin@ansibleserver:/opt/ansible$ vi prep-dev-env.yaml
```

It should look like Example 13-65.

Example 13-65 *A More Feature-Rich Playbook with Conditions*

```
---
  - name: Prep Development Environment
    hosts: infra
    gather_facts: no
    vars:
      ansible_connection: network_cli
      ansible_network_os: nxos
      ansible_become: no
      dev_vlans:
        - { vlan_id: 1000, name: Dev1 }
        - { vlan_id: 1001, name: Dev2 }

    tasks:
      - name: Get Nexus facts
        nxos_facts:
          gather_subset: legacy
        register: data
```

```
      - name: Create Dev VLANs, if VLAN 200 is missing
        cisco.nxos.nxos_vlans:
          config:
          - vlan_id: "{{ item.vlan_id }}"
            name: "{{ item.name }}"
          state: merged
        with_items: "{{ dev_vlans }}"
        when: ("200") not in data.ansible_facts.ansible_net_vlan_list

      - name: Delete the decommissioned NTP server 10.1.1.100
        cisco.nxos.nxos_ntp:
          server: 10.1.1.100
          state: absent

      - name: Create MOTD banner message
        cisco.nxos.nxos_banner:
          banner: motd
          text: |
            This is my multiline MOTD banner
            that was deployed by an Ansible playbook
          state: present
...
```

Now you can run the Ansible playbook, as in Example 13-66.

Example 13-66 *Running the More Sophisticated Ansible Playbook with Conditionals*

```
(env) ansibleadmin@ansibleserver:/opt/ansible$ ansible-playbook -i inventory
--vault-id dmz@my_vault prep-dev-env.yaml


PLAY [Prep Development Environment] *************************************************
*******************************************************


TASK [Get Nexus facts] **************************************************************
*******************************************************
ok: [n9kv-nxapi-2]
ok: [n9kv-nxapi-1]


TASK [Create Dev VLANs, if VLAN 200 is missing] *************************************
*******************************************************
skipping: [n9kv-nxapi-1] => (item={'vlan_id': 1000, 'name': 'Dev1'})
skipping: [n9kv-nxapi-1] => (item={'vlan_id': 1001, 'name': 'Dev2'})
changed: [n9kv-nxapi-2] => (item={'vlan_id': 1000, 'name': 'Dev1'})
changed: [n9kv-nxapi-2] => (item={'vlan_id': 1001, 'name': 'Dev2'})
```

```
TASK [Delete the decommissioned NTP server 10.1.1.100] ****************************
*******************************************************
ok: [n9kv-nxapi-1]
ok: [n9kv-nxapi-2]

TASK [Create MOTD banner message] *************************************************
*******************************************************
changed: [n9kv-nxapi-2]
changed: [n9kv-nxapi-1]

PLAY RECAP ************************************************************************
*******************************************************
n9kv-nxapi-1               : ok=3    changed=1    unreachable=0    failed=0
skipped=1    rescued=0    ignored=0
n9kv-nxapi-2               : ok=4    changed=2    unreachable=0    failed=0
skipped=0    rescued=0    ignored=0
```

Interpreting the output, you can see that n9kv-nxapi-1 does have VLAN 200, so it skips adding the new VLANs. However, nk9v-nxapi-2 does not have VLAN 200, so it adds the new VLANs 1000 and 1001 (the "changed" results). Neither device has the decommissioned NTP server 10.1.1.100—the **ok** result, not **changed**. The MOTD banner is created on both devices—the **changed** results. You can see the summary results of one change for the first device and two changes for the second device.

Now that you've experienced some Ansible-style IaC, let's get into Terraform, another popular IaC solution.

Terraform Overview

Terraform is another open-source IaC solution that is generally associated with cloud orchestration. It is a relative newcomer to the IaC fold, initially released mid-2014 by HashiCorp (see Figure 13-6). As noted previously, it achieved version 1.0.0 status in the summer of 2021.

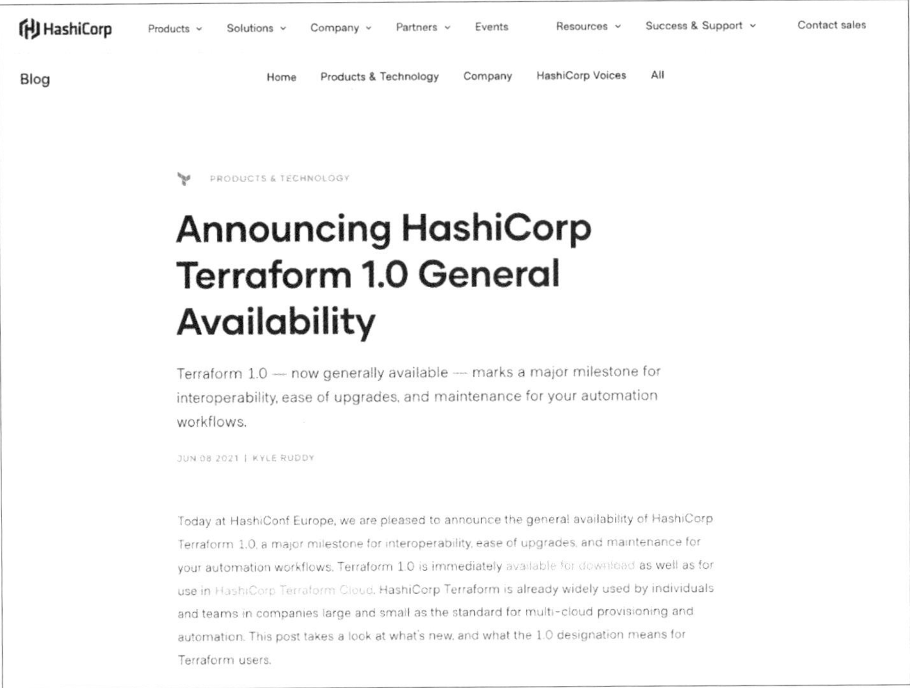

Figure 13-6 *HashiCorp Blog Announcing Terraform v1.0.0 GA Status*

Terraform uses a declarative configuration language known as HashiCorp Configuration Language, or HCL. Terraform designers define their data center infrastructure and/or cloud resources by using "providers" that define a logical abstraction of a product vendor's API and deal with the translation from HCL to the native device's syntax.

Terraform has a great following and application in the cloud space, where managed workloads can be spun up or deleted by defining the desire end state (declarative model) versus the step-by-step process (imperative model).

The Terraform community maintains a repository of providers at https://registry.terraform.io/browse/providers. These pluggable modules can be added to the base Terraform server as your needs grow. The selection is vast: AWS, Kubernetes, Azure, Oracle, Google Cloud Platform, Active Directory, Cisco, and many others.

Let's look at Terraform at a high level. Because the DEVCOR exam focuses more on Ansible, our coverage of Terraform is not as extensive, but it serves to show the power of IaC. If you find yourself doing a lot of cloud-based engineering, especially in spin-up/spin-down of DevTest environments, you will be well served by Terraform.

Installing Terraform

To install Terraform, you can use the same model you used for Puppet and Ansible. In this case, start with a virgin Ubuntu 21.04 server and build up a Terraform server from there.

NOTE Terraform supports Windows (using Chocolatey) and OS X (using Homebrew) also. In this chapter, we show a common Linux example for broader application.

Terraform has a simple client-only architecture that is easily installed. You start by adding HashiCorp's GNU Privacy Guard (gpg) key by downloading it with the **curl** utility and passing it to the **apt-key** utility, adding it to your list of trusted keys. This approach is shown in Example 13-67.

Example 13-67 *Obtaining Hashicorp GPG Keys for Package Management*

```
terraformadmin@terraformserver:~$ curl https://apt.releases.hashicorp.com/gpg | sudo
apt-key add -
[sudo] password for terraformadmin:
  % Total    % Received % Xferd  Average Speed   Time    Time     Time  Current
                                 Dload  Upload   Total   Spent    Left  Speed
100  3195  100  3195    0     0  58090      0 --:--:-- --:--:-- --:--:-- 58090



Progress: [ 80%] [####################################################################
############################.......................]
OK
```

Next, you add the software repository to your local list of authorized sources, as in Example 13-68.

Example 13-68 *Adding the Hashicorp Software Repository to the Package Manager*

```
terraformadmin@terraformserver:~$ sudo apt-add-repository "deb [arch=$(dpkg --print-
architecture)] https://apt.releases.hashicorp.com $(lsb_release -cs) main"
Hit:1 http://us.archive.ubuntu.com/ubuntu focal InRelease
Hit:2 http://us.archive.ubuntu.com/ubuntu focal-updates InRelease
Get:3 https://apt.releases.hashicorp.com focal InRelease [4,419 B]
Hit:4 http://us.archive.ubuntu.com/ubuntu focal-backports InRelease
Hit:5 http://us.archive.ubuntu.com/ubuntu focal-security InRelease
Get:6 https://apt.releases.hashicorp.com focal/main amd64 Packages [31.2 kB]
Fetched 35.7 kB in 1s (64.0 kB/s)
Reading package lists... Done
```

For good measure, Example 13-69 shows how to update the package information from all configured sources.

Example 13-69 *Performing a Package Manager Update*

```
terraformadmin@terraformserver:~$ sudo apt update
Hit:1 https://apt.releases.hashicorp.com focal InRelease
Hit:2 http://us.archive.ubuntu.com/ubuntu focal InRelease
Hit:3 http://us.archive.ubuntu.com/ubuntu focal-updates InRelease
Hit:4 http://us.archive.ubuntu.com/ubuntu focal-backports InRelease
Hit:5 http://us.archive.ubuntu.com/ubuntu focal-security InRelease
Reading package lists... Done
Building dependency tree
Reading state information... Done
All packages are up to date.
```

Then you direct the package installer to install Terraform, as shown in Example 13-70.

Example 13-70 *Using the Package Manager to Install Terraform*

```
terraformadmin@terraformserver:~$ sudo apt install terraform
Reading package lists... Done
Building dependency tree
Reading state information... Done
The following NEW packages will be installed:
  terraform
0 upgraded, 1 newly installed, 0 to remove and 0 not upgraded.
Need to get 32.7 MB of archives.
After this operation, 79.4 MB of additional disk space will be used.
Get:1 https://apt.releases.hashicorp.com focal/main amd64 terraform amd64 1.0.6
[32.7 MB]
Fetched 32.7 MB in 0s (70.9 MB/s)
Selecting previously unselected package terraform.
(Reading database ... 71474 files and directories currently installed.)
Preparing to unpack .../terraform_1.0.6_amd64.deb ...
Unpacking terraform (1.0.6) ...
Setting up terraform (1.0.6) ...
```

For good measure, Example 13-71 shows how to verify the version of Terraform installed.

Example 13-71 *Checking the Installed Version of Terraform*

```
terraformadmin@terraformserver:~$ terraform --version
Terraform v1.0.6
on linux_amd64
```

Using Terraform

Let's use Terraform to do an IaC provisioning use case that deploys new tenants in an ACI environment. Terraform can download and install any provider defined in a configuration file as it initializes the project's working directory.

If you have your own ACI DevTest environment, feel free to use that. If not, the DevNet *ACI Always On* Sandbox Lab is free to use as a shared, public resource at https://devnetsandbox.cisco.com/RM/Diagram/Index/18a514e8-21d4-4c29-96b2-e3c16b1ee62e?diagramType=Topology.

The first thing to do is create a project directory to maintain configuration files and Terraform state information:

terraformadmin@terraformserver:~$ **mkdir aci-create-tenant**

terraformadmin@terraformserver:~$ **cd aci-create-tenant/**

Next, create the Terraform configuration file; ideally, this would be programmatically created and maintained in a git repo. Terraform files are named with a .tf extension by convention.

terraformadmin@terraformserver:~/aci-create-tenant$ **vi**

deploy-test-tenant.tf

Ensure the configuration file contents appear as shown in Example 13-72. Replace the ACI APIC URL and credentials to suit your environment or use the DevNet *Always On* environment, as supplied.

Key Topic

Example 13-72 *A Terraform File to Create an ACI Tenant and App*

```
terraform {
  required_providers {
    aci = {
      source = "ciscodevnet/aci"
    }
  }
}

#configure provider with your cisco aci credentials.
provider "aci" {
  # cisco-aci user name
  username = "admin"
  # cisco-aci password
  password = "!v3G@!4@Y"
  # cisco-aci url
  url      = "https://sandboxapicdc.cisco.com"
  insecure = true
  #proxy_url = "https://proxy_server:proxy_port"
}

resource "aci_tenant" "devcor-test-tenant" {
  name        = "devcor-test-tenant"
  description = "This tenant is created by terraform"
}
```

```
resource "aci_app_profile" "devcor-test-app" {
  tenant_dn   = "${aci_tenant.devcor-test-tenant.id}"
  name        = "devcor-test-app"
  description = "This app profile is created by terraform"
}
```

To make use of Terraform, you must initialize your current working directory. Initializing the directory creates a .terraform subdirectory containing provider information. You may also see a lock file with a .lock.hcl extension. Example 13-73 shows the execution.

Example 13-73 *Initializing a Terraform Project*

```
terraformadmin@terraformserver:~/aci-create-tenant$ terraform init

Initializing the backend...

Initializing provider plugins...
- Finding latest version of ciscodevnet/aci...
- Installing ciscodevnet/aci v0.7.1...
- Installed ciscodevnet/aci v0.7.1 (signed by a HashiCorp partner, key ID
433649E2C56309DE)

Partner and community providers are signed by their developers.
If you'd like to know more about provider signing, you can read about it here:
https://www.terraform.io/docs/cli/plugins/signing.html

Terraform has created a lock file .terraform.lock.hcl to record the provider
selections it made above. Include this file in your version control repository
so that Terraform can guarantee to make the same selections by default when
you run "terraform init" in the future.

Terraform has been successfully initialized!

You may now begin working with Terraform. Try running "terraform plan" to see
any changes that are required for your infrastructure. All Terraform commands
should now work.

If you ever set or change modules or backend configuration for Terraform,
rerun this command to reinitialize your working directory. If you forget, other
commands will detect it and remind you to do so if necessary.
```

Note that the **terraform init** command also downloads the ciscodevnet/aci provider from the Terraform registry.

The next activity is to instruct Terraform to assess the IaC configuration you provided. You use the **terraform plan** command to show the changes necessary to bring the environment in line with the configuration you declared. Terraform connects to the endpoints defined in the configuration file to assess the changes necessary. Example 13-74 shows the execution of **terraform plan**.

Key Topic

Example 13-74 *Executing* **terraform plan**

```
terraformadmin@terraformserver:~/aci-create-tenant$ terraform plan

Terraform used the selected providers to generate the following execution plan.
Resource actions are indicated with the following symbols:
  + create

Terraform will perform the following actions:

  # aci_tenant.devcor-test-tenant will be created
  + resource "aci_tenant" "devcor-test-tenant" {
      + annotation  = "orchestrator:terraform"
      + description = "This tenant is created by terraform"
      + id          = (known after apply)
      + name        = "devcor-test-tenant"
      + name_alias  = (known after apply)
    }

  # aci_tenant.devcor-test-tenant2 will be created
  + resource "aci_tenant" "devcor-test-tenant2" {
      + annotation  = "orchestrator:terraform"
      + description = "This tenant is created by terraform"
      + id          = (known after apply)
      + name        = "devcor-test-tenant2"
      + name_alias  = (known after apply)
    }

  # aci_tenant.devcor-test-tenant3 will be created
  + resource "aci_tenant" "devcor-test-tenant3" {
      + annotation  = "orchestrator:terraform"
      + description = "This tenant is created by terraform"
      + id          = (known after apply)
      + name        = "devcor-test-tenant3"
      + name_alias  = (known after apply)
    }

Plan: 3 to add, 0 to change, 0 to destroy.

───────────────────────────────────────────────────────────────────────────────
─────────────────────────────────────────────────────

Note: You didn't use the -out option to save this plan, so Terraform can't guarantee
to take exactly these actions if you run "terraform
apply" now.
```

If you agree with the assessment of creating three new tenants, you can move to the provisioning mode with **terraform apply**, depicted in Example 13-75.

Example 13-75 *Applying the* Terraform Plan

```
terraformadmin@terraformserver:~/aci-create-tenant$ terraform apply

Terraform used the selected providers to generate the following execution plan.
Resource actions are indicated with the following symbols:
  + create

Terraform will perform the following actions:

  # aci_tenant.devcor-test-tenant will be created
  + resource "aci_tenant" "devcor-test-tenant" {
      + annotation  = "orchestrator:terraform"
      + description = "This tenant is created by terraform"
      + id          = (known after apply)
      + name        = "devcor-test-tenant"
      + name_alias  = (known after apply)
    }

  # aci_tenant.devcor-test-tenant2 will be created
  + resource "aci_tenant" "devcor-test-tenant2" {
      + annotation  = "orchestrator:terraform"
      + description = "This tenant is created by terraform"
      + id          = (known after apply)
      + name        = "devcor-test-tenant2"
      + name_alias  = (known after apply)
    }

  # aci_tenant.devcor-test-tenant3 will be created
  + resource "aci_tenant" "devcor-test-tenant3" {
      + annotation  = "orchestrator:terraform"
      + description = "This tenant is created by terraform"
      + id          = (known after apply)
      + name        = "devcor-test-tenant3"
      + name_alias  = (known after apply)
    }

Plan: 3 to add, 0 to change, 0 to destroy.

Do you want to perform these actions?
  Terraform will perform the actions described above.
  Only 'yes' will be accepted to approve.
```

```
  Enter a value: yes

aci_tenant.devcor-test-tenant2: Creating...
aci_tenant.devcor-test-tenant3: Creating...
aci_tenant.devcor-test-tenant: Creating...
aci_tenant.devcor-test-tenant: Creation complete after 1s [id=uni/
tn-devcor-test-tenant]
aci_tenant.devcor-test-tenant2: Creation complete after 1s [id=uni/
tn-devcor-test-tenant2]
aci_tenant.devcor-test-tenant3: Creation complete after 1s [id=uni/
tn-devcor-test-tenant3]

Apply complete! Resources: 3 added, 0 changed, 0 destroyed.
terraformadmin@terraformserver:~/aci-create-tenant$
```

To verify the creation, you can go to the ACI APIC controller's web UI, as shown in Figure 13-7.

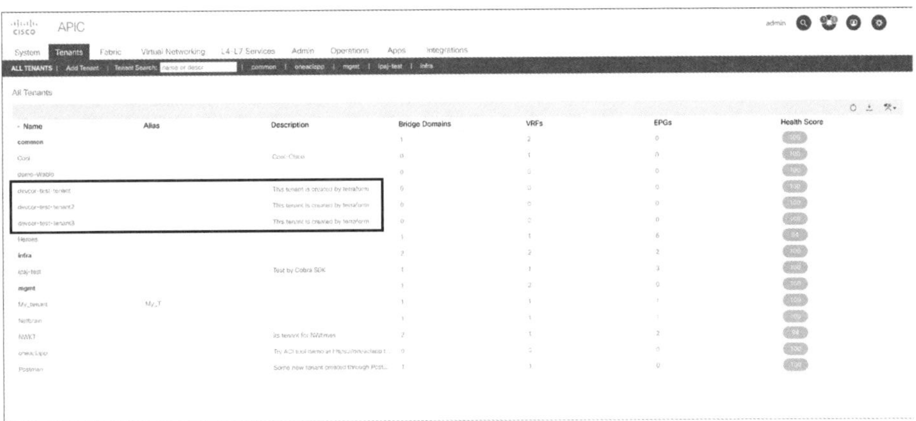

Figure 13-7 *ACI APIC Controller Showing Terraform Provisioning Results*

To glean some more ideas about ACI provisioning, check out the Terraform ACI provider examples on GitHub at https://github.com/CiscoDevNet/terraform-provider-aci/tree/master/examples.

Cisco Solutions Enabled for IaC

Following the default route of hands-on-keyboards or "finger-defined networks," as I like to call it, can be over if you're with us. Embracing Infrastructure as Code provides the opportunity to programmatically define and build your networks, including the compute and cloud-based services you regularly employ.

From open management interfaces, such as NX-API, NETCONF, and RESTCONF; to available agent-based technologies, such as Puppet and Chef; to agentless technologies in Ansible and Terraform, Cisco is providing options. The portfolio is broad with products that support these technologies—routers, switches, servers, collaboration, wireless, security, cloud, and management solutions.

You have the flexibility to align your provisioning and orchestration with the same solutions that are popular in the server/compute domain. Cisco is an active developer in all these communities and has a dedicated developer advocacy team in its DevNet organization. You can engage with them through the following links:

Twitter: @CiscoDevNet

Facebook: https://www.facebook.com/ciscodevnet/

GitHub: https://github.com/CiscoDevNet

Cisco developer forums: https://community.cisco.com/t5/for-developers/ct-p/4409j-developer-home

Exam Preparation Tasks

As mentioned in the section "How to Use This Book" in the Introduction, you have a couple of choices for exam preparation: the exercises here, Chapter 17, "Final Preparation," and the exam simulation questions in the Pearson Test Prep Software Online.

Review All Key Topics

Review the most important topics in this chapter, noted with the Key Topic icon in the outer margin of the page. Table 13-3 lists a reference of these key topics and the page numbers on which each is found.

Table 13-3 Key Topics for Chapter 13

Key Topic Element	Description	Page Number
Section	Imperative and Declarative Models	448
Paragraph	Agent-based technologies	450
Paragraph	Agentless technologies	450
Table 13-2	Puppet Platform Support Matrix	451
Paragraph	Puppet **facter** module	459
Example 13-19	Using Puppet **facter** to Extract **system_uptime**	463
Example 13-34	Puppet Manifest to Change a Device	470
Example 13-50	Creating an Ansible Vault Password	481
Example 13-51	Encrypting Strings for Device Passwords in Ansible	481
Example 13-52	Ansible Inventory File in YAML Syntax	482
Example 13-56	Using Ansible to Obtain JSON-Formatted Device Configuration	485
Example 13-61	Sample nxos-vlan.yml File	488

Key Topic Element	Description	Page Number
Example 13-62	Creating VLANs in an Ansible Playbook	489
Example 13-72	A Terraform File to Create an ACI Tenant and App	497
Example 13-74	Executing **terraform plan**	499
Example 13-75	Applying the **Terraform Plan**	500

Complete Tables and Lists from Memory

Print a copy of Appendix C, "Memory Tables" (found on the companion website), or at least the section for this chapter, and complete the tables and lists from memory. Appendix D, "Memory Tables Answer Key," also on the companion website, includes completed tables and lists to check your work.

Define Key Terms

Define the following key terms from this chapter and check your answers in the glossary:

agentless, agent-based, declarative model, imperative model, Chef, Puppet, Ansible, Terraform, manifest, playbook, spec file, plan

References

URL	QR Code
https://github.com/cisco/cisco-network-puppet-module/blob/develop/docs/README-agent-install.md	
https://github.com/grpc/grpc/issues/21514	
https://puppet.com/docs/puppet/7/core_facts.html	
https://devnetsandbox.cisco.com/RM/Diagram/Index/dae38dd8-e8ee-4d7c-a21c-6036bed7a804?diagramType=Topology	

URL	QR Code
https://www.w3schools.io/file/yaml-introduction/	
https://docs.ansible.com/ansible/latest/reference_appendices/YAMLSyntax.html	
https://docs.ansible.com/ansible/latest/collections/index_module.html	
https://docs.ansible.com/ansible/latest/collections/ansible/builtin/file_module.html#ansible-collections-ansible-builtin-file-module	
https://docs.ansible.com/ansible/latest/collections/cisco/nxos/nxos_command_module.html	
https://docs.ansible.com/ansible/latest/collections/ansible/builtin/copy_module.html#ansible-collections-ansible-builtin-copy-module	
https://docs.ansible.com/ansible/latest/user_guide/playbooks_templating.html	
https://jinja.palletsprojects.com/en/3.0.x/templates/#builtin-filters	

URL	QR Code
https://docs.ansible.com/ansible/latest/user_guide/playbooks_filters.html#network-xml-filters	
https://galaxy.ansible.com/	
https://docs.ansible.com/ansible/latest/collections/ansible/index.html	
https://docs.ansible.com/ansible/latest/collections/cisco/nxos/nxos_vlans_module.html	
https://docs.ansible.com/ansible/latest/collections/cisco/nxos/nxos_ntp_module.html	
https://docs.ansible.com/ansible/latest/collections/cisco/nxos/nxos_banner_module.html	
https://registry.terraform.io/browse/providers	
https://devnetsandbox.cisco.com/RM/Diagram/Index/18a514e8-21d4-4c29-96b2-e3c16b1ee62e?diagramType=Topology	

URL	QR Code
https://github.com/CiscoDevNet/terraform-provider-aci/tree/master/examples	
https://www.facebook.com/ciscodevnet/	
https://github.com/CiscoDevNet	
https://community.cisco.com/t5/for-developers/ct-p/4409j-developer-home	

CHAPTER 14

Software Configuration Management

This chapter covers the following topics:

- **Software Configuration Management (SCM):** In this section we discuss general SCM concepts and how to track all development properties, processes, characteristics, disciplines, and responsibilities of a software product. We also discuss a few of the available systems and decision criteria for choosing the one that fulfills your requirements. In addition, we cover Ansible and Terraform strengths, weaknesses, and decision-making criteria.
- **Business and Technical Requirements:** In this section we cover architectural requirements and how they affect architectural decisions and trade-offs. We also discuss technical debt and how it is created by certain architectural decisions.

This chapter maps to the first part of the *Developing Applications Using Cisco Core Platforms and APIs v1.0 (350-901)* Exam Blueprint Section 5.0, "Infrastructure and Automation," with specific connection to subsections 5.3 and 5.4.

Gathering requirements, building a development plan, and then building an implementation plan, a test plan, and a support plan are a few small tasks of a huge software development project. Diligence, speed, and the ability to correct course are also the basis for achieving success. In this chapter we introduce you to few important concepts for participating in or leading major software development projects and how to ensure that adequate communication, documentation, and interaction with all parties are essential for flawless execution.

At the beginning of this book we focused on helping you understand the functional and nonfunctional requirements. You learned what they are, how they influence the architecture, and what trade-offs you must make to build the best product. But you also learned that architectures could evolve to meet new requirements, or they may also be changed to speed up the go-to-market cycle. Time to market is important to business and marketing stakeholders; however, architecture adherence and diligence are important to engineering teams striving to build high-quality products. Somewhere in between the two lies the perfect world (or the perfect product, if such a thing even exists).

"Do I Know This Already?" Quiz

The "Do I Know This Already?" quiz allows you to assess whether you should read this entire chapter thoroughly or jump to the "Exam Preparation Tasks" section. If you are in doubt about your answers to these questions or your own assessment of your knowledge of the topics, read the entire chapter. Table 14-1 lists the major headings in this chapter and their corresponding "Do I Know This Already?" quiz questions. You can find the answers in Appendix A, "Answers to the 'Do I Know This Already?' Quizzes."

Table 14-1 "Do I Know This Already?" Section-to-Question Mapping

Foundation Topics Section	Questions
Software Configuration Management (SCM)	1–7
Business and Technical Requirements	8

1. Why is software configuration management needed?
   a. To track changes
   b. To track the names of persons or organizations conducting changes
   c. To house data dictionaries
   d. All of these answers are correct.
2. Which of the following is *not* tracked by an SCM?
   a. Design
   b. Implementation
   c. Market data
   d. Release data
3. The following are widely used SCM tools except
   a. Chef
   b. Ansible
   c. Muppet
   d. SaltStack
4. What are the main components of Ansible?
   a. Control node, software node, and management node
   b. Control node, inventory files, playbooks, modules, and managed nodes
   c. Core engine, automation and orchestration engine
   d. Platform, files, inventory, and providers
5. To find the versions of Ansible and Python being used, which command do you execute at the CLI?
   a. **ansible-version**
   b. **ansible-vault -v**
   c. **ansible -version**
   d. **ansible -Show version**
6. There are two approaches to IaC tools: imperative and declarative. What does declarative mean?
   a. The user defines the desired outcome, and the system achieves it.
   b. The user defines all procedures; the system executes them, and they are declared as "Done."
   c. The declared state should be imperatively defined first.
   d. There is no such thing.

7. Terraform uses the declarative approach and has the following simple lifecycle:
   a. Initialize, execute, reset, repeat
   b. Init, plan, apply, destroy
   c. Architect, document, init, apply, delete
   d. Open, execute, reset, close
8. What is technical debt?
   a. A database decision that does not support all quality attributes
   b. Short-term decisions that have long-term consequences
   c. A test environment that facilitates easier testing but simulates a production environment
   d. All of these answers are correct.

Foundation Topics

Software Configuration Management (SCM)

Chapter 1, "Software Development Essentials," defined software architecture to be a set of structures needed to reason about the system. These structures comprise software elements, relations among them, and properties of both. When you inspected several software architecture documents, you likely found very little text explaining rationale and a lot more diagrams with colors and a lot of arrows among the colorful components. You know that you arrived at that architecture as a result of meetings, questionnaires, and interviews with business and technical stakeholders. You know that the rationale exists for all these colors and arrows (on an architectural diagram), but how is it continuously being referenced as you move toward the development cycle? You know for a fact that many technical decisions are made during the development cycle that are not fully captured into the original documentations or specifications. That chapter also discussed how to solve some of these issues through continuous collaboration and frequent communication with Agile processes. However, are you making sure that the proper "feedback loops" exists? Are you updating all aspects or layers of the project?

SCM Definitions and Standards

Configuration management is concerned with keeping track of definitions and standards with defined disciplines and responsibilities. First, you need to define what constitutes a "product" and all documentation related to it. The following are common examples (this is only a partial list):

- Business and functional requirements
- Technical requirements and technical specifications
- Testing (design, cases, automation)
- Support systems
- Source code
- Libraries

- Data dictionaries
- Maintenance documentation
- Modification requests and implementation

You can add other documentations or items to this list, but what you use to represent the architecture's lifecycle may be project- or organization-dependent.

ANSI and IEEE attempted to put on paper what configuration management is. There are a few documents that can help you. A simple and most recent attempt is "The IEEE Standard for Configuration Management in Systems and Software Engineering" (IEEE Std 828.). Figure 14-1 sums it up.

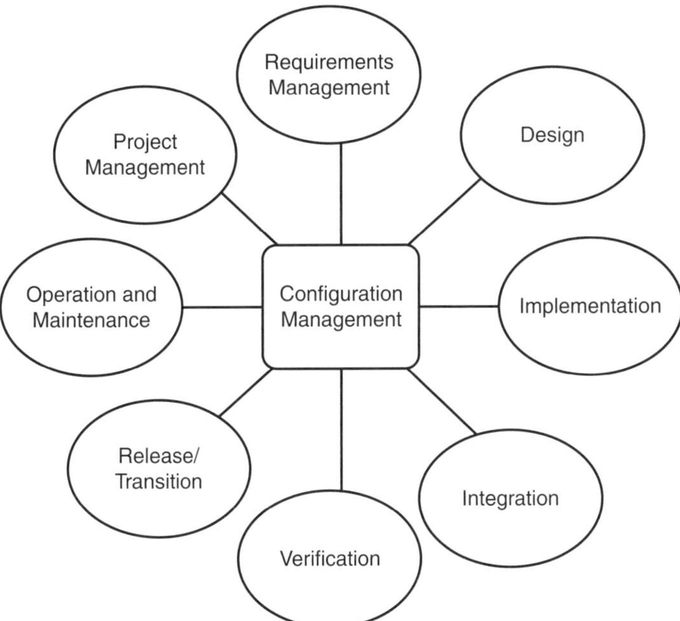

Figure 14-1 *Configuration Management Lifecycle (Source: IEEE Std 828-2012)*

Why Do You Need SCM?

The configuration management process (or system) is essential throughout the product's lifecycle, from inception until its end-of-life stages. DevOps, CI/CD, and Agile development practices are changing how to look at software architecture and how to execute the development and deployment cycles, *but at the same time they're increasing dependence on SCM tools and practices to preserve the integrity of the architecture*. Above and beyond the architecture, there is the massive scale of deployment and provisioning within enterprises (campuses, branches, data centers, and clouds). To move at the speed of business and to ensure consistency within networks, you need to rely on SCMs as a central repository for everything related to the infrastructure and as a single point of truth related to the architecture and how it is being deployed in production.

The general answer to "Why do you need SCM?" can be summarized as follows:

- **Software configuration management (SCM)** decomposes architecture components into deliverables.
- It helps to track changes at the macroscopic level (the entire project).
- It helps with planning the process and duration.
- It helps track status of deployments of subprojects.

Which SCM Process Is Best for You?

In today's distributed environments with a high degree of automation, the question you ask should probably be "Which SCM process is best for **Infrastructure as Code (IaC)** practices?" There are many SCM systems, and each has its own pros and cons. *The best one among all these tools is the one you know, the one your team is comfortable using, or the one your team decided on before you came along.* In addition, if you end up choosing an open-source system, you need to ensure that you have a strong community standing behind it and that it has clear documentation.

Several SCM and automation systems are available. Some are open source, but some aren't, so we want to cover a few of them quickly. Our focus is on the most relevant to our practices of automating network functions and infrastructures. The following names seem to enjoy a high degree of popularity among the infrastructure automation community:

- **Chef:** An excellent SCM and IaC tool with few restrictions. The fact that it uses Ruby is great if you're a fan. But you have no choice here. Chef has good interoperability and integration with major operating systems (Windows included). It's open source but is also available as an enterprise offering. Unlike Puppet and Ansible, Chef does not support Push functionality.
- **Puppet:** An open-source SCM tool. Puppet is mostly used for the server side of the operation; however, it has wider infrastructure capabilities. Puppet is also agent-based and therefore not the preferred choice as compared to the agentless tools. Puppet is known for having excellent reporting and compliance tools, alongside its easy-to-use user interface. You can find more information at https://puppet.com/.
- **Ansible:** See the description in the following section.

Ansible gets the most attention in this chapter because we have found it to be the most popular among the development communities we interact with.

Ansible

Ansible is open source, free, and easy to use. What else do you need? It also integrates with almost all the major infrastructure providers out there. Alongside all the automation and management capabilities, it also provides for an adequate collaboration platform among developers, communities, or departments.

The main reasons that Ansible is a favorite include

- Ease of use (You can get up to speed and get on with your automation journey in a very short time.)

- Secure communication between the nodes and the servers (It uses SSH.)
- Agentless execution
- The ability to run ad hoc commands to execute single tasks once
- Interoperability
- Sizable user community

The main components of Ansible are

- **Control node:** Any machine with Ansible and Python installed can be a control node. The control node is like the engine that runs the automation flow. There can be one or multiple control nodes.
- **Inventory files:** All hosts can be managed or operated by Ansible.
- **Playbooks:** Playbooks are developed in YAML and contain domain-specific language (DSL) for tasks to be executed. YAML is easy to read and understand.

  Figure 14-2 shows a simple playbook that performs two tasks:

  - Show run
  - Backup config to Linux

```
---
- hosts: cisco-ios
  gather_facts: true
  connection: local

  tasks:
   - name: show run
     ios_command:
     commands: show run
     host: "{{ ansible_host }}"
     username: cisco-ios
     password: cisco-ios
     register: config

   - name: Backup config to linux
     copy:
     content: "{{ config.stdout[0] }}"
     dest: "/home/show_run_{{ inventory_hostname }}.txt"
```


Figure 14-2 *A Playbook Showing One Play and Two Tasks*

- **Modules:** Modules are units of code that Ansible executes. There is a high degree of flexibility in modules. You can execute single tasks (single modules) or a group of modules as specified by a playbook.
- **Managed nodes:** These nodes are servers or network devices to be managed by Ansible.

Figure 14-3 shows the flow and interaction among all the components of Ansible.

Key Topic

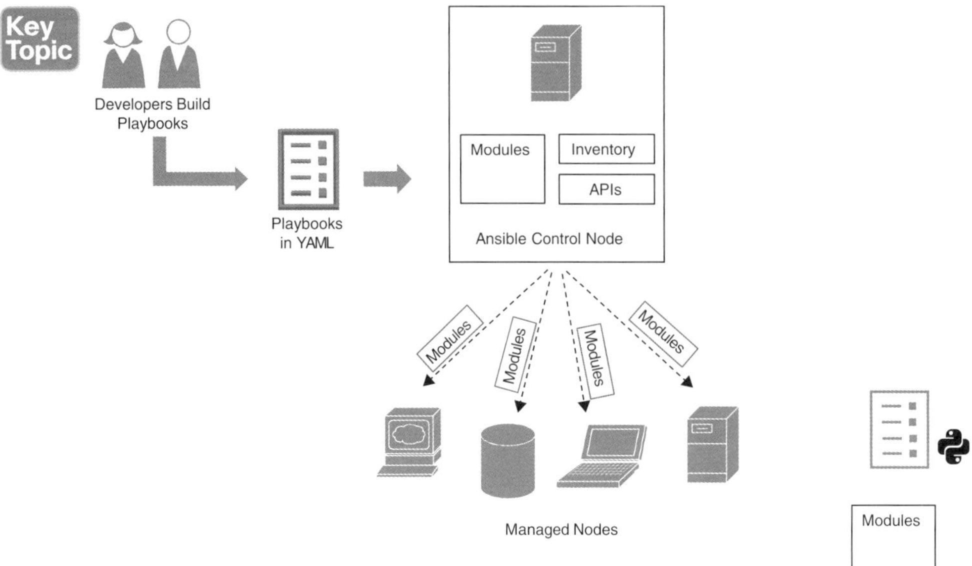

Figure 14-3 *Ansible High-Level Workflow (Simplified View)*

As mentioned earlier, Ansible supports the execution of ad hoc CLI commands like the examples supplied here:

- **ansible:** CLI command for running individual tasks or modules

  Example 14-1 shows **ansible -version** returning the Ansible version as well as the Python version (and the path to all relevant directories).

Example 14-1 *An Ansible CLI Command to Display the Version*

```
testuser@test_machine ~ % ansible -version
ansible [core 2.12.1]
  config file = None
  configured module search path = ['/Users/testuser/.ansible/plugins/modules', '/
usr/share/ansible/plugins/modules']
  ansible python module location = /usr/local/lib/python3.9/site-packages/ansible
  ansible collection location = /Users/testuser/.ansible/collections:/usr/share/
ansible/collections
  executable location = /usr/local/bin/ansible
  python version = 3.9.9 (main, Nov 21 2021, 03:23:44) [Clang 13.0.0
(clang-1300.0.29.3)]
  jinja version = 3.0.3
  libyaml = True
```

- **ansible-playbook:** CLI command or tool for running playbooks against a host
- **ansible-vault:** CLI command for encrypting sensitive data
- **ansible -h:** Help command that shows a number of supported features

NOTE A great deal of information about Ansible is available online, and it is rapidly growing. We recommend you take a look at the open-source data at https://docs.ansible.com/ansible/latest/index.html as well as the Red Hat sponsored sites at https://www.ansible.com/.

Terraform

Terraform is *not* an SCM. This is why it is explained in its own section. It's not unusual for engineers to speak about Terraform and Ansible in the same context and in direct comparison. There is some truth to that, but there are differences in how each tool performs its tasks. There is no doubt Terraform is the most-used Infrastructure as Code (IaC) tool for managing data centers, software-defined networks (SDNs), and cloud assets.

14

Terraform is a secure, efficient, easy-to-use open-source system for building, configuring, and managing infrastructure. Here are a few interesting features:

- It enables you to compose and combine infrastructure resources to build and maintain a desired state.
- It provides for fast and easy deployment because of the declarative approach.

  Declarative means that the user defines the end state and Terraform takes the appropriate actions to achieve the desired outcome. The SCMs we discussed earlier take an *imperative* or *procedural* approach, meaning that the user defines a series of steps or tasks that the system must follow. Ansible uses an imperative approach as a configuration management tool. However, Ansible does have orchestration capabilities using the declarative approach. For this reason, we like to think of Ansible as a hybrid.
- It manages all actions through APIs.
- It provides for rapid deployment and provisioning.
- Agentless management is available for a wide range of systems.
- There are no server-side dependencies.
- You can reuse resources multiple times within a single module.

As seen in Figure 14-4, the Core provides the simplicity and the sophistication for the system. It defines a configuration language (HashiCorp Configuration Language, or HCL), rules of operations, and plug-ins. *Providers*, on the other hand, are an abstraction that uses a plug-in to interact with the cloud service providers. A common example of providers would be Google Cloud (GCP), Microsoft Azure, or Amazon Web Services (AWS).

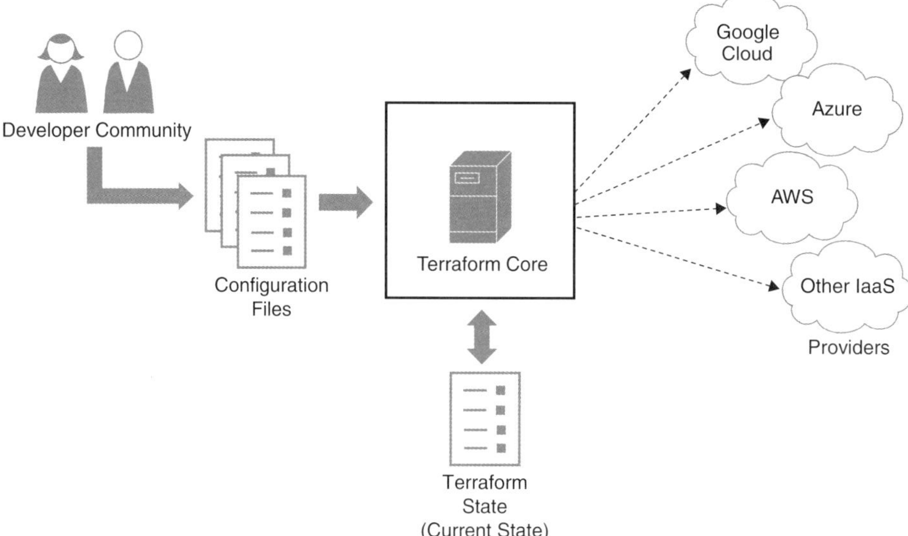

Figure 14-4 *High-Level Terraform Architecture*

Terraform has a simple lifecycle. As a matter of fact, the core Terraform workflow is "write, plan, apply." In practical coding terms, Figure 14-5 through Figure 14-8 explain the lifecycle.

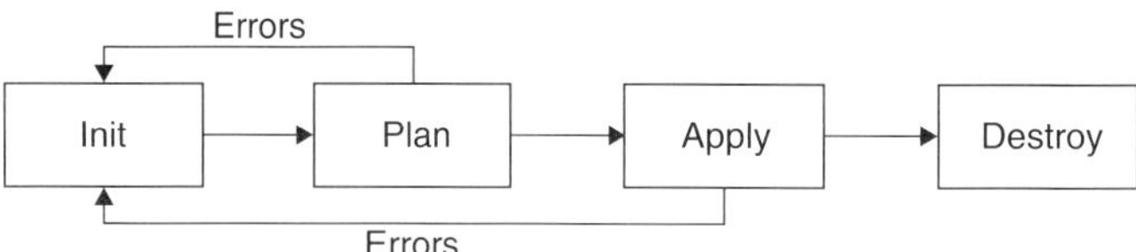

Figure 14-5 *Terraform Lifecycle of IaC*

- **Init:** Initialize workflows and build directories of all configuration files to represent your environments. This is where you write configuration files.

```
# Create repository
$ git init my-infra && cd my-infra

Initialized empty Git repository in /.../my-infra/.git/

# Write initial config
$ vim main.tf

# Initialize Terraform
$ terraform init

Initializing provider plugins...
# ...
Terraform has been successfully initialized!
```

User-Created Terraform Configuration File

e.g., Plugins specific to Cloud Provider

Figure 14-6 *Terraform Initialization Workflow*

- **Plan:** Create the execution plan for desired state(s). During the development cycle, it is recommended to repeatedly run **plan** to flush out errors as you go.

```
# Review plan
$ terraform plan   <------ "Plan" exposes errors

# Make additional edits, and repeat
$ vim main.tf   <------ Additional Edits after error reports
```

Figure 14-7 *Terraform* plan

- **Apply:** Execute changes defined in the plan.

```
$ terraform apply

An execution plan has been generated and is shown below.
# ...

Do you want to perform these actions?
Terraform will perform the actions described above.
Only 'yes' will be accepted to approve.
Enter a value: yes

# ...

Apply complete! Resources: 1 added, 0 changed, 0 destroyed.
```

Figure 14-8 *Terraform* apply

- **Destroy:** Delete older infrastructure resources marked as "Tainted"' after you run **apply**. Figure 14-8 shows "0 destroyed." This result is clearly because the example shows a new or clean implementation where no older configs exist to be destroyed.

The following are a few important Terraform terms:

- **Variable:** This key-value pair is used by Terraform modules to allow customization.
- **Provider:** A provider is an abstraction of the API/service provider, such as AWS, GCP, DNSimple, or Fastly. Providers typically require some sort of configuration data, such as an API key or credential file.
- **Resources:** This term refers to a block of one or more infrastructure objects (compute instances, virtual networks, and so on), which are used in configuring and managing the infrastructure.
- **Data source:** This source is implemented by providers to return information on external objects to Terraform.
- **Output values:** These return values of a Terraform module can be used by other configurations.
- **Interpolation:** Terraform includes a built-in syntax for referencing attributes of other resources. This technique is called *interpolation*. Terraform also provides built-in

functions for performing string manipulations, evaluating math operations, and doing list comprehensions.

- **HashiCorp Configuration Language (HCL):** Terraform's syntax and interpolation are part of an open-source language and specification called HCL.

NOTE A great deal of information about Terraform is available online, and it is rapidly growing. We recommend you take a look at the open-source data at https://www.terraform.io/.

Terraform or Ansible: A High-Level Comparison

As a software engineer and networking expert, you are certain to get the famous "It depends" answer when trying to determine whether to use Terraform or Ansible. Both systems have strengths and limitations. You can argue that a typical SCM system goes above and beyond orchestration. You can also argue that you have room for both. All these ideas are valid, and at the end, your choice may just depend on your organization and the community you're working within.

Table 14-2 presents a simple comparison between Terraform and Ansible. Ansible, which was originally built to be a configuration manager, has evolved to include orchestration capabilities similar to Terraform.

Key Topic

Table 14-2 High-Level Comparative Analysis of Ansible and Terraform

Terraform	Ansible	Implications
Open-source and free	Open-source and free	—
Commercial offerings available	Commercial offerings available	—
Orchestration	Software configuration management	Many similar capabilities, but Ansible has device-level management capabilities independent of orchestration.
Mainly for cloud automation	Mainly for infrastructure automation (including bare metal support by default)	A great deal of similarities.
Development community support	Development community support	Surveying colleagues across enterprises, we hear that Ansible has more support from the community, whereas Terraform has more commercial offerings. (Our sample is small and may not represent the market.)
Declarative	Imperative or procedural (can also be classified as hybrid as some declarative capabilities exist)	Ansible depends on smart engineers and a good understanding of the infrastructure they support.
Stateful: Maintain state of	Stateless	

At the end of the day, you know your organization, the level of collaboration, the level of adherence to process, the politics within your IT group, and what tool serves you best. Which one you choose depends!

Business and Technical Requirements

Previously, we focused on tools or systems for building configuration files for managing infrastructure wherever it may exist (on-premises, off-premises, or in the cloud). One thing we wanted to emphasize along these lines is the "process" or the "project." At some time before you arrived at the orchestration or provisioning state, you must have had an architecture that explains why you need to configure the infrastructure that way and to support what application delivers what business process. So, we want to take you back to the "architecture" talk.

Chapter 2, "Software Quality Attributes," discussed quality attributes (nonfunctional requirements), and you learned that, after you get the functional and business architecture figured out, the most important part of the architecture worthy of your attention is the quality attributes (a.k.a. nonfunctional requirements). That chapter also discussed a few of the quality attributes like

- Maintainability
- Availability
- Usability
- Security
- Performance
- Modularity

A majority of the product failures are due to weak quality attributes. Applications or web apps that fail to meet performance or security thresholds expected by their customers will fail.

So, what do you do about quality attributes?

Architectural Decisions

The answer to the question about quality attributes is simple: List all quality attributes that are most important to your stakeholders in the order of priority and prepare for trade-offs. You will not be able to treat them all the same. For example, you want the highest level of security? In that case, prepare to give up some performance or compromise on usability. These are **architectural decisions** that you must make, and you *must clearly document* them. This is the only way you can get in the mind of the architects and how they arrived at these decisions and what trade-offs you allowed. There are many ways to do this—whether as an extension of your SCM tooling (see the previous section) or through development platforms where the interpretation of the architecture into working code happens. For example,

GitHub provides what's called "Architectural Decision Records" (https://adr.github.io), which are explained as follows:

> An Architectural Decision (AD) is a software design choice that addresses a functional or non-functional requirement that is architecturally significant. An Architecturally Significant Requirement (ASR) is a requirement that has a measurable effect on a software system's architecture and quality. An Architectural Decision Record (ADR) captures a single AD, such as often done when writing personal notes or meeting minutes; the collection of ADRs created and maintained in a project constitute its decision log. All these are within the topic of Architectural Knowledge Management (AKM).

This paragraph sums it up very well. The https://adr.github.io/ site has few interesting articles and blogs from software engineering professionals. It's worth the time to check them out.

Technical Debt

It's natural to discuss **technical debt** after architectural decisions. It is not unusual to work against a go-to-market deadline or against system constraints that require you to make quick or short architectural decisions that may or may not deviate from the main architecture principles. In other words, small or short-term decisions that expedite the development process, if not corrected at a later time, will turn into big or long-term problems. Simply speaking, that's technical debt.

Although the original idea was concerned with the code, rightly so, it was recently expanded to include other aspects of the software development lifecycle (SDLC). In their book *Continuous Architecture in Practice*, Murat Erder, Pierre Pureur, and Eoin Woods categorized technical debt into three distinct categories:

- **Code:** Code written to meet an aggressive timeline and few short decisions at the early stages may make it difficult to maintain and evolve (that is, introduce new features).
- **Architecture:** This comes as a result of architectural decisions made during the software development cycle. This type of technical debt is difficult to measure via tools but usually has a more significant impact on the system than other types of debt. This type of debt affects scalability and maintainability of the architecture.
- **Production infrastructure:** This category of technical debt deals with decisions focused on the infrastructure and code that are used to build, test, and deploy a software system. Build-test-deploy is becoming increasingly integral to software development and is the main focus of DevOps.

Figure 14-9 presents the problem and where it manifests itself and what effect it has on the software quality.

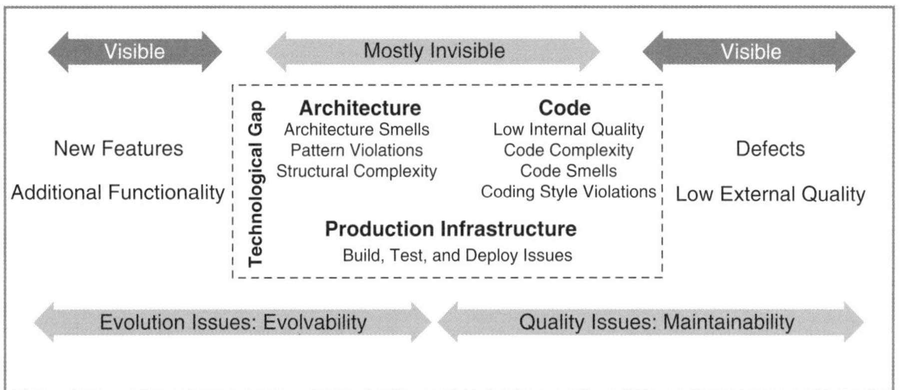

Figure 14-9 *Technical Department Landscape (Source: M. Erder, P. Pureur, & E. Woods, Continuous Architecture in Practice, Addison-Wesley Professional, 2021)*

Technical debt is visible and incurred by choice when you're adding new features. You want to integrate new features quickly to meet market demand or to improve the user experience. Similarly, technical debt is also visible and difficult to deal with when you're troubleshooting technical or quality issues. However, it's almost invisible when you're working on these three categories. Complex architecture is interpreted or simplified by programmers and tested or deployed on an infrastructure also customized for the final product (debt included). This is how technical debt gets compounded and becomes difficult to handle.

A few interesting terms in Figure 14-9 are in the middle section marked "Technological Gap." It clearly shows the bulk of the software development decisions that are made without an immediate visible impact to the quality software. *Architecture Smells* and *Code Smells* are both symptoms of bad decisions, bad code, or bad design that can solve a short-term problem but introduce software quality issues and technical debt that affects the evolvability or maintainability on the long run.

Exam Preparation Tasks

As mentioned in the section "How to Use This Book" in the Introduction, you have a couple of choices for exam preparation: the exercises here, Chapter 17, "Final Preparation," and the exam simulation questions on the companion website.

Review All Key Topics

Review the most important topics in this chapter, noted with the Key Topic icon in the outer margin of the page. Table 14-3 lists a reference of these key topics and the page numbers on which each is found.

Table 14-3 Key Topics for Chapter 14

Key Topic Element	Description	Page Number
Section	SCM Definitions and Standards	510
Section	Ansible	512
Figure 14-3	Ansible High-Level Workflow	514
Section	Terraform	515
Table 14-2	High-Level Comparative Analysis of Ansible and Terraform	518
Section	Architectural Decisions	519
Section	Technical Debt	520

Complete Tables and Lists from Memory

There are no Memory Tables or lists in this chapter.

Define Key Terms

Define the following key terms from this chapter and check your answers in the glossary:

architectural decisions, Ansible, Infrastructure as Code (IaC), software configuration management (SCM), technical debt, Terraform

References

URL	QR Code
https://standards.ieee.org/standard/828-2012.html	
https://www.ansible.com/	

URL	QR Code
https://www.terraform.io/	
Continuous Architecture in Practice: Software Architecture in the Age of Agility and DevOps https://www.informit.com/store/continuous-architecture-in-practice-software-architecture-9780136523567	

CHAPTER 15

Hosting an Application on a Network Device

This chapter covers the following topics:

- **Benefits of Edge Computing:** This section covers the concept of pushing compute functionality to the network edge, closer to the user. We explore the benefits and limitations of edge computing.
- **Application Container Ideas:** This section covers the concept of application containers and how they may be used along with cautions about where they may not be optimal.
- **Platforms Supporting Application Containers:** This section discusses which Cisco products support application containers. You may be able to quickly jump into application containers with the equipment you already have.
- **How to Implement Application Containers:** This section provides an overview of how to implement application containers with provisioning guidelines.
- **Best Practices for Managing Application Containers:** This section covers best practices for managing your deployed application containers. When you get the container bug, your next challenge is how to manage your growing inventory.

This chapter maps to the *Developing Applications Using Cisco Core Platforms and APIs v1.0 (350-901)* Exam Blueprint Section 5.5, "Describe how to host an application on a network device (including Catalyst 9000 and Cisco IOx-enabled devices)."

Application containers are a newish technology with a legacy following Sun Solaris Zones and BSD jails. Around 2000, shared-environment hosting providers developed the notion of FreeBSD jails. They provided partitioning of the operating system into multiple independent systems, or "jails." Each independent environment could have its own IP address and separate configuration for common applications like Apache and mail server. In 2004, Sun Microsystems released Solaris Containers, which also leveraged a common underpinning operating system with separations called "zones."

This chapter provides information on containers running on network devices. You may find suitable use cases in your environment by distributing the computing requirements and data collection for your applications.

"Do I Know This Already?" Quiz

The "Do I Know This Already?" quiz allows you to assess whether you should read this entire chapter thoroughly or jump to the "Exam Preparation Tasks" section. If you are in doubt about your answers to these questions or your own assessment of your knowledge of the topics, read the entire chapter. Table 15-1 lists the major headings in this chapter and their corresponding "Do I Know This Already?" quiz questions. You can find the answers in Appendix A, "Answers to the 'Do I Know This Already?' Quizzes."

Table 15-1 "Do I Know This Already?" Section-to-Question Mapping

Foundation Topics Section	Questions
Benefits of Edge Computing	1–3
Application Container Ideas	4
Platforms Supporting Application Containers	5–6
How to Implement Application Containers	7–10
Best Practices for Managing Application Containers	11

1. Which of the following are examples of Type-1 hypervisors? (Choose two.)
   a. Microsoft Hyper-V
   b. Oracle VM VirtualBox
   c. Parallels Desktop
   d. VMware ESXi
2. Which of the following are examples of Type-2 hypervisors? (Choose two.)
   a. QEMU with KVM
   b. Oracle VirtualBox
   c. VMware Workstation
   d. Citrix XenServer
3. Docker aligns more to operating system containerization versus application containerization.
   a. True
   b. False
4. Application hosting/containerized workloads are well suited for which use cases? (Choose two.)
   a. Where low-latency is not a high priority
   b. Where data sovereignty is a key consideration
   c. Where centralized management is preferred over regional management
   d. Where WAN traffic is metered and cost-prohibitive
5. Application hosting is supported on the Catalyst 9300 at what minimum release?
   a. Cisco IOS-XE 15.0
   b. Cisco IOS-XE 16.2.1
   c. Cisco IOS-XE 17.1.1
   d. Cisco IOS-XE 17.5.1

6. Docker containers are supported on NX-OS–based switches starting at what release?
   a. 6.2.1
   b. 7.0
   c. 9.2.1
   d. 10.1
7. Which of the following are deployment options for Docker containers with IOx-supported Catalyst 9000 series switches? (Choose three.)
   a. Cisco DNA Center
   b. Command-line interface (CLI)
   c. Docker Deployer
   d. IOx Local Manager
   e. Prime KVM
8. What **docker** command is used on a local system to prepare an image for remote hosting in an IOx-capable device?
   a. **docker archive image/latest my_image.tar**
   b. **docker create image/latest my_image.tar**
   c. **docker export image/latest my_image.tar**
   d. **docker save repo/image:latest -o my_image.tar**
9. What Cisco IOS XE command is used to configure an application and enter application hosting configuration mode?
   a. **docker config appid** <*name*>
   b. **app config** <*name*>
   c. **app-config appid** <*name*>
   d. **docker-host app** <*name*>
   e. **app-hosting appid** <*name*>
10. In IOS-XE, what interface is created for application hosting?
    a. interface AppGigabitEthernet0
    b. interface AppGigabitEthernet1/0/1
    c. interface DockerApp0
    d. interface AppHostGigE0
11. The IOx Local Manager centralizes Docker container images for enterprisewide deployments.
    a. True
    b. False

Foundation Topics

Benefits of Edge Computing

Edge computing is a design methodology in which computing resources are shifted from remote, centralized data centers and the cloud to networked devices closer to users at the edge of the network. Edge computing use cases include architecture, applications, and methodologies such as 5G, Internet of Things (IoT), and streaming services.

Some applications have strict requirements for low latency. User experience for voice and video applications suffers when there is lag due to long-distance network paths. Indeed, the longer the distance is, the greater potential for additional hop-counts and routing decision points that make a nondeterministic experience among different invocations. Gaming applications also benefit from low-latency, low-loss networks (according to my son, Every. Single. Day.).

The promise of new 5G networks with higher bandwidth and lower latency even enables intelligent car navigation systems that require the best performance for public safety interests.

The IoT community also benefits from pushing the reception, computation, and analysis of sensor data closer to the device.

Next, let's consider situations where polling at the edge of the network is desirable. In most traditional network management situations, the element management systems (EMSs), plus performance and fault management systems, are centralized, many times in a data center. When those systems are responsible for polling or taking alerts in from hundreds, thousands, or tens of thousands of devices, then extreme amounts of data can be transferred. Additionally, the information is often duplicated or nonurgent. If the data is being collected regularly for trending or accounting purposes, then the collection of every data point may be necessary. However, if not, then great efficiencies of data transfer and retention can be achieved by only transferring data that violates a threshold or policy. Distributing the collection, analysis, and exception-based alerting to the edge can greatly reduce the administrative network management traffic.

Similarly, businesses can save network backhaul costs if their use case can be handled closer to the source. If the information is regional in nature, there may be little need to serve and distribute it from a centralized data store or cloud location.

Not all use cases are practical or economically feasible for edge computing, so careful consideration must be given to the application requirements and costs before distributing workloads. Some business decisions may support edge computing where there are higher concentrations of users who do multimedia streaming, whereas other locations may still be served from consolidated compute farms in a centralized data center because of lower user count.

Virtualization Technologies

Edge computing can be implemented on bare-metal compute nodes near the data consumers; however, the use of compute virtualization technologies is more common for flexibility of service delivery and resource utilization. Several virtualization technologies exist today:

Type-1 and Type-2 hypervisors, **Linux Containers (LXC)**, and Docker **containers**. We cover the nuances of each, but for purposes of the DEVCOR exam, the Cisco support of LXC and Docker container solutions is of key importance. In any of these virtualization methods, a hosting system shares its finite resources with a guest environment that can take a portion of those resources—CPU, memory, or disk—for its own application servicing purposes. The virtualization technologies differ on the level of isolation from the foundational **hypervisor**, or operating system, and that among the separate virtualized environments.

Type-1 Hypervisors

The architecture of Type-1, or native (or bare-metal), hypervisors typically involves the hypervisor kernel acting as a shim layer between the underlying hardware serving compute, memory, network, and storage, from the overlying operating systems. Sample solutions are Microsoft Hyper-V, Xen, and VMware ESXi. Figure 15-1 depicts the architecture involving a **Type-1 hypervisor**.

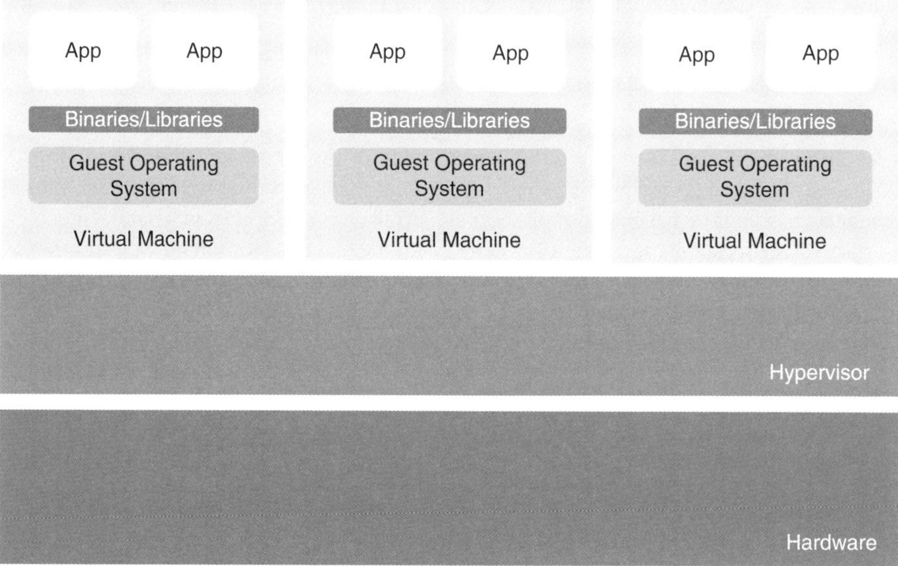

Figure 15-1 *Type-1 Hypervisor Architecture*

The operating systems are truly isolated as virtual machines in this model, allowing for different deployments; separate RedHat, Ubuntu, Windows, FreeBSD, and others are possible. The operating system licensing requirements must be considered, even though virtualized.

Type-2 Hypervisors

The architecture of Type-2, or hosted, hypervisors involves running the hypervisor over the top of a conventional hosted operating system (OS). Other applications, besides the hypervisor, may also run on the hosted OS as other programs or processes. One or more guest operating systems run over the hypervisor. Figure 15-2 shows the architecture of a **Type-2 hypervisor**.

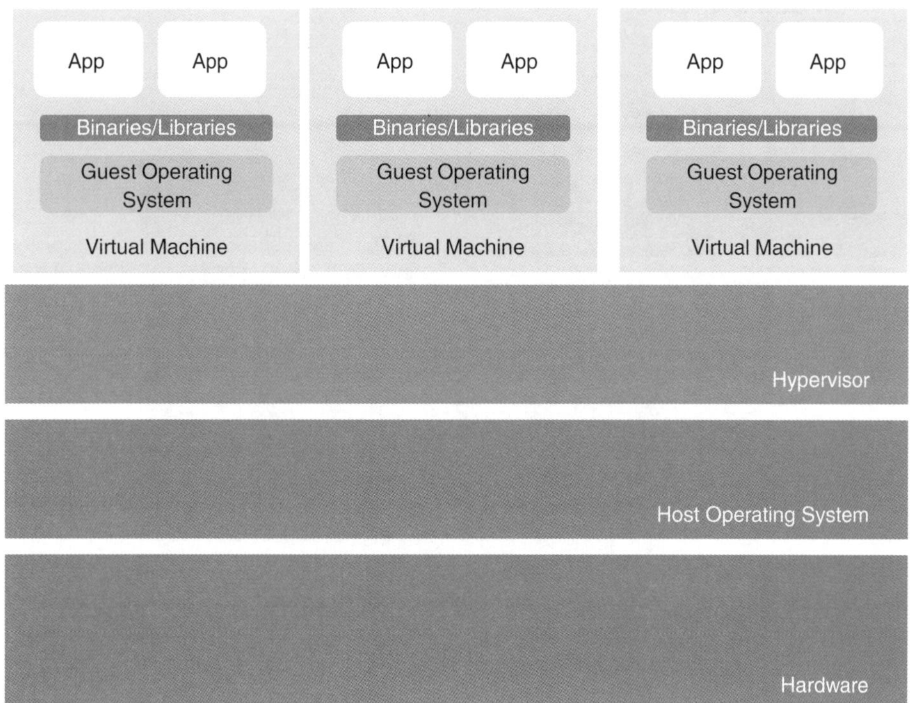

Figure 15-2 *Type-2 Hypervisor Architecture*

Type-2 hypervisors abstract guest OSs from the host OS. Parallels Desktop for Mac, QEMU, Oracle VirtualBox, VMware Player, and VMware Workstation are examples of Type-2 hypervisors.

Linux Containers (LXC)

Linux Containers (LXC) is a type of virtualization realized mid-2008. LXC is operating-system-based, where all container instances share the same kernel of the hosting compute node. The guest operating systems may execute in different user space. This can be manifested as different Linux distributions with the same kernel. An LXC architecture can be seen in Figure 15-3.

LXC provides operating-system-level virtualization as a virtual environment with its own process and network space. Linux kernel release 2.6.24 brought control groups, also known as cgroups, which provide the capability to limit, prioritize, measure, and control resource usage in a collection of processes.

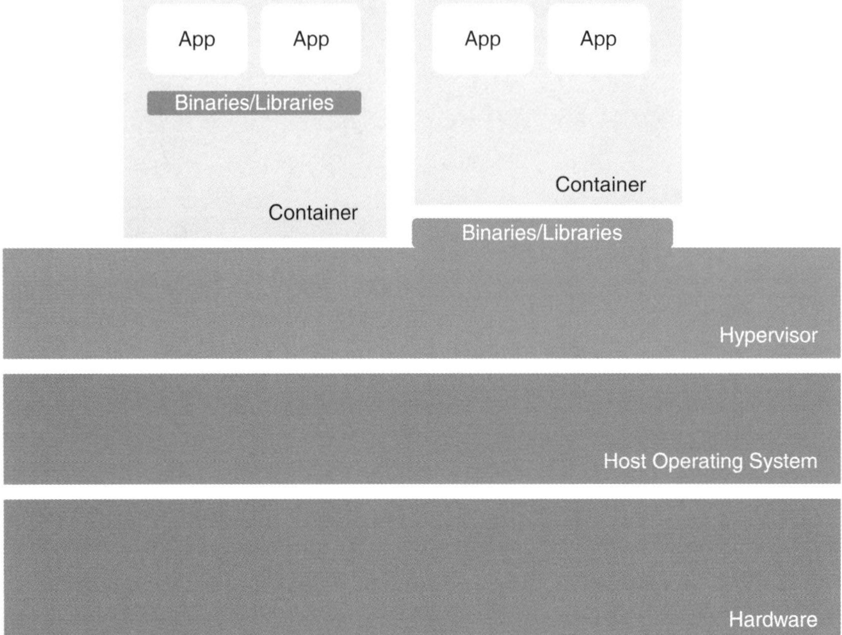

Figure 15-3 *Linux Containers Architecture*

When you're considering virtualization, the isolation, segmentation, and reallocation of resources are important. CPU, memory, storage, and networking are finite resources on host systems, but assigning them efficiently among virtual workloads is desirable.

Namespace isolation is not specifically encompassed in cgroups but is a related Linux kernel feature. The notion of process identifier (PID) namespace isolation allows control of parent processes with its children but restricts it across different parent namespaces. Network namespace isolation restricts physical or virtual network interface controllers, routing tables, and firewall rules. The Mount, or storage, namespace provides isolation across different filesystems, including file ownership, read-write, or read-only attributes. Interprocess communication (IPC) namespace isolation constrains System V IPCs: message queues, semaphores, and shared memory. Additionally, user namespaces isolate among user IDs among namespaces. The mixture and depth of these namespace options provide extreme flexibility for enhancing security and accountability.

Docker Containers

Docker is another type of containerized virtual environment. A Docker runtime is executed on the hosting operating system and controls the deployment and status of the containers. Docker containers are lightweight; you don't have the administrative burden of setting up virtual machines and environments. Docker containers use the host OS but don't have a separate kernel to run the containers; this is shown in Figure 15-4. It uses the same resources as the host OS. Docker also uses namespaces and control groups, as you saw with Linux Containers.

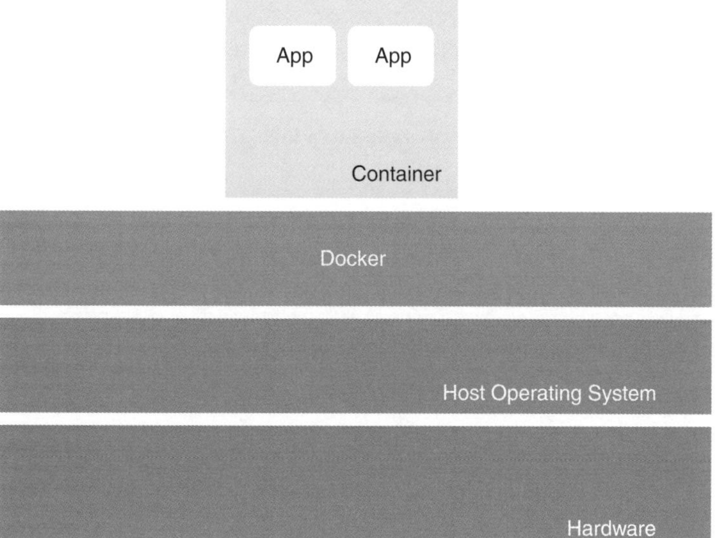

Figure 15-4 *Docker Container Architecture*

When comparing Docker to LXC, note that there is no guest operating system (in a traditional sense). The Docker daemon runs on the hosting OS. It is responsible for creating, executing, and maintaining the containers. By convention, each container runs a process (or application). There are strong affinities for microservices with Docker containers. Each application is isolated from others and executes without affecting them. Each container instance has its own configuration file, Dockerfile, which defines its base image, any layered dependencies, and definitions for copying files/folders and running tasks necessary to build the container to desired specifications.

What are the main differences between LXC and Docker containers? LXC aligns more to operating system containerization, whereas Docker is focused more on application containerization. Many virtualization designers use Docker for single-purpose application virtualization, whereas LXC serves multipurpose OS virtualization services. An administrator could log in to a virtualized LXC environment and create packages dynamically. Docker containers tend to be built-to-function and are less oriented toward dynamic updates or upgrades. If you had a Docker containerize app that needed a newer version of OpenSSL libraries, you would traditionally update the Dockerfile to reflect the updated dependency, spin up the new instance, and deprecate the original one. Docker containers are also ephemeral, so any data you need to retain across invocations must be purposely stored in persistent volumes or databases where the information can be extracted.

Application Container Ideas

When you're considering application container opportunities, here are some relevant questions to ask:

- Where do applications or data need to be restricted to a locale? (data sovereignty, governmental/corporate restrictions)
- Where are you trying to improve user experience by reducing latency due to network distance and routing?
- Where are apps that need to be managed by regional teams only?
- Are you equipped to push management of containers to the edge?

As mentioned in the previous section, an example could be monitoring network stats at the edge, reporting to a central system only when out of norms. This model would relieve network polling requirements, traffic, and data storage from centralized management tools. If your business model doesn't require high detail trending of network statistics, this may be a viable option.

Measuring user experience through availability, latency, packet loss, and responsiveness ensures visibility into what your customers are seeing. Consider the deployment model used with the Cisco IP SLAs feature and the Cisco ThousandEyes technology; they use an agent-based, source-destination deployment. If the monitoring source is as close to the network edge as possible, then you benefit from the closest possible user experience.

When there are clustered users in a locale, it may make sense to keep their local, regional data as close to them as possible. If the data being collected and processed involves personally identifiable information (PII), then country data privacy and sovereignty regulations may apply. In those cases, it makes sense to handle the data in the region without backhauling to a regional or centralized corporate data center or cloud environment, potentially outside the country policy.

Even if the localized or regional data is not governed by data privacy or sovereignty, it may make sense to host the information closer to the interested users. If the "Woolly Worm Festival" is only interesting to consumers in Banner Elk, North Carolina, why store and serve it in a data center in Seattle?

Another common use case for application hosting and containerization is with packet capture applications, such as Wireshark, embedded with a Cisco network switch. Now, no more dragging out a physical packet sniffer device when needing to do deep packet inspection of network traffic!

Syslog event messaging is an important monitoring service. Oftentimes it is used for alerting on failure of a component, but it is also possible to alert on informational events, such as a port or service being used. Security management is another prominent use case for syslog event data. With the diversity of network component failures, informational service reporting, and security notification, syslog event data is often multiplexed to different consuming management applications focused on function or domain. Another idea is to host a local syslog management application in a container to optimize the management traffic and limit redundancies. Other network devices (or application servers) that generate syslog event messages can forward to the containerized syslog receiver.

Platforms Supporting Application Containers

The Cisco Unified Computing System (UCS) and Hyperflex solutions are integrated compute, storage, and networking systems. It is broadly accepted that these "big iron" systems can be run in data centers and can also host bare-metal Docker environments. From an edge computing perspective, it is less likely that they are deployed to an extreme network edge, such as a cellular tower site, unless there are optimal levels of services and user traffic. However, several Cisco platforms do support application hosting or containers. Review the following options for your specific use case.

- The Cisco IC3000 Industrial Compute Gateway running software release 1.2.1 or higher for native Docker support for industrial IoT use cases.
- The Cisco IR809 and 829 platforms running Cisco IOS-XE release 15.6(1)T1 or higher for mobile IoT use cases.
- The Cisco IR1101 Integrated Services Router (ISR) platform running Cisco IOS-XE release 17.2.1 or higher for ARM-based IoT gateway use cases.
- The Cisco IE3400 switch platform running Cisco IOS-XE release 17.2.1 or higher for ruggedized industrial IoT use cases.
- The Cisco IE4000 switch platform running Cisco IOS release 15.2(5)E1 or higher for ruggedized industrial IoT user cases. Note that the IE4010 does not support Cisco IOx.
- The Catalyst 9000 series switch platform running Cisco IOS-XE release 16.2.1 or higher for diverse LAN access deployment use cases. This platform is most generally covered in this book and the DEVCOR exam.
  - Catalyst 9300/L series switches with Cisco IOS XE 16.12.1 release
  - Catalyst 9404 and 9407 switches with Cisco IOS XE 17.1.1 release
  - Catalyst 9410 switches with Cisco IOS XE 17.5.1 release
  - Catalyst 9500 High Performance and 9600 series switches with Cisco IOS XE 17.5.1 release

NOTE The new AppGigabitEthernet interface was introduced on the Catalyst 9300/9400 for dedicated application traffic. Catalyst 9500/9600 switches do not support the AppGigabitEthernet interface. Containers that need external network connectivity must use a management interface through loopback from any front-panel port.

- The CGR1000 Compute Module for CGR1000 series routers running Cisco IOS release 15.6(3)M2 for edge compute enablement on Connected Grid Routers (SmartGrid deployments).
- The Cisco IW6300 heavy duty series access points managed by Cisco Wireless Controller (WLC) release 8.10 or higher.
- The Cisco Nexus series switches running Cisco NX-OS Release 9.2(1) or higher.

How to Implement Application Containers

Cisco IOx (IOs + linuX) is an end-to-end application framework that provides application hosting capabilities of Docker containers in IOS XE-based platforms. Separately, the Cisco Guest Shell is also a specialized container service that allows for embedded Python interpreter and packet capture services. IOx provides lifecycle management of applications and data, including distribution, deployment, hosting, starting, stopping (management), and monitoring. The standard lifecycle phases are seen in Figure 15-5.

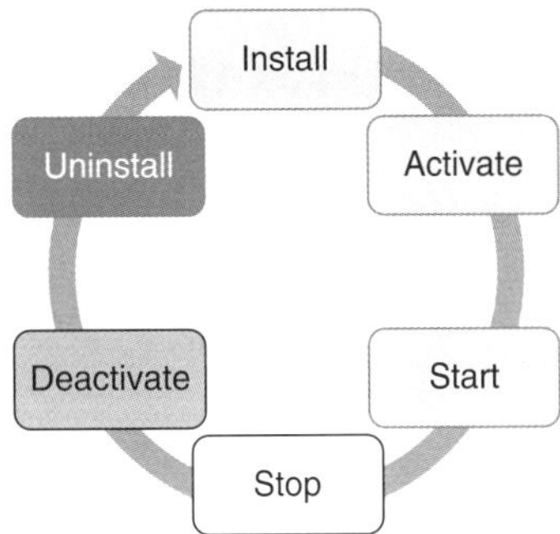

Figure 15-5 *Application Container Lifecycle Phases*

For the purposes of education and demonstration, we show you how to deploy a premade Docker container to a Catalyst 9000 running IOS XE 16.12 (or higher). Later, we show you how to deploy your own custom-developed container and deploy that to the switch. You can use a Catalyst 9000 in your environment—preferably a lab! Follow along on your own device or use a DevNet Sandbox Lab.

NOTE If you prefer to go the DevNet Sandbox Lab route, navigate to https://devnetsandbox.cisco.com and use the search bar to find options with "DNA Center," "IOS XE," or "Catalyst 9." The intent is to find an available lab with Catalyst 9300 platforms running IOS XE 16.12 or higher—17.3, ideally. The Always On labs would be the most immediately available but may not have all the permissions or dependencies needed for these examples (such as SSD flash drives). Alternatively, reservable labs like the ones for DNA Center, including Catalyst 9300s, would provide more access but may also be reserved, requiring you to schedule a timeslot in the future.

There are several steps to implementing a Docker container on a network switch: validate prerequisites, enable the application hosting framework, and install/activate/start the app.

Validating Prerequisites

For a Catalyst 9k switch, ensure you are running at least IOS XE release 16.12.1; release 17.3.3 or higher is preferable, in case you wish to deploy a Cisco ThousandEyes agent as a Docker container image. Example 15-1 provides the process and sample output for validating the running IOS XE release.

Example 15-1 *Validating the IOS XE Software Release Version*

```
cat9k# show version
Cisco IOS XE Software, Version 17.03.03
Cisco IOS Software [Amsterdam], Catalyst L3 Switch Software (CAT9K_IOSXE), Version
17.3.3, RELEASE SOFTWARE (fc7)
Technical Support: http://www.cisco.com/techsupport
Copyright (c) 1986-show 2021 by Cisco Systems, Inc.
Compiled Thu 04-Mar-21 12:32 by mcpre


Cisco IOS-XE software, Copyright (c) 2005-2021 by cisco Systems, Inc.
All rights reserved. Certain components of Cisco IOS-XE software are
[ . . . REMAINING TRIMMED . . . ]
```


Ensure you have a Cisco-certified USB 3.0 Flash Drive installed into the back-panel USB port to host the application hosting files. Part numbers SSD-120G or SSD-240G (for Catalyst 9300) are supported. Example 15-2 shows how to validate the existence of a USB 3.0 Flash Drive using the **dir** and **show inventory** commands.

Example 15-2 *Verifying USB 3.0 Flash Drive Availability*

```
cat9k# dir usbflash1:
Directory of usbflash1:/

13       -rw-        104034816  Jul 29 2021 14:51:49 +00:00  suricata.tar
12       -rw-        793325568  Jul 24 2021 05:32:38 +00:00  snort3.tar
524289   drwx             4096  Jul 19 2021 17:43:22 +00:00  iox_host_data_share
11       -rw-          6052864  Jun 27 2020 11:13:12 +00:00  iperf3.tar

118014062592 bytes total (108672851456 bytes free)
cat9k#
cat9k# show inventory
NAME: "c93xx Stack", DESCR: "c93xx Stack"
PID: C9300-48T         , VID: V02  , SN: FJC********

NAME: "Switch 1", DESCR: "C9300-48T"
PID: C9300-48T         , VID: V02  , SN: FJC********

NAME: "Switch 1 - Power Supply B", DESCR: "Switch 1 - Power Supply B"
PID: PWR-C1-350WAC-P   , VID: V01  , SN: ART********

NAME: "Switch 1 FRU Uplink Module 1", DESCR: "8x10G Uplink Module"
PID: C9300-NM-8X       , VID: V02  , SN: FJZ********

NAME: "usbflash1", DESCR: "usbflash1-1"
PID: SSD-120G          , VID: STP22270NXB, SN: V01
```

At this point, ensure you have the DNA-Advantage subscription licensing enabled:

```
cat9k# show license summary
License Usage:
  License                Entitlement Tag               Count Status
  -----------------------------------------------------------------
  network-advantage     (C9300-48 Network Advan...)       1 IN USE
  dna-advantage          (C9300-48 DNA Advantage)         1 IN USE
```

Enabling Application Hosting Framework

The application hosting framework is not enabled by default. You should enable the IOx service from configuration mode. To do so, use the following IOS XE CLI commands and configuration directives to enable it. IOx takes a few minutes to start. Additional information on the Guest Shell virtual environment, enabled by the IOx Application Hosting Infrastructure, is available at https://www.cisco.com/c/en/us/td/docs/ios-xml/ios/prog/configuration/173/b_173_programmability_cg/guest_shell.html.

```
cat9k# configure terminal
Enter configuration commands, one per line. End with CNTL/Z.
cat9k(config)# iox
cat9k(config)#
```

Verify the application hosting services are running by using the IOS XE CLI command shown in Example 15-3.

Example 15-3 *Verifying the IOx Application Hosting Infrastructure Services*

```
cat9k# show iox-service

IOx Infrastructure Summary:
---------------------------
IOx service (CAF) 1.11.0.5      : Running
IOx service (HA)                : Running
IOx service (IOxman)            : Running
IOx service (Sec storage)       : Not Running
Libvirtd 1.3.4                  : Running
Dockerd 18.03.0                 : Running
Application DB Sync Info        : Available
Sync Status                     : Disabled
cat9k#
```

If the highlighted services do not show as Running, toggle the IOx configuration in config mode with **no iox; iox** to restart the services.

Be patient when you run the following IOS XE CLI command to review the status and list of hosted applications. It may take several minutes for the application hosting environment to be fully ready, even if reporting that no applications are registered.

```
cat9k# sh app-hosting list
No App found
```

Now that you have an environment ready to host a Docker container, you must decide what application to host. Several Cisco-validated open-source options are available at https://developer.cisco.com/app-hosting/opensource/.

You are free to pick other Docker container options, but for this exercise, choose iPerf because it is a useful utility. iPerf3 is an open-source, cross-platform, and CLI-based utility that performs active measurements between iPerf endpoints to gauge bandwidth and loss statistics. It supports IPv4 and IPv6 endpoints.

The first action is to download the iPerf Docker container code to the usbflash1: file-system. We also suggest you familiarize yourself with the project notes from https://hub.docker.com/r/mlabbe/iperf3.

Pulling the Docker image directly from Docker hub to an IOx-enabled Cisco platform is not currently supported. However, you can pull the Docker image down to another system that already has the Docker utilities—a PC, laptop, or Linux VM—and save the Docker image as a tar archive. Example 15-4 shows the process of using a separate computer with Docker installed to pull the iPerf image and save it as a tar file for later transfer to the network device.

Example 15-4 *Using Docker Commands to Pull and Save the iPerf Container Image*

```
[sre@docker-utils Downloads]$ docker pull mlabbe/iperf3
Using default tag: latest
latest: Pulling from mlabbe/iperf3
4c0d98bf9879: Pull complete
c9050d8c9c5a: Pull complete
Digest: sha256:0f5780e6a5dc6a9e0187701ad4540445d8fa08023692e0d930772a654305d167
Status: Downloaded newer image for mlabbe/iperf3:latest
docker.io/mlabbe/iperf3:latest
[sre@docker-utils Downloads]$ docker save mlabbe/iperf3:latest -o iperf3.tar
[sre@docker-utils Downloads]$ ls -l
total 5960
-rw-------. 1 sre sre 6100992 Oct 23 12:11 iperf3.tar
```

You now have several deployment options. You can use Cisco DNA Center, the Cisco IOx Local Manager, or you can do CLI-based actions. We cover each option in the following sections.

Using Cisco DNA Center for App Hosting

Cisco DNA Center Release 1.3.1 introduced the application hosting feature, which allows the upload/import, configuration, and startup of Docker containers in Catalyst IOS XE-based switches. For purposes of this example, you can use Cisco DNA Center Release 2.2.2.3 with a Catalyst 9300-24 running IOS XE 17.3.3.

Step 1. Check that device prerequisites are complete. Navigate to the main DNA Center menu panel to **Provision**, into **Services** and **App Hosting for Switches**, as seen in Figure 15-6.

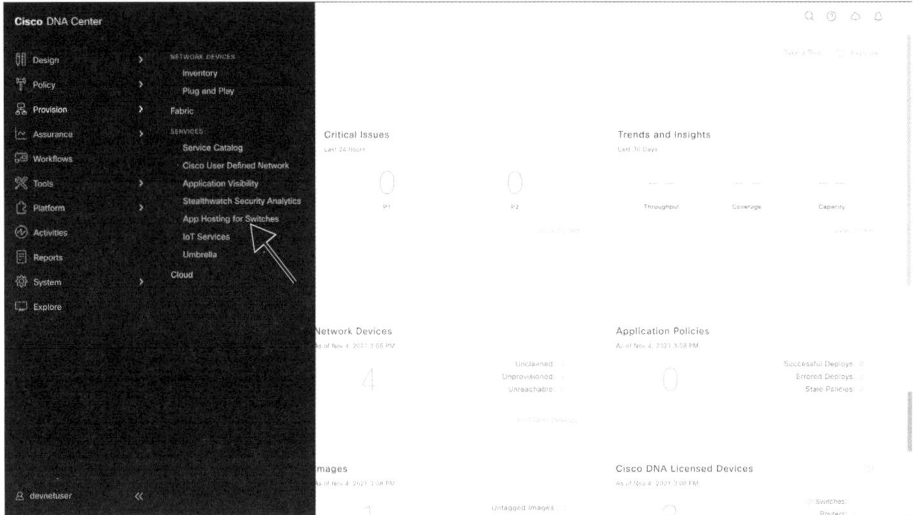

Figure 15-6 *DNA Center App Hosting for Switches Feature*

Click the **All Devices** link in the upper-right corner to review whether the devices meet prerequisites. DNA Center does an assessment and identifies the App Hosting status, as seen in Figure 15-7.

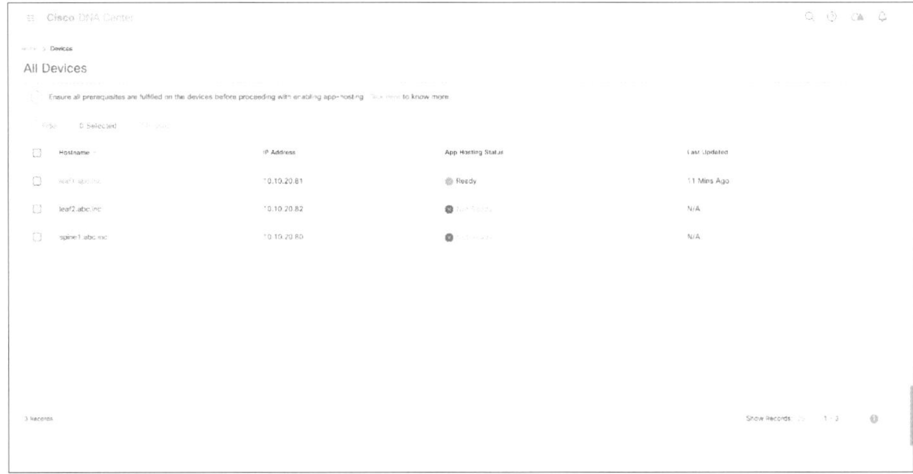

Figure 15-7 *Devices in DNA Center with App Hosting Status*

If devices are Not Ready, you can hover over the status to get a summary of what needs to be fixed. The summary does not list all discrepancies, so you may need to take an iterative approach to fixing each issue until the device becomes fully Ready. The prerequisites are also documented on this portal on the Click Here link in the Information banner. Example 15-5 shows the content of the prerequisites.

Example 15-5 *DNA Center Guidance on Application Hosting Prerequisites*

```
Prerequisites
To enable application hosting on a Cisco Catalyst 9000 device, the following prereq-
uisites must be fulfilled.

1. Configure a secure HTTP server on the switch where the applications will be
hosted.

2. Configure local or AAA based authentication server for the HTTPS user on the
switch. You must configure the username and the password with privilege level 15.

3. Ensure Cisco Catalyst 9300 Series switches are running Cisco IOS XE 16.12.x or
later version and Cisco Catalyst 9400 Series switches are running Cisco IOS XE
17.1.x or later version.

4. Ensure that the device has an external USB SSD pluggable storage. (Only for the
switches of 9300 family)

5. The following example shows a working configuration on a switch.

     prompt# sh run | sec http
     ip http server
     ip http authentication local
     ip http secure-server
     ip http max-connections 16
     ip http client source-interface Loopback0

To verify that the configuration on the switch is correct, open the WebUI on the
switch and ensure that you can log in as the HTTPS user.

6. On Cisco DNA Center, configure the HTTPS credentials while manually adding the
device. The HTTPS username, password, and port number are mandatory for application
hosting. The default port number is 443. You can also edit the device credentials.
If you edit a device that is already managed, resynchronize that device in the
inventory before it is used for application hosting-related actions.
```

Step 2. Upload the container image into the DNA Center App Hosting software repository.

Navigate to the main DNA Center menu panel to **Provision**, into **Services** and **App Hosting for Switches**, as seen in Figure 15-6, resulting in the software repository seen in Figure 15-8. There may or may not be existing app packages based on prior use.

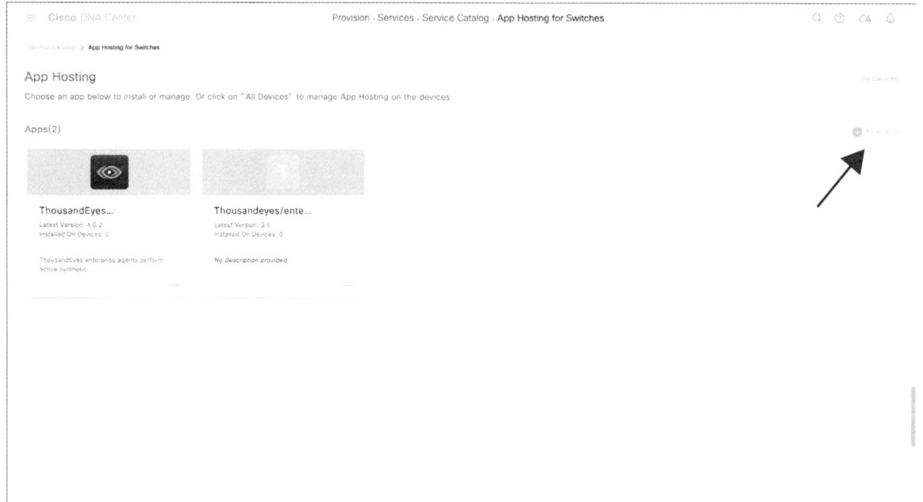

Figure 15-8 *Cisco DNA Center App Hosting Portal*

If you click on the **New App** gadget in the upper-right corner, a new pop-up window appears, like the one in Figure 15-9.

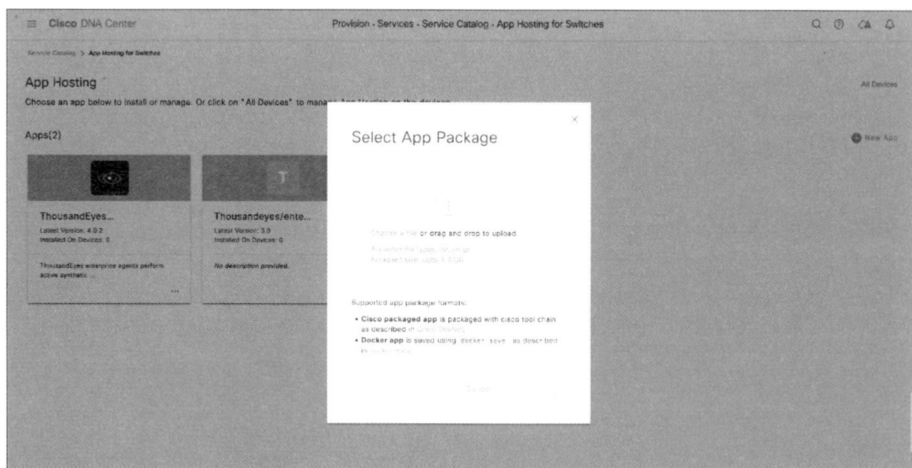

Figure 15-9 *Uploading an App into Cisco DNA Center*

At this point, you can select an App Package (container image) to import into DNAC. Note the supported formats that require using the IOx application package process, as documented at https://developer.cisco.com/docs/

iox/#!package-format/iox-application-package. It is also possible to use a locally derived docker image that was created with the **docker save** command, as previously described in Example 15-4.

Clicking the **Choose a File** link presents a local file chooser where you can navigate your file system to the docker .tar or .tar.gz image. After you select a file, click the **Upload** button and DNA Center then shows a progression of the file upload, as seen in Figure 15-10.

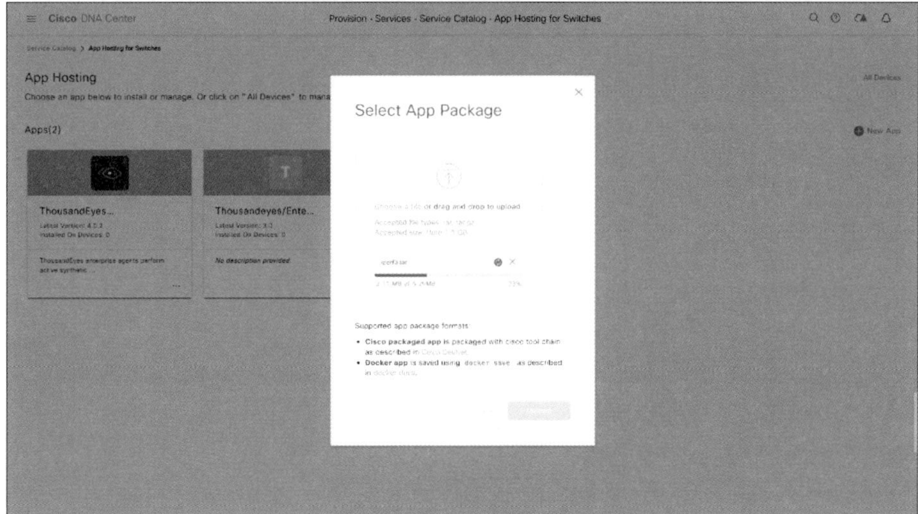

Figure 15-10 *Cisco DNA Center Performing App Hosting Image Import*

When the import into the DNA Center App Hosting repository is complete, the portal updates to show the new app. In this situation, Figure 15-11 depicts this as Mlabbe/Iperf3, the first app in the list.

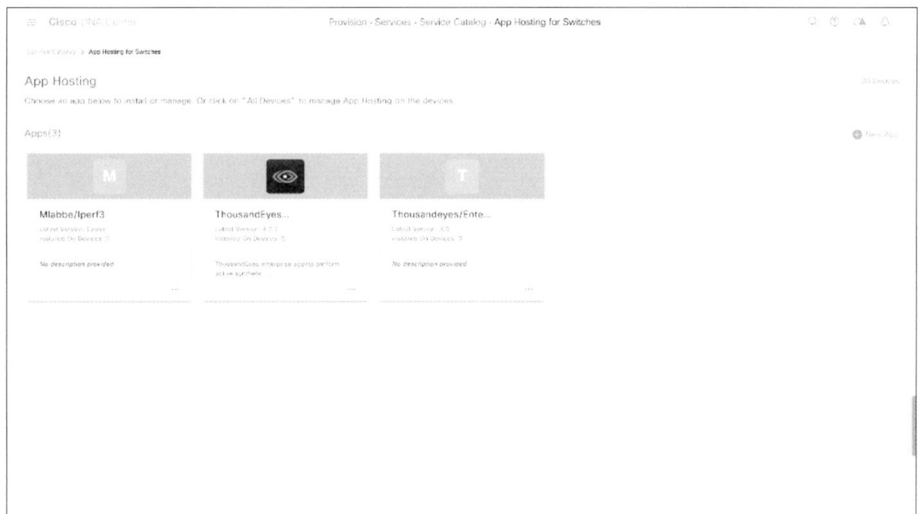

Figure 15-11 *Cisco DNA Center App Hosting After iPerf3 Import*

Step 3. Update container parameters, as necessary.

Some Docker containers offer services that need to be exposed to the host system. iPerf requires a management port, TCP/UDP 5201, to be exposed. At the main app portal, the ellipses (...) icon provides Update and Delete options. Click the **Edit** option to update the Docker Runtime Options, as seen in Figure 15-12.

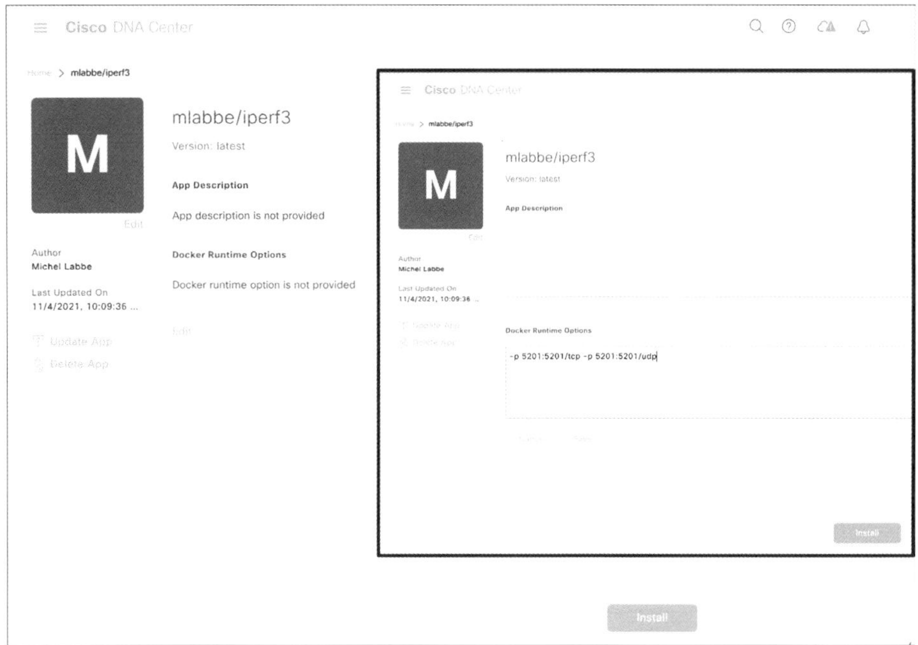

Figure 15-12 *Editing iPerf3 Application Docker Runtime Options*

Specifically, -p 5201:5201/tcp -p 5201:5201/udp must be added to allow the guest container's port listener on TCP/UDP 5201 to be exposed on the hosting switch. iPerf uses this port for management communication between the server and client.

You can then click the **Save** option under the Docker Runtime Options text window and the **Install** button to import the container change. A Success pop-up should appear, acknowledging the update.

Step 4. Select app deployment hosts.

When you return to the main app portal, select the app to install—in this case, **Mlabbe/Iperf3**. A Site Selector presents options to select a building. After you make a selection and click the **Next** button, a Select Switches screen shows options to deploy the app to any preferred switches that are ready. One or more switches can be selected, and the workflow can continue, as seen in Figure 15-13.

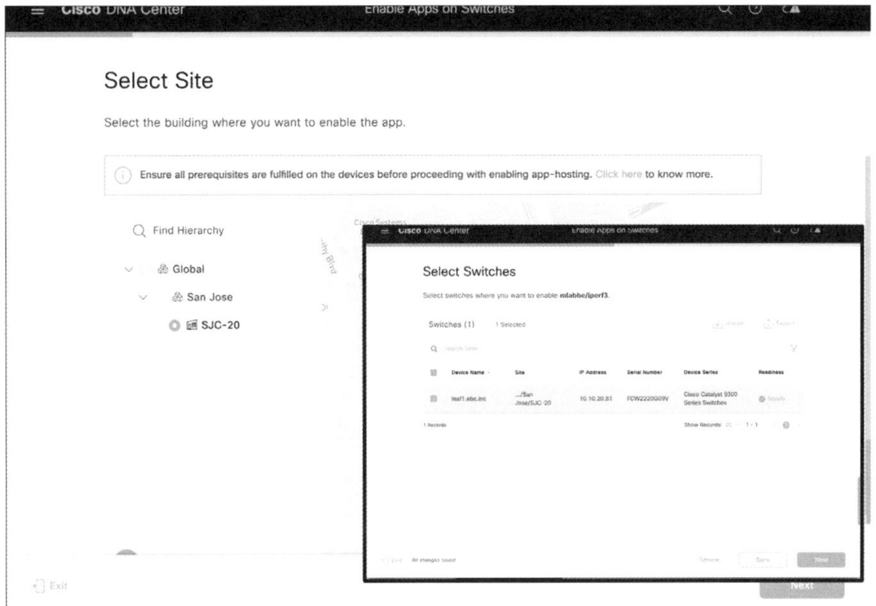

Figure 15-13 *Selecting Devices for App Hosting Deployment in Cisco DNA Center*

Step 5. Configure host-specific deployment options—Network Settings.

The next portal to appear is the Configure App, where Network Settings can be defined. If the app doesn't expose network services or if your environment is appropriately configured to serve DHCP IP addresses, then this step is trivial. In scenarios using static IP addresses, there are several more steps. First, you must click the **Export** button to download a CSV file defining the network specifications. Figures 15-14 and 15-15 show these steps.

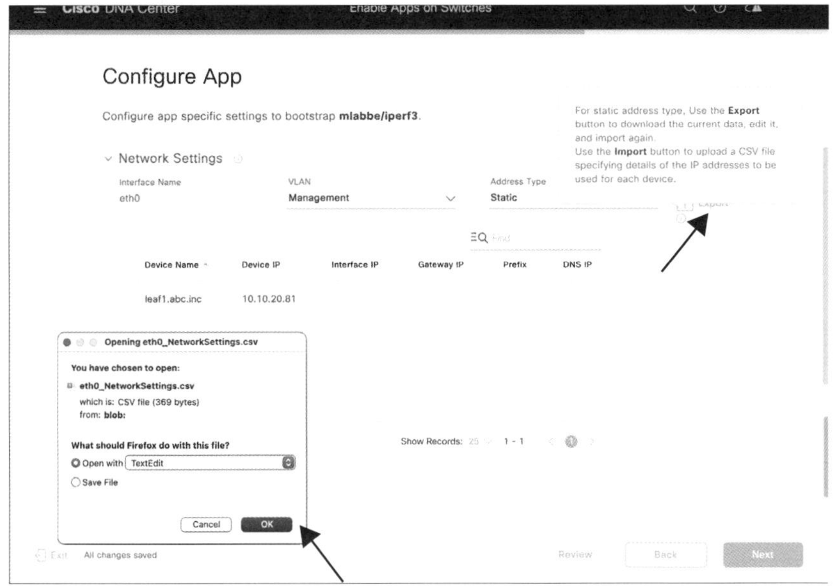

Figure 15-14 *Configuring App Dependencies by Exporting Network Settings*

eth0_NetworkSettings.csv — Edited

```
# Cisco Systems Inc. All Rights Reserved.,,,,,
# Comment starts with #.,,,,,
# Comment and Blank line will be ignored.,,,,,
# Mandatory fields are marked with *.,,,,,
# Gateway IP** field is mandatory for first interface.,,,,,
# Don't change Header Names,,,,,
,,,,,
,,,,,
Host Name*,Device IP*,Interface IP*,Gateway IP**,Prefix*,DNS IP
leaf1.abc.inc,10.10.20.81,10.10.20.101,10.10.20.254,24,
```

Figure 15-15 *Editing Network Settings for Application Hosting Deployment*

After editing the CSV file to suit your needs and saving it, you can return to the DNA Center portal to click **Import Gadget** and upload the modified CSV file. At this point, you can expect to see the Static Network Settings pop-up shown in Figure 15-16.

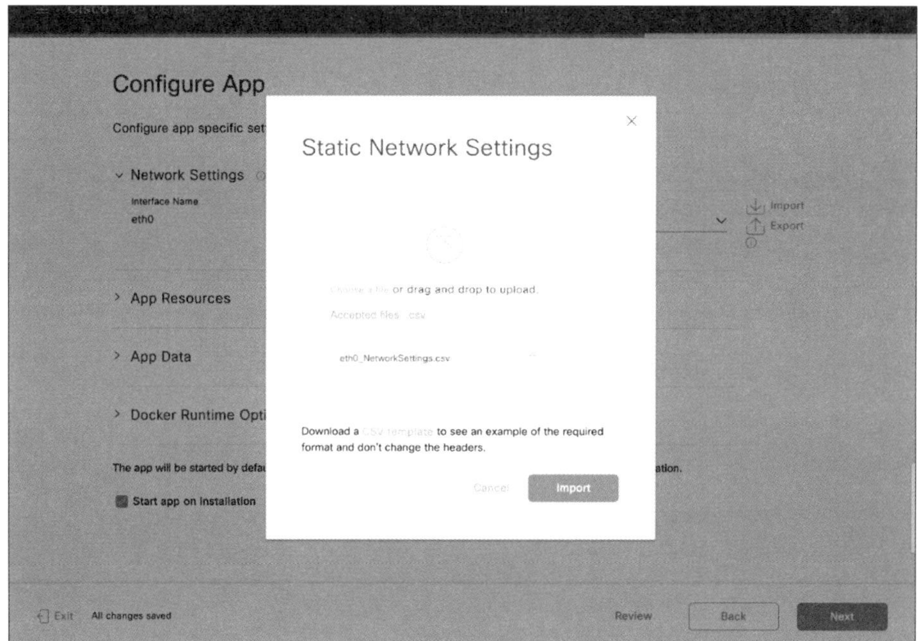

Figure 15-16 *Importing Network Settings for Application Hosting Deployment*

The Network Settings should reflect changes. If desired, you can scroll down and review App Resources, App Data, and Docker Runtime Options. Click the **Next** button to review the deployment on a Summary screen. One more click of the **Next** button takes you to a Provisioning Task.

Step 6. Perform the app-to-host(s) provisioning.

Figure 15-17 depicts the final step: provisioning. Click the **Provision** button to upload the container app to the device(s), configure the docker parameters and network settings, and start the app.

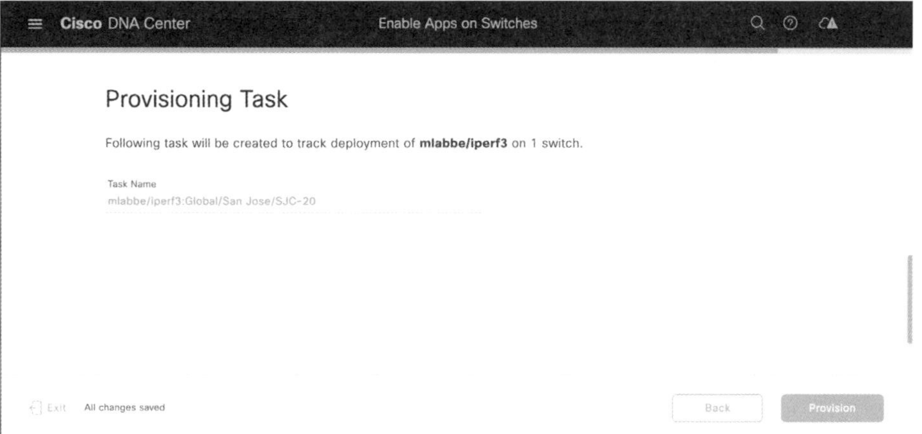

Figure 15-17 *Provisioning iPerf Application Hosting Instance*

The workflow continues to show a provisioning status screen, as seen in Figure 15-18. The amount of time to complete depends on the number of sites, building, switches, and the size of the container apps that must be uploaded to each host switch.

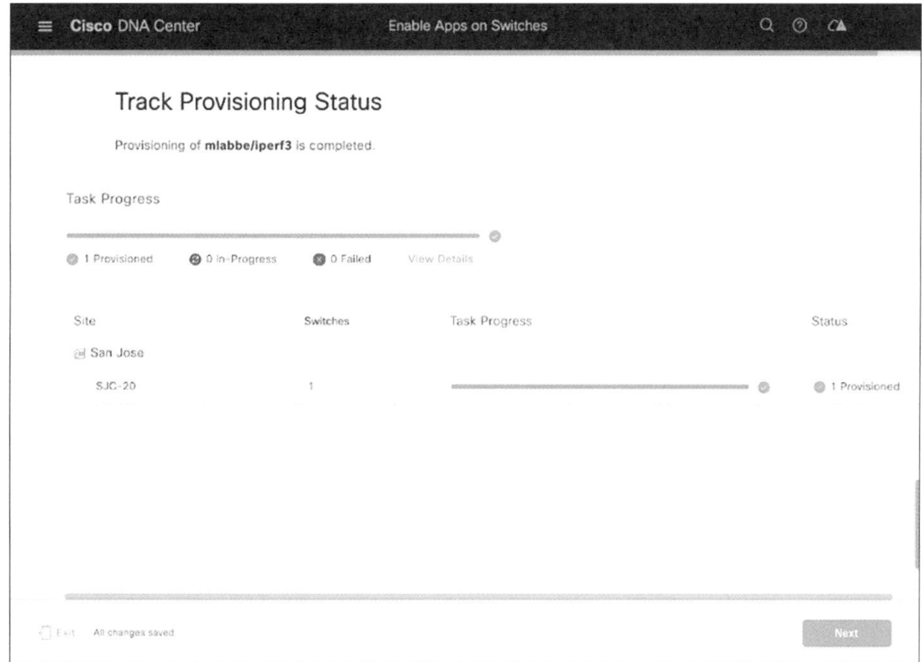

Figure 15-18 *Monitoring iPerf Application Hosting Provisioning Status*

If desired, you can return to the home portal of the App Hosting for Switches function and select the app ellipses icon for the Manage function to review all hosting switches and their status related to the container app. Figure 15-19 shows this portal, and Figure 15-20 shows the selection of a specific hosting switch for its individual app details and status.

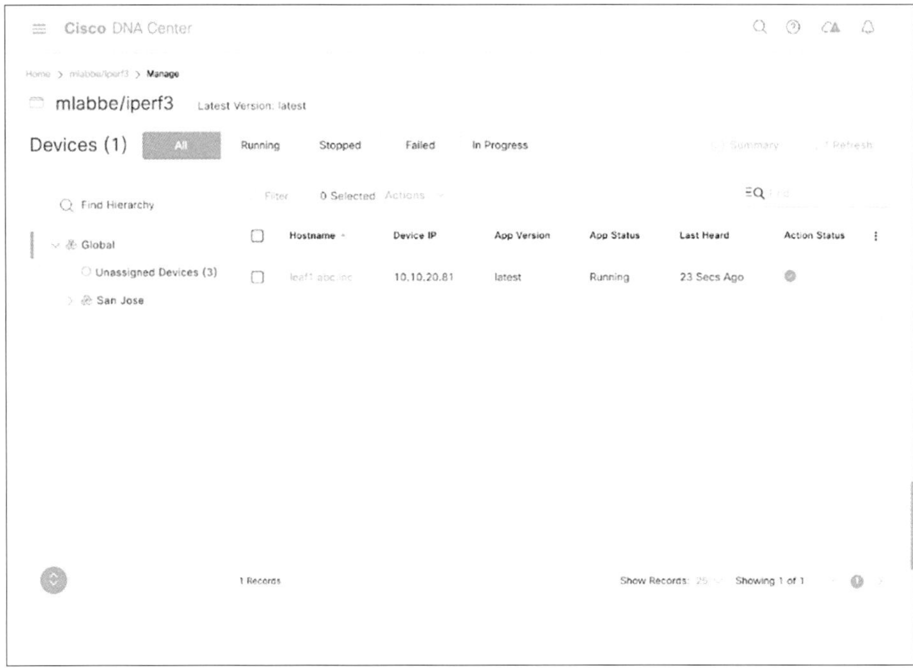

Figure 15-19 *Reviewing the iPerf App-Specific Deployment Inventory*

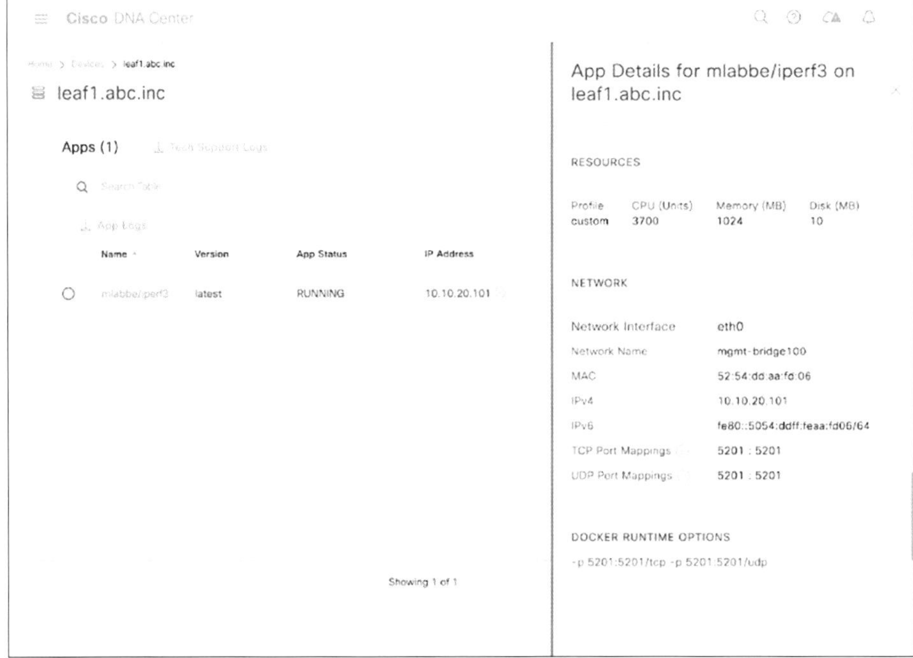

Figure 15-20 *Reviewing the Device-Specific Deployment Parameters of iPerf App*

At this point, you can interact with the container app. Navigate down to the "Interacting with App Hosted iPerf3" section if you prefer. The following sections cover a similar process of getting the container app into the hosting switch using alternative IOx Local Manager or command-line interface methods.

Using Cisco IOx Local Manager for App Hosting

The Cisco IOx Local Manager is a graphical, web-based app that runs local to the Cisco device doing application hosting. For this use case, ensure the device has **ip http secure-server** configured; then log in through a web browser at https://<IP_Address>/iox/login. The login screen appears as shown in Figure 15-21.

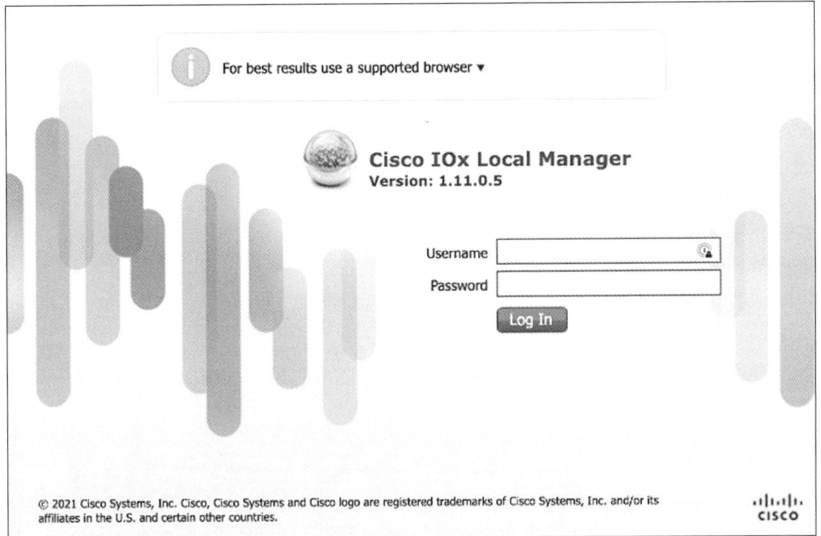

Figure 15-21 *Cisco IOx Local Manager Login Portal*

Use an account with Priv-15 access.

After successful login, for a system with no registered or active Docker container apps, the browser shows this status as in Figure 15-22.

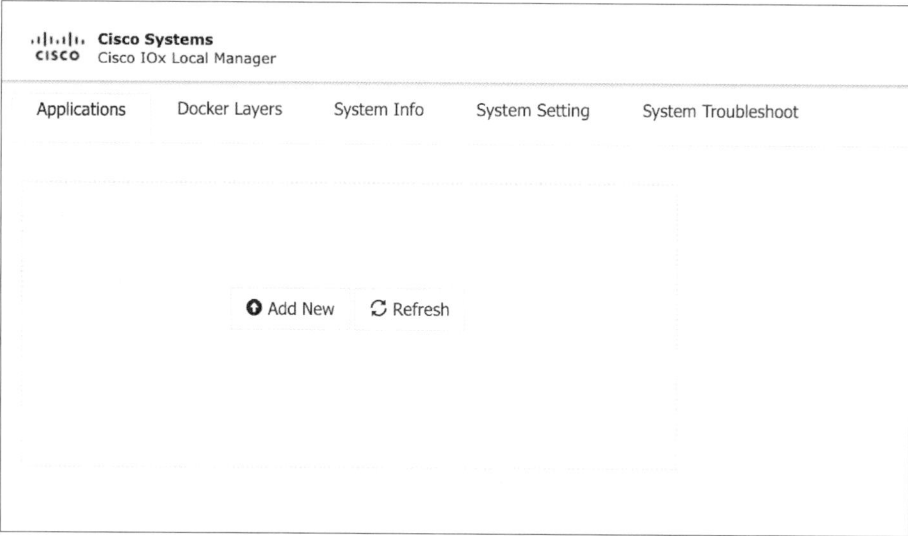

Figure 15-22 *Cisco IOx Local Manager Applications Portal*

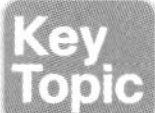

Feel free to click through the IOx Local Manager app tabs for familiarity's sake, but there will be limited information until you deploy an app. Next, click the prominent Add New button in the middle of the Applications tab frame.

A new pop-up window appears, as seen in Figure 15-23. Give the app a name or application ID; then use the Choose File button to navigate to a file selector. Look for the iperf3.tar file that was created earlier from the "docker save" activity.

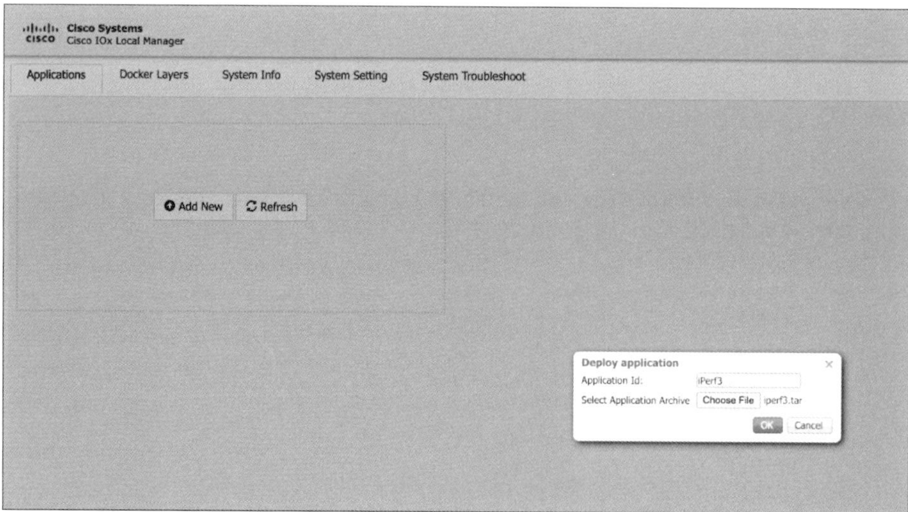

Figure 15-23 *Using Cisco IOx Local Manager to Import iPerf3 App*

After you click the OK button, the system starts importing the Docker app, as seen in Figure 15-24, resulting in the message shown in Figure 15-25.

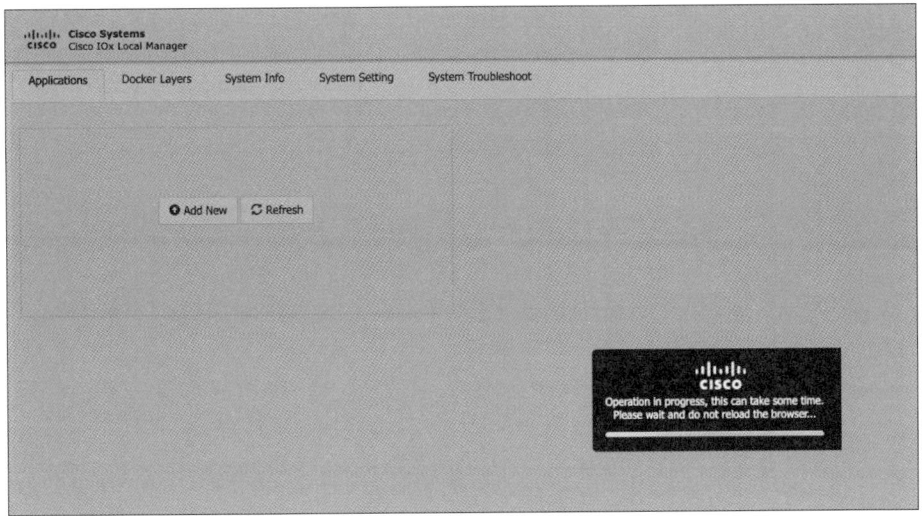

Figure 15-24 *Cisco IOx Local Manager iPerf3 Import Progress*

Cisco Systems
Cisco IOx Local Manager
Applications Docker Layers System Info System Setting System Troubleshoot
Successfully Deployed.
OK
iPerf3
DEPLOYED
No Description Available
TYPE docker
VERSION latest
PROFILE custom
Memory * 50.0%
CPU * 50.0%
Activate Upgrade Delete
Add New Refresh

Figure 15-25 *Cisco IOx Local Manager iPerf3 Import Completion*

At this point, the image is deployed. Next, click the Activate button, as seen in Figure 15-26. Doing so enables you to update the container parameters, as seen in Figure 15-27, where you need to identify the guest app networking and Docker options. Specific to iPerf3, when you want to run as a listening server, you need to pass through a port listener from the Catalyst switch host to the guest app. The settings for the Docker options are

```
--rm -p 5201:5201/tcp -p 5201:5201/udp
```

These are default port settings for iPerf3. Make note if you chose alternative settings.

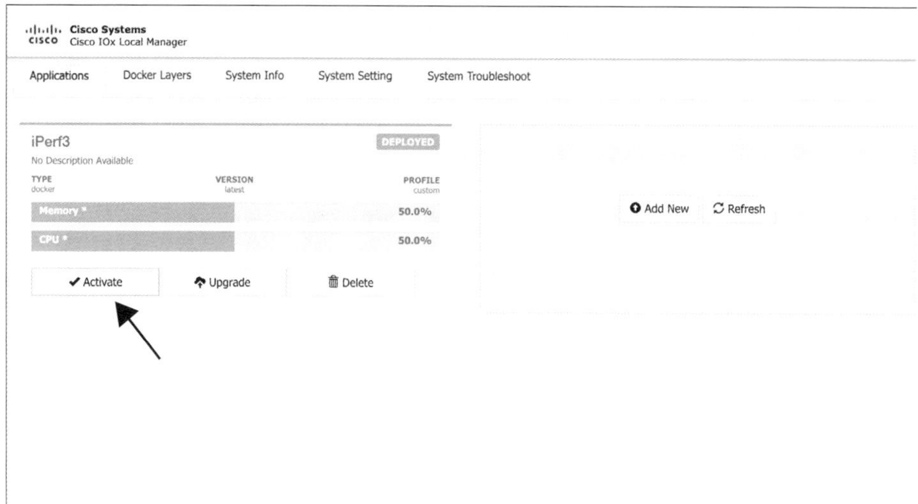

Figure 15-26 *Activating the iPerf3 Image in Cisco IOx Local Manager*

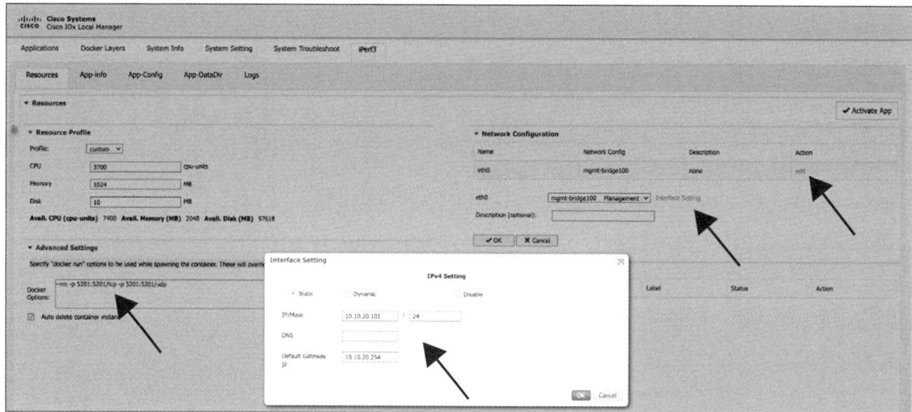

Figure 15-27 *Updating iPerf3 Image Network and Docker Options in Cisco IOx Local Manager*

Now that the Docker container app has the desired guest parameters, you can fully activate it by clicking the Activate App button in the upper-right corner, as seen in Figure 15-28. This shows a processing pop-up, like the one in Figure 15-29.

Figure 15-28 *Activating the iPerf3 App in Cisco IOx Local Manager*

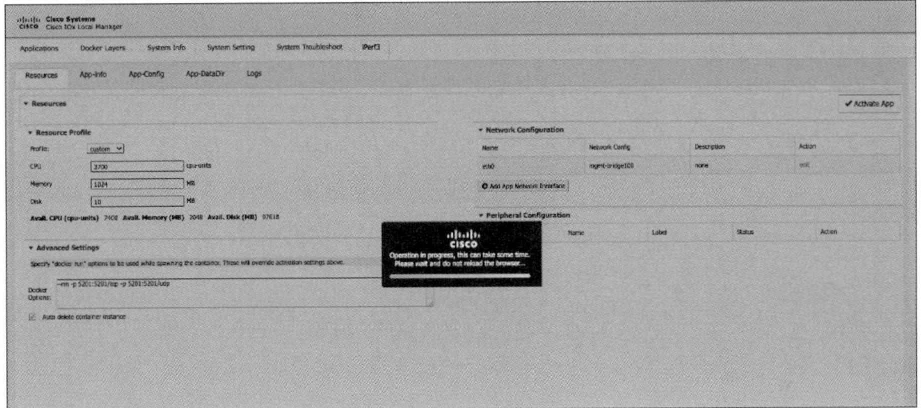

Figure 15-29 *Activation Progress of iPerf3 App in Cisco IOx Local Manager*

With an activated application, you can now start it by clicking the Start button, as shown in Figure 15-30. You then see a processing pop-up, like the one in Figure 15-31.

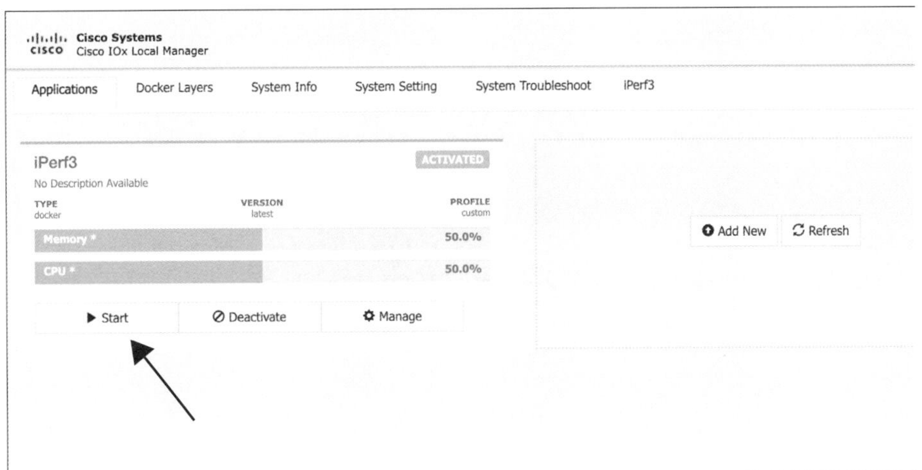

Figure 15-30 *Starting the iPerf3 App in Cisco IOx Local Manager*

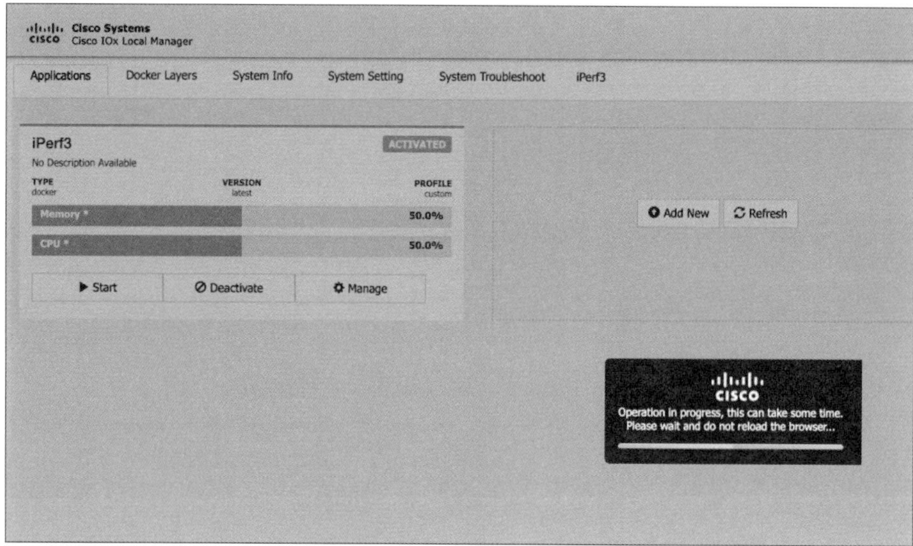

Figure 15-31 *Startup Progress of iPerf3 App in Cisco IOx Local Manager*

Finally, the IOx Local Manager shows a fully running Docker container app, as in Figure 15-32.

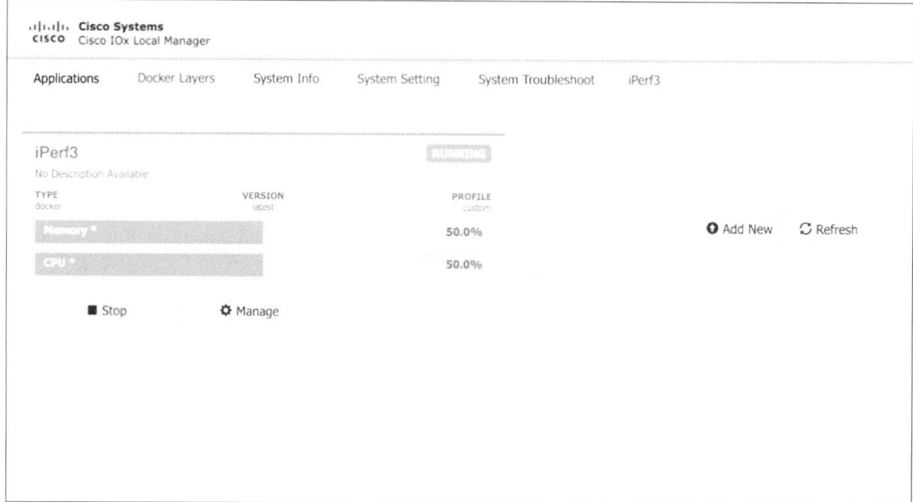

Figure 15-32 *Final Startup Status of iPerf3 App in Cisco IOx Local Manager*

Jump ahead to the "Interacting with App Hosted iPerf3" section to interact with the running Docker container app.

Using the Command-Line Interface for App Hosting

To use the command-line interface for app hosting, you must get the Docker image from the previous "docker save" activity onto the switch filesystem, specifically usbflash1:.

Step 1. Copy the tar file to the switch usbflash1: filesystem using available file transfer protocols, such as TFTP, SCP, FTP, RCP, HTTP, or HTTPS. If you need a refresher, reference this document for Catalyst 9300 and the minimum IOS XE release 16.12 at http://cs.co/9004Jryo2#concept_lqt_ltk_l1b.

Step 2. Configure the AppGigabitEthernet1/0/1 interface.

Application hosting in IOS XE on Catalyst 9300/9400 includes a new AppGigabitEthernet interface, specifically, AppGigabitEthernet1/0/1, which acts as the bridge between the physical switch networking and the virtualized Docker application.

Depending on your use case, you can trunk all switch VLAN traffic, a subset, or just a single VLAN. For this educational use case, you can trunk but allow just one VLAN:

```
!
interface AppGigabitEthernet1/0/1
 switchport trunk allowed vlan 100
 switchport mode trunk
end
```

Step 3. Map any Docker application virtual network (vNIC) interfaces. For this iPerf example, there is only one, but there could be other scenarios where your Docker app may have a "management" interface that is separate from a "sniffer" or "data-traffic" interface. Pay attention to any VLAN, guest IP address, gateway, and Docker resource dependencies.

```
app-hosting appid iPerf3
 app-vnic AppGigabitEthernet trunk
  vlan 100 guest-interface 0
   guest-ipaddress 10.10.20.101 netmask 255.255.255.0
 app-default-gateway 10.10.20.254 guest-interface 0
 app-resource docker
  run-opts 1 "-p 5201:5201/tcp -p 5201:5201/udp"
```

Unpacking this set of commands a bit, you can see that it gives the Docker container app an application ID (appid) of **iPerf3**. You're defining the application virtual network interface card (vNIC) to the AppGigabithEthernet trunk. Correspondingly, it assigns the application's guest-interface, traditionally Ethernet0, as instance 0 mapped to VLAN 100, matching the earlier interface AppGigabitEthernet1/0/1 settings. In this use case, the intention is to give the guest app a static IP address, so the address, netmask, and default gateway should be supplied. DNS is optional. DHCP served parameters are supported. Finally, there is a special consideration to add Docker resource parameters that port forward

TCP and UDP port 5201 externally from the hosting switch to the internal port 5201 of the guest app. This is a default port listener for iPerf3.

Step 4. Install the iPerf3 docker app by referencing its flash file-system location. You can follow the installation with commands to verify the status:

```
cat9k# app-hosting install appid iPerf3 package
usbflash1:iperf3.tar
Installing package 'usbflash1:iperf3.tar' for 'iPerf3'.
Use 'show app-hosting list' for progress.

cat9k# show app-hosting list
App id                                    State
---------------------------------------------------
iPerf3                                    DEPLOYED

cat9k#
```

Again, remember the **show app-hosting list** command may take some time to process.

Step 5. Activate the docker app, referencing it by application ID (appid).

```
cat9k# app-hosting activate appid iPerf3
iPerf3 activated successfully
Current state is: ACTIVATED

cat9k#
```

Step 6. Finally, run the iPerf3 docker app with the **app-hosting start** directive:

```
cat9k# app-hosting start appid iPerf3
iPerf3 started successfully
Current state is: RUNNING
```

Again, you can double-check the status with other app-hosting commands. Example 15-6 shows a couple of commands to verify status.

Example 15-6 *Reviewing Container Status with* **show app-hosting** *Commands*

```
cat9k# show app-hosting list
App id                                    State
---------------------------------------------------------
iPerf3                                    RUNNING
cat9k# show app-hosting detail appid iPerf3
App id                   : iPerf3
Owner                    : iox
State                    : RUNNING
```

```
Application
  Type                    : docker
  Name                    : mlabbe/iperf3
  Version                 : latest
  Description             :
  Path                    : usbflash1:iperf3.tar
  URL Path                :
Activated profile name : custom

Resource reservation
  Memory                  : 1024 MB
  Disk                    : 10 MB
  CPU                     : 3700 units
  VCPU                    : 1

Attached devices
  Type              Name                Alias
  ---------------------------------------------
  serial/shell     iox_console_shell   serial0
  serial/aux       iox_console_aux     serial1
  serial/syslog    iox_syslog          serial2
  serial/trace     iox_trace           serial3

Network interfaces
   ---------------------------------------
eth0:
   MAC address          : 52:54:dd:56:a:40
   IPv4 address         : 10.10.20.101
   Network name         : mgmt-bridge100



Docker
------


Run-time information
  Command                 :
  Entry-point             : iperf3 -s
  Run options in use    : -p 5201:5201/tcp -p 5201:5201/udp
  Package run options   :
Application health information
  Status                  : 0
  Last probe error       :
  Last probe output      :
```

15

Now that you have a fully running iPerf3 Docker application, you can proceed to interacting with the app either as a server endpoint or as an embedded client.

Interacting with App Hosted iPerf3

Regardless of how you deployed the App hosted iPerf3, now you can interact with it. From another system acting as a client, you can send test traffic to the Catalyst 9300 running the iPerf3 Docker app acting as the server endpoint. Figure 15-33 depicts a couple of options:

- A local laptop, server, or virtual machine with the iPerf3 utility as a client, targeting a local Cisco Nexus 9300 running the iPerf3 docker-app in IOx Application Hosting
- A local laptop, server, or virtual machine with the iPerf3 utility as a client *and* the OpenConnect VPN software, targeting a Cisco Sandbox Lab environment with a Cisco Nexus 9300 running the iPerf3 docker-app in IOx Application Hosting

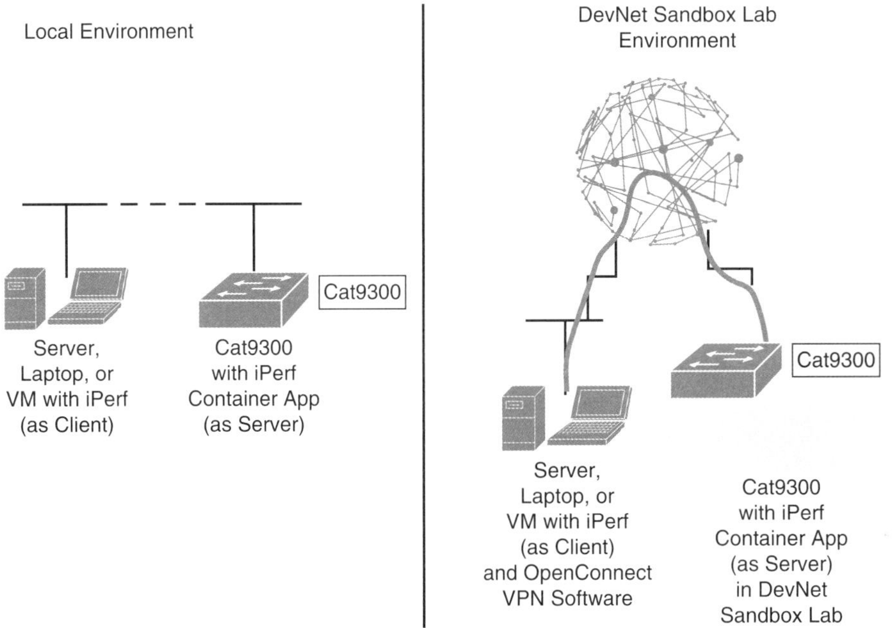

Figure 15-33 *Testing iPerf3 Environment Options*

Either way, Example 15-7 guides you in using the iPerf3 utility on a local system to target the Catalyst 9300 acting as an iPerf3 server. The iPerf deployment on the Catalyst switch enabled server-listener mode based on the Docker runtime options provided in activation and startup.

Example 15-7 *Running the iPerf3 Utility as a Client on the Local System*

```
sre@docker-utils Utilities % ./iperf3 -c 10.10.20.101
Connecting to host 10.10.20.101, port 5201
[  4] local 192.168.254.11 port 56235 connected to 10.10.20.101 port 5201
[ ID] Interval           Transfer     Bandwidth
[  4]   0.00-1.00   sec   935 KBytes  7.65 Mbits/sec
[  4]   1.00-2.00   sec   892 KBytes  7.32 Mbits/sec
[  4]   2.00-3.00   sec  1.12 MBytes  9.37 Mbits/sec
[  4]   3.00-4.00   sec   390 KBytes  3.20 Mbits/sec
[  4]   4.00-5.00   sec   386 KBytes  3.16 Mbits/sec
[  4]   5.00-6.00   sec   387 KBytes  3.17 Mbits/sec
[  4]   6.00-7.00   sec   386 KBytes  3.17 Mbits/sec
[  4]   7.00-8.00   sec   386 KBytes  3.16 Mbits/sec
[  4]   8.00-9.00   sec   386 KBytes  3.16 Mbits/sec
[  4]   9.00-10.00  sec   379 KBytes  3.10 Mbits/sec
- - - - - - - - - - - - - - - - - - - - - - - - -
[ ID] Interval           Transfer     Bandwidth
[  4]   0.00-10.00  sec  5.54 MBytes  4.65 Mbits/sec                  sender
[  4]   0.00-10.00  sec  5.53 MBytes  4.64 Mbits/sec                  receiver

iperf Done.
```

Now let's go from the embedded Docker app running on the switch using iPerf3 *out* to another iPerf3 system running in server (-s) mode. The iPerf project page documents some publicly accessible iPerf servers if you don't have any other systems available (see https://iperf.fr/iperf-servers.php).

Figure 15-34 shows the topology use case options:

- A local laptop, server, or virtual machine with the iPerf3 utility as a server, receiving client traffic from a local Cisco Nexus 9300 running the iPerf3 docker-app in IOx Application Hosting
- A local Cisco Nexus 9300 running the iPerf3 docker-app in IOx Application Hosting as a client, targeting Internet-based iPerf3 servers
- A local laptop, server, or virtual machine with the iPerf3 utility as a server *and* the OpenConnect VPN software, receiving client traffic from a Cisco Sandbox Lab environment with a Cisco Nexus 9300 running the iPerf3 docker-app in IOx Application Hosting as a client

NOTE A Cisco Sandbox environment sending traffic out the general Internet is not displayed in this example because it is not supported.

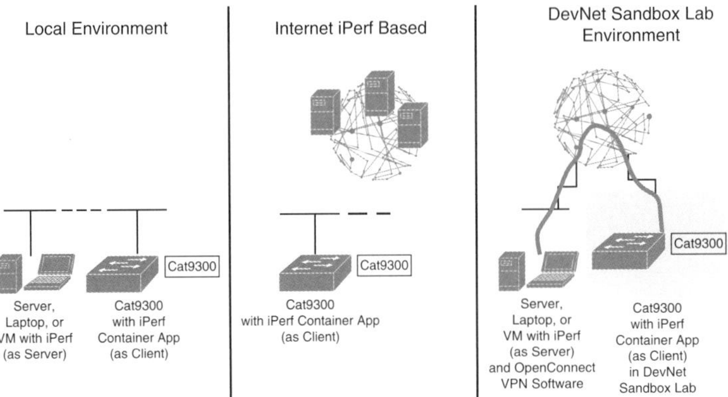

Figure 15-34 *Testing iPerf3 Environment Options with a Catalyst Switch as the Client*

Example 15-8 shows the steps you need to run from the Catalyst 9300 to access the iPerf3 container-app and run the iPerf3 utility. In this example, the server would be the local PC, server, or virtual machine running in server mode with **iperf3 -s** and a local Catalyst 9300 targeting that local system. Sending traffic to Internet-based iPerf servers is possible if your system allows traffic to the Internet.

Example 15-8 *Accessing the Catalyst Switches' iPerf3 Container-App and Running as a Client*

```
cat9k# app-hosting connect appid iPerf3 session
/ $ iperf3 -c 10.10.20.20
Connecting to host 10.10.20.20, port 5201
[  5] local 10.10.20.101 port 59998 connected to 10.10.20.20 port 5201
[ ID] Interval           Transfer     Bitrate         Retr  Cwnd
[  5]   0.00-1.00   sec   114 MBytes   952 Mbits/sec   14    754 KBytes
[  5]   1.00-2.00   sec   112 MBytes   940 Mbits/sec   65    799 KBytes
[  5]   2.00-3.00   sec   112 MBytes   941 Mbits/sec  146    635 KBytes
[  5]   3.00-4.00   sec   112 MBytes   938 Mbits/sec  152    714 KBytes
[  5]   4.00-5.00   sec   112 MBytes   941 Mbits/sec    1    822 KBytes
[  5]   5.00-6.00   sec   112 MBytes   937 Mbits/sec    0    922 KBytes
[  5]   6.00-7.00   sec   113 MBytes   945 Mbits/sec    1   1008 KBytes
[  5]   7.00-8.00   sec   112 MBytes   940 Mbits/sec   22   1.01 MBytes
[  5]   8.00-9.00   sec   109 MBytes   915 Mbits/sec  870    573 KBytes
[  5]   9.00-10.00  sec   110 MBytes   922 Mbits/sec    5    691 KBytes
- - - - - - - - - - - - - - - - - - - - - - - - -
[ ID] Interval           Transfer     Bitrate         Retr
[  5]   0.00-10.00  sec  1.09 GBytes   937 Mbits/sec  1276             sender
[  5]   0.00-10.00  sec  1.09 GBytes   935 Mbits/sec                  receiver


iperf Done.
/ $
```

Now that you have a taste for using traffic testing functions, what other workloads can you think of? Would it be useful to run a local syslog receiver with more advanced filtering and forwarding as a local Docker container app? How about using the robust ThousandEyes Enterprise agent to get much more observability functions?

As one more example of this exciting container functionality, let's build a container in which you run a local syslog receiver in the Catalyst 9300. This container-app will run the popular, feature-rich Syslog-NG utility and do better event message handling, filtering, and forwarding than the native IOS XE can do. You can forward the hosting Catalyst 9300's syslog messages to the container. It is possible to have other devices near the hosting system also forward their messages to the container. You can provide a Syslog-NG configuration file that

- Sends security-focused ACL violations to the security management tools, like Cisco Secure Network Analytics (formerly Stealthwatch)
- Sends all messages to a DNA Center system
- Sends all messages to a secondary logging system for archival purposes
- Sends all messages to a local file within the container-app

This model would be effective for regional collection, filtering, and follow-on forwarding to centralized systems.

First, you need to access a system that has a Docker engine running on it to build a container app. You can use something familiar like Ubuntu, Red Hat Enterprise Linux, or CentOS to build the container. Then use the following commands to create a project directory:

```
sre@docker-utils home/sre % mkdir -p Docker/syslog-ng

sre@docker-utils syslog-ng % cd Docker/syslog-ng

sre@docker-utils syslog-ng % vi Dockerfile
```

Now that you have a vi editor session, you need to create the Dockerfile. Use Example 15-9 for guidance.

Example 15-9 *Dockerfile for Syslog-NG*

```
FROM balabit/syslog-ng:latest

ADD syslog-ng.conf /etc/syslog-ng/syslog-ng.conf

EXPOSE 514/udp
EXPOSE 601/tcp

HEALTHCHECK --interval=2m --timeout=3s --start-period=30s CMD /usr/sbin/syslog-ng-
ctl stats || exit 1

ENTRYPOINT ["/usr/sbin/syslog-ng", "-F"]
```

In Example 15-9 the FROM directive pulls the balabit/syslog-ng:latest image from Dockerhub. You use **ADD** to add a syslog-ng.conf file, which you define in the next step, and mount it to the container's /etc/syslog-ng/syslog-ng.conf location. You then use **EXPOSE** to expose the traditional Syslog UDP/514 port, which is typical for the network equipment, but you also use **EXPOSE** to expose and listen to TCP/601 for any reliable syslog event messages coming from other sources. Then you define a **HEALTHCHECK** function that periodically checks the operation of Syslog-NG. Finally, you use **ENTRYPOINT** to execute the Syslog-NG utility.

The Dockerfile is complete and can be saved, but you need to define the syslog-ng.conf file that was referenced in the Dockerfile before you can build the image. Example 15-10 depicts a suggested syslog-ng.conf file. You can use an editor to create this syslog-ng.conf file in the same directory as the Dockerfile.

Example 15-10 *syslog-ng.conf File*

```
@version: 3.35
@include "scl.conf"

source s_net { default-network-drivers(); };

filter f_ACL-violation {
  match("SEC-6-IPACCESSLOG" value("MESSAGE")) or
  match("SYS-5-PRIV_AUTH_FAIL" value("MESSAGE"))
};

destination d_securityapp { udp("<CiscoSecureNetworkAnalytics>" port(514)); };

destination d_DNAC { udp("<DNACenter>" port(514)); };

destination d_LOGArchive { udp("<LOGArchive>" port(514)); };

destination d_localfile { file("/var/log/${YEAR}.${MONTH}.${DAY}/messages" };

log {
  source(s_net);
  filter(f_ACL-violation);
  destination(d_securityapp);
};

log {
  source(s_net);
  destination(d_DNAC);
  destination(d_LOGArchive);
  destination(d_localfile);
};
```

The first lines of the syslog-ng file are administrative but necessary. If you are pulling a different version of the Syslog-NG utility, then specify the correct version; if newer than v3.35, you can leave as is. The **@include "acl.conf"** is necessary for the network drivers source seen next.

The **source s_net** definition pulls in default network drivers that list to several ports, such as UDP/514, TCP/601, and TCP/6514 (for syslog over TLS). It also includes a standard Cisco parser. You can define other ports to suit your needs.

The **filter f_ACL-violation** definition includes a pattern match for a typical login and ACL violation message with SYS-5-PRIV_AUTH_FAIL and SEC-6-IPACCESSLOG. You can define even more by using additional **or** conditions.

The **destination d_securityapp** definition specifies the target syslog receiver for security messages. Change the entry, including the < >s, to reflect your environment.

The **destination d_DNAC** definition specifies a target syslog receiver for Cisco DNA Center. Change the entry, including the < >s, to reflect your environment.

The **destination d_LOGArchive** definition specifies a target syslog receiver for another Syslog-NG server for archival purposes. Change the entry, including the < >s, to reflect your environment.

The **destination d_localfile** definition specifies a target file, which is in the switch's Docker container in the /var/log/ directory and with subdirectories by Year, Month, and Date. Dynamic directories are created, such as /var/log/2022.01.01/messages, for all incoming syslog event messages received on January 1, 2022.

The first **log** definition takes in messages from the network source and matches any with the ACL-violation filter and then sends to the security app destination.

The second **log** definition takes in messages from the network source and sends all messages to the DNAC, LOGArchive, and localfile destinations. No filter is defined, so no messages are excluded.

Now, you should save the syslog-ng.conf file in the same directory as the Dockerfile.

Example 15-11 shows the process of building the container image.

Example 15-11 *Building the Syslog-NG Container Image*

```
sre@docker-utils syslog-ng % docker build --tag syslog-ng .
Sending build context to Docker daemon  3.584kB
Step 1/6 : FROM balabit/syslog-ng:latest
 ---> 123b82e5cba8
Step 2/6 : ADD syslog-ng.conf /etc/syslog-ng/syslog-ng.conf
 ---> 8890abfd7006
Step 3/6 : EXPOSE 514/udp
 ---> Running in 41667db3e024
Removing intermediate container 41667db3e024
 ---> fd1459249233
Step 4/6 : EXPOSE 601/tcp
 ---> Running in fdae437f557a
Removing intermediate container fdae437f557a
 ---> 7b5691da5b3f
```

```
Step 5/6 : HEALTHCHECK --interval=2m --timeout=3s --start-period=30s CMD /usr/sbin/
syslog-ng-ctl stats || exit 1
Note: overriding previous HEALTHCHECK: [CMD-SHELL /usr/sbin/syslog-ng-ctl stats ||
exit 1]
 ---> Running in 0725d6fa7629
Removing intermediate container 0725d6fa7629
 ---> 817b3135bc93
Step 6/6 : ENTRYPOINT ["/usr/sbin/syslog-ng", "-F"]
 ---> Running in 2a11758cacad
Removing intermediate container 2a11758cacad
 ---> de5f49139a68
Successfully built de5f49139a68
Successfully tagged syslog-ng:latest
sre@docker-utils syslog-ng %
```

Use the **docker save** command previously described to create a .tar image of the container on the local system:

```
sre@docker-utils syslog-ng % docker save syslog-ng > syslog-ng.tar
```

Now, copy the .tar image to the hosting device using DNA Center, IOx Local Manager, or CLI methods described in earlier sections. Also, remember that the UDP/514 port must be exposed. When you have a running image, you should be able to verify it from a terminal session with the hosting switch using the **show app-hosting list** command:

```
cat9k# show app-hosting list

App id                                          State

---------------------------------------------------

syslog_ng                                       RUNNING
```

Then you can access the Syslog-NG container-app with the **app-hosting connect** command:

```
cat9k# app-hosting connect appid syslog_ng session

# cat /var/log/2021.10.26/messages

Oct 26 21:31:11 758d4280b792 syslog-ng[1]: syslog-ng starting up;
version='3.31.2'

#
```

Finally, remember to forward the syslog event messages from your hosting system back to the assigned IP address of the Docker container:

```
cat9k(config)# logging host 10.10.20.101 vrf Mgmt-vrf
```

Use a similar **logging host** ***IP_Address*** command on other Cisco network devices to have them forward their syslog event messages to this container-app also. If everything is configured, forwarding, and filtering correctly, you see the securityapp system receiving log messages that are filtered to ACL violations like this:

```
Oct 26 21:15:58.154: cat9300 1895: Oct 26 21:15:58: %SYS-5-PRIV_
AUTH_FAIL: Authentication to Privilege level 15 failed by Bob on
vty0 (192.168.1.14)

Oct 26 21:00:07.958: cat9300 1896: Oct 26 21:00:07: %SEC-6-
IPACCESSLOGDP: list stop-ping denied icmp 192.168.1.230 ->
192.168.1.11 (0/0), 51packets

Oct 26 21:05:07.980: cat3560 5943: Oct 26 21:05:07: %SEC-6-
IPACCESSLOGDP: list stop-ping denied icmp 192.168.1.230 ->
192.168.1.11 (0/0), 162 packets
```

The other systems that are not filtered receive messages like this:

```
Oct 26 20:54:43.492: cat9300 1894: Oct 25 20:54:42: %SYS-5-
CONFIG_I: Configured from console by admin on vty0 (192.168.1.230)

Oct 26 21:15:58.154: cat9300 1895: Oct 26 21:15:58: %SYS-5-PRIV_
AUTH_FAIL: Authentication to Privilege level 15 failed by Bob on
vty0 (192.168.1.14)

Oct 26 21:00:07.958: cat9300 1896: Oct 26 21:00:07: %SEC-6-
IPACCESSLOGDP: list stop-ping denied icmp 192.168.1.230 ->
192.168.1.11 (0/0), 51packets

Oct 26 21:03:02.903: cat9300 1897: Oct 26 21:03:02: %SYS-5-
CONFIG_I: Configured from console by admin on vty0 (192.168.1.230)

Oct 26 21:05:07.980: cat3560 5943: Oct 26 21:05:07: %SEC-6-
IPACCESSLOGDP: list stop-ping denied icmp 192.168.1.230 ->
192.168.1.11 (0/0), 162 packets

Oct 26 21:07:40.747: cat3560 5944: Oct 26 21:07:40: %LINK-3-
UPDOWN: Interface GigabitEthernet0/5, changed state to down

Oct 26 21:07:45.235: cat3560 5945: Oct 26 21:07:45: %LINK-3-
UPDOWN: Interface GigabitEthernet0/6, changed state to down

Oct 26 21:07:45.492: cat3560 5946: Oct 26 21:07:45: %SYS-5-
CONFIG_I: Configured from console by admin on vty0 (192.168.1.230)
```

Using this model allows you to create a more sophisticated syslog event management process than is available in the native IOS-XE software.

Best Practices for Managing Application Containers

Some basic practices around the administration of the application hosting containers focus on inventory management. If you are using Cisco DNA Center to manage and deploy your containers, then the inventory is already centrally managed and monitored. If you use the embedded Cisco IOx Local Manager or CLI models, then you should consider implementing a centralized software repository to manage the .tar and .tar.gz files and facilitate version control. The centralized software repository can also serve to host the images via TFTP or SCP, if desired. It is also suggested that you need a database or spreadsheet of which applications and versions are being deployed to which switches.

For containerized apps that store files, plus syslog event messages, binary software images, database components, and so on, it is also a best practice to routinely monitor the usage of the switch's usbflash1: filesystem. Monitoring the flash disk usage by container-app is best, but at a minimum, you should retrieve the whole flash disk usage to know when "spring cleaning" is necessary.

Availability monitoring of the container-apps is trivial if the apps expose an IP address to ping or if they have APIs accessible for polling. If you are in control of the development and deployment of the container-apps, consider building API endpoints that expose the app name, version, resource deployment, uptime, CPU/memory/interface, and disk usage.

Performance monitoring of the container-apps depends on the embedded instrumentation and telemetry. If the container-app has a lightweight Linux foundation with shell access, then a simple Ansible script that accesses it via SSH to run relevant performance commands would be appropriate. If you are in control of the development and deployment of the container-apps, consider using a gRPC or AMQP message bus approach to stream telemetry and messages from the remote app to a centralized collection and monitoring system.

Fault monitoring of the container-apps is like the performance monitoring aspect: it depends on the embedded instrumentation and telemetry. If the container-app is generating log messages, then ensure a function like syslog-ng or logger is creating outbound copies for collection, archiving, and analysis.

Security management of the container-apps varies on the services deployed in the container. Remember that containers are not full-blown operating systems. The docker daemon and Cisco IOx hosting services provide some protections. If your container-app provides a shell access, then you should use basic practices of good password management, prioritizing public key authentication over passwords. Be mindful of the ports and services exposed from the container-app to the hosting device. In a containerized database scenario, you might consider the application-level configuration protections: encryption, RBAC, and table/schema partitioning. If the container-app is running a more feature-rich base like Ubuntu Linux and the app data is sensitive or proprietary, it may make sense to implement host-based firewalls like iptables, firewalld, or UFW. Note, however, that Docker does manipulate and control many networking interactions, so you need to review documentation associated with the version of dockerd running on the host. Nginx, haproxy, and other proxy use common with containers prevents the container-app from seeing the remote IP address, so dynamic tracking and blocking tools (such as fail2ban) are not effective without using Layer-2/bridging connectivity. Finally, it might be warranted to run a container-app firewall appliance and chain the other container-app traffic through it. Keep in mind the best practices learned with traditional, hardware-based architectures because many are possible to implement with virtualized software.

As mentioned earlier, inventory and asset management are important. Keeping track of container-app versions to ensure the latest with the newest features, bug fixes, and patches is an additional administrative task. Routine asset scans to validate the asset tracking system or CMDB are desirable.

Exam Preparation Tasks

As mentioned in the section "How to Use This Book" in the Introduction, you have a couple of choices for exam preparation: the exercises here, Chapter 17, "Final Preparation," and the exam simulation questions in the Pearson Test Prep Software Online.

Review All Key Topics

Review the most important topics in this chapter, noted with the Key Topic icon in the outer margin of the page. Table 15-2 lists a reference of these key topics and the page numbers on which each is found.

Table 15-2 Key Topics for Chapter 15

Key Topic Element	Description	Page Number
Section	Type-1 Hypervisors	528
Section	Type-2 Hypervisors	528
Section	Linux Containers (LXC)	529
Section	Docker Containers	530
Paragraph	Enabling application hosting framework	536
Step	Uploading an image to DNAC	540
Paragraph	Uploading an image to IOx Local Manager	548
Step	Installing an image via CLI	554
Example 15-8	Accessing the Catalyst Switches' iPerf3 Container-App and Running as a Client	558

Complete Tables and Lists from Memory

There are no memory tables or lists in this chapter.

Define Key Terms

Define the following key terms from this chapter and check your answers in the glossary:

hypervisor, Type-1 hypervisor, Type-2 hypervisor, Linux Containers (LXC), container

References

URL	QR Code
https://devnetsandbox.cisco.com/	
https://www.cisco.com/c/en/us/td/docs/ios-xml/ios/prog/configuration/173/b_173_programmability_cg/guest_shell.html	
https://developer.cisco.com/app-hosting/opensource/	
https://hub.docker.com/r/mlabbe/iperf3	
https://developer.cisco.com/docs/iox/#!package-format/iox-application-package	
http://cs.co/9004Jryo2#concept_lqt_ltk_l1b	
https://iperf.fr/iperf-servers.php	

CHAPTER 16

Cisco Platforms

This chapter covers the following topics:

- **Webex:** This section covers practical examples of using the Webex API and SDKs.
- **Firepower:** This section covers practical examples of using the Firepower Management Center APIs.
- **Meraki:** This section covers practical examples of using the Meraki API and SDKs.
- **Intersight:** This section covers practical examples of using the Intersight API and SDKs.
- **UCS Manager:** This section covers practical examples of using the UCS Manager API and SDKs.
- **DNA Center:** This section covers practical examples of using the DNA Center API and SDKs.
- **App Dynamics:** This section covers practical examples of using the AppDynamics API.

This chapter does not map to a specific section of the *Developing Applications Using Cisco Core Platforms and APIs v1.0 (350-901)* Exam Blueprint. However, the examples in this chapter may be instructional for other components of the exam. Specifically, it is beneficial for you to understand the common product application programming interfaces, how they authenticate, and some basic function methods. This chapter provides those examples that should augment your continuous learning process.

"Do I Know This Already?" Quiz

The "Do I Know This Already?" quiz allows you to assess whether you should read this entire chapter thoroughly or jump to the "Exam Preparation Tasks" section. If you are in doubt about your answers to these questions or your own assessment of your knowledge of the topics, read the entire chapter. Table 16-1 lists the major headings in this chapter and their corresponding "Do I Know This Already?" quiz questions. You can find the answers in Appendix A, "Answers to the 'Do I Know This Already?' Quizzes."

Table 16-1 "Do I Know This Already?" Section-to-Question Mapping

Foundation Topics Section	Questions
Webex	1–2
Firepower	3–4
Meraki	5–6
Intersight	7–8
UCS Manager	9–10
DNA Center	11–12
AppDynamics	13–14

1. The Webex SDK is available for what frameworks?
   a. iOS
   b. Android
   c. Java
   d. Python
   e. All of these answers are correct.
2. Where can you publish a Webex bot using the Webex REST API?
   a. Apple App Store
   b. Google Play Store
   c. Webex App Hub
   d. Windows App Store
3. What authentication headers are generated using the api/fmc_platform/v1/auth/generatetoken endpoint within the FMC API?
   a. X-authorization
   b. X-bearer, X-refresh
   c. X-auth-access-token, X-auth-refresh-token
   d. X-fmc-device-auth, X-fmc-device-refresh
4. How does the Firepower Management Center handle concurrent logins with the same username/password combination to the FMC portal, API explorer, and API?
   a. All logins can be used concurrently.
   b. Only one session is supported to the FMC at one time, regardless of access method.
   c. FMC supports a session to the FMC web UI and another to either the API explorer or logged in to the REST API.
   d. None of these answers are correct.

5. Which one of the following would be a correct authentication body for the Meraki Dashboard v1 API?

   a.

   ```
   {
       "Authentication": "Basic <MERAKI_DASHBOARD_API_KEY>"
   }
   ```

   b.

   ```
   {
   "Authentication": "Bearer <MERAKI_DASHBOARD_API_KEY>"
   }
   ```

   c.

   ```
   {
   "Authorization": "Bearer <MERAKI_DASHBOARD_API_KEY>"
   }
   ```

   d.

   ```
   {
   "Authorization": "Basic <MERAKI_DASHBOARD_API_KEY>"
   }
   ```

6. Which of the following is the correct method invocation for the Meraki Python SDK to obtain device information from a specific organization?
   a. api.organizations.getOrganizationDevices(organization_id)
   b. api.devices.getDevices(organization_id)
   c. api.getOrganizationDevices()
   d. api.organizations.<orgid>.getOrganizationDevices()
7. What pieces of information must be present to successfully authenticate to the Intersight REST API?
   a. Username and password
   b. API key and password
   c. MD5-encoded bearer token
   d. API key and private key
8. What tools or SDKs exist to interact with the Intersight APIs?
   a. REST APIs
   b. Python SDK, PowerShell SDK
   c. Ansible, Terraform
   d. All of these answers are correct.

9. What data format(s) of request and response are supported by the UCS Manager API?
   a. JSON only
   b. XML only
   c. JSON and XML
   d. RESTCONF
10. Which statement about the UCS PowerTool is correct?
   a. It is supported only on Windows operating systems.
   b. It requires a manually collected API key to connect to the UCS Manager instance.
   c. It allows output to be filtered to only specific object values.
   d. It displays output data in native XML format by default.
11. Direct REST API usage with DNA Center requires which type of header?
   a. An authorization header with a basic authentication string
   b. An authentication header with a basic authentication string
   c. A bearer token authentication header
   d. An OAuth token authorization header
12. What is the name of the community-supported Python SDK that should be pip installed and imported into your Python script for DNA Center SDK usage?
   a. **ciscodnacsdk**
   b. **dnacsdk**
   c. **ciscodnac**
   d. **dnacentersdk**
13. In AppDynamics authorization, what is the difference in usage between client secrets and temporary access tokens? (Choose two.)
   a. The client secret is generated through the API.
   b. A client secret is used to generate a short-lived access token via the API.
   c. The temporary access token is generated in the WebUI and is generally a longer-term assignment.
   d. The client secret can be defined by the user.
   e. The temporary access token can be defined by the user.
14. In what format is the AppDynamics API default output encoded?
   a. JSON
   b. SAML
   c. XML
   d. YAML

Foundation Topics

Webex

Webex by Cisco is the industry's leading collaboration platform, providing users with a secured unified experience of meeting, calling, and messaging in one app. Webex brings virtual meetings to life by allowing users to stay connected with video conferencing that's engaging, intelligent, and inclusive. Webex Calling provides a fully integrated, carrier grade cloud phone system that keeps users connected from anywhere. Webex Messaging keeps the work flowing between meetings by bringing everyone together with secure and intelligent messaging organized by workstreams. The Webex Events portfolio delivers solutions for any occasion, any size audience, anywhere—from town halls and customer webinars to multisession conferences and networking events.

Webex provides an extensive set of REST APIs and SDKs to build Webex-embedded apps, bots, integrations, widgets, or guest issuer apps. These APIs and SDKs provide your applications with direct access to the Cisco Webex platform, which includes a suite of features and applications for performing administrative tasks, meetings, calling, messaging, device configuration, and Webex Assistant. Webex provides SDKs for iOS, Android, Web Apps, Node.js, and Java. Several other community-developed SDKs are available for other languages.

Enabling the Webex REST API/SDK Access

To start using the Webex REST APIs and SDKs, you must have an access token. This access token is used to identify you as the requesting user.

Step 1. You need a Webex account backed by Cisco Webex Common Identity (CI). You can sign up for a free Webex account at https://www.webex.com/.

Step 2. Using your Webex credentials, access the developer dashboard at https://developer.webex.com/ (see Figure 16-1).

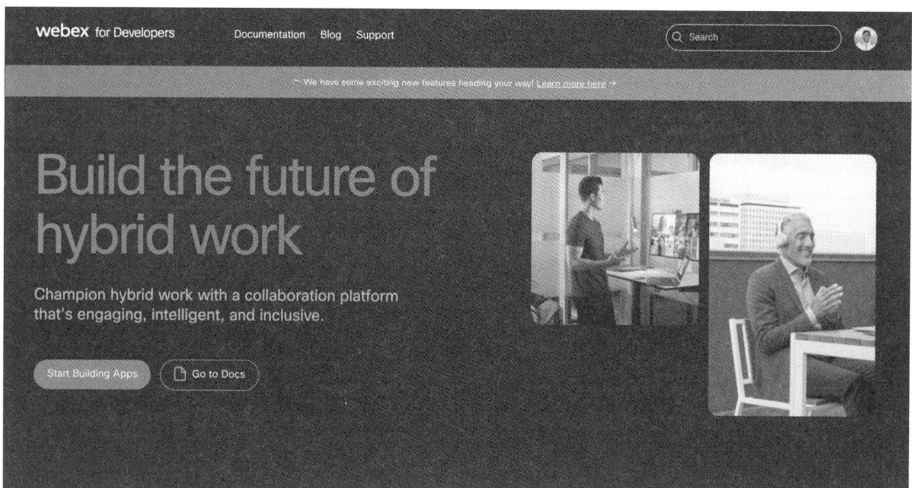

Figure 16-1 *Webex Developer Website*

Step 3. Navigate through the menus by selecting **Start Building Apps > Create a New App** (see Figure 16-2).

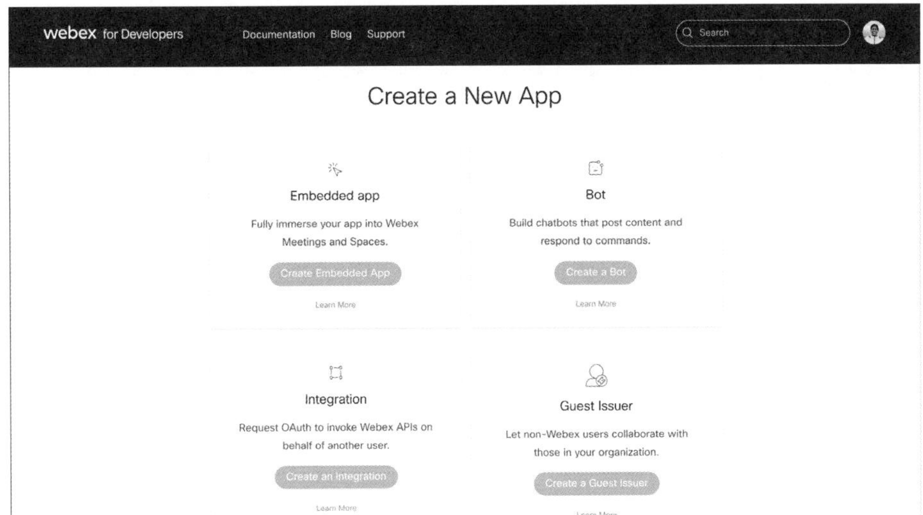

Figure 16-2 *The Dashboard*

Step 4. After creating the application, you are assigned a personal access token (PAT) based on the application type. A bot access token is issued for bot applications, and an OAuth access token is issued for integrations or guest issuer applications.

Step 5. You can review existing access tokens for your apps by navigating through **Profile Photo or Avatar > My Webex Apps** (see Figure 16-3).

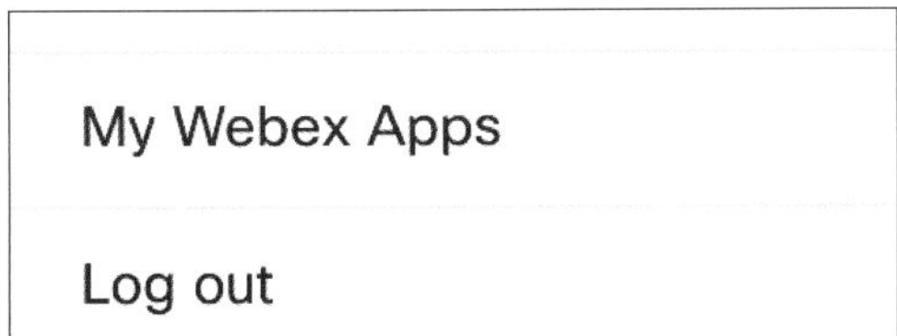

Figure 16-3 *Navigation Menu for Webex Apps*

Webex API Documentation

The Webex REST APIs and SDKs are officially documented at https://developer.webex.com/docs/platform-introduction.

Webex API tutorials and structured lab lessons are available on Learning Labs by Cisco DevNet and can be accessed at https://developer.cisco.com/learning/tracks/collab-cloud (see Figure 16-4).

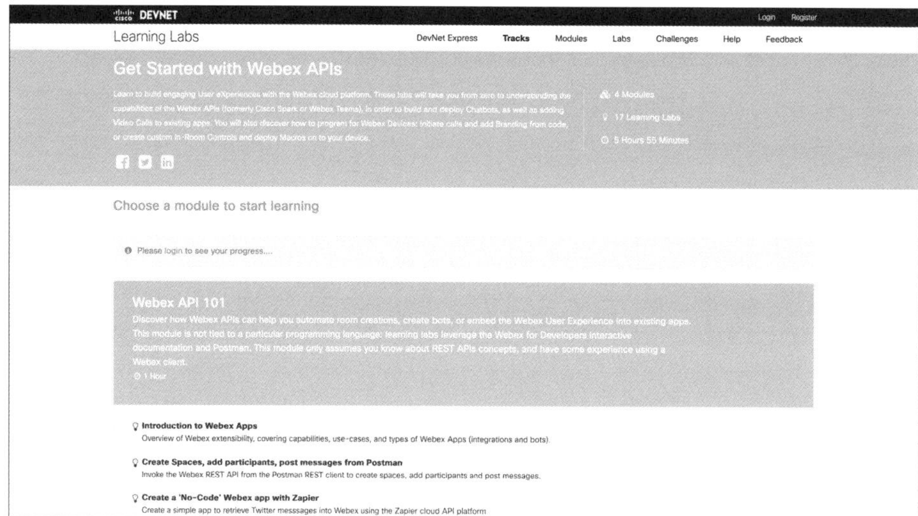

Figure 16-4 *Webex Developer Tutorials by Cisco*

The Webex API Support team is available to help you with API questions and can be reached at https://developer.webex.com/support (see Figure 16-5).

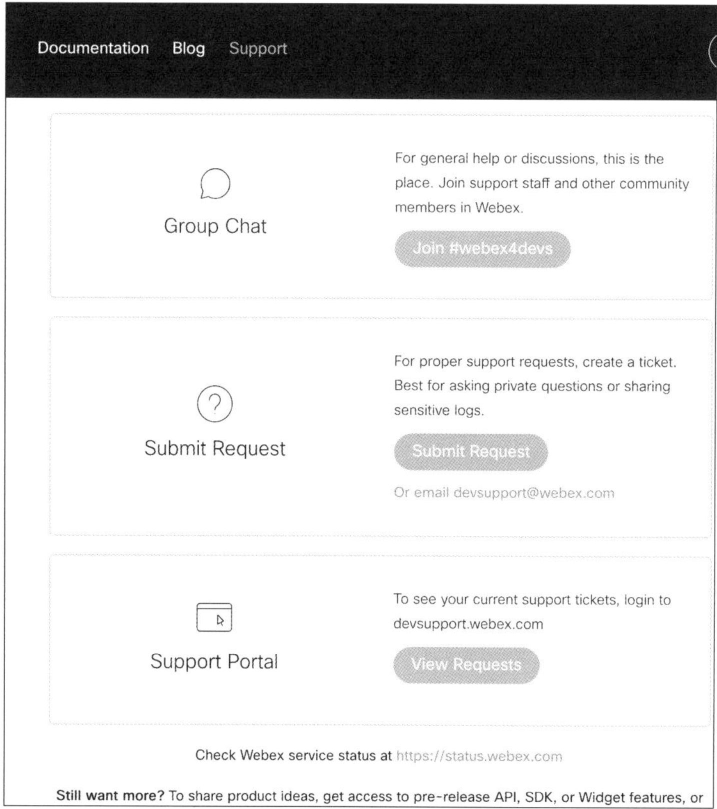

Figure 16-5 *Webex Developer Support*

When your Webex bot or integration is ready, you can publish it on Webex App Hub, where existing Webex users can browse the App Hub and find your apps (see Figure 16-6).

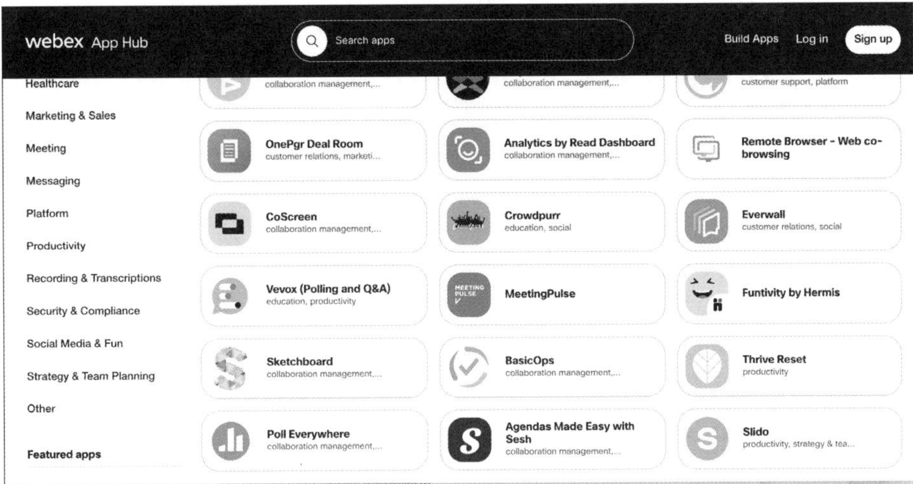

Figure 16-6 *Existing Webex Apps (App Hub)*

You can access the Webex App Hub submission process at https://developer.webex.com/docs/app-hub-submission-process.

16

API Examples

Using the Webex REST API (documented at https://developer.webex.com/docs/getting-started) or through Postman collections (available at https://github.com/CiscoDevNet/postman-webex) is simple. The first activity is to understand the Webex API authentication process. When you make requests to the Webex REST API, an authentication HTTP header is used to identify you as the requesting user. The header must include an access token—whether a personal access token, bot token, or OAuth token—as described previously. The token is supplied as bearer authentication, sometimes called token authentication.

```
{
 'Authorization': 'Bearer ****************************************
***********
************_***_********-****-****-****-************'
}
```

It is important to note that personal access tokens are time-limited to 12 hours after you log in to the site. You can extract your PAT from the getting-started URL at https://developer.webex.com/docs/getting-started.

As a simple example, let's assume that you want to determine what Webex rooms a bot is part of. You can find the Webex REST API for Messaging and Rooms directly at https://developer.webex.com/docs/api/v1/rooms (see Figure 16-7).

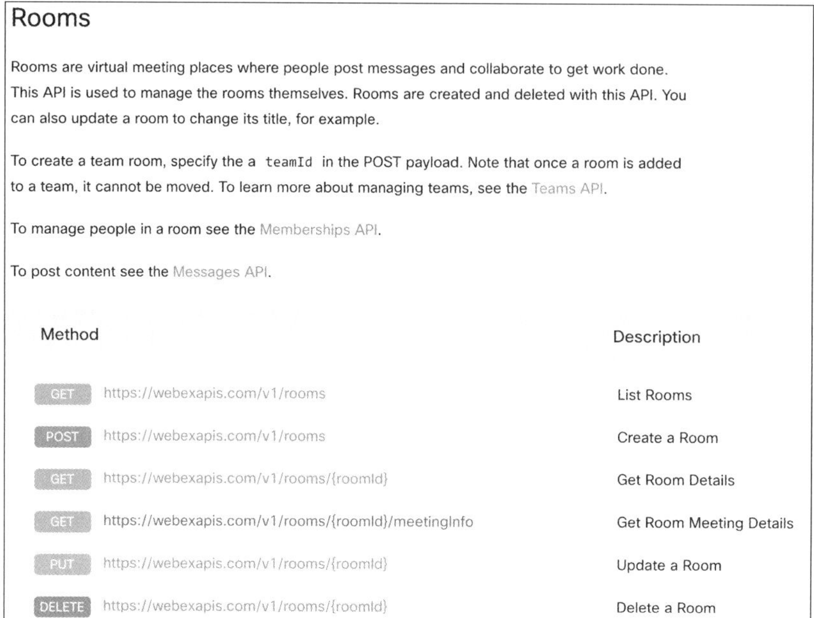
Rooms

Rooms are virtual meeting places where people post messages and collaborate to get work done. This API is used to manage the rooms themselves. Rooms are created and deleted with this API. You can also update a room to change its title, for example.

To create a team room, specify the a `teamId` in the POST payload. Note that once a room is added to a team, it cannot be moved. To learn more about managing teams, see the Teams API.

To manage people in a room see the Memberships API.

To post content see the Messages API.

Method		Description
GET	https://webexapis.com/v1/rooms	List Rooms
POST	https://webexapis.com/v1/rooms	Create a Room
GET	https://webexapis.com/v1/rooms/{roomId}	Get Room Details
GET	https://webexapis.com/v1/rooms/{roomId}/meetingInfo	Get Room Meeting Details
PUT	https://webexapis.com/v1/rooms/{roomId}	Update a Room
DELETE	https://webexapis.com/v1/rooms/{roomId}	Delete a Room

Figure 16-7 *Webex Personal Room API*

A GET API call to the endpoint at https://developer.webex.com/docs/api/v1/rooms/list-rooms results in the desired information.

Example 16-1 shows how a Python script can serve as a template for obtaining this room information for an access token that is supplied via an environment variable—a more secure way of using that credential versus hard-coding it in the script.

Example 16-1 *Obtaining Personal Room Information*

```
import requests
import os
import json
import pprint

# Get environment variables
ACCESS_TOKEN = os.getenv('WEBEX_ACCESS_TOKEN')

pp = pprint.PrettyPrinter(indent=4)

url = "https://webexapis.com/v1/rooms"

payload={}
headers = {
  'Authorization': 'Bearer ' + ACCESS_TOKEN
}
```

```
fimi
response = requests.request("GET", url, headers=headers, data=payload)

json_response = json.loads(response.text)
pp.pprint(json_response)
```

By running this script, you obtain the output shown in Example 16-2.

Example 16-2 *Output of Running the Script Shown in Example 16-1*

```
(.venv) sre@pythonserver DEVCOR % export WEBEX_ACCESS_TOKEN=*****…'
(.venv) sre@pythonserver DEVCOR % python getWebexRooms.py
{   'items': [   {   'created': '2020-07-16T17:43:03.982Z',
                     'creatorId': 'Y2lz*****…',
                     'id': 'Y2lz*****…',
                     'isLocked': False,
                     'lastActivity': '2020-08-05T20:51:35.741Z',
                     'ownerId': 'Y2lz*****…',
                     'title': 'Firstname Lastname',
                     'type': 'direct'},
                 {   'created': '2020-03-26T13:39:27.664Z',
                     'creatorId': 'Y2lz*****…',
                     'id': 'Y2lz*****…',
                     'isLocked': False,
                     'lastActivity': '2021-06-10T19:29:13.440Z',
                     'ownerId': 'Y2lz*****…',
                     'teamId': 'Y2lz*****…',
                     'title': Development',
                     'type': 'group'},
                 {   'created': '2019-10-30T18:51:05.869Z',
                     'creatorId': 'Y2lz*****…',
                     'id': 'Y2lz*****…',
                     'isLocked': False,
                     'lastActivity': '2020-06-24T22:10:03.317Z',
                     'ownerId': 'Y2lz*****…',
                     'teamId': 'Y2lz*****…',
                     'title': 'Alerts',
                     'type': 'group'}]}
```

16

SDK Examples

The Webex software development kit is available for iOS, Android, Web Apps, Node.js, and Java, making it easy for you to integrate Webex functionalities within your own mobile and web applications (see Figure 16-8). In addition to these, you can access community-developed SDKs for other language applications on GitHub at https://github.com/CiscoDevNet/awesome-webex-client-sdk.

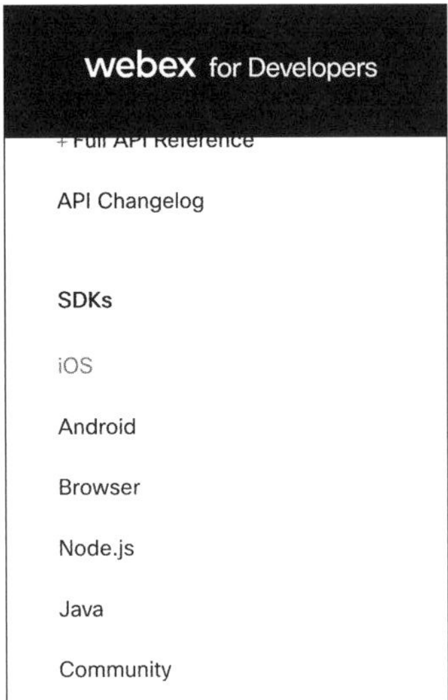

Figure 16-8 *Webex SDK Menu*

Extensive Webex SDK documentation for each platform is accessible on the developer dashboard. SDK documentation includes a detailed getting started guide, installation steps, demo apps, versions, features, requirements, limitations, and troubleshooting details.

You need to set up your Xcode environment to a minimum of Xcode 13 (released in 2019). At the time of writing (2021), Xcode 15 is the latest release. The Webex iOS SDK can be obtained from https://developer.webex.com/docs/sdks/ios. As of December 2021, the current iOS SDK version is 3.2.

Assuming you already have an Xcode project, such as MyWebexApp, for your iOS app, here are the steps to integrate the Webex iOS SDK into your Xcode project using CocoaPods:

Step 1. Install CocoaPods:

```
gem install cocoapods
```

Step 2. Set up CocoaPods:

```
pod setup
```

Step 3. Create a new file, Podfile, with the content shown in Example 16-3 in your MyWebexApp project directory.

Example 16-3 *Webex iOS SDK Integration*

```
source 'https://github.com/CocoaPods/Specs.git'

use_frameworks!

target 'MyWebexApp' do
  platform :ios, '13'
  pod 'WebexSDK'
end
```

```
target 'MyWebexAppBroadcastExtension' do
    platform :ios, '13'
    pod 'WebexBroadcastExtensionKit'
end
```

Step 4. Install the Webex iOS SDK from your MyWebexApp project directory:

```
pod install
```

Step 5. To your app's Info.plist, add the **GroupIdentifier** entry with the value as your app's GroupIdentifier. This step is required so that you can get a path to store the local data warehouse.

Step 6. If you plan to use the WebexBroadcastExtensionKit, you also need to add a **GroupIdentifier** entry with the value as your app's GroupIdentifier to your Broadcast Extension target. This step is required so that you can communicate with the main app for screen sharing.

Step 7. Modify the Signing & Capabilities section in your Xcode project, as shown in Figure 16-9.

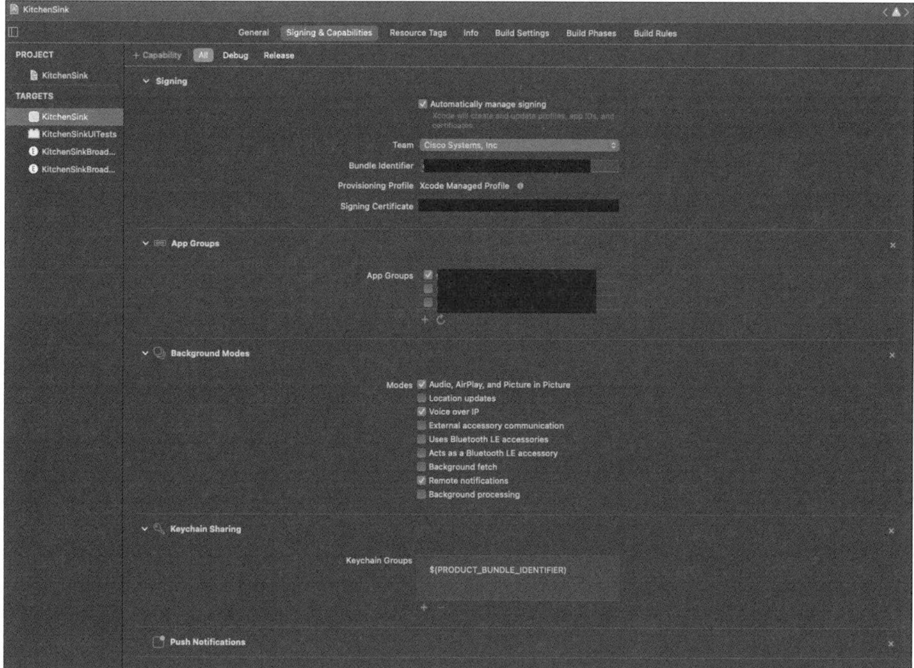

Figure 16-9 *Configuration of Webex iOS SDK in Xcode*

You can find a sample app that implements this SDK with source code at https://github.com/webex/webex-ios-sdk-example. This example showcases how to consume the APIs and is not meant to be a production-grade app.

The following examples show how to use the iOS SDK in your iOS app:

Step 1. Create the Webex instance using Webex ID authentication (OAuth-based), as shown in Example 16-4.

Example 16-4 *Creating an Instance Using Webex ID*

```
let clientId = "$YOUR_CLIENT_ID"
let clientSecret = "$YOUR_CLIENT_SECRET"
let scope = "spark:all" // space separated list of scopes. spark:all is always
required
let redirectUri = "https://webexdemoapp.com/redirect"

let authenticator = OAuthAuthenticator(clientId: clientId, clientSecret: clientSe-
cret, scope: scope, redirectUri: redirectUri, emailId: "user@example.com")
let webex = Webex(authenticator: authenticator)
webex.enableConsoleLogger = true
webex.logLevel = .verbose // Highly recommended to make this end-user configurable
in case you need to get detailed logs.

webex.initialize { isLoggedIn in
        if isLoggedIn {
            print("User is authorized")
        } else {
            authenticator.authorize(parentViewController: self) { result in
            if result == .success {
                print("Login successful")
            } else {
                print("Login failed")
            }
        }
```

Step 2. Create the Webex instance with Guest ID authentication (JWT-based), as shown in Example 16-5.

Example 16-5 *Creating a Webex Instance*

```
let authenticator = JWTAuthenticator()
let webex = Webex(authenticator: authenticator)

webex.initialize { [weak self] isLoggedIn in
        guard let self = self else { return }
        if isLoggedIn {
            print("User is authorized")
        } else {
           authenticator.authorizedWith(jwt: myJwt) { result in
                switch result {
```

```
                case .failure(let error):
                    print("JWT Login failed")
                case .success(let authenticated):
                    if authenticated {
                        print("JWT Login successful")
                    }
                }
            })
        }
    }
```

Step 3. Use the Webex service as shown in Example 16-6.

Example 16-6 *Creating a Webex Service*

```
webex.spaces.create(title: "Hello World") { result in
    switch result {
    case .success(let space):
        // ...
    case .failure(let error):
        // ...
    }
}

// ...

webex.memberships.create(spaceId: spaceId, personEmail: email) { result in
    switch result {
        case .success(let membership):
            // ...
        case .failure(let error):
            // ...
        }
    }
}
```

Step 4. Make an outgoing call, as shown in Example 16-7.

16

Example 16-7 *Making a Call*

```
webex.phone.dial("coworker@example.com", option: MediaOption.audioVideo(local: ...,
remote: ...)) { result in
    switch result {
    case .success(let call):
        call.onConnected = {
            // ...
        }
        call.onDisconnected = { reason in
            // ...
        }
    case .failure(let error):
        // failure
    }
}}
```

Step 5. Enable Background Noise Removal (BNR):

```
webex.phone.audioBNREnabled = true
```

You can access more examples showing how to use the Webex iOS SDK at https://github.com/webex/webex-ios-sdk/blob/master/README.md.

Firepower

Firepower Threat Defense (FTD) is the Cisco next-generation firewall (NGFW) solution, providing not only a traditional L3/L4 security policy, but also L7 application inspection and a comprehensive IDS/IPS, leveraging the Cisco Snort acquisition. These devices can be managed individually, using Firepower Device Management (FDM), or using a central management platform called Firepower Management Center (FMC). Although both tools can be used, they cannot be used concurrently (the use of FDM removes the ability to manage the device using FMC and vice versa). Additionally, when opting to use FDM rather than FMC, the management functions (and subsequent APIs supporting the functions) are diminished or smaller in number. As such, this discussion focuses on the FMC APIs.

The REST APIs provided within FMC cover the complete operations and management of the devices under FMC, the deployed security policy, and configuration objects.

Enabling API/SDK Access to Firepower

Access to the FMC REST API is enabled through a setting within the FMC WebUI, as shown in the following steps:

Step 1. Log in to the FMC WebUI using your username and credentials.

Step 2. Navigate through **System > Configuration > REST API Preferences > Enable REST API.**

Step 3. Click the **Enable REST API** check box, as shown in Figure 16-10.

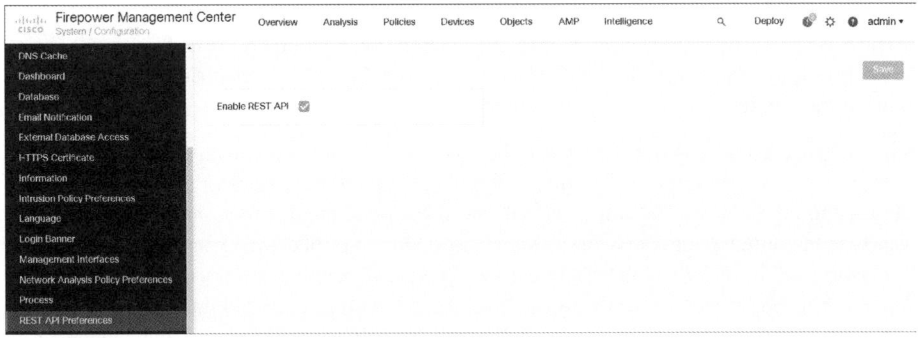

Figure 16-10 *Enabling the REST API Within FMC*

Step 4. Click **Save**. You should see a dialog box indicating that the settings were saved successfully.

Firepower API Documentation

Firepower Management Center API documentation is available through the on-box API explorer accessible through https://<FMC-IP>/api/api-explorer/, the main screen of which is shown in Figure 16-11. Access to the API explorer is protected via the same username and password credentials that are used to log in directly to the FMC WebUI. When you are logged in, the authorization and refresh token are generated and placed into the variables within the interactive API browser. This allows anyone accessing the API browser to execute live calls on the FMC, see the API call (in cURL format) and responses to the call, and view sample payloads. The OAS 3.0 spec (in JSON format) can also be downloaded from this portal.

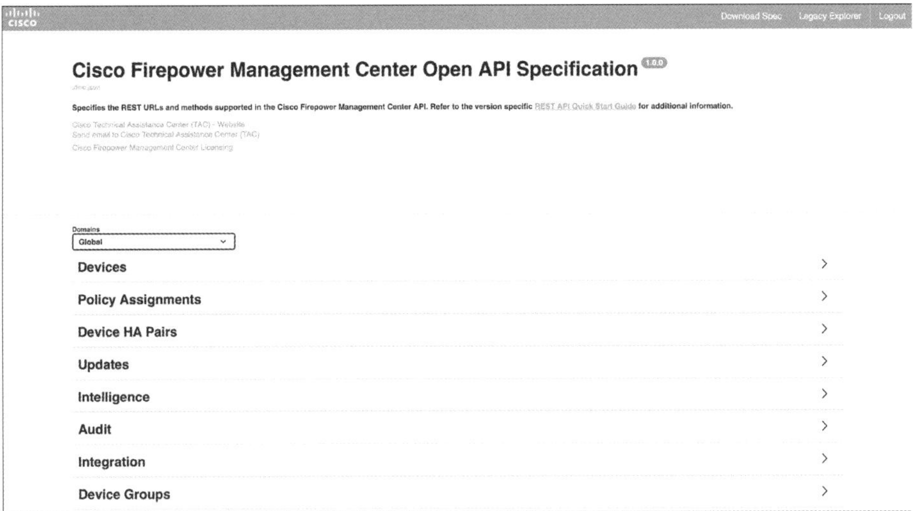

Figure 16-11 *Cisco FMC REST API Explorer*

16

The DevNet team offers several labs focused on exploring and utilizing the FMC REST API. There is also a reservable FMC Sandbox available for learning and testing the API. This Sandbox provides a view into the FMC UI as well as the APIs, while ensuring security and preventing the Sandbox from being sabotaged.

Another helpful resource is the Postman collection, which allows you to import all public API resources into a common utility that is popular with software developers. The Postman collection can be accessed and imported into your Postman environment at https://www.postman.com/ciscodevnet/workspace/cisco-devnet-s-public-workspace/collection/8697084-bf06287b-a7f3-4572-a4d5-84f1c652109a?ctx=documentation (or following the QR code in the "References" section at the end of this chapter) and clicking the Cisco Secure Firewall Management collection, as seen in Figure 16-12. You can then fork this collection into your personal collection for editing and use.

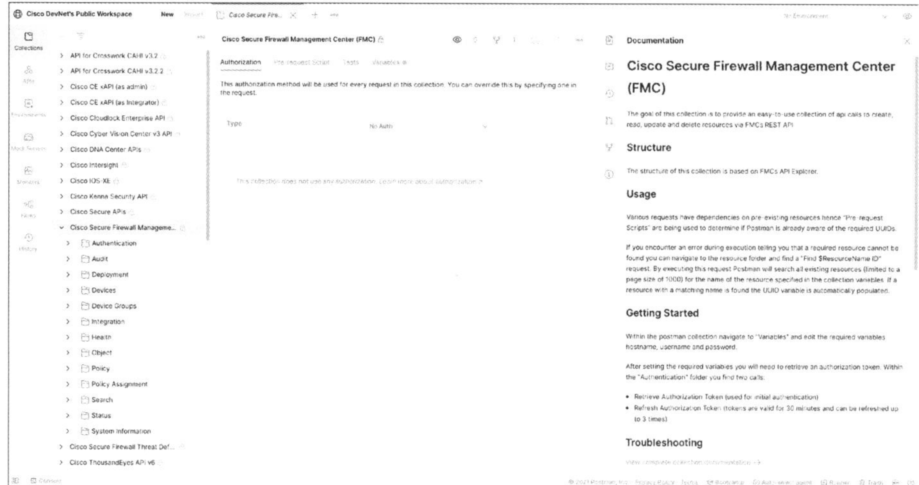

Figure 16-12 *Cisco FMC Postman Collection*

Unlike many other Postman collections, the FMC collection does not leverage an environment to store all variables. Instead, the collection has variables defined within the collection itself, illustrated in Figure 16-13. When you use the collection, you should set the environment in the upper-right corner of the Postman window to No Collection to ensure that overlapping variables are not used and overwritten in the requests. Any required values, such as hostname, username, and password, need to be changed to reflect the target endpoint prior to use.

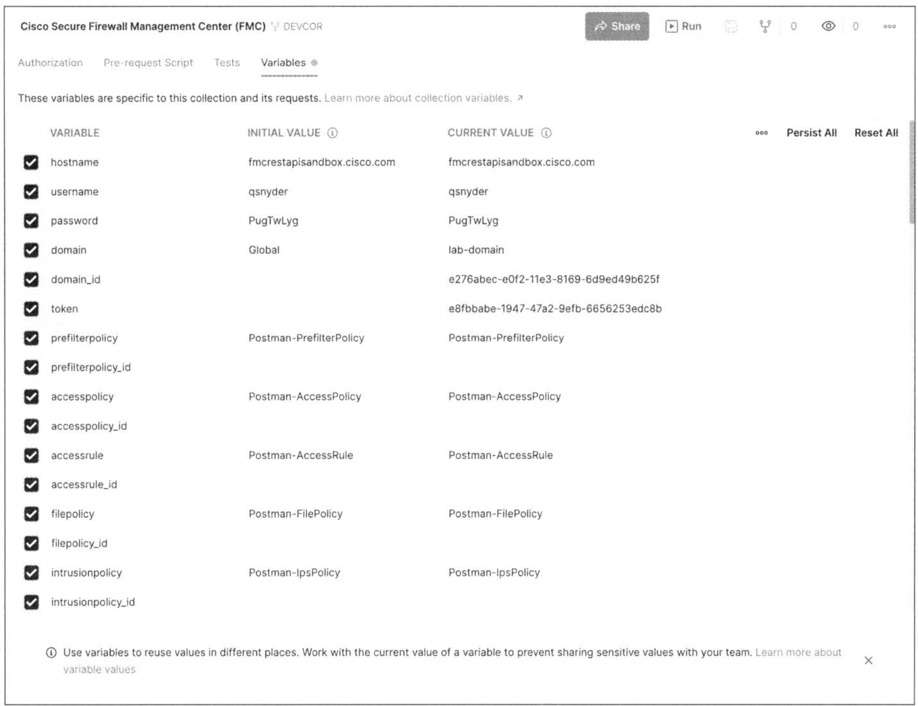

Figure 16-13 *Cisco FMC Postman Collection Variables*

By inspecting the collection, you can see that a variety of requests exist, from devices and device groups, system information, device health, status of deployment tasks, and the FMC object management of different objects within the FMC configuration universe. However, prior to sending any request toward the FMC, the calling station must be authenticated. You do this by using the request in the **Authentication > Retrieve Authorization Token** within the collection. This request sends a Base64-encoded string of the username and password to the /api/fmc_platform/v1/auth/generatetoken/ URI. When inspecting the Tests tab within the request, you can see that it stores the response headers **X-auth-access-token** and **X-auth-refresh-token** to variables within the environment. For all other requests, the value of **X-auth-access-token** is set as a header value; this serves as the authentication mechanism.

One other consideration when using the Postman collection is that the FMC does not distinguish between sessions via the WebUI and those made via the API. If the same user credentials are supplied to the API as a currently logged-in session to the WebUI, the FMC disconnects the web user. Alternatively, if a session is currently using the API and a login using the same credentials is attempted using the web, a dialog box asks if the active session is to be ended.

The FMC does not have an official SDK, though some unofficial repositories that contain SDK skeletons do exist. Although they are out of scope for this book, the API of the FMC can be accessed directly using Python and the **requests** library. This method, however, requires you to manually handle the authorization header to process any requests. First, you should set up a Python virtual environment (despite the requirements for accessing the FMC to be only the **requests** library). Example 16-8 demonstrates the steps required to create this virtual environment.

Example 16-8 *Creating a Python Virtual Environment to Access the FMC REST API*

```
dev » mkdir devcor-fmc

dev » python -m venv venv

dev » source venv/bin/activate

[venv] dev » pip install requests
Collecting requests
  Using cached requests-2.26.0-py2.py3-none-any.whl (62 kB)
Collecting urllib3<1.27,>=1.21.1
  Using cached urllib3-1.26.7-py2.py3-none-any.whl (138 kB)
Collecting certifi>=2017.4.17
  Using cached certifi-2021.10.8-py2.py3-none-any.whl (149 kB)
Collecting idna<4,>=2.5
  Using cached idna-3.3-py3-none-any.whl (61 kB)
Collecting charset-normalizer~=2.0.0
  Using cached charset_normalizer-2.0.9-py3-none-any.whl (39 kB)
Installing collected packages: urllib3, idna, charset-normalizer, certifi, requests
Successfully installed certifi-2021.10.8 charset-normalizer-2.0.9 idna-3.3
requests-2.26.0 urllib3-1.26.7
```

After creating the virtual environment, you can create the code to gather the authorization token for the FMC, as shown in Example 16-9.

Example 16-9 *Python Code for FMC API Authorization*

```
import argparse
import json
import requests

from requests.packages.urllib3.exceptions import InsecureRequestWarning
requests.packages.urllib3.disable_warnings(InsecureRequestWarning)

def get_token(fmcIP, path, user, password):
    try:
        r = requests.post(f"https://{fmcIP}/{path}", auth=(f"{user}",
            f"{password}"), verify=False)
    except requests.exceptions.HTTPError as e:
        raise SystemExit(e)
   except requests.exceptions.RequestException as e:
        raise SystemExit(e)
```

```
    required_headers = ('X-auth-access-token', 'X-auth-refresh-token',
'DOMAIN_UUID')
    result = {key: r.headers.get(key) for key in required_headers}
    return result

if __name__ == "__main__":
    parser = argparse.ArgumentParser(
        formatter_class=argparse.RawDescriptionHelpFormatter)
    parser.add_argument("user", type=str, help ="Valid FMC Username")
    parser.add_argument("password", type=str, help="Valid FMC Password")
    parser.add_argument("ip_address", type=str, help="IP of FMC")
    args = parser.parse_args()

    user = args.user
    password = args.password
    ip = args.ip_address
    token_path = "/api/fmc_platform/v1/auth/generatetoken"

    header = get_token(ip, token_path, user, password)
```

This code gathers the appropriate headers from the response and stores them as a header variable for use in subsequent requests against the API. You need to use this header value to gather additional information against the FMC API. You do so by appending the sample code shown in Example 16-10 to the request in Example 16-9.

Example 16-10 *Gathering FMC Version Using the REST API and Python*

```
   version_path = f"/api/fmc_platform/v1/info/serverversion"

    try:
        r = requests.get(f"https://{ip}/{version_path}", headers=header,
            verify=False)
    except requests.exceptions.HTTPError as e:
        raise SystemExit(e)
    except requests.exceptions.RequestException as e:
        raise SystemExit(e)

    try:
        print(json.dumps(r.json(), indent=2))
    except Exception as e:
        raise SystemExit(e)
```

When this code is combined and run, output like that shown in Example 16-11 is received. Keep in mind that the exact output will vary depending on the version of code running on the FMC within your environment.

Example 16-11 *Output from Gathering the FMC Version Using the REST API*


```
{
  "links": {
    "self": "https://198.19.10.120/api/fmc_platform/v1/info/
serverversion?offset=0&limit=1"
  },
  "items": [
    {
      "serverVersion": "6.7.0 (build 65)",
      "geoVersion": "2021-01-25-002",
      "vdbVersion": "build 340 ( 2020-12-16 00:13:46 )",
      "sruVersion": "2021-01-20-001-vrt",
      "type": "ServerVersion"
    }
  ],
  "paging": {
    "offset": 0,
    "limit": 1,
    "count": 1,
    "pages": 1
  }
}
```


Using the header variable passed in as part of the GET request does work (otherwise, the code shown in Example 16-11 would not return the FMC version). However, it is a generally accepted practice to leverage the **.session()** method within the requests library to ensure a persistent HTTP session instead of creating a new request with each new URI. This approach works fine because the header value is passed in as part of the GET request to the system version URI. However, when you use the requests module, you can leverage the header as part of a persistent session. Doing so removes the need for sending the header with each request, increasing performance, and removing the need to have as much duplicated code within the script.

Example 16-12 *Using the* **.session()** *Method to Query Multiple API Endpoints on the FMC Using Python*

```
import argparse
import json
import requests

from requests.packages.urllib3.exceptions import InsecureRequestWarning
requests.packages.urllib3.disable_warnings(InsecureRequestWarning)

def get_token(fmcIP, path, user, password):
    try:
```

```
        r = requests.post(f"https://{fmcIP}/{path}", auth=(f"{user}",
            f"{password}"), verify=False)
    except requests.exceptions.HTTPError as e:
        raise SystemExit(e)
    except requests.exceptions.RequestException as e:
        raise SystemExit(e)

    required_headers = ('X-auth-access-token', 'X-auth-refresh-token',
'DOMAIN_UUID')
    result = {key: r.headers.get(key) for key in required_headers}
    return result

if __name__ == "__main__":
    parser = argparse.ArgumentParser(
        formatter_class=argparse.RawDescriptionHelpFormatter)
    parser.add_argument("user", type=str, help ="Valid FMC Username")
    parser.add_argument("password", type=str, help="Valid FMC Password")
    parser.add_argument("ip_address", type=str, help="IP of FMC")
    args = parser.parse_args()

    user = args.user
    password = args.password
    ip = args.ip_address
    token_path = "/api/fmc_platform/v1/auth/generatetoken"

    header = get_token(ip, token_path, user, password)
    UUID = header["DOMAIN_UUID"]

    version_path = f"/api/fmc_platform/v1/info/serverversion"
    device_path = f"/api/fmc_config/v1/domain/{UUID}/devices/devicerecords?
expanded=True"

    sess = requests.Session()
    sess.headers.update({'X-auth-access-token': header["X-auth-access-token"],
'X-auth-refresh-token': header["X-auth-refresh-token"]})

    try:
        resp1 = sess.get(f"https://{ip}/{version_path}", verify=False)
        resp2 = sess.get(f"https://{ip}/{device_path}", verify=False)
    except requests.exceptions.HTTPError as e:
        raise SystemExit(e)
    except requests.exceptions.RequestException as e:
        raise SystemExit(e)
```

16

```
    try:
        print(json.dumps(resp1.json(), indent=2))
        print()
        print("*************")
        print()
        print(json.dumps(resp2.json(), indent=2))
    except Exception as e:
        raise SystemExit(e)
```

By adding (or changing) the highlighted sessions, you are able to define the headers to be sent toward the API endpoint only once. These values are then used for all subsequent requests calling that instance of the **.session()** method, without declaring explicit header values each time. Multiple requests can use the same instance and store the response within different variables to be accessed later. The results of the script look like Example 16-13 (depending on devices connected to the FMC).

Example 16-13 *Responses from Querying the FMC Version and Managed Device APIs*


```
{
  "links": {
    "self": "https://198.19.10.120/api/fmc_platform/v1/info/
serverversion?offset=0&limit=1"
  },
  "items": [
    {
      "serverVersion": "6.7.0 (build 65)",
      "geoVersion": "2021-01-25-002",
      "vdbVersion": "build 340 ( 2020-12-16 00:13:46 )",
      "sruVersion": "2021-01-20-001-vrt",
      "type": "ServerVersion"
    }
  ],
  "paging": {
    "offset": 0,
    "limit": 1,
    "count": 1,
    "pages": 1
  }
}

*************

{
  "links": {
    "self": "https://198.19.10.120/api/fmc_config/v1/domain/
e276abec-e0f2-11e3-8169-6d9ed49b625f/devices/devicerecords?o
ffset=0&limit=3&expanded=True"
  },
```

```
  "items": [
    {
      "id": "15c6c338-4f6e-11eb-845c-b89f5b28ebea",
      "type": "Device",
      "links": {
        "self": "https://198.19.10.120/api/fmc_config/v1/domain/
e276abec-e0f2-11e3-8169-6d9ed49b625f/devices/devicerecor
ds/15c6c338-4f6e-11eb-845c-b89f5b28ebea"
      },
      "name": "NGFWBR1",
      "description": "NOT SUPPORTED",
      "model": "Cisco Firepower Threat Defense for VMWare",
      "modelId": "A",
      "modelNumber": "75",
      "modelType": "Sensor",
      "healthStatus": "green",
      "sw_version": "6.7.0",
      "healthPolicy": {
        "id": "c253737c-2b73-11eb-960a-bf3ad063ddd4",
        "type": "HealthPolicy",
        "name": "Initial_Health_Policy 2020-11-20 21:02:54"
      },
      "accessPolicy": {
        "name": "Branch Access Control Policy",
        "id": "00505697-87b7-0ed3-0000-034359738978",
        "type": "AccessPolicy"
      },
      "advanced": {
        "enableOGS": false
      },
      "hostName": "ngfwbr1.dcloud.local",
      "license_caps": [
        "THREAT",
        "MALWARE",
        "URLFilter"
      ],
      "keepLocalEvents": false,
      "prohibitPacketTransfer": false,
      "ftdMode": "ROUTED",
      "metadata": {
        "readOnly": {
          "state": false
        },
```

```
        "inventoryData": {
          "cpuCores": "1 CPU (4 cores)",
          "cpuType": "CPU Pentium II 2700 MHz",
          "memoryInMB": "8192"
        },
        "deviceSerialNumber": "9A1V2FD3L7A",
        "domain": {
          "name": "Global",
          "id": "e276abec-e0f2-11e3-8169-6d9ed49b625f",
          "type": "Domain"
        },
        "isPartOfContainer": false,
        "isMultiInstance": false,
        "snortVersion": "2.9.17 (Build 200 - daq12)",
        "sruVersion": "2021-01-20-001-vrt",
        "vdbVersion": "Build 340 - 2020-12-16 00:13:46"
      }
    },
<...output omitted for brevity...>
```

For further exploration of the FMC API, Cisco DevNet provides several learning modules dedicated to Firepower APIs, including Threat Defense, Device Manager, Management Center, and others. You can find these modules at https://developer.cisco.com/learning/modules?keywords=firepower.

Meraki

Cisco's acquisition of Meraki in 2012 has proven to be popular with those desiring a cloud-managed solution of software-defined WAN devices, switches, wireless access points, security, and IoT solutions. Even with simplified management and monitoring, the Meraki solutions have a robust set of APIs and SDKs that are appealing to companies looking to extract even more functionality from their cloud-managed assets.

The APIs span the gamut of provisioning functions, monitoring and performance values, and inventory whether your perspective is at an organization, network, or device level. The API also provides an architecture that reflects product types: Appliance, Camera, Cellular Gateway, Switch, Wireless, Insight (traffic analytics), and Sm (Systems Manager, Mobile Device Manager).

The APIs and Python SDK are useful for custom application development, guest Wi-Fi insights, location services, and sensor management.

Enabling API/SDK Access to Meraki

To use the Meraki Dashboard API or Python SDK, you must first obtain an API key. This secure credential is used in your Python scripts, Postman, REST API calls, or other programmatic use accessing the Meraki cloud API gateway.

Step 1. Access your Meraki dashboard at http://dashboard.meraki.com.

Step 2. Navigate through **Organization > Settings** down to the Dashboard API access section.

Step 3. Ensure the Enable Access to the Cisco Meraki Dashboard API option is selected, as shown in Figure 16-14.

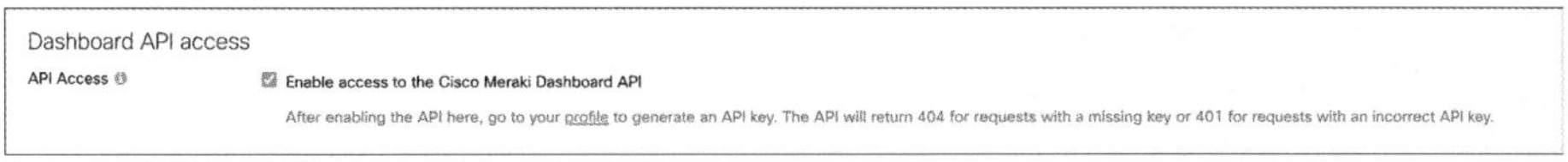

Dashboard API access

API Access

☑ Enable access to the Cisco Meraki Dashboard API

After enabling the API here, go to your profile to generate an API key. The API will return 404 for requests with a missing key or 401 for requests with an incorrect API key.

Figure 16-14 *Meraki Dashboard API Access Option*

Step 4. Click the **Profile** hyperlink to navigate to your personal profile portal. Scroll down to the API Access section, as shown in Figure 16-15.

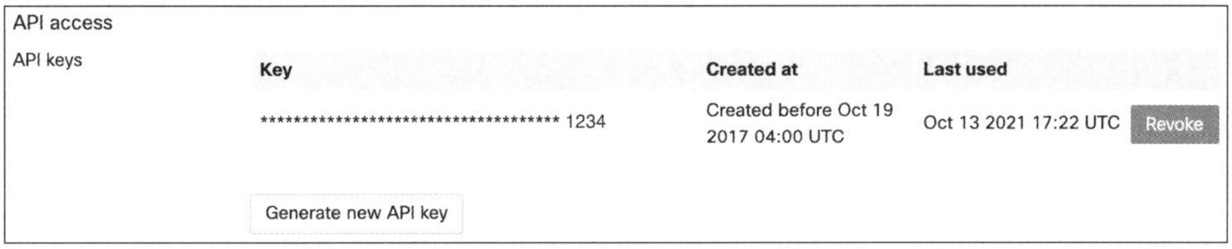

API access

API keys

Key	Created at	Last used	
************************************ 1234	Created before Oct 19 2017 04:00 UTC	Oct 13 2021 17:22 UTC	Revoke

Generate new API key

Figure 16-15 *Meraki API Key Settings*

If your portal shows an existing key, search your secure password repository for a key ending in the same last four digits as shown. In this example, you would search for keys ending in 1234.

If you have no existing key, or if you've forgotten your prior key, then it is simple to generate a new key by clicking the **Generate New API Key** button.

Step 5. If you generated a new key, remember to store it in your secure password repository. If you do a lot of development with API keys, it's inefficient to regenerate keys and impact several applications because of unrecorded credentials, so develop a discipline of secure credential storage.

Meraki API Documentation

The Meraki Dashboard API is officially documented at https://developer.cisco.com/meraki/api-v1/.

The DevNet team offers many learning labs that can familiarize you with the API. There is also a DevNet Sandbox Lab for accessing an always-on environment that is useful for training when you don't have Meraki equipment or prefer not to use your environment.

Another helpful resource is the Postman collection, which allows you to import all public API resources into a common utility that is popular with software developers. The Postman collection can be accessed and imported into your Postman environment at https://www.postman.com/meraki-api?tab=collections.

At this time, v1.15 is the latest to download and import, as shown in Figure 16-16.

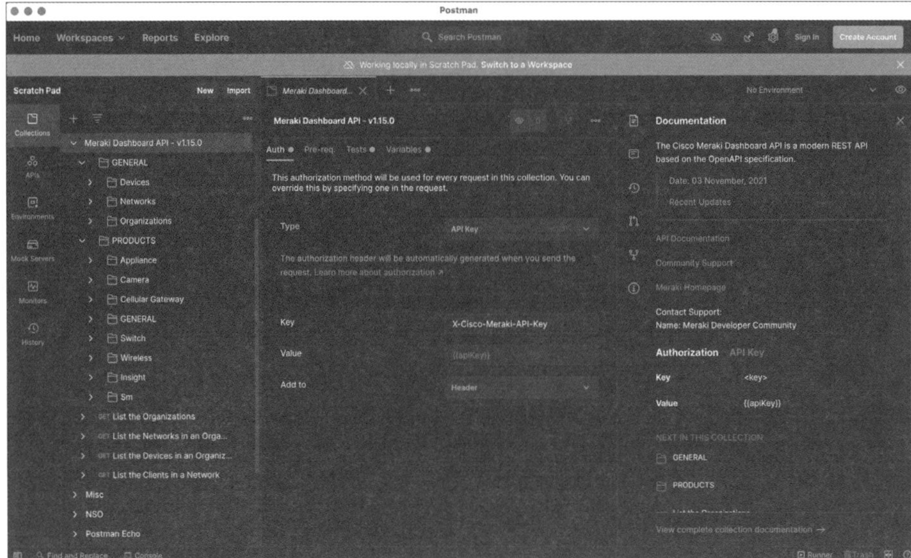

Figure 16-16 *Postman Application with Meraki Dashboard API*

Perusing the Postman collection hierarchy, you can see the following categories:

- **General:** Involving organizational, network, and device-level resources
- **Products:** Involving product-specific resources, such as appliances, cameras, and cellular gateways

Within each category, further Configure and Monitor subdivisions allow for specific functions related to provisioning and management.

Meraki SDK Documentation

Meraki's Python SDK is an easy-to-use solution that relieves you of routine coding tasks regarding API authentication, data encoding, pagination, rate limiting, and error handling. Understanding the API resources is important and useful; it is simplified in using tools like Postman, but you will find that the SDK provides even more benefits. Because the documentation is extensive and accessible, SDK use is encouraged.

You need to set up your Python environment to a minimum of Python v3.7 (released in the summer of 2018). As of Fall 2021, Python 3.10 is the latest, so for the love of all that is good and super(), use a recent release! Also, consider using a virtual environment (venv) when setting up your project.

You can easily obtain the Meraki SDK through the Python Package Index (PyPi) project at https://pypi.org/project/meraki/.

A quick method would be to use the steps shown in Example 16-14.

Example 16-14 *Creating a Meraki Project from the CLI*

```
myserver Python % mkdir MyProject
myserver Python % cd MyProject
myserver MyProject % python3 -m venv .venv
myserver MyProject % source .venv/bin/activate
(.venv) myserver MyProject % pip install meraki
Collecting meraki
  Downloading meraki-1.15.0-py3-none-any.whl (416 kB)
     |████████████████████████████████| 416 kB 573 kB/s
Collecting requests
  Using cached requests-2.26.0-py2.py3-none-any.whl (62 kB)
Collecting aiohttp
  Downloading aiohttp-3.8.1-cp39-cp39-macosx_10_9_x86_64.whl (574 kB)
     |████████████████████████████████| 574 kB 34.3 MB/s
Collecting attrs>=17.3.0
  Downloading attrs-21.2.0-py2.py3-none-any.whl (53 kB)
     |████████████████████████████████| 53 kB 7.1 MB/s
Collecting charset-normalizer<3.0,>=2.0
  Downloading charset_normalizer-2.0.8-py3-none-any.whl (39 kB)
Collecting yarl<2.0,>=1.0
  Downloading yarl-1.7.2-cp39-cp39-macosx_10_9_x86_64.whl (121 kB)
     |████████████████████████████████| 121 kB 21.3 MB/s
Collecting multidict<7.0,>=4.5
  Downloading multidict-5.2.0-cp39-cp39-macosx_10_9_x86_64.whl (45 kB)
     |████████████████████████████████| 45 kB 11.8 MB/s
Collecting async-timeout<5.0,>=4.0.0a3
  Downloading async_timeout-4.0.1-py3-none-any.whl (5.7 kB)
Collecting frozenlist>=1.1.1
  Downloading frozenlist-1.2.0-cp39-cp39-macosx_10_9_x86_64.whl (81 kB)
     |████████████████████████████████| 81 kB 26.5 MB/s
Collecting aiosignal>=1.1.2
  Downloading aiosignal-1.2.0-py3-none-any.whl (8.2 kB)
Collecting typing-extensions>=3.6.5
  Downloading typing_extensions-4.0.0-py3-none-any.whl (22 kB)
Collecting idna>=2.0
  Downloading idna-3.3-py3-none-any.whl (61 kB)
     |████████████████████████████████| 61 kB 14.5 MB/s
Collecting urllib3<1.27,>=1.21.1
  Downloading urllib3-1.26.7-py2.py3-none-any.whl (138 kB)
     |████████████████████████████████| 138 kB 25.9 MB/s
Collecting certifi>=2017.4.17
  Downloading certifi-2021.10.8-py2.py3-none-any.whl (149 kB)
     |████████████████████████████████| 149 kB 2.1 MB/s
```

```
Installing collected packages: typing-extensions, multidict, idna, frozenlist, yarl,
urllib3, charset-normalizer, certifi, attrs, async-timeout, aiosignal, requests,
aiohttp, meraki
Successfully installed aiohttp-3.8.1 aiosignal-1.2.0 async-timeout-4.0.1 attrs-
21.2.0 certifi-2021.10.8 charset-normalizer-2.0.8 frozenlist-1.2.0 idna-3.3 mer-
aki-1.15.0 multidict-5.2.0 requests-2.26.0 typing-extensions-4.0.0 urllib3-1.26.7
yarl-1.7.2
(.venv) myserver MyProject %
```

Now the environment is ready for the follow-on SDK examples. Note the authorization methods available in the next section.

Meraki Authorization

The Meraki Dashboard API requires a REST request header parameter, X-Cisco-Meraki-API-Key, for authorization in each request.

The JSON representation of this parameter is

```
{
    "X-Cisco-Meraki-API-Key": <MERAKI_DASHBOARD_API_KEY>
}
```

If you use the curl command-line tool, it would appear as

```
curl https://api.meraki.com/api/v1/<request_resource> \
  -H 'X-Cisco-Meraki-API-Key: <MERAKI_DASHBOARD_API_KEY>'
```

The Python SDK method, without follow-on processing, would appear as

```
import meraki


# Use the shell environment variable method for more secure
# implementation as a leading practice, e.g.
# $ export MERAKI_DASHBOARD_API_KEY=****1234
Dashboard = meraki.DashboardAPI()
```

The newer and current Dashboard API v1 supports bearer authentication using the authorization header parameter. This is generally preferred over using bespoke header parameters.

The JSON representation of this parameter is

```
{
    "Authorization": "Bearer <MERAKI_DASHBOARD_API_KEY>"
}
```

If you use the curl command-line tool, it would appear as

```
curl https://api.meraki.com/api/v1/<request_resource> \
  -L -H 'Authorization: Bearer <MERAKI_DASHBOARD_API_KEY>'
```

The Python SDK method handles authorization without change, assuming the shell environment variable is configured correctly, so the previous example is still applicable.

When using the Postman API platform and after having imported the Meraki collection, as described previously, you see the overall collection has a default predefined authentication method, as shown in Figure 16-17.

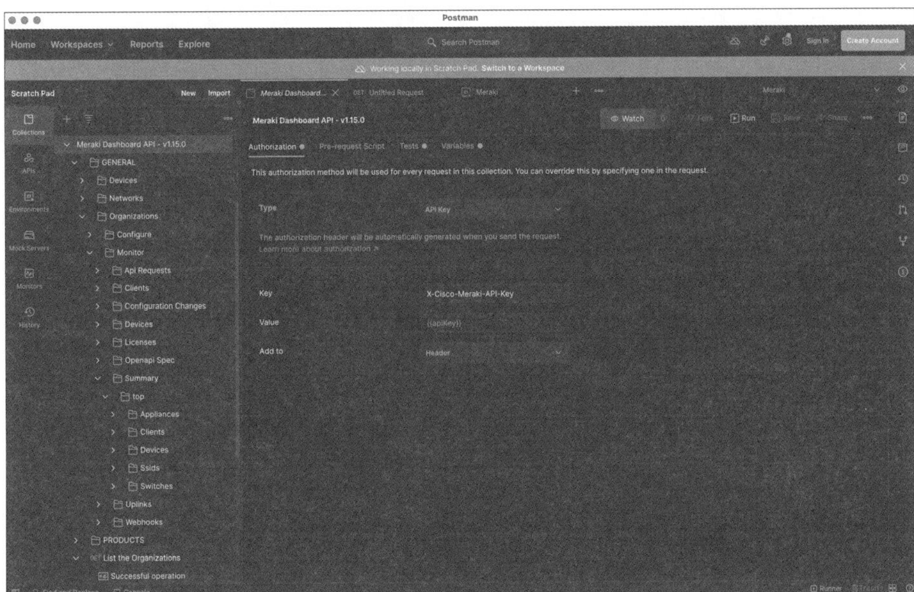

Figure 16-17 *Configuring Meraki Authorization Settings in Postman*

In the upper-right corner, you need to ensure you create a Meraki environment that has a key-value pairing of **apiKey** with your personal API key. It is also suggested you create a key-value pairing of **organizationId** with whatever numeric string represents your specific organization ID of interest. See Figure 16-18, for example.

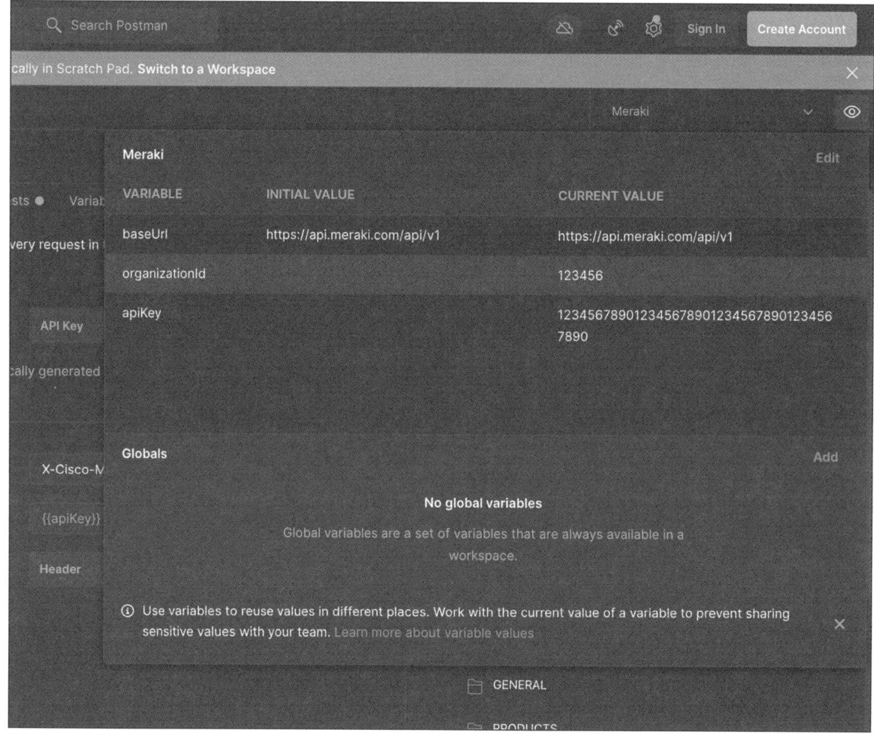

Figure 16-18 *Creating Meraki Environment Variables in Postman*

If you are unsure of your organization ID, one of the first API endpoints to poll would be

```
GET https://api.meraki.com/api/v1/organizations
```

This poll should result in output like that shown in Figure 16-19 using Postman.

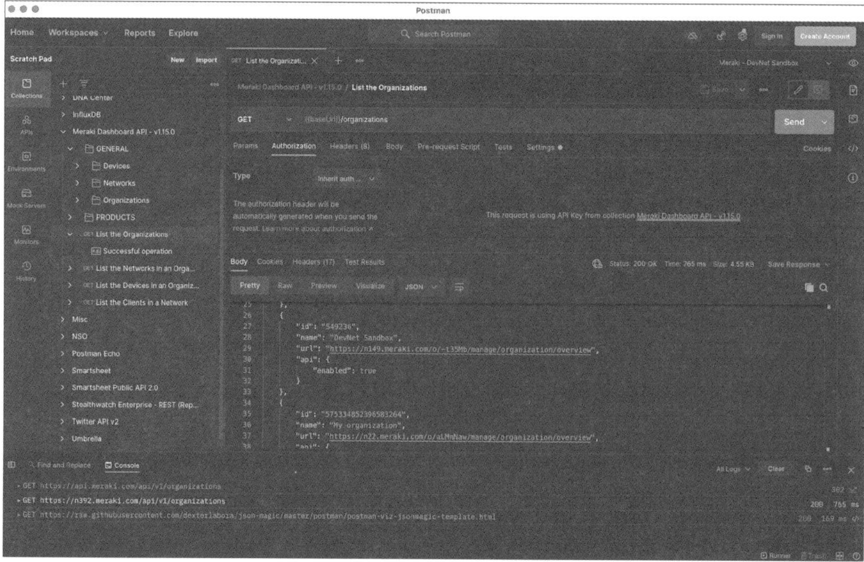

Figure 16-19 *Using Postman to Poll Meraki Organizations*

From this output, you can see the organization name DevNet Sandbox has the ID **549236**. Knowing and retaining your specific organization ID help make Meraki polling more efficient and specific.

The following simple script extracts Meraki devices in a cloud-managed environment. You start by maintaining the Meraki API key in a shell environment variable. This is a more secure method over storing it in a Python script variable.

```
export MERAKI_DASHBOARD_API_KEY=1234567890…
```

Then you create a new Python script in a virtual environment:

```
vi GetMerakiDevices.py
```

Next, you create the contents of the file as shown in Example 16-15.

Example 16-15 *Python Script to Extract Meraki Devices in the Organization*

```
import meraki
import pprint

pp = pprint.PrettyPrinter(indent=4)

organization_id = '549236'

dashboard = meraki.DashboardAPI()
my_devices = dashboard.organizations.getOrganizationDevices(organization_id,
total_pages='all')

pp.pprint(my_devices)
```


Executing the script provides a structured output view of devices, as shown in Example 16-16.

Example 16-16 *Execution and Output of GetMerakiDevices.py*

```
(.venv) myserver MyProject % python GetMerakiDevices.py
[   {   'address': '',
        'configurationUpdatedAt': '2021-10-26T04:49:57Z',
        'firmware': 'Not running configured version',
        'lanIp': None,
        'lat': 37.4180951010362,
        'lng': -122.098531723022,
        'mac': 'e0:55:3d:10:42:8a',
        'model': 'MR84',
        'name': '',
        'networkId': 'L_6468294…….',
       'notes': '',
        'productType': 'wireless',
       'serial': 'Q2EK-….-….',
        'tags': [],
        'url': 'https://n1**.meraki.com/DNSMB3-jxxxxxat/n/hW2vCavc/manage/nodes/
new_list/2466567013****'},
```

```
    {   'address': '',
        'configurationUpdatedAt': '2021-11-29T17:57:48Z',
        'firmware': 'Not running configured version',
        'lanIp': None,
        'lat': 37.****951010362,
        'lng': -122.****31723022,
        'mac': 'e0:55:3d:10:**:**',
        'model': 'MR84',
        'name': '',
        'networkId': 'L_64682949648*****',
        'notes': '',
        'productType': 'wireless',
        'serial': 'Q2EK-****-****',
        'tags': [],
        'url': 'https://n149.meraki.com/DNSMB1-wireless/n/XhipOdvc/manage/nodes/
new_list/246656701****'},
    {   'address': '',
        'configurationUpdatedAt': '2021-11-28T16:21:51Z',
        'firmware': 'Not running configured version',
        'lanIp': None,
        'lat': 34.****4579899,
        'lng': -117.****867527,
        'mac': '34:56:fe:a2:**:**,
        'model': 'MV12WE',
        'name': '',
        'networkId': 'L_64682949648*****',
        'notes': '',
        'productType': 'camera',
        'serial': 'Q2FV-****-****',
        'tags': [],
        'url': 'https://n149.meraki.com/DNENT1-vxxxogmai/n/o4tztdvc/manage/nodes/
new_list/575482438****'
/*** Abbreviated output ***/
]
(.venv) myserver MyProject %
```

For other SDK (and API) insights, you can find the interactive Meraki API documentation at https://developer.cisco.com/meraki/api-v1/#!get-device.

It serves as a great resource for planning your Python development strategy on Meraki equipment.

If you're looking to get deep into the guts of the SDK, the project is maintained on GitHub at https://github.com/meraki/dashboard-api-python.

Specifically, this directory shows a lot of detail on the API methods: https://github.com/meraki/dashboard-api-python/tree/master/meraki/api.

Intersight

Intersight is the Cisco cloud-enabled management platform for on-premises compute. Rather than relying on local connectivity to the server management portal (UCSM or CIMC), Intersight enables remote, API-enabled capabilities via secured connections between devices and the Intersight cloud. Although Intersight provides a powerful management platform for server infrastructure, enabling ease of logging, proactive TAC/RMA cases, and hardware compatibility lists based on the OS/hypervisor running on the server, it also allows administrators and operators to utilize purpose-built applications powered by the cloud to manage and operate their server infrastructure in a faster, orchestrated manner.

Because Intersight is API-driven, you can use a robust set of REST APIs in lieu of the graphical web interface. You can use these APIs to interact with not only the Cisco hardware controlled by Intersight but also the management of Kubernetes clusters, workflow orchestration, and third-party hardware platforms connected to Intersight. Additionally, the Intersight APIs are designed using the Open API Specification version 3 (OASv3) standard, enabling them to be easily translated into SDKs for various languages, as well as modules and providers for third-party automation and orchestration tools, such as Ansible and Terraform.

Enabling API Access to Intersight

16

API access to Intersight is not enabled by default; it must be enabled on a per-user basis. Additionally, if a user manages multiple accounts, access must be enabled for that user per account because an API key pair is scope-limited to a single account. The process to enable API access generates an API key, as well as an API secret, both of which are required to access the Intersight API.

Step 1. Log in to the Intersight portal at http://www.intersight.com. Login requires an account if you do not already have one.

Step 2. In the upper-right corner of the Intersight UI, click the user and then the account, as highlighted in Figure 16-20.

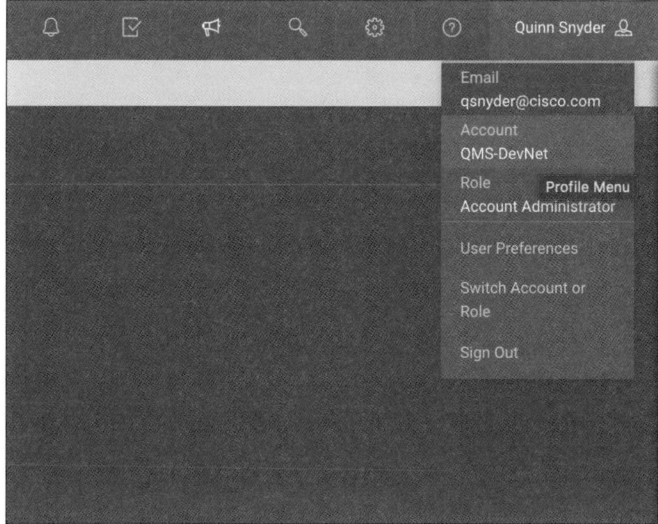

Figure 16-20 *Accessing Intersight User Account*

Step 3. Click the **API Keys** menu item toward the bottom of the account management window. This brings up the API key management screen, where you can create a new API key by clicking the **Generate API Key** button.

Step 4. Within the resulting dialog box, you provide a name for the API key pair, as well as which version of key you want to generate. At the time of this writing, the OASv2 schema will suffice for most users, though you can create both key types within the account (see Figure 16-22). The "legacy" version uses RSA private keys, whereas the newer version uses elliptical curve private keys.

Figure 16-21 shows the generation of the API keys, and Figure 16-22 shows all generated API keys for that user account.

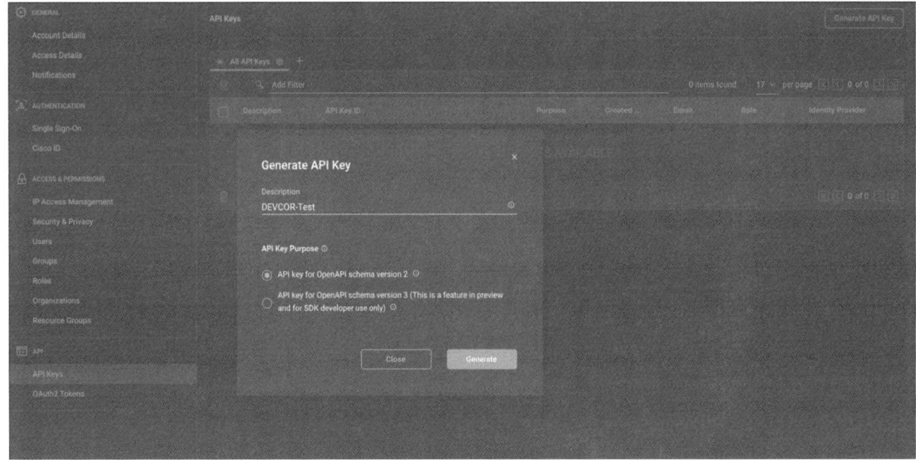

Figure 16-21 *Generating Intersight API Keys*

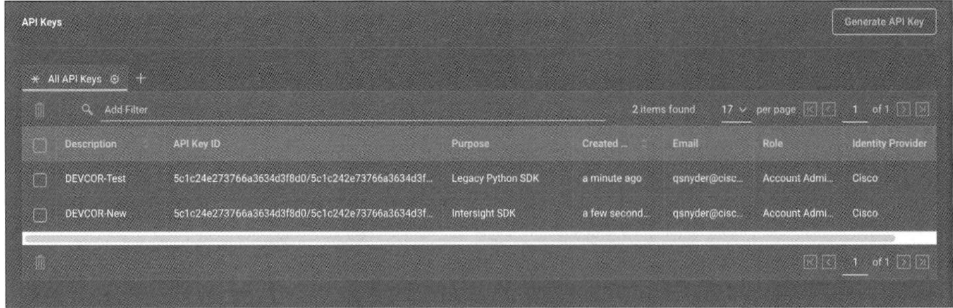

Figure 16-22 *Viewing Generated Intersight API Keys for a User Account*

If a previous API key and secret have been generated, there is no way to recover them if they are not documented. In this instance, a new API key and secret need to be created prior to using the API or SDK.

Step 5. If you generated a new key, remember to store it in your secure password repository. If you do a lot of development with API keys, it's inefficient to regenerate keys and impact several applications because of unrecorded credentials, so develop a discipline of secure credential storage. Ensure that both the API key and secret are kept and labeled together because API keys and secrets are generated in pairs and cannot be mismatched with other generated key/secret pairs.

Intersight API Documentation

All documentation related to Intersight programmability is documented at https://intersight.com/apidocs/introduction/overview/. The documentation includes the behavior of the APIs, a canonical reference guide for all exposed API endpoints, and a download page for the OAS documents (in various formats) as well as SDKs, Ansible modules, and Terraform providers.

The DevNet team offers several different Learning Labs that are focused around the learning and use of the Intersight API and its integrations. There are also several Sandbox Labs to complement the Learning Labs. These Sandboxes provide either a virtualized environment that can be claimed within Intersight (to test the control plane and APIs only) or a physical hardware domain that can support virtualized and containerized workloads.

Another helpful resource is the Postman collection, allowing you to import all public API resources into a common utility that is popular with software developers. The Postman collection can be accessed and imported into your Postman environment at https://documenter.getpostman.com/view/30210/SVfWN6Yc (or following the QR code in the "References" section at the end of this chapter).

When you click the Run in Postman button at the upper left of the window, a copy of this collection is added to your local instance of Postman (either installed on your local machine or using the cloud version).

To use this collection, you should create an environment that includes **api-key-id** with a value set to the created API key from the previous steps, as well as a **secret-key** value with the full output of the generated secret key (including the **begin** and **end** RSA lines with dashes). An example of these values filled into the Postman collection is shown in Figure 16-23.

DevNet Intersight Edit

VARIABLE	INITIAL VALUE	CURRENT VALUE
api-key-id	5c1c24e273766a3634d3f8d0/5c1c242e7376 6a3634d3f02e/61a927537564612d33b9d2b e	5c1c24e273766a3634d3f8d0/5c1c242e737 66a3634d3f02e/61a927537564612d33b9d 2be
secret-key	-----BEGIN RSA PRIVATE...	-----BEGIN RSA PRIVATE...

Figure 16-23 *Adding api-key and secret-key Values to the Postman Collection for Intersight*

Intersight must have devices added in order for you to manage them. If you're reserving the DevNet Sandbox for Intersight, which contains a pair of UCS Platform Emulators (UCSPEs), these devices should be claimed in order to receive data into Intersight, which requires the device's DeviceID and claim code. You can find them within the UCSPE by clicking the Admin menu on the left side of the screen and then Device Connector at the bottom of the submenu screen, as shown in Figure 16-24. The time-sensitive claim code is refreshed every five minutes.

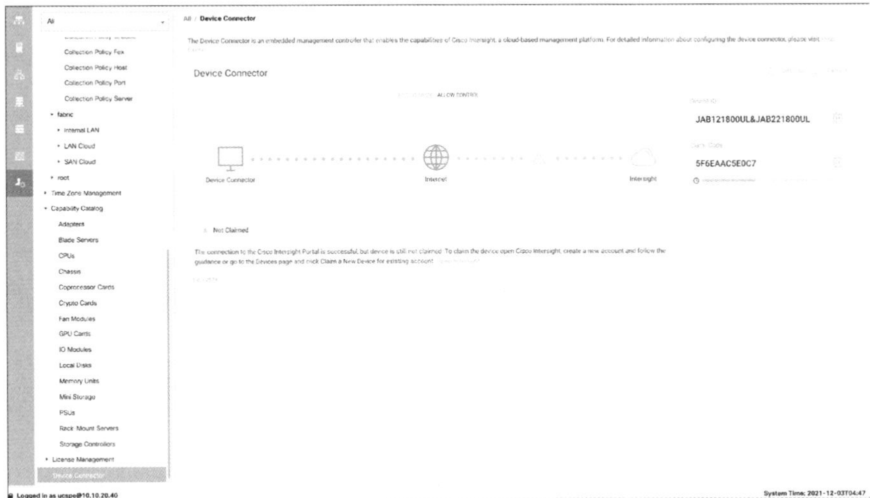

Figure 16-24 *UCS Manager Intersight Claim Code*

You can claim the device with the Postman collection, using the Device Claim request under the Device Claiming folder. After you add the DeviceID and claim code to the body of the request, you can send them to Intersight to initiate the device claim process. Inserting the DeviceID into the Serial Number field and the claim code in the Security Token field of the request body yields a payload similar to Figure 16-25. The claim can also be verified in Intersight under Targets.

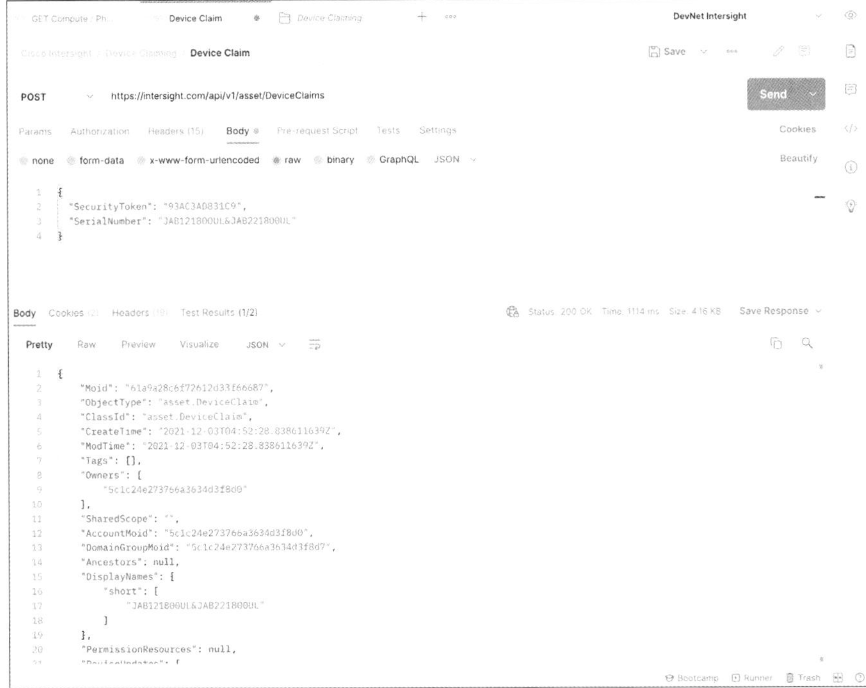

Figure 16-25 *Claiming UCS Manager Instances Using the Postman Collection for Intersight*

The rest of the Postman collection is focused on various tasks, including activities around server profiles, vMedia policies, boot policies, and NTP policies. The collection is not exhaustive, especially because the capabilities within Intersight have been under constant development and some features require additional licensing, but it should suffice when you're getting familiar with the REST API of the platform.

Intersight SDK Documentation

The Intersight SDK provides a level of both abstraction and completeness in interacting with Intersight, without the tedium of interacting directly with API endpoints. The SDK also handles the transition of the v2 API key method to v3 seamlessly because the appropriate methods have been coded directly into the SDK. The SDK is written to support Python, but PowerShell commandlets, Ansible modules, and Terraform providers all exist to manage Intersight through any workflow. Through the API Documentation page, you are able to download the JSON and YAML API schemas to create SDKs in languages outside of Python.

Using a recent version of Python (3.9.7 in this example), you can set up an environment to support the Intersight SDK. If you use a Python virtual environment, the process would look like the code in Example 16-17.

Example 16-17 *Setup for Python Virtual Environment for Intersight*

```
devcor-intersight » python -m venv venv

devcor-intersight » source venv/bin/activate

[venv] devcor-intersight » pip install intersight
Collecting intersight
  Downloading intersight-1.0.9.4903.tar.gz (12.1 MB)
     |████████████████████████████████| 12.1 MB 10.0 MB/s
Collecting urllib3>=1.25.3
  Using cached urllib3-1.26.7-py2.py3-none-any.whl (138 kB)
Collecting python-dateutil
  Downloading python_dateutil-2.8.2-py2.py3-none-any.whl (247 kB)
     |████████████████████████████████| 247 kB 10.6 MB/s
Collecting pem>=19.3.0
  Downloading pem-21.2.0-py2.py3-none-any.whl (8.8 kB)
Collecting pycryptodome>=3.9.0
  Downloading pycryptodome-3.11.0-cp35-abi3-macosx_10_9_x86_64.whl (1.5 MB)
     |████████████████████████████████| 1.5 MB 1.9 MB/s
Collecting six>=1.5
  Using cached six-1.16.0-py2.py3-none-any.whl (11 kB)
Using legacy 'setup.py install' for intersight, since package 'wheel' is not
installed.
Installing collected packages: six, urllib3, python-dateutil, pycryptodome, pem,
intersight
    Running setup.py install for intersight ... done
Successfully installed intersight-1.0.9.4903 pem-21.2.0 pycryptodome-3.11.0 python-
dateutil-2.8.2 six-1.16.0 urllib3-1.26.7
```

Intersight Authorization

Authorization requirements using the Python SDK are like those required for using the Postman collection: everything is generated using the API and secret keys. However, authenticating directly using the key and secret is not possible (as evidenced by the Pre-request Script within the Intersight Postman collection). Plus, both the v2 and v3 API key methods can be used to authenticate to the Intersight cloud. The Intersight SDK repository within the CiscoDevNet organization (https://github.com/ciscodevnet/intersight-python) has a sample script to authenticate to the Intersight API. This script can be added to Python code as a function or created as a standalone Python file that can be imported into a subsequent Python script. Example 16-18 provides sample Intersight authorization code that can handle both types of API keys generated from the Intersight portal.

Example 16-18 *Intersight Authorization Python Code*

```
import intersight
import re



def get_api_client(api_key_id, api_secret_file, endpoint="https://intersight.com"):
    with open(api_secret_file, 'r') as f:
        api_key = f.read()

    if re.search('BEGIN RSA PRIVATE KEY', api_key):
        # API Key v2 format
        signing_algorithm = intersight.signing.ALGORITHM_RSASSA_PKCS1v15
        signing_scheme = intersight.signing.SCHEME_RSA_SHA256
        hash_algorithm = intersight.signing.HASH_SHA256

    elif re.search('BEGIN EC PRIVATE KEY', api_key):
        # API Key v3 format
        signing_algorithm = intersight.signing.
ALGORITHM_ECDSA_MODE_DETERMINISTIC_RFC6979
        signing_scheme = intersight.signing.SCHEME_HS2019
        hash_algorithm = intersight.signing.HASH_SHA256

    configuration = intersight.Configuration(
        host=endpoint,
        signing_info=intersight.signing.HttpSigningConfiguration(
            key_id=api_key_id,
            private_key_path=api_secret_file,
           signing_scheme=signing_scheme,
            signing_algorithm=signing_algorithm,
            hash_algorithm=hash_algorithm,
            signed_headers=[
```

```
                intersight.signing.HEADER_REQUEST_TARGET,
                intersight.signing.HEADER_HOST,
                intersight.signing.HEADER_DATE,
                intersight.signing.HEADER_DIGEST,
            ]
        )
    )

    return intersight.ApiClient(configuration)
```

This code handles the computations that occurred in the Pre-request Script within the Postman collection, showing the value of an SDK because the SDK can abstract API complexity away from a user, allowing the user to focus on the end result of the code. Adding additional code to apply or retrieve configuration becomes somewhat trivial, given how the SDK is organized. Referencing the API documentation on intersight.com and the samples within the GitHub repository, you can make some assumptions within the code to achieve the desired outcomes. Assuming that you want to receive all alarms within Intersight, you can start by looking at the API docs. You can see that this falls inside the **cond/Alarms** API path, shown in Figure 16-26.

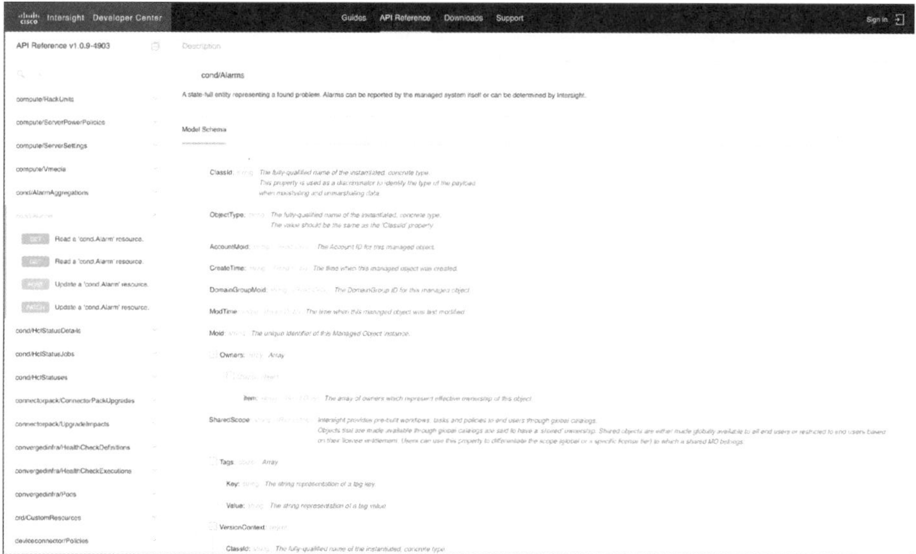

Figure 16-26 *Finding the API Path to Query Alarms in Intersight*

Looking at the samples within the GitHub repository (based on retrieving the boot policy), you can assume that you need to leverage the **CondApi()** method to get a list of alarms. You can glean the exact Pythonic path by analyzing the specific code within the module, or by importing the module into an API and viewing the available methods.

When you put this all together, a code sample to gather the alarms can be similar to that shown in Example 16-19. This code assumes that you have set the Intersight API key as an environment variable within your system.

Example 16-19 *Gathering Intersight Alarm Status Using the Intersight Python SDK*

```
import intersight
import os
import re
from intersight.api import cond_api
from pprint import pprint


def get_api_client(api_key_id, api_secret_file, endpoint="https://intersight.com"):
    with open(api_secret_file, 'r') as f:
        api_key = f.read()

    if re.search('BEGIN RSA PRIVATE KEY', api_key):
        # API Key v2 format
        signing_algorithm = intersight.signing.ALGORITHM_RSASSA_PKCS1v15
        signing_scheme = intersight.signing.SCHEME_RSA_SHA256
        hash_algorithm = intersight.signing.HASH_SHA256

    elif re.search('BEGIN EC PRIVATE KEY', api_key):
        # API Key v3 format
        signing_algorithm = intersight.signing.
ALGORITHM_ECDSA_MODE_DETERMINISTIC_RFC6979
        signing_scheme = intersight.signing.SCHEME_HS2019
        hash_algorithm = intersight.signing.HASH_SHA256

    configuration = intersight.Configuration(
        host=endpoint,
        signing_info=intersight.signing.HttpSigningConfiguration(
            key_id=api_key_id,
            private_key_path=api_secret_file,
            signing_scheme=signing_scheme,
            signing_algorithm=signing_algorithm,
            hash_algorithm=hash_algorithm,
            signed_headers=[
                intersight.signing.HEADER_REQUEST_TARGET,
                intersight.signing.HEADER_HOST,
                intersight.signing.HEADER_DATE,
                intersight.signing.HEADER_DIGEST,
            ]
        )
    )

    return intersight.ApiClient(configuration)

api_key = os.environ.get('INTERSIGHT_KEY')
```

```
api_key_file = "/Users/qsnyder/Downloads/SecretKey.txt.old.txt"

api_client = get_api_client(api_key, api_key_file)

api_instance = cond_api.CondApi(api_client)

try:
    api_response = api_instance.get_cond_alarm_list()
    pprint(api_response)
except intersight.ApiException as e:
    print("Exception calling alarm list: %s\n" % e)
```

The output of this code is lengthy and includes a lot of superfluous information regarding the alarms seen by Intersight that may or may not be appropriate for the given application. Looking through the examples within the GitHub README, you can see that selectors are supported, allowing you to parse the resulting query without needing to run through the machinations of JSON parsing using keys and values. By changing the code to include query selectors, you can filter the information returned as part of the response, as shown in Example 16-20.

Example 16-20 *Using Query Selectors Within the Intersight SDK*

```
import intersight
import re
from intersight.api import cond_api
from pprint import pprint



def get_api_client(api_key_id, api_secret_file, endpoint="https://intersight.com"):
    with open(api_secret_file, 'r') as f:
        api_key = f.read()

    if re.search('BEGIN RSA PRIVATE KEY', api_key):
        # API Key v2 format
        signing_algorithm = intersight.signing.ALGORITHM_RSASSA_PKCS1v15
        signing_scheme = intersight.signing.SCHEME_RSA_SHA256
        hash_algorithm = intersight.signing.HASH_SHA256

    elif re.search('BEGIN EC PRIVATE KEY', api_key):
        # API Key v3 format
        signing_algorithm = intersight.signing.
ALGORITHM_ECDSA_MODE_DETERMINISTIC_RFC6979
        signing_scheme = intersight.signing.SCHEME_HS2019
        hash_algorithm = intersight.signing.HASH_SHA256
```

```
    configuration = intersight.Configuration(
        host=endpoint,
        signing_info=intersight.signing.HttpSigningConfiguration(
            key_id=api_key_id,
            private_key_path=api_secret_file,
            signing_scheme=signing_scheme,
            signing_algorithm=signing_algorithm,
            hash_algorithm=hash_algorithm,
            signed_headers=[
                intersight.signing.HEADER_REQUEST_TARGET,
                intersight.signing.HEADER_HOST,
                intersight.signing.HEADER_DATE,
                intersight.signing.HEADER_DIGEST,
            ]
        )
    )

    return intersight.ApiClient(configuration)

api_key = "5c1c24e273766a3634d3f8d0/5c1c242e73766a3634d3f02e/61a927537564612d33b9d
2be"
api_key_file = "/Users/qsnyder/Downloads/SecretKey.txt.old.txt"

api_client = get_api_client(api_key, api_key_file)

api_instance = cond_api.CondApi(api_client)
query_selector="CreationTime,Description"

try:
    api_response = api_instance.get_cond_alarm_list(select=query_selector)
    pprint(api_response)
except intersight.ApiException as e:
    print("Exception calling alarm list: %s\n" % e)
```

The results are filtered to include only the creation time and the description of the alarm. This data is still incredibly raw, as you can see in Example 16-21, and can benefit from formatting the date, for instance, but it illustrates the query selection available within the SDK.

Example 16-21 *Raw Returned Response from the Use of Query Selectors*

```
{'class_id': 'cond.Alarm',
'creation_time': datetime.datetime(2021, 12, 2, 17, 21, 8, 115000, tzinfo=tzutc()),
'description': 'Connection to Adapter 1 eth interface 1 in '
               'server 4 missing',
'moid': '61a9a2a265696e2d3216210a',
'object_type': 'cond.Alarm'},
```

Further examples using the Intersight SDK are available at https://github.com/CiscoDevNet/intersight-python-utils. Although the structure of the Python code differs (creating the authentication using **credentials.py** and formatting the time using **helpers.py**), the classes and methods are the same.

Additionally, it is possible to interact with Intersight outside of the SDK, using the Ansible modules and Terraform providers. They could be useful if you're automating changes to the Intersight-managed infrastructure using Infrastructure-as-Code (IaC) principles. You can find links to these specific pieces on the Intersight API docs page or at https://galaxy.ansible.com/cisco/intersight (Ansible) or https://registry.terraform.io/providers/CiscoDevNet/intersight/latest (Terraform). Although neither one provides as complete coverage as the SDK, they both cover a majority of the use cases and can provide a higher level of abstraction than the SDK, allowing infrastructure developers to focus on the outcome more than the code.

UCS Manager

Cisco Unified Computing System Manager (UCS Manager or UCSM) provides a single point of management for all UCS form factors, including blades and rack-mount servers. By connecting the devices to the UCS Fabric Interconnects, you can centralize device profiles, network configuration, and systems management through a single plane. UCSM configuration is provided through a well-documented model, known as the Management Information Tree (MIT). This model exposes all configuration objects available within the UCSM UI through API endpoints.

While the UI and capabilities have been expanded since its initial release in 2009, UCSM's APIs were designed during a time in which "unspoken standards" hadn't been fully decided, so if you have used OAS-compliant APIs, using UCSM may feel a bit clunky because the data returned is only available via XML. However, a fully documented API explorer tool, called Visore, is included on each UCSM instance. Additionally, several different tools available to interact with the UCSM API don't require complex parsing of XML, but simply knowledge of Python or PowerShell. Ansible modules are also available for UCSM via Ansible Galaxy.

Enabling API Access to UCS Manager

API access to the UCS Manager is enabled by default, with no option within the UI to disable the access.

UCS Manager API Documentation

UCS Manager has several different locations for referencing API documentation. You can view online references without access to a UCSM platform (or platform emulator) directly on Cisco's website via https://www.cisco.com/c/en/us/td/docs/unified_computing/ucs/sw/api/b_ucs_api_book.html. This reference contains background and sample information on using the API, including the object model reference, filters, sample XML payloads, and descriptions of which classes are exposed via API. While not interactive, this resource serves as a canonical reference for the API endpoints within the platform.

The second resource available for the API reference exists within the UCSM itself. By accessing the Visore API browser at http://<UCSM-IP>/visore.html, you open an interactive tool that allows you to navigate and view the UCS Management Information Tree, which is the model upon which all UCS interactions (via API or UI) are built. Figure 16-27 shows the Visore landing page when you first access the tool.

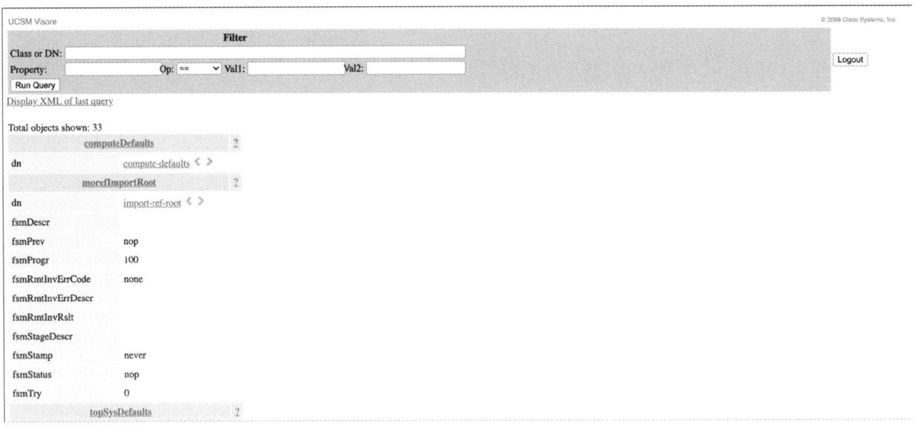

Figure 16-27 *UCSM Visore Landing Page*

While the full MIT may take some time to understand, Visore can help with the relationship between parent and child managed objects (MOs). If you search for **topSystem** in the search bar at the top of the Visore page, you are taken to a new page with a single entry on it—the topSystem class—which is the top-level object for all UCS devices within the UCSM domain (shown in Figure 16-28). This page also provides two key tools for exploring UCS APIs: (a) the ability to view the XML of the previous query and (b) a complete doc page for that MO/class.

Display XML of last query

Total objects shown: 1

topSystem	?
address	192.168.111.7
currentTime	2021-12-06T22:24:26.089
descr	
dn	sys
ipv6Addr	::
mode	cluster
name	UCSPE-192-168-111-7
owner	
site	
systemUpTime	00:03:26:37

Figure 16-28 topSystem *MO Page Within Visore*

When you click the ? next to the **topSystem** link, you are taken to a simple text page documenting the MO. Within this documentation are the "contained" and "container" hierarchies, which document what the parent MO of this object is and which MOs are children of this object, both of which are provided in a tree-style format. This information allows you to understand the distinguished name (DN) path to access each configuration item within the UCS MIT. Below the hierarchy tables is the properties table, which is what is output when this specific MO is queried. This page is shown in Figure 16-29.

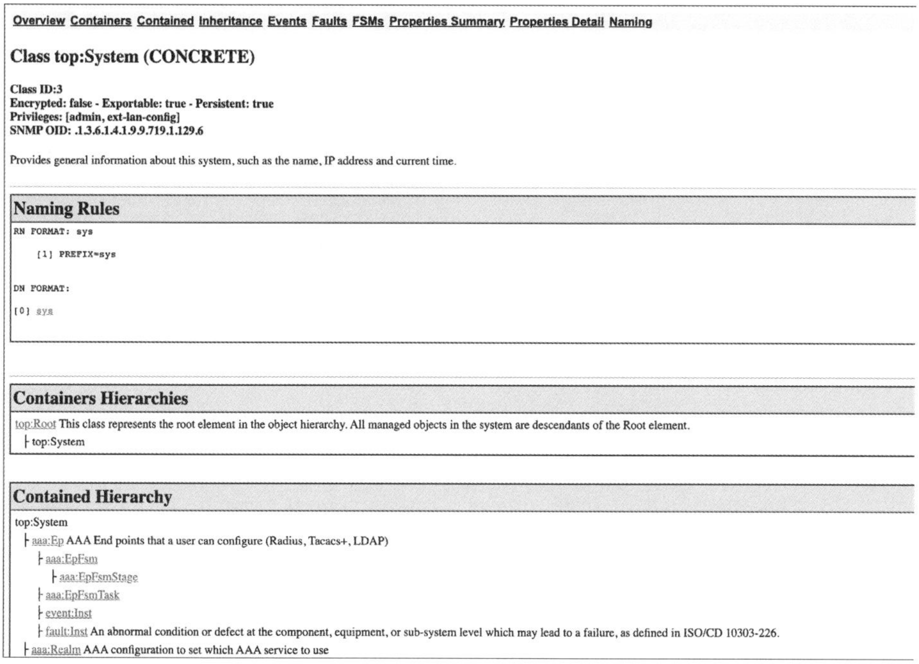

Overview Containers Contained Inheritance Events Faults FSMs Properties Summary Properties Detail Naming
Class top:System (CONCRETE)
Class ID:3
Encrypted: false - Exportable: true - Persistent: true
Privileges: [admin, ext-lan-config]
SNMP OID: .1.3.6.1.4.1.9.9.719.1.129.6
Provides general information about this system, such as the name, IP address and current time.
Naming Rules
RN FORMAT: sys
[1] PREFIX=sys
DN FORMAT:
[0] sys
Containers Hierarchies
top:Root This class represents the root element in the object hierarchy. All managed objects in the system are descendants of the Root element.
├ top:System
Contained Hierarchy
top:System
├ aaa:Ep AAA End points that a user can configure (Radius, Tacacs+, LDAP)
├ aaa:EpFsm
├ aaa:EpFsmStage
├ aaa:EpFsmTask
├ event:Inst
├ fault:Inst An abnormal condition or defect at the component, equipment, or sub-system level which may lead to a failure, as defined in ISO/CD 10303-226.
├ aaa:Realm AAA configuration to set which AAA service to use

Figure 16-29 topSystem *MO Documentation*

Returning to the Visore page for the **topSystem**, you can see that the keys shown on the left side of the column align with what was seen under the properties section of the doc page, and the values reflect the current state at the time the page was generated, indicating that, while not in the OAS style of more recently created tools, it is an interactive API browser for UCS.

The other important piece to Visore is the ability to generate the XML query that produced the output seen on-screen. Using this feature, you are able to

- Understand what XML query needs to be sent to generate a desired payload.
- Provide a check to ensure that the information being received is as to be expected from the query.

As a result, you can quickly understand and develop queries to glean the desired information from the API. Figure 16-30 illustrates the XML required to generate a query for the **topSystem** MO.

UCSM Visore

Filter

Class or DN:

Property: Op: == Val1: Val2:

Run Query

Display XML of last query

```
<configResolveClass cookie="null" inHierarchical="false" classId="topSystem"/>
```

Figure 16-30 *XML Query for the* ***topSystem*** *MO*

Although UCSM does not have a published Postman collection, you can easily get started by querying the API directly via cURL. This query can then be translated into a Postman request if so desired for reuse. We explore both methods of querying the API so that you gain familiarity with the steps required for translation.

All API queries to UCSM are sent toward the URL http://<UCSM-IP>/nuova. This URL serves as the single entry point for all requests, with the delineation of which MO to query/configure being defined within the payload of the API request. However, UCSM requires a two-step authentication process to access the API: an initial step using the username and password to gather a cookie/token that is then copied into the body of all subsequent requests to validate that the user is authorized to access the API.

To gather the cookie, you must first send a payload of the username and password of the UCSM to the **aaaLogin** method. You can accomplish this using cURL by entering the following:

```
» curl -d "<aaaLogin inName='ucspe' inPassword='ucspe'>
</aaaLogin>" http://192.168.111.7/nuova
```

In this example, the username and password are passed in the request to the IP address of the UCSM at the API entrypoint. UCSM responds with a payload similar to the following:

```
<aaaLogin cookie="" response="yes" outCookie="1638850563/999f4f8e-
d32a-442c-b108-2084603ea17c" outRefreshPeriod="600" outPriv="aaa,
admin,ext-lan-config,ext-lan-policy,ext-lan-qos,ext-lan-security,
ext-san-config,ext-san-policy,ext-san-security,fault,operations,
pod-config,pod-policy,pod-qos,pod-security,read-only" outDomains=
"org-root" outChannel="noencssl" outEvtChannel="noencssl"
outSessionId="" outVersion="4.1(2c)" outName=""> </aaaLogin>
```

This response provides several pieces of information, such as the UCSM version, the permissions assigned to the user who authenticated to the API, the domain of the user, and, most importantly, the cookie that will be used for subsequent API authentication. This value is given by the **outCookie** tag and includes everything after the slash (/) within the tag body (everything before the slash [/] is the current time of the request given in UNIX epoch time, which allows you to correlate the start time of the cookie validity with the time at which the cookie expires because the refresh period is provided within the **aaaLogin** body).

After the cookie is received, you can place it in the XML query of another API request. The cookie is added to the request as given by the View XML Request link within Visore. To query the **topSystem** MO, you would enter a request like the following:

```
» curl -d "<configResolveClass cookie="999f4f8e-d32a-442c-b108-
2084603ea17c" inHierarchical="false" classId="topSystem"/>"
http://192.168.111.7/nuova
```

This request generates the same data as seen in the Visore viewer, but with XML tag delineation:

```
<configResolveClass cookie="999f4f8e-d32a-442c-b108-
2084603ea17c" response="yes" classId="topSystem"> <outCon-
figs>  <topSystem address="192.168.111.7" currentTime="2021-12-
07T04:18:08.080" descr="" dn="sys" ipv6Addr="::" mode="cluster"
name="UCSPE-192-168-111-7" owner="" site="" systemUp-
Time="00:09:20:19"/> </outConfigs> </configResolveClass>
```

The XML can be difficult to read at times, especially when it is all placed together on a single line and especially if the MO query includes many child objects and classes of the parent. However, when you use command-line tools, you are able to format the resulting response without having to either save it locally or copy/paste to another tool. By piping the output of the response to **xmllint**, you can print formatted output directly to stdout, similar to what is shown in Example 16-22.

Example 16-22 *Formatting UCSM XML Responses Using* **xmllint**

```
» curl -d "<configResolveClass cookie="999f4f8e-d32a-442c-b108-2084603ea17c"
inHierarchical="false" classId="topSystem"/>" http://192.168.111.7/nuova | xmllint
--format -
  % Total    % Received % Xferd  Average Speed   Time    Time     Time  Current
                                 Dload  Upload   Total   Spent    Left  Speed
100   449  100   345  100   104  11638   3508 --:--:-- --:--:-- --:--:-- 21380
<?xml version="1.0"?>
<configResolveClass cookie="999f4f8e-d32a-442c-b108-2084603ea17c" response="yes"
classId="topSystem">
  <outConfigs>
    <topSystem address="192.168.111.7" currentTime="2021-12-07T04:45:32.208"
descr="" dn="sys" ipv6Addr="::" mode="cluster" name="UCSPE-192-168-111-7" owner=""
site="" systemUpTime="00:09:47:43"/>
  </outConfigs>
</configResolveClass>
```

This same process can be followed for all classes and MOs available within the UCSM API.

It is possible to translate the cURL requests from the CLI to be used in Postman and have Postman store the cookie as an environment variable to be used for subsequent requests. To do so, follow these steps:

Step 1. Open Postman. Create a new environment and collection.

Step 2. Within the environment, create a variable for the IP address of the UCSM and assign it an IP address. Create a placeholder variable with no value to store the resulting cookie, as seen in Figure 16-31.

Figure 16-31 *Placeholder Variable Created Within Postman for the UCSM Cookie*

Step 3. Create a new POST request, pointing to the API entrypoint address (http://UCSM-IP/nuova). Add the same XML payload to include the username and password of the UCSM, in XML format, as in Figure 16-32.

Figure 16-32 *XML Payload to Authenticate to the UCSM API*

Step 4. The final piece is to add a test to capture the **outCookie** value from the XML response, strip the epoch time, and store the cookie value into a variable for use in subsequent API calls. You add this code (written in JavaScript) to the Tests tab within the login request (shown in Figure 16-33):

```
var responseJson = xml2Json(responseBody);

var withTime = responseJson.aaaLogin.$.outCookie;

var removeEpoch = withTime.indexOf('/');

var removeEpochAndSlash = removeEpoch + 1;

var withoutTime = withTime.substr(removeEpochAndSlash, withTime.
length);

postman.setEnvironmentVariable("cookie", withoutTime);
```

Figure 16-33 *Creating the Test to Gather the UCSM API Cookie from the Response Payload*

Step 5. After you save the request, you can send it toward the UCSM. When the response is received, the full XML body is displayed within the response window, but the cookie value is stored within the environment (you can confirm this by clicking the **Environment Quick Look** button next to the environment name in the upper right of the Postman window).

Step 6. The final step is to transpose the **topSystem** request to Postman, similar to what is shown in Figure 16-34. You do this by creating a new POST request to the same URL as the login (remember, UCSM does not have unique entrypoints within the API; the returned data is determined by the class and classID within the XML payload). The value for **cookie** is then replaced with the newly created cookie variable within the UCS Postman environment. The response from the request is formatted similarly to the **xmllint** formatted request from the cURL command line.

```
<configResolveClass cookie="{{cookie}}" inHierarchical="false"
classId="topSystem"/>
```

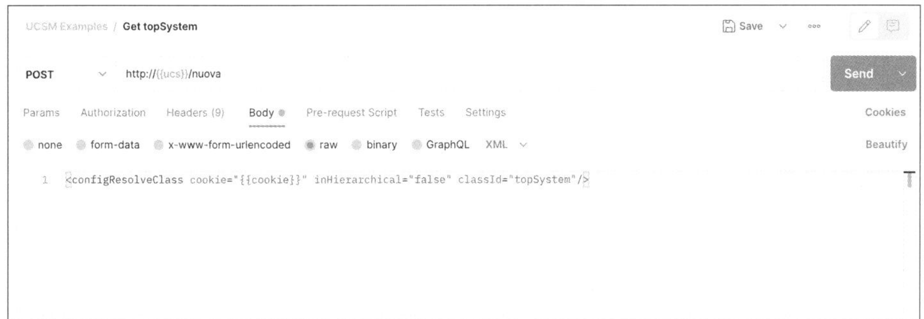

Figure 16-34 *Using the Newly Gathered UCSM API Cookie to Query the* **topSystem** *MO*

The DevNet team offers several different Learning Labs that enable you to learn and use the UCSM API and SDKs that accompany the same Sandbox used for Intersight exploration. Using this singular Sandbox, you can explore both the original UCSM platform and the next-generation compute management system, Intersight.

Python SDK Documentation

Two SDKs are available to interact with the UCSM API: Python and PowerShell. Both of these SDKs greatly reduce the friction in interacting with the API because you can use the tooling within the language you are most familiar with to extract information from UCSM. The installation of both SDKs is covered in this section.

The Python SDK for UCSM is written to provide a Pythonic wrapper around the interactions with the API and to provide methods and classes for data extraction from the individual MOs. The UCSM SDK supports the full range of CRUD operations within the UCS MIT, conversion of UI paths to Python code, and configuration backup and restore. It also supports other operational tasks, such as starting an IP KVM session and capturing tech support bundles. Complete documentation is located at https://ucsmsdk.readthedocs.io, and the GitHub repository for the SDK is located at https://github.com/CiscoUcs/ucsmsdk. The UCM SDK is supported through Python 3.9.

Using a recent version of Python (3.9.7 in this example), you can set up an environment to support the UCSM SDK. If you use a Python virtual environment, the process would be like that shown in Example 16-23.

Example 16-23 *Creating a Python Virtual Environment for Accessing the UCSM API*

```
devcor-ucsmsdk » python -m venv venv

devcor-ucsmsdk » source venv/bin/activate

[venv] devcor-ucsmsdk » pip install ucsmsdk
Collecting ucsmsdk
  Downloading ucsmsdk-0.9.12-py2.py3-none-any.whl (6.5 MB)
     |████████████████████████████████| 6.5 MB 5.2 MB/s
Requirement already satisfied: setuptools in ./venv/lib/python3.9/site-packages
(from ucsmsdk) (57.4.0)
Collecting pyparsing
  Downloading pyparsing-3.0.6-py3-none-any.whl (97 kB)
     |████████████████████████████████| 97 kB 16.0 MB/s
Requirement already satisfied: six in ./venv/lib/python3.9/site-packages (from
ucsmsdk) (1.16.0)
Installing collected packages: pyparsing, ucsmsdk
Successfully installed pyparsing-3.0.6 ucsmsdk-0.9.12
```

When the SDK is installed, it may be beneficial to explore the SDK using the Python REPL (or **bpython** package) to understand how objects are created and accessed. You can enter the code to connect to a UCSM as shown in Example 16-24.

Example 16-24 *Accessing the UCSM SDK from* **bpython**

```
[venv] devcor-ucsmsdk » bpython
bpython version 0.22.1 on top of Python 3.9.7 /Users/qsnyder/dev/devcor-intersight/
venv/bin/python
>>> import ucsmsdk.ucshandle as handler
>>> ucs_session = handler.UcsHandle("10.10.20.40", "ucspe", "ucspe")
>>> ucs_session.login()
True
```

This code connects the SDK to the UCSM instance. When it is connected, you can begin to explore simple queries of MOs within the MIT. Carrying forward the **topSystem** example, you can explore several ways to access the information from this MO. The SDK supports accessing objects by classID, like you did using the XML queries. You do this using the **query_classid()** method, as shown in Example 16-25.

Example 16-25 *Querying the* **topSystem** *MO Using the UCSM SDK in* **bpython**

```
>>> classObject = ucs_session.query_classid("topSystem")
>>> type(classObject)
<class 'list'>
>>> print(classObject)
[<ucsmsdk.mometa.top.TopSystem.TopSystem object at 0x1032d0f10>]
>>> print(type(classObject[0]))
<class 'ucsmsdk.mometa.top.TopSystem.TopSystem'>
>>> print(classObject[0])

Managed Object                  :       TopSystem
--------------
class_id                        :TopSystem
address                         :10.10.20.40
child_action                    :None
current_time                    :2021-12-07T23:24:11.870
descr                           :
dn                              :sys
ipv6_addr                       :::
mode                            :cluster
name                            :UCSPE-10-10-20-40
owner                           :
rn                              :sys
sacl                            :None
site                            :
status                          :None
system_up_time                  :05:06:16:51


>>> print(classObject[0].name)
UCSPE-10-10-20-40
```

Note that the object created is of class **list** and needs to be indexed to correctly print the output. When the root of the object is accessed, the full table of information is presented in a much easier-to-digest form than the XML payload from the cURL/Postman calls. Additionally, any individual item can be accessed by accessing the method called by the name of the MO (such as **.name** to gather hostname information).

The UCSM SDK also supports accessing MOs by the distinguished name (DN) path within the MIT. Recall Figure 16-28, which is a snapshot of the Visore page for the topSystem classID, or the output from Example 16-25. Within this table, there is a reference for the DN, the unique path from the top level of the MIT to the specific MO. If you choose to access the **topSystem** object by DN using the SDK, the code would look like that shown in Example 16-26.

16

Example 16-26 *Querying the* **sys** *DN Using the UCSM SDK*

```
>>> dnObject = ucs_session.query_dn("sys")
>>> print(type(dnObject))
<class 'ucsmsdk.mometa.top.TopSystem.TopSystem'>
>>> print(dnObject)

Managed Object                  :       TopSystem
--------------
class_id                        :TopSystem
address                         :10.10.20.40
child_action                    :None
current_time                    :2021-12-07T23:44:43.755
descr                           :
dn                              :sys
ipv6_addr                       :::
mode                            :cluster
name                            :UCSPE-10-10-20-40
owner                           :
rn                              :sys
sacl                            :None
site                            :
status                          :None
system_up_time                  :05:06:37:23



>>> print(dnObject.name)
UCSPE-10-10-20-40
```

This example looks similar to queries done by classID, but the resulting output object does not need to be indexed; it is ready to be accessed in full or through a method to gather the specific values needed. To carry this example one level deeper, you can query a specific **computeRackUnit** by DN. You can utilize Visore to gather the DN and query it, with results similar to Example 16-27.

Example 16-27 *Querying a Specific UCS Server by DN Using the UCSM SDK*

```
>>> dnComputeRack = ucs_session.query_dn("sys/rack-unit-10")
>>> print(dnComputeRack)

Managed Object                  :       ComputeRackUnit
--------------
class_id                        :ComputeRackUnit
admin_power                     :policy
admin_state                     :in-service
asset_tag                       :
assigned_to_dn                  :
association                     :none
```

```
availability                          :available
available_memory                      :49152
check_point                           :discovered
child_action                          :None
conn_path                             :A,B
conn_status                           :A,B
descr                                 :
discovery                             :complete
discovery_status                      :
dn                                    :sys/rack-unit-10
enclosure_id                          :0
fan_speed_config_status               :
fan_speed_policy_fault                :no
flt_aggr                              :2
fsm_descr                             :
fsm_flags                             :
fsm_prev                              :DiscoverSuccess
fsm_progr                             :100
fsm_rmt_inv_err_code                  :none
fsm_rmt_inv_err_descr                 :
fsm_rmt_inv_rslt                      :
fsm_stage_descr                       :
fsm_stamp                             :2021-12-02T17:24:55.696
fsm_status                            :nop
fsm_try                               :0
id                                    :10
int_id                                :86468
kmip_fault                            :no
kmip_fault_description                :
lc                                    :discovered
lc_ts                                 :1970-01-01T00:00:00.000
local_id                              :
low_voltage_memory                    :not-applicable
managing_inst                         :A
memory_speed                          :not-applicable
mfg_time                              :not-applicable
model                                 :HX220C-M5SX
name                                  :
num_of40_g_adaptors_with_old_fw       :0
num_of40_g_adaptors_with_unknown_fw:0
num_of_adaptors                       :2
num_of_cores                          :16
num_of_cores_enabled                  :16
num_of_cpus                           :2
num_of_eth_host_ifs                   :0
```

```
num_of_fc_host_ifs            :0
num_of_threads                :16
oper_power                    :off
oper_pwr_trans_src            :unknown
oper_qualifier                :
oper_qualifier_reason         :N/A
oper_state                    :unassociated
operability                   :operable
original_uuid                 :1b4e28ba-2fa1-11d2-e00a-b9a761bde3fb
part_number                   :
physical_security             :chassis-open
policy_level                  :0
policy_owner                  :local
presence                      :equipped
revision                      :0
rn                            :rack-unit-10
sacl                          :None
serial                        :RK93
server_id                     :10
slot_id                       :0
status                        :None
storage_oper_qualifier        :unknown
total_memory                  :49152
usr_lbl                       :
uuid                          :1b4e28ba-2fa1-11d2-e00a-b9a761bde3fb
vendor                        :Cisco Systems Inc
version_holder                :no
veth_status                   :A,B
vid                           :0
```

You can see that this method of accessing the API provides a much cleaner interface for gathering information and selecting specific pieces of information from the API. Finally, because the SDK opens a persistent session connection to the UCSM, it is good programmatic practice to close the connection before exiting the REPL:

```
>>> ucs_session.logout()
True
>>> exit()
```

PowerShell SDK Documentation

The PowerShell SDK (also known as the UCS PowerTool) is a PowerShell-based alternative to interacting with the UCSM API. It follows the traditional PowerShell syntax of "verb + noun" commandlet syntax and provides a low barrier to entry for those looking to automate UCSM who already have experience with PowerShell, such as Windows systems administrators. However, because PowerShell has been released as a cross-platform application, it is possible to leverage the UCS PowerTool on Linux and macOS systems. See the following

URLs for your system OS. Each URL is also available in QR code format in the "References" section at the end of this chapter:

- **Linux:** https://docs.microsoft.com/en-us/powershell/scripting/install/installing-powershell-on-linux?view=powershell-7.2
- **macOS:** https://docs.microsoft.com/en-us/powershell/scripting/install/installing-powershell-on-macos?view=powershell-7.2
- **Windows:** https://docs.microsoft.com/en-us/powershell/scripting/install/installing-powershell-on-windows?view=powershell-7.2

It is also possible to run PowerShell as a container within the Docker runtime. This capability provides portability across systems without worrying about installation permissions (assuming Docker is installed). Although this method is demonstrated in the following examples, the steps performed after the container is running apply to any operating system.

You can download the (Linux-based) PowerShell core container from Microsoft's DockerHub page and run it in interactive mode by using the process shown in Example 16-28.

Example 16-28 *Pulling the Docker PowerShell Container*

```
~ » docker pull mcr.microsoft.com/powershell
Using default tag: latest
latest: Pulling from powershell
7b1a6ab2e44d: Pull complete
f738ed9de711: Pull complete
68dfbdc8ea02: Pull complete
501a0230e302: Pull complete
Digest: sha256:bbf28e97eb6ecfcaa8b1e80bdc2700b443713f7dfac3cd648bfd3254007995e2
Status: Downloaded newer image for mcr.microsoft.com/powershell:latest
mcr.microsoft.com/powershell:latest

~ » docker run -it mcr.microsoft.com/powershell
PowerShell 7.2.0
Copyright (c) Microsoft Corporation.

https://aka.ms/powershell
Type 'help' to get help.

PS />
```

When the container is running in interactive mode, the process to install the UCS PowerTool is the same within the container as it would be in a bare-metal OS, as seen in Example 16-29.

Example 16-29 *Installing the UCS PowerTool into the Running Docker PowerShell Container*

```
PS /> Install-Module -Name Cisco.UCSManager

Untrusted repository
You are installing the modules from an untrusted repository. If you trust this
repository, change its InstallationPolicy value by running the Set-PSRepository cmd-
let. Are
you sure you want to install the modules from 'PSGallery'?
[Y] Yes  [A] Yes to All  [N] No  [L] No to All  [S] Suspend  [?] Help (default is
"N"): y
```

After the prompt to install the module, you may be prompted to accept several different license agreements. After you accept them, you can use the UCS PowerTool to work with the UCSM API. First, you must import the module, and then you must establish a connection to the UCSM, as shown in Example 16-30.

Example 16-30 *Connecting to a UCSM Instance Using UCS PowerTool*

```
PS /> Import-Module Cisco.UCSManager
PS /> Connect-Ucs -Name 10.10.20.40

cmdlet Connect-Ucs at command pipeline position 1
Supply values for the following parameters:
Credential
User: ucspe
Password for user ucspe: *****


NumPendingConfigs             : 0
Ucs                           : UCSPE-10-10-20-40
Cookie                        : 1638934478/e08f56e8-f796-49c8-8496-e4760882c6d0
Domains                       : org-root
LastUpdateTime                : 12/8/2021 3:35:28 AM
Name                          : 10.10.20.40
NoSsl                         : False
NumWatchers                   : 0
Port                          : 443
Priv                          : {aaa, admin, ext-lan-config, ext-lan-policy…}
PromptOnCompleteTransaction   : False
Proxy                         :
RefreshPeriod                 : 600
SessionId                     :
TransactionInProgress         : False
Uri                           : https://10.10.20.40
```

```
UserName                     : ucspe
Version                      : 4.0(4c)
VirtualIpv4Address           : 10.10.20.40
WatchThreadStatus            : None


PS />
```

When you're connected to the UCS, you are able to perform all standard CRUD operations. However, to compare similar examples, continue gathering **topSystem** data. Gathering the same information is simple enough because there is a noun built for most classIDs within the PowerTool, as shown in Example 16-31.

Example 16-31 *Querying the* **topSystem** *MO Using UCS PowerTool*

```
PS /> Get-UcsTopSystem


Address        : 10.10.20.40
CurrentTime    : 2021-12-08T03:37:04.720
Descr          :
Ipv6Addr       : ::
Mode           : cluster
Name           : UCSPE-10-10-20-40
Owner          :
Sacl           :
Site           :
SystemUpTime   : 05:10:29:44
Ucs            : UCSPE-10-10-20-40
Dn             : sys
Rn             : sys
Status         :
XtraProperty   : {}
```


It's also possible to extract the raw XML data, in addition to the formatted table of data, by using the **-Xml** switch, with results similar to those shown in Example 16-32.

Example 16-32 **topSystem** *Output in XML Format*

```
PS /> Get-UcsTopSystem -Xml
==>UCSPE-10-10-20-40:<configResolveClass classId="topSystem" cookie="1638934478/
e08f56e8-f796-49c8-8496-e4760882c6d0" inHierarchical="false" />
<==UCSPE-10-10-20-40: <configResolveClass cookie="1638934478/e08f56e8-f796-49c8-
8496-e4760882c6d0" response="yes" classId="topSystem"> <outConfigs>  <topSys-
tem address="10.10.20.40" currentTime="2021-12-08T03:38:58.207" descr="" dn="sys"
ipv6Addr="::" mode="cluster" name="UCSPE-10-10-20-40" owner="" site="" systemUp-
Time="05:10:31:38"/> </outConfigs> </configResolveClass>
```

```
Address       : 10.10.20.40
CurrentTime   : 2021-12-08T03:38:58.207
Descr         :
Ipv6Addr      : ::
Mode          : cluster
Name          : UCSPE-10-10-20-40
Owner         :
Sacl          :
Site          :
SystemUpTime  : 05:10:31:38
Ucs           : UCSPE-10-10-20-40
Dn            : sys
Rn            : sys
Status        :
XtraProperty  : {}
```

By piping the command output to the **Select-Object** command, you can print only the desired fields of information (similar to accessing the specific methods within the Python SDK):

```
PS /> Get-UcsTopSystem | Select-Object Name


Name
----
UCSPE-10-10-20-40
```

It is also possible to query specific paths within the API. All the filters and query parameters are accepted, as well as filtering-specific commands by DN, much like finding a specific compute rack unit within the overall **computeRackUnit** classID, as shown in Example 16-33.

Example 16-33 *Accessing a Specific Server Instance Using the UCS PowerTool*

```
PS /> Get-UcsRackUnit -dn sys/rack-unit-10


AdminPower                    : policy
AdminState                    : in-service
AssetTag                      :
AssignedToDn                  :
Association                   : none
Availability                  : available
AvailableMemory               : 49152
CheckPoint                    : discovered
ConnPath                      : {A, B}
ConnStatus                    : {A, B}
Descr                         :
Discovery                     : complete
DiscoveryStatus               :
```

```
EnclosureId                   : 0
FanSpeedConfigStatus          :
FanSpeedPolicyFault           : no
Id                            : 10
KmipFault                     : no
KmipFaultDescription          :
Lc                            : discovered
LcTs                          : 1970-01-01T00:00:00.000
LocalId                       :
LowVoltageMemory              : not-applicable
ManagingInst                  : A
MemorySpeed                   : not-applicable
MfgTime                       : not-applicable
Model                         : HX220C-M5SX
Name                          :
NumOf40GAdaptorsWithOldFw     : 0
NumOf40GAdaptorsWithUnknownFw : 0
NumOfAdaptors                 : 2
NumOfCores                    : 16
NumOfCoresEnabled             : 16
NumOfCpus                     : 2
NumOfEthHostIfs               : 0
NumOfFcHostIfs                : 0
NumOfThreads                  : 16
OperPower                     : off
OperPwrTransSrc               : unknown
OperQualifier                 :
OperQualifierReason           : N/A
OperState                     : unassociated
Operability                   : operable
OriginalUuid                  : 1b4e28ba-2fa1-11d2-e00a-b9a761bde3fb
PartNumber                    :
PhysicalSecurity              : chassis-open
PolicyLevel                   : 0
PolicyOwner                   : local
Presence                      : equipped
Revision                      : 0
Sacl                          :
Serial                        : RK93
ServerId                      : 10
SlotId                        : 0
StorageOperQualifier          : unknown
TotalMemory                   : 49152
UsrLbl                        :
```

16

```
Uuid                       : 1b4e28ba-2fa1-11d2-e00a-b9a761bde3fb
Vendor                     : Cisco Systems Inc
VersionHolder              : no
VethStatus                 : A,B
Vid                        : 0
Ucs                        : UCSPE-10-10-20-40
Dn                         : sys/rack-unit-10
Rn                         : rack-unit-10
Status                     :
XtraProperty               : {}
```

Finally, when the interaction is complete, it is good programmatic practice to close the connection with the UCSM:

```
PS /> Disconnect-Ucs


Ucs        : UCSPE-10-10-20-40
InCookie   : 1638937107/e815357b-1047-49ab-8620-27b6e78a41c7
Name       : 10.10.20.40
OutStatus  : success
SessionId  :
Uri        : https://10.10.20.40
Version    : 4.0(4c)
```

Additional UCS Manager Programmability Resources

Cisco DevNet maintains a comprehensive library of Learning Labs to help you understand the UCS Python SDK and the UCS PowerTool:

- **Introduction to the UCS Python SDK:** https://developer.cisco.com/learning/modules/ucs-python-sdk-introduction
- **Introduction to the UCS PowerTool:** https://developer.cisco.com/learning/modules/ucs-powertool-introduction
- **Intermediate PowerTool and Python SDK:** https://developer.cisco.com/learning/modules/ucs-programmability-intermediate

DNA Center

The Cisco DNA Center solution is the controller for enterprise fabric deployments. It serves as the follow-on management solution from Prime Infrastructure. DNA Center provides configuration management, software image management, performance and fault monitoring, and inventory tracking. Traditional route/switch and wireless inventory can be managed. DNA Center serves as an on-premises management solution with open and extensible APIs that complement your intent-based networking (IBN) requirements.

The DNA Center APIs span provisioning, monitoring, performance, and inventory functions and are generally broken into Intent and Integration APIs, Event and Notification Webhooks, and a multivendor SDK, as shown in Figure 16-35.

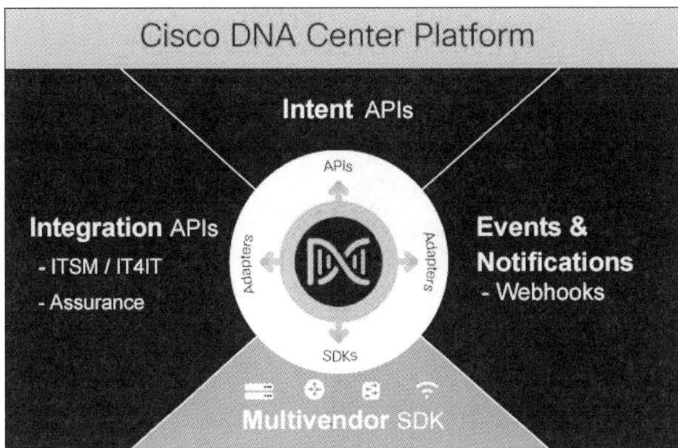

Figure 16-35 *Cisco DNA Center Platform*

The northbound Intent API provides functional capabilities of the DNA Center platform related to policy-based abstraction of business intent. The RESTful API provides GET, POST, PUT, and DELETE operations and uses JSON-structured data. The obligatory authentication function provides for a security token that aligns privileges to the REST API user. The remaining categories are aligned to inventory, provisioning, monitoring, and software maintenance functions, as shown in the Postman representation in Figure 16-36.

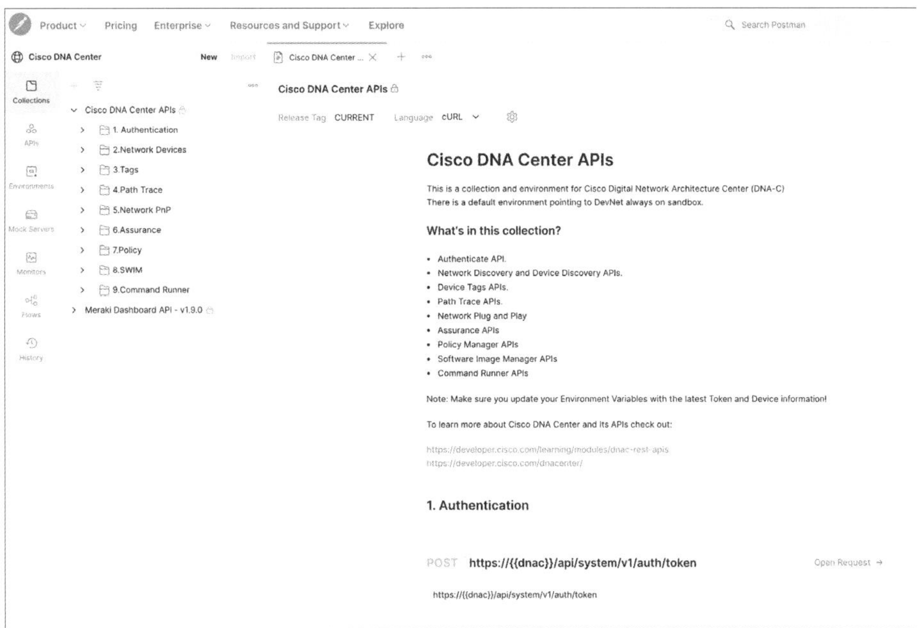

Figure 16-36 *Cisco DNA Center API Documentation from Postman*

The APIs and Python SDK are useful for custom application development, extracting network and service information, provisioning, and software maintenance.

Enabling API/SDK Access to DNA Center

To use the DNA Center API or Python SDK, you must first ensure the REST API feature is enabled. Within the DNA Center portal, navigate to the upper-right menu gadget (which appears as three parallel, horizontal lines). Next, select Platform and then Manage. Figures 16-37 through 16-39 show this progression.

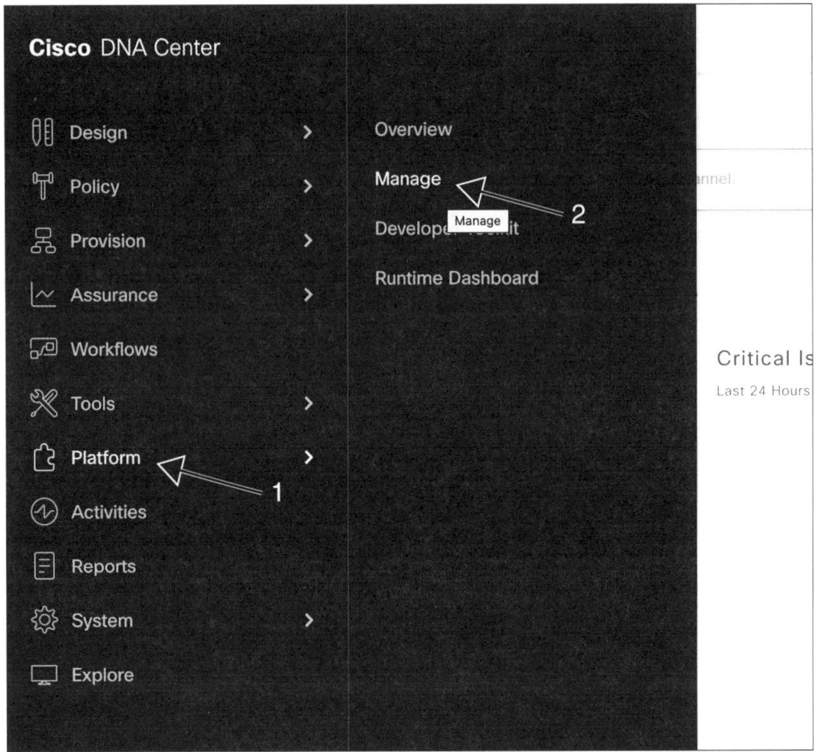

Figure 16-37 *Cisco DNA Center Platform > Manage*

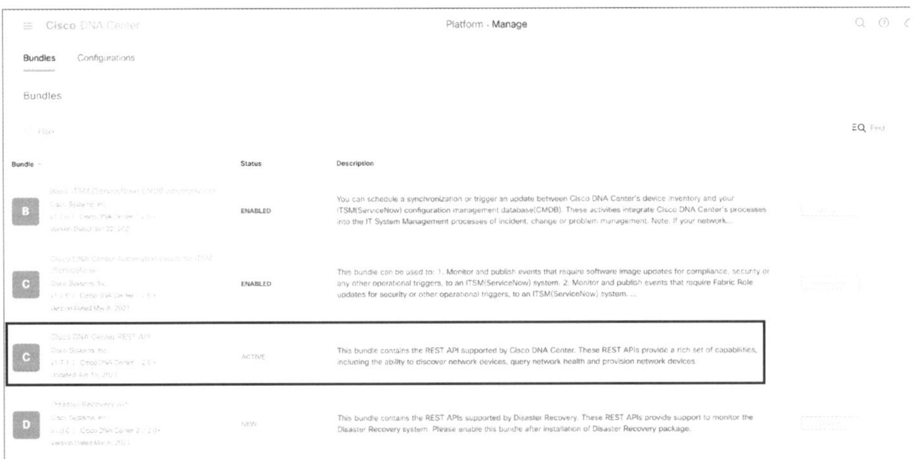

Figure 16-38 *Cisco DNA Center REST API Bundle*

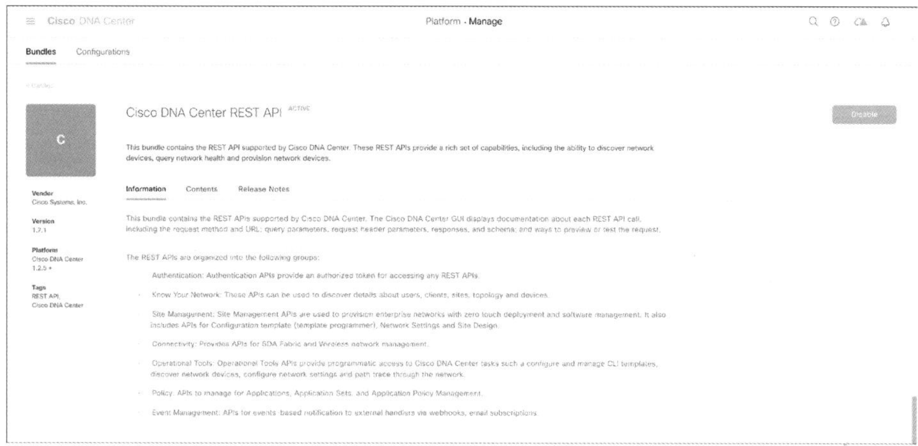

Figure 16-39 *Cisco DNA Center REST API Bundle Documentation*

If the Cisco DNA Center REST API feature does not show ACTIVE, you can turn it on from the Bundles page (shown in Figure 16-38) by clicking the Enable button.

DNA Center API Documentation

The latest DNA Center API is officially documented at https://developer.cisco.com/docs/dna-center/. At the time of this writing, v2.2.3 is the latest. Note that since v2.2.2 of the API, there are now generic function methods separated from software-defined access (SDA) methods.

The northbound Intent API authentication domain provides security and aligns privileges to REST API user accounts.

The Know Your Network domain provides access to information about clients, sites, topology, devices, and issues. Site Management methods include Site Design, Network Settings, Software Image Management (sometimes called SWIM), Device Onboarding (sometimes called Plug and Play, or PnP), and Configuration Templates. Connectivity methods enable you to configure and manage fabric wired and non-fabric wireless networks. Operational tasks and tools extend functionality of

- **Command Runner:** Supports CLI command retrieval and execution
- **Network Discovery:** Enables you to execute network inventory scans
- **Path Trace:** Provides flow analysis between two endpoints in the network
- **Tasks:** Enables you to initiate activities via an API request, including status and completion results
- **Tags:** Assigns named attributes to devices for ease of searching

Policy management aligns business intent in a simplified representation to network- or device-specific configurations that account for device type, operating system, and network role/function.

Event Management provides custom notification functions when specific alerts are triggered in DNA Assurance, configuration management, or software image management events.

On the southbound perspective, Multivendor Support is provided through an SDK allowing DNA Center to manage third-party devices.

Events and Notifications are supported eastbound to offer notification handling with other IT Service Management systems.

Finally, westbound Integration API capabilities address the need to glue DNA Center together with other management tools in the broader IT Service Management ecosystem.

The DevNet team provides many Learning Labs that can familiarize you with the API. There is also a DevNet Sandbox Lab for accessing an always-on environment useful for training when you don't have an existing DNA Center environment or prefer not to use your own. You can access this link at https://devnetsandbox.cisco.com/RM/Topology and enter **dna** in the search box to see the current lab catalog. The catalog is shown in Figure 16-40.

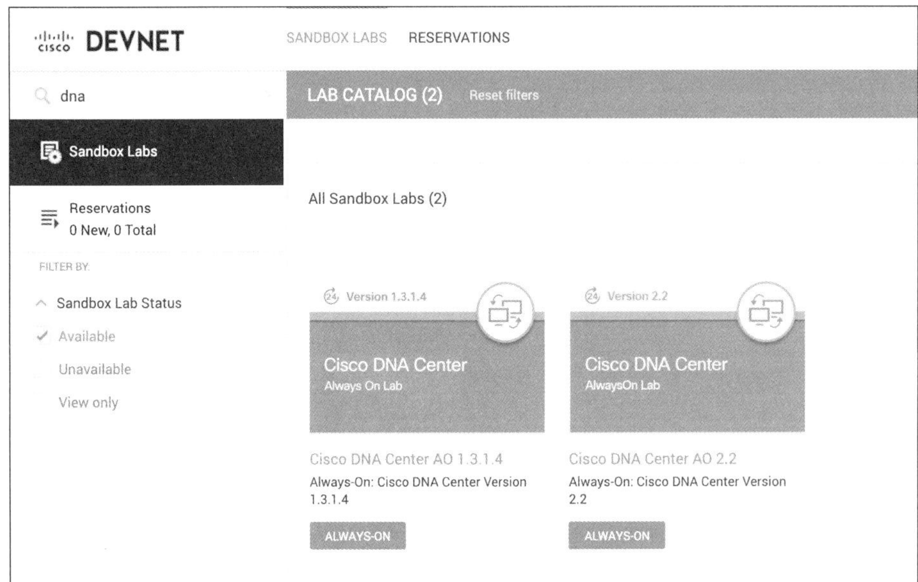

Figure 16-40 *Cisco DevNet Sandbox Labs for DNA Center*

The DNA Center REST API requires BASIC access authentication, depending on Base64 encoding of the username and password concatenated with a colon (:). For example, with the username **Aladdin** and password **open sesame**, Base64-encoding the string '**Aladdin:open sesame**' would provide

```
QWxhZGRpbjpvcGVuIHNlc2FtZQ==
```

Therefore, the authorization HTTP header you use is

```
Authorization: Basic QWxhZGRpbjpvcGVuIHNlc2FtZQ==
```

To build the Base64 authorization string on Windows, you install OpenSSL and use the following instructions, or obtain a Base64-encoding utility (preferably an offline one!).

To build the Base64 authorization string on Mac/Linux, you use built-in openssl binaries and execute

```
echo -n 'USERNAME:PASSWORD' | openssl base64
```

A helpful resource is the Postman collection, which allows you to import public API resources into a common utility that is popular with software developers. You can access the Postman collection and import it into your Postman environment at https://www.postman.com/ciscodevnet/workspace/cisco-dna-center/collection/382059-634a2adf-f673-42eb-8c36-290f38e37971?ctx=documentation. (Because that's a monster URL, a QR code representation is provided in the "References" section at the end of the chapter.)

Figure 16-41 shows the organization of the DNA Center REST API, as described earlier.

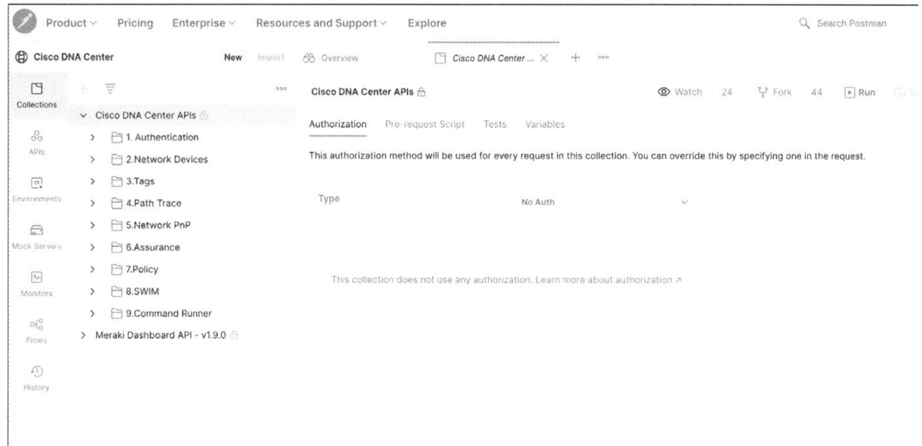

Figure 16-41 *Cisco DNA Center Postman Collection*

While the web-based Postman is useful for cloud-based endpoints, you may find a need for a local, inside network instance on your laptop. If you highlight the Cisco DNA Center APIs heading and click the ellipsis icon (...), you find an Export option that extracts the Postman collection to a JSON file. The JSON file can then be imported into your Postman app. Figure 16-42 shows this result. You can further navigate into the Authentication POST request.

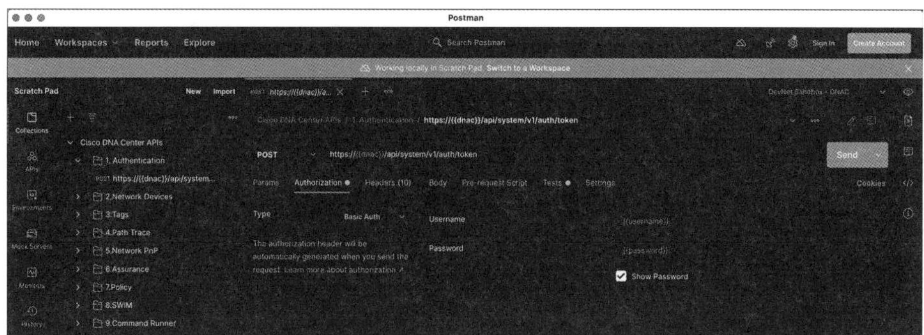

Figure 16-42 *Cisco DNA Center Postman Collection Inside Postman App*

Several Postman environment variables are used. They need to be reconciled for the collection to be used. To do so, you create a new environment by clicking the Environments menu option from the left navigation panel. Click the plus (+) icon in that fly-out menu option to create a new environment. Fill in the environment settings as shown in Figure 16-43.

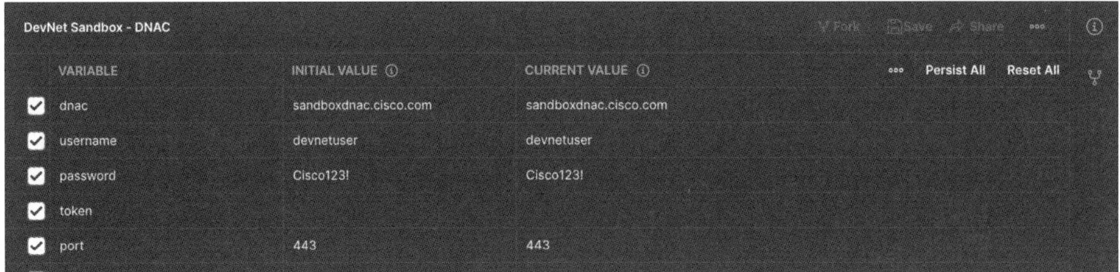

Figure 16-43 *Postman Environment Settings for Cisco DNA Center on DevNet Sandbox Lab*

The settings in Figure 16-43 are for the DevNet Always On DNAC 2.2 Sandbox. Feel free to use it for your education or create another environment with settings relevant to your DNA Center. As you hover over the {{variable}} entries, you should note that Postman shows a pop-up with the variable resolved.

If you return to the Authentication request and click the Send button (on the right), note the completion of a request for an API token. The Tests tab has been filled with simple JavaScript code to extract the API response and create a new token environment variable. If you navigate back to the Environment section, you can see the new entry.

A nice feature of Postman is the Translate to Code feature. Along the right navigation column, the </> icon represents this feature. Click this icon to create a code snippet. A Python-Requests version is suggested and results in the code shown in Example 16-34.

Example 16-34 *Default Postman Translate to Code Output*

```
import requests

url = "https://sandboxdnac.cisco.com/api/system/v1/auth/token"

payload = ""
headers = {
  'Authorization': 'Basic ZGV2bmV0dXNlcjpDaXNjbzEyMyE='
}

response = requests.request("POST", url, headers=headers, data=payload)

print(response.text)
```

Because we prefer more secure coding practices, we suggest that you do *not* put credentials and authorization codes inside your script. The possibility of posting this into an open GitHub repository is a risk too great! So, we suggest the following method: put your username and password in shell environment variables and tweak the script to read them. Here is an example providing similar functionality to the Postman generic code snippet but with a touch better security:

```
$ export DNAC_USER=devnetuser
$ export DNAC_USERPASSWORD=Cisco123!
```

The full script is shown in Example 16-35.

Example 16-35 *A More Refined Python Script for DNA Center as Template*

```
import requests
import os
import base64

url = "https://sandboxdnac.cisco.com/api/system/v1/auth/token"

# Get environment variables
USER = os.getenv('DNAC_USER')
PASSWORD = os.environ.get('DNAC_USERPASSWORD')

payload = ""

response = requests.request("POST", url,  auth=HTTPBasicAuth(USER, PASSWORD),
data=payload)

print(response.text)
```


Running the script results in the following.

```
(.venv) sre@pythonserver DEVCOR % python dnac-getauth.py
{"Token":"eyJhbGciOiJSUzI1NiIsInR5cCI6IkpXVCJ9..."}
```

You now have a template for a script to do other DNA Center REST API work.

DNA Center SDK Documentation

DNA Center's Python SDK is an easy-to-use solution that relieves you of routine coding tasks regarding API authentication, data encoding, pagination, rate limiting, and error handling. The SDK is community supported and is shared from the PyPI project or GitHub from the following URLs:

https://pypi.org/project/dnacentersdk/

https://github.com/cisco-en-programmability/dnacentersdk

Understanding the foundational API resources is important and useful. It is simplified in using tools like Postman; however, you will find that the SDK provides even more benefits. Because the documentation is extensive and accessible, SDK use is encouraged. You can find the authoritative docs for the DNA Center SDK at https://dnacentersdk.readthedocs.io/en/latest/.

You can find additional helpful guidance on DevNet at https://developer.cisco.com/docs/dna-center/#!python-sdk-getting-started/pip-install.

For purposes of this example, we consider the latest version, 2.4.1, released December 1, 2021. To get started, set up your Python environment to a minimum of Python v3.6 (released December 2016). As of Fall 2021, Python 3.10 is the latest release. Using a recent release is recommended, but if you have a current environment at version 3.6 or higher, that is sufficient. Also, consider using a virtual environment (venv) when setting up your project.

The quick install method uses the PyPi project to obtain the **dnacentersdk** package, as shown in Example 16-36.

Example 16-36 *Creating a Cisco DNA Center SDK Project*

```
myserver Python % mkdir MyDNACProject
myserver Python % cd MyDNACProject
myserver MyDNACProject % python3 -m venv .venv
myserver MyDNACProject % source .venv/bin/activate
(.venv) myserver MyDNACProject % pip install dnacentersdk
Collecting dnacentersdk
  Downloading dnacentersdk-2.4.1-py3-none-any.whl (2.4 MB)
     |████████████████████████████████| 2.4 MB 2.7 MB/s
Collecting requests<3.0.0,>=2.25.1
  Using cached requests-2.26.0-py2.py3-none-any.whl (62 kB)
Collecting requests-toolbelt<0.10.0,>=0.9.1
  Downloading requests_toolbelt-0.9.1-py2.py3-none-any.whl (54 kB)
     |████████████████████████████████| 54 kB 9.6 MB/s
Collecting fastjsonschema<3.0.0,>=2.14.5
  Downloading fastjsonschema-2.15.1-py3-none-any.whl (21 kB)
Collecting future<0.19.0,>=0.18.2
  Downloading future-0.18.2.tar.gz (829 kB)
     |████████████████████████████████| 829 kB 4.3 MB/s
Collecting idna<4,>=2.5
  Using cached idna-3.3-py3-none-any.whl (61 kB)
Collecting urllib3<1.27,>=1.21.1
  Using cached urllib3-1.26.7-py2.py3-none-any.whl (138 kB)
Collecting certifi>=2017.4.17
  Using cached certifi-2021.10.8-py2.py3-none-any.whl (149 kB)
Collecting charset-normalizer~=2.0.0
  Downloading charset_normalizer-2.0.9-py3-none-any.whl (39 kB)
Using legacy 'setup.py install' for future, since package 'wheel' is not installed.
Installing collected packages: urllib3, idna, charset-normalizer, certifi, requests,
requests-toolbelt, future, fastjsonschema, dnacentersdk
    Running setup.py install for future ... done
Successfully installed certifi-2021.10.8 charset-normalizer-2.0.9 dnacentersdk-2.4.1
fastjsonschema-2.15.1 future-0.18.2 idna-3.3 requests-2.26.0 requests-toolbelt-0.9.1
urllib3-1.26.7
WA
```

Now your environment is ready for the follow-on SDK examples. The next section addresses authorization. If you haven't already covered the DNA Center REST API enablement steps, go back to the "Enabling API/SDK Access to DNA Center" section. You must ensure that the feature is enabled and that you have a user (with password) defined.

SDK Authorization

The DNA Center SDK enables you to obtain the username and password credentials via environment variables, which is recommended over putting your credentials inside your Python script. For example, if you're using the DevNet Always On Sandbox Lab for DNA Center, these would be the applicable environment variables:

```
export DNA_CENTER_USERNAME=devnetuser

export DNA_CENTER_PASSWORD=Cisco123!

export DNA_CENTER_BASE_URL=https://sandboxdnac.cisco.com:443
```

Now you can build a sample Python script that uses the SDK. You can reference the API docs from the community portal to see the various functions and options. At the time of this writing, this link refers to the latest API information:

https://dnacentersdk.readthedocs.io/en/latest/api/api.html#dnacenterapi-v2-2-3-3

Navigating down to the Devices section would be a safe approach and would result in practical information you might want to obtain for putting into an asset management system. Specifically, you can use the **devices.get_device_list()** method for this first approach. Now, create the Python script in Example 16-37 as getDNACdevicelist.py in your virtual environment.

Example 16-37 *Python Script to Extract Cisco DNA Center Devices*

```
from dnacentersdk import DNACenterAPI
import pprint

pp = pprint.PrettyPrinter(indent=4)

api = DNACenterAPI()

my_devices = api.devices.get_device_list()
for device in my_devices.response:
    pp.pprint(device)
```

This simple script imports the necessary libraries: the DNA Center SDK and pretty print. It configures the pretty print feature to indent four spaces. You create the DNA Center session, passing authentication credentials via the environment variables previously set. You then call the devices group **get_device_list()** and store the list into a **my_devices** variable. Finally, you pretty print out the list device by device.

Now you can execute the script shown in Example 16-38.

Example 16-38 *Executing and Observing getDNACdevicelist.py*

```
(.venv) myserver MyDNACProject % python getDNACdevicelist.py
{   'apEthernetMacAddress': None,
    'apManagerInterfaceIp': '',
    'associatedWlcIp': '',
    'bootDateTime': '2021-07-09 13:31:59',
    'collectionInterval': 'Global Default',
    'collectionStatus': 'Managed',
    'description': 'Cisco Controller Wireless Version:8.5.140.0',
    'deviceSupportLevel': 'Supported',
    'errorCode': None,
    'errorDescription': None,
    'family': 'Wireless Controller',
    'hostname': 'c3504.abc.inc',
    'id': '6b741b27-f7e7-4470-b6fc-d5168cc*****',
    'instanceTenantId': '5e8e896e4d4add00ca2*****',
    'instanceUuid': '6b741b27-f7e7-4470-b6fc-d5168cc*****',
    'interfaceCount': '0',
    'inventoryStatusDetail': '<status><general code="SUCCESS"/></status>',
    'lastUpdateTime': 1639144079982,
    'lastUpdated': '2021-12-10 13:47:59',
    'lineCardCount': '0',
    'lineCardId': '',
    'location': None,
    'locationName': None,
    'macAddress': 'ac:4a:56:6c:**:**',
    'managedAtleastOnce': True,
    'managementIpAddress': '10.10.20.51',
    'managementState': 'Managed',
    'memorySize': '3735302144',
    'platformId': 'AIR-CT3504-K9',
    'reachabilityFailureReason': '',
    'reachabilityStatus': 'Reachable',
    'role': 'ACCESS',
    'roleSource': 'AUTO',
    'serialNumber': 'FOL250*****',
    'series': 'Cisco 3500 Series Wireless LAN Controller',
    'snmpContact': '',
    'snmpLocation': '',
    'softwareType': 'Cisco Controller',
    'softwareVersion': '8.5.140.0',
    'tagCount': '0',
    'tunnelUdpPort': '16666',
    'type': 'Cisco 3504 Wireless LAN Controller',
    'upTime': '154 days, 0:16:55.00',
    'uptimeSeconds': 13312136,
```

```
    'waasDeviceMode': None}
{   'apEthernetMacAddress': None,
    'apManagerInterfaceIp': '',
    'associatedWlcIp': '',
    'bootDateTime': '2021-10-28 18:10:20',
    'collectionInterval': 'Global Default',
    'collectionStatus': 'Managed',
    'description': 'Cisco IOS Software [Amsterdam], Catalyst L3 Switch '
                   'Software (CAT9K_IOSXE), Version 17.3.3, RELEASE SOFTWARE '
                   '(fc7) Technical Support: http://www.cisco.com/techsupport '
                   'Copyright (c) 1986-2021 by Cisco Systems, Inc. Compiled '
                   'Thu 04-Mar-21 12:32 by mcpre',
    'deviceSupportLevel': 'Supported',
    'errorCode': None,
    'errorDescription': None,
    'family': 'Switches and Hubs',
    'hostname': 'leaf1.abc.inc',
    'id': 'aa0a5258-3e6f-422f-9c4e-9c196db*****',
    'instanceTenantId': '5e8e896e4d4add00ca2*****',
    'instanceUuid': 'aa0a5258-3e6f-422f-9c4e-9c196db*****',
    'interfaceCount': '0',
    'inventoryStatusDetail': '<status><general code="SUCCESS"/></status>',
    'lastUpdateTime': 1639144220380,
    'lastUpdated': '2021-12-10 13:50:20',
    'lineCardCount': '0',
```


So, you can see the SDK simplified a lot of actions behind the scenes: authentication, data encoding, error handling, and rate limiting. You could, of course, go directly to the REST API, but you would still need to perform these functions. The SDK reduces the code requirements for developers, like you.

AppDynamics

AppDynamics (a.k.a. AppD) is a cloud-enabling, full-stack application performance monitoring (APM) solution. It is used in a multicloud world to improve performance through visibility and detection of issues via real-time monitoring. AppD provides end-to-end visibility of application traffic, enabling developers and architects to deploy and manage solutions with assurance. It also uses machine learning in executing automated root-cause analysis. AppD agents in your environment discover and track individual transactions with servers, databases, and other application dependencies. The user experience is tracked and can be attributed to specific code blocks, database calls, name resolution, or other dependencies. The insight can be mapped to business metrics, providing deep insight into impact and severity.

As a rich APM solution, AppD has an extensive API. We cover some of the basics for authentication and basic information gathering, but a whole book could be written about the depth of its API. The AppDynamic APIs are documented at https://docs.appdynamics.com/21.12/en/extend-appdynamics/appdynamics-apis.

The system provides for short-term, API-generated access tokens that expire within five minutes by default or for longer-term, UI-generated temporary access tokens that can be defined by the administrator for hour, day, or year expirations. You can define your API clients by logging in to your AppDynamics portal and accessing the gear icon in the upper-right corner. From the drop-down navigation panel, select Administration. Then on the left tab option, select API Clients. Next, click the Create (or +) button and define your client name with an optional description. Click the Generate Secret button and the copy gadget to the left of it. Make sure to retain this client secret in a secure password manager. Furthermore, click the Add (+) button under Roles and select the appropriate roles for the API user. Finally, click Save in the upper-right corner. Figure 16-44 depicts the steps just described.

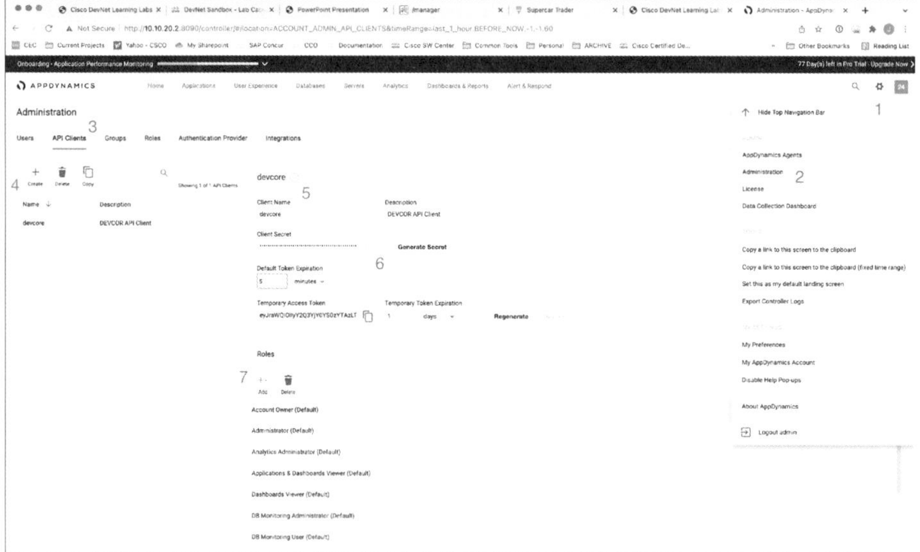

Figure 16-44 *Generating a Temporary Access Token in AppDynamics*

Authentication with the longer-term, WebUI-generated client secret is done as described in the next process.

A POST operation is created to the controller with the following characteristics:

- **URL:** https://<CONTROLLER_HOST>:8090/controller/api/oauth/access_token
- **Header Content-Type:** 'application/vnd.appd.cntrl+protobuf;v=1'
- **Payload Data:** x-www-form-urlencoded of

```
grant_type=client_credentials

client_id=<APIUserName>@<CustomerName>

client_secret=<ClientSecret>
```

An example curl utility equivalent would be

```
curl -X POST -H "Content-Type: application/vnd.appd.
cntrl+protobuf;v=1" "http://<CONTROLLER_HOST>:8090/controller/
```

```
api/oauth/access_token" -d 'grant_type=client_
credentials&client_id=<APIUserName>@<CustomerName>&client_
secret=<ClientSecure>'
```

The output results in the following:

```
appserver[centos]$ curl -X POST -H "Content-Type: application/
vnd.appd.cntrl+protobuf;v=1" "http://****:8090/controller/api/
oauth/access_token" -d 'grant_type=client_credentials&client_
id=devcore@customer1&client_secret=fa42bc81-f3a8-4cbd-
9ac7-******'

{"access_token": "eyJraWQiOiIyY2Q3YjY0YS0zYTAzLTRiNzMtYmN
lMS02MjgwZTVmMzAyMTMiLCJhbGciOiJIUzI1NiJ9.****M",
"expires_in": 300}

appserver[centos]$
```

A Postman utility equivalent is provided in Figure 16-45.

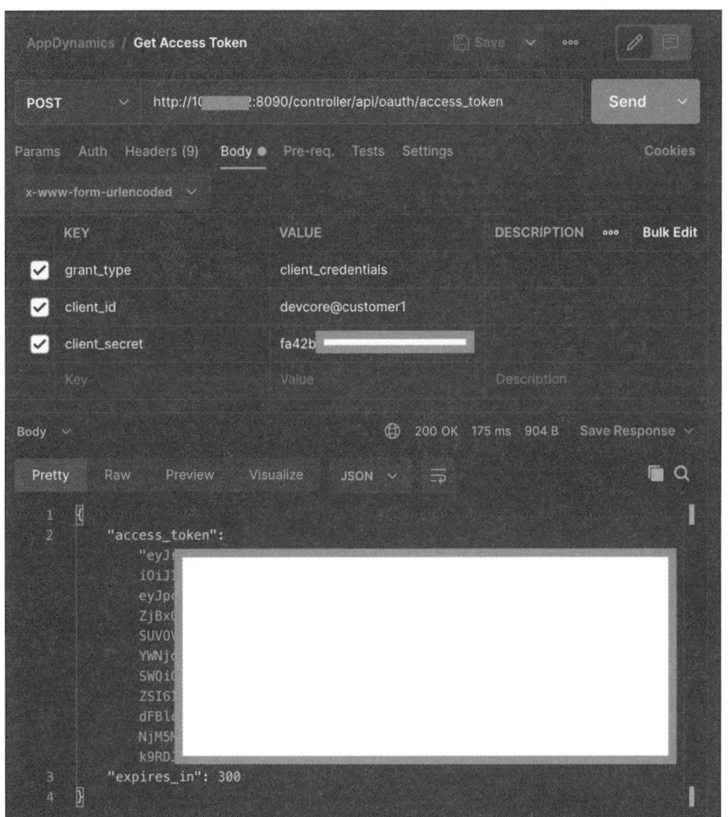

Figure 16-45 *Using Postman to Generate AppDynamics Access Token*

Additionally, this Python script would be a helpful baseline for progressing to other API methods. You can set the following environment variables to perform a more secure authentication method:

```
$ export APPD_CONTROLLER=10.10.20.2:8090
$ export APPD_API_USER=devcore
$ export APPD_CUSTOMER=customer1
$ export APPD_CLIENT_SECRET=fa42bc81-f3a8-4cbd-9ac7-cf9766bcd93d
```

The full script is shown in Example 16-39.

Example 16-39 *Python Script to Generate an AppDynamics Access Token*

```
import os
import requests

# Get environment variables
APPD_CONTROLLER = os.getenv('APPD_CONTROLLER')
APPD_API_USER = os.getenv('APPD_API_USER')
APPD_CUSTOMER = os.getenv('APPD_CUSTOMER')
APPD_CLIENT_SECRET = os.getenv("APPD_CLIENT_SECRET")

url = f'http://{APPD_CONTROLLER}/controller/api/oauth/access_token'

payload = f'grant_type=client_credentials&client_id={APPD_API_USER}%40{APPD_
CUSTOMER}&client_secret={APPD_CLIENT_SECRET}'
headers = {
             'Content-Type': 'application/x-www-form-urlencoded'
          }

response = requests.request("POST", url, headers=headers, data=payload)
data = response.json()
access_token = data['access_token']

print(access_token)
```

This script, when executed, generates the following:

```
appserver[centos]$ python3 getAppDToken.py
eyJraWQiOiIyY2Q3YjY0YS0zYTAzLTRiNzMtYmNlMS02MjgwZTVmMzAyMTMiLCJhbG-
ciOiJIUzI1NiJ9.****
appserver[centos]$
```

With a slight addition to the authentication template, as shown in Example 16-40, you can move on to getting all the web applications that AppDynamics is currently monitoring.

Example 16-40 *Python Script to Get AppDynamics Applications*

```
import os
import requests

# Get environment variables
APPD_CONTROLLER = os.getenv('APPD_CONTROLLER')
APPD_API_USER = os.getenv('APPD_API_USER')
APPD_CUSTOMER = os.getenv('APPD_CUSTOMER')
APPD_CLIENT_SECRET = os.getenv("APPD_CLIENT_SECRET")

url = f'http://{APPD_CONTROLLER}/controller/api/oauth/access_token'

payload = f'grant_type=client_credentials&client_id={APPD_API_USER}%40{APPD_
CUSTOMER}&client_secret={APPD_CLIENT_SECRET}'
headers = {
             'Content-Type': 'application/x-www-form-urlencoded'
          }

response = requests.request("POST", url, headers=headers, data=payload)
data = response.json()
access_token = data['access_token']


url2 = f'http://{APPD_CONTROLLER}/controller/rest/applications'
headers2 = { 'Authorization': 'Bearer ' + access_token }
response2 = requests.request("GET", url2, headers=headers2)
print(response2.text)
```

This script would result in the following simple output:

```
appserver[centos]$ python3 getAppDapplications.py
<applications><application>
  <id>6</id>
  <name>Supercar-Trader</name>
  <accountGuid>2cd7b64a-3a03-4b73-bce1-6280e5f30213</accountGuid>
</application>
</applications>
```

Note the API's default output is XML. If you prefer JSON, you can append the URL with **?output=JSON.**

You can make additional enhancements to this script by using the API to extract the applications involved and the nodes of those applications with detailed information, as shown in Example 16-41. This enhancement may be useful for documentation purposes.

Example 16-41 *Python Script to Get AppDynamics Application Nodes*

```
import os
import requests
import xml.etree.ElementTree as ET

# Get environment variables
APPD_CONTROLLER = os.getenv('APPD_CONTROLLER')
APPD_API_USER = os.getenv('APPD_API_USER')
APPD_CUSTOMER = os.getenv('APPD_CUSTOMER')
APPD_CLIENT_SECRET = os.getenv("APPD_CLIENT_SECRET")

url = f'http://{APPD_CONTROLLER}/controller/api/oauth/access_token'

payload = f'grant_type=client_credentials&client_id={APPD_API_USER}%40{APPD_
CUSTOMER}&client_secret={APPD_CLIENT_SECRET}'
headers = {
             'Content-Type': 'application/x-www-form-urlencoded'
          }

response = requests.request("POST", url, headers=headers, data=payload)
data = response.json()
access_token = data['access_token']


url2 = f'http://{APPD_CONTROLLER}/controller/rest/applications'
headers2 = { 'Authorization': 'Bearer ' + access_token }
response2 = requests.request("GET", url2, headers=headers2)
print(response2.text)

root = ET.ElementTree(ET.fromstring(response2.text))
for app in root.findall('application'):
    appname = app.find('name').text
    print(appname)
    url3 = f'http://{APPD_CONTROLLER}/controller/rest/applications/{appname}/nodes'
    response3 = requests.request("GET", url3, headers=headers2)
    print(response3.text)
```

Executing this script results in the output shown in Example 16-42.

Example 16-42 *Executing and Observing getAppDAppNodes.py*

```
appserver[centos]$ python3 getAppDAppNodes.py
<applications><application>
  <id>6</id>
  <name>Supercar-Trader</name>
  <accountGuid>2cd7b64a-3a03-4b73-bce1-6280e5f30213</accountGuid>
</application>
</applications>
Supercar-Trader
<nodes><node>
  <id>300</id>
  <name>Web-Portal_Node-01</name>
  <type>Other</type>
  <tierId>10</tierId>
  <tierName>Web-Portal</tierName>
  <machineId>301</machineId>
  <machineName>appserver.localdomain</machineName>
  <machineOSType>Linux</machineOSType>
  <machineAgentPresent>false</machineAgentPresent>
  <appAgentPresent>true</appAgentPresent>
  <appAgentVersion>Server Agent #21.11.0.33247 v21.11.0 GA compatible with 4.4.1.0
r7f7d2e9ac67aabc2b2b39b7b6fcf9b071104bf79 release/21.11.0</appAgentVersion>
  <agentType>APP_AGENT</agentType>
</node>
<node>
  <id>302</id>
  <name>Inventory-Services_Node-01</name>
  <type>Other</type>
  <tierId>11</tierId>
  <tierName>Inventory-Services</tierName>
  <machineId>301</machineId>
  <machineName>appserver.localdomain</machineName>
  <machineOSType>Linux</machineOSType>
  <machineAgentPresent>false</machineAgentPresent>
  <appAgentPresent>true</appAgentPresent>
  <appAgentVersion>Server Agent #21.11.0.33247 v21.11.0 GA compatible with 4.4.1.0
r7f7d2e9ac67aabc2b2b39b7b6fcf9b071104bf79 release/21.11.0</appAgentVersion>
  <agentType>APP_AGENT</agentType>
</node>
<node>
  <id>303</id>
  <name>Enquiry-Services_Node-01</name>
  <type>Other</type>
  <tierId>12</tierId>
```

```
  <tierName>Enquiry-Services</tierName>
  <machineId>301</machineId>
  <machineName>appserver.localdomain</machineName>
  <machineOSType>Linux</machineOSType>
  <machineAgentPresent>false</machineAgentPresent>
  <appAgentPresent>true</appAgentPresent>
  <appAgentVersion>Server Agent #21.11.0.33247 v21.11.0 GA compatible with 4.4.1.0
r7f7d2e9ac67aabc2b2b39b7b6fcf9b071104bf79 release/21.11.0</appAgentVersion>
  <agentType>APP_AGENT</agentType>
</node>
```

In this output, you can see a lot of helpful information related to server name, operating system type, whether the AppD agent is installed, and what version, along with other characteristics.

We encourage you to continue to investigate the AppD API for extracting information that may be beneficial to your projects.

Exam Preparation Tasks

As mentioned in the section "How to Use This Book" in the Introduction, you have a couple of choices for exam preparation: Chapter 17, "Final Preparation," and the exam simulation questions on the companion website.

References

URL	QR Code
https://www.postman.com/ciscodevnet/workspace/cisco-dna-center/collection/382059-634a2adf-f673-42eb-8c36-290f38e37971?ctx=documentation	
https://www.postman.com/ciscodevnet/workspace/cisco-devnet-s-public-workspace/collection/8697084-bf06287b-a7f3-4572-a4d5-84f1c652109a?ctx=documentation	
https://documenter.getpostman.com/view/30210/SVfWN6Yc	

URL	QR Code
https://docs.microsoft.com/en-us/powershell/scripting/install/installing-powershell-on-linux?view=powershell-7.2	
https://docs.microsoft.com/en-us/powershell/scripting/install/installing-powershell-on-macos?view=powershell-7.2	
https://docs.microsoft.com/en-us/powershell/scripting/install/installing-powershell-on-windows?view=powershell-7.2	

CHAPTER 17

Final Preparation

The first 16 chapters of this book cover the technologies, protocols, design concepts, and considerations required to be prepared to pass the Developing Applications Using Cisco Core Platforms and APIs v1.0 DevNet Professional 350-901 DEVCOR Exam. Although these chapters supply the detailed information, most people need more preparation than simply reading the first 16 chapters of this book. This chapter details a set of tools and a study plan to help you complete your preparation for the exams.

This short chapter has two main sections. The first section lists the exam preparation tools useful at this point in the study process. The second section lists a suggested study plan now that you have completed all the earlier chapters in this book.

Getting Ready

Here are some important tips to keep in mind to ensure you are ready for this rewarding exam!

- **Build and use a study tracker:** Consider taking the exam objectives shown in each chapter and building yourself a study tracker! This will help ensure you have not missed anything and that you are confident for your exam! As a matter of fact, this book offers a sample Study Planner as a website supplement.
- **Think about your time budget for questions in the exam:** When you do the math, you realize that on average you have one minute per question. Although this does not sound like enough time, realize that many of the questions are very straightforward, and you will take 15 to 30 seconds on those. This builds time for other questions as you take your exam.
- **Watch the clock:** Check in on the time remaining periodically as you are taking the exam. You might even find that you can slow down pretty dramatically as you have built up a nice block of extra time.
- **Get some ear plugs:** The testing center might provide them, but get some just in case and bring them along. There might be other test takers in the center with you, and you do not want to be distracted by their screams. Some people have no issue blocking out the sounds around them, so they never worry about this, but it is an issue for some.
- **Plan your travel time:** Give yourself extra time to find the center and get checked in. Be sure to arrive early. As you test more at that center, you can certainly start cutting it closer time-wise.
- **Get rest:** Most students report success with getting plenty of rest the night before the exam. All-night cram sessions are not typically successful.
- **Bring in valuables but get ready to lock them up:** The testing center will take your phone, your smart watch, your wallet, and other such items. They will provide a secure place for them.

- **Take notes:** You will be given note-taking implements, so do not be afraid to use them. You might try jotting down any questions you struggled with. You then can memorize them at the end of the test by reading your notes over and over again. Make sure to have a pen and paper in the car. You can write down the issues in there just after the exam. After you get home with a pass or fail, you can research those items!

Tools for Final Preparation

This section lists some information about the available tools and how to access the tools.

Pearson Cert Practice Test Engine and Questions on the Website

Register this book to get access to the Pearson IT Certification test engine (software that displays and grades a set of exam-realistic, multiple-choice questions). Using the Pearson Cert Practice Test Engine, you can either study by going through the questions in Study Mode or take a simulated (timed) DevNet Professional 350-901 DEVCOR exam.

The Pearson Test Prep practice test software comes with two full practice exams. These practice tests are available to you either online or as an offline Windows application. To access the practice exams that were developed with this book, please see the instructions in the card inserted in the sleeve in the back of the book. This card includes a unique access code that enables you to activate your exams in the Pearson Test Prep software.

Accessing the Pearson Test Prep Software Online

The online version of this software can be used on any device with a browser and connectivity to the Internet, including personal computer, tablets, and smartphones. To start using your practice exams online, simply follow these steps:

Step 1. Go to http://www.PearsonTestPrep.com.

Step 2. Select **Pearson IT Certification** as your product group.

Step 3. Enter your email/password for your account. If you don't have an account on PearsonITCertification.com or CiscoPress.com, you need to establish one by going to PearsonITCertification.com/join.

Step 4. In the My Products tab, click the **Activate New Product** button.

Step 5. Enter the access code printed on the insert card in the back of your book to activate your product.

Step 6. When the product is listed in your My Products page, click the **Exams** button to launch the exam settings screen and start your exam.

Accessing the Pearson Test Prep Software Offline

If you wish to study offline, you can download and install the Windows version of the Pearson Test Prep software. There is a download link for this software on the book's companion website, or you can just enter this link in your browser:

http://www.pearsonitcertification.com/content/downloads/pcpt/engine.zip

To access the book's companion website and the software, simply follow these steps:

Step 1. Register your book by going to PearsonITCertification.com/register and entering the ISBN: **9780137370443**.

Step 2. Respond to the challenge questions.

Step 3. Go to your account page and select the **Registered Products** tab.

Step 4. Click the **Access Bonus Content** link under the product listing.

Step 5. Click the **Install Pearson Test Prep Desktop Version** link under the Practice Exams section of the page to download the software.

Step 6. When the software finishes downloading, unzip all the files on your computer.

Step 7. Double-click the application file to start the installation, and follow the on-screen instructions to complete the registration.

Step 8. When the installation is complete, launch the application and select the **Activate Exam** button on the My Products tab.

Step 9. Click the **Activate a Product** button in the Activate Product Wizard.

Step 10. Enter the unique access code found on the card in the sleeve in the back of your book and click the **Activate** button.

Step 11. Click **Next** and then the **Finish** button to download the exam data to your application.

Step 12. You can now start using the practice exams by selecting the product and clicking the **Open Exam** button to open the exam settings screen.

Note that the offline and online versions synch together, so saved exams and grade results recorded on one version are available to you on the other as well.

Customizing Your Exams

When you are in the exam settings screen, you can choose to take exams in one of three modes:

- Study Mode
- Practice Exam Mode
- Flash Card Mode

Study Mode enables you to fully customize your exams and review answers as you are taking the exam. This is typically the mode you would use first to assess your knowledge and identify information gaps. Practice Exam Mode locks certain customization options, as it is presenting a realistic exam experience. Use this mode when you are preparing to test your exam-readiness. Flash Card Mode strips out the answers and presents you with only the question stem. This mode is great for late-stage preparation when you really want to challenge yourself to provide answers without the benefit of seeing multiple-choice options. This mode does not provide the detailed score reports that the other two modes do, so you should not use it if you are trying to identify knowledge gaps.

In addition to these three modes, you can select the source of your questions. You can choose to take exams that cover all of the chapters, or you can narrow your selection to just a single chapter or the chapters that make up specific parts in the book. All chapters are selected by default. If you want to narrow your focus to individual chapters, simply deselect all the chapters and then select only those on which you wish to focus in the Objectives area.

You can also select the exam banks on which to focus. Each exam bank comes complete with a full exam of questions that cover topics in every chapter. The two exams printed in the book are available to you as well as two additional exams of unique questions. You can have the test engine serve up exams from all four banks or just from one individual bank by selecting the desired banks in the exam bank area.

There are several other customizations you can make to your exam from the exam settings screen, such as the time of the exam, the number of questions served up, whether to randomize questions and answers, whether to show the number of correct answers for multiple-answer questions, or whether to serve up only specific types of questions. You can also create custom test banks by selecting only questions that you have marked or questions on which you have added notes.

Updating Your Exams

If you are using the online version of the Pearson Test Prep software, you should always have access to the latest version of the software as well as the exam data. If you are using the Windows desktop version, every time you launch the software, it checks to see if there are any updates to your exam data and automatically downloads any changes that were made since the last time you used the software. This requires that you are connected to the Internet at the time you launch the software.

Sometimes, due to many factors, the exam data may not fully download when you activate your exam. If you find that figures or exhibits are missing, you may need to manually update your exams.

To update a particular exam you have already activated and downloaded, simply select the **Tools** tab and select the **Update Products** button. Again, this is an issue only with the desktop Windows application.

If you wish to check for updates to the Pearson Test Prep exam engine software, Windows desktop version, simply select the **Tools** tab and select the **Update Application** button. This ensures you are running the latest version of the software engine.

Premium Edition

In addition to the free practice exam provided on the website, you can purchase additional exams with expanded functionality directly from Pearson IT Certification. The Premium Edition of this title contains an additional two full practice exams and an eBook (in both PDF and ePub format). In addition, the Premium Edition title also has remediation for each question to the specific part of the eBook that relates to that question.

Because you have purchased the print version of this title, you can purchase the Premium Edition at a deep discount. There is a coupon code in the book sleeve that contains a one-time-use code and instructions for where you can purchase the Premium Edition.

To view the premium edition product page, go to www.informit.com/title/9780137370344.

Chapter-Ending Review Tools

Chapters 1 through 16 each provide several features in the "Exam Preparation Tasks" section at the end of the chapter. You might have already worked through them in each chapter. It can also be useful to use these tools again as you make your final preparations for the exam.

Suggested Plan for Final Review/Study

This section lists a suggested study plan from the point at which you finish reading through Chapter 16, until you take the Developing Applications Using Cisco Core Platforms and APIs v1.0 DevNet Professional 350-901 DEVCOR Exam. Certainly, you can ignore this plan, use it as is, or just take suggestions from it.

The plan uses two steps:

Step 1. **Review key topics and DIKTA? questions:** You can use the table that lists the key topics in each chapter, or just flip the pages looking for key topics. Also, reviewing the DIKTA? questions from the beginning of the chapter can be helpful.

Step 2. **Use the Pearson Cert Practice Test engine to practice:** The Pearson Cert Practice Test engine can be used to study using a bank of unique exam-realistic questions available only with this book.

Summary

The tools and suggestions listed in this chapter have been designed with one goal in mind: to help you develop the skills required to pass the Developing Applications Using Cisco Core Platforms and APIs v1.0 DevNet Professional 350-901 DEVCOR Exam. This book has been developed from the beginning to not just tell you the facts but to also help you learn how to apply the facts. No matter what your experience level leading up to when you take the exams, it is our hope that the broad range of preparation tools, and even the structure of the book, helps you pass the exam with ease. We hope you do well on the exam!

APPENDIX A

Answers to the "Do I Know This Already?" Questions

Chapter 1

1. D. Software architecture includes functional and business requirements and nonfunctional requirements, which include building blocks and structures. All of these answers relate to this concept.
2. B. Although the synchronous data link control is a real communication protocol created in the 1970s for IBM Mainframe computer connectivity, the correct response here is software development lifecycle. At the time of this writing, social data language controller does not exist.
3. A. Functional requirements define the functionality and business purpose of an application. Answer B is incorrect because high availability is an attribute of the application and is considered part of the nonfunctional requirements. How to develop an application and what programming language to use are not part of the functional requirements.
4. D. Scalability, modularity, and high availability are part of a long list of nonfunctional requirements briefly discussed in this chapter and in more detail in Chapter 2, "Software Quality Attributes."
5. B. Flexibility, speed, and collaboration among the various independent teams are the main characteristics of Agile development.
6. D. The Lean process relies on rapid development and a lot less planning at the early stages of the development cycle. Answers A, B, and C are clear characteristics of the Lean development model.
7. D. DevOps has four metrics for assessing performance. Three are listed here, and the fourth one is mean time to response.
8. C. White-box testing is different from black-box testing in that full knowledge of the system under testing is needed; that's also a requirement of unit testing.
9. D. Code reviewers should be looking at a variety of aspects or concepts related to high-quality code, including functionality, complexity, naming, testability of code, style, and the presence of proper comments and documentation.
10. B. Patterns ensure consistency of coding practices and the approach or context of the solution. They are meant to reduce complexity (not increase it). There are various patterns to choose from, and you should choose one that works well with the context of the architecture you're working on.

Chapter 2

1. D. As you will learn later, nonfunctional requirements, like scalability, availability, and security, define the success of your application, and it is to attract and maintain the user base. The other answers, independently, do not define quality. Quality is a combination of several applicable attributes. A bug-free application with slow access or slow transaction times is not considered high quality because it does not address all predefined quality attributes.
2. D. Functional requirements, in a way, dictate the limitations and measurability of nonfunctional requirements. For example, if you build a globally accessed application to be hosted from a centralized data center in the US, you cannot require transaction times to be less than 50 milliseconds, knowing very well that Internet latency for a user in Europe or Australia is higher than 100 milliseconds.
3. A. It is safe to assume that *nonfunctional requirements* and *quality attributes* are the same. Scalability, availability, flexibility, and other "-ilities" are referred to by software developers.
4. D. These attributes are all qualities of a software application and should clearly be defined and measurable.
5. B. The degree to which a system is operational and accessible when needed for use is how we measure availability. Answers A and C are incorrect because they give half the answer.
6. D. The ISO/IEC 25010 attempts to tabulate the most common quality attributes based on relevance, and all the answers here are correct.
7. C. Whether they are called *chunks* or *blocks* does not matter; the emphasis here is on the interaction among the various blocks and how they each contribute to the big picture.
8. D. When two or more functions are dependent on each other or share functions or datasets, they're closely coupled. Independence or dependence is a form of coupling. In simple terms, *loosely coupled* means there is a degree of independence. *Tightly coupled* means there is a degree of dependence.
9. A. *Coupling* is used to refer to relationships among modules, and *cohesion* is used for relationships and interactions within a module. Cohesion within a module indicates that all elements needed for a specific computation within a function are included and done within the module. There is no dependence on other elements.
10. D. Answers A, B, and C are all examples of horizontal scalability. Adding servers to an application either through clustering or load balancing is an example of scaling out and subsequently an example of horizontal scaling.
11. D. The type of redundancy you use is a pure design dilemma and trade-off. The type of standby depends on your functional and nonfunctional requirements.
12. D. Hello packets are exchanged between two systems to inform each other of their state. The packets may be as simple as a heartbeat or may carry more details about failing subcomponents.

Chapter 3

1. D. Maintainability of software depends on various factors, including proper comments, documentation, and modular design. A modular design without adequate documentation is useless.
2. D. Structured programming is the traditional way of using a set of functions and is not a characteristic of object-oriented programming.
3. C. SOLID is software design principles for building maintainable code. The five SOLID principles are discussed in detail in the "Maintainability Design and Implementation" section.
4. B. The text of the question is a simple definition of the open-closed principle (or OCP).
5. E. The dependency inversion principle states that high-level modules should not depend on low-level modules. Both should depend on abstractions, and abstractions should not depend on details. Details should depend on abstractions.
6. D. Latency, round-trip time, and throughput are all indicators of performance. Monitoring these parameters may also be an indicator of system- or network-related issues that need attention or further optimization.
7. B. Network oversubscription is the safest answer. You can also argue that oversubscribed wireless systems lead to the same effect.
8. A and B. Both caching and rate limiting are ways to manage system load and prevent performance degradations and outages. Echo replies can measure latency but are not related to managing load in this question. Open Shortest Path First (OSPF) is a routing protocol.
9. D. Observability is a combination of logging, metrics, and tracing. They are all part of the three answers A, B, and C.
10. C. The three pillars of observability are logging, metrics, and tracing. The other answers are not related.
11. B and C. Relational databases store data in rows and columns like spreadsheets, whereas nonrelational databases have four different types: one of them is document-oriented stores designed for storing, managing, and retrieving document-oriented information. The other types of nonrelational databases are key-value stores, wide-column stores, and graph stores.

Chapter 4

1. D. Although the primary use of version control is to track code changes, version control, in practice, is often used to store configuration, release, and deployment information.
2. B. GitHub adds development workflow functionality associated with Git. This functionality includes pull requests, review/approvals, searchability, and tags. GitHub is a repository hosting service toolset that includes access control and collaboration features. GitLab is a repository hosting manager toolset developed by GitLab Incorporated.

3. D. A version control system is used for managing the code base, streamlining the development process, and tracking all changes. It also tracks who made the changes.
4. B. When a file is deleted, it can no longer be modified. There are many ways conflicts can be generated. When two programmers commit changes to the same line, for example, a merge conflict can be generated. Two developers opening the same file does not cause a conflict; however, two developers saving changes to the same area of a file may cause a conflict.
5. B and C. A branching strategy needs to define the types of branches and all the rules governing usage by the development team. In addition, every developer has to agree to the strategy. These are basic branching and branching strategy concepts, and no successful branching can be achieved without them. All developers need to understand branching strategies; otherwise, conflicts will continually arise.

Chapter 5

1. A. You can use the PATCH request to require partial resources or to modify an existing resource. Answers B and D are incorrect because a GET request retrieves resource details and Delete removes resources. There is no cancel HTTP method, which means answer C is incorrect.
2. B. The PUT method is idempotent; it is not safe because changes can be made, resulting in misconfiguration and errors if the wrong details are sent to a resource. It replaces whatever exists at the target URL with something else. Answers A and C are incorrect because they are not safe and idempotent. Answer D is incorrect because an HTTP PUT method will modify but not remove (delete) resources.
3. A. With application/x-www-form-urlencoded, the keys and values are encoded in key-value tuples separated by an ampersand (&), with an equal sign (=) between the key and the value. Answer B is incorrect because multipart/form-data is a special type of body whereby each value is sent as a block of data. Answers C and D are incorrect because the request body format is not indicated as XML.
4. C. Swagger is a set of open-source tools for writing REST-based APIs. It enables you to describe the structure of your APIs so that machines can read them. Answers A, B, and D are incorrect because multiple languages can be used to document APIs with Swagger UI, and it can support more than browser/Postman testing.
5. A and C. REST represents Representational State Transfer; it is a relatively new aspect of writing web APIs. Answer B and D are incorrect because REST/RESTful APIs are not sets of rules that developers follow when they create their APIs.

   RESTful refers to web services written by applying REST architectural concepts; they are called RESTful services. They focus on system resources and how the state of a resource should be transported over the HTTP protocol to different clients written in different languages. In a RESTful web service, HTTP methods like GET, POST, PUT, and DELETE can be used to perform CRUD operations.
6. A. In the context of transaction processing, the acronym ACID refers to the four key properties of a transaction: atomicity, consistency, isolation, and durability.

7. B. SOAP is defined as an XML-based protocol. It is known for designing and developing web services as well as enabling communication between applications developed on different platforms using various programming languages over the Internet. It is both platform and language independent. Answers A and C are not correct because SOAP only allows XML and has built-in error handling. Although SOAP can be stateless by default, it is possible to make SOAP stateful by changing the code on the server; this makes D incorrect.

8. A. NETCONF/YANG provides a standardized way to programmatically update and modify the configuration of a network device; this makes B incorrect. YANG is the modeling language that describes the configuration changes. NETCONF is the protocol that applies the changes to the relevant datastore (such as running, saved) on the device. Answers C and D are incorrect because NETCONF can also update and modify the running configuration of a network device and does not have an irreplaceable attribute operation.

9. A, B, C, and D. A client/server architecture is made up of clients, servers, and resources, with requests managed through HTTP. The most common formats found in modern APIs are JavaScript Object Notation (JSON) and Extensible Markup Language (XML). A uniform interface exists between components so that information is transferred in a standard form. Communication is stateless, meaning no client information is stored between GET requests, and each request is separate and unconnected.

10. A, B, C, D. gRPC is a modern, open-source remote-procedure call (RPC) framework that can run in any environment. gRPC is built on http/2, which makes it very lean and ideal in low latency, with support for multiple languages such as Java, Python, and Go. gRPC enables client and server applications to communicate transparently and makes it easier to build connected systems.

Chapter 6

1. B. A software development kit (SDK) helps speed up and improve the adoption and developer experience of an API. Answer A is incorrect because asynchronous API performance refers to overall throughput. Answers C and D could be partially correct; B has the correct two main benefits of an API SDK.

2. C. The OpenAPI Specification (OAS) defines a standard programming language–agnostic interface to RESTful APIs, which allows both humans and computers to discover and understand the capabilities of the service without access to source code, documentation, or through network traffic inspection. Answers A, B, and D are incorrect as OpenAPI Specification (OAS) for RESTFUL APIs.

3. A and B. An API client abstracting and encapsulating all the necessary REST API endpoints calls for authenticating. Other resources might include code samples, testing and analytics, and documentation. Answers C and D are incorrect because both headers and parameters are additional or optional options.

4. D. The bearer token is an opaque string, which is generated by the server response to a developer login request, and not intended to have any meaning to clients using it.

Answers A, B, and C are incorrect because OAuth uses a single string, which has no meaning and may be of varying lengths.

5. A. True. A WebSocket uses a bidirectional protocol, in which there are no predefined message patterns such as request/response. The client and the server can send messages to each other.

6. A. The back-end infrastructure already exists within an organization and is used as a foundation for defining the API. This means that answers B and C are incorrect. Answer D is incorrect because a mock server is not a back-end infrastructure but is rather a fake server.

7. A and C. Outside-in API design allows for a lot more elasticity than inside-out API design, covering more use cases in single API calls, thus leading to fewer APIs being made by the consumer and less traffic on the wire and back-end systems for the provider. Answers B and C are incorrect because outside-in does not increase API adoption rate, and in an outside-in approach to API design the UI is often the first to be built.

8. A. True. The HTTP endpoints indicate how you access the resource, whereas the HTTP method indicates the allowed interactions (such as GET, POST, or DELETE) with the resource. HTTP methods should not be included in endpoints.

9. A and B. With page-based pagination, the developer can choose to view the required number of pages and items on the page. This could be a single page or a preset range of pages. An API could allow the developer to select a starting page—for example, page 10 through page 15. This is referred to as offset pagination. Answers C and D are incorrect because page-based is often used when the list of items is of a fixed and predetermined length.

10. E. Rate limiting protects an API from inadvertent or malicious overuse by limiting how often each developer or account can call the API. Rate limiting is also used for scalability, performance, monetization, authentication, and availability.

Chapter 7

1. C. The idea is that DevOps is a cultural shift to enable cross-functional teams experienced in a variety of areas to develop and operate an application in production. Answers A, B, and D are aspects of DevOps but need not occur if DevOps is adopted (they are somewhat optional).

2. B. DevOps and SRE share a common outcome, to deliver higher uptimes and reliability to an application or service—and the use of tooling/observability/training/etc. to help enable that uptime and resilience. DevOps encourages cross-functional teams, whereas SRE encourages a separate team to liaise between development and operations. Answer A is incorrect because it is generally looked at as part of SRE as a new team is instituted. Answer D is generally looked at as part of DevOps culture. Answer C is incorrect because the two overlap.

3. D. CI is meant to build/compile the code, perform standard unit testing against the code, and then ensure there are no security holes against the dependencies or developed code. Answer A refers to deployment of an application. Answers B and C refer

to the act of application development and merging of code branches (which need not have a CI component).

4. B. CI/CD pipeline definition files are generally written in YAML. Answers A and C can represent the same information as YAML, but it is not used. Answer D is a programming language and is not used to define the pipelines.
5. C. Pilot covers the specific methods in which applications can be deployed via CD. Answers A, B, and D are valid ways to release applications or incremental updates to applications to an environment (production, test, etc.).
6. B. This question specifically discusses what the name *serverless* means as it pertains to the focus on the underlying infrastructure needed to deploy an app. Answer A is incorrect because we still need to use servers. Answer C is incorrect because there does need to be packaging.
7. A and D. There is a discussion around the levels of abstraction and the benefits provided versus the trade-offs. As we abstract away management of the underlying infra in the cloud, we don't have to worry about the details of the platforms, but we must conform to the cloud provider in what is allowed and exposed from the abstraction, which is the opposite of answers B and C.
8. D. The idea of the 12-factor app is to create a set of standards and recommendations to be followed when designing an application meant to be deployed across multiple clouds. Answer A is incorrect because they are not specific "tests" that can be run. Answer B is incorrect because the 12 aspects don't directly deal with user experience. These rules don't just apply to a CI/CD pipeline, so answer C is also incorrect.

Chapter 8

1. B. Information system security can be summed up in three fundamental components: confidentiality, integrity, and availability.
2. A and D. The data is either at rest (for example, stored on a hard drive or a database) or in motion (for example, flowing or in transit though the network between two nodes). You may encounter some references that use a third state called in use, indicating that data is being processed by a CPU or a system. As for encryption and clear text, data can be in motion and encrypted, or clear text while it's in motion or at rest.
3. D. Data at rest is stored on a hard drive, tape, database, or in other ways.
4. A. PII refers to personally identifiable information. The other answers do not apply or relate to the topic.
5. B. GDPR gives European Union (EU) citizens control over their own personal data. It gives citizens the right to withdraw consent, to have easier access to their data, to understand where their data is stored, and to know if their data has been compromised by a cyberattack within 72 hours, depending on the relevance of the attack.
6. D. IT secrets are used as "keys" to unlock protected applications or application data. Passwords, account information, and API keys are examples. A VIN is not considered a secret because it is always displayed on every car's windshield.

7. B. The main responsibility of a certificate authority (CA) is issuing and signing certificates. Certificates are used to protect account and personal information.
8. D. Injection attacks are common and are one of the main issues that OWASP warns about. Injection attacks can come in different formats, such as database, LDAP, or OS command injections.
9. D. A PoH (or Proof of History) attack is not a cryptographic attack. It is closely related to Blockchain and crypto currency. Brute-force, statistical, and implementation attacks are types of cryptographic attacks.
10. C. There is no such thing as a four-legged authorization. The most common authorization flows are two-legged and three-legged. The three-legged OAuth flow requires four parties: the authorization server, client application, resource server, and resource owner (end user).

Chapter 9

1. C. Option C has the common categories of the PDIOO model in the correct order. The other options are contrived or out of order.
2. A. SNMPv3 uses the MD5 or SHA authentication method. Option B is incorrect for SNMPv3 but is correct for SNMPv1 and 2c. Option C is incorrect; there is no key-based authentication. Option D is incorrect; AES-128 is a function of data encryption, not authentication.
3. B. Option B is the proper expansion of the acronym, as defined by Google, which coined the term. The other options are contrived.
4. C. OOB stands for out-of-band networking, which is a way to partition management/administrative traffic from other traffic. Segment routing and VLANs are technologies used to segment or partition traffic, but they are generally or more commonly used with user traffic. Answer A is incorrect because FWM (firewall management) firewalls are useful for restricting traffic, but firewall management is not a type of network for separating administrative traffic from other production traffic.
5. B. PnP is a common and recommended process for zero-touch deployments. Options A and D are contrived answers. Option C is a user-initiated feature common to SMB products.
6. A. Intent-based networking is aligned to business requirements that are easily translated into policies reflecting native device configurations. All the other options are incorrect; the software image of a device does not make it intent-based; the routing protocols do not make a network intent-based, even if the routing protocols are defined similarly in an IBN; and AI does not intuit business requirements. It may inform you of what is more predominant or what is out of the norm.
7. D. NETCONF is an IETF working group specification and protocol standardized to normalize configuration management across multiple vendors using XML schemas and YANG models. Option A is incorrect; it is a contrived answer. Option B is incorrect; XML was the first (and consistent) data encoding method for NETCONF. Option C is incorrect; it is a contrived answer. Python may be used to implement NETCONF-based management, but it is only an option.

8. C. Two-factor or multifactor authentication relies on something a user knows, such as a password with proof of who they are (for example, a hardware token, mobile app response, or something else in their possession). Options A and B are contrived answers. Option D is incorrect; although an organization may use 2FA/MFA to allow access to Webex, it is not the definition of what 2FA/MFA is. Likewise, the current model of programmatically accessing Webex (via API) does not use 2FA/MFA.

9. B. Embedded management is often found in sophisticated ITSM environments; however, it should be augmented by off-box monitoring (EMS, cloud-native monitoring systems) to have a broader perspective. If a network node using embedded management (and only embedded management) goes down, it lacks reporting/notification.

Chapter 10

1. B. In environments where devices perform different functions using a model to define a device's configuration and desired state, model-driven management is highly efficient and effective. Answers A, C, and D are incorrect. Templates can be effective but are less flexible. They also require more routine maintenance, especially as software images change. Atomic-driven management is a contrived answer, and generally, managing devices atomically (one by one) leads to a higher degree of maintenance. Distributed EMSs also is a contrived answer. Having multiple element management systems *can* be less efficient, especially when they are not integrated or used.

2. B. Software, infrastructure, and operations are defined by Google's catalyst of this role. Answers A, C, and D are incorrect. Firmware is not a focus (while software image management *may* be addressed). While close, answer C puts more focus on network engineering than SRE promotes. Likewise, traffic and SecOps are not general focus areas for SRE (although security can be a component of it).

3. D. Agile promotes requirements gathering, adaptive (and collaborative) planning, quick delivery, and a CI/CD approach. Answers A, B, and C are incorrect. The "defined process" part implies a rigorous structure that is inflexible; this is not Agile. Although Agile does provide flexibility, it does not give developers a "free pass" without accountability. Answer C reflects more of a test-driven methodology.

4. A. Kanban provides a more visual, graphical approach of software development; many people attribute the "board" and "cards" approach to identify work and progress. Answers B, C, and D are incorrect. Neither Agile nor Waterfall is specifically a visual, graphical-based approach to software development. Answer D is contrived. Although the term *illustrative* does imply a visual, graphical approach, it is the Kaban methodology that is the accepted industry term.

5. A. Concurrency provides the ability to do lots of tasks at once, and parallelism is defined as working with lots of tasks at once. Answers B, C, and D are incorrect. Exchanging implies swapping away from tasks; switching also implies changing focus among tasks. The threading part of answer C is accurate, but the sequencing part is incorrect. Answer D is the opposite of answer A.

6. A. OpenAPI was previously known as Swagger. Answers B, C, and D are incorrect. REST was never known as the CLI, but it's funny. SDN was catalyzed in the Clean

Slate project, but it is broader than RESTful web services. OpenWeb and CORBA are not specifications for RESTful web services.

7. C. Basic authentication takes a concatenation of username and password with a colon (:) separating them, and Base64 encodes the string. The **openssl** utility is helpful for performing that function. Answers A, B, and D are incorrect. Basic authentication does not use the **md5** hash function. There is no specification of what encoding method to use with the **openssl** utility. Also, basic authentication does not use the ampersand (&) to join the username and password.

8. B. XML is the Extensible Markup Language. Answers A, C, and D are incorrect. It is not extendable or machine. Nor is it extreme or machine or learning—but it sounds fun. Likewise, it is not extraneous or modeling.

9. D. JSON records and objects are denoted with curly braces. Answers A, B, and C are incorrect. Angle braces are seen in XML, not JSON. Square brackets note lists in JSON, not records. Simple quotes note strings in JSON, not records.

10. B. HEAD and GET methods in REST operations are both idempotent (able to be run multiple times receiving the same result). Answers A, C, and D are incorrect. In A and C, POST is not idempotent (both need to be for the correct answer). In D, PATCH is not idempotent, but HEAD is idempotent (both need to be for the correct answer).

11. A and C. REST and JDBC are APIs. Answers B and D are incorrect. RMON is a legacy management protocol. SSH is a useful protocol, but it is predominately used for human interaction with a device; it is not optimal for programmatic use as an API would be.

Chapter 11

1. B. The Internet Engineering Task Force (IETF) created the NETCONF working group in May 2003 to tackle the configuration management problem across vendors. Option A is incorrect because the ANSI organization is a private nonprofit organization that oversees the development of voluntary consensus standards for products, services, processes, systems, and personnel in the United States. It did not initiate the work for NETCONF. Option C is incorrect because the ITU is a specialized agency of the United Nations responsible for all matters related to information and communication technologies, but it did not initiate the work for NETCONF. Option D is incorrect because the TM Forum is a global industry association for service providers and their suppliers in the telecommunications industry; it did not initiate the work for NETCONF.

2. D. The IETF RFC defining NETCONF initially was RFC 4741 in December 2006. RFC 6241 provided updates to the base protocol in June 2011. Option A is incorrect because they are related to SNMP. Option B is incorrect because they are related to SNMP. Option C is incorrect because they are related to RESTCONF.

3. A. Model-driven configuration management allows for the definition of relationship and desired configuration distinctives across networks/devices/services. Answers B, C, and D are incorrect. A model describes network/device/service relationships and

configures them with consideration of the interdependencies, not segmentation or isolation. Answer C is a contrived answer that plays on remote control devices sometimes being called models. Answer D is incorrect because an inference engine is part of a machine-learning solution that decides solutions from the rules and knowledge base; it might not reflect true intent. A model provides specific guidance.

4. C. Cisco IOS XE requires the **netconf-yang** configuration command to enable NETCONF. The other answers use incorrect syntax.
5. C. NETCONF uses IANA-assigned TCP port 830, as defined in RFC 6242. Answer A is incorrect because it is the standard port for HTTP protocol over TLS/SSL. Answer B is incorrect because it is the standard port for UDP-based HTTP protocol over TLS/SSL. Answer D is incorrect; although the port number 830 is accurate, the UDP transport protocol is incorrect.
6. B. The end-of-message framing sequence for a NETCONF RPC over an SSH session is]]>]]>, as defined in RFC 6242, Section 4.3. The other options are incorrect; they are not the ending sequences for a hello exchange.
7. C. NETMOD is the IETF working group, and YANG serves as a data modeling language to characterize configuration, state, and administrative functions. Answers A, B, and D are incorrect. There is not a focus or catalyst with firmware image management. There is no complementary YIN encoding method.
8. A. YANG definition files are made of module declarations, containers of objects, lists of objects, and individual leaf items. Answer B is incorrect because there is no spine item. Answer C is incorrect because there are no spine or interconnect items.
9. D. The Accept header identifies the requester's intent to receive data in a specific format. The value of application/yang-data+json is correct for JSON-encoded data coming from a YANG-enabled endpoint. Answer A is incorrect because the header is not Content-Type and the value is not application/json. Answer B is incorrect because the header is not Content-Type, even as the value is correct. Answer C is incorrect because it has the correct header type of Accept but the value of application/json is incorrect.
10. C. The HTTP PUT operation, used by NETCONF, would be appropriate for update/replace operations. Another option is the PATCH operation, but it is not supplied as an option. Answer A is incorrect because GET operations retrieve data from APIs. Answer B is incorrect because POST operations set data for APIs. Answer D is incorrect because DELETE operations remove data from APIs.

Chapter 12

1. D. SNMPv3 uses MD5/SHA for authentication and DES/3DES/AES for encryption and data security. MDT gRPC has SSL/TLS integration and promotes its use to authenticate the server and encrypt the data exchanged between client and server. These capabilities afford similar data security. Answer A is incorrect because SNMPv1 uses community string authorization and no encryption, which affords little security. MDT can provide TLS. Answer B is incorrect because SNMPv2c uses community string authorization and no encryption, which affords little security. Answer C is incorrect because answers A and B are.

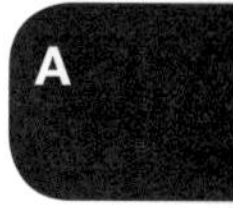

2. B. MDT uses the HTTP/2 application protocol. Answer A is incorrect because MDT uses the more advanced HTTP/2 application protocol rather than HTTP. Answer C is incorrect because SPDY was an original experimental protocol, but HTTP/2 became the final model. Answer D is incorrect because MDT does not use secure copy (SCP). Answer E is incorrect because MDT does not use secure FTP (sFTP).

3. A. In MDT, the device is the authoritative source of the telemetry. In dial-out mode, the device pushes telemetry to the receiver/collector. Answer B is incorrect because it describes dial-in mode with an inaccurate representation of the device being passive. Answer C is incorrect because it describes a dial-in mode model. Answer D is incorrect because in dial-out mode the telemetry receiver is still considered a server. Answer E is incorrect because it describes dial-in mode where the receiver dials in to the network device and subscribes dynamically to one or more sensor paths.

4. C. When building a telemetry dial-out configuration, you must create a destination group, sensor group, and subscription. Answer C is not a major task because flow spec is not necessary and is a contrived detractor reminiscent of OpenFlow. Answers A, B, and D are incorrect because they are major tasks needed to configure telemetry dial-out.

5. C. Google Protocol Buffers (or protobufs) is the correct answer. Answers A, B, and D are incorrect because they are contrived answers. Answer E is incorrect because it is a contrived answer of a legacy protocol, Gopher, with other unaffiliated terms.

6. D. A sensor path is a combination of YANG data model for the feature of interest with the specific metric node (leaf, leaf-list, container, and so on). Answer A is incorrect because a sensor path is not related to SNMP. Answer B is incorrect because a sensor path is more than a hierarchy to an interface/module/interface. Answer C is incorrect because a sensor path does not define the receiving telemetry collector settings.

7. B and D. YANG data models are published on GitHub by de facto convention across several vendors and standards bodies. They are also published and searchable on yangcatalog.org, an IETF project since 2015's IETF 92 YANG Model Coordination Group and Hackathon. Answer A is incorrect because YANG models are not published to stackoverflow. Answer C is incorrect because YANG models are not published to yang.org.

8. D. The TIG stack is Telegraf, InfluxDB, and Grafana. Answers A, B, and C are incorrect because none of the references map to TIG stack actual definitions.

9. C. The on-change MDT policy provides for event-driven telemetry, which pushes metrics only on change. A periodic policy pushes telemetry at a predefined interval and can repeat nonchanging values, which leads to poor disk usage and processing overhead. Answer A is incorrect because periodic frequency is not a frugal deployment policy. Answer B is incorrect because it is a reference to a database export process. Answer D is incorrect because MDT does not use gzip for compression or policy.

10. B. The most accurate estimation of disk and processing utilization is gleaned from baselining the traffic volume and receiver CPU after the subscriptions are configured and then extrapolating over time. Answers A and C are incorrect because the data

size and payload can vary; there is no static equation. Answer D is incorrect because there is no such calculator.

Chapter 13

1. C. IaC solutions come as both declarative and imperative modeled solutions. Answer A is incorrect because IaC solutions can be declaratively modeled. Answer B is incorrect because IaC solutions can be imperatively modeled. Answer D is incorrect because IaC solutions can be declaratively or imperatively modeled.
2. E. An imperative model is a programming paradigm that uses implicit commands and flow directives that change a device or environment's state. Answer A is correct but not only by itself, as answer C is also correct. Answer B is incorrect; imperative model solutions do describe control flow. Answer C is correct but not only by itself, as answer A is also correct. Answer D is incorrect because it contains answer B, which is incorrect.
3. D. A declarative model is a programming paradigm that expresses the desired state of a device or environment but does not describe the control flow. Answer A is correct but not only by itself, as answer B is also correct. Answer B is correct but not only by itself, as answer A is also correct. Answer C is incorrect because it describes an imperative model solution. Answer E is incorrect because it contains the incorrect answers A and C.
4. B. This response provides the correct definition of both items. Provisioning generally refers to the action of performing device changes, whereas configuration management refers to the function or concept. Answer A is incorrect because the ZTD function is zero touch deployment, not zero task deployment. Answer C is incorrect because ZTD does not implement XModem for file transfer. Answer D is incorrect because configuration management does not require Gateway Load Balancing Protocol.
5. A, C, and E. Chef is agent-based, Puppet supports both modes, and Ansible is agentless, depending on the SSH feature of a device. Answer B is incorrect because Chef requires an agent. Answer D is incorrect because Ansible does not require an agent; it is agentless.
6. B. The Puppet Facter tool's default output is to JSON. Answer A is incorrect because Puppet Facter output defaults to JSON, not ANSI. Answer C is incorrect because Puppet Facter's output defaults to JSON, not XML. Answer D is incorrect because Puppet output defaults to JSON, not YAML.
7. C. A Puppet configuration or definition file is called a manifest. Answer A is incorrect because the file used to define Puppet operations/definitions/parameters is called a manifest. Answer B is incorrect because the Puppet file for operations/definitions/parameters is not a DDL; it is a manifest. Answer D is incorrect because it is the operations/definition/parameters file for Ansible, not Puppet.
8. A and C. Ansible playbooks support YAML and INI data exchange format. The YAML style allows for greater functionality with key-value definitions. Answers B and D are incorrect because Ansible playbooks support YAML and INI, not JSON, and zsh is a type of shell.

9. C. The YAML style of Ansible playbooks allows for inline references to Ansible Vault parameters. Answer A is incorrect because INI format does not allow for inline references of Ansible Vault definitions. Answers B and D are incorrect because they are not valid data exchange formats for Ansible inventory files.

10. C. You use **terraform init** to initialize a project working directory. The **terraform plan** command reads the configuration file and compares it to the current state, and the **terraform apply** command deploys the desired state. Answers A, B, and D are incorrect because they are not valid Terraform commands.

Chapter 14

1. D. Tracking changes, along with who made them, and housing the data repositories are all functions of the SCM.
2. C. Almost everything related to the software product is tracked by the SCM. The market research data related to the marketability of your product may not be tracked by the SCM.
3. C. Chef, Ansible, and SaltStack are examples of an SCM. Muppet is not an SCM and should not be confused with Puppet, which is an SCM.
4. B. Ansible has five main components: the control node, inventory files, playbooks, modules, and managed nodes.
5. C. The CLI command **ansible -version** displays both software versions. The other commands do not work. We recommend that you familiarize yourself with the help command: **ansible -h**.
6. A. Terraform is an example of a declarative Infrastructure as Code (IaC) automation and orchestration tool. Ansible is an example of an imperative one.
7. B. One of the strengths of Terraform is its simplicity and straightforward lifecycle. The lifecycle is init, plan, apply, and destroy.
8. D. Technical debt consists of decisions made to satisfy short-term goals but have long-term consequences. The first three answers are examples of that. A bad database decision is a test environment that's not representative of the production environments.

Chapter 15

1. A and D. Microsoft Hyper-V and VMware ESXi are Type-1 hypervisors. They are characterized as bare-metal hypervisors acting as a software layer between the underlying hardware and the overlying virtual machines (with self-contained operating systems and applications). Answer B is incorrect because Oracle VM VirtualBox is a Type-2 hypervisor running over the top of another operating system, such as Microsoft Windows, macOS, or Linux. Answer C is incorrect because Parallels Desktop is a Type-2 hypervisor running over the top of macOS.
2. B and C. Oracle VirtualBox and VMware Workstation are Type-2 hypervisors. They are characterized as being installed over a foundational operating system and providing virtualized operating system service to overlying guest virtual machines. Answers

A and D are incorrect because QEMU with KVM and Citrix XenServer are considered Type-1 hypervisors.

3. B. False. Docker aligns more to application containerization. LXC aligns more to operating system containerization.

4. B and D. Moving workloads to the network edge with application hosting/containerization can help with data sovereignty requirements and reduce costs where WAN traffic is metered and cost-prohibitive. Answer A is incorrect because application hosting/containerization can be used where low latency is desirable. Answer C is incorrect because application hosting/containerization is more suited to distributed solutions.

5. B. Cisco IOS-XE release 16.2.1 is the minimum version supporting application hosting and Docker containers. Answers A, C, and D are incorrect because application hosting is supported on Catalyst 9300 at a minimum of Cisco IOS-XE 16.2.1.

6. C. Cisco NX-OS release 9.2.1 is the minimum version supporting Docker containers. Answers A, B, and D are incorrect because Docker containers are supported on NX-OS–based switches starting on release 9.2.1.

7. A, B, and D. Docker containers can be deployed on IOx-supported Catalyst 9000 series switches with Cisco DNA Center, the command-line interface, or the IOx Local Manager. Answer C is incorrect because there is no such Docker Deployer deployment option. Answer E is incorrect because there is no such Prime KVM deployment option.

8. D. The **docker save** command is used to create an image that can be copied to another system for import (for example, **docker load** in traditional environments). This process is necessary to prepare an image from a local Docker system for import into Cisco DNA Center, IOx Local Manager, or a network device CLI. Answer A is incorrect because there is no **docker archive** command. Answer B is incorrect because the **docker create** command creates a writeable container layer over the specified image and prepares it for running the specified command. Answer C is incorrect because the **docker export** command exports a container's filesystem, not the image, as a tar archive.

9. E. The Cisco IOS XE command **app-hosting appid <*name*>** is used to configure an application and enter application hosting configuration mode. It was introduced in IOS XE 16.12.1 on the Cisco Catalyst 9300 series switches. Answers A and D are incorrect because these commands are not supported in Cisco IOS XE. Answers B and C are incorrect because no such command syntax exists.

10. B. The interface AppGigabitEthernet1/0/1 is created for application hosting. It is used to trunk or pass specific VLAN traffic into the Docker environment. Answer A is incorrect because it is an incomplete interface reference. Answers C and D are incorrect because they are not legitimate interface references.

11. B. False. The IOx Local Manager manages the Docker container lifecycle of a single hosting device. It is a best practice to create a central software repository for container image tracking, archiving, and distribution.

Chapter 16

1. E. Webex SDKs are available for Apple iOS, Google Android, Java, and Python environments, along with several other platforms and languages not mentioned here.
2. C. You can publish a Webex bot in the Webex App Hub. The other sites will have the complete application. Subcomponents like bots and APIs will be posted at the Webex App Hub.
3. C. X-auth-access-token and X-auth-refresh-token are returned in the response to a POST request with a valid FMC username and password. None of the other answers are returned in the API response from an FMC login.
4. B. Access to the FMC is supported with only one concurrent login using a username, regardless of the method used to access the FMC.
5. C. Meraki Dashboard v1 API uses the bearer token authentication with the API key. Answer A is incorrect because the Meraki Dashboard v1 API does not use HTTP authentication; it uses bearer token authentication with the API key. Also, the header key is not Authentication; it is Authorization. Answer B is incorrect because the header key is not Authentication; it is Authorization. Answer D is incorrect because the Meraki Dashboard v1 API does not use HTTP authentication; it uses bearer token authentication with the API key.
6. A. You can find organization-level device information via the SDK under **<*api_session*>.organizations.getOrganizationDevices(orgId)**. Answer B is incorrect because there is no **api.device.getDevices** method. Answer C is incorrect because **api.getOrganizationDevices** is not a correct method; it is subordinate to organizations. Answer D is incorrect because it is a contrived method—Meraki does not use the orgid inside the method path.
7. D. The API key and private key are required to compute the hash values that are sent to the REST API with every request.
8. D. You can find the list of supported tools and SDKs on the Downloads page of the online Intersight API documentation.
9. B. The UCS API only supports XML output natively. SDKs and other tools display the output in different formats through text manipulation on the output.
10. C. You can filter the output from running a command by invoking **| Select-Object <*value*>** after the command. Answer A is incorrect because the PowerTool is supported across different platforms. Answer B is incorrect because the PowerTool does not use an API key to connect to a UCSM instance (it uses a username/password combination). Answer D is incorrect because the PowerTool can also display output information in more ways than just the native XML output through formatting.
11. A. The DNA Center REST API requires an authorization header with basic access authentication. Answer B is incorrect because the authorization header is used with basic authentication for DNA Center REST API access. Answer C is incorrect because DNA Center does not use bearer token authentication; it uses HTTP authentication. Answer D is incorrect because DNA Center does not use OAuth token authentication; it uses HTTP authentication.

12. D. The Cisco DNA Center SDK package is called **dnacentersdk** on PyPI. Answers A, B, and C are incorrect because they are contrived examples.

13. B and C. The client secret is used to generate a short-lived (generally five-minute) access token created via the API. The temporary access token is created in the Web-UI and generally is used for longer-term access. Answer A is incorrect because AppDynamics does not generate the client secret through the API. Answer D is incorrect because the AppDynamics client secret is generated for the user. Answer E is incorrect because the AppDynamics temporary access token is generated for the user.

14. C. The default output of the AppDynamics API is XML. You can specify that it use JSON by appending **'?output=JSON'** to the calling URL. Answer A is incorrect because the AppDynamics API data can be retrieved by appending **'?output=JSON'** to the calling URL, but it is not the default encoding. Answer B is incorrect because SAML is an open standard for exchanging authentication and authorization data between an identity provider and a service provider. It is not an encoding method for API data from AppDynamics. Answer D is incorrect because YAML is a data encoding method commonly used for configuration file declarations, but it is not the data encoding method used for the AppDynamics API.

APPENDIX B

Cisco DevNet Professional DEVCOR 350-901 Exam Updates

Updates

Over time, reader feedback allows Pearson to gauge which topics give our readers the most problems when taking the exams. To assist readers with those topics, the authors create new materials clarifying and expanding on those troublesome exam topics. As mentioned in the Introduction, the additional content about the exam is contained in a PDF on this book's companion website, at http://www.ciscopress.com/title/9780137370443.

This appendix is intended to provide you with updated information if Cisco makes minor modifications to the exam upon which this book is based. When Cisco releases an entirely new exam, the changes are usually too extensive to provide in a simple update appendix. In those cases, you might need to consult the new edition of the book for the updated content. This appendix attempts to fill the void that occurs with any print book. In particular, this appendix does the following:

- Mentions technical items that might not have been mentioned elsewhere in the book
- Covers new topics if Cisco adds new content to the exam over time
- Provides a way to get up-to-the-minute current information about content for the exam

Always Get the Latest at the Book's Product Page

You are reading the version of this appendix that was available when your book was printed. However, given that the main purpose of this appendix is to be a living, changing document, it is important that you look for the latest version online at the book's companion website. To do so, follow these steps:

Step 1. Browse to www.ciscopress.com/title/9780137370443.

Step 2. Click the **Updates** tab.

Step 3. If there is a new Appendix B document on the page, download the latest Appendix B document.

NOTE The downloaded document has a version number. Comparing the version of the print Appendix B (Version 1.0) with the latest online version of this appendix, you should do the following:

- **Same version:** Ignore the PDF that you downloaded from the companion website.
- **Website has a later version:** Ignore this Appendix B in your book and read only the latest version that you downloaded from the companion website.

Technical Content

The current Version 1.0 of this appendix does not contain additional technical coverage.

GLOSSARY

A

agent-based Technologies that do require additional software modules or functions to perform work. Agent-based technologies might not be able to experience the breadth of functionality needed using existing, embedded functions like SSH. Therefore, the agent extends the functionality desired through its installed software/module. Early Puppet and Chef implementations required agents to be installed on the managed nodes.

agentless Technologies that do not require additional software modules or functions to perform work. Oftentimes agentless technologies depend on existing functionality, such as SSH or NETCONF, to act as the endpoint's processing receiver. Common agentless solutions in network IT are Ansible, Terraform, and recent Puppet and Chef implementations.

Ansible An agentless configuration management tool that enables IaC, software provisioning, and application deployment. Ansible was acquired by RedHat in 2015. It was initially released in 2012 and is written mainly in Python. Ansible uses playbooks written in YAML to define tasks and actions to perform on managed endpoints.

API inside-out design A type of design that commences with the infrastructure or database followed by the back-end classes and services. The user interface (UI) is typically the last bit to get built.

API outside-in/user interface (API first approach) A type of design that begins with UI creation, and then the APIs are built with the database schema.

application performance monitoring (APM) A discipline or tool set for measuring various granular parameters related to performance of application code, runtime environments, and interactions.

architectural decision A software design choice that addresses a functional or nonfunctional requirement that is architecturally significant.

C

caching The capability to store data as close as possible to the users so that subsequent or future requests are answered faster.

certificate authority (CA) Third-party or neutral organization that certifies that other entities communicating with each are in fact who they say they are.

Chef A company and tool name for a configuration management solution written in Ruby. Initially released in 2009, it supports configuration management for systems, network, and cloud environments. It also supports CI/CD, DevOps, and IaC initiatives. A recipe defines how a Chef server manages environment configuration. Progress acquired Chef mid-2020.

clustering A technology for combining multiple servers (or resources), making them appear as a single server.

cohesion In software engineering, the interaction and relationships within a module and the ability for a module to complete its tasks within the module.

cold standby A redundancy concept in which a redundant resource is available as a spare and is ready to take over in case of failure of the active resource.

container A type of lightweight virtualization where the workload uses an underpinning operating system kernel. A container is an image constructed of all necessary runtime libraries, code, and local storage and is portable. Docker containers are a de facto implementation and are the foundation for stateless microservice architectures.

content delivery network/content distribution network (CDN) A geographically distributed network of proxy servers and their data centers. The goal is to provide high availability and performance by distributing the service spatially relative to end users.

continuous delivery (CD) The automated process involved in moving the software that has passed through the continuous integration pipeline to a state in which it is moved to a staging area for live testing. This often involves packaging the software into a format in which it can be deployed and moving the resulting package to a remote repository or fileshare.

continuous integration/continuous deployment (CI/CD) A software development concept in which the lifecycle or process flow of development follows a prescribed path of testing, integration validation, archiving, code scanning, vulnerability checking, and automated publication to software repositories.

control plane The conceptual layer of network protocols and traffic that involve path determination and decision-making.

coupling The relationships and interaction between various modules.

cross-site scripting (XSS) A type of injection attack in which attackers inject malicious scripts into a web application to obtain information about the application or its users.

D

data at rest A data state in which data is being stored in a database, hard drive, or tape.

data in motion A data state in which data is in transit between two nodes.

data plane The conceptual layer of network protocols and traffic that involve the actual user traffic. Forwarding decisions are followed in the data plane.

declarative model A style of programming, network engineering, and more broadly, IT management that expresses the logic and desired state of a device or network, instead of describing the control flow.

DevOps A portmanteau of *development* and *operations*; the name for a methodology in which collaboration and cross-functional teams are formed with both software developers as well as infrastructure operations personnel. This methodology focuses on rapid development and deployment principles, such as CI/CD and Agile software development, with an idea that the combination of teams leads to greater empathy between individuals, leading to higher uptime and support of the end application or service.

dial-in A model-driven telemetry model where the subscribing telemetry receiver initiates a telemetry session with the telemetry source, which streams the telemetry data back.

dial-out A model-driven telemetry mode where the telemetry source configures a destination, sensor path, and subscription defining the metrics to be streamed to the receiving telemetry collector. The telemetry source initiates the session.

digital certificate Also known as a certificate; a file that verifies the identity of a device or user and enables data exchange over encrypted connections.

E

event-driven telemetry (EDT) A mode of telemetry that initiates the sending of metrics on-change rather than by periodic cadence.

Extensible Markup Language (XML) A data-encoding method and markup language defining rules in a form that is humanly readable but also programmatic. There are synergies among HTML and XML for creating stylesheets that are dynamic to different device capabilities for representing content. Generally, JSON is preferred in more recent cloud and infrastructure development.

F

format The way that data is represented, such as JSON and XML.

functional requirements The conditions that specify the business purpose of the functionality of software or an application.

G

General Data Protection Regulation (GDPR) A regulation that gives European Union (EU) citizens control over their own personal data.

Google Remote Procedure Call (gRPC) An open-source, high-performance RPC framework released by Google in 2015. gRPC uses HTTP/2 for transport with TLS and token-based authentication. The HTTP/2 support provides low latency and scalability.

gRPC Network Management Interface (gNMI) A Google innovation to provide a standardized management interface for configuration management and telemetry functions. gNMI provides the mechanism to install, change, and delete the configuration of network devices, and also to view operational data. The content provided through gNMI can be modeled using YANG. gRPC carries gNMI and provides the means to define and transmit data and operation requests.

H

hypervisor Software that creates and executes virtual machines (VMs). A hypervisor enables a host system to support multiple guest VMs by virtually sharing and allocating its resources, such as CPU, memory, and storage.

I

imperative model A style of programming, network engineering, and more broadly, IT management that uses exact steps or control statements to define a desired state. This model requires operating system syntax knowledge for operation and provisioning.

Infrastructure as Code (IaC) The act of defining one or more pieces of infrastructure (network, compute, storage, platform, and so on) through configuration files that are deployed using programming languages or higher-level configuration management platforms (such as Terraform).

injection attack A common type of attack discussed by OWASP. When user data is not frequently validated, then injection or extraction of sensitive records is possible.

intent-based networking (IBN) A networking concept where business requirements or intent are translated to native network device configurations and syntax. Using simple language that maps intent to complex networking characteristics is a key principle.

J

JavaScript Object Notation (JSON) A data-encoding method that is easy for humans to read and is conducive to programmatic use.

K

Kubernetes An open-source container management and operations platform, originally created by Google. Kubernetes provides the foundational infrastructure and APIs such that applications and supporting services (such as clustering and distributed file storage) are able to run across one or more hosts.

L

latency The length of time taken for a system to complete a specified task.

Linux Containers (LXC) A type of virtualization that was realized mid-2008. LXC is operating-system-based where all container instances share the same kernel of the hosting compute node. The guest operating systems may execute in a different user space. This can be manifested as different Linux distributions with the same kernel.

load balancing Sometimes generically used as server load balancing; a technique for distributing load among a number of servers or virtual machines for the purpose of scalability, availability, and security.

logging Reporting of events, their timestamp, and severity.

M

management plane The conceptual layer of network protocols and traffic that involve the administrative functions of a network device, such as Network Time Protocol (NTP), syslog event messaging, SNMP, and NETCONF.

manifest A configuration file used by Puppet, written in a Puppet-specific language like Ruby. The files define resources and state to be provisioned on a managed device and typically uses a .pp extension.

mean time between failures (MTBF) How likely it is for a system to fail and what events can contribute to the failure.

mean time to repair or mean time to recovery (MTTR) How much time is needed for the system to recover from failure or for the issue causing the failure to be repaired.

method The intent of an API call; often referred to as a "verb." It describes the operations available, such as GET, POST, PUT, PATCH, and DELETE.

metrics System performance parameters. Latency, response time, sessions per second, and transactions per second are examples of metrics.

model-driven telemetry (MDT) A function that uses data models, such as YANG, to represent configuration and operational state. Associated with streaming telemetry, MDT provides a structure for defining telemetry receivers, sensor paths (metrics), and subscriptions necessary to encode and transport the data.

multiprocessing Processing independent tasks using additional processors.

multithreading Dividing tasks or requests into threads that can be processed in parallel.

N

NETCONF The Network Configuration Protocol (NETCONF) is a network management protocol developed and standardized by the IETF as RFC 4741, later revised as RFC 6241. It enables functionality to provision, change, and delete the configuration of network devices through remote procedure calls of XML-encoded data.

Network Configuration Protocol (NETCONF) An IETF working group standard and protocol. It allows cross-vendor management focused on configuration and state data.

nonfunctional requirements The conditions that describe how a system should perform the functions described in the functional requirements.

O

object The resource a user is trying to access. It is often referred to as a "noun" and is typically a Uniform Resource Identifier (URI).

observability The ability to measure the state of a system based on the output or data it generates (i.e., logs, metrics, and traces).

Open Authentication (OAuth) An open standard defined by IETF RFC 6749. Two versions are in use today: OAuth 1.0 and 2.0. OAuth2.0 is not backward compatible with OAuth 1.0 (RFC 5849). OAuth is designed with HTTP in mind and allows users to log in to multiple sites or applications with one account.

Open Web Application Security Project (OWASP) A nonprofit organization working to improve software security through community-led open-source projects that develop tools, resources, and training.

OpenAPI Specification (OAS) Formerly known as the Swagger Specification, this is a powerful format for describing RESTful APIs. A standard, programming language–agnostic interface description for HTTP APIs.

P

pagination The process of splitting data sets into discrete pages with a set of paginated endpoints. Therefore, an API call to a paginated endpoint is called a paginated request. API endpoints paginate their responses to make the result set easier to handle.

personally identifiable information (PII) Any information that can be used to identify a person—name, password, Social Security number, driver's license number, credit card number, address, and so on.

plan Specific to Terraform, a command process that creates an execution plan allowing a designer to review changes Terraform would make to an environment.

playbook A configuration file used by Ansible, written in YAML. It defines the tasks and actions to be performed in provisioning or management functions.

Power-On Auto-Provisioning (POAP) A network function that enables a device to bring itself to a minimum level of functionality on a network through intuited and configuration-guided mechanisms during bootup.

public key infrastructure (PKI) A type of asymmetric cryptography algorithm that requires the generation of two keys. One key is secure and known only to its owner. It is called the *private* key. The other key, called the *public* key, is available and known to anyone or anything that wishes to communicate with the private key owner.

Puppet A software configuration management tool that uses a declarative language to describe configuration state. It was released in 2005 and written in C++, with rewrites in Clojure and Ruby in 2014. Puppet uses a manifest to describe system resources and state using Puppet's declarative language or a Ruby domain-specific language. Puppet has a utility called **facter**, used to discover system information.

R

rate limiting Limiting requests or controlling the rate at which they are passed to the processor.

remote-procedure call (RPC) A software communication protocol that a system uses to request a service from another system located in another part of a network without having to understand the network's details. RPC is used to call other processes on the remote systems as if it exists on the local system.

REST (Representational state transfer) A software architectural style that conforms to constraints for interacting with APIs. RESTful APIs are commonly used to GET or POST/PUT data with a device for obtaining state or changing configuration.

RESTCONF An evolution of the use of NETCONF to use RESTful API equivalencies.

round-trip time (RTT) The time taken for round-trip travel between two network nodes or the length of time taken to complete a set of tasks.

S

sensor-path The unique path of a YANG model and the hierarchy/structure required to identify a configuration item or metric.

serverless The abstraction of the underlying infrastructure from the application or service being run on the infrastructure. This abstraction enables operations personnel to focus on the outcome of the application being served, rather than the supporting operating system, patching, and system and software dependencies, which are placed under the responsibility of the cloud provider.

service-level agreement (SLA) A commitment made by the system architect (owner or operator) that the system will be up for a specified period.

site reliability engineering (SRE) A functional concept catalyzed by Google in which network operations personnel maintain software development skills with the intent of developing network monitoring and management solutions necessary to sustain IT operations.

software architecture The set of structures needed to reason about the system, which comprise software elements, relations among them, and properties of both.

software configuration management (SCM) A discipline or framework for tracking architecture and development processes and changes. A number of automation and orchestration tools are available to simplify the process.

software-defined networking (SDN) A concept of network abstraction, virtualization, and programmability that enables networks to be more resilient, scalable, and programmatic. The concept of network controllers with control plane and data plane separation is a key concept. Virtualization or abstraction of functions and services is another key concept.

software development kit (SDK) A collection of software development tools in one installable package. An SDK is created by products alongside their APIs to make APIs more accessible.

software development lifecycle (SDLC) A process or framework for designing and implementing software.

SOLID Object-oriented software design principles, which include the single responsibility principle (SRP), open-closed principle (OCP), Liskov's substitution principle (LSP), interface segregation principle (ISP), and dependency inversion principle (DIP).

source code manager A specific platform implementation of a VCS protocol that enables tracking, management, and collaboration of source code. Common git-based SCMs include GitHub, BitBucket, and GitLab.

spec file Specific to Ansible, a YAML-based file that defines the XML/XPath syntax used to map XML-structured data to JSON for use in playbooks.

subscription A desired session between telemetry source and receiver defining the desired sensor(s)/metric(s), encoding, destination, and frequency.

SwaggerHub A part of the Swagger toolset; it includes a mix of open-source, free, and commercial tools. SwaggerHub is an integrated API development platform, which enables the core capabilities of the Swagger framework to design, build, document, and deploy APIs. SwaggerHub enables teams to collaborate and coordinate the lifecycle of an API. It can work with version control systems such as GitHub, GitLab, and Bitbucket.

T

technical debt A term used to describe short-term decisions that can possibly affect the quality of the software on the long run.

Terraform An Infrastructure-as-Code solution created by HashiCorp, initially released in 2014 to manage IT resources in the public or private cloud, network devices, or SaaS endpoints using providers to translate the desired state and intent to device-native syntax. Terraform works from the known state of deployed resources and can safely provision environments idempotently using Create, Read, Update, Delete (CRUD) actions.

throughput The amount of load (utilization) a system is capable of handling during a time period.

tracing The ability to track multiple events or a series of distributed events through a system.

Transport Layer Security (TLS) TLS is a successor to Secure Sockets Layer protocol. It provides secure communications on the Internet for such things as e-mail, Internet faxing, and other data transfers. Common cryptographic protocols are used to imbue web communications with integrity, security, and resilience against unauthorized tampering.

Type-1 hypervisor Architecture that typically involves the hypervisor kernel acting as a shim-layer between the underlying hardware serving compute, memory, network, and storage, from the overlying operating systems. Sample solutions are Microsoft Hyper-V, Xen, and VMware ESXi.

Type-2 hypervisor Architecture that involves running the hypervisor over the top of a conventional, hosted operating system (OS). Other applications, besides the hypervisor, may also run on the hosted OS as other programs or processes. One or more guest operating systems run over the hypervisor.

version control A process for tracking and managing changes of code or files during the development process.

version control system (VCS) A specific protocol-based system that allows for source code to be tracked, checked in, and worked on in a collaborative manner. A VCS specifically refers to the higher-level protocol, such as git or subversion, rather than a specific platform implementation of the protocol.

web scraping Data scraping used for extracting data from websites. Also known as web harvesting or web data extraction.

YANG A data modeling language for the definition of data sent from NETCONF and RESTCONF. It was released by the NETMOD working group of the IETF as RFC 6020 and later updated in RFC 7950. YANG can model configuration data or network element state data.

Z

zero-touch provisioning (ZTP) A network function that enables an unconfigured device to bring itself to a defined level of functionality on a network through configurations provided via file servers.

Index

A

B

C

E

F

G

H

I

J

K

L

M

N

O

P

Q

R

S

T

U

V

W

Z

Exclusive Offer – 40% OFF

Cisco Press Video Training

livelessons

ciscopress.com/video

Use coupon code **CPVIDEO40** during checkout.

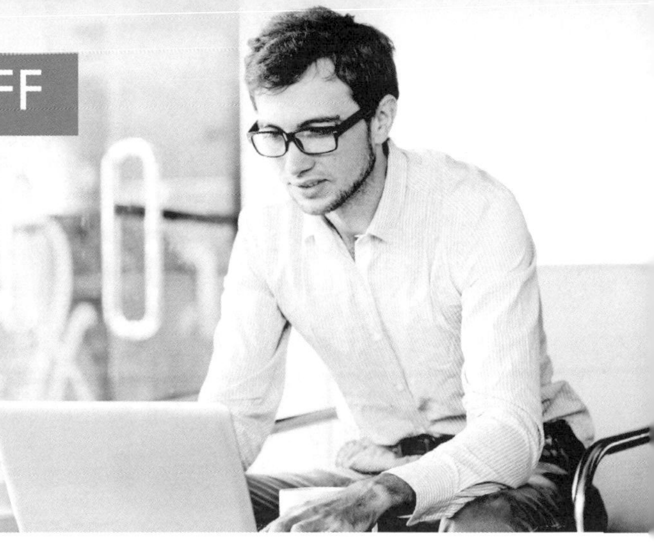

Video Instruction from Technology Experts

Advance Your Skills

Get started with fundamentals, become an expert, or get certified.

Train Anywhere

Train anywhere, at your own pace, on any device.

Learn

Learn from trusted author trainers published by Cisco Press.

Try Our Popular Video Training for FREE!

ciscopress.com/video

Explore hundreds of **FREE** video lessons from our growing library of Complete Video Courses, LiveLessons, networking talks, and workshops.

Cisco Press ciscopress.com/video

ALWAYS LEARNING PEARSON

REGISTER YOUR PRODUCT at CiscoPress.com/register

Access Additional Benefits and SAVE 35% on Your Next Purchase

- Download available product updates.
- Access bonus material when applicable.
- Receive exclusive offers on new editions and related products. (Just check the box to hear from us when setting up your account.)
- Get a coupon for 35% for your next purchase, valid for 30 days. Your code will be available in your Cisco Press cart. (You will also find it in the Manage Codes section of your account page.)

Registration benefits vary by product. Benefits will be listed on your account page under Registered Products.

CiscoPress.com – Learning Solutions for Self-Paced Study, Enterprise, and the Classroom

Cisco Press is the Cisco Systems authorized book publisher of Cisco networking technology, Cisco certification self-study, and Cisco Networking Academy Program materials.

At CiscoPress.com you can

- Shop our books, eBooks, software, and video training.
- Take advantage of our special offers and promotions (ciscopress.com/promotions).
- Sign up for special offers and content newsletters (ciscopress.com/newsletters).
- Read free articles, exam profiles, and blogs by information technology experts.
- Access thousands of free chapters and video lessons.

Connect with Cisco Press – Visit CiscoPress.com/community

Learn about Cisco Press community events and programs.

Cisco Press

ALWAYS LEARNING

PEARSON